The **MICHELIN** Guide

New York City

RESTAURANTS
2015

Michelin Travel Partner

Société par actions simplifiées au capital de 11 288 880 EUR
27 Cours de l'Ile Seguin - 92100 Boulogne Billancourt (France)
R.C.S. Nanterre 433 677 721

© **Michelin, Propriétaires-Éditeurs**

Dépôt légal septembre 2014

Printed in Canada - septembre 2014
Printed on paper from sustainably managed forests

Compogravure : Nord Compo à Villeneuve d'Ascq (France)
Impression et Finition : Transcontinental (Canada)

Dear Reader

We are thrilled to present the tenth edition of our MICHELIN guide to New York City.

Our dynamic team has spent this year updating our selection to wholly reflect the rich diversity of New York City's restaurants. As part of our meticulous and highly confidential evaluation process, our inspectors have anonymously and methodically eaten through all five boroughs to compile the finest in each category for your enjoyment. While the inspectors are expertly trained food industry professionals, we remain consumer-driven and provide comprehensive choices to accommodate your comfort, tastes, and budget. Our inspectors dine, drink, and lodge as "regular" customers in order to experience and evaluate the same level of service and cuisine that you would as a guest.

We have expanded our criteria to reflect some of the more current and unique elements of New York City's dining scene. Don't miss the tasty "Small Plates" category, highlighting places with a distinct style of service, setting, and menu; as well as the "Under $25" listing, which includes an impressive choice at great value.

Additionally, you may follow our Inspectors on Twitter @ MichelinGuideNY as they chow their way around town. They usually tweet daily about their unique and entertaining food experiences.

Our company's founders, Édouard and André Michelin, published the first MICHELIN guide in 1900, to provide motorists with practical information about where they could service and repair their cars, find quality accommodations, and a good meal. Later in 1926, the star-rating system for outstanding restaurants was introduced, and over the decades we have developed many new improvements to our guides. The local team here in New York City eagerly carries on these traditions.

We truly hope that the MICHELIN guide will remain your preferred reference to New York City's restaurants.

Contents

The MICHELIN Guide

"This volume was created at the turn of the century and will last at least as long".

This foreword to the very first edition of the MICHELIN Guide, written in 1900, has become famous over the years and the Guide has lived up to the prediction. It is read across the world and the key to its popularity is the consistency in its commitment to its readers, which is based on the following promises.

→ Anonymous Inspections

Our inspectors make anonymous visits to hotels and restaurants to gauge the quality offered to the ordinary customer. They pay their own bill and make no indication of their presence. These visits are supplemented by comprehensive monitoring of information—our readers' comments are one valuable source, and are always taken into consideration.

→ Independence

Our choice of establishments is a completely independent one, made for the benefit of our readers alone. Decisions are discussed by the inspectors and the editor, with the most important decided at the global level. Inclusion in the guide is always free of charge.

→ The Selection

The Guide offers a selection of the best hotels and restaurants in each category of comfort and price. Inclusion in the guides is a commendable award in itself, and defines the establishment among the "best of the best."

How the MICHELIN Guide Works

→ Annual Updates

All practical information, the classifications, and awards, are revised and updated every year to ensure the most reliable information possible.

→ Consistency & Classifications

The criteria for the classifications are the same in all countries covered by the Michelin Guides. Our system is used worldwide and is easy to apply when choosing a restaurant or hotel.

→ The Classifications

We classify our establishments using 🟍🟍🟍🟍-🟍 and 🏨🏨🏨🏨-🏠 to indicate the level of comfort. The ❀❀❀-❀ specifically designates an award for cuisine, unique from the classification. For hotels and restaurants, a symbol in red suggests a particularly charming spot with unique décor or ambiance.

→ Our Aim

As part of Michelin's ongoing commitment to improving travel and mobility, we do everything possible to make vacations and eating out a pleasure.

How to Use This Guide

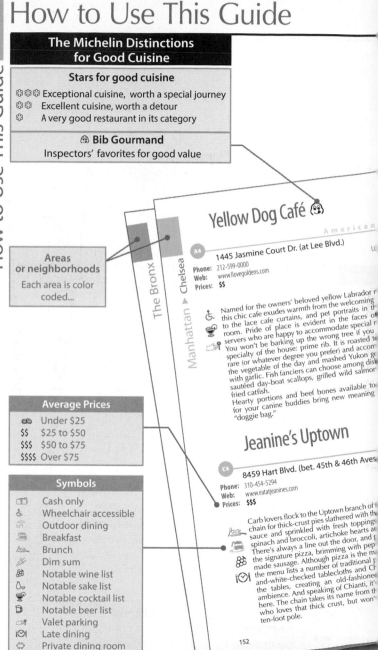

The Michelin Distinctions for Good Cuisine

Stars for good cuisine

✿✿✿ Exceptional cuisine, worth a special journey
✿✿ Excellent cuisine, worth a detour
✿ A very good restaurant in its category

⊛ Bib Gourmand
Inspectors' favorites for good value

Areas or neighborhoods
Each area is color coded...

The Bronx ▶ Chelsea

Manhattan

Yellow Dog Café ⊛

American

A4 1445 Jasmine Court Dr. (at Lee Blvd.)

LU

Phone: 212-599-0000
Web: www.Ilovegoldens.com
Prices: $$

Named for the owners' beloved yellow Labrador r
this chic cafe exudes warmth from the welcoming
to the lace cafe curtains, and pet portraits in th
room. Pride of place is evident in the faces of
servers who are happy to accommodate special r
You won't be barking up the wrong tree if you
specialty of the house: prime rib. It is roasted te
rare (or whatever degree you prefer) and accom
the vegetable of the day and mashed Yukon go
with garlic. Fish fanciers can choose among dis
sautéed day-boat scallops, grilled wild salmon
fried catfish.
Hearty portions and beef bones available to
for your canine buddies bring new meaning
"doggie bag."

Jeanine's Uptown

C4 8459 Hart Blvd. (bet. 45th & 46th Aves

Phone: 310-454-5294
Web: www.eatatjeanines.com
Prices: $$$

Carb lovers flock to the Uptown branch of t
chain for thick-crust pies slathered with th
sauce and sprinkled with fresh toppings
spinach and broccoli, artichoke hearts ar
There's always a line out the door, and f
the signature pizza, brimming with pep
made sausage. Although pizza is the ma
the menu lists a number of traditional f
and-white-checked tablecloths and Cl
the tables, creating an old-fashioned
ambience. And speaking of Chianti, it'
here. The chain takes its name from th
who loves that thick crust, but won'
ten-foot pole.

152

Average Prices

⊜	Under $25
$$	$25 to $50
$$$	$50 to $75
$$$$	Over $75

Symbols

🍴	Cash only
ⓖ	Wheelchair accessible
🌿	Outdoor dining
🍳	Breakfast
🥂	Brunch
🥢	Dim sum
🍷	Notable wine list
🍶	Notable sake list
🍸	Notable cocktail list
🍺	Notable beer list
🚗	Valet parking
🌙	Late dining
⟷	Private dining room

Restaurant Classifications by Comfort

More pleasant if in red

X	Comfortable
XX	Quite comfortable
XXX	Very comfortable
XXXX	Top class comfortable
XXXXX	Luxury in the traditional style
▦	Small plates

Map Coordinates

Sonya's Palace ✿ ✿

Italian XXXX

Manhattan ▶ Chelsea

A4 100 Reuther Pl. (at 30th Street)   Dinner daily

Phone: 415-867-5309
Subway: 14th St – 8 Av
Web: www.sonyasfabulouspalace.com
Prices: $$$

Home cooked Italian never tasted so good than at this unpretentious little place. The simple décor claims no big-name designers, and while the Murano glass light fixtures are chic and the velveteen-covered chairs are comfortable, this isn't a restaurant where millions of dollars were spent on the interior.

Instead, food is the focus here. The restaurant's name may not be Italian, but it nonetheless serves some of the best pasta in the city, made fresh in-house. Dishes follow the seasons, thus ravioli may be stuffed with fresh ricotta and herbs in summer, and pumpkin in fall. Most everything is liberally dusted with Parmigiano Reggiano, a favorite ingredient of the chef.

For dessert, you'll have to deliberate between the likes of creamy tiramisu, ricotta cheesecake, and homemade gelato. One thing's for sure: you'll never miss your nonna's cooking when you eat at Sonya's.

153

San Francisco ▶ Nob Hill

...s.)

Lunch daily

retriever,
waitstaff
e dining
friendly
guests.
der the
edium
ied by
inged
ch as
pan-

ome
erm

meat with a

107

er,
aff
ing
dly
ts.
the
ium
d by
nged
ch as
pan-

home
e term

zza X

at dinner only

cal pizzeria
use marinara
n as organic
ncetta.
ns rave about
i and house-
traction here,
f will. Red:
bottles adorn
lian restaurant
wine of choice
er's daughter.
h meat with a

Where to Eat

Manhattan

Chelsea

DIVERSITY IN DINING

Chelsea is a charming residential neighborhood combining modern high-rises and sleek lofts with classic townhouses and retail stores aplenty. To that end, this nabe is a shopper's paradise, offering everything from computer stores and high fashion boutiques, to **Chelsea Market**, the city's culinary epicenter. And let's not forget the art: the neighborhood's once-dilapidated warehouses and abandoned lofts are now home to more than 200 prominent galleries as well as the artists who contribute to them, resulting in a burgeoning cultural scene. To feed its well-educated and art-enthusiastic residents, and out-of-towners on pilgrimage, Chelsea teems with casual cafeterias. Old-world Puerto Rican luncheonettes that used to dot Ninth Ave. (rest easy as **La Taza de Oro** still remains) have now given way to mega-hip temples of fusion fare—where diners are accommodated in stylish digs

and the cocktail carte packs a potent punch. Carousers party until last call at such high-energy hangouts as **1 OAK**, launched by greenmarket-obsessed, Chef Alex Guarnaschelli's Butter Group. Patrons of this hot spot may jump ship to the likes of **Marquee**, but remain loyal to late-night stalwarts like **Robert's Steakhouse @ Scores New York**. Nestled inside The Penthouse Executive Club, it's really all about the "meat" at this flesh fortress, where gentlemen seem far more lured by char-rich steaks on plates than the ladies on their laps.

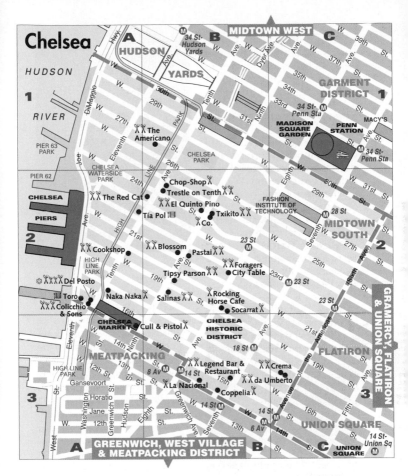

Chelsea

MIDTOWN WEST

HUDSON YARDS

HUDSON RIVER

GARMENT DISTRICT

MIDTOWN SOUTH

GRAMERCY, FLATIRON & UNION SQUARE

FLATIRON

UNION SQUARE

MEATPACKING

CHELSEA HISTORIC DISTRICT

GREENWICH, WEST VILLAGE & MEATPACKING DISTRICT

These insomnious hordes can also be seen swinging to live salsa at **Son Cubano**, an Old Havana-inspired supper club whose superb mojitos and Spanish small plates will have you shouting *viva la Cubanos* before the night is out.

THE HIGH LINE

Located above Manhattan's mean streets and atop an elevated freight railroad, **The High Line** is a lengthy public space with a large presence in Chelsea. Populated by yuppies and young families, and punctuated by acres of indigenous greenery as well as unexpectedly stunning views of the Hudson, this city-center oasis also offers unique respites for refreshment. **Bubby's High Line** is a perpetual favorite for its impressive repertoire of food and drink. Envision rambling locals ordering off a kid's menu; or late-night carousers devouring "midnight brunch" and you will begin to understand what this neighborhood is all about. Too rushed to dwell over dessert? Their retail store sells pastries and ice cream sandwiches to-go, after

15

which a shot of single-origin drip espresso at **Blue Bottle Coffee Café** is not just fitting, but first-class. As history would have it, the last functional freight train that passed through The High Line had cars filled with meat. It therefore seems only natural that **Delaney Barbecue's Smokeline** also has a station here. This down-home shack may only prepare simple, straightforward food, but it makes for a fantastic pit stop en-route to **The Taco Truck**—churning out Mexican street eats during the summer heat. Nearby, **Terroir at The Porch** is an open-air, full-service café with small plates, wine, and beer to boot. Seal such stellar sips with a cooling kiss from **L'Arte del Gelato**.

In 1997, the 1898 Nabisco factory reopened as **Chelsea Market**, a fabled culinary bazaar whose brick-lined walkways are now cramped with stores selling everything from lemons to lingerie. Carb-addicts begin their culinary excursion here at the likes of now-expanded **Amy's Bread**, where artisan-crafted loaves are as precious as crown jewels. Then they might layover at **Bar Suzette** for an array of undeniably excellent, very fluffy crêpes. Meanwhile, the calorie-counters collect at **Beyond Sushi** for healthy, tasty renditions of the Japanese staple, wrapped here in black rice and topped with creamy tofu. From Asian signatures to everyday Italian, **Buon Italia** will not only help stock your pantry for a night in with *nonna*, but sates those inevitable hunger pangs while you're at it—a stand upfront sells cooked foods and sandwiches to crowds on the run. Other welcome members to this epicurean community include **Dickson's Farmstand** for house-made pâté; sweet sanctum **Sarabeth's** or **Fat Witch Bakery** for goodies and holiday gifts; as well as **Ronnybrook Milk Bar**, a milk and shakes shop-turned-full service restaurant. Keep sipping your way north and close the deal over at **The Grill at La Piscine** (stunningly set on the rooftop of Hôtel Americano) with a bite of any kind but sure sip of *vino*!

The Americano

Contemporary 🍴🍴

B1

518 W. 27th St. (bet. Tenth & Eleventh Aves.)

Subway: 23 St (Eighth Ave.)　　　　　　　　　Lunch & dinner daily
Phone: 212-216-0000
Web: www.hotel-americano.com
Prices: $$$

Within its all-mesh metal façade, the Hotel Americano's namesake restaurant is a striking home to contemporary dining in far west Chelsea, just steps from the High Line. A citron banquette seems to pop in the slick setting, which combines floor-to-ceiling windows, glossy walls, and a polished concrete floor.

A talented team behind the line strives—and succeeds—in preparing delicious Latin fare with French flair. Menu options include delicate empanadas stuffed with Oaxacan cheese and wild mushrooms, or succulent lobster fried tempura-style and set on a complex sauce of fruity *chile pasilla* and dried corn. Some classics remain wonderfully familiar, as in the tarte Tatin made from local Golden Delicious apples, topped with a dollop of crème fraîche.

Blossom

Vegan 🍴🍴

B2

187 Ninth Ave. (bet. 21st & 22nd Sts.)

Subway: 23 St (Eighth Ave.)　　　　　　　　　Lunch & dinner daily
Phone: 212-627-1144
Web: www.blossomnyc.com
Prices: $$

Unpretentious and welcoming, this is a vegan favorite with spot-on spicing and delicious surprises. The cream-colored interior is dim with dark velvet curtains and votive candlelight reflected in round mirrors. The vibe may seem moody come evening, but the staff is always warm and affable.

Huge portions and the bold flavors of smoked tempeh, spinach, pine nuts, and cremini mushrooms prove the power of vegetables to dedicated carnivores. Follow this with meaty and woodsy grilled seitan, glazed with violet-mustard and served over a mélange of roasted salsify and sautéed kale surrounded by horseradish cream. Come dessert, try the hand-churned cashew ice cream or a lemony cheesecake with a mixed berry reduction and coconut-cookie crust.

Chop-Shop

Asian

B2

254 Tenth Ave. (bet. 24th & 25th Sts.)

Subway: 23 St (Eighth Ave.)
Phone: 212-820-0333
Web: www.chop-shop.co
Prices: $$

Lunch Mon– Sat
Dinner nightly

Now an über-hip scene, this far west strip of Chelsea has been attracting its fair share of affluent locals and a flurry of dashing eateries; Chop-Shop is part of that evolution. Outfitted in reclaimed pine, vintage lights, and concrete floors, it has an industrial look but is awash with sunlight thanks to soaring windows.

The eclectic menu roams Asia with deliciously balanced and infinitely varied plates. Subtlety reigns in an avocado-tofu summer roll paired with peanut curry sauce or crunchy salt-and-pepper shrimp, while Chinese water spinach with fermented tofu cream delivers an intense punch of flavor. Fried rice with salmon and peas is less than classic but more than popular. Rich tastes and silky textures meld beautifully in coconut crème caramel.

Co.

Pizza

B2

230 Ninth Ave. (at 24th St.)

Subway: 23 St (Eighth Ave.)
Phone: 212-243-1105
Web: www.co-pane.com
Prices: $$

Lunch Tue-Sun
Dinner Daily

Head to Co. for something other than those Naples-aping pizzerias that have come to monopolize the whole of New York. A serious destination for its dedicated take on pies, this carb haven pays equal attention to the dough and toppings, with outstanding results. These are the ways of celebrated baker and chef, Jim Lahey, who perfected his yeasty, smoky flavors at Sullivan Street Bakery (a few doors away) and is NYC's resident expert on bread-making.

Amid wood-paneled walls, wine racks, and modern-looking mirrors, crowds savor innovative combinations, such as spicy merguez with smoked pepper sauce, pecorino, and mint on a puffy crust. Nightly specials include a creamy leek and celeriac soup, finished with olive oil and freshly ground black pepper.

Colicchio & Sons

A2

American

85 Tenth Ave. (bet. 15th & 16th Sts.)

Subway: 14 St - 8 Av
Phone: 212-400-6699
Web: www.craftrestaurantsinc.com
Prices: $$$$

Lunch & dinner daily

This stunning, smart Chelsea-meets-Meatpacking outpost highlights the renowned talent of Chef Tom Colicchio. The front "Tap Room" boasts an impressive beer list, small plates with big prices, and cords of chopped wood resting on chrome shelves to fuel the wood-burning oven. The sophisticated back dining room offers moon-shaped leather banquettes, a glass wine hall, and a bird's-eye mural of the neighborhood.

Meals are simple but beguilingly delicious, as in beautifully ridged ricotta cavatelli tossed with silky leeks, *cavolo nero*, and a bit of heat from fiery chili peppers. Desserts might feature a wonderfully firm cream cheese panna cotta with blackberry gelée, cashew brittle, chai ice cream, and a surprising little coriander shortbread.

Cookshop

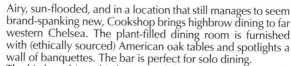

A2

American

156 Tenth Ave. (at 20th St.)

Subway: 23 St (Eighth Ave.)
Phone: 212-924-4440
Web: www.cookshopny.com
Prices: $$

Lunch & dinner daily

Airy, sun-flooded, and in a location that still manages to seem brand-spanking new, Cookshop brings highbrow dining to far western Chelsea. The plant-filled dining room is furnished with (ethically sourced) American oak tables and spotlights a wall of banquettes. The bar is perfect for solo dining.

The kitchen drives this locavare philosophy with energy and skill. A cooling late-summer tomato soup is a smooth balance of sweet and tart flavors, enhanced with tangy lemon-basil and riesling. House-made *lasagnetti* highlights the best of the season with high-minded Italian style, through tight, wavy ridges of pasta beautifully dressed in delicate pesto. Save room for sweet treats like peanut butter Bavarian with Concord grape *granite* and milk ice cream.

Coppelia

Latin American ✗

B3

207 W. 14th St. (bet. Seventh & Eighth Aves.)

Subway: 14 St (Seventh Ave.)
Phone: 212-858-5001
Web: www.coppelianyc.com
Prices: $$

Lunch & dinner daily

Think of ultra-casual Coppelia as a favorite anytime Latin-American diner, ready to please with its enormous menus served 24 hours a day, seven days a week. The space is long and narrow, with a dining counter for solo guests, checkerboard floors, booths, and cheery yellow walls. Late at night, this place is hopping.

Sometimes their dishes can be inconsistent, but nevertheless grow in popularity as the sun goes down. Highlights at this unique spot include *churrasco*, a smoky and perfectly seasoned skirt steak with sweet fried plantains and tender, earthy black beans simmered with aromatics; or snacks like *croquetas de queso*, fried until crunchy and oozing piping hot melted cheese. Dessert might include a fluffy, light, and milk-soaked *tres leches* cake.

Crema

Mexican ✗✗

C3

111 W. 17th St. (bet. Sixth & Seventh Aves.)

Subway: 18 St
Phone: 212-691-4477
Web: www.cremarestaurante.com
Prices: $$

Lunch & dinner daily

There seems to be an air of comfort surrounding lovely Crema—especially at dinner. Bare marble tables, warm yellow walls, and a cactus garden surround a front banquette, strewn with pillows and overlooking 17th Street. The bar displays glass vats of sangria and mixes a vast array of refreshing cocktails, like the *delirio* combining gin, cucumber, white cranberry juice, and freshly muddled lime.

From the kitchen, find wonderfully complex Mexican dishes, as in the *caldo de habas*, a thick and rich fava bean soup that is crimson-red, smoky, and very spicy. The *pastel Azteca* arrives as a tall ramekin laying tortillas, shredded chicken, beans, corn, and an array of cheeses with *salsa roja* and a drizzle of truffle oil. The $15.95 lunch is a fantastic value.

Cull & Pistol

A3

75 Ninth Ave. (in Chelsea Market)

Subway: 14 St - 8 Av
Phone: 646-568-1223
Web: www.cullandpistol.com
Prices: $$$

Lunch daily
Dinner Mon — Sat

Named for a lobster that's missing either one or both claws, Cull & Pistol is a full-fledged seafood haven that resides next to Chelsea Market's Lobster Place and is replete with reclaimed wood tables, brushed steel chairs, and a zinc-topped raw bar. If that isn't alluring enough, they also boast craft beer to go with a meal that is sure to sate any seafood lover.

Comforting New England classics like chowders and lobster rolls are on offer, but don't pass up the spectacular clams and oysters—a briny, heavenly selection collected from up and down the Eastern coast. Other excellent items include *fideos negros* tossed in squid ink, braised *seppia*, and garlic aïoli; or copious amounts of clams with caramelized shallots and tasso ham over grilled ciabatta.

da Umberto

C3

107 W. 17th St. (bet. Sixth & Seventh Aves.)

Subway: 18 St
Phone: 212-989-0303
Web: www.daumbertonyc.com
Prices: $$$

Lunch Mon — Fri
Dinner Mon — Sat

There is a finely tuned harmony to dining at such classic New York restaurants as da Umberto. The Italian menu seems familiar and unpretentious, the kitchen makes no mistakes, and the ingredients are superb; but what actually sets it apart is an ability to serve exactly what you crave without seeming trite or predictable. Even the look is a perfectly conjured mix of dark woods, creaky floors, a lavish antipasto bar, and impeccably timed servers.

The daily risotto special may be glistening with a rich duck ragù beneath a slowly melting slice of Parmesan. When the dessert cart rolls its way to the table, expect a surprising array of excellent house-made sweets, like Italian cheesecake or their legendary tiramisu dusted with cinnamon and fresh berries.

Del Posto ⌘

Italian

85 Tenth Ave. (at 16th St.)

Subway: 14 St - 8 Av
Phone: 212-497-8090
Web: www.delposto.com
Prices: $$$$

Lunch Mon – Fri
Dinner nightly

Del Posto's prime Manhattan location is pricelessly situated beneath the Highline, across from the Chelsea Market and glimmering high-rises. A sloping staircase, inlaid marble floors, and polished woods ensure that the interior is just as posh. Where the sheer vastness of the space might have rendered it cold, rotund balconies, fabric-covered walls, and exquisitely dressed windows add charm and texture. Service is impeccable, reserved, and well-timed—if a seat is vacated, a silver cloche instantly covers the food.

Yes, this can all seem as theatrical and old-timey as that tuxedo-clad pianist tickling the ivories, but it is nonetheless opulent.

The large Italian menu focuses on the seasons, but is loaded with deliciously humble dishes like crisp *porchetta* stuffed with pork and herb-seasoned liver atop braised cabbage. Highlights include a rather stylish *vitello tonnato*, the delicate veal skillfully cut across the grain and topped with a decadently creamy sauce counterpoised with a host of tart, sour capers as well as black squid-ink croutons. Desserts here marry the sweet and savory in unexpected and refreshing ways, as in pumpkin cake with sage gelato, candied pumpkin, and brown butter.

El Quinto Pino

Spanish ✗✗

401 W. 24th St. (bet. Ninth & Tenth Aves.)

Subway: 23 St (Eighth Ave.)
Phone: 212-206-6900
Web: www.elquintopinonyc.com
Prices: $$

Lunch Tue – Sun
Dinner nightly

Blend Barcelona tapas with New York creativity and get this beloved Chelsea baby from Alex Raij and Eder Montero. It recently tripled its footprint, making even more of an impression in the area's crowded landscape of tapas restaurants. Still packed, guests can now forgo balancing drinks on a skinny bar and relax in a properly romantic dining room adorned with wool tapestries.

Choose a wine from the chalkboard and dive into the deconstructed yet sublime flavors. Supple and smoky calamari delivers surprise after surprise with squid jus, Parmesan, and black garlic all perfectly balanced with umami. Intensely aromatic, earthy, and excellent, the *arroz brut de conejo* stuffs "dirty" rice and rabbit into tender cabbage beautifully braised in saffron broth.

Foragers City Table

Contemporary ✗✗

300 W. 22nd St. (at Eighth Ave.)

Subway: 23 St (Eighth Ave.)
Phone: 212-243-8888
Web: www.foragerscitygrocer.com
Prices: $$

Lunch Sat – Sun
Dinner Tue – Sat

Chef Nickolas Martinez shows off his impressive pedigree at this Chelsea charmer, where the staff is dutiful and the foodies are leaning iPhones over the counter to get shots of The Action. The style is minimalist and industrial with hardwood tables and unencumbered windows. Foragers City Table may as well be located in California's wine country. Thankfully it's here, and it's delicious.

Start with snacks like panko-fried spring onions served with tangy and peppery Meyer lemon crème fraîche. Then, move on to *orechiette* bathed with rabbit Bolognese, fresh fava beans, brown beech mushrooms, and *Parmigiano Reggiano*. Pickled daikon with crushed peanuts and lemongrass aïoli pair beautifully with soft-shell crab. Finish with a minty berry-yogurt parfait.

La Nacional

Spanish 🍴

B3

239 W. 14th St. (bet. Seventh & Eighth Aves.)

Subway: 14 St (Seventh Ave.)
Phone: 212-243-9308
Web: N/A
Prices: $$

Lunch & Dinner daily

A quirky relic of New York's past and beloved by its most talented Spanish chefs, La Nacional transcends its roots as a private cultural club with authentic dishes served in an ageless setting. The comfortable bar and dining room on the ground floor of the 19th century Spanish Benevolent Society building speak to a bygone era.

Well-made traditional dishes prize simplicity: *arroz negro* swimming with an ocean's worth of seafood and squid ink *sofrito* sports a perfectly crispy *soccarat* bottom. Succulent seared lamb chops brushed with tangy *chimichurri* need nothing more than roasted potatoes and olive oil-tossed green beans for accompaniment. An over-easy egg fried in olive oil, placed atop chorizo and toasted bread, is luxurious, smoky, and rich.

Legend Bar & Restaurant

Chinese 🍴🍴

B3

88 Seventh Ave. (bet. 15th & 16th Sts.)

Subway: 14 St
Phone: 212-929-1778
Web: www.legendrestaurant88.com
Prices: 🐝

Lunch & Dinner daily

While Legend may offer a nice variety of Asian fare, just stick to the Sichuan specialties and be thoroughly rewarded. Find one of the many highlights in supremely flavorful and tender Chong Qing spicy chicken, loaded with viciously good dried chiles. The house duck is a traditional presentation of roasted and crisped meat with wraps as well as a host of accoutrements, including crushed peanuts, fragrant herbs, scallions, and very tasty plum sauce. Bok choi with black mushrooms is a crunchy, simply delicious departure from the intensity of other dishes you may face here.

The dining room has a certain hip and chic feel that fosters a lively happy hour scene. Colorful fabrics, striped walls, and statues of deities make for an attractive space.

Naka Naka

Japanese ✗

A2

458 W. 17th St. (bet. Ninth & Tenth Aves.)

Subway: 14 St - 8 Av   Dinner Tue – Sat
Phone: 212-929-8544
Web: www.nakanakany.com
Prices: $$$

Like a graceful ballet, Naka Naka's kimono-draped servers, lustrous pearl-hued lanterns, and elegant calligraphy create a dance that instantly transports you from Chelsea to Japan. Housed in a timeworn tenement building amid high-rise condos, the soothing atmosphere draws a largely urban crowd, slung in the low wooden seats of this hidden gem.

There is a melody to the food as well, beginning with aged, unfiltered sake. Dishes include cold soba topped with flaky fish tempura and the signature Naka Naka box, an ever-changing selection of exceptional tempuras, rice, and miso-dressed tuna. Salty, briny, mouth-coating flavors soon climax with bites of the vibrant sea urchin and downright perfect salmon roe sushi, worthy of its own Kyoto temple.

Pastai

Italian ✗✗

B2

186 Ninth Ave. (bet. 21st & 22nd Sts.)

Subway: 23 St (Eighth Ave.)   Lunch & dinner daily
Phone: 646-688-3463
Web: www.pastainyc.com
Prices: $$

Chef Melissa Muller-Daka hits her stride with this very charming enterprise. Pastai is a darling among the Ninth Avenue natives and evokes a rustic and airy feel, styled with whitewashed brick, slate walls, and wooden communal tables. Milk bottles serving as water pitchers and bright flower arrangements complete the look.

Freshly made pastas are the main draw, with about ten different varieties made from locally sourced whole grains. Start with a dive into decadent *arancini siciliani*, pork and fontina cheese-stuffed rice balls fried until crisp and set in a pool of tomato sauce. Then, try *piattini di pasta*, such as *bucatini* tossed in saffron and cauliflower ragù, studded with golden raisins and pine nuts, and sprinkled with toasted Parmesan breadcrumbs.

The Red Cat

American ✗✗

B2

227 Tenth Ave. (bet. 23rd & 24th Sts.)

Subway: 23 St (Eighth Ave.)
Phone: 212-242-1122
Web: www.theredcat.com
Prices: $$

Lunch & Dinner daily

By 6 P.M. any night of the week, area gallerists and anyone else with a yen for sophisticated food and cocktails are already packed in—just as they have been for 15 years. With Moorish lanterns, Mediterranean hues, and dark lighting, its funky décor conjures a Bohemian past with equally creative dishes. Here, innovative combinations act like a mixed media canvas, ready to engage each sense. Curry-spiked emulsion lays the groundwork for the crunch of golden chicken croquettes. Deeply seasoned pan-seared salmon gets an unexpectedly earthy preparation of spicy mushrooms and a bold *guajillo* pepper sauce with oregano and sweet roasted garlic. Pleasing desserts include individual pumpkin cheesecake over pear butter topped with *pepitas* and bits of chestnut.

Rocking Horse Cafe

Mexican ✗

B2

182 Eighth Ave. (bet. 19th & 20th Sts.)

Subway: 14 St - 8 Av
Phone: 212-463-9511
Web: www.rockinghorsecafe.com
Prices: $$

Lunch & dinner daily

Rainbow flags draped over the awning, the silhouette of a horse's head, and a red garage door that opens to Eighth Avenue are among the first signs you've arrived at the Rocking Horse Cafe. Inside, a shimmering blue mosaic wall and linen-covered tables lend sophistication. Lunchtime is calm when compared to the dinner hours, when music blares and service rushes to keep up with a room that is suddenly cramped with wall-to-wall people. Still, the bar is a fun stop for serious margaritas

Whether modern or traditional, this Mexican fare satisfies the soul. Expect a succulent, bone-in lamb shank, braised with chipotle and rich with myriad flavors; or fluffy-crisp yucca cake. The freshly grated coconut flan is a perfect rendering of the classic.

27

Salinas

B2

136 Ninth Ave. (bet. 18th & 19th Sts.)

Subway: 18 St
Phone: 212-776-1990
Web: www.salinasnyc.com
Prices: $$$

Dinner nightly

Salinas is undeniably sexy. Step beyond the wrought-iron gates and squeeze your way past the bar to find the dusky scene. The patio dining room is where fashionistas nestle like pretty young things on button-tufted banquettes amid bunches of pink roses and flickering votives. A retractable glass roof shields the attractive Brazilian walnut floors and limestone walls from the outside elements.

The Spanish cuisine of Chef Luis Bollo, a native of San Sebastian, sparkles with coastal influences. Tapas are muy creative and include *boquerones* over delicate toast strips spread with smashed avocado. The *fideos negros y crujientes* is an ink-stained mound of toasted vermicelli, cuttlefish, and aïoli foam grandly stirred together upon presentation.

Socarrat

B2

259 W. 19th St. (bet. Seventh & Eighth Aves.)

Subway: 18 St
Phone: 212-462-1000
Web: www.socarratrestaurants.com
Prices: $$$

Lunch & dinner daily

Tapas bars have been taking over the city, yet Socarrat—named for the delicious crust of rice that forms at the bottom of a pan—is a worthy addition by virtue of its irresistible paella. Like its siblings, this is a friendly and familiar spot, where long communal tables are packed with your newest old friends and tapas-loving locals. Glossy walls reflect the room's gentle light, while mirrors and portraits lend depth and color.

Octopus rounds crowned with spices is a perfect opener for paella Socarrat, a crisp layer of caramelized rice mingled in a fragrant stock with spicy chorizo and briny clams. Happy Hour keeps everyone beaming by pairing the likes of *croquetas de setas* (mushrooms) or crispy pork belly with sangria, either red or white.

Tía Pol

A2

Spanish

205 Tenth Ave. (bet. 22nd & 23rd Sts.)

Subway: 23 St (Eighth Ave.)
Phone: 212-675-8805
Web: www.tiapol.com
Prices: ⊜⊜

Lunch Tue – Sun
Dinner nightly

Tapas may have taken over Chelsea's storefronts, but stepping into this small plates paradise, you'll do a double take and wonder if this is Barcelona. The dimly lit, narrow room packs in wine-guzzling guests awaiting just a few tables. Busy servers uncork bottles and stream in and out of the open kitchen with Spanish classics like hand-shaved *jamón* and piquillo peppers. It's entertainment for the waiting game, which is always part of the experience at this ten-year-old staple.

First bites say everything, and the fluffy wedge of tortilla, with its dab of garlicky aïoli, sets the standard for here and beyond. Don't miss the skirt steak, the most flavorful meat on the menu and a frequent special, served with potatoes and pickled red onions.

Tipsy Parson

B2

American

156 Ninth Ave. (bet. 19th & 20th Sts.)

Subway: 18 St
Phone: 212-620-4545
Web: www.tipsyparson.com
Prices: $$

Lunch & dinner daily

With its masculine bar shelved with books and premium spirits, dining room decorated with bric-a-brac, and French doors looking out on to a garden, Tipsy Parson conjures homey and familiar comfort. Imagine dining at an old friend's house, starting with drinks in the living room and ending on the back porch.

The distinct Southern bent is clear from such beginnings as a trio of spreads including pimento cheese, deviled tasso ham, and black eyed pea salad with house-made crackers; or deviled eggs judiciously loaded with tarragon. Oysters are marvelously crisp and served with Old Bay mayo flecked with cornichons. For dessert, the Tipsy Parson is a trifle-like and boozy wonder of brandy-soaked almond cake, vanilla custard, and brandied berries.

Toro

A2

Spanish

85 Tenth Ave. (entrance at 15th St. & Eleventh Ave.)

Subway: 14 St - 8 Av Dinner Mon – Sat
Phone: 212-691-2360
Web: www.toro-nyc.com
Prices: $$

Boston's Ken Oringer and Jamie Bissonnette make their talented NY debut at this local haunt, perfectly positioned in west Chelsea. The industrial space faces a buzzing highway, but inside the thick wood doors, young diners (and drinkers) notice nothing but the warm brick-walled space and rows of cured hams. This vibrant scene creates a cozy atmosphere for outstanding *pintxos*, paellas, and a *reserva*-fueled wine list.

Be sure to try the decadent *bocadillo de erizos*. The sandwich's bombastic flavors of sea urchin, pickled mustard seeds, and miso butter may only be rivaled by the prized, smoky *pimentón de la Vera* on the grilled purple cauliflower—a feast for all the senses. For dessert, the goat's milk yogurt mousse is refreshing and unusually delicious.

Trestle on Tenth

B2

Contemporary ✕✕

242 Tenth Ave. (at 24th St.)

Subway: 23 St (Eighth Ave.) Lunch & dinner daily
Phone: 212-645-5659
Web: www.trestleontenth.com
Prices: $$

Everything is low-key and *très* chic at this Swiss-inflected favorite on a prime corner of western Chelsea. While the exterior looks like some tavern of yesteryear, the inside has a rustic-urban, NY-via-Scandanavia feel, minimally dressed with contemporary art along rough brick walls, blond woods, and clean lines.

Seeking out the *metzgete* ("butcher's affair") in January is a must. Other dishes might include thick, juicy slices of smoked and roasted pork loin atop potato galette and pork jus with a haunting whiff of mustard. The *nusstorte* is a Swiss-style caramel-walnut tart that is an ideal close to any rich, meat-focused meal here.

Through the secret garden in back, discover the Rocket Pig for a carefully packed "pignic" (pork sandwich) to-go.

Manhattan ▲ Chelsea

Txikito

Spanish ✗✗

B2

240 Ninth Ave. (bet. 24th & 25th Sts.)

Subway: 23 St (Eighth Ave.)   Dinner nightly
Phone: 212-242-4730
Web: www.txikitonyc.com
Prices: **$$**

Start off with a "gin tonic" and taste what the fuss is all about. Always packed, delicious, and passionate, this Basque spot conveys a world of regional cuisine, thanks to Chefs Alex Raij and Eder Montero. Colorful touches and a chalkboard of daily specials lend an informal Spanish feel. Closely spaced tables remind you that you're in New York.

The Basque menu offers both small and large plates that often seem simple but are rich, tasty, and downright special—don't miss the anchovies! Their worthy signature octopus carpaccio (*pulpo*) is cut into remarkably thin slices, dressed in lemon, marjoram, and *piment d'Espelette*. If the umami-rich *laminas de setas*—citrus-marinated king oyster mushrooms offset with salty Marcona almonds—is available, get it.

Couverts (✗... ✗✗✗✗✗)
indicate the level of
comfort found at a
restaurant. The more
✗'s, the more upscale a
restaurant will be.

Chinatown & Little Italy

As different as chow mein and chicken cacciatore, these two neighborhoods are nonetheless neighbors and remain as tight as thieves. In recent years, their borders have become increasingly blurred, with Chinatown gulping up most of Little Italy. In fact, rumor has it that New York cradles the maximum number of Chinese immigrants in the country; and settlers from Hong Kong and mainland China each bring with them their own distinct regional cuisines.

EAT THE STREETS

Chowing in Chinatown can be both delectable and delightfully affordable. Elbow your way through these cramped streets to find a flurry of food markets, bubble tea cafés, bakeries, and eateries. Freshly steamed pouches of chicken, seafood, pork, and beef are all the rage at **Vanessa's Dumpling House**, a neighborhood fixture featuring a long counter packed with a longer line of hungry patrons. There is plenty more of deliciousness to be had in this 'hood—from feasting on freshly pulled noodles; ducking into a parlor for a scoop of avocado or black sesame ice cream; and breezing past a market window with crocodile meat on display (claws included!). Speaking of markets, **New Kam Man** is a bustling bazaar teeming with everything from woks and china, to wontons, tea, and oyster sauce.

Over on Mulberry Street, **Asia Market Corp.** is a sight for sore eyes as shelves spill over with Malaysian, Indonesian, Filipino, and Thai specialties. The space may be tight, but the display of imported goods is tantalizing at all times. Find celebrity chefs at other Asian storefronts, haggling over the freshest fish and quality produce, before sneaking under the Manhattan Bridge for a crusty *bánh mì*. From chilies to curry pastes, **Bangkok Center Grocery** boasts every ingredient necessary for a Thai-themed dinner—not to mention those

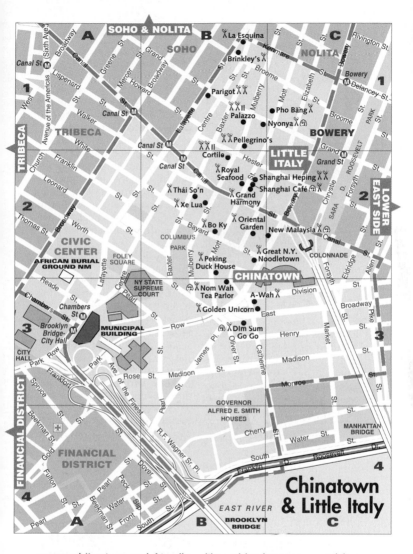

Chinatown & Little Italy

Map labels:

SOHO & NOLITA

A B C

La Esquina
Brinkley's
SOHO
NOLITA
Rivington St.
Kenmare St.
Bowery
Delancey St.

Parigot
Palazzo
Pho Bâng
Nyonya
BOWERY
Pellegrino's

Cortile
LITTLE ITALY
Grand St.

Royal Seafood
Shanghai Heping
Shanghai Café
Thái So'n
Grand Harmony
Xe Lua
LOWER EAST SIDE

Bo Ky
Oriental Garden
New Malaysia

COLUMBUS PARK
Great N.Y. Noodletown
CIVIC CENTER
AFRICAN BURIAL GROUND NM
Peking Duck House
CHINATOWN
COLONNADE

NY STATE SUPREME COURT
Nom Wah Tea Parlor
A-Wah

Golden Unicorn

Brooklyn Bridge-City Hall
MUNICIPAL BUILDING
Dim Sum Go Go

CITY HALL

GOVERNOR ALFRED E. SMITH HOUSES

MANHATTAN BRIDGE

FINANCIAL DISTRICT

EAST RIVER
BROOKLYN BRIDGE

expat publications and friendly owner! Fans of Cantonese cuisine join the queue outside **Big Wong King**, where comfort food classics (think congee and roast duck) are just as outstanding as the setting is ordinary. **Amazing 66** is a brightly lit, bi-level local darling with two dining rooms serving one menu starring the

likes of lamb's tongue and live eel. Dishes here arrive almost as swiftly as the crowds go in and out, naturally making it a spot where taste and efficiency are of superlative quality. Dim sum is obligatory and weekend brunch is a longtime tradition at **Jing Fong**. Take the escalator up a floor to arrive at this massive

mainstay, where the service is gruff but the Hong Kong-style treats are nothing short of genuine. For a more snug setting, date-night duos are sure to adore **Tai Pan Bakery** for their delectable array of pastries that promises to set hearts on fire. The exquisitely light, always-moist, and subtly sweet sponge cake at **New Kam Hing Coffee Shop** has made it a worthy competitor in the "Best bakeries around town" contest; just as artisan bakeshop, **Fay Da**, has been serving its classic Chinese treats complete with a modern twist to the community for near-infinity. Klezmer meets Cantonese at the **Egg Rolls and Egg Creams Festival**, an annual summer street celebration honoring the neighboring Chinese and Jewish communities of Chinatown and the Lower East Side. Every year during Chinese New Year, partygoers pack these festive streets, with dragons dancing down the avenues accompanied by costumed revelers and firecrackers.

LITTLE ITALY

The Little Italy of Scorsese's gritty *Mean Streets* is slowly vanishing into what may now be more aptly called Micro Italy. The onetime stronghold of a large Italian-American population has dwindled today to a mere corridor—Mulberry Street between Canal and Broome. But, the spirit of its origins still pulses in century-old markets, cramped delis, gelato shops, and mom-and-pop trattorias. Seasoned palates love **Piemonte Ravioli** for incredible homemade sauces amid dried and fresh pastas, available in all shapes with a variety of fillings. **Alleva Dairy** (known for homemade ricotta) is the oldest Italian cheese store in the country; and **Di Palo Fine Foods** struts imported *sopressata*, *salumi*, and cheeses. Primo for pastries and espresso, fans never forget to frequent **Ferrara's Bakery and Café** on Grand Street. During warmer months, Mulberry Street becomes a pedestrian zone with one big alfresco party—the **Feast of San Gennaro** is particularly raucous. While these days you can get better Italian food elsewhere in the city, tourists and old-timers still gather to treasure and bathe in the nostalgia of this nabe.

A-Wah

B3

Chinese ✗

5 Catherine St. (bet. Division St. & East Broadway)

Subway: Canal St (Lafayette St.)
Phone: 212-925-8308
Web: www.awahrestaurant.com
Prices: ⊖⊖

Lunch & dinner daily

An incredibly popular member of NYC's diverse culinary scene, simple, tiny, and singularly focused A-Wah fires up a vast array of Hong Kong-style comfort foods from ginger chicken feet to sautéed pea leaves. The region's tasty take on *lo mein* is a total departure from the familiar version. Here, find a platter of thin noodles topped with pork or duck, served with a side of delicate, comsommé-like broth for dipping.

However, the biggest treat is the fantastic *bo zai fan*: rice cooked to crunchy perfection in a clay pot and crowned with ginger, scallions, and a mind-boggling choice of seventeen toppings like frog, pork, and preserved vegetables. These dishes and their tasty burnt-rice sides are made even better with a thick and sweet house-made soy sauce.

Bo Ky

B2

Chinese ✗

80 Bayard St. (bet. Mott and Mulberry Sts.)

Subway: Canal St (Lafayette St.)
Phone: 212-406-2292
Web: N/A
Prices: ⊖⊖

Lunch & dinner daily

If you're drawn to those bare bones sort of places where food quality, beyond-warm service, and value speak for itself, this is your Chinatown slam dunk. Bo Ky's steamed-up windows (from the succulent meats roasting inside) are an invitation to come in and get cracking on a perfect bowl of wonton and noodle soup.

Crispy, skinned and exquisitely juicy chicken drizzled with dark soy and served beside chili-studded *nuoc cham* may be the closest local sib to the Hong Kong classic, presented here with a Vietnamese touch. Its textural interplay is as first-rate as the house specialty itself— a crispy fried shrimp-and-scallion roll wrapped in bean curd skin. Spice fiends can turn up the heat at home—their secret-recipe addictive sauces are for sale by the jar!

35

Brinkley's

B1

406 Broome St. (bet. Centre & Lafayette Sts.)

Subway: Spring St (Lafayette St.)   Lunch & dinner daily
Phone: 212-680-5600
Web: www.brinkleysnyc.com
Prices: $$

Brinkley's seems to be the provincial "pub" for everyone from students and hipsters to executives looking for a thirst quencher and bite after work. This easy and informal spot wears a boho-chic look with metallic stools lining a zinc-topped bar, a black-and-white checked floor, and burgundy leather booths. The team fits the casual, neighborhood feel of its vibrant yet rather noisy surroundings.

Find such straightforward delights as a grilled chicken salad with walnuts, grapes, and red onion in a shallot vinaigrette. Then, move on to a deliciously crusty lobster club filled with bacon and avocado, served with sweet potato fries. A taste of their moist bread pudding topped with whipped cream will ensure some very simple, homespun bliss.

Dim Sum Go Go 🎭

B3

5 East Broadway (at Chatham Sq.)

Subway: Canal St (Lafayette St.)   Lunch & dinner daily
Phone: 212-732-0797
Web: N/A
Prices: $$

Winning dim sum and crazy good Cantonese are the stars at this bi-level space. The rooms are dressed with contemporary touches like metal chairs, bright white walls, and geometric shaped tables. Speedy service ensures that ravenous appetites are quickly sated. Treat yourself to delectable dim sum day or night here—their vast array may induce torturous fits of indecision. Hunker down for steamer baskets of tender, almost opaque dough filled with bright pea shoots, sweet shrimp-and-chive, or fatty duck. Excellent pan-fried pork and vegetable dumplings are worth an order and baked roast pork buns are famous for good reason.

Be sure to include choices from their outstanding Cantonese menu with a unique variety and better quality than most of the neighbors.

Golden Unicorn

B3

Chinese 🍴

18 East Broadway (at Catherine St.)

Subway: Canal St (Lafayette St.)   Lunch & dinner daily
Phone: 212-941-0911
Web: www.goldenunicornrestaurant.com
Prices: $$

This age-old dim sum parlor, spread over many floors in an office building, is one of the few Cantonese spots that actually has the space and volume to necessitate its parade of steaming carts brimming with treats. While Golden Unicorn's system is very efficient and part of the spectacle, arrive early to nab a seat by the kitchen for better variety and hotter items. A helpful brigade of suited men and women roam the space to offer the likes of exquisitely soft roast pork buns, or congee with preserved egg and shredded pork. Buzzing with locals and visitors, it is also a favorite among families who appreciate the kid-friendly scene as much as the delectable, steamed pea shoot and shrimp dumplings, pork *siu mai*, and rice rolls stuffed with shrimp.

Grand Harmony

B2

Chinese 🍴

98 Mott St. (bet. Canal & Hester Sts.)

Subway: Canal St (Lafayette St.)   Lunch & dinner daily
Phone: 212-226-6603
Web: N/A
Prices: 🍜

With every seat filled before noon and dim sum carts roaming the sea of famished diners, Grand Harmony's expansive columned hall echoes the commotion of Chinatown. Naturally, they must be doing something right, so snag a seat upon arrival and flag those nimble women as they direct their carts through the labyrinth of tables.

Resting upon these coveted carts is a plethora of solid dim sum. Friendly servers parade the likes of beautifully crisp bean curd skin stuffed with vegetables, shrimp, and pork; congee studded with bits of dried fish and scallions; and juicy shrimp and chive dumplings all at an unbelievably good price. Leave room for what lies on the dessert cart, like fried sweet sesame balls or creamy coconut jelly to finish this feast.

Great N.Y. Noodletown

28 Bowery (at Bayard St.)

Subway: Canal St (Lafayette St.)
Phone: 212-349-0923
Web: N/A
Prices: 😊😊

Lunch & dinner daily

When heading to Great N.Y. Noodletown, invite plenty of dining companions to share those heaping plates of roasted meats and rice and noodle soups served at this bargain favorite. Locals stream in until the 4:00 A.M. closing bell for their great Cantonese fare—food is clearly the focus here, over the brusque service and unfussy atmosphere. Guests' gazes quickly pass over the imitation wooden chairs to the rest on the crispy skin of suckling pig and ducks hanging in the window.

These dishes are huge, so forgo the rice and opt instead for deliciously chewy noodles and barbecue meats. Incredible shrimp wontons, so delicate and thin, and the complex, homemade *e-fu* noodles demonstrate technique and quality to a standout level that is rarely rivaled.

Il Cortile

125 Mulberry St. (bet. Canal & Hester Sts.)

Subway: Canal St (Lafayette St.)
Phone: 212-226-6060
Web: www.ilcortile.com
Prices: $$

Lunch & dinner daily

Beyond this quaint and charming façade lies one of Little Italy's famed mainstays, ever-popular with dreamy eyed dates seeking the stuff of Billy Joel lyrics. The expansive space does indeed suggest a nostalgic romance, with its series of Mediterranean-themed rooms, though the most celebrated is the pleasant garden atrium (*il cortile* is Italian for courtyard), with a glass-paneled ceiling and abundant greenery.

A skilled line of chefs present a wide array of familiar starters and entrées, from eggplant *rollatini* to chicken Francese; as well as a range of pastas, such as *spaghettini puttanesca* or *risotto con funghi*. Several decades of sharing family recipes and bringing men to one bent knee continues to earn Il Cortile a longtime following.

Manhattan ▶ Chinatown & Little Italy

Il Palazzo

B1

Italian ✗✗

151 Mulberry St. (bet. Grand & Hester Sts.)

Subway: Canal St (Lafayette St.)
Phone: 212-343-7000
Web: N/A
Prices: $$

Lunch & dinner daily

A touristy crowd-pleaser, Il Palazzo is mecca for red-sauce signatures served with flair. The "palatial" space features a nice front dining room that leads to a very inviting glass-enclosed garden flooded with windows and natural light. The décor feels throwback to old-school Little Italy.

While its neighbors have moved to the boroughs, Il Palazzo continues to loom large thanks to competent service and good, satisfying food. Bread dunked in olive oil is tasty, but leave extra room for gargantuan artichokes stuffed with mozzarella and garlic—a bomb of flavor and *abbondanza*. *Pappardelle alla casalinga* tossed with porcinis and prosciutto will draw everyone's fork for a twirl, so don't bother with half portions. Go for the whole shebang.

La Esquina

B1

Mexican ✗

114 Kenmare St. (bet. Cleveland Pl. & Lafayette St.)

Subway: Spring St (Lafayette St.)
Phone: 646-613-7100
Web: www.esquinanyc.com
Prices: $$

Lunch & dinner daily

When La Esquina opened it was a breath of bright air, offering enjoyably fresh cuisine that stood tall among the paltry selection of Manhattan Mexican. Thankfully, the city's south-of-the-border dining scene has evolved since then. However, La Esquina remains a worthy option. More playground than restaurant, the multi-faceted setting takes up an iconic downtown corner and draws a hip crowd to the grab and go taqueria, 30-seat café, and lively subterranean dining room and bar amplified by a nightly DJ soundtrack.

The spirit here is not just alive but kicking with classic renditions of tortilla soup; *mole negro enchiladas* filled with excellently seasoned chicken; as well the likes of *carne asada* starring black Angus sirloin with *mojo de ajo*.

New Malaysia

C2

46-48 Bowery (bet. Bayard & Canal Sts.)

Subway: Canal St (Lafayette St.)
Phone: 212-964-0284
Web: N/A
Prices: ☞

Lunch & dinner daily

Mad for Malaysian? Head to this lively dive, sequestered in a Chinatown arcade. Proffering some of the best Malaysian treats in town, including all the classics, New Malaysia sees a deluge of regulars who pour in for a massive offering of exceptional dishes. Round tables cram a room furnished with little more than a service counter. Still, the aromas wafting from flaky *roti canai* and Melaka crispy coconut shrimp keep you focused on the food.

Capturing the essence of this region are fast (brusque?) servers who deliver abundant yet authentic bowls of spicy-sour *asam laksa* fragrant with lemongrass; *kang-kung belacan*, greens infused with dried shrimp and chili; and *nasi lemak*, the national treasure starring coconut rice, chicken curry, and dried anchovies.

Nom Wah Tea Parlor

B3

13 Doyers St. (bet. Bowery & Pell St.)

Subway: Canal St (Lafayette St.)
Phone: 212-962-6047
Web: www.nomwah.com
Prices: ☞

Lunch & dinner daily

Even after a renovation, this "parlor" continues to thrive as a retro dive replete with truly awful service. But keep reading, because the supremely delicious food and unreal value more than make up for Nom Wah's many flaws.

Dim sum is the main draw at this busy neighborhood diner, where small groups fill the dining counter and pack into pleather booths for the likes of pan-fried dumplings stuffed with ground pork and sweet shrimp. Scallion pancakes flaunt outstanding texture; fried shrimp wrapped in bean curd unites top product with heavenly flavor; and noodles sautéed with superior soy is a salt fiends dream. Bring hungry friends and expect lots of leftovers, because the simple pleasures here have been known to thrill even the most ardent epicurean.

Nyonya ⓦ

Malaysian ☓

199 Grand St. (bet. Mott & Mulberry Sts.)

Subway: Canal St (Lafayette St.)　　　　　Lunch & dinner daily
Phone: 212-334-3669
Web: www.ilovenyonya.com
Prices: $$

Nyonya prides itself with a comfortable setting composed of brick walls and wood tables, but everyone's really here for the food, which is always on the money. The adept staff is eager to steer you through the varied menu—and sometimes even away from such daring and delicious dishes as *asam laksa*, an exceptionally spiced and intensely sour broth floating with lemongrass, ground fish, and thick, round noodles.

Asians and other hungry locals pack this haunt for seemingly simple yet deeply satisfying items like *achat* (pickled vegetables tossed with turmeric and peanuts); *mee siam* (noodles stir-fried with tofu, eggs, and shrimp in a chili sauce); or pungent beef *rendang*. Crispy prawns garnished with curry-infused toasted coconut are nothing short of wow!

Oriental Garden

Chinese ☓

14 Elizabeth St. (bet. Bayard & Canal Sts.)

Subway: Canal St (Lafayette St.)　　　　　Lunch & dinner daily
Phone: 212-619-0085
Web: www.orientalgardenny.com
Prices: $$

A daily destination for dim sum, Oriental Garden is a treasure among tourists, foodies, and wealthy Chinese residents. The place is known to get packed as crowds pour in for top-notch dumplings, whose prices seem to escalate with its popularity. So, be sure to reserve ahead for a seat in this group-friendly den, decked with kitschy fish tanks and food photo-covered menus boasting delicious dim sum.

Set menus are widely appealing and have been known to unveil such tasty crowd-pleasers as steamed watercress and pork dumplings; crispy fried shrimp wontons; and crab claws. Equally worthy (read: safe) options include a duo of lettuce wraps with minced duck and pork served with hoisin; or one massive oyster cooked in its shell with classic black bean sauce.

Parigot

B1

155 Grand St. (at Lafayette St.)

Subway: Canal St (Lafayette St.)   Lunch & dinner daily
Phone: 212-274-8859
Web: N/A
Prices: $$

Parigot is a *trés* charming bistro on (now mega trendy) Grand Street. Owned and operated by Chef Michel Pombet and partner, Catherine Amsellem, the French cooking is classic yet fine-tuned for its downtown crowd. However, the warm, time-worn décor stays true to its roots. Tables are topped with paper and crayons to entertain the kids in tow.

Service is adept, and locals seem to feel their *joie de vivre* as the place is always abuzz. The vast, straightforward, and hearty menu is an equal draw with exquisitely rich onion soup bobbing beneath sliced *croûtes* and melted cheese. The superb duck confit is set over a sautéed mushrooms, haricot verts, and salsify. Pâté is wonderously pork-y, rich, perfectly seasoned, and paired with grilled country bread.

Peking Duck House

B2

28 Mott St. (bet. Chatham Sq. & Pell St.)

Subway: Canal St (Lafayette St.)   Lunch & dinner daily
Phone: 212-227-1810
Web: www.pekingduckhousenyc.com
Prices: $$

Only rookies open the menu at Peter Luger steakhouse—and the same ought to apply to any restaurant named after a menu item. So, while you may stumble onto a few gems like the sautéed string beans with minced pork, the bird is the word at this convivial and group-friendly joint.

Despite its rather odd name, the Peking Duck House is a touch classier than her Chinatown sisters, with a contemporary polish that won't frighten your Midwestern cousin. Service may slow down at the more elegant midtown location, but both wheel out the golden brown duck with proper flare, and carve it into crisp-skinned mouthwatering slices. Your job is easy: fold into fresh pancakes, sprinkle with scallion, cucumbers, and a dash of hoisin sauce...then devour.

Pho Băng

C1

Vietnamese ✗

157 Mott St. (bet. Broome & Grand Sts.)

Subway: Bowery
Phone: 212-966-3797
Web: N/A
Prices: 👛

Lunch & dinner daily

Hangover? Craving? In need of a quick, tasty meal? Pho Băng is where it's at for restorative bowls of bubbling *pho*, served up in a flash and on the cheap. Park it in the simple space and start with a plate of delicious fried Vietnamese spring rolls (*cha gio*) served with lettuce and mint leaves for wrapping; or try the tasty rice "crêpe" (*bahn cuon nhan thit cha lua*) stuffed with black mushrooms, pork, sprouts, and ham—a real treat and rare find here in New York, so don't skip it.

Finally, follow the lead of your fellow diners and slurp up one of seventeen varieties of hearty *pho*. Try the *pho tai gau*—fresh eye of round plus brisket and rice noodles in a flavorful beef broth, served with sprouts, basil, and lemon, all for less than eight bucks.

Royal Seafood

B2

Chinese ✗

103 Mott St. (bet. Canal & Hester Sts.)

Subway: Canal St (Lafayette St.)
Phone: 212-219-2338
Web: N/A
Prices: 👛

Lunch & dinner daily

Bright, chaotic, and jam-packed with a multi-generational Chinese crowd, this well-priced favorite has dim sum lovers lined up and waiting in droves. Dinnertime brings a quieter vibe, along with an extensive Cantonese menu. The sizable room is decked with round tables draped in pink linens and kitschy Chinese touches. This communal scene has friends and strangers alike dining side by side.

Join the masses and feast on the likes of steamed dumplings, nicely crafted and filled with mushrooms, vegetables, ground pork and peanut, or seafood and greens. The shrimp wrapped in yellow bean curd skin are crisply fried, not at all greasy, and completely delicious. Pan-fried wontons are thin and delicate yet exploding with flavor from garlic and chives.

Shanghai Café 😊

Chinese ✗

B2

100 Mott St. (bet. Canal & Hester Sts.)

Subway: Canal St (Lafayette St.)
Phone: 212-966-3988
Web: N/A
Prices: 😊😊

Lunch & dinner daily

This quirky café is a Chinatown stalwart. Busy booths line one wall, while big round tables are popular for gathering families. Note the dumpling station upfront, where agile chefs assemble their mouthwatering parcels.

Regulars know to arrive early for lunch to make the most of their vast menu, appetizing to vegetarians and omnivores alike. Servers are remarkably capable, balancing trays of addictive steamed juicy buns and cold dried bean curd, or soft rice cakes stir-fried with chicken and shrimp. The "queen" mushroom is sized for a king, its thick slices cooked until tender and bathed in an umami-rich brown sauce. The salty pork slices and fresh, crunchy bamboo shoots arrive in a broth so nourishing that you will slurp to the last drop.

Shanghai Heping

Chinese ✗✗

B2

104 Mott St. (bet. Canal and Hester Sts.)

Subway: Canal St (Lafayette St.)
Phone: 212-925-1118
Web: N/A
Prices: $$

Lunch & dinner daily

Head downtown to fully appreciate the swank Shanghai Heping—a stylish and contemporary restaurant decked out in lime green accents, faux-granite tabletops, and tiled floors. Friendly staff and a proficient chef ensure tasty renditions of Shanghainese dishes.

Quality ingredients and great skill shine through menu items like chilled and crunchy-salty bamboo shoots braised in a soy-based brown sauce abundant with Chinese spices; and knots of chewy tofu skin stewed with pork belly cubes in a rich, velvety sauce, wonderfully flavored with cloves, star anise, and ginger. Large slices of green opo squash (long gourd) sautéed in garlic sauce are so tender, delicate, and simply tasty that you might just see them atop every table in the house.

Thái Sơn

B2

V i e t n a m e s e ✗

89 Baxter St. (bet. Bayard & Canal Sts.)

Subway: Canal St (Lafayette St.) Lunch & dinner daily
Phone: 212-732-2822
Web: N/A
Prices: 🥜

Thái Sơn is by far the best of the bunch in this Vietnamese quarter of Chinatown. It's neither massive nor fancy, but it's bright, clean, and perpetually in business. One peek at the specials on the walls (maybe golden-fried squid strewn with sea salt) will have you begging for a seat in the crammed room.

Speedy servers scoot between groups of City Hall suits and Asian locals as they order the likes of *cha gio*, pork spring rolls with *nuac cham*; or *goi cuon*, fantastic summer rolls filled with poached shrimp and vermicelli. Naturally, *pho* choices are abundant, but the real star of the show is *pho tai*—where raw beef shavings are cooked to tender perfection when combined with a scalding hot, savory broth replete with herbs, sprouts, and chewy noodles.

Xe Lua

B2

V i e t n a m e s e ✗

86 Mulberry St. (bet. Bayard & Canal Sts.)

Subway: Canal St (Lafayette St.) Lunch & dinner daily
Phone: 212-577-8887
Web: www.xeluarestaurantnyc.com
Prices: 🥜

For fantastic Vietnamese food, make your way into Xe Lua. Their décor features a basic Southeast Asian tropical theme, but chopstick tins, soup spoons, and enticing condiments decorate the table and return all focus to the food—which is always a winner and delivered at wonderful value.

Efficient servers speed around regulars and suits, but keep your eyes fixed on the laminated menu brimming with pictures. Fried spring rolls (*cha gio*) with ground pork served with lettuce, mint, and *nuoc cham*; or *goi du du*, a spicy papaya salad tossing carrots and cashews in a salty dressing exemplify their tasty repute. *Pho tai* elicits gratified sighs, served as a steaming bowl of spiced beef broth bobbing with noodles, thinly sliced beef, and crunchy bean sprouts.

East Village

Long regarded as the capital of counter-culture, the East Village has been home to squatters, rioters, and was a shadier incarnation of Tompkin's Square Park. But today, it is safer, cleaner, and livable. Cheap walk-ups sheltering aspiring musicians and models may be a thing of the past, but its revitalization hasn't resulted in a downturn in self-expression or creativity. Reflecting the independent, outspoken spirit for which this 'hood is known, the East Village offers an utterly distinctive dining landscape.

CHEAP EATS

Budget-friendly bites abound in these parts. Family-run **Veselka**, located in the heart of this neighborhood, has been serving traditional Ukrainian specialties for over 60-years, representing the area's former eastern European population. After a night of bar-hopping and other mischief, grab a restorative hit of salt and fat at **Pomme Frites**, where double-cooked Belgian fries are heightened by black truffle mayo; or at **Crif Dogs** for a deep-fried hot dog served until 4:00 A.M.

ONE HIT WONDERS

A number of food-related endeavors are the product of laser-focused culinary inspiration. **Porchetta** is a smash for its rendition of crackling-skinned pork sandwiches. Meanwhile, **The Nugget Spot**, rolled out by Chef/owner Jason Hairston, fries up crunchy morsels of chicken, pork, and fish. Find these iconic, crisp, and comforting bites served up with such outstanding sauces as the "Shhh" for instance—a secret creation with a near-cultish following. **S'mac** is known for lip-smacking variations of everyone's favorite comfort food,

mac n cheese; and **Luke's Lobster** has expanded into a city-wide network offering rolls stuffed with crustaceans fresh from Maine. For ramen, Japanese-import **Ippudo** doles out steaming bowlfuls in a raucous setting. In need of cheese? The creamy slice that started a sensation can be found at **Artichoke Pizza** on 14th Street. Drawing incognito celebrities for pots of fondue, **The Bourgeois Pig** prepares a fantastic range of fromage; while **East Village Cheese** boasts a quality selection without the gourmet shop mark-up.

A TASTE OF ASIA

The sensory assault around St. Mark's Place offers an immersion in Asian flavors that is delightfully kitschy and incredibly worthwhile. Duck into **Boka** for Korean fried chicken or follow the scent of *takoyaki* frying and sizzling *okonomiyaki* at **Otafuku**. Look for the red paper lanterns of hip *yakitori* spots like **Taisho**; or keep your taste buds tingling at divey *izakayas* like **Village Yokocho**. Among this area's sultry sake dens, none rival the outrageous offering at subterranean **Decibel**.

A SWEET SIDE

Badass 'tude and savory dishes aside, the East Village also has a deliciously sweet side. **Moishe's Bake Shop** is a Kosher treat where challah, rugelach, and light-as-air marble sponge cake have been prepared since 1978. Established in 1894, **Veniero's Pasticceria & Caffé** offers another taste of the Old World. This friendly staple draws long lines, especially around holiday time, for traditional Italian baked goods. David Chang's dessert darling, **Momofuku Milk Bar**, turns out a spectrum of insanely unique takes on dessert (imagine the likes of pastrami

a listing of creamy indulgences together with frozen pops perfect for summertime.

COCKTAIL HOUR

The craft cocktail movement has taken firm root in this capital of "cool," where a number of subtly (and even undisclosed) locations offer an epicurean approach to mixology. **Death & Co.** is a dimly lit lair on East 6th, but if this hot-as-hell spot is packed, seek out the secret passageway inside **Crif Dogs** to access **PDT** or Please Don't Tell—where cocktail connoisseurs rave over Benton's Old-Fashioned made with bacon-infused bourbon and maple syrup. Cached behind a wall in a Japanese restaurant, **Angel's Share's** natty bartenders shake and stir for a civilized crowd. **Mayahuel's** mescal- and tequila-based creations offer a south-of-the-border spin, whereas **Pouring Ribbons**, a

pockets or "Compost" cookies) as well as soft-serve ice cream in seasonal flavors. **Big Gay Ice Cream** started life as a truck with a name that's hard to forget, but has gone brick and mortar near Tompkins Square Park (and now in the West Village as well). Junkies come here for signatures

including the Salty Pimp or Bea Arthur—a swirl of vanilla, *dulche de leche*, and crushed Nilla wafers. Finally, no self-respecting local can forget about **Puddin'**, an unlikely success that peddles

second-floor lounge, has a list devoted to vintage Chartreuse. For *vino*, **Terroir** is a wine geek's dream run by Hearth partners Chef Marco Canora and sommelier Paul Grieco.

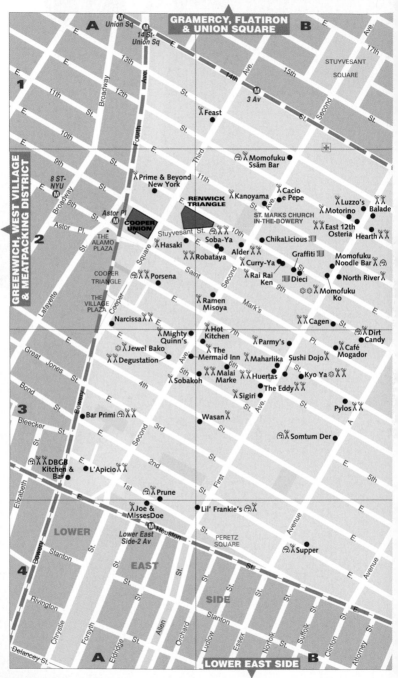

A   Union Sq   B

14 St-
Union Sq

STUYVESANT
SQUARE

E. 17th St.
E. 15th St.
E. 14th St.
3 Av

E. 13th St.
E. 12th St.
E. 11th St.
E. 10th St.
Broadway
Fourth Ave.
Second Ave.

1

Feast

Momofuku
Ssäm Bar

GREENWICH, WEST VILLAGE & MEATPACKING DISTRICT

8 ST-
NYU

Prime & Beyond
New York

RENWICK
TRIANGLE

Kanoyama   Cacio
e Pepe

Luzzo's
Motorino   Balade

Astor Pl

COOPER
UNION

ST. MARKS CHURCH
IN-THE-BOWERY

East 12th
Osteria   Hearth

THE
ALAMO
PLAZA

Astor Pl.

Hasaki

Stuyvesant St.

Soba-Ya

Alder

ChikaLicious

2

COOPER
TRIANGLE

Porsena

Robataya

Curry-Ya

Graffiti

Momofuku
Noodle Bar

THE
VILLAGE
PLAZA

Saint

Rai Rai
Ken

Dieci

North River

Momofuku
Ko

Lafayette
Cooper
Square

Narcissa

Ramen
Misoya

Mark's

Cagen

Mighty
Quinn's

Hot
Kitchen

Parmy's

Dirt
Candy

Great   Jones   St.

Jewel Bako

The
Mermaid Inn

Maharlika

Sushi Dojo

Café
Mogador

Degustation

Malai
Marke

Huertas

Kyo Ya

Bond   St.

Sobakoh

Sigiri

The Eddy

3

Bar Primi

Wasan

Pylos

Bleecker   St.

Somtum Der

DBGB
Kitchen &
Bar

L'Apicio

Elizabeth
Bowery

Prune

Lil' Frankie's

Joe &
MissesDoe

LOWER

Houston

Lower East
Side-2 Av

PERETZ
SQUARE

Avenue

EAST

Supper

4

Stanton

SIDE

Rivington

Chrystie   Forsyth   Eldridge   Allen   Orchard   Ludlow   Essex   Norfolk   Suffolk   Clinton   Attorney

Delancey St.

A   Stanton   B

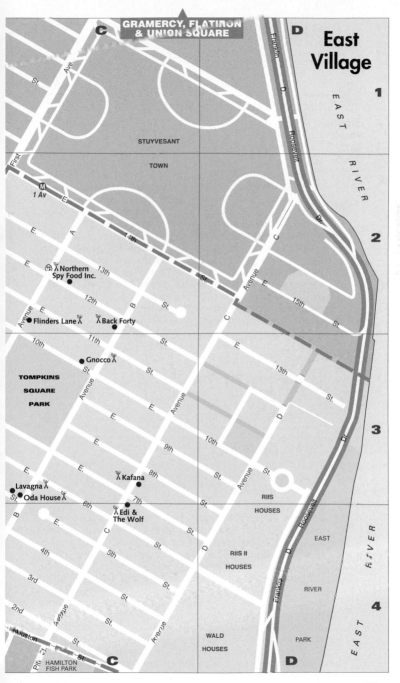

East Village

GRAMERCY, FLATIRON & UNION SQUARE

STUYVESANT
TOWN

EAST
RIVER

M 1 Av

Northern Spy Food Inc.

Flinders Lane   Back Forty

Gnocco

TOMPKINS
SQUARE
PARK

Kafana

Lavagna
Oda House

Edi &
The Wolf

RIIS
HOUSES

RIIS II
HOUSES

EAST

RIVER

WALD
HOUSES

PARK

EAST RIVER

HAMILTON
FISH PARK

Alder

B2

157 Second Ave. (bet. 9th & 10th Sts.)

Subway: Astor Pl
Phone: 212-539-1900
Web: www.aldernyc.com
Prices: $$

Lunch Sun
Dinner nightly

Celebrated Chef Wylie Dufresne's latest venture brings modernism to the hip heart of downtown. After opening to much fanfare, it's still loud, crammed, and enthusiastic, but far easier to get a seat at the attractive bar or table reservation. In short, Alder is a destination for foodies of every age.

It is also a place for adventurous palates seeking cuisine that is unabashedly contemporary—though it can be just plain weird or unbalanced at times. The kitchen exemplifies creativity in perfectly cooked and expertly seasoned sea scallops set atop a winter-vegetable ragout mixed with grains, offering an immaculate contrast of textures and flavors. For dessert, try a carrot cake-meets-sundae, with clumps of cake, cream cheese ice cream, and candied pecans.

Back Forty

C2

190 Ave. B (at 12th St.)

Subway: 1 Av
Phone: 212-388-1990
Web: www.backfortynyc.com
Prices: $$

Lunch Sat – Sun
Dinner nightly

Chef/owner Peter Hoffman sates city slickers seeking the country life with this popular tavern's array of fresh-from-the-farm themed preparations. The casual setting evokes heartland charm with tables topped by brown paper mats displaying the menu, walls adorned with found objects and agricultural tools, as well as an inviting backyard dining area.

Though it's billed as a grass-fed burger joint, the menu offers much more than spicy homemade ketchup. Starters feature garden-fresh ingredients; while seasonality and sustainability drives the rest of the menu with the likes of Catskill trout *a la plancha* and East Coast hake with local clams and salsa verde. The SoHo location resides at the corner previously occupied by Savoy (also from the same chef).

Balade

B2

Lebanese ✗✗

208 First Ave. (bet. 12th & 13th Sts.)

Subway: 1 Av
Phone: 212-529-6868
Web: www.baladerestaurants.com
Prices: ☜☜

Lunch & dinner daily

Honing in on the cuisine of Lebanon, Balade is a welcoming and tasty Middle Eastern experience fronted by a cheerful red awning. The spotless room is accented with tile, brick, and wood; and each table bears a bottle of private label herb-infused olive oil.

The menu begins with a glossary of traditional Lebanese ingredients and the explanation that *Balade* means "fresh, local." The meze; grilled meat-stuffed sandwiches; and Lebanese-style pizzas called *manakeesh* topped with the likes of lean ground beef, chopped onion, and spices are all fresh-tasting indeed. House specialties are also of note, like the *mujaddara crush*—a platter of lentils and rice topped with crispy fried onions as well as a salad of cool, chopped cucumber and tomato.

Bar Primi ☺

A3

Italian ✗✗

325 Bowery (at 2nd St.)

Subway: Bleecker St
Phone: 212-220-9100
Web: www.barprimi.com
Prices: $$

Lunch & dinner daily

Chef Andrew Carmellini has added this pasta-centric trattoria to his clutch of inspired operations. A tomato-red awning highlights the two-floor space designed by Taavo Somer, which features whitewashed brick walls, tawny leather banquettes, and a communal table topped with terra cotta pots of greenery.

Bensonhurst-native Chef Sal Lamboglia uses first rate ingredients to produce two categories of toothsome strands and shapes. Traditional preparations bring the likes of bucatini with lamb *all'Amatriciana*; while seasonal inspiration includes *fiore di carciofi*, a coiled tube of artichoke cream, dressed with diced fatty bacon and pecorino. The menu is bolstered by small plates like fontina-stuffed meatballs in a thick *sugo* as well as rotating daily specials.

Cacio e Pepe

Italian 🍴

182 Second Ave. (bet. 11th & 12th Sts.)

Subway: 3 Av   Dinner nightly
Phone: 212-505-5931
Web: www.cacioepepe.com
Prices: $$

With its subdued temperament and pleasant service, this casual and charming Italian *gioia* can be trusted to satisfy, from the warm greeting everyone receives upon entering right down to the cannoli—a lovely finale to any meal here. The rustic menu of traditional Roman dishes features a house specialty from which the establishment takes its name: homemade *tonnarelli* tossed with pasta water, olive oil, cracked black pepper, and a showering of pecorino. Yet there is much more to be discovered, such as cuttlefish over soft polenta or *bucatini all'Amatriciana.*

The wine list is short but carefully selected to highlight less-familiar producers in the most notable Italian regions. In warm weather, the pretty backyard garden makes for an idyllic dining area.

Café Mogador

Moroccan 🍴

101 St. Mark's Pl. (bet. First Ave. & Ave. A)

Subway: 1 Av   Lunch & dinner daily
Phone: 212-677-2226
Web: www.cafemogador.com
Prices:

The key to Café Mogador's longterm success is its popular array of tasty, crowd-pleasing Moroccan favorites. Open from morning to night, breakfast offers the likes of Middle Eastern eggs, any style, with sides of hummus and *tabouli*. Lunch adds heartier fare like a grilled chicken kebob with tart pickles and tahini-slicked Arabic salad stuffed into a warm and tender pita, served with French fries. Dinner focuses on Moroccan specialties like *bastilla*, grilled *merguez*, and meatball tagine with saffron sauce and couscous.

Opened back in 1983, Café Mogador continues to thrive and has recently received a fresh coat of paint to brighten the laid-back, coffee-house setting.

A second outpost of this beloved café is flourishing in Williamsburg.

Cagen

B2

Japanese 〉〈〉〈

414 E. 9th St. (bet. Ave. A & First Ave.)

Subway: Astor Pl Dinner Tue – Sun
Phone: 212-358-8800
Web: www.cagenrestaurant.com
Prices: $$$

Chef Toshio Tomita has set up shop at Kajitsu's former address. This minimally altered dining room is quiet and serene, with an 8-seat counter offering the finest seats in the house.

Omakase is the best way to get introduced to Chef Tomita's talents. Assorted nibbles set up the arrival of superb sashimi. Beautifully knifed slices sparkle brighter when dressed with wasabi grated over shark skin, reduced soy sauce, and bright *chimichurri*—a touch of fusion that signals the chef's 16 years working for Nobu. Next up is the fantastic soba made from hand-ground, Japanese buckwheat and followed by a shot of warm *soba-yu* (cooking liquid). A fried dish, say King crab tempura with jalapeño mayonnaise, grilled fish, and sushi concludes this repast.

ChikaLicious

B2

Contemporary 〉〈〉〈

203 E. 10th St. (bet. First & Second Aves.)

Subway: Astor Pl Dinner Thu – Sun
Phone: 212-475-0929
Web: www.chikalicious.com
Prices: ⊖⊖

Named for Pastry Chef/owner Chika Tillman, this sweet spot presents an all-encompassing dessert experience that somehow manages to impress without overkill. The chic white space offers counter seating overlooking a lab-clean kitchen where the team prepares elegant jewels that start as butter, sugar, and chocolate. À la carte is offered, but the best way to appreciate this dessert bar is to select the prix-fixe. Feasts here may begin with an amuse-bouche of Darjeeling tea gelée with milk sorbet; followed by a mascarpone semifreddo topped with espresso granita. Then finish with pillowy cubes of coconut-marshmallow *petits fours*.

Dessert Club across the street tempts with delish cookies, cupcakes, and shaved ice for a grab-and-go fix.

Curry-Ya

B2

Japanese ✗

214 E. 10th St. (bet. First & Second Aves.)

Subway: Astor Pl

Phone: 866-602-8779

Web: www.nycurry-ya.com

Prices: 🍜

Lunch & dinner daily

Complex, warming, and perfumed with fruity sweetness, slow-cooked *wafuu* (or Japanese-style) curry is a highly popular national treat. Tantalizingly draped over a mound of steamed short grain rice, each bowl calls for one of the kitchen's tasty embellishments such as panko-crusted fried shrimp, pan-fried hamburger steak, Berkshire pork, or chicken *katsu*. The brief menu also offers inspiring starters like flavor-packed tofu skin or green bean salad tossed with Parmesan and a crushed-olive dressing.

Brought to you by Bon Yagi (also of Rai Rai Ken, a few doors away), this local jewel has 14-seats along a white marble counter lined with bowls of pickles and dried onion flakes. The space may seem simple but it's a spectacular destination to dig in and enjoy.

DBGB Kitchen & Bar 😋

A3

French ✗✗

299 Bowery (bet. First & Houston Sts.)

Subway: Lower East Side - 2 Av

Phone: 212-933-5300

Web: www.dbgb.com

Prices: $$

Lunch & dinner daily

Über chef, Daniel Boulud, shakes off some of his signature upmarket panache with this downtown favorite. The fun-for-all brasserie joins a lively bar area to a rear dining room, open kitchen, and chef's table. The space recalls the Bowery's history as a hub for restaurant supplies: dry goods are prominently shelved, bathroom walls are papered with vintage cookware catalogs, and gleaming copper pots (engraved with the names of famed French chefs) are on display.

Luxe burgers and a globally inspired lineup of house-made sausages are all popular. But go on to explore other dishes like the lunch prix-fixe offering decadent country pâté, ricotta and spinach ravioli in Vermont veal Bolognese, as well as a lemon bar with meringue bits and blueberry sorbet.

Degustation

Spanish 🍴

A3

239 E. 5th St. (bet. Second & Third Aves.)

Subway: Astor Pl

Phone: 212-979-1012

Web: www.degustation-nyc.com

Prices: $$

Dinner nightly

With its slate-tiled walls and cozy lighting, this well-loved tapas bar is of the most elegant degree—and a romantic escape from the fray for couples on date night. Counter seating surrounds the spotless and very serious kitchen of Chef Nicholas Licata, and dapper proprietor Jack Lamb is a colorful presence.

The skillfully rendered and enticingly presented small plates are ever-evolving. Expect hot and crunchy *croquetas* oozing with mushroom-infused cream; or zesty *boquerones* dressed with yuzu peel and breadcrumbs. Sunchokes are roasted whole and sent forth with pumpernickel "soil" and an addictive mound of "funyons." For a fantastic finale, cubes of seared pineapple are composed with white chocolate sponge cake and intensely green lime granita.

Dieci

Fusion

B2

228 E. 10th St. (bet. First & Second Aves.)

Subway: Astor Pl

Phone: 212-387-9545

Web: www.dieciny.com

Prices: $$

Dinner nightly

Dieci fuses Italian and Japanese cuisines for a successful marriage of taste and creativity. Springy ramen clutching spicy lamb Bolognese is a perfect example of this flavorful union. The tiny step-down setting is easy to miss but conquers its spatial challenge with comfortable seats. Find foodies centered around a dining counter that juts out from the kitchen; a handful of small tables also bolster the accommodations.

A unique array of small plates includes buffalo mozzarella with uni and yuzu foam, and steamed buns filled with Berkshire pork belly. Meanwhile, entrées go on to include miso-glazed cod set atop an appealing wild mushroom risotto fortified by a poached egg. Desserts are equally impressive, as in a silky Earl Grey crème brûlée.

Dirt Candy ⊛

B3

Vegetarian ✗

430 E. 9th St. (bet. First Ave. & Ave. A)

Subway: 1 Av
Phone: 212-228-7732
Web: www.dirtcandynyc.com
Prices: $$

Dinner Tue – Sat

From her vantage point behind the line, Chef/owner Amanda Cohen keeps a watchful eye on every one of her 18 guests as she skillfully crafts vegetarian fare for a voracious crowd of followers. The room is tiny, but attractively designed with sustainability in mind.

Devotees and skeptics alike can't help but find Dirt Candy's meatless menu intriguing and downright tasty. An entrée simply titled "Beans" brings semi-firm tofu poached in coconut milk, topped by a pyramid of al dente long beans, tempura sea beans, and spiced coconut milk sauce. Meanwhile, "Cauliflower" reveals battered florets arranged on a tender waffle with horseradish-spiked buttermilk sauce. Eggplant ingeniously finds its way into a tiramisu embellished with rosemary cotton candy.

East 12th Osteria

B2

Italian ✗✗

197 First Ave. (at 12th St.)

Subway: 1 Av
Phone: 212-432-1112
Web: www.east12osteria.com
Prices: $$

Lunch Sat – Sun
Dinner nightly

On the one hand, this is a straightforward little corner trattoria. On the other, Chef Roberto Deiaco's exciting cooking is a delicious presentation of Italian tastes and technique. The front of house is run by the chef's wife, who lends a personal and intimate air that's hard to fake and increasingly rare. The room glows with good vibes that radiate across the hardwood floor, marble bar, and tin ceiling.

Contemporary highlights accent the Northern Italian-focused menu of *fritto di mare* neatly piling hot and delicately crisp calamari, red mullet, jumbo shrimp and a zucchini blossom. *Tagliolini all'uovo* is twirled with basil pesto, *ricotta salata*, and black truffle; and slowly braised veal cheeks is coddled with *pinot bianco gremolata* sauce and polenta.

The Eddy

B3   Contemporary ✕✕

342 E. 6th St. (bet First & Second Aves.)

Subway: 2 Av   Dinner nightly
Phone: 646-895-9884
Web: www.theeddynyc.com
Prices: $$

If this innovative arrival is any indication, Curry Row could become the city's newest restaurant strip. Headlined by Chef Brendan McHale, formerly of Jack's Oyster Bar, the wee bistro is defined by a serious bar and well-managed dining area.

The Eddy's menu defies easy categorization and offers cleverly constructed cooking. Fried beef tendons are a puffed and crunchy snack dabbed with charred onion cream and sweet trout roe. Delicate ricotta gnocchi with toasted hazelnuts showcases spring's sweet peas and pickled ramps, while golden spotted tile fish is seared and plated with squid ink hollandaise, saffron broth, rice beans, and braised artichokes. Cardamom panna cotta with rhubarb granita and olive oil relays the menu's spirit to the finish line.

Edi & The Wolf

C4   Austrian ✕

102 Ave. C (bet. 6th & 7th Sts.)

Subway: 1 Av   Lunch Sat – Sun
Phone: 212-598-1040   Dinner nightly
Web: www.ediandthewolf.com
Prices: $$

Chefs Eduard Frauneder and Wolfgang Ban, the dynamic duo behind Seäsonal, have brought their wares downtown with this *heuriger*—a casual neighborhood wine tavern popular throughout Austria. The dark and earthy den is chock-full of reclaimed materials including a 40-foot rope salvaged from a church, now culled above the tiny bar.

The crux of the offerings is comprised of small and shared plates such as cured and dried *landjäger* sausage, accompanied by house-made mustard and pickles. Entrées fall under the heading of "schnitzel & co." and offer a highly recommended wiener schnitzel, which starts with a pounded filet of heritage pork encased in an incredibly delicate and crunchy coating, finished with an Austrian-style potato salad and lingonberry jam.

Feast

B1

102 Third Ave. (bet. 12th & 13th Sts.)

Subway: 3 Av
Phone: 212-529-8880
Web: www.eatfeastnyc.com
Prices: $$

Lunch Sat – Sun
Dinner Mon – Sat

This recent arrival with the straightforward but promising moniker is a rustic, textbook amalgam of wood, brick, and tiles.

The kitchen is confidently led by an alum of Veritas who has devised several prix-fixe menus, served family style. These might be based on the farmer's market or even a nose-to-tail meal of lamb, including merguez stew; and a lasagna layering shank, broccoli rabe, and goat cheese. If you're not up for a whole feast, dine à la carte on meaty, ocean-fresh oysters capped by cocktail sauce aspic; or a *nouveau* take on incredibly tender chicken and "dumplings" of liver-stuffed pan-fried gnocchi and wisps of crisped skin. End with the awesome Valrhona chocolate pudding—leaving a single dark chocolate cookie crumb behind is impossible.

Flinders Lane

C2

162 Ave. A (bet. 10th & 11th Sts.)

Subway: 1 Av
Phone: 212-228-6900
Web: www.flinderslane-nyc.com
Prices: $$

Dinner nightly

Two Melbourne natives bring Australian dining to the East Village with this whimsical bistro. Flinders Lane hosts a convivial set in a petite room that's trademark downtown, with its mix of industrial and rustic touches.

A strong Asian accent is woven throughout the menu, which also hails inspiration from Australia's Greek and Italian immigrants. Moist seaweed combined with avocado, snake beans, and roasted red pepper is a pop of flavors, brightened by a soy sauce- and toasted sesame oil-dressing. Grilled naan with *tandoori*-style rabbit is especially tasty thanks to its marinade of spiced yogurt and quick-pickled green mango garnish. And for as refreshing a dessert as you're likely to ever come across, order the coconut jelly with watermelon.

Gnocco

C3

Italian ✕

337 E. 10th St. (bet. Aves. A & B)

Subway: 1 Av
Phone: 212-677-1913
Web: www.gnocco.com
Prices: $$

Lunch Sat – Sun
Dinner nightly

This charming, mural-lined Alphabet City trattoria lies across from Tompkins Square Park and its panoply of activity— youngsters shooting hoops, strolling dog-walkers, and local characters overcome by the urge to express themselves.

The namesake *gnocco* are crispy, deep-fried pillows of dough served with a platter of shaved Italian meats. That might be prelude to a thin-crusted pizza; house-made whole-wheat *tubetti integrale* tossed with chickpeas, cherry tomatoes, and diced smoked pancetta; or pork loin braised in milk with rosemary and garlic. After such a hearty meal, a light homespun finish is in order as in a plate of freshly baked almond *cantucci* paired with a glass of chilled *vin santo*.

The shaded back terrace is a popular hangout come summer.

Graffiti

B2

Contemporary

224 E. 10th St. (bet. First & Second Aves.)

Subway: 1 Av
Phone: 212-464-7743
Web: www.graffitinyc.com
Prices: $$

Dinner Tue – Sat

Credibly doted on since it's inception in 2007, this cub of Chef/owner Jehangir Mehta is still going strong and baby boy is quite the dreamboat. Dressed with tightly-packed square communal tables and beaded ceiling lights, petite Graffiti may be dimly lit, but an exposed brick wall glossed with a metallic finish and hugging framed mirrors is all brightness.

Feeding a pack of 20 on newspaper wrapped tables are Indian-inspired sweet and savory small plates of watermelon and feta salad cooled by a vibrant mint sorbet; eggplant buns spiked with toasty cumin; green mango *paneer*; and a zucchini-hummus pizza. If you forget to order the addictive green chili shrimp, you can hit "Mehtaphor" in the Duane Street Hotel for a taste of this spicy delight.

Hasaki

210 E. 9th St. (bet. Second & Third Aves.)

Subway: Astor Pl   Lunch Wed – Sun
Phone: 212-473-3327   Dinner nightly
Web: www.hasakinyc.com
Prices: $$

Since the mid-eighties, this local darling has been going strong thanks to its high quality ingredients, skilled kitchen, and excellent value. For under $20, the soba lunch set will warm the heart of any frugal fan of Japanese cuisine. This generous feast features a bowl of green tea noodles in hot, crystal-clear dashi stocked with wilted water spinach and fish cake, accompanied by lean tuna *chirashi*, yellowtail, and *kanpyo*. The *ten-don*, a jumbo shrimp tempura served over rice, is just as enticing. The à la carte offerings draw crowds seeking delish sushi as well as a host of tasty cooked preparations; a Twilight menu is nice for early birds.

The dining room has a clean and spare look, with seating available at a number of wood tables or sizable counter.

Hearth

403 E. 12th St. (at First Ave.)

Subway: 1 Av   Lunch Sat – Sun
Phone: 646-602-1300   Dinner nightly
Web: www.restauranthearth.com
Prices: $$$

Housed in the happening East Village, Hearth's glass panes allow glimpses into their animated yet sophisticated room. Walls padded with fabric panels lend a soft touch to the warm, comfortable space, styled with wine festival prints and maps. Service is either friendly and knowledgeable or totally checked out.

The dining counter is a great place to absorb the kitchen's controlled chaos as they carefully prepare unique classics with increasingly contemporary style. Crispy veal sweetbreads finished in a *piccata* sauce reach high levels of artistry. *Lesso misto*, gently cooked chicken, sausage, and veal bathed in tawny *brodo*, is luscious and flavorful. And the wine list is as enticing as a carrot cake sundae layered with cream cheese mousse and whipped cream.

Hot Kitchen

B3

Chinese ✗

104 Second Ave. (bet. 6th & 7th Sts.)

Subway: Astor Pl
Phone: 212-228-3090
Web: www.hotkitchenny.com
Prices: $$

Lunch & dinner daily

Hot Kitchen brings a dash of fiery Sichuan cooking to a neighborhood already rife with international options. Whitewashed brick walls accented by chili-red beams and ebony furnishings detail the tidy space.

Steer clear of the Chinese-American portion of the menu, and instead, partake in Hot Kitchen's offering of classic Sichuan dishes bolstered by a portion of well-made house specialties. Expect the likes of wok-fried quail liberally seasoned with cumin and salt; steamed whole fish slathered in a deluge of minced pickled red peppers; and shredded crispy duck studded with green onions and fried fresh ginger. Hot Kitchen uses the seasons to influence its roster of specials that have featured an autumnal bowl of braised spareribs with yam.

Huertas

B3

Spanish ✗✗

107 First Ave. (bet. 6th & 7th Sts.)

Subway: Astor Pl
Phone: 212-228-4490
Web: www.huertasnyc.com
Prices: $$$

Lunch Sat – Sun
Dinner Tue – Sat

A festive spirit fronts this Basque country-inspired den, where *pintxos* are passed around in the bar. This is the kind of place that honors authentic sips like *kalimotxo* (red wine and cola), *vermut* (Catalan for vermouth), and sherry, so don't expect to see pitchers of sangria being bandied about.

The proper dining room in the back is where the highly recommended tasting menu is served. This reasonably priced prix-fixe stimulates with small bites like sardine *conserva* served on buttered crostini with shaved radish; and may be followed by softly scrambled eggs drizzled with ruby shrimp jus, or seared lamb loin with greenmarket produce and crushed black olives. A chocolate custard topped with whipped cream and crushed Marcona almonds is heaven on a plate.

Jewel Bako ✿

A3

Japanese ✖

239 E. 5th St. (bet. Second & Third Aves.)

Subway: Astor Pl
Phone: 212-979-1012
Web: www.jewelbakosushi.com
Prices: $$$

Dinner Mon – Sat

Except for a tiny window of light, Jewel Bako does little to draw you in, lending an almost furtive, subterranean feel to its narrow entrance. Inside, this long space is lined with intimately spaced wooden tables. The upholstered banquettes are filled with a comfortably casual and convivial crowd, while solo diners seem to adore the dining counter that surrounds the expert team. The chefs here are busy, very passionate, and provide a wealth of culinary entertainment.

Painstaking detail is clear from the colorful glasses to the smiling staff's ability to explain the finer points of each preparation.

Their menu showcases the remarkable quality of each fish, which seem to have arrived straight from Japan. Expect to sample a range of original appetizers like oysters with micro greens and refreshing citrus juice or smooth salmon tartare in crisp pastry. Bluefin tuna, tender octopus, and plump sweet shrimp sashimi are all firm and glossy, with wasabi root grated tableside. Each grain of slightly sticky rice is cooked precisely and combined with barracuda, eel, and scallop for superb sushi. To close, try creamy green jasmine ice cream, sandwiched between crunchy chocolate cookies.

Joe & MissesDoe

A4

Contemporary ✗

45 E. 1st St. (bet. First & Second Aves.)

Subway: 2 Av
Phone: 212-780-0262
Web: www.chefjoedoe.com
Prices: $$

Lunch Sat – Sun
Dinner Tue – Sun

Chef Joe and Jill Doe have revamped their earnest establishment with a tweaked menu and pared down interior look. Gone are the knickknacks that were previously sprinkled throughout this small room, which now seats about 30 at a single row of tables and long bar counter.

From his station in the open kitchen, the chef gives American cuisine a creative re-working. Broccoli meets *skordalia* in an appetizer of caramelized florets dressed with grated pecorino, sliced almonds, pistachios, and toasted garlic. Beef brisket is slow-braised then griddled, and plated with house-made steak sauce and spicy radish chow-chow. A sundae of chocolate chip banana bread with vanilla ice cream and bananas Foster sauce is yet another example of this enjoyable hybrid cuisine.

Kafana

C3

Eastern European ✗

116 Ave. C (bet. 7th & 8th Sts.)

Subway: 1 Av
Phone: 212-353-8000
Web: www.kafananyc.com
Prices: $$

Lunch Sat-Sun
Dinner nightly

Traditional Serbian cuisine, a rarity in these parts, is the specialty at this heartwarming Alphabet City café. The intimate space is outfitted with exposed brick walls hung with mirrors and vintage photographs, rough-hewn wood tables, and boldly patterned banquettes. Carnations and votive candles pretty the room.

Begin a meal with an assortment of air-dried or smoked meats and tall slices of savory pies like the *gibanica* stuffed with tart feta layered in excellent phyllo. Other authentic and hearty treats include *ćevapi* (grilled minced meat kebabs) as well as wonderfully rustic stews combining lamb and wilted spinach, or beans with smoked baby back ribs. Kafana's regional wine list features a selection of orange wines from Slovenia and Croatia.

Kanoyama

Japanese ✕

175 Second Ave. (at 11th St.)

Subway: 3 Av
Phone: 212-777-5266
Web: www.kanoyama.com
Prices: $$

Dinner nightly

Offering an impressive lineup of excellent quality and deftly prepared fish, this popular and permanently packed sushi den is housed in a space that may be simply decorated but is spotless and well-maintained. The kitchen's focus here is on a parade of pristine cuts that are bolstered by a passage of daily items such as rich baby shad from Japan and tender, mild American white bonito. Also find a generous listing of plump, briny oysters; starters such as *wakasagi* tempura (fried baby smelts) sprinkled with green tea-salt; and a handful of cooked entrées. The value-conscious omakase is highly recommended.

Besides being tempting, the website is very informative: it presents diverse fish facts, photos, and recommendations for seasonality and preparation.

L'Apicio

Italian ✕✕

13 E. 1st St. (bet. Bowery & Second Ave.)

Subway: 2 Av
Phone: 212-533-7400
Web: www.lapicio.com
Prices: $$

Lunch Sat – Sun
Dinner nightly

The talented team behind L'Artusi has headed east to open this modern trattoria in a dramatically transformed quarter of the East Village, where luxury rentals now dominate. Rustic yet glossy, L'Apicio provides a chic den for young movers-and-shakers to kick back and unwind after a demanding day. Come for a snack or a meal; the menu's format leaves it up to you. Find the likes of a watercress salad with avocado, both roasted and raw carrots, swiped with spiced yogurt and crushed pistachios; or polenta *alla spianatora*, golden-yellow cornmeal topped with a savory stew of rock shrimp, tomato, and bacon. Come dessert, the chocolate *crostata* arrives as a warm ganache in a neatly fluted and wonderfully crumbly cookie crust, paired with *stracciatella* gelato.

Kyo Ya ✿

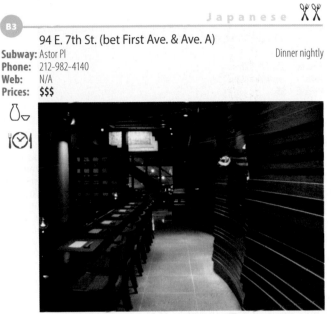

Japanese XX

B3

94 E. 7th St. (bet First Ave. & Ave. A)

Subway: Astor Pl
Phone: 212-982-4140
Web: N/A
Prices: $$$

Dinner nightly

In the basement level of a classic walk-up smack in the midst of a hip-artsy downtown neighborhood, Kyo Ya looks and feels like a secret hideaway cloaked in undulating wood and dark slate. The height of professionalism and hospitality, the staff is not merely attentive but appreciative of your presence at their table—or perhaps at one of the prized chef's counter stools for kaiseki dining, where mesmerizing craft is exhibited.

This is a place where traditional cuisine is prepared with modern flair, and Japanese is the moneyed clientele's mother tongue.

Refinement pervades every element of every dish, like the delicate, slightly tart pickled cabbage potage with chewy tri-colored taro root-potato *dango* and pale green strips of simmered vegetables finished with a dab of miso. The sashimi of the day may feature a fresh oyster with sautéed onion and *yuzu kosho oroshi* swimming in ponzu; simmered firefly squid and celery topped with salty *karashi*-miso and pickled plum; or tender raw octopus. Clay pots reveal fragrant dashi cooked with woodear mushrooms, carrots, turnips, and bobbing with a tiny melting ball of excellent mozzarella as well as the quenelle-like shrimp dumpling, *ebishinjo*.

Lavagna

C3

545 E. 5th St. (bet. Aves. A & B)

Subway: 2 Av
Phone: 212-979-1005
Web: www.lavagnanyc.com
Prices: $$

Lunch Sat – Sun
Dinner nightly

Instantly evidencing Lavagna's popularity is its steady stream of regulars who seem smitten with this delightfully discreet trattoria. Open since 1999, the staff is ever gracious, greeting guests by name, but the same courtesy is offered to first-timers as well. A wood-burning oven flickers in the elfin kitchen, thereby elevating Lavagna's sense of snug comfort.

Speaking of snug, the Italian menu offers a terse listing of *pizzette*, perhaps capped with roasted mushrooms, fontina, and white truffle oil. Antipasti unveils cool, shaved octopus massaged with fresh lemon and extra virgin olive oil; while entrées vie for center stage as in an al dente twirl of *fedelini fini* with slow-cooked tomatoes and toasted garlic slices; or oven-roasted fish, flambéed tableside.

Lil' Frankie's 😊

B4

19 First Ave. (bet. 1st & 2nd Sts.)

Subway: 2 Av
Phone: 212-420-4900
Web: www.lilfrankies.com
Prices: 🍝🍝

Lunch Sat– Sun
Dinner nightly

Frank Prisinzano's pizzeria combines a series of intimate rooms for a laid-back vibe that's perfectly in step with the neighborhood. An open kitchen is in one room, a pizza oven in another, and a third boasts a wall of window panels that open for alfresco dining. Framed photos and colorful vinyl tablecloths add character.

The Neapolitan-style pizza is always a hit, perhaps topped with bright tomato sauce, fresh mozzarella, and slices of spicy salami. Also savor the likes of fava bean purée with dandelion greens for a thick and homey soup. Garlic bread, baked pasta of the day, and whole eggplant with *pepperoncino* oil are all flame-kissed creations from the wood-burning oven. Stop by during weekend brunch for "killer" pancakes made with buckwheat flour.

Luzzo's

Pizza ✗

B2

211-13 First Ave. (bet. 12th & 13th Sts.)

Subway: 1 Av
Phone: 212-473-7447
Web: www.luzzospizza.com
Prices: $$

Lunch & dinner daily

The reason why decade-old Luzzo's continues to claim top ranking among the city's artisanal pizzerias is the handiwork of Naples-born executive *pizzaiolo* Michele Luliano (also of Ovest Pizzoteca) and his well-trained minions. Fashioned in the Neapolitan manner, these mouthwatering, smoke-kissed pies are made with a blend of flours, slick of San Marzano tomatoes, and creamy blobs of fresh mozzarella (or *mozzarella di bufala*) and baked in one of the city's last remaining coal-fired ovens. Sample from more than 20 variations on offer including the crisp, old-fashioned *quadrata* squares, or a pizza *fritta* stuffed with cheese, sauce, and ham. A mirror hung at the front of the slender, rustic space offers a view of the pizza-making action in the back.

Maharlika

Filipino ✗

B3

111 First Ave. (bet. 6th & 7th Sts.)

Subway: Astor Pl
Phone: 646-392-7880
Web: www.maharlikanyc.com
Prices: $$

Lunch & dinner daily

The décor may not be a highlight, but Maharlika's cordial staff and focus on traditional Filipino cooking shine through the low-tech setting.

The easiest way to describe the food here is to say it is hearty and meaty. Prepare yourself for *kare kare*, a stew of oxtail braised in peanut butter-enriched sauce; or Pampangan-style sizzling *sisig*, a hot skillet heaped with a trio of pig parts (ear, snout, and belly), arranged around a fried egg, and stirred together tableside. The chicken and waffle combines crispy pieces of light and dark meat served atop a waffle made with *ube* flour, with contrasting embellishments like anchovy butter and *macapuno* syrup, crafted from thick, caramelized coconut juice.

Also stop by the younger offshoot, Jeepney.

Malai Marke

Indian 🍴🍴

B3

318 E. 6th St. (bet. First & Second Aves.)

Subway: Astor Pl
Phone: 212-777-7729
Web: www.malaimarke.com
Prices: $$

Lunch & dinner daily

Now settled on the scene is Malai Marke, where owner Shiva Natarajan showcases an appealing room that displays a bit of flash and dispels the notion that Curry Row is not a destination for fine Indian cooking. Polished copper pans hang from brick walls, shiny black tiles accent the space, a dining counter expands seating options, and the kitchen is in full view.

The moniker translates to "extra cream" in Hindi tea-stall slang, a rich embellishment that inspires this regionally focused food. A feast here features *paneer tikka* brushed with thick cream and fresh herbs, or fish *moilee* simmered in coconut milk, spiced with red chili, turmeric, and black mustard seeds. *Makka roti*, griddled corn flatbreads; and coconut rice studded with flecks of *papadum* are excellent accompaniments.

The Mermaid Inn

Seafood 🍴

A3

96 Second Ave. (bet. 5th & 6th Sts.)

Subway: Astor Pl
Phone: 212-674-5870
Web: www.themermaidnyc.com
Prices: $$

Dinner nightly

This laid-back and inviting seafood spot has been a neighborhood favorite for over a decade now, spawning locations in Greenwich Village and the Upper West Side. A steady stream of guests lines the bar early for the super-sized "Happiest of Happy Hours" with freshly shucked oysters, snack-sized fish tacos, and other specially priced bites. For a hearty plate after your nosh, try blackened catfish dotted with crawfish butter alongside hushpuppies, or the lobster roll with Old Bay fries. On Sunday nights, look out for lobsterpalooza—a whole lobster accompanied by grilled corn on the cob and steamed potatoes.

At the end of your meal there's no need to deliberate over dessert. A demitasse of perfect chocolate pudding is presented compliments of the house.

Mighty Quinn's

A3

103 Second Ave. (at 6th St.)

Subway: Astor Pl   Lunch & dinner daily
Phone: 212-677-3733
Web: www.mightyquinnsbbq.com
Prices: ⊜⊜

Mighty Quinn's luscious treats were previously served only at Smorgasburg, Brooklyn's open-air foodie market. But these can now be enjoyed at this permanent stage for Chef/pitmaster Hugh Mangum. The sturdy location features terrazzo floors, whitewashed brick walls, and salvaged spruce tables (repurposed from the renovated Puck building). Service is totally casual, but that's hardly a complaint. After all, this is a barbecue joint, so you will need to place your order at the counter before sitting. Naturally raised, slow-smoked meats beckon as brisket, sausage, or pulled pork. All are offered by the pound or as a portion, naked or piled high in an egg-yellow bun. Everything is good, but the insanely tender pulled pork sandwich is simply irresistible.

Momofuku Noodle Bar ☺

B2

171 First Ave. (bet. 10th & 11th Sts.)

Subway: 1 Av   Lunch & dinner daily
Phone: 212-777-7773
Web: www.momofuku.com
Prices: $$

This is the one that started it all. David Chang's first-born remains a temple of hipster comfort food and rocks from the time its doors open. Two dining counters and a handful of communal tables furnish the honey-hued room, though the genteel staff deftly maximizes the minimal real estate.
Noodle Bar's gutsy menu is fashioned with Asian street food in mind. Steamed buns filled with tender pork brisket, horseradish mayonnaise, and pickled onion; or a bowl of springy ramen doused with a ginger-scallion sauce are just two examples of the crew's signature work. Blackboards display the day's specials and soft-serve flavors, as in the awesomely creamy Ritz cracker and peanut butter swirl, served with a pinch of sea salt and Concord grape compote.

Momofuku Ko ✿ ✿

B2

Contemporary ✗

163 First Ave. (bet. 10th & 11th Sts.)

Subway: 1 Av
Phone: 212-500-0831
Web: www.momofuku.com
Prices: $$$$

Lunch Fri – Sun
Dinner nightly

Dinner here is an exhilarating thrill ride, which comes as a happy surprise since it's precluded by so little fanfare. Case in point: the impressively democratic reservation system, handled solely online and free from any degree of influence. The spot has become a venue of international acclaim, and its twelve measly stools no longer fit the bill.

Team Chang will soon be working their magic in bigger digs nearby, at Extra Place, but the troupe remains the same. Until then, settle into one of the dozen seats, let the beverage liason suggest a glass of *vino*, and wait for the brilliant cuisine to arrive.

Hozon, a fermented paste, lends luscious umami to chopped, raw diver sea scallops rolled in a sheet of daikon and set in a pool of liberally salted tomato water. Chilled honeydew soup poured over sea urchin, cucumber, and avocado is more refreshing than a Polar Vortex, even with its sprinkle of Korean chili powder. The procession is in constant evolution, but those with some knowledge of Ko's repertoire will be delighted to discover classics like sea bass crudo splashed with spicy poppy seed-flecked buttermilk, and foie gras torchon shaved over lychees, pine nut brittle, and Riesling gelée.

Momofuku Ssäm Bar 🐷

Contemporary ✗

B2

207 Second Ave. (at 13th St.)

Subway: 3 Av
Phone: 212-254-3500
Web: www.momofuku.com
Prices: $$

Lunch & dinner daily

Momofuku Ssäm Bar will always be a darling among trendy New Yorkers who can routinely be found clamoring at the bar or packing their low-slung tables. This minimalist favorite may be staffed with brisk servers, yet its appetizing menu (especially those steamed buns filled with juicy pork belly) encourages lingering. Lunches are ideal for professionals on the run.

Ssäm Bar's unique blend of Asian and Western flavors accounts for its popularity. Taste the likes of rotisserie duck tucked with duck-and-pork sausage beneath the skin and cooked to crispy perfection. When joined with chive pancakes and sweet hoisin, the dish is elevated to global fame. Best to follow such creativity with a beautifully sweet and salty truffle filled with chocolate-pretzel cake.

Motorino

Pizza ✗

B2

349 E. 12th St. (bet. First & Second Aves.)

Subway: 1 Av
Phone: 212-777-2644
Web: www.motorinopizza.com
Prices: ⊜⊜

Lunch & dinner daily

Mathieu Palombino's Neapolitan-style pizzeria has been successfully churning out a spectrum of tasty pies for some years now. Simply beautified with white marble-topped tables, a pressed-tin ceiling, and bold green-and-white striped walls, the room's blackboard specials convey the product-focused sensibility that is applied here—fresh ramps have been a seasonally tuned topping.

Cold and hot antipasti (an octopus salad tossed with potatoes, celery, and chili oil; or roasted peppers with capers and parsley) bolster the mouthwatering pizza selection. This may be topped with the likes of *fior di latte*, caramelized Brussels sprouts, and diced bits of pancetta.

The Brooklyn brother has been sending fans back across the bridge.

Narcissa

Contemporary   ✗✗

A2

21 Cooper Sq. (at 5th St.)

Subway: Astor Pl
Phone: 212-228-3344
Web: www.narcissarestaurant.com
Prices: $$

Lunch Sat-Sun
Dinner nightly

The brainchild of André Balazs and Chef John Fraser, Narcissa lends a sleek, downtown twist on farm-to-table dining. Tucked into the Standard East Village, this tony space makes a fresh design statement with warm wood finishes, caramel leather-trimmed seating, and a modern open kitchen offering close-up views of the action.

The product-focused menu yields some show-stopping results, like the carrots Wellington: roasted carrots, fresh from the restaurant's farm in Hudson Valley, wrapped in puff pastry and finished with cocoa nibs and walnuts. Steamed black bass is presented with creamy curry sauce, lentils, and diced dried apricots; and the sundae of silken olive oil ice cream dabbed with lemon curd and thyme whipped cream is a delightful finale.

Northern Spy Food Co. 😀

American   ✗

C2

511 E. 12th St. (bet. Aves. A & B)

Subway: 1 Av
Phone: 212-228-5100
Web: www.northernspyfoodco.com
Prices: $$

Lunch & dinner daily

Under the steady stewardship of founding partner Christophe Hille, this noteworthy Alphabet City café continues to entice on every level—from the product-driven cooking to the country-chic decor. Reclaimed hickory floors and salvaged wood tabletops fill the petite room, accented in framed mirrors, touches of vintage wallpaper, and a splash of robin's egg blue paint.

The kitchen easily pleases with brunch-like midday meals. Dinnertime really shines, perhaps beginning with pork sticky rolls drizzled with a parsnip glaze to snack on while awaiting top-quality farm-raised lamb, prepared two ways. This single dish might feature fanned slices of loin and a collard-wrapped bundle of spoon-tender shoulder, plated with savory granola and a swipe of thick yogurt.

North River

B2

Contemporary ✕

166 First Ave. (bet. 10th & 11th Sts.)

Subway: 1 Av
Phone: 212-228-1200
Web: www.northriverny.com
Prices: $$

Lunch Sat – Sun
Dinner nightly

Steps away from perpetual scene-stealers like Momofuku Noodle Bar and Hearth, North River deserves a spotlight all its own. This unassuming entry boasts an intimate space where pretty wallpaper and botanical prints add charm to simple whitewashed brick.

Don't let the rustic-chic setting fool you; the kitchen here produces food that's nothing short of vibrant. Sweet morsels of roasted crawfish are dressed with rich crustacean-infused butter sauce and given a seasonal accent with tender ramps. A lamb stew hinting of rosemary is served as braised then crispy fried nuggets of meat nestled in soft polenta dotted with crushed black olives. Even the vegetable dishes—finely diced turnips glazed with fermented black bean paste, for example—are smartly rendered.

Oda House

C3

Eastern European ✕

76 Ave. B (at 5th St.)

Subway: 2 Av
Phone: 212-353-3838
Web: www.odahouse.com
Prices: $$

Lunch & dinner daily

For a taste of something different, this inviting café serves intriguing specialties from Georgia. That country's proximity to Russia, Turkey, and Armenia results in a vibrant and enticingly diverse cuisine that Oda House does proud.

A liberal use of fragrant spices, cheese-filled breads, kebabs, and slow-cooked meats typify the kitchen's preparations. Classic dishes include *satsivi*, boiled chicken served cool in a creamy walnut sauce seasoned with warm spices, accompanied by *gomi*, hominy grits in a mini cauldron studded with morsels of rich, stretchy *sulgani* cheese. Balance out the hearty fare with a fresh, perfectly dressed garden salad.

The vibe is simple and rustic with pumpkin-stained stucco walls, exposed brick, and wood furnishings.

Parmy's

Persian 🍴

125 First Ave. (bet. 7th St. & St. Marks Pl.)

Subway: Astor Pl   lunch & dinner daily
Phone: 212-335-0207
Web: www.parmyspersianfusion.com
Prices: $$

In a neighborhood with a world of dining options to choose from, this simple room stands out. Here, rugs hang on walls the color of red clay and the smell of Persian cooking fills the air.

Char-grilled kabobs of marinated meat plated with basmati or couscous and luscious stews fragrant with sweet spices are at the heart of Parmy's menu. But before you dig in, whet your palate with creamy yogurt-based spreads, refreshing salads, or a cool and invigorating bowlful of *turshi* (finely diced pickled vegetables in a deep yellow-tinted sauce tasting of dried mint). Then, move on to *khoresh bademjan*—a hearty portion of braised lamb chunks wrapped in roasted eggplant slices and served in a pool of light tomato sauce seasoned with *ghooreh* or sour grapes.

Porsena

Italian 🍴🍴

21 E. 7th St. (bet. Second & Third Aves.)

Subway: Astor Pl   Lunch Sat-Sun
Phone: 212-228-4923   Dinner nightly
Web: www.porsena.com
Prices: $$

Sara Jenkins' fans gather at Porsena, where her flavorful and approachable style to Italian food shines bright. Casual and rustic, Porsena has an unplanned yet true sense of place. The dining room is divided into two intimate spaces tightly packed with snug tables, in true East Village style. Snagging the coveted chef's table situated before the semi-open kitchen is enough to start a foodie fight.

Expect such sumptuous standards as brandied chicken liver pâté paired with pickles; perfectly cooked octopus infused with smoked paprika and served beside roasted fingerlings; or raw milk curd, a creamy-pungent cheese with a compote of *agretti* and chilies. Massive *anelloni* with spicy lamb sausage, mustard greens, and breadcrumbs is wow-inducing.

Prime & Beyond New York

A2

90 E. 10th St. (bet. Third & Fourth Aves.)

Subway: Astor Pl   Dinner nightly
Phone: 212-505-0033
Web: www.primeandbeyond.com
Prices: $$$

This location of the Fort Lee, NJ original brings great steak to the East Village. Appropriate for this locale, the setting eschews the standard men's club swagger of most steakhouses for a look that's spare and cool. Despite the chillax vibe, expect to see suits; the meat is that good. In fact, it's procured from the same purveyor that supplies Peter Luger and Keens.

Aged in-house for six weeks, the USDA Prime Porterhouse is presented hot off the grill but well rested, richly flavored, tender, and juicy. Myriad cuts satisfy all preferences, while sides like kimchi, spicy scallion salad, and fermented cabbage stew are especially appealing and honor the owners' heritage. Heartwarming Korean-style soups and stews are wonderful wintertime favorites.

Prune 🆕

A3

54 E. 1st St. (bet. First & Second Aves.)

Subway: 2 Av   Lunch Sat-Sun
Phone: 212-677-6221   Dinner nightly
Web: www.prunerestaurant.com
Prices: $$

Chef Gabrielle Hamilton's sterling little bistro has long bewitched the city's foodies who cram its bar and row of tables. Unpretentious cooking in a room branded by pops of purple is Prune's hallmark, and a completely revised menu shines with newfound inspiration.

"Straw and hay" pasta—fresh strands of egg and boiled linguine—is sauced with chicken livers and diced green tomatoes, while deep-fried rabbit is seasoned with romesco salt, and sided with buttermilk dressing. For the most simple yet epic finale ever, the season's best peaches are lightly sugared and laid over warm buttered toast.

Prune's daiquiri (a zesty combination of three rums garnished with a vanilla bean swizzle stick that perfumes each sip) is proof of serious cocktail creativity.

Pylos

B3

Greek ✗✗

128 E. 7th St. (bet. First Ave. & Ave. A)

Subway: Astor Pl
Phone: 212-473-0220
Web: www.pylosrestaurant.com
Prices: $$

Lunch Wed – Sun
Dinner nightly

Taking its name from the Greek translation of "made from clay," this contemporary taverna features a ceiling canopy of suspended terra-cotta pots and whitewashed walls with lapis-blue insets. The restrained décor produces a chic Mediterranean vibe that perfectly suits its lusty, home-style, and deliciously refined cuisine—courtesy of noted Greek food authority, Diane Kochilas.

Moussaka, a luscious comfort favorite, is beautifully presented here as a dome filled with layers of browned meat and silky eggplant, encrusted in slender potato slices, finished with a layer of golden-browned béchamel. Sides may include *spanakorizo*, wilted spinach rice flecked with feta crumbles; whereas a custard-filled phyllo drenched in mountain honey ends things sweetly.

Rai Rai Ken

B2

Japanese ✗

218 E. 10th St. (bet. First & Second Aves.)

Subway: Astor Pl
Phone: 212-477-7030
Web: N/A
Prices: ⊜⊜

Lunch & dinner daily

Rai Rai Ken isn't quite what it used to be—it's bigger and much more comfortable. Just a few doors east of its former location, this room boasts a fresh and tidy look with blonde wood seating plus signature red vinyl stools. An array of pots remain bubbling and steaming behind the counter.

Rest assured the menu's star attraction—those thin and toothsome ramen noodles—are just as delicious, served with four near-addictive, fantastically complex broth variations: *shio*, *shoyu*, miso, and curry. Each bowlful is chock-full of garnishes, like slices of roasted pork, boiled egg, nori, fishcake, and a nest of springy noodles. Grab a business card before leaving as loyal diners are rewarded with a complimentary bowl after ten visits.

Ramen Misoya

B2

Japanese ✗

129 Second Ave. (bet. St. Marks Pl & 7th St.)

Subway: Astor Pl
Phone: 212-677-4825
Web: www.misoyanyc.com
Prices: 🍴🍴

Lunch & dinner daily

With 30 locations worldwide, Ramen Misoya brings its trademark ambrosial bowlfuls to New York City. The earthy dining area dons a bamboo-lined ceiling as well as a TV monitor that is internally looped to broadcast the kitchen's every move.

The ramen offering here differentiates itself by centering on a trio of miso-enriched broths: *shiro* is a white miso fermented with rice *koji* (starter); *kome-miso* is richer tasting; and *mame-miso* is a strictly soybean product. The mouth-coating soup is delicious alchemy. Each slurp is a multifaceted distillation of pork and chicken bones with savory-salty-sweet notes, stocked with excellent noodles, vegetables, and the likes of panko-crusted shrimp tempura, fried ginger chicken, or slices of house-made *cha-su*.

Robataya

B2

Japanese ✗✗

231 E. 9th St. (bet. Second & Third Aves.)

Subway: Astor Pl
Phone: 212-979-9674
Web: www.robataya-ny.com
Prices: $$

Dinner Tue-Sun

Irasshaimase! This is the kind of intensely authentic place where welcomes are shouted to guests upon entering. At peak times, wait among Japanese expats and young couples lining the sidewalk. Aim straight for the counter to appreciate the theatrics of it all, where orders are acknowledged with more shouts flying from Japanese servers to chefs. The energy is high, but so are the standards for their expertly grilled meats and vegetables.

Kneeling cooks use long wooden paddles to deliver dishes hot off the robata, like *gyu tataki*, seared beef filet topped with tobiko and scallions on a bed of red onions with ponzu. Technical mastery is clear in a salt-packed sea bream's subtle smoky flavors emphasizing the delicacy of such white, flaky fish.

Sigiri

B3

91 First Ave. (bet. 5th & 6th Sts.)

Subway: 1 Av
Phone: 212-614-9333
Web: www.sigirinyc.com
Prices: 🍛🍛

Lunch & dinner daily

S

Just off of Curry Row, Sigiri offers a sweetly spiced taste of Sri Lanka in an area abounding with Indian dining. This second-floor room may be plain, but is very tidy with tables dressed in colorful linens that pop against the brownish walls. Stir-fried and slow-cooked specialties are sought-after here, as in the pork black curry featuring an ink-dark sauce of roasted spices, chilies, black pepper, ginger, and cloves. The string hopper *kotthu* is deliciously traditional, served as a fluffy heap of rice noodles sautéed with bits of white meat chicken and an array of fresh vegetables with a small dish of vibrant coconut curry.

Alcohol is not served, but a number of soft drinks are offered and guests are welcome to bring their own wine or beer.

Sobakoh

B3

309 E. 5th St. (bet. First & Second Aves.)

Subway: 2 Av
Phone: 212-254-2244
Web: www.sobakoh-nyc.com
Prices: 🍛🍛

Lunch & dinner daily

♿

Before entering Sobakoh, stop for a minute to appreciate Chef/owner Hiromitsu Takahashi, sequestered to his temperature- and humidity-controlled glass booth, forming layers of organically grown buckwheat flour dough into first-rate noodles. This ritual is performed several times daily by the smiling chef and is the foundation of the seasonally arranged offerings at this Japan-meets-East Village soba spot. Service can be sluggish, so start with a classic snack, like the refreshing daikon salad dressed with yuzu, wasabi, and bonito flakes. Then dive into your bowlful of *uni ikura soba*—chilled buckwheat noodles heaped with creamy sea urchin and plump salmon roe.

The inexpensive prix-fixe offered nightly is even cheaper before 7:00 P.M.

Soba-Ya ☺

B2

Japanese ✗✗

229 E. 9th St. (bet. Second & Third Aves.)

Subway: Astor Pl
Phone: 212-533-6966
Web: www.sobaya-nyc.com
Prices: ☺☺

Lunch & dinner daily

In a neighborhood replete with tempting Japanese dining options, Soba-Ya has been sating noodle cravings with awesome buckwheat soba and hearty udon—all homemade daily—for more than a decade. Enterprising co-owner Bon Yagi, also of Curry-Ya, favors authenticity over flash in his establishments, and this popular soba spot fashioning a traditional aesthetic is no exception.

Sit among the largely Japanese lunchtime clientele to savor and slurp cold, refreshing soba attractively served in a red-black bento box. Find it neatly stocked with the likes of dashi-poached vegetables, fresh and deliciously glazed salmon, or crisp shrimp tempura. Complete this meal with a pot of hot broth added to your remaining soy-based dipping sauce for a warming finish.

Somtum Der ☺

B3

Thai ✗

85 Ave A. (bet. 5th & 6th Sts.)

Subway: 2 Av
Phone: 212-260-8570
Web: www.somtumder.com
Prices: $$

lunch & dinner daily

Fun, funky, and as impressive as that massive mortar and pestle used to grind ingredients for the city's best green papaya salad, Somtum Der is cool, distinctive, and remarkably authentic. Step into this mod space and ogle over the Northern Thai somtum station, bursting with jars of peanuts, chilles, dried shrimp, and dark paste used to dress that wonderful eponymous dish.

The cuisine of Thailand's Isaan region dominates the menu here, with pungent, spicy, and fresh flavors including lemongrass and mint. Those seductive pickled bamboo shoots make for a memorable cold dish, tossed with scallion and a mysterious undertone of delicious fish sauce. Meanwhile, the excellent and unique marinated raw shrimp spreads serious chili fire, then cools down with mint.

Supper 😊

B4

156 E. 2nd St. (bet. Aves. A & B)

Subway: 1 Av
Phone: 212-477-7600
Web: www.supperrestaurant.com
Prices: $$

Lunch Sat – Sun
Dinner nightly

Supper manages to exude a vibe that's as laid-back and lively as the 'hood it resides in, making it an inviting spot to while away a few lazy hours with great wine and even better Italian bites. Add to that a truly great value, and it's hard not to fall head-over-heels in love with this joint.

Intimacy prevails in the back, while the front room is packed with a hip crowd watching the chefs whip up such spoils as grilled country bread with a deliciously gamey chicken liver spread or panzanella—a flavorful toss-up of olive oil *croûtes*, black kale, tomatoes, and capers in a red wine vinaigrette. Taste is at the forefront in *spaghetti al limone*, with a touch of cream and tons of Parmesan. Grilled polenta with sautéed wild mushrooms is Italy-incarnate.

Sushi Dojo

B3

110 First Ave. (bet. 6th & 7th Sts.)

Subway: Astor Pl
Phone: 646-692-9398
Web: www.sushidojonyc.com
Prices: $$

Dinner Tue – Sat

Chef David Bouhadana follows up his stint at Sushi Uo and some time in Japan to head up this winning *sushi-ya*. A 14-seat counter and handful of tables outfit this pleasant room, where the congenial chef sends forth an impressive array of morsels.

The chef's choice menu is highly recommended and offers very good value for the masterful skill and high quality of fish. This is immediately clear in the nigiri presentation that has included Tasmanian trout, cherry salmon from Japan, and a trio of *maguro* (lean, medium, and fatty). Beyond the sushi menu, sample dishes like house-made cold tofu served with yuzu salt; and *kaki-age*, a light and crisp tempura-fried combination of delicate *mizuna*, seaweed, squid, and shrimp with green-tea salt.

Wasan

Japanese ※

B3

108 E. 4th St. (bet. First & Second Aves.)

Subway: 2 Av
Phone: 212-777-1978
Web: www.wasan-ny.com
Prices: $$

Dinner nightly

The Tokyo-born team of Chef Ryota Kitagawa and Kakusaburo Sakurai both spent time in the kitchen of the Waldorf-Astoria's pioneering Inagiku. Their pedigree is evident in this intimate room, offering excellent food and service.

A unique rendition of Japanese cooking includes the house salad of lettuces, radish, seaweed and slivered chayote presented in a delicately crisp, edible bowl made from wheat and corn flour. The ingredients are tossed at the table, resulting in a lovely presentation that's strewn with crisped bits. Delightful house-pickled vegetables include salt-pickled Napa cabbage, sweet-and-sour shavings of watermelon radish, and Brussels sprouts in curry vinegar. And with its foundation of *hijiki* seaweed rice, the lush *unagi* bowl is a treat.

Look for our symbol 🍇, spotlighting restaurants with a notably wine list.

Financial District

New York City's Financial District is home to some of the world's largest corporations. Previously cramped with suits of all stripes, this buzzing business center is becoming increasingly residential thanks to office buildings being converted into condos and a sprouting culinary scene. Every day like clockwork, Wall Street warriors head to lunch-only stalwarts like **Delmonico's** for their signature Angus boneless ribeye. If that's too heavy on the heart (or expense account), change course to **Nixtamalito**, the popular lunch kiosk at 1 Centre Street turning out authentic yet inexpensive Mexican flavors like slow-cooked carnitas wrapped in light, fluffy tortillas.

NOSTALGIC NIGHTS

At sundown, bring a picnic basket and catch the Shearwater for a memorable sail around Manhattan. Alternatively, step aboard **Honorable William Wall**, the floating clubhouse of the Manhattan Sailing Club, anchored in the New York harbor from May through October every year. Not only does this gorgeous platform let you get up, close, and personal with Lady Liberty herself, but it also proffers a perfect view of the evening sailboat races—don't forget to have a drink while you're at it! Although there are several other voyages showcasing Gotham City in all its glory, visitors to this district remain eternally impressed by the **Champagne City Lights Cruise** of Manhattan, where you can sip on bubbly or beer as you take in the sights of beautiful and expansive Battery Park City. During the summer, weekend trips to Governor's Island—a lush parkland featuring playing fields and hills—are not just popular but make for wonderful

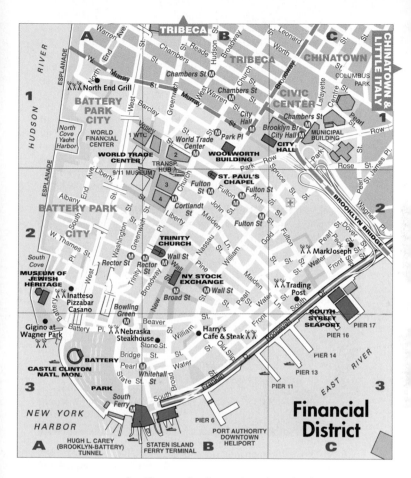

Financial District

escapes among families and friends alike. In fact, all of the city's carnivores make sure to convene here every October for their hugely famous and always delicious **Festival Meatopia**.

BIGHT BITES

Recently recuperated public markets also point to the residential boom in this quarter. Case in point: the burgeoning **Staten Island Ferry Whitehall Terminal Greenmarket** (open on Tuesdays and Fridays) is

housed within the large and well-designed Staten Island Ferry Terminal, and deserves plenty of praise for sourcing local and farm-fresh produce to the community. tindependent vendors

BARS & BEVVIES GALORE

Despite the destruction wreaked by Hurricane Sandy, restaurants downtown seem to have bounced back into buzzing mode with finance whizzes drowning their worries in martinis, and reviewing portfolios over burgers and beer. One of the neighborhood's largest tourist draws, **South Street Seaport**, is flanked by a collage of fantastic eateries and convivial, family-friendly bars. The legendary **Fraunces Tavern** is a fine specimen on Pearl Street that includes a restaurant and museum paying homage to early American

well-conceived décor and small plates. If the ground floor's sawdust proves too rustic for your taste, head up to the Taproom for a whiff of elegance. While here, take a moment to sip on homemade punch and peruse the cocktail menu, a work of art in and of itself. Wash down their Irish-influenced eats with the same nation's drink of choice at South Street's **Watermark Bar**. Speaking of bars, Beekman

history. While they proffer an impressive selection of brews and cocktails, crowds also flock here for comprehensive brunch, lunch, and dinner specials. Plus happy hour is always hopping, with over 130 craft beers and ciders on offer. Thanks to such flourishing destinations, buttoned-up suits have learned to loosen their ties and chill out with the locals over drinks at **The Deadrabbit Grocery & Grog**. This delightful, multi-award-wining watering hole has been drawing city slickers to Water Street as much for their specialty cocktails as their

Beer Garden Beach Club Revelers lounge in style at **Livingroom Bar and Terrace**, accommodated in the sleek W Hotel, and accoutered with towering windows set above specially designed seats that afford unobstructed views of the glimmering Manhattan skyline. By cooking up classic plates in conjunction with a litany of enticing martinis, this hot spot remains a coveted summer venue for concerts, corporate events, and other celebrations.

Jamaican food sensation **Veronica's Kitchen** carries on the food cart craze in the FiDi

events like the **Stone Street Oyster Festival** play to this district's strengths—what better way to lift your spirits and celebrate the local Blue Point harvest in September than by slurping up meaty and briny oysters outdoors on narrow, sinuous, and very charming Stone Street?

IN MEMORIAM

Leaving aside this abundance of food and festivity, memorials and monuments also form a large part of the fabric of the Financial District today. Occupying 18 acres at the World Trade Center, The National September 11 Memorial & Museum pays tribute to the attacks in 2001. Similarly, The Irish Hunger Memorial, complete with a rural landscape and an abandoned cottage, serves as both a metaphor to the Great Irish Famine as well as a reminder that hunger still prevails in the world today.

with its flavorful spectrum of Caribbean classics including the likes of smoky jerk and tender stewed chicken. Similarly, **Alan's Falafel Cart** on Cedar Street is an exquisite haunt for a pick-me-up minus the sticker shock. **Financier Patisserie** presents tantalizing sweets known to leave a lasting impression on Stone Street; and need only be topped by a cuppa' coffee at one of the vendors nearby. Finally, food-focused

Gigino at Wagner Park

Italian ✗✗

20 Battery Pl. (in Wagner Park)

Subway: Bowling Green
Phone: 212-528-2228
Web: www.gigino-wagnerpark.com
Prices: $$

Lunch & dinner daily

Holed up in Battery Park is this culinary jewel that is routinely frequented by downtown residents. Its cave-like entrance leads to a quiet, serene area as well as an open terrace rife with incredible views that all New Yorkers would treasure. This is the sort of place to kick back and enjoy the calm in a bustling city, while sipping from an intelligent, well-priced wine list.

The food is just as precise and refined, thanks to a kitchen that understands the provenance of each dish. Find evidence of this in potato gnocchi bobbing in a slow-cooked, tomato *sugo* dotted with tiny beef meatballs. Don't forget to give *spaghetti del Padrino* with *colatura*, anchovies, beets, and escarole a rightful whirl if only for its tempting garlic essence.

Harry's Cafe & Steak

American ✗✗

1 Hanover Sq. (bet. Pearl & Stone Sts.)

Subway: Wall St (William St.)
Phone: 212-785-9200
Web: www.harrysnyc.com
Prices: $$

Lunch & dinner Mon – Sat

Nestled beneath the historic Hanover building, Harry's presents two distinct experiences. The casual Cafe and bar stand at the entrance, packed wall to wall with Wall Street suits haunting their local watering hole. Dining here is both cozy and communal, in an atmosphere that promises a fun time. Harry's Steak sits behind the Cafe, with its own bar and a series of snug rooms for a more intimate evening.

Begin with a classic starter, like mushrooms stuffed with sweet, succulent lobster; but everyone really comes for the steak. Here, a prime hanger steak is perfectly seared, juicy, and tender—impressive for this particular cut—served with homemade béarnaise. There is no room left for disappointment, but maybe enough for the pecan bread pudding.

Inatteso Pizzabar Casano

A2

I t a l i a n ✗✗

28 West St. (at 2nd Pl.)

Subway: South Ferry
Phone: 212-267-8000
Web: www.inattesopizzabar.com
Prices: $$

Lunch & dinner daily

Manhattan has no shortage of pizza. But shockingly, the touristy, banker-packed Battery Park City lacked a proper wood-fired pizza until the arrival of Inatteso. Tucked away, it features stunning views of the Statue of Liberty and Ellis Island from the south end of the bar. Any seat in the brightly lit, wood-paneled room provides a glimpse of the oven and scents of a blistering crust.

The 12-inch margherita pie expresses pure pizza-making skill through soft, fluffy dough with a touch of semolina and knobs of *fior di latte*. It's not entirely traditional but completely enjoyable. The menu doesn't stop at pizza, and neither should you. Sample pasta like orechiette with broccoli rabe and pan-roasted mahi mahi with sweet and sour eggplant caponata.

MarkJoseph

C2

S t e a k h o u s e ✗✗

261 Water St. (bet. Peck Slip & Dover St.)

Subway: Fulton St
Phone: 212-277-0020
Web: www.markjosephsteakhouse.com
Prices: $$$

Lunch Mon – Fri
Dinner nightly

Feared never to reopen after Hurricane Sandy, this smart steak haven has reclaimed its rightful place among the faithful haunts of local residents and carnivores in town. Restored to its dark wood-paneled glory, with a wine cellar display and white tablecloths, this traditional den looks like a clubby Wall Street scene. Expect to see a crowd of suits discussing stocks, shares, and sports scores, of course.

The quality of USDA Prime beef is paramount here, but the culinary technique is just another reason why this steakhouse succeeds. Steaks are perfect medium rare, brushed with sweet melting fat, seasoned with salt, and perhaps served with a gravy boat of béarnaise sauce. Finish off with a classic slice of pecan pie topped with whipped cream.

Nebraska Steakhouse

B3

15 Stone St. (bet. Broad & Whitehall Sts.)

Subway: Bowling Green
Phone: 212-952-0620
Web: www.nebraskasteakhousenyc.com
Prices: $$$

Lunch & dinner Mon – Fri

A classic New York destination, Nebraska Steakhouse remains a fixture in the otherwise downtrodden, post-Superstorm Sandy FiDi. This rather brash yet classic watering hole with equally brazen diners hovering around a tiny, narrow, and well-soaked bar evokes that old-timey city tavern scene. The vibe is lively, drinks are strong, and steaks are expertly handled.

Finding the door isn't a cakewalk and manipulating the crowd takes some negotiating, but rest assured that the end result is worth it. Yes, those steaks are on-point, but smoked trout salad followed by 22-ounces of tender and juicy grilled lamb Porterhouse chops never fails to sate.

In contrast to the gruff service, a pecan pie studded with chocolate chips and heavy cream is so sweet.

North End Grill

A1

104 North End Ave. (at Murray St.)

Subway: Chambers St (West Broadway)
Phone: 646-747-1600
Web: www.northendgrillnyc.com
Prices: $$$

Lunch & dinner daily

Brought to you by über restauranteur Danny Meyer, this downtown stunner is quickly becoming the table of choice for Goldman Sachs' tycoons and waterfront-dwelling families. The décor seems sleek with midnight-blue banquettes and black-and-white landscapes, but wood salvaged from Wyoming snow fences, impressive service, and over 100 bottles of Scotch whiskey warm the striking setting.

The menu ranges from a raw bar selection, charcuterie, and salads including Maine crab tossed with grapefruit, celery stalks, and pink peppercorns. A quail egg surrounded by a dollop of paddlefish caviar is decadence incarnate. Also save room for a shatteringly crisp clam flatbread pizza, sealed by salted-honey bread pudding with caramel sauce and buttermilk sherbet.

Trading Post

C2 — American XX

170 John St. (at South St.)

Subway: Fulton St — Lunch & dinner Mon – Sat
Phone: 646-370-3337
Web: www.tradingpostnyc.com
Prices: **$$**

In the historic building that previously housed Yankee Clipper, Trading Post is a massive and stylish reprieve from those nearby pubs and quick-serve joints. It occupies three floors, including a whiskey cellar, first-floor bar, and more upscale second floor with water views, tufted leather banquettes, orange wingback chairs, and an elegant library.

The menu complements the setting with a wealth of top products, found in creamy corn chowder made with briny, tender blue crab; or an heirloom tomato salad nestled among feta and watermelon, finished with balsamic vinaigrette. Also sample more novel items, such as the substantial cornmeal-crusted skate with caramelized pineapple. The coveted crème brûlée is perfectly classic and absolutely delicious.

Bib Gourmand
indicates our inspectors'
favorites for good value.

Gramercy, Flatiron & Union Square

Anchored around the members-only Gramercy Park, this neighborhood of the same name is steeped in history, classic beauty, and tranquility. Even among thoroughbred NYers, most of whom haven't set foot on its private paths, the park's extreme exclusivity is the stuff of legends—because outside of the residents whose homes face the square, Gramercy Park Hotel guests are among the few permitted entrance.

baked pastries and—in true New York City fashion—pretzel croissants. Old-timers love the warm chocolate *babka* from **Breads Bakery**, but for those who prefer a little spice, head north to **Curry Hill**. This exotic stretch brings Indian flavors to the big city by way of authentic, budget-friendly restaurants. While some may be focused on the greasy takeout formula, foodies and home cooks know to head to **Foods of India** for

Bounded by touristy Union Square and the fashionably edgy Flatiron District, this quiet enclave also boasts of beautiful brownstones, charming cafés, and haute hotels. Channel your inner Dowager Countess of Grantham as you nibble on dainty finger sandwiches at the refreshed **Lady Mendl's Tea Salon**, a Victorian-style parlor tucked inside the Inn at Irving Place. Stroll a few blocks only to discover assorted pleasures at **Maury Rubin's City Bakery**, a prominent haunt for fresh-

choice ingredients. **Kalustyan's** is an equally celebrated spice emporium showcasing such exceptional products as orange blossom water and over thirty varieties of dried whole chilies.

FLATIRON DISTRICT

Named after one of the city's most notable skyscrapers, the Flatiron District is a commercial hub-turned-residential mecca. Engulfed with trendy clothing stores and chic establishments, the area today is a colorful explosion of culture and shopping. A few blocks to the west, find the welcoming Madison Square Park, complete with its own unique history and vibe. It is therefore only fitting that park visitors are greeted by the original outpost of burger flagship, **Shake Shack**, serving its signature fast food from an ivy-covered kiosk. While burgers and Chicago-style dogs are popular, their house-made custard has patrons fixated and checking the online "custard calendar" weekly for favored flavors.

Tourists looking to trend it up should hang with the cool kids and expats at the Ace Hotel. While some may gather around **No. 7 Sub Shop** for a quick bite, others take their sip from **Stumptown Coffee Roasters** to savor in the hipster-reigning lobby. Equally nifty, NoMad hotel is home to Gotham's first **sweetgreen**. Socialites watching their waistline along with "Silicon Alley" staffers can't get enough of their cold-pressed juices and frozen yogurt. A long way from clean tastes and on to bold bites, barbecue addicts remain eternally committed to the **Big Apple Barbecue Block Party** held every June. This weekend-long event features celebrity pit masters showing off their "smoke" skills to hungry aficionados. One of the district's most frequented spectacles is **Eataly NY**, founded by Oscar Farinetti but brought stateside by Mario Batali and Joe Bastianich. This *molto* glam marketplace incorporates everything Italiano under one roof, including a dining hall with delish eats, regional specialties, and aromatic food stalls.

UNION SQUARE

Nearby Union Square is an important historic landmark characterized by a park with playgrounds and tiered plazas that occasionally host political protests and rallies. Today it may be best known for its year-round **Greenmarket**, heaving with a pristine collection of seasonal produce, and held on Mondays, Wednesdays, Fridays, and Saturdays. Beyond the market, find a bottle of fine wine to complement your fresh farm-to-table meal from either **Union Square Wines and Spirits**, or **Italian Wine Merchants**. Further evidence of this *piazza*'s reputation as the center of Manhattan's culinary scene, is the thriving presence of **Whole Foods** and the city's very first **Trader Joe's**, all within just blocks of one another.

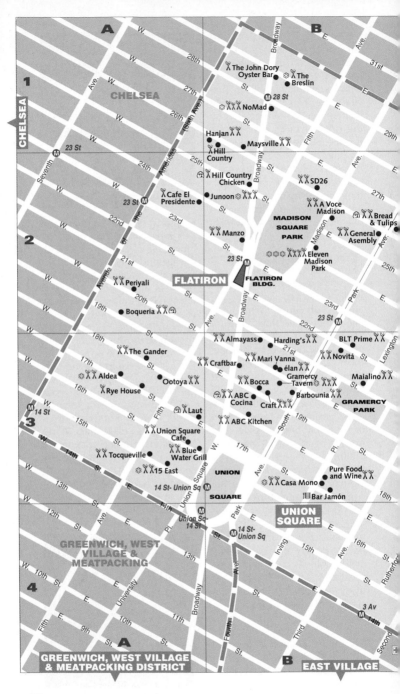

A

B

CHELSEA

CHELSEA

1

The John Dory Oyster Bar

The Breslin

28 St

NoMad

Hanjan

Maysville

Hill Country

Hill Country Chicken

SD26

Cafe El Presidente

Junoon

A Voce Madison

Bread & Tulips

MADISON SQUARE PARK

General Asembly

Manzo

2

Eleven Madison Park

Periyali

FLATIRON

FLATIRON BLDG.

23 St

Boqueria

23rd

23 St

Almayass

Harding's

BLT Prime

The Gander

Mari Vanna

Novitá

Craftbar

élan

Aldea

Ootoya

Bocca

Gramercy Tavern

Maialino

Rye House

ABC Cocina

Barbounia

GRAMERCY PARK

Laut

Craft

3

ABC Kitchen

Union Square Cafe

Tocqueville

Blue Water Grill

15 East

Pure Food and Wine

UNION

Casa Mono

14 St- Union Sq

SQUARE

Bar Jamón

UNION SQUARE

Union Sq

14 St

GREENWICH, WEST VILLAGE & MEATPACKING

14 St- Union Sq

3 Av

4

GREENWICH, WEST VILLAGE & MEATPACKING DISTRICT

A

B

EAST VILLAGE

94

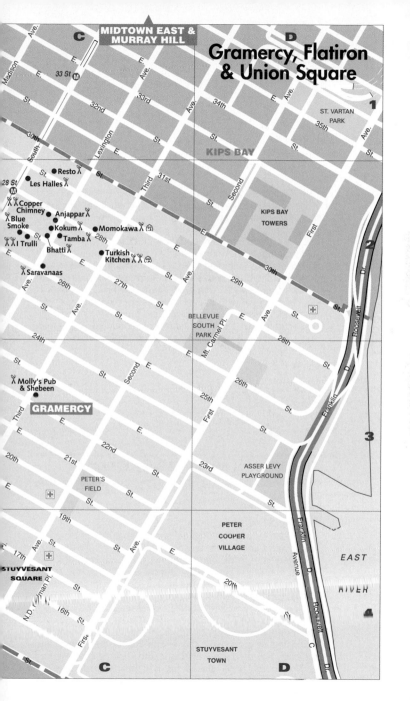

Gramercy, Flatiron & Union Square

C   **D**

1

Madison Ave.

E. 33 St Ⓜ

E.

32nd St.

33rd St.

E. 34th St.

E. Ave.

ST. VARTAN
PARK

35th

Ave.

St.

KIPS BAY

30th

South

Lexington

Third

31st St.

Second

First

● Resto Ⓧ

28 St Ⓜ

St. ● Les Halles Ⓧ

**KIPS BAY
TOWERS**

Ⓧ Ⓧ Copper
Chimney ●

● Anjappar Ⓧ

Ⓧ Blue
Smoke

● Kokum Ⓧ

● Momokawa Ⓧ

Ⓧ Ⓧ I Trulli

St. ● Tamba Ⓧ

E. 28th

E.

Bhatti Ⓧ

● Turkish
Kitchen Ⓧ Ⓧ

E. 30th St.

Ⓧ Saravanaas

27th

29th

2

Roosevelt Dr.

26th

Ave.

St.

E. Ave.

St.

✚

Ⓧ

St.

Franklin D.

Ave.

St.

St.

24th

BELLEVUE
SOUTH
PARK

Mt. Carmel Pl.

E. 28th

St.

St.

St.

Ⓧ Molly's Pub
& Shebeen ●

Second

E.

25th

First

26th

St.

3

Third

GRAMERCY

22nd

E.

E.

St.

20th

21st

E.

23rd

ASSER LEVY
PLAYGROUND

St.

Franklin

E.

PETER'S
FIELD

St.

St.

St.

✚

Roosevelt

Avenue

19th

PETER
COOPER
VILLAGE

EAST

17th

St.

St.

Ave.

E.

RIVER

✚

**STUYVESANT
SQUARE**

Rutherford Pl.

20th

St.

N.D.

16th

St.

First

STUYVESANT
TOWN

St.

C   **D**

ABC Cocina

B3

38 E. 19th St. (bet. Broadway & Park Ave. South)

Subway: 23 St (Park Ave. South)   Lunch & dinner daily
Phone: 212-677-2233
Web: www.abccocinanyc.com
Prices: $$

ABC Cocina stands in stark contrast to her wholesome and whitewashed cousin next door, ABC Kitchen. Markedly sexy, this space favors a vampy backdrop furnished with black and magenta lacquered café chairs and metal tables topped by red flowers and bottles of habanero hot sauce.

Accents from Latin America and beyond lilt the menu of small plates, perhaps including sweet potato empanadas delicately crafted and imbued with smoked cherry pepper, paired with lemon yogurt sauce. Tamarind-marinated black sea bass is slender and neat with its lusciously crisped mottled skin still attached, dressed with tart juice and smoky-sweet chipotle barbecue sauce. The *tres leches* cake coddled with green apple foam and gooey *cajeta* is an illuminating finish.

ABC Kitchen

B3

35 E. 18th St. (bet. Broadway & Park Ave. South)

Subway: 23 St (Park Ave. South)   Lunch & dinner daily
Phone: 212-475-5829
Web: www.abckitchennyc.com
Prices: $$

Chef Jean-Georges Vongerichten's signature dining chez ABC Carpet and Home began at this rustic yet glossy farm-to-table venue. A hit since opening, the room is an absolute scene. The pretty people are almost as pretty as the room. Service never impresses, but that is of little importance to this gregarious gaggle of devotees. Tables are accented with flowers and soy-based candles, which cast a glow on each plate.

Expect the fresh flavors of ruby-red line-caught tuna sashimi marinated in ginger-soy sauce, sparked by fresh mint and red chili. Bowtie pasta with kasha and veal meatballs slicked with reduced, herb-infused jus is a hearty treat. Desserts may elicit cheers, especially the creamsicle tart—an orange-infused rendition of *gâteau Basque*.

Aldea ❀

M e d i t e r r a n e a n 🍴🍴

31 W. 17th St. (bet. Fifth & Sixth Aves.)

Subway: 14 St - 6 Av
Phone: 212-675-7223
Web: www.aldearestaurant.com
Prices: $$$

Lunch Mon – Fri
Dinner Mon – Sat

Prepare to leave the chaos of Manhattan behind the moment you set foot into Chef George Mendes' slick temple to Mediterranean flavors.

The resto's moniker is Portuguese for village, and the look is a vision of seaside dining by way of a Flatiron loft. Glass panels, pale birch wood, and shades of blue compose the slender dining room, which is augmented by a mezzanine seating area and chef's counter that seats six beneath a dramatic chandelier.

Mendes has honed his craft under the talents of David Bouley, Alain Ducasse, and Kurt Gutenbrunner, and the chef's Portuguese-American background is reflected in his unique carte. *Petiscos*, or snacks, like organic egg filled with whipped *bacalhau*, potato foam, and black olive "dirt" preclude expertly filleted Portuguese sardines served *escabèche*-style with date vinegar, olive oil, and crispy quinoa. Also delicious is Aldea's house signature *arroz de pato*: beautifully rendered short-grain rice studded with tender duck breast, confit, and crisped skin; as well as smoky chorizo, briny olives, and the sweet punch of dried apricots. For dessert, honey and olive oil are transformed into a warm pudding streaked with cinnamon ice cream and chocolate.

Almayass

B3

24 E. 21st St. (bet. Broadway & Park Ave. South)

Subway: 23 St (Park Ave. South)   Lunch & dinner daily
Phone: 212-473-3100
Web: www.almayassnyc.com
Prices: $$

Hot or cold, fresh and flavorful—the extensive choice of meze at Almayass showcases the riches of Lebanese cuisine accented by Armenian influences, thereby reflecting the heritage of this family-run operation with global outposts. A selection from the spreads and dips is a must, as in the *moutabbal*—eggplant seasoned with lemon, sesame paste, and garlic, redolent of smoke, and topped with jewel-like pomegranate seeds. Other items to seriously consider include *subereg* (a baked dish of four cheeses); oven-baked *mantee* traditional; or charbroiled beef kebabs laced with sour cherries.

Polished wood accents, vivid artwork, servers attired in candy-hued shirts, and tables sized for feasting produce a distinctly upscale vibe within this delicious dining room.

Anjappar

Indian

C2

116 Lexington Ave. (at 28th St.)

Subway: 28 St (Park Ave. South)   Lunch & dinner daily
Phone: 212-265-3663
Web: www.anjapparusa.com
Prices: $$

Step inside this Curry Hill standout to unearth a dining room that is festive without being kitschy. Carved woodwork and a palette of red and ivory embolden the tasteful setting.

Specializing in the cuisine of the Chettinad region, this south Indian kitchen showcases freshly ground spice blends and a particular fondness for eggs. This is clear in items like *nattukozi* (country chicken) *biryani* featuring a fluffy mound of fragrant basmati stuck with a hard-boiled egg and pieces of bone-in chicken, sided by onion gravy, chopped fresh onion, and tomato-studded *raita*. Also sample the *meen kolambu* or chunks of kingfish in a brick-red curry redolent with mustard seeds, coarse ground black peppercorns, red chilies, and bits of fresh and aromatic curry leaf.

A Voce Madison

B2

Italian ✗✗

41 Madison Ave. (entrance on 26th St.)

Subway: 28 St (Park Ave. South)
Phone: 212-545-8555
Web: www.avocerestaurant.com
Prices: $$$

Lunch Mon – Fri
Dinner Mon-Sat

With a terrace overlooking Madison Sq. Park, this is a modern beacon of *Italia* in the city. Its elegant dining room, with swivel chairs and abstract paintings, invites stylish patrons to dine on substantial cooking in a casual-chic setting. Changes in the kitchen have created a few inconsistencies in food pacing, yet the menu remains impressive and NY'ers love it all the same.

Pass over the pastas for more inventive items like Mediterranean sea bass, pan-seared with green onions and paired with artichoke hearts in a lemon-olive oil reduction; or agnolotti filled with lemony ricotta and bathed in a light dressing. Finish with a subtle panna cotta and sip of *vino*.

Shopaholics should savor a plate of pasta at A Voce Columbus in the Time Warner Center.

Barbounia

B3

Mediterranean ✗✗

250 Park Ave. South (at 20th St.)

Subway: 23 St (Park Ave. South)
Phone: 212-995-0242
Web: www.barbounia.com
Prices: $$

Lunch & dinner daily

Big and bold, this Mediterranean brasserie highlights the flame-kissed cooking of sunnier climes. Fat columns, arched openings, and pillow-lined banquettes make the sprawling space seem cozy, but Barbounia's most appetizing feature is Chef Amitzur Mor's open kitchen, equipped with a wood-burning oven.

Irresistible bread, served hot from the oven, begins a meal here that should certainly focus on meze and hot appetizers like charred octopus. Entrées include brick oven-baked branzino with salsa verde, and hanger steak *souvlaki* with black lentil and jasmine rice pilaf. The weekday lunch prix-fixe is a boon to business diners, offering three courses that may end with caramelized milk-coffee gelato crowned by shredded halva and puffed rice brittle.

Bar Jamón

Manhattan ▶ Gramercy, Flatiron & Union Square

B3

Spanish 🍽

125 E. 17th St. (at Irving Pl.)

Subway: 14 St - Union Sq
Phone: 212-253-2773
Web: www.barjamonnyc.com
Prices: $$

Lunch & dinner daily

A nibble at tiny but terrific Bar Jamón, with its brilliant by-the-glass list of Spanish wines (shared with big sister Casa Mono next door), may convince you that Chef Andy Nusser is the unsung hero of the Batali empire. Though the restaurant is the size of a closet, everything is done deliciously and with panache.

This mouthwatering menu so creatively breaks the tired tapas mold that arrival more than 15 minutes past opening almost guarantees a wait. Luscious slices of *jamón serrano* or the famed *ibéríco* from Spain's *pata negra* (black hoofed) pigs; as well as a long list of cheeses and accompaniments star on their menu of small plates. Wash this all down by more than 600 choices of Spanish wine. A *cuarto* from the impressive list is de rigueur.

Bhatti

C2

Indian ✗

100 Lexington Ave. (at 27th St.)

Subway: 28 St (Park Ave. South)
Phone: 212-683-4228
Web: www.bhattinyc.com
Prices: 🪙

Lunch & dinner daily

This Northern Indian eatery is praised for its array of tasty grilled meats and kebabs that emerge from the *bhatti* (open-fire grill). Quality ingredients and a skilled kitchen combine with delicious results as in *haryali choza*, nuggets of white meat chicken marinated in an herbaceous blend of mint, cilantro, green fenugreek, chilies, and hung curd; or the unique house specialty *gilauti kebab*, made from fragrantly spiced lamb ground so fine and incredibly tender that it's almost pâté-smooth. Hearty dishes like *khatte baigan*, silky chunks of eggplant stewed in a tangy onion-tomato masala and garnished with pickled ginger root, wrap up such temptations.

The room is kitsch-free and tasteful with dark wood furnishings set against red-and-gold wallpaper.

BLT Prime

Steakhouse ✕✕

B3

111 E. 22nd St. (bet. Lexington Ave. & Park Ave. South)

Subway: 23 St (Park Ave. South)　　　　　　　　　Dinner nightly
Phone: 212-995-8500
Web: www.bltprime.com
Prices: $$$

Prime Angus beef broiled at 1700 degrees fahrenheit, dabbed with herb butter, and presented on sizzling hot cast iron is the reason this Gramercy steakhouse continues to bask in unbridled success. Power brokers are found unwinding at the bar and downing classic cocktails before settling into taupe banquettes trimmed with gleaming zebrawood tables. The menu is printed on brown craft paper, but is also grandly displayed on a huge wall-mounted board.

Steak may be the most popular option, but this kitchen's talent runs deep. Sautéed Dover sole with soy-caper brown butter satisfies non-meat desires. The nightly prix-fixe has included beautifully done wild Scottish partridge, wrapped in pancetta and plated with melted Savoy cabbage and apple cider jus.

Blue Smoke

American ✕

C2

116 E. 27th St. (bet. Lexington Ave. & Park Ave. South)

Subway: 28 St (Park Ave. South)　　　●　　　Lunch & dinner daily
Phone: 212-447-7733
Web: www.bluesmoke.com
Prices: $$

With its distinct roadhouse feel, Blue Smoke is a down-home treat. Carefully calculated rough edges aside, this is a Danny Meyer restaurant where everyone is truly welcome, from serious suits to Björn-strapped young 'uns.

The faint smell of hickory and applewood used to infuse the meat seeps into the dining room and instantly whets the appetite. Pulled pork, beef brisket, and baby back ribs are all irresistible, but don't overlook the applewood-smoked chicken—a revelation of moist, ivory meat under a layer of gorgeously bronzed skin. Dishes are tasty enough on their own, but the tabletop caddy of sauces allows customized embellishment. Save room for their home-spun sweets, like a kick-ass slice of chocolate layer cake, served with ice-cold milk.

Blue Water Grill

A3

Seafood ✗✗

31 Union Sq. West (at 16th St.)

Subway: 14 St - Union Sq
Phone: 212-675-9500
Web: www.bluewatergrillnyc.com
Prices: $$

Lunch & dinner daily

Facing the Union Square Greenmarket, perennially popular Blue Water Grill is housed in a former, century-old bank, whose grand rooms now bustle with eager guests and a well-trained service team. Still, it retains a stately air with its soaring molded ceiling, gleaming marble floors, and windows overlooking the terraced dining area, ideal for warmer weather.

The crowd-pleasing menu focuses on seafood, but offers something for everyone. Highlights include a raw bar and sushi or maki selections; as well as fish entrées, simply grilled or accented with international flavors, as in big eye tuna with miso-black garlic vinaigrette. Find live jazz nightly in the downstairs lounge; or private group dining in the Vault Room, a former repository for gold bullion.

Bocca

B3

Italian ✗✗

39 E. 19th St. (bet. Broadway & Park Ave. South)

Subway: 23 St (Park Ave. South)
Phone: 212-387-1200
Web: www.boccanyc.com
Prices: $$

Lunch Mon – Fri
Dinner nightly

It's not the newest kid on the block, but this established Italian claims new fame since the arrival of Chef James Corona. Bocca's Roman-accented cuisine hits the right notes in meals that should absolutely begin with the first-rate *tonnarelli cacio e pepe*. This luscious tangle of pasta is tossed with freshly cracked black pepper and cheese, then dramatically arrives to the table in a giant wheel of hollowed Pecorino Romano. The superb quality of that dish is no surprise, considering the owners also run Cacio e Pepe in the East Village. The *porchetta alla Romana* is just as lovely, crisp-skinned and tender, accompanied by red onion marmalade and rapini.

Parchment-hued walls hung with movie posters conjure Fellini's Roma and frame the pleasant setting.

Boqueria 🎅

A2

Spanish 🍴🍴

53 W. 19th St. (bet. Fifth & Sixth Aves.)

Subway: 18 St (Seventh Ave.)
Phone: 212-255-4160
Web: www.boquerianyc.com
Prices: $$

Lunch & dinner daily

Named after Barcelona's famed market, Boqueria does that vibrant emporium proud with an array of ingredient-driven tapas. Their tortilla Española is a true classic, served as a towering wedge of organic eggs, tender potatoes, and sweet onions. Kale reaches new heights as a sweet and earthy salad tossed with a rainbow of cumin-roasted carrots, toasted sunflower seeds, pomegranate arils, and lush swipe of tangy *labne*. Bombas *de la Barceloneta* are crunchy, beef-stuffed potato croquettes plated with salsa verde and silken, garlicky aïoli.

Envision high banquettes amid creamy hues, a white marble bar area filled with wooden boards of Spanish cheeses, olives in terra-cotta bowls, and crowds cooing over classic tapas like *pan con tomate. Delicioso.*

Bread & Tulips 🎅

B2

Italian 🍴🍴

365 Park Ave. South (at 26th St.)

Subway: 28 St (Park Ave. South)
Phone: 212-532-9100
Web: www.breadandtulipsnyc.com
Prices: $$

Lunch Mon – Fri
Dinner Mon – Sat

A cordial greeting and personal escort down to this lower level Hotel Giraffe dining room is a promising start to an inspired meal. Exposed brick, darkly polished wood, and smart arrangements create an air of seclusion to match the room's contemporary good looks (never mind the low ceiling and lack of windows).

The menu offers an array of brick oven baked pizzas as well as small plates of au courant Mediterranean cooking like homemade organic ricotta and grilled octopus. A chilled beet salad mixes creamy goat cheese, young watercress, pink grapefruit, and toasted pistachios. Freshly made pastas are known to gratify, especially the pristine squid ink tagliatelle with tender calamari, diced chorizo, herbed breadcrumbs, and white wine *salsa bianco.*

The Breslin ⭐

Gastropub ✗

B1

16 W. 29th St. (bet. Broadway & Fifth Ave.)

Subway: 28 St (Broadway)　　　　　　　　　　　　Lunch & dinner daily
Phone: 212-679-1939
Web: www.thebreslin.com
Prices: $$$

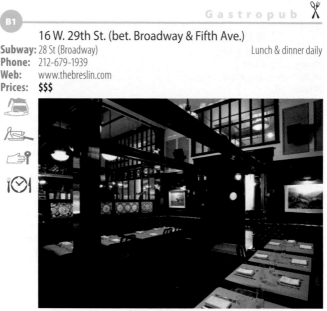

Not sure you've come to the right place? Just look for those new media hotties climbing out of black cars, and know that you've arrived at The Breslin. Attached to the markedly hip Ace Hotel, this uber-stylish gastropub, known for its pretty patrons and perpetual buzz, is a place to see and be seen.

Booths tucked into nooks on one side of the room are by far the best seats in the house, but all is not lost if you can't nab one. Close-knit tables adorned with white china and rustic wooden boards are equally inviting, with views of the open kitchen. If your welcome was a bit…well lukewarm… you'll find that the tee- and tattoo-donning staff warms up as service progresses—not unlike one's appreciation for the chef's outstanding creations.

Parmesan and fried parsley leaves gild the romaine leaves in a delicious, very garlicky Caesar salad; just as a coiled link of terrifically flavored merguez is perfectly finished with smoky marcona almond aïoli. Meanwhile, warm and milky burrata gains great flavor and texture when kissed by nutty hazelnut pesto. Clementine cake frosted with mascarpone and dates is a sweet example of how this kitchen elevates seemingly simple eats to thoroughly stellar treats.

Cafe El Presidente

M e x i c a n ✗

30 W. 24th St. (bet. Fifth & Sixth Aves.)

Subway: 23 St (Sixth Ave.)
Phone: 212-242-3491
Web: www.cafeelpresidente.com
Prices: 😊😊

Lunch & dinner daily

With its colorful interior signage and indoor/outdoor aesthetic, this tasty taqueria near Madison Square Park could easily pass for a Mexico City hot spot. Soaring ceilings cover an open kitchen and tortilla-production station where disks of masa—the foundation for an enticing lineup of tacos—are turned out at a steady clip.

Café El Presidente's attention to both quality and creativity is impressive, and proof is in the tacos *especiales*: wilted Swiss chard combined with roasted poblano chiles and sautéed yellow onion; or a spread of black bean purée topped with diced roasted sweet potato and dusting of *cotija*. For the ultimate conclusion, go for *Gringa Madison*, a rich pairing of pork *al pastor* and melted Chiuhuahua spiked with freshly chopped cilantro.

Copper Chimney

I n d i a n ✗✗

126 E. 28th St. (bet. Lexington Ave. & Park Ave. South)

Subway: 28 St (Park Ave. South)
Phone: 212-213-5742
Web: www.copperchimneynyc.com
Prices: $$

Lunch & dinner daily

Copper Chimney is a pleasing and tasteful retreat from Curry Hill's sassier options. Polite service and a dining room of pale gray walls and buff-colored banquettes soothe the spirit. But, one peek at the expansive menu is sure to entice your palate. The regional offerings bring extensive choice, with myriad vegetarian and *tandoori* specialties. Mild but flavorful curries like *dalchi* may feature salmon in a pale orange sauce that is thick as *dal* and seasoned with mustard seeds, curry leaves, and whole dried red chilies. *Baigan bartha* is a sumptuous blend of roasted and mashed eggplant cooked with onions, tomatoes, and spices. Breads served hot off the *tawa* are a must, like the *aloo paratha* which is pillowy soft and stuffed with spiced potatoes.

Casa Mono ❀

Spanish ✗✗

B3

52 Irving Pl. (at 17th St.)

Subway: 14 St - Union Sq
Phone: 212-253-2773
Web: www.casamononyc.com
Prices: $$$

Lunch & dinner daily

Still lording over its primo little corner of Irving Place, Casa Mono is small, jammed, and 100% New York…but in a Spanish kind of way. Inside, tight-knit tables seem to grunt under the numbers of mouthwatering plates everyone is tempted to order. Locals flock here Monday through Friday, before the weekend's destination diners begin to arrive. The dining counter cannot be reserved, but clockwork service means that seats turn quickly. Staff may favor efficiency to pleasantries, but so be it. The food is awesome.

Dishes are creative and ambitious renditions of Spanish tapas, but each was clearly crafted with pleasure in mind. Even their humble *patatas bravas* attain new heights, as a pan of fingerling potatoes that have been steamed, crisped in olive oil, then tossed with tomato *mojo* and aïoli. It is impossible to come here and not order certain dishes such as razor clams *a la plancha* in finger-licking garlicky parsley sauce; and big, messy piles of *fideos* with clams and chorizo.

Rabbit displays innovation and stunning skill, with each cut prepared a different way—fried, barbecued, and roasted— served with creamy habanero *cuajada* and lightly pickled, subtly spiced "Mono kimchee."

Craft

B3

American ✗✗✗

43 E. 19th St. (bet. Broadway & Park Ave. South)

Subway: 14 St - Union Sq
Phone: 212-780-0880
Web: www.craftrestaurantsinc.com
Prices: $$$$

Dinner nightly

This first and most original venture of renowned Chef Tom Colicchio opened back in 2001, yet its look is timeless. Housed in a former department store built in 1886, the setting is masculine yet cozy, lofty yet intimate. Terra-cotta columns, bare-bulb lights, and gleaming copper serving pieces filled with farm-fresh ingredients are among the iconic signatures here. It's still tough to get a reservation, so there is time to save up for your meal.

The menu's laissez-faire conceit allows diners to design their own meal from lists that group ingredients by their method of preparation. Raw bigeye tuna with Meyer lemon zest or roasted quail dabbed with balsamic might lead to a single braised beef short rib coupled with decadent potato gratin.

Craftbar

B3

Contemporary ✗✗

900 Broadway (bet. 19th & 20th Sts.)

Subway: 14 St - Union Sq
Phone: 212-461-4300
Web: www.craftrestaurantsinc.com
Prices: $$

Lunch & dinner daily

This first Craft spin-off proudly displays its pedigree with simple yet elegant ingredient-focused cooking presented in a chic and lofty domain that respects the bones of its Flatiron locale. With its extensive menu of something for everyone, there is no wonder that this place packs a lively crowd.

Diners nibble on addictive, cheese-flecked breadsticks while perusing a menu that presents snacks, local cheeses, *salumi*, and small plates like a flavor-packed bowl of marinated Montauk squid dressed with a fish sauce vinaigrette, spicy mayonnaise, pickled Fresno chilies, and cool cucumber. A handful of pastas are offered among the large plate selection, such as squid-ink *chitarra* tangled with seafood, red wine *soffritto*, and mustard greens.

élan

Contemporary ✕✕

B3

43 E. 20th St. (bet. Broadway & Park Ave. South)

Subway: 23 St (Park Ave. South)   Dinner nightly
Phone: 646-682-7105
Web: www.elannyc.com
Prices: $$$

Diners of a certain age will remember Chef David Waltuck's trailblazing Chanterelle, which closed in 2009 after a commendable 30 years on the NYC restaurant scene. His new residence, housed in the former Veritas space has been tweaked to feature a gallery-style bar that showcases the works of emerging artists, plus a dining room of silver-striped banquettes and walls hung with foxed mirrors.

Global accents influence much of the cooking, as in duck breast paired with crispy vegetable spring rolls and sauced with smoky jus. The pine nut-studded seafood sausage is a classic, plated with sauerkraut and grainy mustard beurre blanc, and a sundae of cherry pit-infused ice cream—complete with cherry sorbet and almond cake—is a shining example of seasonality.

The Gander

Contemporary ✕✕

A3

15 W. 18th St. (bet. Fifth & Sixth Aves.)

Subway: 14 St - Union Sq   Lunch & dinner daily
Phone: 212-229-9500
Web: www.thegandernyc.com
Prices: $$

A step up in elegance from sibling Recette, The Gander's pale tones, burlap ceiling pendants, and ivory terrazzo floor flow from the front lounge to a back dining area. The very hospitable service team ensures that while the vibe can seem energetic, it is still family-friendly and pleasant for conversation.

The menu flaunts Chef Jesse Schenker's signature whimsy—a lobster "roll" is a roulade of tender tail meat filled with shrimp mousse over toasted brioche. Kitchen talent is clear in unique and inspired pasta courses, like delicate *tortelli* filled with earthy puréed beets, set in a pool of coconut cream and goat yogurt. Desserts may include a creative take on crème brûlée made with crème anglaise mousse, chocolate ganache, and bits of crunchy bacon.

Eleven Madison Park ✿ ✿ ✿

Contemporary ✗✗✗✗

B2

11 Madison Ave. (at 24th St.)

Subway: 23 St (Park Ave. South)
Phone: 212-889-0905
Web: www.elevenmadisonpark.com
Prices: $$$$

Lunch Thu – Sat
Dinner nightly

All the imposing art deco grandeur a former bank can offer soars to new heights at Eleven Madison Park. With ceilings high enough to tempt the laws of physics and a quarry's worth of granite, this is one of the city's most elegant settings. In any other hands, it might seem heavy or serious, but this service team goes beyond impeccable timing and lock-step precision; staff members take time with guests and strive to make each experience here unique.

Chef Daniel Humm's storied menu is a sophisticated tribute to New York food history, with smart references pervading a dizzying array of small plates. Find a superb mix of tastes and softness in the fresh oyster in shallot mignonette with an intensely refreshing potato sherbet, bits of domestic caviar, crème fraîche ice cream, and crusty potato chips. Local and of-the-moment ingredients shine in a Hudson Valley foie gras terrine cured with orange and chamomile that melts in the mouth—a perfect contrast to the onion foam and asparagus salad topped with a crisp orange-dusted tuile.

Save yourself for dessert, when New York's best Baked Alaska (ever) is torched tableside with aged rum, strawberries, toasted almonds, and strawberry coulis.

109

15 East 🏵

15 E. 15th St. (bet. Fifth Ave. & Union Sq. West)

Subway: 14 St - Union Sq
Phone: 212-647-0015
Web: www.15eastrestaurant.com
Prices: $$$

Lunch & dinner Mon — Sat

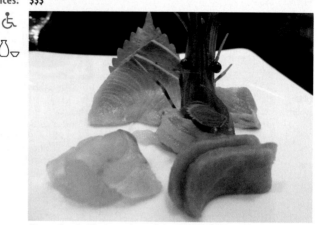

On a classic Flatiron slice of the city, find this deeply focused temple of sushi and sashimi. The front counter area is bright with natural elements, sculpture, colorful pillows on the windowsill, and a counter made of a single piece of wood with glass cases to peer into the chef's refrigerated section. Beyond the *sakabayashi* gently dividing the space in two, enter the narrow dining room lined with windows, bare tables and upholstered banquettes. The crowd is young, diverse, and very comfortable.

Tremendous care and skill is exhibited in the meticulously selected serving vessels that enhance the beauty of each morsel; of course, that level of care starts with the ingredients. Envision octopus that has been "beaten" 500 times, braised in soy, and served with sea salt to complement its good flavor with remarkable tenderness. The omakase sashimi may yield a parade of fresh Tasmanian salmon, wonderfully fatty *chu-toro*, or striped jack fish. Standout sushi is made with superb rice that highlights the flavors of kampachi or amberjack with yuzu-lemon.

Word to the wise: if you happen to spy another diner scoring a course that you were not offered, just ask for it—the chef will gladly oblige.

Manhattan ▶ Gramercy, Flatiron & Union Square

General Assembly

Contemporary 🍴🍴

B2

360 Park Ave. South (at 26th St.)

Subway: 28 St (Park Ave. South)
Phone: 212-951-7111
Web: www.generalassemblyrestaurant.com
Prices: $$$

Lunch Mon – Fri
Dinner nightly

Thanks to a country-chic redesign by avroKO, General Assembly has been transformed into a market-driven brasserie that opens into a series of separate dining areas with soaring ceilings. Among the new nooks is the softly lit Lillet Room, a downstairs event space—one of a few—that's shelved solely with bottles of the French aperitif.

Chef Craig Koketsu lets the season guide the expansive roster of cuisine, which starts off with a sharable platter of crudité stocked with flatbread and spreads like house-made ricotta drizzled with local honey and white bean tinted with smoked tomato. Other highlights include rabbit saddle wrapped in excellent pastry for a novel take on the Wellington; and meaty lamb ribs with a sticky gloss of smoked cherries.

Hanjan

Korean 🍴🍴

B1

36 W. 26th St. (bet. Broadway & Sixth Ave.)

Subway: 28 St (Broadway)
Phone: 212-206-7226
Web: www.hanjan26.com
Prices: $$

Lunch Mon-Fri
Dinner nightly

The latest from Chef Hooni Kim is similar in scale to his Hell's Kitchen hot spot, Danji. Here, find an entryway bar leading to a clutch of tables surrounding the communal centerpiece. The low-lit room is accented by an array of white ceramic crockery neatly arranged against shades of grey.

Korean small plates headlined under "Traditional" and "Modern" delight palates with vibrant flavors. The scallion pancake stuffed with squid is incredible—this lacy crisp heap is served with a fiery dipping sauce. Skewers of freshly butchered chicken are served hot off the grill with a walnut-and-chili paste; while a boneless pig's foot is slowly braised to take on a sweet-salty sheen and is presented with a blend of chopped kimchi and fermented shrimp paste.

111

Gramercy Tavern ✿

Contemporary 🍴🍴🍴

B3

42 E. 20th St. (bet. Broadway & Park Ave. South)

Subway: 23 St (Park Ave. South)
Phone: 212-477-0777
Web: www.gramercytavern.com
Prices: $$$

Lunch Mon – Fri
Dinner nightly

Cloaked in Americana and the scent of wood smoke, Gramercy Tavern is such an unspoiled rendition of old New York that were it not for the electric bulbs in the iron chandeliers, you might forget we are in the 21st century. The front "tavern" area is always pleasantly bustling and offers one of the city's premium options for solo dining at the bar. Period portraits, wood beams, and velvet curtains accent the series of smaller dining rooms, all staffed by expert yet very friendly servers.

From start to finish, this is a restaurant that bears a steady hand to excel with precision and finesse. Begin with a smooth and silky butternut squash soup, served with braised yet still snappy Brussels sprouts, tangy Granny Smith apple cubes, fresh chives, and enjoyable notes of subtle bitterness from toasted pumpkin seeds.

Perfectly seasonal standouts have shown moist and meaty duck breast set over parsnip purée, crushed hazelnuts, and Puy lentils. Composition and combination are paramount in the tarte Tatin, its flaky and marvelously buttery crust bearing caramelized apples topped with green apple *granite* and batons of fresh apple—the contrast of temperature and flavor offer a knockout finale.

Harding's

A m e r i c a n   ✗✗

B3

32 E. 21st St. (bet. Broadway & Park Ave. South)

Subway: 23 St (Park Ave. South)
Phone: 212-600-2105
Web: www.hardingsnyc.com
Prices: $$

Lunch daily
Dinner Mon-Sat

A bowl of cream-free plum tomato purée drizzled with fragrant thyme olive oil, partnered with a grilled cheddar cheese sandwich perfectly portrays Harding's comforting yet up-to-date appeal. The lofty setting feels more yesteryear than tomorrow, with creaky wood planks underfoot, walls dressed with butter-yellow damask wallpaper, foxed mirror accents, and a giant American flag affixed to the exposed brick wall.

The kitchen keeps up the good work with a menu that includes the likes of a Waldorf salad dressed with creamy blue cheese buttermilk; or striped bass, slow-cooked then pan-seared, plated with shaved planks of roasted fennel and foamy bacon essence. The deconstructed rendering of lemon meringue pie is a sweet and satisfying finish.

Hill Country

B a r b e c u e   ✗

B1

30 W. 26th St. (bet. Broadway & Sixth Ave.)

Subway: 28 St (Broadway)
Phone: 212-255-4544
Web: www.hillcountryny.com
Prices: $$

Lunch & dinner daily

Manhattan's Hill Country offers as succulent a barbecue experience as one can hope for without actually stepping onto the rolling hills of central Texas. This rollicking roadhouse proudly displays its Lone Star heritage throughout; the lower level doubles as a live country music venue and the ground floor is arranged with counters dispensing the mouthwatering victuals.

Consider your meat options, but don't fret 'cause it's all good, whether you choose lean (or moist) brisket, pork ribs, or smoked chicken to name just a few of the treats. Have your meal ticket stamped, then pick from a plethora of sides and sweets to complete your meal.

Downtown Brooklyn recently welcomed its own Hill Country Barbecue, adjacent to the Hill Country Chicken offshoot.

Hill Country Chicken 🐥

A m e r i c a n ✗

B2

1123 Broadway (at 25th St.)

Subway: 23 St (Broadway)
Phone: 212-257-6446
Web: www.hillcountrychicken.com
Prices: 🍲

Lunch & dinner daily

Gussied up in a happy palette of sunny yellow and sky blue, this 100-seat homage to deep-fried down-home country cooking serves exemplary fried chicken offered in two varieties. The "classic" sports a seasoned, golden brown skin; "Mama El's" is skinless and cracker-crusted. Both are available by the piece or as part of whimsically named meals, like the "white meat solo coop."

Step up to the counter and feast your eyes on cast-iron skillets of chicken, as well as sides like creamy mashed potatoes, pimento macaroni and cheese, or grilled corn salad with red peppers and green onion. And then there's pie. More than 12 assortments, baked in-house and available by the slice, whole, or blended into a milkshake for a drinkable take on "à la mode."

I Trulli

I t a l i a n ✗✗

C2

122 E. 27th St. (bet. Lexington Ave. & Park Ave. South)

Subway: 28 St (Park Ave. South)
Phone: 212-481-7372
Web: www.itrulli.com
Prices: $$

Lunch Mon – Fri
Dinner nightly

I Trulli has been celebrating the wine and food of Southern Italy's Puglia region for the past two decades. From its roaring fireplace to the breezy outdoor garden, this place oozes warmth and the country-chic ambience is always comfortable. Wood furnishings, marble, and white tableclothes outfit the dining room, which is linked through a small hallway to a second dining room and the adjacent Enoteca. Service is engaging and pleasantly old school.

I Trulli takes pride in its pastas, made in-house and on full view in the open kitchen. Selections have included silken rounds of *ravioli d'Olivia* stuffed with ricotta cheese, cloaked in a creamy pistachio sauce. Entrées are appropriately rustic and might feature crispy fried rabbit or roasted chicken.

The John Dory Oyster Bar

B1

1196 Broadway (at 29th St.)

Subway: 28 St (Broadway)
Phone: 212-792-9000
Web: www.thejohndory.com
Prices: $$

Lunch & dinner daily

Brought to you by Chef April Bloomfield and company, this oyster bar occupies a blue-chip, corner spot in the untouchably cool Ace Hotel. The style is vintage with aquatic accents: floor-to-ceiling windows flood the space with light, while black-tiled columns, copper tables, and crayon-bright green and blue bar stools complete the look.

The unpretentious and modern menu showcases impeccable seafood. An assortment from the raw bar may feature whelks with parsley and garlic butter; east- and west-coast oysters shucked before your very eyes; and top quality shellfish with a lemon-and-shallot sauce. On the menu, find semolina soup with Nantucket bay scallops, or Spanish mackerel with crunchy cilantro-squid crackers. Sadly, service can be indifferent.

Kokum

C2

106 Lexington Ave. (bet. 27th & 28th Sts.)

Subway: 28 St (Park Ave. South)
Phone: 212-684-6842
Web: www.kokumny.com
Prices: $$

Lunch & dinner daily

The specialties of India's southern coastline are the focus at restaurateur Shiva Natarajan's latest. Named after the tart tropical fruit, Kokum is prettified by a mural of fishing boats on a sandy stretch and exposed filament bulbs reflecting warmly off bronzed mirror panels.

Delights from Kerala, Chennai, and Mangalore anchor the menu. Roasted in a banana leaf with diced tomato and spices, the fish *pollichathu* is infused with sweetness and accompanied by fried tapioca root. *Kori gassi* is chicken in a rich curry containing plenty of dried red chilies but tempered by coconut milk and flecked with curry leaf. Carb fans can't resist the fragrant mound of vegetable biryani, drizzled with saffron butter, topped with fried onions and crushed *papadum*.

Junoon ✿

Indian 𝗫𝗫𝗫

B2

27 W. 24th St. (bet. Fifth & Sixth Aves.)

Subway: 23 St (Sixth Ave.)
Phone: 212-490-2100
Web: www.junoonnyc.com
Prices: $$$

Lunch & dinner daily

Attention to detail is what sets Junoon far apart from its *desi* brethren. The façade appears dramatic, but once through those ebony doors, the cavernous setting is welcoming and rich with treasures from the subcontinent. The large bar exudes class and fun, with two antique *jhoolas* (swings) crafted from Burmese teak. Walk through a 200-year-old wooden arch and carved panels beyond, seemingly afloat in a reflecting pool, to enter the amber-tinted dining room where tables are luxuriously spaced. Head downstairs to glimpse the glass-walled room displaying a market's worth of spices.

Junoon presents a contemporary vision of Indian cuisine, begining with a thick octopus tentacle sent to the tandoor oven, emerging crisped, charred, incredibly tender, served with pickled purple potato and herb oil. *Murg lababdar* tastes of pure elegance in seared and braised de-boned chicken drenched in a sweetly spiced, deeply flavored tomato and onion gravy.

The toothsome Kashmiri lotus root dumplings, *nadru kofte*, are enriched with house-made *paneer* and poached in a creamy curry spiced with fenugreek. *Daal tadka* is a mouthwatering infusion of yellow split peas, chickpeas, turmeric, cumin, and chilies.

Laut 🍜

A3

15 E. 17th St. (bet. Broadway & Fifth Ave.)

Subway: 14 St - Union Sq
Phone: 212-206-8989
Web: www.lautnyc.com
Prices: $$

Lunch Mon-Fri
Dinner nightly

Laut is a unique Malaysian restaurant that is at once cheerful and authentic yet never challenging or inaccessible. It is likewise true to its downtown spirit, in a room that features dim lighting and exposed brick prettied with chalk drawings of orchids and water lilies.

The personable staff and menu of Southeast Asian delights are as steady as the constant crowd. Popular choices include *roti telur*, a thin and slightly crisped yet pliable pancake stuffed with scrambled eggs, onions, and peppers, paired with fragrant chicken curry and coconut dipping sauce. The *nasi lemak* is a dome of coconut rice surrounded with sweet chili shrimp, hard-boiled egg, roasted peanuts, and dried anchovies for mixing into an outrageously good mélange of Malaysian flavors.

Les Halles

C2

411 Park Ave. South (bet. 28th & 29th Sts.)

Subway: 28 St (Park Ave. South)
Phone: 212-679-4111
Web: www.leshalles.net
Prices: $$

Lunch & dinner daily

Named for the famed Parisian marketplace, this Les Halles is better known locally for birthing New York's *enfant terrible*, Tony Bourdain. The writer and chef-turned TV personality may be globe-trotting, but his legend remains part of the fabric here. Gaze up those worn wooden columns to sense this brasserie's storied history and age. Tightly knit tables generate competing conversations; checkered terrazzo floors and hardwood do little to buffer the hum.

Expect many *ooh-la-las* over very tasty *gratinée des Halles*, a French onion soup with melted cheese capping croutons soaked in a rich beef broth. Waiters are courteous yet quick in delivering timeless dishes like *steak au poivre* crusted with black peppercorns and coupled with deliciously crisp frites.

Maialino

B3

2 Lexington Ave. (at 21st St.)

Subway: 23 St (Park Ave South)
Phone: 212-777-2410
Web: www.maialinonyc.com
Prices: $$

Lunch & dinner daily

Maialino is a trattoria, but only in theory. As the dining room of the Gramercy Park Hotel designed by the Rockwell Group, and overseen by service maestro Danny Meyer, there's nothing rustic or humble about it. The setting buzzes from day to night, and has established itself as a preferred watering hole for every sort of influencer.

Chef Nick Anderer's menu of Roman-inspired delights brings the upscale scene down to earth with an assortment of hearty preparations, like unctuous honeycomb *trippa alla Trastaverina* braised in a spicy tomato sauce. Enticing pastas include fat tubes of *paccheri* dressed with silky white beans, pleasantly bitter escarole, and a touch of rosemary. Come dessert, the curiously light ricotta-based panna cotta cannot be missed.

Manzo

B2

200 Fifth Ave. (at 23rd St.)

Subway: 23 St (Broadway)
Phone: 212-229-2180
Web: www.eataly.com
Prices: $$$

Lunch & dinner daily

Eataly New York (brought to you by Mario Batali and friends) is a perpetually bustling emporium brimming with Italian products. The rollicking scene rarely lets up and navigating through the hordes of visitors entranced by the sights and scents of the abundance on offer may prove to be overwhelming for some.

For sit down dining, steer yourself straight toward Manzo, tucked away from the fray. "Beef" in Italian, Manzo offers a meaty take on this country's cuisine. *Paste* are numerous and impressively prepared; and the weekday lunch prix-fixe is highly recommended—baby artichokes with plump cranberry beans; charred New York strip with Barbaresco vinaigrette; and silken vanilla panna cotta. Pair your meal with a pour from the comprehensive wine selection.

Mari Vanna

B3

41 E. 20th St. (bet. Broadway & Park Ave. South)

Subway: 23 St (Park Ave South)
Phone: 212-777-1955
Web: www.marivanna.ru/ny
Prices: $$

Lunch & dinner daily

The bar is stocked with urns of house-infused vodka (apricot, seaberry, and cucumber-dill to name just a few) and the main dining room is often fully occupied by large groups. Despite the revelry, the ambience at Mari Vanna persuades its occupants to sit back and enjoy themselves in the shabby-chic room, done in a bleached palette complemented by embroidered seat backs and glowing chandeliers.

Traditional Russian specialties abound with an Olivier salad, *salo* (house-smoked fatback), borscht, and plump *pelmeni* served with herbed butter and sour cream. The kitchen's serious effort shines through in entrées like *golubtzi*, featuring two neat bundles of braised cabbage stuffed with fragrant ground beef and rice, then draped with a lush coat of tomato cream.

Maysville

B1

17 W. 26th St. (bet. Broadway & Sixth Ave.)

Subway: 23 St (Sixth Ave.)
Phone: 646-490-8240
Web: www.maysvillenyc.com
Prices: $$

Lunch & dinner daily

Manhattan now has a bourbon temple to call its own with Sean Joseph's offshoot of Brooklyn's beloved Char No. 4. Named after the Kentucky port town and birthplace of bourbon, Maysville tends to exceed expectations in its catalog of American whiskey.

The amber-hued room is sure to sooth any Manhattanite starting to feel culturally overshadowed by that borough across the river. Inside find a long bar, triptych of charcoal horse sketches, and skilled team led by an ex-Gramercy Tavern sous-chef preparing Southern food. Appetizers are quite interesting as in cubes of crispy grits nestled in bourbon aïoli and topped with ruffles of salty country ham; or fried, black pepper-flecked veal sweetbreads plated with capers, fingerlings, and fennel.

Molly's Pub & Shebeen

C3

Gastropub ✗

287 Third Ave. (bet. 22nd & 23rd Sts.)

Subway: 23 St (Park Ave. South)
Phone: 212-889-3361
Web: www.mollysshebeen.com
Prices: ⊜⊜

Lunch & dinner daily

A stop at Molly's Pub & Shebeen isn't just for celebrating St. Patrick's Day-style revelry the remaining 364 days of the year. The utterly charming setting, friendly service, and heartwarming fare make it much more than the standard Irish watering hole. First established in 1895, this framework has had various incarnations but has been sating a loyal following since 1964. Wood smoke perfumes the air, rustic furnishings are arranged on a sawdust-covered floor, and a seat at the original mahogany bar couldn't be more welcoming. The ambience of this pub (or *shebeen*, which is an illicit drinking establishment) has few peers.

Stick with the list of house specialties (lamb stew, corned beef and cabbage, and Shepherd's pie) for an authentic experience.

Momokawa ☺

C2

Japanese ✗

157 E. 28th St. (bet. Lexington & Third Aves.)

Subway: 28 St (Park Ave. South)
Phone: 212-684-7830
Web: www.momokawanyc.com
Prices: $$

Lunch & dinner daily

By offering the comforting tastes of authentic Japanese cooking (the kind that people yearn for on a daily basis), Momokawa reminds us that sushi is for special occasions. Favored by expats and area residents, it's the type of place Tokyo salarymen might frequent before the long commute home. Ascend the winding staircase to discover a tidy room with counter seats and booths that can become private thanks to ceiling-mounted bamboo shades.

The range of tasty plates reveal *goma*-tofu, a dimpled round of sesame tofu topped with a bit of uni and freshly grated wasabi; as well as *satsuma-age*, tasty pan-fried fish cakes. Other satisfying courses include *ochazuke-mentai*, rice topped with spicy cod roe and nori, over which guests pour a savory green tea broth.

NoMad ✿

Contemporary ✕✕✕

B1

1170 Broadway (at 28th St.)

Subway: 28 St (Broadway)
Phone: 347-472-5660
Web: www.thenomadhotel.com
Prices: $$$

Lunch & dinner daily

While Chef Daniel Humm and Will Guidara's Eleven Madison Park plays the role of virtuoso, there's a distinct rock star attitude at work in this dining pleasure palace at the NoMad hotel.

The focal point of the multifaceted setting—designed by Jacques Garcia—is the Atrium, which is a stately glass-roofed area with French limestone flooring, dark wood, and acid-green armchairs. Adding to this hip restaurant's charms are private dining under the cupola on the 12th-floor rooftop, a snug alcove complete with a working, French chateau-like fireplace, as well as the newly installed NoMad Bar. Custom-made ceramic pieces in earthy shades present the kitchen's set of astonishing à la carte works. Fresh tagliatelle slicked with Meyer lemon butter and dotted with King crab is a luscious example of restraint; while roasted butternut squash goes for gusto with a stuffing of *morcilla* and garnishes of dried apple and crisped *jillnoa. Beef filet* is roasted to medium rare until sports sweet potato (both a purée and crunchy, salted chips of skin) and bone marrow-enriched bordelaise sauce.

Malted chocolate ganache is a bombshell finale, so smooth and silken, paired with malted milk ice cream and warm fondant.

Novitá

B3

Italian ✗✗

102 E. 22nd St. (bet. Lexington Ave. & Park Ave. South)

Subway: 23 St (Park Ave South)
Phone: 212-677-2222
Web: www.novitanyc.com
Prices: $$

Lunch Mon – Fri
Dinner nightly

This delightfully unpretentious trattoria is located on the ground floor of an art deco residential building that dates back to 1928. Novitá may have only opened in 1994, but elegant touches honor its tony Gramercy locale, with flowers dressing up the interior and canvas umbrella-topped tables outside. The dining room combines large, bright windows with pale yellow walls and a warm, autumnal-hued banquette. The staff's air of friendly formality suits the room. Enjoyable house-made pasta might feature *strozzapreti* tossed in fragrant basil pesto. Equally pleasing is a salad of *rucola*, avocado, and warm calamari. Other options include entrées like the black pepper-crusted tuna with lemon sauce, or a bittersweet chocolate-speckled semifreddo for dessert.

Ootoya

A3

Japanese ✗✗

8 W. 18th St. (bet. Fifth & Sixth Aves.)

Subway: 14 St (Sixth Ave.)
Phone: 212-255-0018
Web: www.ootoya.us
Prices: $$

Lunch & dinner daily

Welcome to this first stateside location of a Tokyo-based chain with more than 300 outlets throughout Asia. A slender dining counter dominates the back section of the rectangular space that also offers table service and a mezzanine seating area. The attractive minimalist design and gracious staff put aside any fears of chain-dining.

Ootoya's angle on Japanese cuisine is hearty portions of comforting *yoshoku*-style (Western-influenced) preparations such as grilled Washu beef burger with demi-glace; pork loin *katsu*; and house-made curry sauce. The *teishoku* (set meal) is a fine lunchtime option, especially when it features hefty morsels of excellent quality, deep-fried *buta kurozu* pork dabbed in sweet-and-sour sauce made from aged rice vinegar.

Periyali

A2

Greek ✗✗

35 W. 20th St. (bet. Fifth & Sixth Aves.)

Subway: 23 St (Sixth Ave.)
Phone: 212-463-7890
Web: www.periyali.com
Prices: $$$

Lunch Mon – Fri
Dinner nightly

Aegean sensibilities and vibrant Mediterranean flavors are dished out with panache at this Greek mainstay, in operation and thriving since 1978. A glinting school of abstract metal fish artfully commands one wall, while an intimate rear seating area glows like a pale pink sunset in the room's evening light. The petite space can get packed with a dressy, European crowd.

First-rate cooking may begin with fresh and crisp *horiatiki salata* sporting creamy feta and powerfully fragrant dried oregano; or the small but pleasingly robust *sikotakia me fakes*, chicken livers sautéed with rosemary laid over a bed of lentils. The reliably decadent moussaka layers crisped potato slices, ground lamb, roasted eggplant, and béchamel so creamy that it verges on fluffy.

Pure Food and Wine

B3

Vegan ✗✗

54 Irving Pl. (bet. 17th & 18th Sts.)

Subway: 14 St - Union Sq
Phone: 212-477-1010
Web: www.purefoodandwine.com
Prices: $$

Lunch & dinner daily

Going strong for more than a decade, it's safe to say the conceit of vegan/raw dining is more than just a passing trend. Owner Sarma Melngailis has positioned this restaurant into a brand supported by cookbooks, a devoted Twitter following, and retail products from the adjacent juice bar and takeout shop.

The plant based creations served in this brownstone dining room are never heated above 118 degrees Fahrenheit. In order to preserve vitamins, minerals, and enzymes. The clever and very enjoyable lineup includes corn and sun-dried tomato tortilla wraps stuffed with cilantro guacamole and cashew sour cream. The zucchini- and heirloom tomato-lasagna has been a signature since day one. Sake and organic/biodynamic wines complement the unique menu.

Resto

Contemporary ✗

C2

111 E. 29th St. (bet. Lexington Ave. & Park Ave. South)

Subway: 28 St (Park Ave. South)
Phone: 212-685-5585
Web: www.restonyc.com
Prices: $$

Lunch & dinner daily

Vibrant cooking, a winning ambience, and an inviting marble bar have made this brasserie a perpetual neighborhood favorite. Despite numerous kitchen shakeups, the talented team behind the line always lands on its feet and continues to turn out a roster of worthwhile temptations. Moules frites are a hold-over from when Belgian cooking dominated the menu, but contemporary plates have included charred squid salad with citrus segments and shaved sunchokes; *cavatelli* with creamy fontina cheese, shaved Brussels sprouts, and toasted pine nuts; and pork shoulder steak with fava bean *gribiche*.

For an array of meaty treats washed down by global brews, head next door to sister spot The Cannibal, which has a second, thriving outpost in midtown's Gotham Market West.

Rye House

American ✗

A3

11 W. 17 St. (bet. Fifth & Sixth Aves.)

Subway: 14 St (Sixth Ave.)
Phone: 212-255-7260
Web: www.ryehousenyc.com
Prices: $$

Lunch & dinner daily

As its name would suggest, Rye House offers a tavern-inspired look and easygoing vibe fueled by an impressive selection of amber liquor. The front bar provides a comfortable seat from which to sip a mint julep or single-malt Scotch, but those who wish to dine sacrifice the bar's ambience for the back area's greater comfort and enjoy the kitchen's concise and enjoyably prepared selection of playful pub grub.

The small plate offerings include the likes of crunchy and well-seasoned fried dill pickle slices, Sloppy Joe sliders, and drunken mussels bathed in Belgian-style ale. The list of entrées may be short but items such as roasted chicken dressed with spoonbread, braised greens, and buttermilk-enriched jus prove this is food to be savored.

Saravanaas

C2

Indian ✗

81 Lexington Ave. (at 26th St.)

Subway: 28 St (Park Ave. South)   Lunch & dinner daily
Phone: 212-679-0204
Web: www.saravanabhavan.com
Prices: ⬤⬤

With its corner location and attractive two-room setting, Saravanaas emerges from the Curry Hill pack. The brightly lit room is set with lacquered tables and high-backed ivory upholstered chairs that seem a far cry from the taxi driver-favored cafeterias dotting this strip of Lexington.

The reason this beloved Gramercy location is forever bustling with locals and tourists is for vegetarian food that is as good as it is serious, with a wide array of specialties, curries, breads, and weekend-only *biryani* on offer. However, table-long *dosas*, paired with a plethora of chuntneys (think coconut and chili) and fiery *sambar* are *the* main attraction. Don't miss the *aloo paratha*: this butter-drenched, puffy flatbread filled with spiced potatoes is excellent.

SD26

B2

Italian ✗✗

19 E. 26th St. (bet. Fifth & Madison Aves.)

Subway: 28 St (Park Ave. South)   Lunch & dinner Mon-Sat
Phone: 212-265-5959
Web: www.sd26ny.com
Prices: $$

Run by Tony May and his daughter Marisa, SD26 is spacious enough to allow the distinct experiences of having a drink at the bar, a snack in the lounge, or a full meal in the dining room. The sleek setting is idyllically suited to its contemporary diners.

The offerings are as wide-ranging as the space, and patrons here will find the possibilities seemingly endless. Platters of ribbon-thin cured meats and imported cheeses are a popular kickoff. Many pastas are freshly made in-house before being embellished with the likes of chickpea purée and rosemary oil, or a beguilingly simple and lovely fresh tomato sauce. Entrées are equally tantalizing as in grilled, lemon-cured cod served over a hearty and enticingly soft buckwheat-speckled polenta *taragna*.

Tamba

C2

103 Lexington Ave. (bet. 27th & 28th Sts.)

Subway: 28 St (Park Ave. South)	Lunch Mon – Sat
Phone: 212-481-9100	Dinner nightly
Web: www.tambagrillandbar.com	
Prices: $$	

Tamba's food may be very good, but the genuine hospitality delivered by owner Mr. Malik and his cadre of servers is memorable. These are the touches that set it well above its Curry Hill brethren.

Billed as an Indian grill, many dishes are char-kissed and arrive fresh from the tandoor like succulent *jalpari* (jumbo shrimp); mint *paneer tikka*; or *haryali* kebab, skewered chunks of white meat chicken marinated in an herbaceous coriander-mint purée served over a bed of salad greens and browned onions. Other favorites include *channa saag*, toothsome chickpeas and finely chopped spinach simmered in onion, tomato, ginger, and fragrant spices. Tamba's special naan is studded with bits of *tandoori* chicken and is a delicious complement to everything on the menu.

Tocqueville

A3

1 E. 15th St. (bet. Fifth Ave. & Union Sq. West)

Subway: 14 St - Union Sq	Lunch Mon – Sat
Phone: 212-647-1515	Dinner nightly
Web: www.tocquevillerestaurant.com	
Prices: $$	

Be it lunch or dinner, few New York restaurants convey the civility found at Tocqueville, courtesy of Chef Marco Moreira and his wife Joann Makovitzky. The serene, butterscotch-colored room features spaciously arranged tables draped with starched linen and laden with sparkling cutlery and stemware.

Tocqueville's location, just steps away from the Union Square Greenmarket, influences its seasonally driven menu. A salad of frisée, shaved celery, and roasted local pear arranged with slices of nutty Cato Farm cheddar is a delightful starting point. House-made silken tofu presented with ginger-infused mushroom broth demonstrates the kitchen's global inspiration. Excellent desserts may offer a candied chestnut Napolean garnished with brandy sorbet.

Turkish Kitchen 😋

C2

386 Third Ave. (bet. 27th & 28th Sts.)

Subway:	28 St (Park Ave. South)	Lunch Sun – Fri
Phone:	212-679-6633	Dinner nightly
Web:	www.turkishkitchen.com	
Prices:	😋😋	

Long heralded for its tasty cuisine and good value, Turkish Kitchen is a jewel-toned mainstay boasting a lively scene and attentive service staff, ready to walk newcomers through the extensive offerings. The wide array of appetizers is best tackled with the help of friends, whether starting with vine leaves stuffed with rice, pine nuts, and black currants; house-made yogurt with cucumber, mint, and dill; or phyllo scrolls stuffed with feta.

However, the four-course prix-fixe at lunch is a perfectly proportioned and well-priced weekday indulgence. Expect the likes of a cool and crisp shepherd's salad; smear of roasted eggplant with warm flatbread; cabbage stuffed with rice and ground beef; and honey-drizzled semolina cake to end this sumptuous spread.

Union Square Cafe

A3

21 E. 16th St. (bet. Fifth Ave. & Union Sq. West)

Subway:	14 St - Union Sq	Lunch & dinner daily
Phone:	212-243-4020	
Web:	www.unionsquarecafe.com	
Prices:	$$$	

Danny Meyer's first-born may have opened back in 1985, but still gets lots of love today from locals and tourists. Come for lunch or come for dinner, but this institution is sure to be mobbed. Despite the crush, there are few other service teams better at making each and every diner feel like a cherished guest. The multi-level setting is bright, cheerful, and features a comfortable bar—great for solo dining.

The menu is hailed for its broad appeal, seasonal salads and starters lead to expertly prepared pastas like *spaghetti Siciliano* with swordfish meatballs and spicy tomato sauce. Memorable entrées have included sea scallops wrapped in thin sheets of crisped and salty prosciutto, arranged with roasted beets, shell beans, and creamy *stracciatella* purée.

Once occupied by struggling artists, poets, and edgy bohemia, Greenwich Village today continues to flourish as one of New York City's most artsy hub. With Washington Square Park and NYU at its core, this area's typically named streets wear an intellectual spirit, as seen in its many cafés, indie theaters, and music venues.

ASSORTED PLEASURES

Mamoun's has been feeding students for decades with some of the best falafel in town. Area residents however have been known to experience similar gratification at **Taïm**, featuring updated renditions; chasing down this savory snack with one of their smoothies is a must. So are the creamy concoctions at the humble **Peanut Butter & Co.** Whether in the mood to linger awhile or pick up a jar to-go, find yourself rubbing shoulders with natives craving authentic Spanish flavors at nearby **100 Montaditos**. Captivating the culinary elite on Bleecker Street are the satisfying *desi* delights at **Bombay Duck Co.** If their prawn-fry and chili cheese toasties are too spicy for your palate, opt for delicate rice- and lentil-flour crêpes served with much character and flair at food truck sensation, **N.Y. Dosas**. But if craving crêpes in their original, faithful form along with other excellent French goodies, pass by **Patisserie Claude**, or unearth a slice of Italy by way of old-time bakeries and butchers settled here. **Faicco's Pork Store** as well as **Ottomanelli & Sons Meat Market** have been tendering their treats for over 100 years now. Take home a sampling of perfectly seasoned sausages or

tray of arancini—even though the staff prefer (insist?) that one must be eaten warm, before leaving the store. Setting aside the dusty floors and minimal décor, **Florence Meat Market** in operation for over 70 years, is every gourmand's go-to spot for Christmas goose, Newport steak, and so much more. And really, what goes best with meat? Cheese, of course, with **Murray's Cheese Shop** initiating hungry neophytes into the art and understanding of their countless varieties. Completing Italy's culinary terrain in Greenwich Village is **Raffetto's**, whose fresh, handmade pastas never cease to please. Hopping countries and bringing a smack of London to this section is **A Salt & Battery**. Here, fish and chips are crafted from the finest ingredients, but if you prefer poultry, dive into the original, always reliable

outpost of **Dirty Bird To Go** for deliciously moist rotisserie chicken. No Village jaunt is complete without pizza, with some of the finest to be found coal-fired and crisp, only by the pie, at **John's of Bleecker Street**. **Joe's** is another local delight that dishes up traditional thin-crust selections, which promise to leave you with a lifetime addiction. Finish this carb and cheese extravaganza with a uniquely textured scoop from **Cones**, available in surprisingly tasty flavor combinations...even watermelon!

WEST VILLAGE

Located along the Hudson River and extending all the way down to Hudson Square, the West Village is predominately residential, marked by angular streets, quaint shops, and charming eateries. Once known as "Little Bohemia," numerous old-fashioned but resilient food favorites continue to thrive here and offer a taste of old New York. For a nearly royal treat, stop by **Tea & Sympathy** for high tea, followed by a full Sunday supper featuring roast beef and Yorkshire pudding. Correspondingly, **Press Tea** serves up global flavors topped with Big Apple flair. Pair the Mont Blanc Wild Himalayan with an Earl Grey cupcake to understand what all the fuss is about. Over on Commerce Street, fans are swooning over **Milk & Cookies'** unapologetically sinful goodies. These are reputedly as sensational as the breakfast and burgers always on offer at **Elephant & Castle**. The influential **James Beard Foundation** is also situated steps away, in a historic 12th Street townhouse that was once home to the illustrious food writer. Sound all too stuffy and Tex-Mex more your speed? Join the raucous twenty-something's set at **Tortilla Flats**. Known as much for Bingo Tuesdays as for their house margaritas, it's a guaranteed good time.

Manhattan's love for brunch is a thrilling and time-tested affair that flourishes in this far west stretch. Find evidence of this at **La Bonbonniere**, a pleasant little diner whose brazen and beautiful creations are excelled only by their absurdly cheap prices. Pack a basket with egg specialties and enjoy a picnic among the urban vista of roller skaters and runners at Hudson River Park. While strolling back through bustling Bleecker Street, let the overpowering aromas of butter and sugar lead you to the original and endlessly decadent **Magnolia Bakery**. Proffering over 128 handmade treats, this official sweet spot is a darling among tourists and date-night duos. Not far behind, **Li-Lac** is the city's oldest chocolate house dispensing the best hand-crafted treats and chocolate-covered

NEW YORK CITY

pretzels in town—take your pick between dark and milk! Beyond bakeries, the bar scene in the West Village is always abuzz. Late-night carousers pound through an assortment of pints at the **Rusty Knot**, while reveling in cheap eats and fantastic live talent. Equally expert mixologists can be found pouring "long drinks and fancy cocktails" at **Employees Only**; just as bartenders reach inventive heights at **Little Branch**—where an encyclopedic understanding of the craft ensures dizzying results.

At the foot of Christopher Street and atop the Hudson River waterfront, **Pier 45** is a particularly lovely destination for icy cold drinks, hot dogs, and sunbathing.

MEATPACKING DISTRICT

Further north is Manhattan's notoriously chichi Meatpacking District. Once home to slaughterhouses, prostitution services, and drug dens, today MePa is packed with savvy locals, trendy tourists, and moneyed B&T types. Thanks to the rave reviews and success of the High Line—an abandoned 1934 elevated railway that is now a 19-block-long lush park—these once-desolate cobblestoned streets now cradle the city's edgiest clubs and restaurants. As if in defiance of these cautious times, luxury hotels, "starchitect" high-rises, and festive bistros have risen; and fashionable minions cannot imagine being elsewhere. The Standard hotel is the social hub with beer and bratwursts ruling the roost every summer at **Biergarten**. Come fall, young hipsters soak up the scene at open-air café, **Kaffeeklatsch**, a pop-up shop promising hot beverages for freezing skaters doing the rounds at Standard Plaza—a public square-turned-ice skating rink. Located in the shadow of this haute hotel, **Hector's Café** is a modest holdout feeding the few remaining meatpackers—usually until 4:00 A.M.

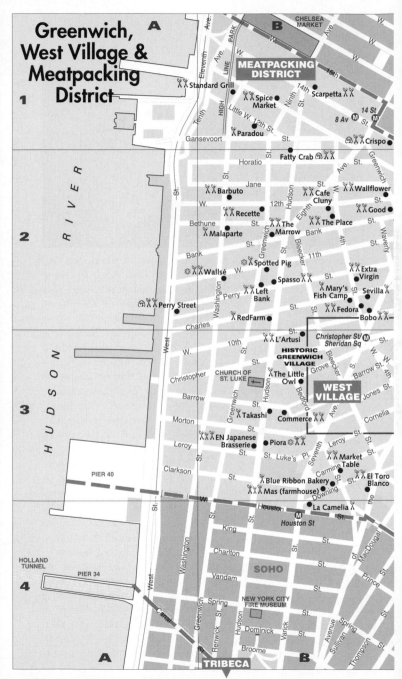

Greenwich, West Village & Meatpacking District

CHELSEA MARKET

MEATPACKING DISTRICT

Standard Grill

Spice Market

Scarpetta

14 St

8 Av

Paradou

Crispo

Gansevoort St.

Horatio St.

Fatty Crab

Jane St.

Barbuto

Cafe Cluny

Wallflower

Recette

The Marrow

The Place

Good

Bethune St.

Malaparte

Bank St.

Spotted Pig

Extra Virgin

Wallsé

Spasso

Mary's Fish Camp

Sevilla

Perry St.

Left Bank

Fedora

Perry Street

Bobo

RedFarm

Charles St.

L'Artusi

Christopher St/ Sheridan Sq

HISTORIC GREENWICH VILLAGE

CHURCH OF ST. LUKE

The Little Owl

WEST VILLAGE

Takashi

Commerce

EN Japanese Brasserie

Piora

Market Table

Blue Ribbon Bakery

El Toro Blanco

Mas (farmhouse)

La Camelia

Houston St

SOHO

HOLLAND TUNNEL

PIER 34

NEW YORK CITY FIRE MUSEUM

TRIBECA

132

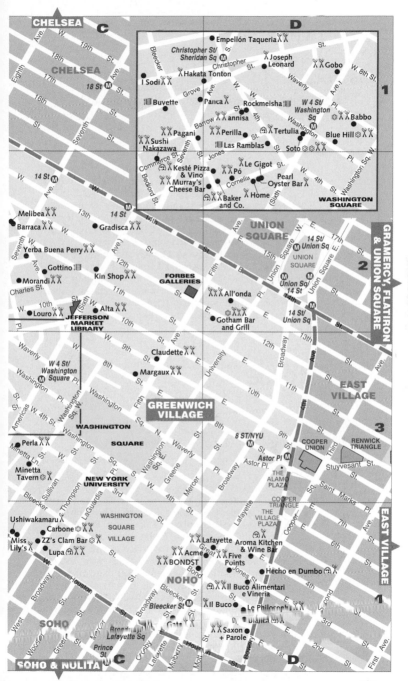

CHELSEA C D

CHELSEA

Empellón Taquería ✕✕

Christopher St/
Sheridan Sq Ⓜ Christopher St. ✕ Joseph
Leonard ✕✕ Gobo W. 8th St.

18 St Ⓜ ✕ Hakata Tonton
✕ I Sodi ✕ Waverly

🍴 Buvette Panca ✕ Rockmeisha🍴 W 4 St/ 1
Washington
✕ annisa Sq ❄ ✕✕ Babbo

✕✕ Pagani ✕ Perilla ❄✕ Tertulia Blue Hill❄✕✕

✕✕ Sushi 🍴 Las Ramblas Soto ❄❄✕
Nakazawa Jones St. ✕ Le Gigot

🍴✕ Kesté Pizza ✕✕ Pó
& Vino ✕ Pearl WASHINGTON
✕ Murray's Cornelia Oyster Bar SQUARE
Cheese Bar ✕ Home
✕✕ Baker
and Co.

Melibea ✕✕✕ 13th
14 St Ⓜ 14th St.

Barraca ✕✕ W. ✕✕ Gradisca ✕✕ UNION
SQUARE
14 St/
Yerba Buena Perry ✕✕ Union Sq 2

Gottino🍴 15th UNION
SQUARE
Morandi ✕✕ Kin Shop ✕✕ FORBES Union Sq Ⓜ
Charles St. GALLERIES Ⓜ 14 St

✕✕✕ All'onda 14 St/
W. 10th St. ✕✕ Alta ✕✕ Union Sq Ⓜ
Louro ✕✕ JEFFERSON ❄✕✕✕
MARKET Gotham Bar
LIBRARY and Grill

Claudette ✕✕ 12th
W 4 St/ 8th
Washington ● Margaux ✕✕ EAST
Square VILLAGE

GREENWICH 3
VILLAGE 8 ST/NYU Ⓜ COOPER RENWICK
● Perla ✕✕ Astor Pl Ⓜ UNION TRIANGLE
WASHINGTON Astor Pl. THE
Minetta SQUARE ALAMO
Tavern ❄ PLAZA

NEW YORK COOPER
UNIVERSITY TRIANGLE
THE
VILLAGE
Ushiwakamaru ✕ WASHINGTON PLAZA
Carbone ❄ ✕✕ SQUARE
Miss VILLAGE Aroma Kitchen
Lily's ✕ ZZ's Clam Bar ❄✕ ✕ Lafayette & Wine Bar
Lupa ✕✕ ✕✕ Acme ✕✕ Five Hecho en Dumbo ❄✕
✕✕ BONDST Points 1
NOHO
🍴✕✕ Il Buco Alimentari
e Vineria
Bleecker St Ⓜ ✕ Il Buco Le Philosoph✕✕
SOHO Bianca ❄✕
Gato 🍴✕ ✕✕ Saxon
Prince + Parole
St
SOHO & NOLITA C D

133

Acme

D4

9 Great Jones St. (bet. Broadway & Lafayette St.)

Subway: Broadway - Lafayette St
Phone: 212-203-2121
Web: www.acmenyc.com
Prices: $$

Lunch Sat – Sun
Dinner nightly

NoHo is no stranger to *Vogue*-ready waitresses, but Acme's reincarnation two years ago produced an inventive Nordic culinary nirvana, equal parts rustic brasserie and sultry lounge. Naturally, the crowds came and never left its metal-topped bar and pine-green banquettes. One could stare at the gorgeously lit backdrop of bottles, but grab a Foxy Brown and contemplate the innovative menu.

Chef Mads Refslund brings his Danish sensibility to many dishes, including lightly cured mackerel finished with grated horseradish. But he also leaves room for comforting fusion dishes like Johnny Cakes—an American classic-turned-fun ensemble of thin cornbread flapjacks, accompanied by sweet, porky confit, as well as an assortment of crispy pig ears and pickled veggies.

All'onda

D2

22 E. 13th St. (bet. Fifth Ave. & University Pl.)

Train: 14 St (Seventh Ave.)
Phone: 212-231-2236
Web: www.allondanyc.com
Prices: $$$

Lunch Mon-Fri
Dinner nightly

This two-story, all-glass façade located just off bustling Union Square would be best described as dramatic. From its rich wood striations that line the walls to the standout black bowls and etched glass, this former tavern space is now a thriving Italian restaurant—though surprises abound with hints of Japan in many dishes that are more fun than mind-blowing.

Chef Chris Jaeckle whips up serious pastas, such as the highly creative hand-rolled *garganelli* with peekytoe crab, tarragon, and punchy *yuzu kosho*. Purple, dark, and stormy *lumache* are equally arresting when paired with a rich braised duck ragù that boasts the unexpected flavor combination of chocolate and Treviso endive to balance both deeply rich and bitter components.

Alta

C2

Contemporary ❌❌

64 W. 10th St (bet. Fifth & Sixth Aves.)

Subway: Christopher St - Sheridan Sq   Dinner nightly
Phone: 212-505-7777
Web: www.altarestaurant.com
Prices: $$

From an ivy-cloaked façade to the complex menu items, Alta seems to imply mystery. Inside its brick townhouse, this attractive and comforting scene mixes antique Moorish floors, splashes of yellow, and a cozy wood-burning fireplace. The second level looks like a balcony but is just as packed thanks to the kitchen's excellent menu selection.

These small plates have featured pillowy lamb meatballs in a pool of charred red-pepper sauce, or uni draped over crostini covered with a shimmering sheet of Ibèrico bacon. Wok-seared *taglierini* reveals cuttlefish slivers sautéed with crispy garlic chips.

First-rate ingredients are surpassed only by thoughtful combinations in desserts like silky *pot de crème* capped in pistachio powder—a midsummer night's dream.

annisa

D1

Fusion ❌❌

13 Barrow St. (bet. Seventh Ave. South & W. 4th St.)

Subway: Christopher St - Sheridan Sq   Dinner nightly
Phone: 212-741-6699
Web: www.annisarestaurant.com
Prices: $$$

Chef Anita Lo's hallowed establishment is *the* definition of casual sophistication. Large windows at the bar look out onto the historic Greenwich Village street, and the elevated dining room is warmed by blonde wood furnishings and the glow of burnt orange fabrics.

Asian inspiration factors heavily in annisa's carte of worldly preparations and include appetizers of buttervelvet squid zinged by Thai basil, chili, and lime, or plump mussels arranged with saffron oil, *salsa verde*, crispy bits of chorizo, and green chickpeas. *Koji*-marinated Berkshire pork loin is temptingly arranged with simmered daikon, smoked avocado purée, and a raw egg yolk. Sip while you sup, as the wine list pours a rarefied selection that applauds female wine makers and vineyard owners.

Aroma Kitchen & Wine Bar 🎭

D4

Italian 𝓧

36 E. 4th St. (bet. Bowery & Lafayette St.)

Subway: Bleecker St   Dinner Mon – Sat
Phone: 212-375-0100
Web: www.aromanyc.com
Prices: $$

When dolled-up crowds pack this cobblestoned street, the staff rises to the occasion with true Italian hospitality. Despite the trendy surrounds, authenticity is paramount as orange-framed doors are flung open to reveal lovely rustic rooms and a quiet, contemporary aura. The front area presents mirrors, a wood bar, and hefty shelves of interesting wines.

Beyond brick archways, a communal table in the dining room is ideal for savoring summer's bounty beautifully showcased in *scafata di verdure*, a *zuppa* bobbing with *quadrettini* dressed in a bright vegetable ragù. Flavorful bites of *strascinati* are tossed with sublime Moliterno cheese, lamb sausage, and smoky red peppers. A scoop of *stracciatella* gelato or the daily *sorbetto* ensures an exalted finish.

Baker & Co. 🎭

D2

Italian 𝓧𝓧

259 Bleecker St. (bet. Cornelia & Jones Sts.)

Subway: W 4 St - Wash Sq   Lunch & dinner daily
Phone: 212-255-1234
Web: www.bakernco.com
Prices: $$

The latest brainchild of the team behind the wildly popular Emporio, brand-new Baker & Co. makes a big mark on NYC's Italian-American scene. From the exposed brick walls and wood-lined banquettes to the backyard garden and Faema espresso machine, the rustic, honest restaurant feels comfortable enough to spread out pappardelle with veal cheek ragù and seasonal daily specials like watermelon gazpacho. A rich, sweet soup spiked with tomatoes, it bobs with lumps of crabmeat and cooling cucumber.

The menu, though, leans more toward traditional Italian dishes. Dig into the braised rabbit meatballs, paired with shaved ricotta and *tonnato*-style aïoli, as well as *garganelli* bathed in a saffron *brodetto* and topped with peekytoe crab accompanied by *bottarga*.

Babbo ✣

D1

Italian ✗✗

110 Waverly Pl. (bet. MacDougal St. & Sixth Ave.)

Subway: W 4 St - Wash Sq
Phone: 212-777-0303
Web: www.babbonyc.com
Prices: $$$

Lunch Tue – Sat
Dinner nightly

After many distinguished years in New York's culinary scene, Babbo continues to flourish, now more than ever. This sweet, bi-level dining room in quaint Waverly Place flaunts an old-world mix of shuttered windows, wrought-iron railings, and hefty wooden armchairs. Despite the historical setting and attentive service, its insane popularity and loud tunes can lead to sensory overload. For better or worse, Chef Mario Batali's classic rock playlist still thumps through dinner (lunchtime is subdued with smoother jazz). The bar is very lively and sometimes rowdy.

The menu delivers what it has long been hailed for: creative yet rustic Italian fare made with stellar skill and extraordinary ingredients. Many dishes have been their own classics for over a decade, like beef cheek ravioli, a shining signature of succulent meat wrapped in silky pasta sheets and bathed in a subtle *Castelmagno* cheese- and black truffle-reduction. Among the entrées, find beautifully composed poached pork *tonnato* in a delicate yet assertive tuna-and-mayonnaise sauce counterpoised with tart caperberries.

Sweet finales include a delightfully warm and moist rosemary-olive oil cake, with a scoop of melting olive oil gelato.

Barbuto

B2

775 Washington St. (at 12th St.)

Subway: 14 St - 8 Av
Phone: 212-924-9700
Web: www.barbutonyc.com
Prices: $$

Lunch & dinner daily

Those who wax poetic on the virtues of the perfect roast chicken need look no farther. Located on a quiet stretch of the West Village just steps from MePa, Chef Jonathan Waxman's Barbuto plays up its locale and industrial bones with concrete flooring, painted-over brick walls, and garage doors that open up to create an atmospheric indoor/outdoor vibe.

Still, that chicken is what best expresses Barbuto's refined simplicity—the roasted bird has a coarse pepper-freckled auburn skin and tender ivory flesh moist with flavorful juices, further enhanced by a splash of bright and briny salsa verde. This dish is admirably supported by the likes of grilled octopus salad with fennel and pink grapefruit or a cookie-like chocolate hazelnut *crostata*.

Barraca

C2

81 Greenwich Ave. (at Bank St.)

Subway: 14 St - 8 Av
Phone: 212-462-0080
Web: www.barracanyc.com
Prices: $$

Lunch Fri– Sun
Dinner nightly

The team behind Latin American Rayuela and Macondo turn their attention towards Spain with this precious spot. Barraca flaunts a rustic air complete with padded wooden banquettes, a beamed ceiling, and bright blue chairs. The staff is enthusiastic and sharply attired in long, dark denim aprons.

At the center of the menu, find a roster of six paellas for two, such as the mouthwateringly fragrant and crisped *roja de carabineros*. Infused with red shrimp stock and scattered with Gulf, rock, and red shrimp, it is the color of terra-cotta. Tapas like chicken and oyster mushroom *croquetas*, flatbreads, and entrées round out the selection that is best washed down by one of the excellent sangrias—think Rioja swirled with Aperol, cherry liqueur, and dried chili.

Bianca 🐷

D4

Italian 🍴

5 Bleecker St. (bet. Bowery & Elizabeth St.)

Subway: Bleecker St
Phone: 212-260-4666
Web: www.biancanyc.com
Prices: $$

Dinner nightly

Curtained windows lead the way to this winsome hideaway which, as evidenced by the always full dining room, enjoys a strongly favorable standing as *the* destination for homestyle Italian dining. Plank floors, an open kitchen, and delicate floral-rimmed china arranged along the walls produce a cherished timeless appeal.

The menu proves simplicity is always satisfying. There is no arguing with a bowl of homemade *tagliatelle* tossed with wild mushrooms sautéed in olive oil and fresh herbs offered as a special; followed by *pollo al balsamico*—chicken poached in balsamic vinegar, set over fresh salad greens, and dressed with a wonderfully restrained sauce. Tiramisu is given a clever and rich twist by chocolate chip-studded mascarpone mousse filling.

Blue Ribbon Bakery

B3

Contemporary 🍴

35 Downing St. (at Bedford St.)

Subway: Houston St
Phone: 212-337-0404
Web: www.blueribbonrestaurants.com
Prices: $$

Lunch & dinner daily

The origin of this very New York bistro begins with the discovery of an abandoned brick oven that brothers Eric and Bruce Bromberg found in the basement of a bodega. This sparked the idea for a bakery, and in 1998 Blue Ribbon Bakery joined the duo's family of popular and impressive dining venues. The sunny corner spot charms with mustard yellow walls and creaky wood-plank flooring; downstairs the heady aroma of freshly baked bread wafts throughout exposed brick alcoves.

Excellent sandwiches star on the roster of lunchtime fare, like shrimp salad with roasted tomato mayonnaise tucked into slices of lightly toasted challah. Dinner brings eclectic possibilities like asparagus vinaigrette, grilled sardines, fried chicken, and ice cream parlor desserts.

Blue Hill ✿

American ✕✕

D1

75 Washington Pl. (bet. Sixth Ave. & Washington Sq. Park)

Subway: W 4 St - Wash Sq
Phone: 212-539-1776
Web: www.bluehillfarm.com
Prices: $$$

Dinner nightly

Chef Dan Barber's iconic venue remains the paragon of farm-to-table dining in Manhattan by virtue of its seasonal lineup of exemplary product. Everything on the menu is sourced from the Stone Barns Center (home to Blue Hill's Westchester farm) as well as a number of local farmers.

The intimate quarters of this former speakeasy has been hosting a devoted foodie following for an impressive 15-years, and service in the cocoa-brown and burnt orange-splashed room, where fresh flowers and candlelight cast a romantic spell, remains excellent.

Blue Hill's innovative cooking showcases the astounding quality stocked in the larder and allows vegetables to shine regardless of the season. Beets, florets of blanched broccoli and cauliflower, and Seckel pear—shaved, poached, and caramelized—came together in a vibrant winter salad, and a tower of roasted carrots, hit with nuggets of unctuous bone marrow and sided by creamed spinach and mashed potatoes, was a luscious and satisfying entrée. Refreshing desserts highlight still more of the season's best, as was the case with torn bits of almond sponge cake coupled with sweet, poached citrus segments and refreshing lemon ice cream.

Bobo

B2

Contemporary ✗✗

181 W. 10th St. (at Seventh Ave.)

Subway: Christopher St - Sheridan Sq
Phone: 212-488-2626
Web: www.bobonyc.com
Prices: $$

Lunch Sat – Sun
Dinner nightly

This resilient Village paragon continues to reign as a prime spot for fine dining. What's all the fuss about? It could be the relishable show courtesy of a skilled kitchen that divulges delicacies like Niman Ranch pork cheeks Provençal, braised with tomato, olives, and served over succulent lemon-infused cavatelli; sides like broccoli rabe *a la plancha*; or sweets like carrot cake with candied pecans and cream cheese ice cream.

Others maintain that it is most definitely Bobo's charming setting—located in a century-old townhouse—designed to feel warm and very whimsical. If none of these sound appealing, have faith that there's no place finer to spend a sultry evening sipping an excellent cocktail than in their quaint back garden.

BONDST

C4

Japanese ✗✗

6 Bond St. (bet. Broadway & Lafayette St.)

Subway: Bleecker St
Phone: 212-777-2500
Web: www.bondstrestaurant.com
Prices: $$$

Dinner nightly

There's no denying that BONDST is still trendy after all these years; it even manages to stay sexy with sheer fabric panels, wispy tree branches, dark leathers, and private spaces. The three-story interior fills nightly with a very European crowd. (Romantics head downstairs; Bacchanalians go up.)

High quality fusion dishes may seem more crowd-pleasing than inventive, but are nonetheless delicious. Behind the wood sushi bar, the buzzing kitchen rolls mountains of maki, like paper-thin slices of pristine scallops balanced with a thick soy-jalapeño sauce and *yuzu kosho*. The *soba nomi* "risotto" is a wickedly rich and unmissable dish of glistening buckwheat soba folded with trout butter, king crab, and shrimp beneath a thatch of bonito flakes and gold paper.

Buvette

French 🍽

C1

42 Grove St. (bet. Bedford & Bleecker Sts.)

Subway: Christopher St - Sheridan Sq
Phone: 212-255-3590
Web: N/A
Prices: $$

Lunch & dinner daily

Wonderfully inviting and proudly French, Chef Jody Williams' *gastrothéque* serves delicious Gallic small plates all day, so there is always a reason for a visit. A white marble dining counter set before polished stemware and bottles of wine dominates the petite, brick-walled room. Everything seems alive with chatter and jazz.

Buvette's snacks focus on French classics, as in silken batons of leek drizzled with stimulating Dijon vinaigrette; or a *croque forestier*, filled with béchamel, oven-dried tomato, wild mushrooms, and Gruyère seasoned with *herbes de Provence*. It goes without saying that a glass of wine is practically mandatory, say a flinty Bourgogne Aligoté chosen off the blackboard selection, framed within the outline of France?

Cafe Cluny

Contemporary ✗✗

B2

284 W. 12th St. (at W. 4th St.)

Subway: 14 St - 8 Av
Phone: 212-255-6900
Web: www.cafecluny.com
Prices: $$

Lunch & dinner daily

A longtime favorite downtown watering hole, Cafe Cluny's mien is a difficult-to-achieve fusion of intimacy, sophistication, and insouciance. The main room is embellished with celebrity caricatures and a wall of shadowy bird cutouts that come alive in the evening candlelight. The back room is a tad more subdued and boasts butterflies behind glass and room-lengthening mirrors.

The kitchen continues to shine bright under the pilotage of Chef Phillip Kirschen-Clark and his inspired team. They can be found routinely turning out such fine fare as artichokes *barigoule* braised in white wine and miso; and *cavatelli* abundantly sauced with luscious lobster bisque. Their classic lemon bar is decidedly adult, topped with Chartreuse ice cream and basil ribbons.

Carbone

Italian ✗✗

181 Thompson St. (bet. Bleecker & Houston Sts.)

Subway: Houston St
Phone: 212-254-3000
Web: www.carbonenewyork.com
Prices: $$$$

Lunch Mon-Fri
Dinner nightly

When the boys behind Carbone decided to leave intact the original sign for Rocco's restaurant—its predecessor dating back to the 1920s—it put nostalgia front and center. That sense of history pervades the entire space, from the vintage police buttons sewn into tufted banquettes to the tiled floor inspired by a certain restaurant scene from *The Godfather*. The very professional and unobtrusive service team is dressed to the natty nines in burgundy suits, and oldies but goodies play in the background.

Mid-century Italian-American cooking may be where the menu begins, but the ingredients, skill, and well-researched inspiration surpasses that of most any *nonna*. Here, taste an assortment of young, chilled, and neatly chopped red and golden beets *Siciliana* mixed with orange segments and dressed with earthy and creamy pistachio pesto. Plump and meaty scallops *Francese* are egg-dipped and pan-fried until gently crisped and golden, then sliced and covered with enriched white-wine sauce, finished with sweet and simple peas, pea greens, and chives.

A proper New York cheesecake is light, smooth, and goes down impossibly easy, complemented with a layer of lemon curd and buttery cookie crumb crust.

Claudette

Mediterranean ✗✗

C3

24 Fifth Ave. (at 9th St.)

Subway: W 4 St - Wash Sq

Phone: 212-868-2424

Web: www.claudettenyc.com

Prices: $$

Dinner nightly

&

Tucked into a stunning residential stretch of Fifth Avenue with views of Washington Square Park, Claudette fills this nabe's restaurant void with its marvelous Mediterranean fare. The bright room, with a marble bar and reclaimed wood floors, is highlighted by wine cask light fixtures, shelves of cocktail books, and tables piled high with colorful plates of chicken tagine.

A Provençal-spirited menu features elegant dishes by Chef Koren Grieveson, who uses garden-fresh herbs for hand-made *chitarra* and fiery red jalapeños to top soft-shell crabs. Her *bouillabaisse en croûte*, a buttery puff pastry filled with chunks of monkfish, octopus, and mussels in an aromatic sauce of red pepper, garlic, and herbs, exemplifies Claudette's quintessential, hearty fare.

Commerce

Contemporary ✗✗

B3

50 Commerce St. (near Barrow St.)

Subway: Christopher St - Sheridan Sq

Phone: 212-524-2301

Web: www.commercerestaurant.com

Prices: $$

Lunch Fri – Sun
Dinner nightly

Meandering down Commerce Street transports you from busy, modern city to quaint, small town, where the Cherry Lane Theater and this market-driven restaurant add to the charm. Honoring its long history, the space nods to an art deco past comprised of bold murals above a Brunswick bar, bronze sconces, and subway tiles for a uniquely New York feel.

Heather Bortnem, the talented baker, delivers an absolutely unavoidable bread basket, stuffed with house-baked goods, like the red pepper- and sun dried tomato-popover or flaky brioche. This in turn sets the tone for Long Island duck, whose pecan crust gently contrasts the tender breast meat, set over a bed of savory seasonal vegetables. Here, it's all about refined rustic cuisine for a little big town.

Crispo

B1

Italian ✕✕

240 W. 14th St. (bet. Seventh & Eighth Aves.)

Subway: 14 St (Seventh Ave.) Dinner nightly
Phone: 212-229-1818
Web: www.crisporestaurant.com
Prices: $$

Convivial Crispo is a breath of fresh, rustic air. A protruding façade shelters its terrazza, while the back garden decked in smooth river stones feels warmer. The inside is dark and low-slung with brick walls, mosaic floors, and wrought-iron seats set around tiny, round tables. A plating station and kitchen reside in the back, as the full bar hums up front.

Courteous waiters attend to neatly arranged tables groaning beneath refined yet peasant-hearty food. Angel hair pasta is twirled around fresh seafood and then tossed in a fresh cherry tomato-cream sauce. Three tender lamb chops s*cottaditto* (glistening with an herb-olive oil marinade) and served beside a goat cheese-polenta cake, could be sealed with a kiss of passion fruit or coconut sorbet.

El Toro Blanco

B3

Mexican ✕✕

257 Sixth Ave. (bet. Bedford & Downing Sts.)

Subway: Houston St Lunch & dinner daily
Phone: 212-645-0193
Web: N/A
Prices: $$

Warm sunset hues shade this Mexican charmer, from the partners behind Burger & Barrel. Polished woods, russet terrazzo flooring, and glossy orange tiles provide a pretty backdrop. So embrace that beachy state of mind and start with a margarita; followed by Baja-style black bass ceviche; or an open-faced Sonoran cheese crisp. Entrées feature regional specialties as in marinated and fried chunks of Berkshire pork shoulder *carnitas Michoacán* with refried beans and shaved cabbage slaw dressed in bright Serrano chiles and fresh lime juice, complete with a stack of excellent tortillas.

Save room for the dressed up take on *tres leches*, a sweet milk-sopped round of sponge cake with caramelized banana, a scoop of *dulce de leche* ice cream and dollop of meringue.

Empellón Taqueria

Mexican ✗✗

D1

230 W. 4th St. (at 10th St.)

Subway: Christopher St - Sheridan Sq
Phone: 212-367-0999
Web: www.empellon.com
Prices: $$

Lunch Thu-Sat
Dinner nightly

Owning a primo Village corner, Alex Stupak has turned this casual taqueria into a totally happening spot—on Saturdays, the small place bursts with night owls from all over the city. Along with upbeat tunes and ever-flowing Mezcal, this restaurant has as much spirit as it does spice.

Of course, the flavor is abundant in dishes that can be terrifically delicious (if equally messy to eat). The *sopes* are a must, perhaps filled with enticingly salty and tasty refried black beans and a poached quail egg. Outrageously good queso melts Chihuahua cheese with any of the four toppings, especially the green chorizo, for pure gooey pleasure. Don't miss house salsas like smoked cashew or tomatillo-chipotle, even if it means paying extra as they're worth every penny!

EN Japanese Brasserie

Japanese ✗✗✗

B3

435 Hudson St. (at Leroy St.)

Subway: Houston St
Phone: 212-647-9196
Web: www.enjb.com
Prices: $$$

Lunch & dinner daily

Cloaked in darkness and steeped in grandeur, this contemporary West Village *izakaya* is a sexy go-to spot when the urge for sushi, soba, and stone-grilled meats strikes. Sprawling and boisterous, EN sets a swanky scene with soaring heights, natural materials, and custom trimmings.

The open kitchen pays homage to authentic Japanese palates, but also reveals ingenuity. Tofu is made fresh hourly and served as a quivering silken scoop drizzled with *wari-joyu* (soy sauce and dashi). This specialty is an absolute must. The chef's sashimi selection may bring Scottish salmon, Pacific bigeye tuna, and Kona kampachi, all incredibly fresh.

For a more private experience, bypass the masses and book your own crowd for kaiseki dinner in a tatami room.

Extra Virgin

B2

M e d i t e r r a n e a n

259 W. 4th St. (at Perry St.)

Subway: Christopher St - Sheridan Sq
Phone: 212-691-9359
Web: www.extravirginrestaurant.com
Prices: $$

Lunch Tue – Sun
Dinner nightly

Consistently good with an easygoing attitude, this longstanding neighborhood gem is a hit with everyone from young families and ladies-who-brunch, to the dog-owners enjoying sidewalk seating. Fresh flowers, blue-velvet barstools, and canvas paintings make it the perfect fusion of casual and classy; rock music lightens the mood.

Pristine olive oils march from the kitchen as if to whet the appetite for a parade of Mediterranean classics to pair with food-friendly Italian wines. Start with butternut squash ravioli bathed in brown butter-mascarpone sauce, or the beautifully textured halibut on herbed tomato carpaccio for an instant return to summer. Roasted Brussels sprouts combine with caramelized apples to cut the enticing richness of fatty pancetta.

Fatty Crab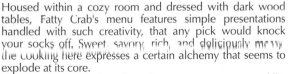

B2

M a l a y s i a n XX

643 Hudson St. (bet. Gansevoort & Horatio Sts.)

Subway: 14 St - 8 Av
Phone: 212-352-3592
Web: www.fattycrew.com
Prices: $$

Lunch & dinner daily

Housed within a cozy room and dressed with dark wood tables, Fatty Crab's menu features simple presentations handled with such creativity, that any pick would knock your socks off. Sweet, savory, rich, and deliciously messy, the cooking here expresses a certain alchemy that seems to explode at its core.

The carte is concise, but there are no misses. Hits included Malay fish fry, a bowl of Tamaki rice ladled with wondrously funky crab curry and topped with strips of delicate fish deep-fried in turmeric-seasoned batter. A side of braised collard greens sauced with *sambal*, anchovies, and pounded red chilies is fantastically strong.

Their indoors and outdoors fills up fast, so arrive early for dinner. Come for lunch and have the whole place to yourself.

Fedora

Contemporary 🍴🍴

B2

239 W. 4th St. (bet. Charles & 10th Sts.)

Subway: Christopher St - Sheridan Sq

Phone: 646-449-9336

Web: www.fedoranyc.com

Prices: $$

Dinner nightly

An ode to the New York old guard, Fedora still attracts the creative, the moneyed and the young. It's a sort of dreamlike supper club where well-crafted cocktails flow into endless conversations, the words absorbed into the crevices of the original carved wooden bar as they have for generations. No longer a renowned literati haunt, Fedora remains an attractive homage to the Village of yore.

Tuck your bag and coat into the cubby above the banquette and set off on an adventure in contemporary cuisine, one that mixes barbecue cream with smoked salmon and highlights the distinctive wines of Jura. This builds to the excellent and gargantuan crispy duck with perfectly lacquered skin accented by a date-barbecue sauce that's pure hedonistic inspiration.

Five Points

American 🍴🍴

D4

31 Great Jones St. (bet. Bowery & Lafayette St.)

Subway: Bleecker St

Phone: 212-253-5700

Web: www.fivepointsrestaurant.com

Prices: $$

Lunch & dinner daily

It may resemble a simple farm-to-table restaurant, but there is great energy at Five Points. The historic 19th century building with sidewalk seating along the cobblestoned street ensures an idyllic setting. Inside, the ample bar's glass shelves gleam with milk bottles, chalkboards list happy hour specials, and the stream of diners is always steady.

The eye-catching open kitchen sets the bar high with starters like intensely flavored smoked white fish heaped precariously atop crostini. Other dishes strive to respect their origins, like hearty and balanced house-made semolina *maccheroni* tossed with potato cubes, crunchy green beans, and authentically judicious amounts of fragrant basil pesto "Lobster Mondays" are a downright steal for $24.

Gato

C4

Mediterranean ✕✕

324 Lafayette St. (bet. Bleecker & Houston Sts.)

Subway: Bleecker St.
Phone: 212-334-6400
Web: www.gatonyc.com
Prices: $$

Dinner nightly

It's been nearly a decade since Bobby Flay opened a restaurant in NY, and Gato has the famed chef's recipe down. With soaring arched brick ceilings, exposed brass fixtures, and views of Crosby Street, this hip hangout exudes a slick downtown sensibility.

In fact, the cozy lounge and massive wooden bar are so cool, you may never make it to the dining room—which is fine, because the beautifully composed small plates pack plenty of flavor. Case in point: quail egg and creamy uni atop a tender artichoke on a plate dressed up with dots of oils and shellfish reduction. Lamb tenderloin needs hardly any marinade thanks to the top-quality meat, a rich pink center, and salsa verde; while smoky eggplant balances earthy and sweet with Manchego and balsamic vinegar.

Gobo

D1

Vegetarian ✕✕

401 Sixth Ave. (bet. 8th St. & Waverly Pl.)

Subway: W 4 St - Wash Sq
Phone: 212-255-3902
Web: www.goborestaurant.com
Prices: ⊜⊜

Lunch & dinner daily

Need a tasty and tranquil timeout from Manhattan's hustle and bustle? Gobo is your place. Sit down, take a cleansing breath and ponder the restful décor. Muted colors and warm wood accents dominate the airy dining room, which offers a view of your meal being prepared from the open kitchen.

Gobo's value-minded menu starts off with healthy beverages like organic juices, soy milk smoothies, and unfiltered ginger ale. Their "food for the five senses" tempts even those who would disavow any vegetarian tendencies, with starters like scallion pancakes with mango salsa; or house-made hummus with carrots and wonton chips. Larger plates might follow with spicy stir-fried Vietnamese rice noodles with crisp pea pods, bright broccoli, bean sprouts, and tofu.

Good

American XX

B2

89 Greenwich Ave. (bet. Bank & 12th Sts.)

Subway: 14 St - 8 Av
Phone: 212-691-8080
Web: www.goodrestaurantnyc.com
Prices: $$

Lunch Tue – Sun
Dinner nightly

Creamy walls and lime green wainscoting frame this cozy and comfortable little slice of Americana that has been pleasing Greenwich Village residents since 2000. Good also happens to be great for date night—the intimate bar pours top-shelf spirits and the muted dining room is dressed with crisp white linens. Everything has a certain serenity, even when it's bubbling at happy hour.

Chef/owner Steven J. Picker's menu puts his own signature on tempting seasonal cooking. Beautifully seared squid and Japanese eggplant grilled until silky are adorned with summer beans, cherry tomatoes, and mint. Turkey scallopini is crisp and light, set atop a bed of frisée, shaved celery, and *ricotta salata*. Long live the tortilla-crusted, jalapeño-kicked mac and cheese!

Gottino

Italian

C2

52 Greenwich Ave. (bet. Charles & Perry Sts.)

Subway: Christopher St - Sheridan Sq
Phone: 212-633-2590
Web: N/A
Prices:

Lunch & dinner daily

No matter the time of day, there is an adept team preparing an assortment of snacks in Gottino's inviting space amid picture-perfect baskets of fruit. A white marble dining counter dominates this charming *salumeria*, dolled up with exposed brick and a few knobby wood tables.

The mood is so gracious that it's best to set aside a couple of hours. Nosh on the likes of farro salad dotted with roasted and diced butternut squash, a generous showering of finely grated Parmesan, and the deliciously fresh note of celery leaves. Or, go for something heartier—crêpes stuffed with prosciutto and *robiola*, warm and oozing. Be sure to check the wall-mounted blackboard promoting Gottino's all-Italian wine list, offering pours by the glass or carafe.

Gotham Bar and Grill ❀

American 𝕏𝕏𝕏

D2

12 E. 12th St. (bet. Fifth Ave. & University Pl.)

Subway: 14 St - Union Sq

Phone: 212-620-4020

Web: www.gothambarandgrill.com

Prices: $$$

Lunch Mon – Fri
Dinner nightly

Warm, personable, and genuine, Gotham Bar and Grill has everything a New York restaurant needs to stand the test of time. Inside, towering floral arrangements and lofty ceilings hung with massive fabric fixtures soften the room's appearance. The interior is vast, but the sunken dining area, elevated bar, and smartly divided room feel more classic than overdone. The service team exemplifies on-the-ball excellence.

This kitchen's distinctive American seasonal cooking is in clear balance from start to finish. Begin with the simple-sounding tuna tartare combining chopped yellowfin and shiso surrounded by Japanese cucumber, enlivened with miso-ginger vinaigrette. Move on to explore seasonal risotto, showcasing wintery mushrooms or perhaps a summery feast of sweet shrimp, chive, and fava bean tomato. Butter-filled soft-shell crabs are a feat of technical perfection, with body and crisped legs set over sautéed vegetables and a light citrus-soy reduction. Desserts alone are worth a visit, especially to indulge in the famously dense chocolate cake, served warm with a scoop of luscious salted-almond ice cream and cracked cocoa nibs.

The "greenmarket" prix-fixe lunch offers great value and quality.

151

Gradisca

Italian ✗✗

C2

126 W. 13th St. (bet. Sixth & Seventh Aves.)

Subway: 14 St (Seventh Ave.)   Dinner nightly
Phone: 212-691-4886
Web: www.gradiscanyc.com
Prices: $$

If one could choose an Italian mother, it would be *"mamma,"* the pasta maker at Gradisca. Walking into this quaint brownstone is like taking a step into a trattoria in Emila Romagna, complete with Fellini posters, napkin-covered bread baskets, and a smiling bartender pouring a glass of violet-scented sangiovese.

Pasta plays front and center here and is luckily always handmade. Gorgeous, rose-shaped tortellini are stuffed with mounds of *prosciutto* and spinach, before being finished by a perfect plum tomato sauce. *Secondi* are also a must and may include the sublime *cotoletta alla Bolognese*, a perfectly breaded and pan-fried free-range chicken cutlet topped with a creamy truffle-béchamel sauce and served with a warm spinach *budino*.

Hakata Tonton

Japanese ✗

D1

61 Grove St. (bet. Bleecker St. & Seventh Ave.)

Subway: Christopher St - Sheridan Sq   Dinner nightly
Phone: 212-242-3699
Web: N/A
Prices: $$

A novel cuisine has taken root in New York. Enter this tiny red and yellow dining room to be educated in this other facet of the Japanese culinary repertoire: *tonsoku* (pigs' feet, ears, and the like).

Varied *tonsoku* dishes may include luxurious slow-roasted pork or *oreilles du cochon* (French in name only) which are an explosion of crunchy, cool, creamy, sweet, sticky, and vinegary flavors. Truer to its Italian roots, *tonsoku* carbonara is made with smoky bacon and is a good choice for wary newbies. A "rare cheesecake" of piped cheese and sour cream is a very smart and absolutely delicious take on the traditional dessert.

The plain-Jane décor sits in stark contrast to the rich and porky fare that diners will come rushing back for.

Hecho en Dumbo

Mexican ✗

D4

354 Bowery (bet. 4th & Great Jones Sts.)

Subway: Bleecker St
Phone: 212-937-4245
Web: www.hechoendumbo.com
Prices: $$

Lunch Sat – Sun
Dinner nightly

Sitting towards the top of NYC's rapidly improving Mexican food scene is Chef and Mexico City native Daniel Mena's spirited cantina. Venture through the exposed brick, salvaged wood, classically downtown dining room to peek at the open kitchen and counter where the tasting menu is offered (to those who reserve in advance).

A trio of excellent salsas and warm tortilla chips is a mouthwatering beginning to this authentic cooking. Indulge in a hearty, alder wood-smoked feast for two in the *parillada Yucateca*, featuring a gnaw-worthy Berkshire pork chop and 14-day dry-aged NY strip with warm Edam cheese topped in olives, capers, and puréed almonds. Mexican traditions shine in cinnamon-infused *capirotada* bread pudding with coconut crème anglaise.

Home

American ✗

D2

20 Cornelia St. (bet. Bleecker & W. 4th Sts.)

Subway: W 4 St - Wash Sq
Phone: 212-243-9579
Web: www.homerestaurantnyc.com
Prices: $$

Lunch & dinner daily

This intimate Cornelia Street dining room has persevered through the years and continues to offer great tastes of Americana in a setting that is welcoming and warm—all apt characteristics for an eatery called Home. Everyone seated in their black spindleback chairs or back garden seats is happy to see this unassuming, unpretentious whitewashed little space thriving.

This kitchen honors sourcing and seasonality in its range of comforting specialties that have included a freshly prepared vegan purée of tomato and sweet basil representing the soup of the day; and a hearty oyster po'boy featuring hefty, briny, cornmeal-crusted Willapa Bay oysters and spice-tinged rémoulade on a fresh ciabatta roll alongside a tangle of Old Bay-sprinkled shoestring fries.

153

Il Buco

D4

47 Bond St. (bet. Bowery & Lafayette St.)

Subway: Bleecker St
Phone: 212-533-1932
Web: www.ilbuco.com
Prices: $$

Lunch Mon – Sat
Dinner nightly

It's hard to find a more charming restaurant than Il Buco. What started as a rustic antique shop in 1994 has evolved through the years into this beloved enoteca that looks as if it was plucked straight from the Italian countryside. The dining room is decorated with polished copper pots, flowers arranged in metal pails, and platters of fruit. An amalgam of farmhouse tables large enough to offer communal-style seating adds to the unabashedly convivial spirit.

Product-obsessed cooking rules the menu here, in a large array of seasonal small plates, house-made pasta and preparations highlighting artisanal ingredients. Expect entrées like stuffed saddle of New York state rabbit set atop rich Anson Mills polenta, with slender gold and orange carrots.

Il Buco Alimentari e Vineria 😊

D4

53 Great Jones St. (bet. Bowery & Lafayette St.)

Subway: Bleecker St
Phone: 212-837-2622
Web: www.ilbucovineria.com
Prices: $$

Lunch & dinner daily

This is the kind of authentic cooking and setting that makes us all wish we were Italian. Start with a stroll through the *alimentari* to pick up some *crema di pistachio* or a whole pork hind. The meticulously conceived dining area is no bigger than a barn and almost as rustic. Step down a few stairs to admire the copper roof, open kitchen, and gargantuan light fixture, which sets a picturesque backdrop for indulging in cheeses and house-cured meats.

Their slow-roasted porchetta vies to be the best in town, served in a round roll slathered with *salsa verde* and loaded with arugula. Skillfully crafted pastas may toss excellent olive oil, poached favas, pecorino, and cracked pepper. Finish with Meyer lemon *sorbetto*—a shining reflection of Italian tradition.

I Sodi

C1

Italian

105 Christopher St. (bet. Bleecker & Hudson Sts.)

Subway: Christopher St - Sheridan Sq   Dinner nightly
Phone: 212-414-5774
Web: www.isodinyc.com
Prices: $$

Manhattan has classic Italian and new Italian, but not many *thoughtful* Italian restaurants. Tuscan native Rita Sodi is out to change that with this trattoria. She consciously selected every aspect of the design, from the heavy linen napkins to the thick, striated glass windows that hide the modern space from the marauding groups of young people on Bleecker.

Inside this oasis, Negronis prep palates for al dente rigatoni and hearty, meat-focused dishes like the *coniglio in porchetta*. This exceptional rabbit preparation combines bacon-wrapped loin with a sweet wine- rosemary- and garlic-sauce. The herbal quality of such savoriness brings out the almost austere nature of the lean rabbit, showing how truly intuitive and innovative Italian cooking can be.

Joseph Leonard

D1

Contemporary

170 Waverly Pl. (at Grove St.)

Subway: Christopher St - Sheridan Sq   Lunch & dinner daily
Phone: 646-429-8383
Web: www.josephleonard.com
Prices: $$

No bigger than your average studio apartment, Joseph Leonard has a big personality and is insanely popular for good reason. From the antique mirrors to the nightly crowds, this contemporary American has nailed the heart and soul of Greenwich Village to become a regular spot for sipping well-sourced wines with friends and chomping down on wonderfully crisp rock shrimp fritters.

The recognizable dishes are expertly prepared, fueled by top-notch ingredients and a kitchen that knows how to handle a pan roasted chicken—arriving crisp-skinned and deliciously tender. Even humble Brussels sprouts get special treatment with a kick of *sriracha*. Finish it all off with monkey bread made with eggy-buttery brioche and a brilliantly subtle hint of maple.

Kesté Pizza & Vino 😊

D2

271 Bleecker St. (bet. Cornelia & Jones Sts.)

Subway: W 4 St - Wash Sq
Phone: 212-243-1500
Web: www.kestepizzeria.com
Prices: 💰💰

Lunch & dinner daily

A runaway success since day one, Kesté takes the craft of making Neapolitan-style pizza to epic heights. *Pizzaiolo* Roberto Caporuscio first opened and established Keste's reputation, even though he has now handed over this custom-built, wood-fired, volcanic stone *forno* to his very capable daughter, Giorgia.

Pizzas may be listed under two headings, but every pie (including gluten-free) is built upon a nicely salted, faintly tangy, gorgeously puffy crust with a delicately charred *cornicione* (raised edge). Pizza *speciale* feature creative ingredients like pistachio pesto or butternut squash purée; while *pizze rosse* are topped with excellent homemade mozzarella, imported tomatoes, and an array of meat or vegetables. Weekday lunches showcase panini.

Kin Shop

C2

469 Sixth Ave. (bet. 11th & 12th Sts.)

Subway: 14 St (Seventh Ave.)
Phone: 212-675-4295
Web: www.kinshopnyc.com
Prices: $$

Lunch & dinner daily

Chef Harold Dieterle combines an ingredient-driven focus with his love for Thai cuisine at this modern venture, which takes its name from the Thai word "to eat." Salads, noodles, and curries are always creative, so listen for the nightly specials—maybe a coconut milk soup with chili oil or chicken meatballs in green curry.

The inexpensive express lunch set is offered on weekdays and has featured a stir-fry of aquatic vegetables; and skate braised in a jungle curry of red chilies, funky crab paste, Kaffir lime leaf, and pickled green peppercorns. A scoop of Thai coffee-chocolate ice cream with sweet condensed milk is a perfectly cooling finish.

The exotic dining room boasts whitewashed brick, batik canvases, and a beachy color scheme.

La Camelia

B4

Mexican ✗

64 Downing St. (bet. Bedford & Varick Sts.)

Subway: Houston St
Lunch & dinner daily
Phone: 212-675-7060
Web: www.lacamelianyc.com
Prices: $$

Vibrant little La Camelia stays under the radar, despite the popular happy hour with margaritas *deliciosas* at the ready. The room combines Mexican artifacts, colorful chairs, and a curving red bar that leads to a framed portrait of Frida Kahlo. In the back, a table is set with all the classic accoutrements for their creamy-chunky guacamole made on the spot.

Start off with La Camelia's own take on *cucurucho*, made here with a crisp corn tortillas filled with chorizo, carnitas, tender potatoes, and much more topped with a smoky-sweet *chile de Cascabel* salsa. Flavorful sauces and marinades combine beautifully in the *pescado tikin xic*, comprised of mahi mahi baked in a banana leaf with black rice pilaf, mashed habanero, and a cooling mango jicama salad.

Lafayette

D4

French ✗✗

380 Lafayette St. (at Great Jones St.)

Subway: Bleecker St
Lunch & dinner daily
Phone: 212-533-3000
Web: www.lafayetteny.com
Prices: $$

Chef Andrew Carmellini's buzzy venture is an homage to French cuisine, proffered in a sexy space conceived by Roman and Williams. Counters lined with organic breads and pastries invite patrons to the entryway bakery. From here, the room unfolds into a series of seductive spaces where one finds a rotisserie oven spinning bronzed birds, a backlit bar emitting an amber glow and finishing clad in warm honey and blue tile.

The chef has recruited a remarkable team to direct Lafayette's kitchen as they churn out impressive creations like *pâté maison* bestowed with earthenware crocks of mustard and cornichons; and sea scallops *a la plancha* with a seasonal setup of peas, morels, and turnips. Burnt honey *vacherin* with apricot coulis is nothing short of stellar.

L'Artusi

Italian 🍴🍴

B3

228 W. 10th St. (bet. Bleecker & Hudson Sts.)

Subway: Christopher St - Sheridan Sq
Phone: 212-255-5757
Web: www.lartusi.com
Prices: $$

Lunch Sun
Dinner nightly

L'Artusi's façade may be demure, but this attractive dining room offers a fun, buzz-worthy vibe to elevate its upscale rendition of Italian-rooted food, anchored by small plates. The large space, with gray and ivory stripes aplenty, offers three dining counters, table service, and a quieter mezzanine. An open kitchen adds to the lively air.

The impressive Italian wine list, complete with maps, is laid out with a gravitas that demands attention. The well-versed staff is pleased to suggest the best pairings to complement pastas such as buckwheat *pizzoccheri* with Brussels sprouts, fontina, and sage. Salads of chicory dressed in Parmesan, lemon, and anchovies, or crudo plates of beef carpaccio with horseradish *crema* are wonderful ways to start a meal here.

Las Ramblas

Spanish 🍴

D1

170 W. 4th St. (bet. Cornelia & Jones Sts.)

Subway: Christopher St - Sheridan Sq
Phone: 646-415-7924
Web: N/A
Prices: ⊜⊜

Lunch Sat – Sun
Dinner nightly

Sandwiched among a throng of attention-seeking storefronts, mighty little Las Ramblas is easy to spot, just look for the crowd of happy, munching faces. The scene spills out onto the sidewalk when the weather allows.

Named for Barcelona's historic commercial thoroughfare, Las Ramblas is a tapas treat. A copper-plated bar and collection of tiny tables provide a perch for snacking on an array of earnestly prepared items. Check out the wall-mounted blackboard for *especiales*. Bring friends (it's that kind of place) to fully explore the menu which serves up delights such as succulent head-on prawns roasted in a terra-cotta dish and sauced with cava vinegar, ginger, and basil; or béchamel creamed spinach topped by a molten cap of Mahón cheese.

Left Bank

Contemporary ✕✕

B2

117 Perry St. (at Greenwich St.)

Subway: Christopher St - Sheridan Sq
Phone: 212-727-1170
Web: www.leftbanknewyork.com
Prices: $$

Dinner nightly

Left Bank may have plenty of local competition, but few have the attentive and considerate service combined with such a lively bar scene. With its faux-farmhouse décor and a rather bucolic corner location, it is a go-to neighborhood haunt. Happy hour specials bring them in, but the bar bites make them stay.

Every dish on the menu is pleasing, from the buttery lobster puffs perched on champagne cream to the perfectly crafted Mongolian dumplings, full of spicy lamb, cabbage, and onion with a cool soy-lime dipping sauce. The lovely farfalle with fresh favas, sunchoke, spring onion, and chili is bound by a sprinkling of nutty *Parmigiano*. Top it off with deliciously simple desserts, like a wedge of ricotta cheesecake and a properly poached Bosc pear.

Le Gigot

French ✕

D2

18 Cornelia St. (bet. Bleecker & W. 4th Sts.)

Subway: W 4 St - Wash Sq
Phone: 212-627-3737
Web: www.legigotrestaurant.com
Prices: $$

Lunch & dinner Tue – Sun

As classically beautiful and intricate as the *Metro* signs of Paris, this *petit resto* is dedicated to honoring The City of Light. Modeled after the Left Bank bistro Polidor, the iconic interior features parquet floors, zinc-topped tables, and antique mirrored walls. The room fills quickly with regulars and the dedicated staff graciously greet them all by name.

The food is roundly beloved, with such classics as generous charcuterie platters that include sausage, duck rillettes, silky smooth chicken liver, and hearty country pâtés. The excellent bœuf Bourguignon is a comforting dish of braised beef cubes, carrots, potatoes, button mushrooms, sweet shallots, and plenty of bacon. Come dessert, tarte Tatin smells of apples and heaven (but with extra butter).

Le Philosophe

French XX

D4

55 Bond St. (bet. Bowery & Lafayette St.)

Subway: Bleecker St
Phone: 212-388-0038
Web: www.lephilosophe.us
Prices: $$

Lunch Sat – Sun
Dinner nightly

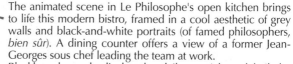

The animated scene in Le Philosophe's open kitchen brings to life this modern bistro, framed in a cool aesthetic of grey walls and black-and-white portraits (of famed philosophers, *bien sûr*). A dining counter offers a view of a former Jean-Georges sous chef leading the team at work.

Blackboard panels display the daily specials and hail the kitchen's purveyors. The cooking is proudly traditional and excels at giving French stalwarts a light touch. The classic duck *a l'orange* is a tender, rosy-fleshed breast under perfectly golden-crisped skin, plated with potato mousseline, baby turnips, and a tawny, citrus-infused sauce that hits just the right note of tartness.

Wine may seem the way to go, but Le Philosophe has a great beer selection to boot.

The Little Owl

American X

B3

90 Bedford St. (at Grove St.)

Subway: Christopher St - Sheridan Sq
Phone: 212-741-4695
Web: www.thelittleowlnyc.com
Prices: $$

Lunch & dinner daily

Perched on a winsome corner of the West Village, Chef Joey Campanaro's The Little Owl continues to hold a dear place in the hearts of diners near and far who appreciate that simple food and great food can be one and the same. The broccoli soup (a pure, silky purée enriched with a trace of cream and crowned by a crouton of bubbling, aged cheddar) is among the best examples of this.

The small corner room is quaint and despite this establishment's popularity, the service team is completely attitude-free. The wee kitchen is on display, and the focused crew turns out a rousing roster of preparations that may bear an affinity for Mediterranean cuisine such as seared cod with *bagna cauda* vinaigrette, and gravy meatball sliders, a hands-down house specialty.

Louro

Contemporary ✗✗

C2

142 W. 10th St. (bet. Greenwich Ave. & Waverly Pl.)

Subway: Christopher St - Sheridan Sq

Phone: 212-206-0606

Web: www.louronyc.com

Prices: $$

Lunch Sun
Dinner nightly

Louro is a tempting and very creative respite, a world away from Caesar salads and burgers. Here, find truly imaginative cooking through the lens of Chef David Santos. It doesn't hurt that the chef briefly ran an underground nightime destination and continues to offer Nossa Mesa—a supper club with an anti-establishment streak. The menu always stimulates, so dig into roasted heirloom carrot salad with toasted miso dressing; hand-cut *tagliatelle* tossed in spicy octopus Bolognese ragù with a hint of tasty goose pancetta; or beautifully seared Spanish mackerel with fresh, crunchy hearts of palm and smoked pineapple purée.

The room's soothing palette showcases foxed mirror panels and trompe l'oeil wallpaper portraying shelves of books lining the walls.

Lupa 😊

Italian ✗✗

C4

170 Thompson St. (bet. Bleecker & Houston Sts.)

Subway: W 4 St - Wash Sq

Phone: 212-982-5089

Web: www.luparestaurant.com

Prices: $$

Lunch & dinner daily

One of the best places for a solid plate of pasta, Lupa fits in snugly between the fire escape-clad walk-ups and charming boutiques along these streets. A modestly decorated spot named for the she-wolf who raised Romulus and Remus, this gem carries an air of relaxed sophistication. It's where neighbors can gather for polite conversation over quartinos of Ligurian wine or the massive collection of *amari*.

If it's a lovely place to sit, it's a stellar place to dine. Textbook-perfect pasta shines here, with luscious *bucatini all' amatriciana* earning its mark among Lazio classics as well as the beguilingly simple yet stunning *cacio e pepe*. Entrées may sometimes miss the mark, but dessert more than makes up for it—try the unique cardamom panna cotta.

Malaparte

B2

Italian ✗

753 Washington St. (at Bethune St.)

Subway: 14 St - 8 Av
Phone: 212-255-2122
Web: www.malapartenyc.com
Prices: $$

Lunch Sat – Sun
Dinner nightly

Tucked away on a quiet, tree-lined street just a short walk away from the Highline and Meatpacking District glitz, Malaparte nails its charmingly rustic ambience. The interior offers an intimate number of seats in a room that is graciously attended.

The food here is anything but an afterthought. In fact, the inexpensive, home-style Italian cuisine is the kind of fare one can return to enjoy regularly. Fresh salads and thin-crust pizzas are fine starters, while the short list of pasta is impressive as in spinach and artichoke lasagna layering fresh made sheets of pasta *verde* with wilted spinach, sliced artichokes, and creamy béchamel. The coffee crème caramel is a lovely finale, especially when sitting outside on a warm summer evening.

Margaux

C3

Mediterranean ✗✗

5 W. 8th St. (bet. Fifth & Sixth Aves.)

Subway: W 4 St - Wash Sq
Phone: 212-321-0111
Web: www.margauxnyc.com
Prices: $$

Lunch & dinner daily

Calling all pretty young things: the fashionable Marlton Hotel is now home to one of the best bar-cum-restaurants around Washington Sq. Park. Walk through its posh lobby, past the sleek espresso station and massive wooden bar (complete with brass footrests—it's that kind of place), to enter Margaux, a 20th century-inspired Parisian bistro. The elegant, well-curated décor includes molded ceilings and floral tiles imported from Argentina, but you'll want to make a beeline for the dreamy, skylight-covered garden room.

Settle in and order an innovative cocktail like the Artichoke Tea, a blend of Cynar, tea syrup, lemon, and cava, as well as a plate of juicy rotisserie chicken with smashed sweet potatoes, tangy *urfa biber* pepper, and powerful green *harissa*.

Market Table

B3

54 Carmine St. (at Bedford St.)

Subway: W 4 St - Wash Sq
Phone: 212-255-2100
Web: www.markettablenyc.com
Prices: $$

Lunch & dinner daily

Sophisticated cooking is on display at this urbane café brought to you by partners Joey Campanaro and Mike Price. The two-room charmer is bright and cheerful during the day, then warm and intimate at night. The décor features wood and leather furnishings, red brick walls shelved with wine bottles, and an open kitchen on display behind an inviting counter.

The kitchen continues to embrace an innovative face thanks to Executive Chef David Standridge as well as his spirited and consistently enjoyable menu. Try the incredibly tender octopus *a la plancha* with rich, herbaceous salsa verde and creamy red romesco; or grilled sea bream with olive *nage*. Desserts may include French toast spread with almond butter, set beside ricotta gelato and huckleberry sauce.

The Marrow

B2

99 Bank St. (at Greenwich St.)

Subway: 14 St (Seventh Ave.)
Phone: 212-428-6000
Web: www.themarrownyc.com
Prices: $$

Lunch Sat – Sun
Dinner nightly

Chef Harold Dieterle's popular venture with business partner Alicia Nosenzo is a harmonious pairing of German and Italian cuisines reflecting the talented chef's heritage. This far West Village dining room buzzes nightly and is chicly done in a dramatic palette of red and brown.

Each side of the family receives equal representation in the listing of inspired cooking. Pretzel rolls accompanied by whole grain mustard and olive oil are a perfect prelude to, well, anything. What may follow are the rich *baccalà gnudi* cleverly dressed with a buttery sauce, pine nuts, golden raisins, and herbed breadcrumbs; or juniper-braised lamb neck served with rutabaga purée and braised red cabbage. Warm stout gingerbread with honey ice cream is a lovely finish.

Mary's Fish Camp

B2

Seafood ✗

64 Charles St. (at W. 4th St.)

Subway: Christopher St - Sheridan Sq
Phone: 646-486-2185
Web: www.marysfishcamp.com
Prices: $$

Lunch & dinner Mon – Sat

Yes, Mary's serves lobster rolls. And yes, they are overflowing with succulent chunks of meat, slathered in mayonnaise, and piled onto a buttery, toasty hot dog bun.

However, there are other many other treats to be had at this highly trafficked West Village fish shack, where global accents spice up the seafood. Explore the likes of shrimp toast with scallion ginger sauce, market fish tacos, Portuguese sardine *bánh mì*, and *pozole* with Florida red snapper. The fried clam roll, spread with chunky tartar sauce and piled high with hot and crispy clams, brings things back home. The majority of seating is offered along a curving stainless steel counter facing the kitchen. Hand-scrawled blackboards, red gingham napkins, and scuffed floors set the stage.

Mas (farmhouse)

B3

Contemporary ✗✗✗

39 Downing St. (bet. Bedford & Varick Sts.)

Subway: Houston St
Phone: 212-255-1790
Web: www.masfarmhouse.com
Prices: $$$

Dinner nightly

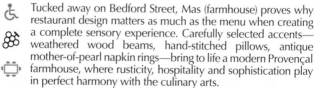

Tucked away on Bedford Street, Mas (farmhouse) proves why restaurant design matters as much as the menu when creating a complete sensory experience. Carefully selected accents— weathered wood beams, hand-stitched pillows, antique mother-of-pearl napkin rings—bring to life a modern Provençal farmhouse, where rusticity, hospitality and sophistication play in perfect harmony with the culinary arts.

Poached shrimp floats in an apple-ginger bath topped with radish, for a cooling yet spicy amuse-bouche to arouse the appetite. This may be followed by delicate fillets of Long Island fluke served over hearts of palm with smoky and earthy shiitake mushrooms. That attention to detail and mouth-filling flavor keeps you engaged, charmed, and absolutely satisfied.

Melibea

C2

2 Bank St. (at Greenwich St.)

Subway: 14 St (Seventh Ave.)
Phone: 212-463-0090
Web: www.melibeanyc.com
Prices: $$

Dinner nightly

An ambitious interpretation of Mediterranean flavors can be found at this darling, where Chef Pep Coronado has teamed up with restaurateur and Spanish compatriot Héctor Sanz (of Rayuela and Macondo) to present diners with a host of fine fare.

To drink, a cocktail arranged from under the headings linen, silk, velvet, and leather is recommended while settling down to take in the well-done interior that incorporates beautiful sienna banquettes, Moorish tiles, and walnut floors. And to eat, preparations include petals of salmon and scallop carpaccio dressed with salmon roe and an unexpected yet utterly enjoyable scoop of savory almond ice cream; or a luscious chicken entrée marinated in Syrian spices and plated with lentils and dried figs in lemon gravy.

Miss Lily's

C4

132 W. Houston St. (at Sullivan St.)

Subway: Houston St
Phone: 646-588-5375
Web: www.misslilysnyc.com
Prices: $$

Lunch Sat – Sun
Dinner nightly

Jamaica is the muse at this buzzy Serge Becker boîte. Up front, the look suggests a longstanding take out joint, complete with orange Formica booths, linoleum flooring, and a backlit menu board above the open kitchen. Stacks of fresh produce are a bright touch and used for Melvin's Juice Box preparations. The back room features playful lighting of curved black leather booths accented in red, green, and gold. Reggae record jackets line the walls and a thumping playlist fills the room.

Don't expect much from the service and you won't be disappointed. However, the food is very enjoyable, as in charred and smoky jerk chicken; pasture-raised curry goat; and richly spiced, bright yellow curried vegetables wrapped in warm and tender *roti*.

Minetta Tavern ❀

Gastropub ✗

C3

113 MacDougal St. (at Minetta Ln.)

Subway: W 4 St - Wash Sq
Phone: 212-475-3850
Web: www.minettatavernny.com
Prices: $$$

Lunch Wed – Sun
Dinner nightly

Minetta Tavern serves up a heaping dose of nostalgia that New Yorkers can't get enough of. Neon signage out front marks the spot of this Greenwich Village institution, which was founded in 1937 as an Italian restaurant subsequent to its time as a speakeasy.

Vintage portraits of original owner Eddie "Minetta" Sieveri posing with stars line the walls of the back dining room, where black-and-white checkerboard flooring and a vivid mural of Washington Square Park frame tables set along red leather banquettes. Up front, the original oak bar is a highly coveted perch for savoring a juicy Black Label burger and skillfully-crafted cocktail.

But for all of its atmosphere, Chef William Brasile and his team produce a lineup of classically-rooted specialties that ensure style doesn't trump substance. A slab of chilled oxtail and foie gras terrine with poached leeks is a decadent way to begin, and fillet of trout meunière, sizzling in browned butter, is crowned with sweet chunks of crabmeat, diced lemon, and tiny brioche croutons. Dessert is equally fantastic, so be sure to leave room. If offered, gâteau Basque filled with vanilla pastry cream gives the stellar coconut cake some competition.

Morandi

Italian XX

C2

211 Waverly Pl. (bet. Charles St. & Seventh Ave. South)

Subway: 14 St (Seventh Ave.)   Lunch & dinner daily
Phone: 212-627-7575
Web: www.morandiny.com
Prices: $$$

From first sight, this prominent West Village location does much to resemble a farmhouse or cantina. Wood panels, antique tiles, tin ceilings, and shelves displaying straw-covered bottles of Chianti conjure an American's idyllic dream of Italy. The food is a more genuine reflection.

Decadent beginnings might include tart and very crisp fried olives stuffed with meat. Plates of fried artichokes brightened with preserved lemon are unmissable, especially when paired with a choice of hand-stretched focaccia. Long twists of *busiate al ragù di pesce spada* are tossed with swordfish and excellent spicy almond pesto. Nightly specials showcase the likes of *vitello alla Milanese* with a crust so perfect and piping-hot, that it threatens to shatter with a fork.

Murray's Cheese Bar

American XX

D2

264 Bleecker St. (bet. Leroy & Morton Sts.)

Subway: W 4 St - Wash Sq   Lunch Tue – Sun
Phone: 646-476-8882   Dinner nightly
Web: www.murrayscheesebar.com
Prices: $$

A turophile's dream come true, this cheese bar is built for people who just want to eat really amazing cheese. The upscale space, decked with subway tiles, whitewashed wood tables, and lacquered chairs, is a natural extension of neighboring Murray's Cheese, the famed Greenwich Village purveyor of phenomenal dairy products.

With a category to suit every craving (fresh, soft-ripened, washed-rind, semi-firm, and blue) the bar's extensive menu has it all, from buttery Pyrenéese Brebis to funky and heady gorgonzola *cremificato*. For a truly indulgent meal, add a glass of wine (*nebbiolo* with that rich gorgonzola), *salumi* (from American purveyors like D'Artagnan and Olli), slow-simmered lamb meatballs, and phenomenal cheeses served with sweet apricot compote.

Pagani

C1

Italian ✗✗

289 Bleecker St. (at Seventh Ave.)

Subway: Christopher St - Sheridan Sq
Phone: 212-488-5800
Web: www.paganinyc.com
Prices: $$

Lunch & dinner daily

With witty cocktails, cured meats, and *rustico nuovo* décor, Pagani brings an extra dose of Italian charm to Bleecker Street, and a good one at that. Flauting a vibrant scene of locals guzzling indigenous wines and Averna-steeped drinks, this brainchild of Massimo Lusardi targets a younger mentality where authenticity and creativity go hand-in-hand.

His family may own several other restaurants, but sizeable portions of house-made pasta with updated embellishments (think: *montasio* cheese topping a decadent ragù of veal and pork) highlight balance and excellence. Just as veal shoulder arrives unbelievably fragrant and tender with herb-rubbed, toasted bread; rigatoni with braised rabbit and sweet carrots feel like a match made in culinary heaven.

Panca

C1

Peruvian ✗

92 Seventh Ave. South (bet. Bleecker & Grove Sts.)

Subway: Christopher St - Sheridan Sq
Phone: 212-488-3900
Web: www.pancany.com
Prices: $$

Lunch & dinner daily

Panca's sedate setting is a fine contrast to its highly trafficked location. Citron walls are complemented by a stacked stone bar area lined with bottles of pisco. Tucked away in the corner, find the *cebiche* station where fresh cuts of fish are transformed into zesty *cebiches* such as shrimp in lime juice with toothsome hominy and barely ripe yet perfectly tart mango. If you choose to sit on the sidewalk, be prepared to give up the dining room's tranquility.

Traditional specialties are a draw here, like *lomo saltado*, slivers of ribeye stir-fried with onions, tomatoes, *aji amarillo*, and soy sauce. However, the chicken is a crowd-pleasing favorite—rotisserie-roasted and incredibly flavorful, it fills the room with a mouthwatering aroma.

Paradou

French 🍴

8 Little W. 12th St. (bet. Greenwich & Washington Sts.)

Subway: 14 St - 8 Av
Phone: 212-463-8345
Web: www.paradounyc.com
Prices: $$

Lunch Sat – Sun
Dinner Tue – Sun

Paradou offers a bit of Provence and a welcome respite from the spate of gargantuan, too-cool-for-school dining halls populating the Meatpacking District. Here, a casual yet energetic crowd revels in the carefree, distinctly French spirit while relaxing over crisp glasses of champagne and supping on plates of foie gras or bowls of *moules du jour*.

Most guests choose to head to the patio which doubles Paradou's seating capacity, but the intimate dining room is lovely as well. Regardless of your seat, the menu offers classic cooking, as in lamb ribs drizzled with truffle honey; sides such as cassoulet beans showered with herbed breadcrumbs presented in a cast iron skillet; and finales such as warming apple crêpes spiked with Calvados.

Pearl Oyster Bar

Seafood 🍴

18 Cornelia St. (bet. Bleecker & W. 4th Sts.)

Subway: W 4 St - Wash Sq
Phone: 212-691-8211
Web: www.pearloysterbar.com
Prices: $$

Lunch Mon – Fri
Dinner Mon – Sat

It's not hard to find a lobster roll in this city, and for that we can thank Rebecca Charles. This winsome seafood spot—inspired by her grandmother and childhood summers spent in Maine—has been going strong since 1997. Its success has assured many like-minded spin-offs.

The two-room setting offers a choice of counter seating or table service. The wood furnishings and white walls are low-key but beachy memorabilia perk up the space. The classic New England menu offers plates of chilled seafood and smaller dishes like johnnycake topped with thinly sliced smoked salmon. Entrées include that signature roll sided by shoestring fries, or lobster (boiled or grilled) served with corn pudding. A hot fudge sundae is a deliciously nostalgic finish.

Perilla

Contemporary ✗✗

9 Jones St. (bet. Bleecker & W. 4th Sts.)

Subway: W 4 St - Wash Sq
Phone: 212-929-6868
Web: www.perillanyc.com
Prices: $$

Lunch Sat – Sun
Dinner nightly

Low-key, casual, and classic, Perilla is simply a comfortable place to be—solo diners seek out the welcoming bar. Observe that the designer zebrawood tables are signed on the edge and then understand this place's level of care and dedication to detail. The subdued lighting, plush banquettes, and cream-colored walls lend a calm vibe despite the clubby music.

The kitchen combines quality ingredients with experimental flair, resulting in dishes that are pleasing but can be overly flavorful. Sample pasta like house-made *garganelli* with smoky *guanciale*, paprika, spring onion, piney-crunchy fiddlehead fern, and sweet octopus. The Long Island duck breast is cooked to gorgeous pink and served with roasted beets and savory baklava layering duck confit and greens.

Perla

Italian ✗✗

24 Minetta Ln. (at Sixth Ave.)

Subway: W 4 St - Wash Sq
Phone: 212-933-1824
Web: www.perlanyc.com
Prices: $$$

Lunch Wed – Sun
Dinner nightly

Well-deserving of its popularity, Perla nails that rustic chic dining experience with a wood-beamed wine vault, hipster-cool servers, and solid cooking. Tucked along a narrow street, the restored tavern pumps out top-notch Italian to a slew of regulars packed onto red leather banquettes. This is in large part thanks to a very skilled kitchen equipped with an army of dedicated cooks.

Delicious, fresh pastas are a hit, such as the egg-based *maltagliati* tossed with braised pork shoulder, escarole, freshly shelled beans, and grated *Parmigiano*. Lighter dishes are comparably good, with sides like pan-seared mushrooms or the salad of lightly toasted hazelnuts, funky, creamy gorgonzola, juicy pear cubes, and rosettes of smoky speck over crisp kale.

Perry Street 🏠

A2

Contemporary ✕✕

176 Perry St. (at West St.)

Subway: Christopher St - Sheridan Sq
Phone: 212-352-1900
Web: www.perrystreetrestaurant.com
Prices: $$

Lunch & dinner daily

Chef Jean-Georges Vongerichten's son, Cedric, is the king of the castle in this Richard Meier-designed building. Perry Street, named for the block on which it is set, is a mid-century, glamorous dining room that is ideal for a sophisticated meal. Look for the sunlight that streams onto creamy leather by way of large windows overlooking the Hudson River. It's perhaps the best lunch option in town, not only for the sumptuous setting and welcoming vibe, but (of course) the menu.

The Vongerichtens fill their dishes with surprises, as in grilled oyster mushrooms with Hass avocados tossed with charred jalapeño, dill, cracked pepper, and gray salt. Expect spicy flavor combinations, on display in the golden-fried chicken with a wallop of scotch bonnet sauce.

The Place

B2

American ✕✕

310 W. 4th St. (bet. Bank & 12th Sts.)

Subway: 14 St - 8 Av
Phone: 212-924-2711
Web: www.theplaceny.com
Prices: $$

Lunch Sat – Sun
Dinner nightly

Set deep within the West Village, The Place is the kind of cozy, grotto-style den that makes you feel all grown-up. Rendezvous-like, guests climb below street level to find a bar aglow with flickering votive candles. Wander back a bit, and you'll find rustic beams and white tablecloth seating; two outdoor terraces beckon when the sun shines.

The guileless name of this "place" and timeless look of its century-old setting is nicely juxtaposed by a wholly American menu that roams from east to west: duck confit-filled parcels with grain mustard and braised red cabbage is a lovely autumnal treat, while entrées please year-round with dishes like a cheddar-capped Shepherd's pie; Long Island duck breast with tamarind sauce; and Cuban-style pork chops.

Piora ✿

B3

Contemporary 🍴🍴

430 Hudson St. (bet. Morton St. & St. Luke's Pl.)

Subway: Christopher St - Sheridan Sq
Phone: 212-960-3801
Web: www.pioranyc.com
Prices: $$$

Lunch & dinner Mon – Sat

Piora's façade blends beautifully into its charming surrounds. A mini entry delivers you to the end of its marble bar, swarming with well-heeled beauties sipping on a superior list of Japanese-influenced libations. In the back is a plush-white dining room, whose petite size is surpassed only by a super sleek vibe. Here, simplicity is truly the peak of elegance, and glossy wood floors star alongside leather-topped tables and black-paned windows.

The theme is crystal clear: captivate crowds with careful presentations, sophisticated plates, and a polished staff. Then cue their diverse team with an Italian-American chef (Chris Cipollone), Korean-born owner, and Japanese head bartender, and know that you're in for the best from this land. Think of a slow-cooked egg served with salty potatoes and a crispy chicken wing for terrific flavor and texture; or tender grilled octopus deliciously spiced with *gochujang*. If such supreme pairings don't knock your socks off, *bucatini* with black garlic and king crab promises ambition, skill, and pure pleasure—as does the poussin, offset with unique citrus sauces.

Sweet whipped cream encircled by mango pavlova makes for a tasty, fun, and fantastic finale.

Pó

D2

31 Cornelia St. (bet. Bleecker & W. 4th Sts.)

Subway: W 4 St – Wash Sq
Phone: 212-645-2189
Web: www.porestaurant.com
Prices: $$

Lunch Wed – Sun
Dinner nightly

This longtime neighborhood favorite, opened in 1993, continues to attract a devoted following for its understated yet sophisticated ambience and creative Italian fare. During the day, the slender dining room is light and breezy, especially in warmer weather when the front door is propped open and ceiling fans swirl overhead. At night, this quaint spot tucked away on tree-lined Cornelia St. feels timeless and utterly romantic.

Frittate, panini, and pastas are available at lunch. The dinner menu features a contemporary slant that may include starters like house-cured tuna dressed with white beans, artichokes, and chili-mint vinaigrette; freshly made gnocchi draped with lamb ragù; and entrées that include grilled skirt steak with gorgonzola butter.

Recette

B2

328 W. 12th St. (at Greenwich St.)

Subway: 14 St - 8 Av
Phone: 212-414-3000
Web: www.recettenyc.com
Prices: $$$

Lunch Sun
Dinner nightly

At Recette, the atmosphere is quaint and buzzy; the talented kitchen is firing up sophisticated, playful dishes designed for sharing; and the chef's playlist is famous in its own right. Perched on an historic West Village corner, it becomes quickly packed with regulars and newcomers alike. The tiny space is styled with dark wood tables, twinkling votives, and white-paneled floor-to-ceiling windows.

Feast on a fantastic array of generously portioned small plates (you might need fewer than you think). The flow of courses reveals cod fritters nestled in lamb sausage ragù and doused with curry aïoli; exquisite duck breast atop beluga lentils and maitake mushrooms; or "Buffalo" sweetbreads—a twist on wings—complete with Valdeón blue cheese dipping sauce.

RedFarm

B2

529 Hudson St. (bet. Charles & 10th Sts.)

Subway: Christopher St - Sheridan Sq
Phone: 212-792-9700
Web: www.redfarmnyc.com
Prices: $$

Lunch Sat – Sun
Dinner nightly

The hot spot for upscale (and of the moment) Chinese food, RedFarm packs in the flavor, the noise, as well as the people. On any given night, the line will snake out the door, and a wait is inevitable to score a seat at their communal table in this industrial space. It's worth any hassle, though, when you sit down to experience the farm-to-table, Asian-fusion concept from big names in the business like Joe Ng & Ed Schoenfeld.

The freewheeling kitchen relishes experimenting with local ingredients. Try the bright green pea-leaf and shrimp dumplings, which stand out beautifully in their near-translucent casing; or wok-fried Dungeness crab and crawfish in a thick and spicy basil-ginger sauce.

For some Peking duck fun, head downstairs to Decoy.

Rockmeisha

D1

11 Barrow St. (bet. Seventh Ave. South & W. 4th St.)

Subway: Christopher St - Sheridan Sq
Phone: 212-675-7775
Web: N/A
Prices: 🍜🍜

Dinner Tue-Sun

Regional specialties hailing from the chef's homeland of Kyushu, the large island in Southern Japan, are the way to go at this laid-back, fun, and tasty *izakaya*.

Like its name, the menu takes on a musical theme in listing its dishes as "goldies" which may reveal *takosu*, thick slices of dense octopus bobbing in a refreshing yuzu-zested soy-vinegar sauce. Their "greatest hits" might feature the *tonsoku*, a crispy pork foot that is unctuous to the point of being voluptuous, accompanied by raw cabbage and a dab of citrusy-spicy *yuzu kosho* to cut the richness.

The intimate space is decorated with a touch of kitsch (think poison warning signs), curious little cartoon drawings lining the walls, and rock music pulsing in the background, of course.

Saxon + Parole

D4

316 Bowery (at Bleecker St.)

Subway: Bleecker St
Phone: 212-254-0350
Web: www.saxonandparole.com
Prices: $$$

Lunch Fri – Sun
Dinner nightly

Brought to you by such key players as Executive Chef Brad Farmerie and the AvroKO Hospitality Group, Saxon + Parole is named after two 19th century racehorses. Inside, this handsome setting employs a limited use of color, but showcases rich wood tones and warm lighting to achieve a suitably clubby atmosphere.

The crowd-pleasing menu, founded on grilled meats and fresh seafood, boasts beginnings like a pot of velvety portobello mushroom mousse capped by a sheen of whiskey and black truffle jelly; and entrées such as whole-roasted branzino stuffed with Parmesan and smoked paprika-seasoned panko, sided by Brussels sprouts in chili-caramel. Desserts play a deliciously whimsical note, as in steamed Christmas pudding with hard-sauce ice cream.

Scarpetta

B1

355 W. 14th St. (bet. Eighth & Ninth Aves.)

Subway: 14 St - 8 Av
Phone: 212-691-0555
Web: www.scottconant.com
Prices: $$$

Dinner nightly

As stiletto-clad women navigate the clubby Meatpacking District's cobblestone streets, Chef Scott Conant maneuvers Scarpetta's kitchen, crafting excellent Italian-style dishes. Sexy describes both the clientele and the atmosphere of the mahogany and marble dining room serving what is a welcome reprieve from the area's overpriced, mediocre fare. Start the party with the irresistible, house-made *stromboli*, studded with smoked mozzarella and salami—any restaurant that dedicates this kind of attention to a bread basket is serious and doesn't disappoint. The hand-crafted spaghetti *pomodoro* is a glorious celebration of fresh tomatoes, basil, and Grana Padano. Oven-roasted halibut cloaked in decadent *lardo* with Romanesco cauliflower is sinfully brilliant.

Sevilla

B2

Spanish ✕

62 Charles St. (at W. 4th St.)

Subway: Christopher St - Sheridan Sq   Lunch & dinner daily
Phone: 212-929-3189
Web: www.sevillarestaurantandbar.com
Prices: $$

With a long and colorful history since first opening its doors in 1941, charmingly nostalgic Sevilla remains a rarity among Manhattan's dining scene. The roaming menu harks back to traditional Spanish fare, heaping and hearty; the kind enjoyed long before our commonplace exposure to the cuisine became focused on small plates.

The majority of Sevilla's reasonably priced dishes are built around simply prepared seafood and chicken dressed with a number of primary sauces featuring almond, garlic, wine, and the prominent green sauce—parsley-packed and punched with garlic. Starters include the *ajo* soup, a clear chicken broth infused with the nutty essence of roasted garlic and enriched with egg; while the smooth, classic flan is a fitting finale.

Spasso

B2

Italian ✕✕

551 Hudson St. (at Perry St.)

Subway: Christopher St - Sheridan Sq   Lunch & dinner daily
Phone: 212-858-3838
Web: www.spassonyc.com
Prices: $$

The refined far West Village has no dearth of Italian restaurants, and Spasso distinguishes itself not only with its ornate, white wood-framed windows, but an inviting ambience and stellar service. It's the friendly corner spot with a marble bar where you can sip a glass of *nebbiolo* and chat with the chefs, or simply dine solo on bowls of fresh *paste*.

The basics are here with squid ink *spaghettini* with *mosciame* or air-dried tuna (a specialty of Sardinia); and tripe ragù over tagliatelle. But creative dishes, like giardiniera-laced beef tartare also star, as a tangy twist on the traditional. Speaking of twists, *affogato* offers quite the kick with ice cream that can be "choked" with sherry, amaro, or rye whisky before drizzling it with a shot of espresso.

Soto ✿✿

D1

357 Sixth Ave. (bet. Washington Pl. & W. 4th St.)

Subway: W 4 St   Wash Sq   Dinner Mon – Sat
Phone: 212-414-3088
Web: N/A
Prices: $$$

Culinary dominance, unmistakable skill, and absolute discipline permeate every angle of this modest storefront. This is not some flashy temple to sushi, but an authentic and visually restrained rendering of a traditional Japanese restaurant. If the sterile look (with little more than blonde wood and bright lighting to embellish) seems too antiseptic, then remember that this is a place that prides itself on precise preparations of raw seafood. Does the staff fear their stern, formidable Chef Sotohiro Kosugi? Maybe.

Knife skills are paramount and every element is at its precise temperature, as these adept cooks coax each morsel of fish into a single bite that vies to be remembered as New York's best sushi. Composed dishes are not only strikingly beautiful, but may prove to be your favorite of the night finely minced and impossibly rich bigeye tuna with avocado coulis, caviar, minced chives, threads of fried daikon, and nori with a sesame-ponzu sauce. The unctuous uni cocktail combines soy reduction and fresh wasabi with icy-cold sea urchin.

Elegant plates have included ebi tartare, showcasing the fresh flavors of sweet, raw shrimp with ginger, caviar, nori, and shiitake dashi.

Spice Market

Asian ✗✗

B1

403 W. 13th St. (at Ninth Ave.)

Subway: 14 St - 8 Av   Lunch & dinner daily
Phone: 212-675-2322
Web: www.spicemarketnewyork.com
Prices: $$

This former warehouse turned sexy Asian street food lair has spawned offshoots in London and Qatar, further facilitating Chef Jean-Georges Vongerichten's global reach. But here in NYC, the 2004 original is a 12,000 square-foot fantasy glammed up by carved wooden arches, jewel-toned fabrics, a teak pagoda, and sarong-wrapped staff. The scene still thumps nightly, crammed with fun-loving grazers supping on faraway specialties all crafted with the chef's trademark élan. The carte divulges a savory romp: shatteringly crispy shrimp spring rolls; salt and pepper skate; polished copper bowls of pork *vindaloo*; and fried rice crowned by a sunny-side up egg ringed with gingery breadcrumbs.

Come to eat. Come to drink. Spice Market rarely disappoints.

Standard Grill

Contemporary ✗✗

B1

848 Washington St. (bet. Little W. 12th & 13th Sts.)

Subway: 14 St - 8 Av   Lunch & dinner daily
Phone: 212-645-4100
Web: www.thestandardgrill.com
Prices: $$

Calling the Standard Grill a scene is an understatement. Tucked beneath the High Line in the hugely popular Standard Hotel, this clubby-chic grill blends black-and-white tiles, wood-framed windows overlooking Washington Street, and sidewalk seating with classic New York style. Modern downtown esthetics are reflected in their cadre of beautiful servers donning 1970s vintage plaid uniforms.

Given its prime location, hip crowd, and sprawling layout, one might expect the food to falter but the culinary team doesn't disappoint. Baked macaroni hits a homerun with its creamy blend of trumpet mushrooms, smoky roasted cauliflower, and tangy *taggiasca* olives; as does the Southern-style Atlantic swordfish, grilled and topped with a lemon- and green olive-salsa.

178

Spotted Pig ✿

B2

314 W. 11th St. (at Greenwich St.)

Subway: Christopher St - Sheridan Sq   Lunch & dinner daily
Phone: 212-620-0393
Web: www.thespottedpig.com
Prices: $$$

Considering its idyllic corner setting—just a few blocks from the Hudson River and in the heart of the dreamy West Village—it's no wonder this well-groomed beau is such a perpetual hit. Barring the too-cool-for-school staff, the bi-level gem is hot and happening, decked out in handsome wood planks, quirky knickknacks, and subdued lighting. Downstairs, a spacious bar is big among carousers; while close-knit tables on the upper level are filled with skinny, stylish types boasting big appetites.

The décor here never tires and neither do those skilled chefs. Lunch tends to be a cozy, quiet affair; whereas evenings are jamming with lines of fans craving such gastropub eats as chicken liver slathered on crusty country bread and drizzled with glugs of delicious olive oil. Another Bloomfield classic features perfectly seasoned pan-seared mackerel, sporting a crackling-crisp skin and perched delicately atop pancetta-studded sweet potatoes.

For dessert, an elevated version of the traditional English banoffee pie (a slice of pastry crust filled with layers of creamy toffee pudding, sliced bananas, whipped cream, and shaved chocolate) has sugar junkies jonesing for more from across the pond.

Sushi Nakazawa

Japanese   ❌❌

C2

23 Commerce St. (bet. Bedford St. & Seventh Ave. South)

Train: Christopher St - Sheridan Sq**Phone:**   Dinner Mon – Sat
212-924-2212
Web: www.sushinakazawa.com
Prices: $$$$

The buzz behind Chef Daisuke Nakazawa's eponymous *sushi-ya* has hordes descending on its tranquil location in hopes of scoring a seat. The comfortably arranged counter is always in demand, while a table in the back room is fine consolation—but might feel like you've been relegated to economy class.

Nakazawa's omakase may display temperature and construction inconsistencies, but the quality of its wildly-sourced lineup is impressive and even stunning. Multiple pieces are presented at once and reveal lightly smoked Chinook salmon sprinkled with Okinawan sea salt, glistening mackerel brushed with *nikiri*, barely cooked blue shrimp from New Caledonia, and lean tuna from Boston kissed with Japanese mustard. A block of excellent *tamago* leaves you wanting more.

Takashi

Japanese   ❌

B3

456 Hudson St. (bet. Barrow & Morton Sts.)

Subway: Christopher St - Sheridan Sq   Dinner nightly
Phone: 212-414-2929
Web: www.takashinyc.com
Prices: $$

Tremendous care, planning, and sourcing of specialty cuts went into cozy Takashi before it ever opened its doors to acclaim. Chef/owner Takashi Inoue honors his Korean ancestry and Osaka upbringing with an array of shamelessly carnivorous *yakiniku* favorites. Walls display cutesy cartoons to clarify exactly what you are eating—like "testicargot."

Creative starters might include the Fashion Week Special, served as a cuffed paper bag of devilishly good collagen chips scented with hibiscus and blood orange. Tables are equipped with gas grills for searing platters of rare cuts, from tender beef cheek to large intestines and every stomach in between. Don't miss homemade desserts, like Madagascar vanilla soft-serve with rice dumplings and salted caramel sauce.

Tertulia 😊

D1

Spanish 🍴

359 Sixth Ave. (at Washington Pl.)

Subway: W 4 St - Wash Sq
Phone: 646-559-9909
Web: www.tertulianyc.com
Prices: $$

Lunch & dinner daily

Hooray for fried food that's totally fun and memorable. Inspired by a *sidreria* or cider house common to Northern Spain, Chef Seamus Mullen's celebrated eatery is a convivial gathering spot. The friendly bar features wooden barrels that dispense Spanish wines, excellent sangria, and of course their ever-coveted ciders.

Cured meats and cheeses bolster the array of tapas like crisp baby eggplant with hazelnut romesco. Open all day, lunch offers a pleasing prix-fixe that may reveal a cool salad of *pardina* lentils mixed with diced cucumber, radicchio, and homemade fresh cheese; or a grilled skirt steak sandwich spread with intense Valdeón cheese alongside spicy pickled veggies and just-fried potato chips. Crispy *churros* are more memorable than a Lorca ode.

Ushiwakamaru

C4

Japanese 🍴

136 W. Houston St. (bet. MacDougal & Sullivan Sts.)

Subway: B'way - Lafayette St
Phone: 212-228-4181
Web: N/A
Prices: $$$$

Dinner Mon – Sat

Arrive early enough and you may find Ushiwakamaru's tables pre-assigned to reserved guests by way of post-its: most nights, this casual basement *sushi-ya* is packed with regulars craving Chef Hideo Kuribara's skillfully crafted morsels.

Sitting at the counter should influence you to indulge in the omakase, along with most of your neighbors. It is more interactive here than found at more traditional *sushi-ya*, allowing diners to tailor the experience based on their budget. Your *itamae* will send forth the likes of a sweet-tasting slice of giant clam, or wild baby yellowtail perched atop warm, loosely packed rice; and sashimi that may feature silver-skinned horse mackerel; or slivers of toothsome octopus tentacles sided by pepper-flecked sea salt.

Wallflower

B2

235 W. 12th St. (bet. Greenwich Ave. & W. 4th St.)

Subway: 14 St (Seventh Ave.)   Dinner nightly
Web: www.wallflowernyc.com
Prices: $$

When a Daniel restaurant veteran opens a casual little cocktail lounge and dining room, the locals will come and never leave. Xavier Herit spent seven years as head bartender at the renowned spot, and his expertise clearly shows in the impressive wine list and complex cocktails—he even crafts a house-made pinot noir syrup for the Scotch-based Père Pinard.

The prix-fixe is a true deal in this neighborhood, especially with choices from the raw bar and charcuterie. For heartier fare, try the country pâté or rabbit terrine, both classically prepared and perfectly seasoned. Silky beef short ribs are deeply comforting, garnished with bacon, mushroom, cipollini, and just the right amount of brawny sauce. The coffee-chocolate *pot de crème* is deliciously intense.

Yerba Buena Perry

C2

1 Perry St. (at Greenwich Ave.)

Subway: 14 St (Seventh Ave.)   Lunch Sat – Sun
Phone: 212-620-0808   Dinner nightly
Web: www.ybnyc.com
Prices: $$

As vivacious as a samba, Yerba Buena Perry transports you to a South American paradise, where Latin-inspired dishes cover each table, the bartender never stops shaking celebrated drinks, and loud laughter and music fill the tight space. A longtime favorite, this staff and the kitchen have their choreography down.

Of course the smoky chipotle-laced guacamole is a necessary way to start the meal. Some dishes show Peruvian twists, like jalapeño-soy dressed tuna ceviche with pickled watermelon; as well as Thai basil-jalapeño *ocopa* sauce, a Peruvian tradition, to accompany those thin and crisp butternut squash-and-Manchego empanadas. Don't leave without trying the wow-inducing panko-coated watermelon fries and poblano-infused tomato ketchup.

Wallsé ❀

A u s t r i a n ✗✗

344 W. 11th St. (at Washington St.)

Subway: Christopher St - Sheridan Sq
Phone: 212-352-2300
Web: www.kg-ny.com
Prices: $$$

Lunch Sun
Dinner nightly

Set amid the narrow cobblestone streets and historic houses that lend Greenwich Village that iconic charm, Wallsé's white panels and oversized picture windows couldn't appear more at home. A certain sense of local artistry carries through the subdued black-and-white dining room, where Julian Schnabel paintings (some of the chef) and colorful modern art are prominently displayed. The service staff is friendly and very professional. The well-to-do clientele is sophisticated, not in the least bit stuffy, and here to savor their time and enjoy a very good meal.

Each dish is a smart, precise, and delicious representation of this accomplished kitchen. Some options are enticingly rustic like a traditional braised rabbit with root vegetables and airy-light spaetzle. Others are masterful renditions of classical mid dishes: simmered tarragon and veal tongue that is as decadent as pastrami yet verges on spoon-tender. Freshly grated horseradish, chives, creamed spinach, crème fraîche, and roasted potatoes complete the dish.

When sweet and pulpy paper-thin apples are wrapped in a buttery pastry alongside cinnamon-spiked ice cream, the taste of apple strudel seems like an entirely new experience.

ZZ's Clam Bar ❀

Manhattan ▶ Greenwich, West Village & Meatpacking District

C4

169 Thompson St. (bet. Bleecker & Houston Sts.)

Subway: Spring St (Sixth Ave.)　　　　　　　Dinner Tue – Sat
Phone: 212-254-3000
Web: www.zzsclambar.com
Prices: $$$$

Blink and you'll miss the entry to this diminutive den, secured (seriously!) by a bouncer. Bypass this odd arrival to enter a sharply attired dining nook dotted with white marble tables set within earshot of each other, dark wood panels, and a super-slim counter. A gorgeous bar positioned in the back pours $20 cocktails. Pricey? Yes. But, worth every pretty penny. Plus this is also where those freshly caught shellfish are shucked—a doubleheader, no doubt.

It's all very snug, sleek, and retro inside, but the spotlight never strays from the simple, elegant food—conveyed from a tiny square opening in the wall. Decadence is of the essence in semolina bread spread with crème fraîche and trout roe; while clam ceviche with Aleppo pepper or *saba* crudo with radish and pomegranate transform ostensibly routine ingredients into sublime creations after a glug of pungent olive oil. Beef carpaccio capped with uni and caviar is strange, superb, and luscious all at once. Not far behind, tuna is turned on its head with shaved foie gras, bone marrow, and more of that excellent EVOO.

And with such preciously prepared sips as the Mango, starring bourbon, Aperol, and lime, dessert is but a distant dream.

Harlem, Morningside & Washington Heights

This upper Manhattan pocket is best known for its 1920s jazz clubs that put musicians like Charlie Parker and Miles Davis on the map. Home to Columbia University, this capital of African-American, Latino, and Caribbean culture lives up to its world-renowned reputation as an incubator of artistic and academic greats, having officially cast off the age-old stigma of urban blight. Streets scattered with terrific soul food joints and authentic African markets make it a vibrant and enormously desired destination.

MORNINGSIDE HEIGHTS

Considered an extension of the Upper West Side, park-lined Morningside Heights is frequented for its fantastic breakfasts. Inexpensive eateries are set between quaint brownstones and commercial buildings. When they're not darting to and from classes, resident scholars and ivy-leaguers can be found lounging at the always-aromatic **Hungarian Pastry Shop** with a sweet treat and cup of tea. Special occasions call for an evening gathering at **Lee Lee's Baked Goods**. Rather than be misled by its plain-Jane façade, prepare yourself for serious gratification thanks to the most delicious and decadent rugelach in town. When spring approaches, stroll out onto the terrace and enjoy a bevy in the breeze.

WEST HARLEM

Further north is Harlem, a sanctuary for the soul and stomach. Fifth Avenue divides this region into two very unique sections: West Harlem, a hub for African-American culture; and East Harlem, a pulsating Spanish district also referred to as "El Barrio." Known for its sassy edge, West Harlem is constantly making way for booming gentrification and socio-cultural evolution. One of its most visible borders is

Fairway, a Tri-State area staple that draws shoppers of all stripes. Pick up one of their treats to-go—and sustain you while sifting through the impressive literary collection at The Schomburg Center for Research in Black Culture for a taste of this area's history. When the sun sets over the Hudson River, find locals and sleek tourists slipping into **Patisserie des Ambassades**, where a modern, chic décor does much to draw hordes for breakfast, lunch, and dinner. Not only do the aromas from their fresh-baked croissants, *eclairs au chocolat*, and cream-filled beignets waft down the block, but they also ensure long lines at all times. Every August, **Harlem Week** brings the community together over art, music, and food. Join in the fun and take in some of the most soulful tunes in town. After, if the **All Natural Ice Cream** stand is around, cool off with a cone of red velvet cake ice cream.

Both east and west of Central Harlem, food has always factored heavily into everyday routine, and the choices are as varied as the neighborhood itself. From Mexican and Caribbean, to West African, there are rich culinary delights. **Manna's** on Frederick Douglass Boulevard attracts hungry diners to its soul food steam table, where church groups rub shoulders and share stories with backpacking Europeans. Fried food junkies fantasize over Chef Charles Gabriel's acclaimed buffet and amazing fried chicken at **Charles Country Pan Fried Chicken**. For dangerously spiced yet incredibly tasty Senegalese food, head over to **Africa Kine**, after combing the shelves at **Darou Salam Market** for wide-ranging West African groceries. End the spree at **Harlem Shambles**, a true-blue butcher shop specializing in quality cuts of meat and poultry, guaranteed to enhance every dining experience.

EAST HARLEM

Over in East Harlem, Spanish cuisine enthusiasts and culture pundits never miss a trip to **Amor Cubano** for home-style food. If smoked and piggy *lechon* served with a side of sultry, live Cuban music isn't your idea of a good time, there's always a divine selection of Caribbean eats to be relished at **Sisters**; or juicy jerk chicken at **Winston & Tee Express**. Alternatively, take the time to peruse the taco truck and taqueria scene along "Little Mexico" on East 116th Street, otherwise known as the nucleus of New York City's myriad Mexican communities.

Almost like a vestige of the former Italian population that was once prevalent here, **Rao's** is a culinary landmark. Operated from a poky basement and patronized by bigwigs like Donald Trump and Nicole Kidman, it is one of the city's most difficult tables to secure. The original benefactors have exclusive rights to a seat here and hand off reservations like rent-controlled apartments! For more accessible Italian fare, try **Patsy's Pizzeria**, another stronghold in East Harlem, famous for its coal oven (and sometimes its pizza). **Ottomanelli Wine & Burger Bar** is dependable for freshly ground Prime sirloin burgers dressed with multiple embellishments. Meanwhile, **Hot Bread Kitchen** (located inside **La Marqueta**) and Chef Corey Cova's **Dough Loco**, selling Blue Bottle coffee with maple- and miso-glazed donuts, are considered holy havens among carb addicts.

WASHINGTON HEIGHTS

Housed along the northern reaches of Uptown, Washington Heights offers ample food choices along its steep streets. From Venezuelan food truck sensation **Patacon Pisao**, to restaurants like **Malecon** preparing authentic *morir soñando*, *mangu*, and *mofongo*, this colorful and vivacious neighborhood serves it all. In fact, the Tony award-winning musical *In The Heights* pays tribute to this ebullient district, where Dominican and Puerto Rican communities have taken root. Late-night revelers never tire of the Latin beats blasting through the air here, after which a visit to refreshing Puerto Rican *piragua* carts selling shaved ice in a rainbow of tropical flavors seems not only nourishing, but also necessary. Locals form long lines around the block outside **Elsa La Reina del Chicharrón** for deep-fried and crunchy *chicharrónes*, after which palates are quenched with *jugos naturales*—natural juices made from cane sugar and fresh fruits—for a healthy treat. Need a pinch of sugar after such an abundant savory feast? **Carrot Top Pastries** never fails to entice its patrons with assorted cookies, cakes, and deliciously moist sweet potato pies. Great fish markets and butcher shops also dot these hilly blocks, and less than ten bucks will get you a plate of traditional pernil with rice and beans at any number of diners. Those in-the-know can be seen routinely ducking into **La Rosa Fine Foods** for fresh fish, meat, and vegetables; or **Nelly's Bakery** for a boost from the *café con leche*—perhaps paired with *guayaba con queso* (guava-and-cheese pastry).

Nearby in affluent Inwood, **Piper's Kilt** is a standing relic revered by former German and Irish settlers for accurate renditions of their native cuisines. Settle into a booth at this lively hangout and order a perfect pint to go with such singular items as Irish nachos or a range of "Kilt burgers." It's just like continental Europe, but without the jet lag!

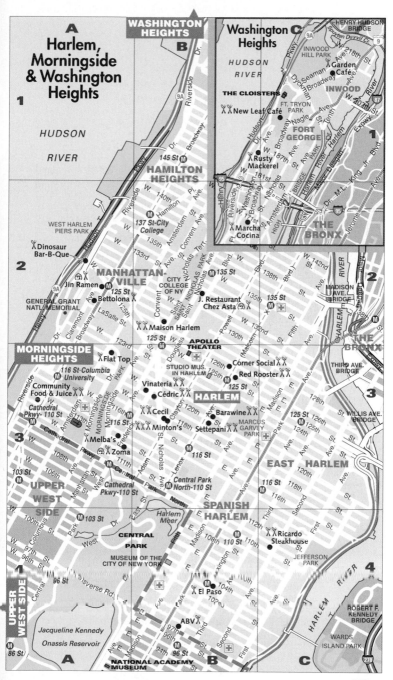

A
Harlem, Morningside & Washington Heights

WASHINGTON HEIGHTS

B

Washington Heights C

HUDSON RIVER

HAMILTON HEIGHTS

THE CLOISTERS

New Leaf Café

INWOOD

INWOOD HILL PARK

Garden Café

FT. TRYON PARK

FORT GEORGE

Rusty Mackerel

Marcha Cocina

THE BRONX

HUDSON RIVER

WEST HARLEM PIERS PARK

Dinosaur Bar-B-Que

MANHATTANVILLE

Jin Ramen

Bettolona

GENERAL GRANT NATL. MEMORIAL

CITY COLLEGE OF NY

J. Restaurant Chez Asta

135 St

MADISON AVE. BRIDGE

THE BRONX

Maison Harlem

APOLLO THEATER

MORNINGSIDE HEIGHTS

Flat Top

116 St-Columbia University

STUDIO MUS. IN HARLEM

Corner Social

Red Rooster

THIRD AVE. BRIDGE

Community Food & Juice

Vinatería

Cédric

HARLEM

Cathedral Pkwy - 110 St

Cecil

Barawine

Minton's

Settepani

MARCUS GARVEY PARK

ST. WILLIS AVE. BRIDGE

Melba's

Zoma

EAST HARLEM

UPPER WEST SIDE

103 St

Central Park North - 110 St

SPANISH HARLEM

CENTRAL PARK

Harlem Meer

MUSEUM OF THE CITY OF NEW YORK

Ricardo Steakhouse

JEFFERSON PARK

HARLEM RIVER

Jacqueline Kennedy Onassis Reservoir

El Paso

ROBERT F. KENNEDY BRIDGE

ABV

WARDS ISLAND PARK

UPPER WEST SIDE

A

B

NATIONAL ACADEMY MUSEUM

C

189

ABV

B4

1504 Lexington Ave. (at 97th St.)

Subway: 96 St (Lexington Ave.)
Phone: 212-722-8959
Web: www.abvny.com
Prices: $$

Lunch Sat – Sun
Dinner nightly

Adam Clark, Michael Cesari, and Corey Cova have leveraged their success at Earl's Beer & Cheese with the more ambitious ABV (alcohol by volume). This Americana gastropub, on a stretch of Lexington Avenue rife with new development, seems amusingly out of place within posh Carnegie Hill. Just think of the setting as part of the story starring picnic tables, soft lighting, and a giant chalkboard citing beers and specials. The semi-open kitchen can be viewed running on all cylinders, preparing chilled tomato soup spiced with chives, charred edamame, and *cotija*. Emblematic of their fresh vision is a pristine scallop ceviche stirred with horseradish and pea leaves; lamb meatballs in an aromatic tomato-cinnamon sauce; and a standout chocolate *pot de crème*.

Barawine

B3

200 Lenox Ave. (at 120th St.)

Subway: 116 St (Lenox Ave.)
Phone: 646-756-4154
Web: www.barawine.com
Prices: $$

Lunch Sat – Sun
Dinner nightly

Amid the leafy, brownstone-lined Mount Morris Park Historic District, Barawine is an inviting newcomer overseen by Fabrice Warin (formerly the sommelier at Orsay). This eye-catching space emanates a warm glow, enticing Lenox Avenue passersby to step in for a drink, snack, and much more. The bar area's communal table is a convivial perch, in addition to the quieter seating in back. Throughout, whitewashed walls attractively double as wine storage.

The crowd-pleasing menu defies classification but offers something for everyone. Expect to enjoy béchamel-enriched macaroni and cheese with diced ham and melted Gruyère; chicken breast with ratatouille and feta; as well as vegan options such as quinoa and grilled tofu salad, and dairy-free chocolate mousse.

Bettolona

A2

Italian ✗

3143 Broadway (bet. LaSalle St. & Tiemann Pl.)

Subway: 125 St (Broadway)
Phone: 212-749-1125
Web: N/A
Prices: $$

Lunch & dinner daily

Morningside Heights' darling gets high marks from Columbia students for pasta and pizza. The little room is crowded with locals fueling up on delightful lasagna *verdi*, meaty linguine Bolognese, or the puffy, crusty delights that emerge from the wood-burning oven. The succulent array includes pizza *affumicata* spread with crushed tomato, fresh cherry tomatoes, smoked fresh mozzarella, and crumbles of sausage. The chicken breast Marsala is stuffed with spinach, fontina, mushrooms, and is a tasty example of their heartier cooking. Lodged under the elevated 1 line, Bettolona is inviting nonetheless with its closely arranged wood tables, brick walls, and rustic mien.

Baby sibling Coccola brings their signature pizza and *panuozzo* up into West Harlem.

Cecil

B3

International ✗✗

210 W. 118th St. (bet. Adam Clayton Bld. & St. Nicholas Ave.)

Subway: 116 St (Frederick Douglass Blvd.)
Phone: 212-866-1262
Web: www.thececilharlem.com
Prices: $$

Lunch Sat – Sun
Dinner nightly

As evidenced by this buzzing newcomer, Harlem continues to prove it's a destination-worthy enclave for serious eats. Neon signage out front marks Cecil's spot and the lounge's provocative artwork gets things off to a sexy start once diners step inside.

Dinner here is a trip around the globe, guided by a menu that spotlights Africa, Asia, South America, and the US South. Skillet fried chicken, dusted with cornmeal for a satisfying crunch, comes plated atop spicy kimchi-inspired slaw; and the *feijoada* is a stoneware pot full of black beans, braised oxtail, and merguez garnished with slivered collard greens and orange segments. Even the wine list has a passport, with an impressive selection of *vino* from black producers under the heading African Diaspora.

Cédric

French ✗✗

B3

185 St. Nicholas Ave. (at 119th St.)

Subway: 116 St (Frederick Douglass Blvd.)   Lunch & dinner daily
Phone: 212-866-7766
Web: www.cedricbistro.com
Prices: $$

Cédric Lecendre's great little bistro is as cool and jubilant as Harlem itself. Marked by red awnings outside, the room is snug and cheerfully adorned with etched mirrors, gold accents, and splashes of rouge. The staff's French accents might hint of Paris, but the black-and-white prints on the walls return you to the landmarks of Manhattan.

This kitchen's updated French bistro classics are universally pleasing. Enjoy thinly sliced endive tossed with walnuts and Roquefort cheese; followed by pan-seared duck breast with a cherry sauce and *gratin Dauphinois*; or hot and juicy grilled hanger steak with caramelized shallots, red wine reduction, and a heap of crispy shoestring frites. Desserts like the *île flottante* are traditional and spot-on.

Community Food & Juice

American ✗✗

A3

2893 Broadway (bet. 112th & 113th Sts.)

Subway: Cathedral Pkwy/110 St (Broadway)   Lunch & dinner daily
Phone: 212-665-2800
Web: www.communityrestaurant.com
Prices: $$

Community Food & Juice is an accomplished restaurant with a deep understanding of its clientele. As part of the sprawl of Columbia University, this address is a godsend for students, faculty, and nearby residents from morning to night. The weekday blueberry pancake breakfast special complete with bottomless cups of coffee is just one reason why it gets so much love. Executive Chef/partner Neil Kleinberg, also of Clinton St. Baking Company, and his brigade turn out joyful fare, including grilled flatbread pizza, spicy shrimp and grits, and sides like carrot hashbrowns.

The setting is accented by grey slate and ivory seating. Although it's spacious with plenty of outdoor options, expect to wait for a table since reservations are not accepted.

Corner Social

B3

A m e r i c a n ✗✗

321 Lenox Ave. (at 126th St.)

Subway: 125 St (Lenox Ave.)
Phone: 212-510-8552
Web: www.cornersocialnyc.com
Prices: $$

Lunch & dinner daily

This high-flying neighborhood now boasts some serious restaurant competition, and Corner Social is only enhancing its reputation as a veritable Harlem dining destination. Much more than a tavern, the pub concept is elevated here with attention to ingredients sourced locally and sustainably farmed. This is a cool, welcoming gathering place that locals are proud to call their own.

On the focused menu, find tasty pulled pork sliders awash in cider vinegar and flecked with red pepper flakes, served alongside fresh, cool coleslaw and tart pickle slices. Fried green tomatoes are thick, sturdy slices dredged in cornmeal and pan-fried to perfection. House-made sweet potato cake is heady with spices and frosted with vanilla for a classic wedge of Americana.

Dinosaur Bar-B-Que

A2

B a r b e c u e ✗

700 W. 125th St. (at Twelfth Ave.)

Subway: 125 St (Broadway)
Phone: 212-694-1777
Web: www.dinosaurbarbque.com
Prices: $$

Lunch & dinner daily

Huge, loud, and perpetually packed, this way west Harlem barbecue hall draws crowds from near and far. The bar area is rollicking, and for that reason kept separate from the dining quarters. There, wood beams and slats, swirling ceiling fans, and oxblood leather booths fashion a comfortable—and quieter—setting.

The scent of wood smoke wafting through the red brick structure (which incidentally once served as a meatpacking warehouse) only heightens the diners' carnivorous cravings. Minimize decision-making and order the Extreme Sampler: a heaping least of apple cider brined smoked chicken, dry-rubbed slow-smoked pork ribs, and lean Creekstone Farms brisket. Add on a creative side or two—perhaps the barbecue fried rice studded with bits of pulled pork?

El Paso

Mexican 🍴

B4

1643 Lexington Ave. (at 104th St.)

Subway: 103 St (Lexington Ave.)   Lunch & dinner daily
Phone: 212-831-9831
Web: www.elpasony.com
Prices: $$

This East Harlem cantina is the largest in an uptown mini-chain serving gratifying south-of-the-border dining. True-blue residents as well as those new to this evolving neighborhood crowd El Paso's affable rooms, where margaritas, ice-cold cerveza, and smiles flow freely. Stucco walls and decorative metal work grace the interior, while the covered back patio has a breezy mien.

Tacos, quesadillas, and ceviche kick off cooking that hits all the right notes. Zesty guacamole is freshly mashed and served up in a *molcajete* with warm tortilla chips. Bold citrus- and tequila-braised *carnitas Michoacanás* are kissed by green chilies and crowningly paired with a bowl of hearty black beans and tender tortillas for wrapping. The silken flan offers a sweet finish.

Flat Top

Contemporary 🍴

A3

1241 Amsterdam Ave. (at 121st St.)

Subway: 116 St (Broadway)   Lunch & dinner daily
Phone: 646-820-7735
Web: www.flattopnyc.com
Prices: $$

Morningside Heights' scholarly set, already familiar with Jin Ramen, has been quick to adopt this bistro from the same team of partners. A mural of the Harlem Viaduct gives the low-key setting a sense of place, while friendly service accentuates the neighborly vibe.

Global accents mark Flat Top's cuisine in starters like a caprese salad with burrata, or shrimp ceviche. Meanwhile entrées have included black pepper-flecked roasted chicken breast. The latter is presented sliced over steamed Yukon gold potatoes and a mouthwatering herb sauce made from puréed cilantro, roasted jalapeños, and hint of cream. For dessert, a dressed-up chocolate cake is layered with whipped ganache, crispy bits of *feuilletine*, and presented with a side of Guinness ice cream.

Garden Cafe

C1

American ✗

4961 Broadway (bet. 207 & Isham Sts.)

Subway: Inwood - 207 St
Phone: 212-544-9480
Web: www.gardencafeny.com
Prices: $$

Lunch & dinner daily

This Inwood favorite continues to be an idyllic getaway from the noisy Broadway hustle just outside its doors. Enter to find brick patches peeking beyond pale yellow walls, dark-wood tables, and flower arrangements. A narrow hall leads to the bucolic garden, which is enclosed and warm in the winter, open and airy during the summer, and entertaining with live music on the weekends.

The food here remains as delightful as the surroundings. The menu crackles with such offerings as blackened, sesame-crusted tuna set atop two fluffy black bean corn cakes; or nutty buckwheat penne tossed with wilted baby spinach, portobello mushrooms, garlic, and olive oil. Hearty turkey meatloaf with green beans and mashed potatoes is everything you crave it to be.

Jin Ramen 🐸

A2

Japanese ✗

3183 Broadway (bet. 125th St. & Tiemann Pl.)

Subway: 125 St (Broadway)
Phone: 646-559-2862
Web: www.jinramen.com
Prices: 🐸🐸

Lunch & dinner daily

All you really need to know is that this is the hands-down best ramen above 59th Street. Sure, decorative elements are simple, and it hardly matters that this little spot is hidden behind the 125th Street station's brick escalator. What comes from the kitchen deserves kudos.

The menu is concise, offering a few items such as house-made *gyoza* for starters. These pan fried shrimp dumplings have a delicate, crisped wrapper and arrive with sesame-seed flecked dipping sauce. *Shio, shoyu,* and miso ramen are all delightful, but the *tonkatsu* ramen is a special treat. The piping hot, almost creamy, mouthcoating distillation of pork bones is deliciously rich and stocked with fragrant *chasu,* pickled bamboo shoots, slivered green onion, and a soft-boiled egg.

195

J. Restaurant Chez Asta

B2

Senegalese ✗

2479 Frederick Douglass Blvd. (bet. 132nd & 133rd Sts.)

Subway: 135 St (Frederick Douglass Blvd.)   Lunch & dinner daily
Phone: 212-862-3663
Web: N/A
Prices: 🪙

Harlem's food scene is exploding, and this sensational Senegalese newcomer is a welcome addition to the party. Enter to find a spirited and generous staff tending to a space outfitted with doily-topped tables, high backed chairs, tile floors, and a massive marble bar.

Exquisitely and authentically prepared dishes range from lamb *mafe*, a rich stew of tender lamb, carrots, and potatoes simmering in decadent peanut butter sauce, served with rice; to the *attiéké*, a tart, fermented cassava root similar in texture to couscous. Senegal's national dish, *thiebou djeun rouge* arrives as a fiery concoction of habanero-stuffed red snapper, yucca, cauliflower, green cabbage, eggplant, and okra, stewed in a tomato-based broth, and served over spicy *jolof* rice.

Maison Harlem

B2

French ✗✗

341 St. Nicholas Ave. (at 127th St.)

Subway: 125 St (St. Nicholas Ave.)   Lunch & dinner daily
Phone: 212-222-9224
Web: www.maisonharlem.com
Prices: $$

Bucolic Paris meets unapologetically cool Harlem at this fun-time spot, where the breezy vibe provides a much needed respite from the phone-toting tourists just east on Lenox. Gorgeous floor-to-ceiling windows, dark red banquettes, and quirky touches like vintage Gallic posters or yellow Mobil T-shirts pinned to the wall, lend a whiff of whimsy.

The bistro-style menu plays around with culinary traditions and the results may include tender duck leg confit, drizzled with orange-cognac sauce, and served with cauliflower gratin; or crispy crab and shrimp cakes atop a green salad. Other playful inventions have revealed grilled daurade fillet matched with an herbaceous lemon sauce and asparagus; or tart lemon curd layered into a rich, buttery crust.

Marcha Cocina

B2

Latin American ⚒

4055 Broadway (at 171st St.)

Subway: 168 St
Phone: 212-928-8272
Web: www.marchanyc.com
Prices: $$

Lunch Fri – Sun
Dinner nightly

Owner/chef duo Freddy and Virgilio de la Cruz have staked their territory in Washington Heights with this cool standout, fit for night owls and diners alike. A back-lit bar, bright yellow banquettes, filament bulbs, and white tables create a sleek look, while the engaging staff ensures a friendly atmosphere. Snack on savory *cocas cangrejos*, Catalan flatbread layered with crabmeat, goat and Manchego cheeses, jalapeño, and cilantro; or linger over amazingly crisp *croquetas* of chopped mushroom, cheddar, and herbs over truffled aïoli. *Platos fuertes* may bring a tender skirt steak in a pool of cheese fondue, topped with bright *chimichurri*, and served with fried yucca. Tasty tapas include scallops *a la plancha*, kissed with caramelized onion and Serrano ham.

Melba's

A3

Southern ⚒

300 W. 114th St. (at Frederick Douglass Blvd.)

Subway: 116 St (Frederick Douglass Blvd.)
Phone: 212-864-7777
Web: www.melbasrestaurant.com
Prices: $$

Lunch & dinner daily

A colorful spirit and Southern classics do much to remind guests of this quickly gentrifying area's flavor, culture, and past. Quaint and lovely Melba's is a place to gather and relax over good food and drinks, from Auntie B's mini-burgers slathered in smoky-sweet sauce to an absolutely perfect fruit cobbler—a golden brown and berry licious height of the pantheon.

Equally important is the swoon-inducing Southern-fried chicken, darkly bronzed, salty sweet, and tender. Thick fillets of fresh flakey tilapia may be densely crusted with crushed pecans and topped in white gravy. Expect surprises here, from the spring rolls with black-eyed peas, collards, and red rice, to a complex Italian *semillion* (ideal for pairing with that fried chicken and waffles).

Minton's

A m e r i c a n XX X

B3

206 W. 118th St. (bet. Adam Clayton Powell Jr. Blvd. & St. Nicholas Ave.)

Subway: 116 St (Lexington Ave.)   Dinner Tue – Sun
Phone: 212-243-2222
Web: www.mintonsharlem.com
Prices: $$$$

This grand jazz club is the sister act to Cecil, located next door. Don a jacket (as recommended for men) and settle into its throwback surroundings to feast and listen to the sweet sounds of live jazz. The art deco interior references Minton's 1938 opening, and black-and-white portraits pay homage to the legendary figures who have graced this stage.

The only distraction from the music is the cooking: an updated take on Southern cuisine that's perfectly suited to this neighborhood haunt's debonair crowd. Smothered lobster and shrimp casserole is richly dressed with pimento cheese grits and crawfish gravy; while hoppin' John pilau, made with Carolina gold rice, fried black-eyed peas, and roasted red pepper purée, is like risotto with a down-home twist.

New Leaf Café

A m e r i c a n XX

C1

1 Margaret Corbin Dr. (in Fort Tryon Park)

Subway: 190 St   Lunch & dinner Tue – Sun
Phone: 212-568-5323
Web: www.newleafrestaurant.com
Prices: $$

Located in a 1930s mansion designed by the Olmstead brothers, New Leaf Café was opened as part of the New York Restoration Project. The inside feels like a large cottage with stone walls and arched windows. Alfresco lunch on the flagstone terrace showcases this high, hilly setting with unparalleled views of the Palisades (squint to find the George Washington Bridge).

The American menu features a fried risotto cake with gooey mozzarella over Tokyo turnips and sweet pea coulis; or a hunk of seared tuna with tiny mushroom-filled ravioli. Profiteroles are a particular treat, filled with vanilla ice cream and drizzled with luscious chocolate sauce.

The gorgeous surrounds and jazz concerts make this a sought-after spot for private events after sun down.

Red Rooster

A m e r i c a n 🍴🍴

B3

310 Lenox Ave. (bet. 125 & 126th Sts.)

Subway: 125 St (Lenox Ave.)
Phone: 212-792-9001
Web: www.redroosterharlem.com
Prices: $$$

Lunch & dinner daily

So many things make Red Rooster special, not the least of which is Chef Marcus Samuelsson whose head-spinning achievements include inventive world-renowned cooking, penning cookbooks, and bringing the New Harlem Renaissance to Lenox Avenue. Downstairs, find live music at Ginny's Supper Club. Up front, The Nook serves sweets and sandwiches to-go. And in the center, the Red Rooster celebrates Harlem, the African-American diaspora, and great food.

Start with a brilliantly simple wedge of crumbly, buttery corn bread. Then, move on to the likes of highly spiced and "dirty" basmati rice with sweet shrimp and swirls of lemon aïoli; or try their interpretation of South African "bunny chow" served as lamb stew on a sesame bun with fried egg and fresh ricotta.

Ricardo Steakhouse

S t e a k h o u s e 🍴🍴

C4

2145 Second Ave. (bet. 110th & 111th Sts.)

Subway: 110 St (Lexington Ave.)
Phone: 212-289-5895
Web: www.ricardosteakhouse.com
Prices: $$

Lunch Fri – Sun
Dinner nightly

Those brioche-like slices of bread coated with spices and pan-fried with garlic are your first clue this insanely popular steakhouse is grander than the neighborhood at large. Beloved by longtime locals, its vibe is genuine, ungentrified East Harlem. Beyond the polished façade and wood-framed doors, find small tables, happy crowds, and on occasion, a sensational DJ.

Even the open kitchen seems happy to be hard at work. Expect portobello mushrooms stuffed with zucchini, tomato, and mozzarella on a bed of greens. Surf and turf items like medallions of grilled filet mignon and jumbo shrimp are doused with a smoky *mojito* sauce; and banana *fritas* are fried to shatter-crisp perfection.

A few blocks north, Ricardo Ocean Grill is also satisfying crowds.

Rusty Mackerel

Fusion ✗

B1

209 Pinehurst Ave. (at W. 187th St.)

Subway: 181 St (Fort Washington Ave.)
Phone: 212-928-4888
Web: www.rustymackerelny.com
Prices: $$

Lunch Sat – Sun
Dinner Tue – Sun

Rusty Mackerel is as comfy as eating at home yet creative enough to keep you contemplating the complex flavors. Living nearby could mean multiple dinners here each week; the miniscule space is typically packed with locals perched on stools by the open kitchen. Destination diners arrive on weekends and reservations are limited, so be sure to to plan ahead.

Boasting a roster of signature dishes including meats from the owners' butcher shop around the corner, the menu offers safe bets like *harissa* chicken as well as free-wheeling riffs like puffed beef tendon with sea salt. Meals culminate in the *spaghettini*, a savory-sweet dish that blends earthy lamb ragù with Turkish apricots and saffron, and give you every reason to trust the mad genius of this kitchen.

Settepani

B3

Italian ✗✗

196 Lenox Ave. (at 120th St.)

Subway: 125 St (Lenox Ave.)
Phone: 917-492-4806
Web: www.settepani.com
Prices: $$

Lunch & dinner daily

Poised within the charming enclave of the Mount Morris Park Historic District, this worthy *ristorante* offers Italian cuisine that is testament to the ascending quality of Harlem dining. The elegant, cream-colored space flaunts art dressed walls, a marble bar, and towering windows draped with silk.

Looking to the north and to the south, the menu here delivers all-around gratification. Begin with insalata *conca d'oro* for a sparkling combination of shaved fennel, red onion, orange segments, and crushed black olives; perhaps followed by *spaghetti di mare* baked in parchment paper, loaded with squid, shrimp, and chopped tomato, plated tableside. The spoon-tender osso buco is garnished with *fregola*, drizzled with lush veal jus, and absolutely delicious.

Vinatería

B3

Italian ✗✗

2211 Frederick Douglass Blvd. (at 119th St.)

Subway: 116 St (Frederick Douglass Blvd.)
Phone: 212-662-8462
Web: www.vinaterianyc.com
Prices: $$

Lunch Sat – Sun
Dinner nightly

Adding to Harlem and its hidden charms is Vinatería, an Italian darling brimming with wines to accompany each sublime bite. Not only is it cozy, but the attractive slate-toned room etched in chalk with scenes of decanters and menu specials will augment your appetite.

The semi-open kitchen in the back unveils such treasures as house-cured sardines with fiery piquillo peppers and crunchy croutons; or a salad of earthy golden and red beets mingled with yogurt, oranges, arugula, crunchy pistachios, tossed with lemon vinaigrette. Herbs plucked from their copper planters may be featured in an impeccably grilled rosemary-marinated pork blade served with rich mashed potatoes; or desserts like citrus-glazed rosemary panna cotta bathed in chamomile grappa.

Zoma

A3

Ethiopian ✗

2084 Frederick Douglass Blvd. (at 113th St.)

Subway: 116 St (Frederick Douglass Blvd.)
Phone: 212-662-0620
Web: www.zomanyc.com
Prices: ⊜⊜

Lunch Sat – Sun
Dinner nightly

Smart, cool, modern, and always welcoming, Zoma may well be this city's most serious Ethiopian restaurant. The crowded bar emits a golden light from below to showcase its premium spirits and the world of dining rooms is filled with locals from this thriving community.

Attention to detail is clear from the steaming hot towel for cleansing your hands to the carefully folded *injera* bread used for scooping up their chopped salads, chunky stews, and saucy vegetables. Unusual starters might include green lentils with a cold and crunchy mix of onions, jalapeños, ginger, white pepper, and mustard seeds. The *doro watt*—a chicken dish of the Amhara people—is a very traditional stew with berbere sauce of sun-dried hot peppers and ground spices.

Lower East Side

The Lower East Side (or LES as locals know it) is one of New York City's most important, energetic, and fast-evolving neighborhoods. Bragging a plethora of shopping, eating, and nightclubs, this high-energy hub proudly retains the personality of its first wave of hard-working immigrants. But, thanks to a steady stream of artists and entrepreneurs over the last few decades as well as a real estate uprising, this area faces constant transformation with an influx of high-rises breaking through trendy boutiques and eminent galleries. And yet, some nooks remain straight up dodgy as if in defiance of such rapid development; while others feel Village-like in stature and spirit.

AROUND THE WORLD

Visit the Lower East Side Tenement Museum for a glimpse of the past before trekking along its enticing, ethnically diverse streets. Then, for a taste of yore, traipse to **Russ & Daughters** on Houston Street for appetizing Kosher including smoked, cured fish and hearty bagels. This nosher's delight was instituted in 1914 but continues to be sought-after

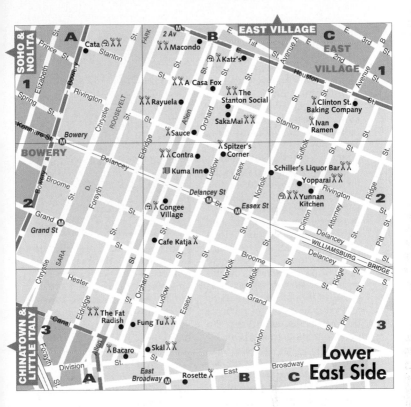

Lower East Side

even today, especially during the holidays when the "ultimate salmon and caviar" package is nothing short of...you guessed it...ultimate! Also inhabiting these streets were German, Italian, and Chinese residents, whose varying cultures have triggered an exposition of diverse and tasty eats plus treats. Find signs of this at **Nonna's LES Pizza** where the red, white, and green squares are known to tug at all the right nostalgic strings. **Palà**, which boasts a vast list of gluten-free and vegan selections, is not far behind with homesick hordes craving their heart-warming pies. If the *pizza al taglio* doesn't take you back to Rome, spend an afternoon

at **Gaia Italian Cafè** breezing through their magazines and biting into delicious *dolci* or perfect biscotti. This warm, inviting spot may be mini in size, but cooks up flavors that are bright, bold, and beautiful. Speaking of which, **Tiny's Giant Sandwich Shop** is equally unpretentious but totally irresistible. Here, sandwiches rule the roost and inventive vegetarian options—like the silly philly portobello—are slung at all times. Ground zero for partygoers, punk rockers, and scholars, this Rivington Street paragon is a rare treat highlighting fresh ingredients and creative presentations. In operation since 1925, **Streit's Matzo Factory** is another resident Rivingtonian frequented for its classic recipes and Passover specials. However, if sweet is what you need, **Economy Candy** is a flourishing emporium that headlines old-time confections. From timeless pleasures to new-fangled pastries, **Bisous Ciao Macarons** gives Stanton Street a bit of French flair thanks to its luxurious namesake goodies. By the 1950s, the ethnic mosaic that defined this district intensified with a surge of new settlers—this time from Puerto Rico and the Dominican Republic. They continue to dot the culinary landscape today, so make sure to savor such authentic, home-style favorites as *mofongo* and *pernil*. Domincan *especiales* and creamy *café con leche* at **El Castillo de Jagua** keep the party pumping from dawn till dusk. After lunch, sate your taste buds with elegantly crafted and exotically flavored chocolates at **Tache Artisan Chocolate**, launched by pastry chef, Aditi Malhotra, and setting hearts aflutter since 2012. If her tequila-infused dark chocolate ganache doesn't leave you love-struck, those French caramel kisses are sure to do the trick.

Rivington Street is a perfect hybrid of the Old World and New Order. During the day, the mood is chill with locals looking to linger at cozy coffee houses. For a nutritious evening pick-me-up, head to **TeaNY** specializing in all things vegan and wonderful including "the cup that cheers," usually served with brunch on weekends. Come sunset, these streets fill with noisy carousers looking to land upon a sleek restaurant or popular party spot.

Further south, Grand Street is home to well-manicured residential complexes scattered amid shops catering to a cadre of deep-rooted residents. While here, carb-addicts should be afraid, very afraid, of **Kossar's Bialys** known for bagels, *biyali* sticks, and *bulkas*; as well as **Doughnut Plant** proffering updated flavors crafted from an age-old recipe. To replicate that classic deli experience at home, pick up pickles to-go from **Pickle Guys**—poised atop Essex Street and stocked with barrel-upon-barrel of these briny treats. Fire escape-fronted Orchard Street is venerated as the original hub of the 'hood. Once dominated by the garment trade with stores selling fabrics and notions, it tells a different tale today with sleek eateries scattered amid trendy boutiques selling handmade jewelry and designer skateboards. Tailors still thrive here today, offering inexpensive, while-you-wait service, after which be sure to stop by sandwich-slinging hot spots like **Black Tree**. Concurrently, **Cup & Saucer** is a teatime treasure serving everything under the sun, whereas new and improved **Dimes** on Division Street is a reliable resource for three square meals a day. It's packed to the rafters at peak hours, so shoppers looking to cool their heels should drop by **Il Laboratorio del Gelato**, located on Ludlow directly off Houston.

ESSEX STREET MARKET

Every self-respecting foodie makes the pilgrimage to **Essex Street Market**, a treasure trove of gourmet delights. Housing first-rate produce merchants, butchers, bakers, and fishmongers all under one roof, this public bazaar further expounds on their expertise by way of cooking demonstrations and wine tastings that keep the crowds coming back for more. Starved shoppers know to calm a craving at **Brooklyn Taco Co.**, **Essex**, or even **Shopsin's General Store**, notorious for its encyclopedic carte and cranky owner. Everything from chocolate (**Roni-Sue's**); ice cream (**Luca & Bosco**); cheese (**Saxelby Cheesemongers**); and coffee (**Davidovich Bakery**) make this pleasure palace an enticing destination for gastronomes and curious palates alike.

A Casa Fox

B1

Latin American ✗✗

173 Orchard St. (bet. Houston & Stanton Sts.)

Subway: 2 Av
Phone: 212-253-1900
Web: www.acasafox.com
Prices: $$

Lunch Sat
Dinner Tue – Sun

This bold and bright darling serves superlative Latin fare with fantastic authenticity and a whole lotta love. This is largely thanks to Chef/owner Melissa Fox, who can be seen in the open kitchen or checking on guests in the snug space, filled with Mexican tiles, wide plank floors, and a warming fireplace.

Be sure to begin any meal with a selection of empanadas, as in pulled pork with caramelized onion, chorizo and aged manchego, or the outstanding *carne enchorizada* (seasoned ground beef with onions, tomatoes, yucca, chayote, and potatoes). Other dishes might include the *camarones a las brazes*, grilled shrimp in sour-orange marinade wrapped in smoky bacon; or chicken *tostones*, its pulled meat on a well-grilled round of corn with *crema* and mango salsa.

Bacaro

A3

Italian ✗

136 Division St. (bet. Ludlow & Orchard Sts.)

Subway: East Broadway
Phone: 212-941-5060
Web: www.bacaronyc.com
Prices: $$

Dinner Tue – Sun

Steal away to this hidden spot, where crumbling brick walls, aged archways, ornate chandeliers, and soft candlelight give the impression of having stepped back in time. The inspiration is a Venetian *bacaro*—counters where folks stand to graze on small bites and sip wine—yet here one dines with ease, seated at distressed wood tables. A visit to the stunning, dark, wood-carved bar and its display of delicate glassware is a worthy detour before ordering up a series of tasty plates. Starters may feature the *sarde en saor*, with the grilled sardines served over caramelized sweet and sour onions, white raisins, pignoli nuts, and thyme. The *cannolicchi* is a noteworthy special, delivering a fresh burst of salinity with each razor clam in garlic-white wine sauce.

Cafe Katja

B2

Austrian 🍴

79 Orchard St. (bet. Broome & Grand Sts.)

Subway: Delancey St
Phone: 212-219-9545
Web: www.cafekatja.com
Prices: $$

Lunch Tue – Sun
Dinner nightly

Beer mugs are clinking and schnapps is flowing at the rustic Cafe Katja. After slowly expanding to neighboring storefronts over the past few years, the owners have now realized its much-deserved grandeur without losing its charm. Expats plus locals are de rigueur here, and routinely stop in for incredibly delicious and unbelievably hearty eats.

Co-chef and owner Erwin Schrottner (who hails from outside Graz) keeps everything authentic, from house-made bratwurst platters to the mustard sour cream. The pretzels arrive straight from Europe as divine carbo-bombs served with *liptauer* cheese and butter. The idea of warm chocolate cake may seem passé, but this rendition with terrifically bittersweet orange marmalade is a treat for all the senses.

Cata 😊

A1

Spanish 🍴🍴

245 Bowery (at Stanton St.)

Subway: 2 Av
Phone: 212-505-2282
Web: www.catarestaurant.com
Prices: $$

Dinner nightly

Raw originality is clear in everything here, from the massive doors and eye-popping red stools to an inspired tapas menu. Sleek brick walls, cement-tiled floors, and dark wood communal tables are beautiful in their simplicity, but the copper work around the bar offers elaborate detail that adds to Cata's complex identity.

Plates may include the smoked *cana de cabra*, a goat cheese hailing from Murcia, Spain, roasted until gloriously gooey and topped with lemon-thyme honey. Curried cauliflower "couscous" is delicious, aromatic, and ingenious. Paella is prepared with traditional Spanish sausage, *butifarra*, and sinfully addictive foie gras. For a distinctive finale, cleanse the palate with grapefruit sorbet and a selection from their unique gin program.

Clinton St. Baking Company

C1

4 Clinton St. (bet. Houston & Stanton St.)

Subway: 2 Av
Phone: 646-602-6263
Web: www.clintonstreetbaking.com
Prices:

Lunch daily
Dinner Mon – Sat

What started as a bakery has become a legend—one that perpetually draws a crowd patiently waiting for ample rewards. A little bit country and little bit food lab, this brunch-focused *bijou* has achieved such success in NY that the owners even have outposts in Japan and Dubai. Leafing through the pastry-driven cookbook is a great way to bide the time. It's a toss-up among popular omelets and egg dishes; thick burgers or BLTs with sugar-cured bacon and hand-cut fries; or just diving straight into a banana-caramel layer cake with vanilla-cream cheese frosting. The textbook-perfect New England clam chowder, brimming with tender bits of pork and briny clams, is pure pleasure.

This expert team of "bakers" will soon be working their magic in bigger digs nearby.

Congee Village

B2

100 Allen St. (at Delancey St.)

Subway: Delancey St
Phone: 212-941-1818
Web: www.congeevillagerestaurants.com
Prices:

Lunch & dinner daily

The menu at Congee Village is vast and its Cantonese focus is clear. The soothing namesake, rice porridge, is well-represented with 30 varieties offering a full spectrum of embellishments, from healthy vegetarian to pig's blood, to name a few. In addition to prized delicacies, find dim sum treats like delicately flaky Hong Kong-style scallion pancakes. Other ample offerings include chicken steamed in lotus leaf with mushrooms and diced Chinese sausage, slicked with soy sauce, ginger, and scallions; bitter melon stir-fried with black bean sauce; or specialties like pork ribs seasoned with shrimp paste and fried until crispy.

From the fringe of Chinatown, the multi-level setting trimmed with bamboo, brick, and stone is well-maintained and inviting.

Contra

Contemporary ✗✗

B2

138 Orchard St. (bet. Delancey & Rivington Sts.)

Subway: 2 Av
Phone: 212-466-4633
Web: www.contranyc.com
Prices: $$

Dinner Tue – Sat

An avant-garde, food-driven spot breathing life into a strip of aging bars, Contra buzzes with young kitchen talent and a fresh attitude toward the direction of this neighborhood. Energetic and welcoming, the dimly lit dining room is long and narrow but features a large communal table crafted from a single tree trunk. This farmhouse look is offset by modern accents and clean, inventive (if at times precious) fare.

This $55 five-course prix-fixe is not merely visually enticing but each dish showcases the kitchen's deep understanding of flavor and contrast. Fresh monkfish is roasted on the bone and served with *broccolini*, and the entire dish is pulled together with succulent claytonia. Elderflower and vanilla ice cream make for a sublime combination.

The Fat Radish

Contemporary ✗✗

A3

17 Orchard St. (bet. Canal & Hester Sts.)

Subway: East Broadway
Phone: 212-300-4053
Web: www.thefatradishnyc.com
Prices: $$

Lunch Tue – Sun
Dinner nightly

This is a true downtown spot—fun, hip, and set on a quiet street. Inside, benches, weathered wood boards, and flowerboxes lend a sense of barnyard chic to the dining room, thereby complementing the menu's fresh and seasonal focus. Yet, what makes The Fat Radish distinctive is that it's neither self-consciously cool nor trendy in concept. It's genuinely good.

Expect the opening salvo to be a crunchy-sharp radish tossed in black olive tapenade. Then, move on to such refined dishes as seared Block Island tuna with mutsumadaun cilantro, mint, and cucumber in a perfectly salty vinaigrette. Dessert may offer a deconstructed chocolate mousse with raspberry compote.

Across the street, The Leadbelly lures legions for its briny oysters and thrilling cocktails.

Fung Tu

Asian ✗✗

22 Orchard St. (bet. Canal & Hester Sts.)

Subway: East Broadway
Phone: 212-219-8785
Web: www.fungtu.com
Prices: $$

Lunch Sun
Dinner Tue – Sun

The obscure zone between Chinatown and the Lower East Side does not conjure images of elegant food, yet this thoughtful spot offers a mountain of unique personality and contemporary fare. Fung Tu's clean lines, red-framed windows, and welcoming black marble bar create an inviting, zen-like space, which looks more like a wine bar than Chinese hangout.

Creativity emanates from the bar as well as the kitchen's myriad snacks. A shatteringly crisp *jian bing* crêpe is folded over braised beef and pickled cucumbers; while micro bok choy massaged in shrimp paste is as memorable as crispy Medjool dates stuffed with shredded duck confit. Inventive flavors abound in slippery wheat noodles drenched in pumpkin seed sauce with smoked trout and hints of chili oil.

Ivan Ramen

Japanese ✗

25 Clinton St. (bet. Houston & Stanton Sts.)

Subway: Delancey St
Phone: 646-678-3859
Web: www.ivanramen.com
Prices: $$

Lunch Mon – Fri
Dinner nightly

Over the last five years, Chef Ivan Orkin's freewheeling take on traditional ramen has earned him a cult following in Tokyo. With the opening of Ivan Ramen, he might just gain it in New York, too. This sleek and modern restaurant on a gentrifying block has distinctive touches: a comic strip illustrates how to properly eat ramen; servers don bright orange shirts; and a garden tempts diners to slurp under the stars.

The excellent ramen is equally unconventional. Ivan uses just-cooked rye noodles for a heartier bite that stands up well to the crimson-colored, spicy chicken broth. In the fiery red chili variety, he adds minced pork, chopped scallions, hard-boiled egg, and a hint of slightly smoky dashi for an inventive salt- and fat-filled dish.

Katz's 🏵

Deli 🍴

B1

205 E. Houston St. (at Ludlow St.)

Subway: 2 Av
Phone: 212-254-2246
Web: www.katzsdelicatessen.com
Prices: 💲💲

Lunch & dinner daily

One of the last-standing, old-time Eastern European spots on the Lower East Side, Katz's is a true NY institution. It's crowded, crazy, and packed with a panoply of characters weirder than a jury duty pool. Tourists, hipsters, blue hairs, and everybody in between flock here, so come on off-hours. Because it's really *that* good.

Walk inside, get a ticket, and don't lose it (those guys at the front aren't hosts—upset their system and you'll get a verbal beating). Then get your food at the counter and bring it to a first-come first-get table; or opt for a slightly less dizzying experience at a waitress-served table.

Nothing's changed in the looks or taste. Matzo ball soup, pastrami sandwiches, potato latkes—everything is what you'd expect, only better.

Kuma Inn

Asian 🍜

B2

113 Ludlow St. (bet. Delancey & Rivington Sts.)

Subway: Delancey St
Phone: 212-353-8866
Web: www.kumainn.com
Prices: 💲💲

Dinner nightly

A veteran of Daniel and Jean-Georges, NYC-born Chef/owner King Phojanakong presents ambrosial pan-Asian bites that reflect the multicultural influences of his Thai-Filipino background.

Come as you are—Kuma Inn doesn't put on airs. The discreetly marked space is set on the second floor of a nondescript walk-up. The menu is best suited for grazing so bring reinforcements to ensure a sampling of the chef's signature items—perhaps cubes of firm tofu sautéed with earthy wood ear mushrooms and fragrant Thai basil sluiced by spicy soy and mirin; slices of Chinese sausage bathed in a Thai chili-lime sauce; or drunken shrimp drizzled with a chili-sparked sake.

Genteel service and a playlist of the chef's favorite tracks add to the mood of this spartan room.

Macondo

B1

157 E. Houston St. (bet. Allen & Eldridge Sts.)

Subway: 2 Av
Phone: 212-473-9900
Web: www.macondonyc.com
Prices: $$

Lunch Sat – Sun
Dinner nightly

Tucked within this bustling stretch of the Lower East Side, Macondo's surrounding never seems to stand still. The front counter opens onto the street and is ideal for a quick bite or cocktail (which can be ordered by the carafe). Beyond this, the dining room has a vague seafaring theme with a few suspended nets, white-washed shelving, and luring dark wood tables.

The rich and dynamic menu may offer dishes that span the Latin culture through *América del Norte*, but everything is prepared with a steady Central American hand. Listed in the "to begin" section, find tender yet crisp calamari tossed with *rocoto* pepper and honey *alioli*. The *tapas del mar* might feature grilled octopus tentacles over a chorizo-studded quinoa salad with mint-basil vinaigrette.

Rayuela

B1

165 Allen St. (bet. Rivington & Stanton Sts.)

Subway: 2 Av
Phone: 212-253-8840
Web: www.rayuelanyc.com
Prices: $$

Lunch Sat – Sun
Dinner Tue – Sun

Patrons entering Rayuela first encounter a sleek concrete bar, colorful displays of decorative bottles, sultry lighting, and a gnarly tree majestically rising in the center of the room. The sexy tree-house aesthetic is not the only thrill served at Rayuela. Their vibrant range of Latin American cuisine pops with creativity.

The guacamole arrives studded with crab and shrimp, and should move from nightly special to permanent menu fixture. The *tamal limeño* is a steamed squid-ink-tinted corn cake, thick and moist, topped with lobster and *rocoto* pepper-pisco sauce. The wonderfully inventive *paella verde* reveals herb-infused Valencia rice packed with shellfish, rabbit, and chicken, licked by tomatillo-poblano aïoli, with an enticing *soccarat*.

Rosette

Contemporary ✗

B3

171 East Broadway (at Canal St.)

Subway: East Broadway
Phone: 212-933-1176
Web: www.rosettenyc.com
Prices: $$

Lunch Sat – Sun
Dinner Mon – Sat

Seriously romantic yet sprawling, Rosette invites both the casual lounger and the discerning diner. Its large couches and 1960s-esque bar call out for a glass of wine and cocktail conversation, while the brick-lined walls and oversized booths of the dining room nestle cozy couples and wood-fired dishes.

Sensual and feminine, the cuisine offers balanced and nuanced flavors in combinations that play with texture. The beautifully scored and roasted avocado with chili-spiked yogurt and bonito flakes is a must-have side dish that proves masterful kitchen skills. Similarly, the locally caught fillet of black cod sees a honey glaze, braised fennel, and artichoke in a tender preparation that's accented with sunflower sprouts and seeds for a touch of crunch.

SakaMai

Japanese ✗✗

B1

157 Ludlow St. (bet. Rivington & Stanton Sts.)

Subway: Delancey St
Phone: 646-590-0684
Web: www.sakamai.com
Prices: $$$

Dinner nightly

A modern *izakaya* like no other, SakaMai sets a new standard for downtown cuisine. With its chic urban style, a curated sake- *shochu*- and whisky-list, and creative dishes, this authentic haunt draws a food- and drink-focused crowd that's more interested in Japanese sips than pints of beer.

Plates are meant to be shared, sashimi are top-notch, and flavors simply impress: a well-seasoned Wagyu steak arrives with roasted vegetables and tasty sauces, while a porcelain sea urchin shell, filled with gently scrambled eggs, caviar, and more sea urchin, is as decadent as it sounds. For an exceptional balance between flavor and texture, try the kanpachi dressed with a chiffonade of shiso, *myoga*, yuzu juice, freshly ground wasabi, and *shoyu* glaze.

Sauce

Italian ✕

78-84 Rivington St. (at Allen St.)

Subway: 2 Av
Phone: 212-420-7700
Web: www.saucerestaurant.com
Prices: ⊜

Lunch Sat – Sun
Dinner nightly

What would you expect from a spot called Sauce? Some serious and very delicious red sauce—naturally! Serving Italian-American comfort food with a nostalgic décor to match, Sauce stays modern with its locale, hipster-friendly playlist, and quirky ambience—the attractive crowd doesn't hurt either. It's a fun meal to say the least.

Pasta is made in-house daily, with specials that feature potato-kale gnocchi or the signature ricotta *cavatelli* drizzled with pecorino. The menu highlights regional specialties from Little Italys across the country, including SF's cioppino and classic *Nuyorkese* tomato gravy like *nonna* used to make. Try the robust Sergio Leone steak smothered in tomato sauce and topped with a fried heritage egg for a whole lotta fun and flavor.

Schiller's Liquor Bar

American ✕✕

131 Rivington St. (at Norfolk St.)

Subway: Delancey St
Phone: 212-260-4555
Web: www.schillersny.com
Prices: $$

Lunch & dinner daily

After ten years, this fantastically retro city favorite is still buzzing with cool crowds and tasty American comfort food—thanks to a focused and skilled kitchen. Plunked on prime Lower East real estate, the commanding bistro's white-tile exterior, striking black- and white-tiled floor, and wrought-iron doors invite groups of friends for cocktails and $1 oyster happy hour at the curved bar.

While the libations aren't standout, they are a nice complement to tried-and-true classics like braised pork tacos folded with pineapple, tomatillos, pickled red onion, and lime crema with a devilish salsa habanera. A braised brisket patty melt with a decadent blend of pepper jack, mustard, and balsamic onions is as faultless as a tart and refreshing Key lime pie.

Skál

Contemporary ✗✗

B3

37 Canal St. (at Ludlow St.)

Subway: East Broadway
Phone: 212-777-7518
Web: www.skalnyc.com
Prices: $$

Lunch Sat – Wed
Dinner nightly

NY's fascination with Nordic cuisine is now ingrained, and Skál is a welcome addition. Designed to evoke an Icelandic-style fishing cottage, reclaimed wood stools line the bar, above which a giant black raven peers out like a Viking. Friendly bartenders shake up a killer cocktail list composed of plenty of artisanal spirits. These sips set the stage for those pickled, fermented, and smoked flavors perfected by Northern Europe.

The standout raw beef has everyone talking (and probably Instagramming); it's a surf-and-turf tartare of sorts where chopped beef mixed with clams is finished with wild onions, fennel fronds, and tiny yellow fennel flowers. Equally stunning, the beetroot dessert's refreshing merengue and dill creates quizzical and lasting memories.

Spitzer's Corner

Gastropub ✗

B2

101 Rivington St. (at Ludlow St.)

Subway: Delancey St
Phone: 212-228-0027
Web: www.spitzerscorner.com
Prices: $$

Lunch & dinner daily

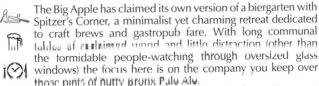

The Big Apple has claimed its own version of a biergarten with Spitzer's Corner, a minimalist yet charming retreat dedicated to craft brews and gastropub fare. With long communal tables of reclaimed wood and little distraction (other than the formidable people-watching through oversized glass windows) the focus here is on the company you keep over those pints of nutty Bronx Palo Alto.

While heartwarming burgers and mac 'n cheese line most tables, there is much more to explore on the menu. Sink your teeth into the skillet of silky meatballs blending beef, veal and Mangalista pork *lardo* with fresh herbs and ricotta simmered in tomato sauce. From flesh to fish, salmon is perfectly cooked and delicately set atop braised lentils and pearl onions.

The Stanton Social

Fusion ✗✗

99 Stanton St. (bet. Ludlow & Orchard Sts.)

Subwy: 2 Av
Phone: 212-995-0099
Web: www.thestantonsocial.com
Prices: $$

Lunch Sat – Sun
Dinner nightly

This hugely favored haunt's low lighting, thumping beats, and beautiful crowd clearly say nightlife lounge, but its roster of pleasing creations establish the kitchen as an expert in flavors and textures. The multi-level room is sexy yet remains timeless despite its age. Those chic, dark leather banquettes provide plenty of space for large groups to kick back to whatever the DJ spins in the second-floor lounge.

This isn't a place for conversation between friends, but rather a large group destination for delicious small plates like crisp red snapper tacos with creamy avocado and zesty mango salsa. Tasty Asian flavors combine seamlessly with chunks of skewered salmon cooked rare and coated in crunchy *sriracha*-infused peas over cold soba and earthy beets.

Yopparai

Japanese ✗✗

151 Rivington St. (bet. Clinton & Suffolk Sts.)

Subwy: Delancey St
Phone: 212-777-7253
Web: www.yopparainyc.com
Prices: $$$

Dinner Mon – Sat

Buzzing into Yopparai is like waltzing into culinary wonder. Secluded above street level, the attentive staff and cozy vibe alone make this Japanese haven a must. Same for the food, which adds immense thrill to the equation.

From the homemade *natto* or amazing, artisanal udon, to the unparalleled flavor from tofu, each dish features a plethora of intricately prepared parts that unite perfectly. While their items are consistently appealing, standouts include *inaniwa* udon, set in a shallow pool of cool dashi topped with thin slices of chicken, tomato, cucumber, and nori accompanied by peanut sauce. The smooth and custardy *yodoufu* is a revelation served warm in a wooden box.

For extra sake fun, drop by Azasu, a group-friendly delight from the same team.

Yunnan Kitchen

Chinese ✗✗

C2

79 Clinton St. (bet. Delancey & Rivington Sts.)

Subway: Delancey St

Dinner Tue-Sun

Phone: 212-253-2527

Web: www.yunnankitchen.com

Prices: $$

Though there's no shortage of affordable Asian meals in the neighborhood, this local standout pays careful attention to the delicate, herbaceous flavors of China's Yunnan province. The communal eatery is welcoming and artfully strewn with memorabilia like heirloom necklaces, embroidered belts, and a framed tiger-print rug from owner Erika Chou's travels.

Hot and cold dishes, along with rice and noodle bowls, represent the diversity of Yunnan cuisine, from the totally unique chrysanthemum leaf salad to the superb salt-and-pepper shrimp transformed by fragrant Kaffir lime leaf. Sausage from New York's own Salumeria Biellese blends with peas and scrambled eggs in fried rice. Cumin, Sichuan pepper, and hot chilies make simple fried potatoes stellar.

Look for our symbol 🍺, spotlighting restaurants with a notable beer list.

Midtown East & Murray Hill

An interesting blend of office buildings, corporate hotels, skyscraping apartments, and beautiful brownstones, Midtown East is one of the city's most industrious neighborhoods. Home to the iconic Chrysler Building and United Nations Headquarters, the vibe here is forever buzzing with suits, students, and old-time New Yorkers. Whether it's that reliable diner around the corner, a gourmet supermarket or fine dining establishment, this region has it all. Residents of neighboring Beekman and Sutton Place are proud of their very own top fishmonger (**Pisacane Seafood**); cheese shop (**Ideal Cheese**); butcher (**L. Simchick Meats**); bagel and lox shop (**Tal Bagels**); and to complete any dinner party, renowned florist (**Zeze**). While **Dag Hammarskjöld Plaza**

Greenmarket may by dwarfed by Union Square, come Wednesdays it presents just the right amount of everything to satisfy locals.

GRAND CENTRAL TERMINAL

Built by the Vanderbilt family in the 19th century, **Grand Central Terminal** is a 21st century foodie sanctuary. Packed to the gills with the same diversity of shopping and dining as the neighborhood itself, it's a perfect microcosm of its eastern midtown home. An ideal day at this titanic train station may begin with a coffee from **Joe's**. Later, stop by one of Manhattan's historic sites, the **Grand Central Oyster Bar & Restaurant**, tucked into the cavernous lower level. This gorgeously renovated seafood treasure prepares shellfish stews,

fresh fish, and of course, an incredible raw bar. Continue the culinary adventure at **Neuhaus**, venerable chocolatiers who craft their delicacies with top-notch ingredients. Or stop by family-owned—and equally renowned—**Li-Lac Chocolates** for such nostalgic confections as dark chocolate-covered pretzels or beautifully packaged holiday gift boxes. Those who meet the dress code should end at **Campbell Apartment**, the restored private office of 1920s railroad mogul John W. Campbell, and one of the area's swankier stops for a famously dry martini. Finally, no trip to this Terminal is complete without a visit to the "whispering gallery" where low, ceramic-tiled arches allow whispers to sound like more like shouts. Just beyond, the loud dining concourse hums with lunch stalls ranging from **Café Spice** for Indian; **Eata Pita** for Middle Eastern; and **Mendy's** for everything kosher. Finish with the sweetest treats in town—red velvet cupcakes at the terminal's very own **Magnolia Bakery** outpost. Those in search of a more deluxe spread should visit the several prized restaurants situated beneath Grand Central's celestial ceiling mural.

Moving on to the market, Eli Zabar has expanded his empire, and continues to proffer the freshest fruits and vegetables at **Eli Zabar's Farm to Table**. But, for an impressive assortment of pastries and cakes, **Eli Zabar's Bread & Pastry** is your best bet. In addition to its numerous fishmongers, butchers, and bakers, you may also find possibly the best spices in the Big Apple here—at one of the market's better-kept secrets, **Spices and Tease**, a boutique store specializing in exotic teas and unique spice blends.

JAPANTOWN

Tucked into a few blocks east of Lexington lies a very sophisticated Japantown, where scores of *izakaya* and restaurants are scattered among hostess clubs. Salarymen can be seen at old-world hangouts like **Riki**, **Ariyoshi**, and **Tsukushi**, or newcomers like **Lucky Cat**. Favored **BentOn Cafe** is a sliver of a lunch respite that may be a retail outpost of a bento delivery service, but presents excellent, daily changing bentos at terrific value. When here, crowds should expect to wait in line, irrespective of arrival time. While Japanese expats with ladies in tow linger over the psuedo-Italian spread at **Aya**, the younger working set may prefer a light bite from **Cafe Zaiya** or **Dainobu** (both bustling deli-cum-markets). **Hinata Ramen** is an all-time favorite for steaming bowls of authentic, top-quality ramen; while **Nikai** is equally well-known for its vast selection. Rice fiends will revel in the selection at **Donburiya**; and carnivores join the snaking lines outside **Katsu-Hama** or **Yakiniku Gen** for delicious grilled meats. Looking to impress your out-of-town guests? Plan a Japanese-themed evening by stocking up on tabletop items, kitchenware,

and other authentic food and beverages from **MTC Kitchen**. This specialty emporium also flaunts a commendable roster of classes and seminars to initiate novices and professionals from near or far. A few blocks south, younger and quieter Murray Hill has its own distinct vibe. Here, fast, casual finds thrive by dint of twenty-somethings craving pizza, cheesesteak, and hot dogs. Supremely sleek and ever-tranquil retreats like The Kitano, Gotham's only Japanese-owned boutique hotel, features everything from fantastic live tunes in the warm and inviting **JAZZ at Kitano** to traditional kaiseki cuisine served at their subterranean restaurant, **Hakubai**.

SWEETS AND SPIRITS

Slightly north, owner and pastry chef extraordinaire, Stephane Pourrez brings fabulous French flair and sweet baked treats to **Éclair** on East 53rd Street. Showcasing an exquisite lineup of pastries, cakes, macarons, and of course, eclairs, this dreamy midtown spot also boasts the flakiest croissants in town. Steps away, savor some bubbly and cool tunes at **Flute**, or indulge in extraordinary wines at petite **Pierre Loti**.

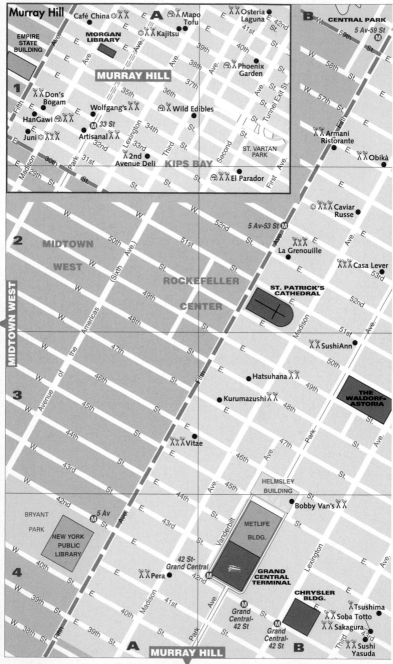

Murray Hill

A

Café China ✗✗
❈✗ Mapo Tofu
❈✗ Kajitsu
✗✗ Osteria Laguna

MORGAN LIBRARY

EMPIRE STATE BUILDING

MURRAY HILL

❈✗ Phoenix Garden

1

✗✗ Don's Bogam
HanGawi ❈✗✗
Juni ❈✗✗✗

Wolfgang's ✗✗
Ⓜ 33 St
Artisanal ✗✗

❈✗ Wild Edibles

ST. VARTAN PARK

✗2nd Avenue Deli

KIPS BAY

❈✗✗ El Parador

B

CENTRAL PARK

5 Av-59 St Ⓜ

✗✗ Armani Ristorante

✗✗ Obikà

❈✗✗✗ Caviar Russe

2

MIDTOWN WEST

5 Av-53 St Ⓜ

✗✗✗ La Grenouille

✗✗✗ Casa Lever

ROCKEFELLER CENTER

ST. PATRICK'S CATHEDRAL

✗✗ SushiAnn

3

● Hatsuhana ✗✗

● Kurumazushi ✗✗

✗✗✗ Vitae

THE WALDORF=ASTORIA

HELMSLEY BUILDING

Bobby Van's ✗✗

4

BRYANT PARK

NEW YORK PUBLIC LIBRARY

5 Av Ⓜ

✗✗ Pera

METLIFE BLDG.

42 St-Grand Central Ⓜ

GRAND CENTRAL TERMINAL

CHRYSLER BLDG.

Grand Central-42 St Ⓜ

Grand Central-42 St Ⓜ

✗ Tsushima

✗✗ Soba Totto
✗✗ Sakagura

✗✗ Sushi Yasuda

MIDTOWN WEST

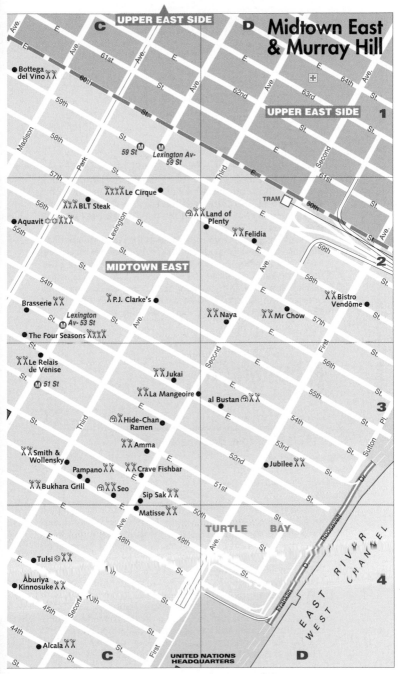

Midtown East & Murray Hill

UPPER EAST SIDE

UPPER EAST SIDE

MIDTOWN EAST

TURTLE BAY

EAST RIVER

WEST CHANNEL

Bottega del Vino

Aquavit

Brasserie

The Four Seasons

Le Relais de Venise

51 St

Smith & Wollensky

Pampano

Bukhara Grill

Tulsi

Aburiya Kinnosuke

Alcala

Le Cirque

BLT Steak

Land of Plenty

Felidia

P.J. Clarke's

Naya

Mr Chow

Bistro Vendôme

Jukai

La Mangeoire

al Bustan

Hide-Chan Ramen

Amma

Crave Fishbar

Jubilee

Seo

Sip Sak

Matisse

59 St

Lexington Av- 59 St

Lexington Av- 53 St

TRAM

UNITED NATIONS HEADQUARTERS

Madison

Park

Lexington

Third

Second

First

Sutton Pl.

Roosevelt Dr.

Franklin

61st
60th
59th
58th
57th
56th
55th
54th
53rd
52nd
51st
50th
49th
48th
45th
44th
62nd
63rd
64th

Aburiya Kinnosuke

C4

213 E. 45th St. (bet. Second & Third Aves.)

Subway: Grand Central - 42 St   Lunch Mon – Fri
Phone: 212-867-5454   Dinner nightly
Web: www.aburiyakinnosuke.com
Prices: $$$

Every bit as authentic in style as in cuisine, Aburiya Kinnosuke offers its elite diners a trip to Tokyo without the tariff. So book ahead for those private nooks or tables separated from the main room by *shoji*. Towards the back, a gleaming action-packed counter wraps around the fiery robata and almighty young cooks.

The staff is good if sometimes amiss as they gush on about an omakase to their global clients. You may be better off sharing a range of enticing items with equally pleasing sips of sake. So, let the kitchen coddle you with terrific toro and sea urchin sashimi; tofu in a light soy bath; or *tskune*—chicken meatball brushed with teriyaki, and set beneath a creamy egg yolk. If *hamachi kama* (yellowtail collar) is on offer, grab it.

al Bustan 😋

D3

319 E. 53rd St. (bet. First & Second Aves.)

Subway: Lexington Av - 53 St   Lunch & dinner daily
Phone: 212-759-5933
Web: www.albustanny.com
Prices: $$

Lebanese specialties are fired up with aplomb at this enticing retreat, where a moneyed Middle Eastern crowd dominates the space along with a stream of locals including diplomats from the UN. Inside, chandeliers hang from a beam-lined ceiling, while neat white leather chairs and glass partitions impart an air of elegance.

The expansive menu boasts a slew of meze, house specials, and a knockout dinner prix-fixe. Let the feasting begin with *samboussek jibneh*, a baked pastry bubbling with salty feta and crisp *fattoush*, tossing crunchy romaine lettuce, cucumber, tomato, and sumac. And that's not all: add on the hugely flavored *sujuk*—spicy beef sausage—sautéed, sliced, and kissed with lemon for that perfect smack of flavor.

Alcala

Spanish ✗✗

C4

246 E. 44th St. (bet. Second and Third Aves.)

Subway: Grand Central - 42 St
Phone: 212-370-1866
Web: www.alcalarestaurant.com
Prices: $$

Lunch Mon – Fri
Dinner nightly

Located steps away from the UN, this chirpy Spanish establishment draws an international clientele whose exuberance often reverberates throughout its cozy quarters. The interior combines buttery yellow walls, hand-painted ceramics, and a petite bar stocked with Spanish wines.

The kitchen focuses its attention on northern specialties that include chilled *esparragos*—plump, white asparagus from Navarra and roasted piquillo peppers dressed with a scallion vinaigrette dotted with minced green olives and hard-cooked egg. Beyond tempting tapas, taste the perfectly seasoned grilled lamb chops sided by a lighter take on potato gratin prepared with olive oil. For dessert, a slice of warm *tarta de Arrese* filled with dense custard is pure decadence.

Amma

Indian ✗✗

C3

246 E. 51st St. (bet. Second & Third Aves.)

Subway: 51 St
Phone: 212-644-8330
Web: www.ammanyc.com
Prices: $$

Lunch Mon – Fri
Dinner nightly

Make your way up a few stairs to enter Amma's home, an elegant parlor arranged with close-knit, white-robed tables set atop carpeted floors. This is indeed Indian food—brought to you in a colonial-style townhouse in frenzied midtown. Amma's "living room" feels bright with big windows, saffron-tinted walls, chaste artwork, and a chandelier twinkling upon an affluent set.

Brimming at lunch with delicacies like *prawn masala* steeped in coconut, Amma becomes romantic at night. In keeping with its mien, warm yet vigilant servers present you with Indian hospitality at its finest—in the form of *tandoori* sea bass with plantain dumplings; *bagharey baingan* (eggplant stuffed with a spicy peanut sauce); and *bhindi ka raita*, all soaked up by a basket of breads.

Aquavit ❀ ❀

Scandinavian ✕✕✕

65 E. 55th St. (bet. Madison & Park Aves.)

Subway: 5 Av - 53 St
Phone: 212-307-7311
Web: www.aquavit.org
Prices: $$$$

Lunch Mon – Fri
Dinner Mon – Sat

Frosted glass chandeliers, a mossy green carpet, the rustic table display of farmhouse cheeses, and furry shags thrown here or there make everyone feel like they've escaped from NY with warm, Scandanavian style. Modern simplicity and a sleek design perspective give the soft-spoken room a quiet formality.

Myriad à la carte, prix-fixe, and tasting menus mean that an array of appetites and budgets can be readily accommodated. But no matter the menu, each highly refined and often ambitious dish is presented as a clever and focused expression of recently promoted Chef Emma Bengtsson's vision.

Begin a springtime feast with sweet and delicate herring fillet topped with perfectly balanced embellishments including trout roe, herbs, horseradish cream, *vasterbotten* cheese, and more. Lush flavors and Nordic roots combine in the Maine lobster with horseradish foam to contrast sweet peas in dill buttermilk with cucumbers and pea shoots. Contemporary desserts may be composed of halved brook cherries with smoked vanilla crème brûlée, sesame and white chocolate "dream cookies," and sesame ice cream. Don't miss the house-infused aquavits, even as they stand in the shadow of their very fine wine program.

Armani Ristorante

B1

Italian ✗✗

717 5th Ave. (at 56th St.)

Subway: 5 Av - 53 St
Phone: 212-207-1902
Web: www.armanirestaurantny.com
Prices: $$$

Lunch daily
Dinner Mon – Sat

At Giorgio Armani's Fifth Avenue restaurant what you're wearing is as important as what you're eating. Overlooking the famous street, models serve as (distracted) staff members and bartenders are pure showstoppers—to no one's surprise. Would you expect anything less of the man whose luxurious Armani Casa furniture lines the space?

His streamlined and modern aesthetic prevails, right down to the glistening, ruby-red tuna tartare. Each cube cut by hand, the sea-fresh fish rolls in truffle oil and chives with briny sea beans and trout roe for a fantastic play on texture. Equally precise, the pan-seared spring flounder is infused with a coriander reduction, fresh porcini, and fennel with an airy foam that looks so good it may as well be Photoshopped.

Artisanal

A1

French ✗✗

2 Park Ave. (entrance on 32nd St.)

Subway: 33 St
Phone: 212-725-8585
Web: www.artisanalbistro.com
Prices: $$

Lunch & dinner daily

It's easy to incorporate (more) cheese into any dish at this midtown spot, regaled for an exceptional selection of decadent fondue. What's tougher is to consistently produce the high-quality classics that this bistro does so well, and with a bit of French flair. The handsome, wood-paneled room invites special occasion celebrations and impressive prix-fixes paired with what keep the crowds returning.

Classic mussels and frites, chicken paillard, and grilled cheese are all sumptuous staples, but for light and fresh flavors, enjoy a lobster salad—a "ladies who lunch" toss-up of poached lobster meat, chunks of avocado, and creamy herb dressing. Smoked salmon rillettes are light yet luscious; and in lieu of dessert, opt for more cheese, of course!

Bistro Vendôme

French 🍴🍴

D2

405 E. 58th St. (bet. First Ave. & Sutton Pl.)

Subway: 59 St   Lunch & dinner daily
Phone: 212-935-9100
Web: www.bistrovendomenyc.com
Prices: $$

The nearby residents of Sutton Place fit Bistro Vendôme, a classic sort of spot where three cozy dining rooms, top-notch service, and excellent food come together seamlessly. Often glimpsed gliding across the restaurant, the husband-and-wife owners warmly cater to locals during pleasant but humming dinner hours. The space makes everyone feel lucky—such solid dining options don't typically exist this far east.

Familiar and well-done classics may include an enjoyably but never over-whelmingly flavorful fish soup sided with Gruyère cheese, *rouille*, and croûtes. The well-executed striped bass arrives with a bed of zucchini cooked in a fragrant tomato-saffron broth; while an *ile flottante* with caramel sauce is like an ode to a Provençal bistro.

BLT Steak

Steakhouse 🍴🍴🍴

C2

106 E. 57th St. (bet. Lexington & Park Aves.)

Subway: 59 St   Lunch Mon – Fri
Phone: 212-752-7470   Dinner nightly
Web: www.bltsteak.com
Prices: $$$$

The best steakhouse in New York City is hotly contested among many contenders, but this handsome retreat sets itself apart with genuine hospitality, great management, and Sunday nights filled with hungry families and friends.

This spot nails crowd-pleasing dishes like addictively hot popovers the size of softballs served to every table, which are extra delicious when drowned in butter and sea salt. Steaks are very good, but sides truly excel, from inch-thick and perfectly crunchy onion rings to umami-rich and salty roasted mushrooms. Even crispy potato skins get the special treatment here—first baked, then deep-fried, and finally topped with bacon, cheese, sour cream, and chives. It may be a precursor to a heart attack, but it's worth every bite.

Bobby Van's

B4

American ✗✗

230 Park Ave. (in East Walkway & 46th St.)

Subway: Grand Central - 42 St
Phone: 212-867-5490
Web: www.bobbyvans.com
Prices: $$$$

Lunch Mon – Fri
Dinner Mon – Sat

Nestled at the base of The Helmsley building near Grand Central lies Bobby Van's, a perennial favorite of the expense-account set. Its classic steakhouse atmosphere—gruff but prompt service, noisy post-work bar scene, and gargantuan portions—is met with commendable dishes that reach beyond the normal chop shop fare.

While the beef speaks for itself, the kitchen's execution takes common combos to the next level: mozzarella and tomatoes are drizzled in flavorful balsamic and olive oil with a chiffonade of basil and shallots; while soft-shell crabs arrive perfectly battered and tempura fried. This massive special, with crisp asparagus and bed of sautéed spinach, showcases great culinary technique and seasonality not expected from a midtown lunch hangout.

Bottega del Vino

C1

Italian ✗✗

7 E. 59th St. (bet. Fifth & Madison Aves.)

Subway: 5 Av - 59 St
Phone: 212-223-2724
Web: www.bottegadelvinonyc.com
Prices: $$$$

Lunch & dinner daily

For true Northern Italian elegance, Bottega del Vino is divine, no matter the time of day. In front, casual Bar Quadronno caters to local business people looking to meet for a European-style breakfast, light lunch, or unbeatable cappuccino. Head to the more formal, rear dining room dressed in white table cloths to savor a very authentic Italian meal.

Veronese influence is clear from the start, with dishes like whole grilled calamari served simply over a bed of arugula drizzled in excellent olive oil with a splash of lemon. The pillowy spinach and potato gnocchi swimming in a creamy sauce with crisp prosciutto and pecorino outdoes most other plates like it in the city. Finish with warm Nutella-filled crêpes served with vanilla ice cream.

Brasserie

C2

Contemporary ✗✗

100 E. 53rd St. (bet. Lexington & Park Aves.)

Subway: Lexington Av - 53 St
Phone: 212-751-4840
Web: www.patinagroup.com
Prices: $$$

Lunch & dinner daily

Sleek and mod Brasserie is an eye-catching spot for corporate lunches, dinner dates, and drinks in between. Guests arrive by descending a short catwalk-like staircase into a room impressively dressed with polished wood panels, slanting green partitions, and white furnishings. And if you're waiting for someone, just keep your eyes on the screens over the bar, which project everyone's entrance.

The menu may be inspired by France but is prepared with contemporary flair. Velvety lobster bisque has the distinct, concentrated flavors of shellfish and is merely dabbed with crème fraîche rather than laden with cream. At dessert, the peaches and cream may arrive as a simple, light, and summertime combination of flaky biscuits and roasted peaches.

Bukhara Grill

C3

Indian ✗✗

217 E. 49th St. (bet. Second & Third Aves.)

Subway: 51 St
Phone: 212-888-2839
Web: www.bukharany.com
Prices: $$$

Lunch & dinner daily

In NYC's ever-expanding realm of Indian dining, Bukhara Grill has stood the test of time with excellence. Glimpse their expert chefs who seem contentedly trapped behind a glass kitchen wall. Featuring a noisy and yuppy set, this three-level space is decorated (albeit oddly) with clunky wooden booths, closely set tables, and private rooms.

Peek into the kitchen for a whiff of *tandoori* treats and Mughlai specialties. *Dahi aloo papri* or spicy potatoes and chickpeas tossed in yogurt and tamarind is a predictably perfect starter. The signature, wickedly creamy *dal* Bukhara will have you coming back for more (tomorrow). Even if the service may range from sweet to clumsy, hand-crafted breads meant to sop up the likes of *sarson ka saag* remain a crowning glory.

Café China ⌘

A1

13 E. 37th St. (bet. Fifth & Madison Aves.)

Subway: 34 St - Herald Sq

Phone: 212-213-2810

Web: www.cafechinanyc.com

Prices: $$

Lunch Mon – Fri

Dinner nightly

An unassuming façade lost in midtown masks this beautiful restaurant, decorated with seductive portraits of 1930s Shanghai starlets, bright red chairs, lush bamboo planters, and a dominating marble-and-dark wood bar. The kitchen may be struggling with popularity, yet on each table find balanced and elegant expressions of Sichuan cuisine that can stand above most in the city—one that avoids the easy umami of monosodium glutamate and egg rolls for balanced, elegant expressions of this region's dishes.

The almost overwhelming menu features dozens of cold and hot appetizers, noodles, entrées, and desserts. From refreshing julienned jellyfish and buoyant *dan dan* noodles tossed with chili oil and minced pork, to aromatic tea-smoked duck, the flavors here often bring complexity than straight heat and the presentations are more feminine than brute.

But that's not to say the kitchen doesn't conduct a fiery affair. Try the flash stir fried crispy chicken spiced with potent red and green chili peppers; or the lip-tingling cumin lamb, an intense, wok-fried dish with Sichuan peppercorns and chili oil. It's a face-melting experience that is as technically authentic as it is devilishly delicious.

231

Casa Lever

Italian ✗✗✗

B2

390 Park Ave. (entrance on 53rd St.)

Subway: Lexington Av - 53 St
Phone: 212-888-2700
Web: www.casalever.com
Prices: $$$$

Lunch Mon – Fri
Dinner Mon – Sat

The modernist design and crowds of corporate denizens give this loud, lively favorite a *Mad Men* feel. Housed in the basement of the iconic Lever House, this sexy, low-lit space is decked with tufted charcoal bucket seats circling red cocktail tables, wood panels, honeycomb-shaped wine racks, and Warhol-esque artwork. The gracious staff is top-notch.

An elegant, Northern Italian menu offers the likes of perfectly roasted, thinly sliced *vitello tonnato* in that unlikely yet incredibly delicious sauce of tuna, capers, and mayonnaise. Linguine with sea urchin, crab meat, crushed tomato, and *peperoncino* is generous and beautifully calibrated. To finish, the contemporary *millefoglie* layers delicate pastry, vanilla Chantilly cream, and raspberry *granite*.

Crave Fishbar

Seafood ✗✗

C3

945 Second Ave. (bet. 50th & 51st Sts.)

Subway: 51 St
Phone: 646-895-9585
Web: www.cravefishbar.com
Prices: $$

Lunch Sun – Fri
Dinner nightly

Just like the raucous bars that populate the neighborhood, this spot is filled to the brim with an exuberant crowd. However this coveted fish bar's sophisticated following aren't interested in bottomless pitchers of beer; they're here to dive into Chef Todd Mitgang's skillfully rendered seafood preparations. Local sea scallops are presented raw and chopped atop slices of roasted sweet potato and dressed with spicy mayonnaise, nori powder, and crumbled house-made oyster crackers. Meanwhile, John Dory has an Indian accent—marinated in spiced yogurt, then roasted and plated with a *chana masala* of green garbanzo beans.

Chow down at the 25-foot marble bar, or head to the back room—a pretty clash of reclaimed timber, floral wallpaper, and plaid upholstery.

Caviar Russe ✿

Contemporary 🗙🗙🗙

B2

538 Madison Ave. (bet. 54th & 55th Sts.)

Subway: 5 Av - 53 St
Phone: 212-980-5908
Web: www.caviarrusse.com
Prices: $$$$

Lunch daily
Dinner Mon – Sat

Following a prompt greeting and quick seating, take your time to admire this dramatic, second-floor shrine to contemporary cuisine glammed-up with a central marble seafood bar, colorful murals, and lavish Murano chandeliers that resemble strings of glass bubbles suspended from a royal blue ceiling. In contrast to the serene and "deep-sea" vibe (completely fitting given the focus on caviar), a large picture window overlooks bustling Madison Avenue and the chichi shoppers who fill it.

Just as rounded booths edge the outer walls, beautiful Bernardaud porcelain-topped tables allow for audible conversations—likely about the staff's proficiency with caviar varieties like Siberian, classic osetra, and delicate osetra, served in mother-of-pearl tasting spoons and matched with warm crêpes and crème fraîche.

A velvety parsnip soup, poured tableside with demi-glace dressed sweetbreads, black truffle-mascarpone cream, and slightly sour sorrel is delicious if not texturally divine. Then, at meal's end, find their luxury-loving clients waiting (with bated breath) for that dense and rich round of chocolate crémeux topped with a quenelle of chocolate-banana ice cream and drips of dark chocolate ganache.

Don's Bogam

A1

17 E. 32nd St. (bet. Fifth & Madison Aves.)

Subway: 33 St
Phone: 212-683-2200
Web: www.donsbogam.com
Prices: $$

Lunch & dinner daily

For a fun and festive night with family and friends, head to Don's Bogam. The food here is fantastic—no wonder this place is perpetually packed. Be sure to reserve ahead as every seat is filled, from the front bar and two-tops to the elevated level of traditional, sunken tables with powerful grills and enormous vents. Go hungry and order platters of immaculate beef and oodles of *soju*.

Novices can rest easy as the gracious staff will guide and grill your way through their classic Korean menu featuring dishes like *japchae*, stir-fried sweet potato noodles in sesame oil with beef, vegetables, and soy sauce; or deep-fried pork *mandu* with a sesame- soy- and scallion sauce. Thinly sliced beef *bulgogi* with mushrooms and carrots is utterly memorable.

El Parador 😊

B2

325 E. 34th St. (bet. First & Second Aves.)

Subway: 33 St
Phone: 212-679-6812
Web: www.elparadorcafe.com
Prices: $$

Lunch Mon– Sat
Dinner nightly

This neighborhood mainstay can boast over fifty years of success. With their fantastic menu, killer margaritas, and dedication to hospitality, El Parador is worthy of its status as a beloved destination. The intimate space is decked with ornate wood chairs, red banquettes, and wood plank ceilings, while white brick walls are hung with artwork and artifacts.

The bountiful menu offers favorites like taco trays and nachos in three varieties, as well as a rotating menu of daily specials (be sure to try the fish of the day). Fill up on *aguachile de camaron*, deliciously classic shrimp ceviche in lime juice and jalapeño; or tender, falling-off-the-bone baby-back ribs, grilled and served with tequila-chili *huajillo* salsa, cabbage slaw, and braised *camote*.

Felidia

D2

Italian

243 E. 58th St. (bet. Second & Third Aves.)

Subway: Lexington Av - 59 St
Phone: 212-758 1479
Web: www.felidia-nyc.com
Prices: $$$

Lunch Mon – Fri
Dinner nightly

Felidia's burnt-orange awning, red brick patio, and tiny olive trees instantly make it the most attractive spot on the block. Inside, the space is bright and warm with a long wood bar, cherry-red leather chairs, and colorful Venetian glass sconces. Expect to glimpse owner and matriarch Lidia Bastianich herself, adding to the friendly ambience.

The consistent menu is composed of top ingredients handled with straightforward care, as in fresh *burrata* topped with a fried egg—its warm, runny yolk drips down to meet perfectly blanched asparagus and crisp bacon; or *cacio e pere* featuring tender ravioli filled with pear purée and finished with showers of pepper. Classic desserts get a fantastic twist, as in tiramisu flavored with limoncello rather than coffee.

The Four Seasons

C2

American

99 E. 52nd St. (bet. Lexington & Park Aves.)

Subway: 51 St
Phone: 212-754-9494
Web: www.fourseasonsrestaurant.com
Prices: $$$$

Lunch Mon – Fri
Dinner nightly

Resolute in its embrace of power and privilege, The Four Seasons is one of Manhattan's most iconic dining rooms. Opened in 1959, this time capsule of mid-century swagger still remains the choice table for the panoply of today's movers and shakers. Whether it's lunch in the Grill Room or dinner in the Pool Room, design aficionados will revel in the beauty of its handsome walnut paneling and sleek Mies van der Rohe furnishings.

This ambience comes at a price, but the food is refined, skillfully prepared, and made with exceptional ingredients. Expect dishes to highlight classical elements, as in luscious Nantucket bay scallops with a black truffle sauce and wild mushrooms; or Dover sole, filleted tableside and presented with a lemon-caper sauce.

HanGawi 😊

K o r e a n 🍴🍴

A1

12 E. 32nd St. (bet. Fifth & Madison Aves.)

Subway: 33 St
Phone: 212-213-0077
Web: www.hangawirestaurant.com
Prices: **$$**

Lunch Mon – Sat
Dinner nightly

Don't worry about wearing your best shoes to HanGawi; you'll have to take them off at the door before settling in at one of the restaurant's low tables. In the serene space, decorated with Korean artifacts and soothed by meditative music, it's easy to forget you're in midtown Manhattan.

The menu is all vegetarian, in keeping with the philosophy of healthy cooking to balance the *um* and *yang*. You can quite literally eat like a king here starting with vermicelli delight (sweet potato noodles), perfectly crisp kimchi and mushroom pancakes, devastatingly delicious tofu clay pot in ginger sauce, and the regal kimchi stone bowl rice made fragrant with veggies. Of course, you'll have to rejoin the crowds outside. Still, it's nice to get away...now and Zen.

Hatsuhana

J a p a n e s e 🍴🍴

B3

17 E. 48th St. (bet. Fifth & Madison Aves.)

Subway: 47-50 Sts – Rockefeller Ctr
Phone: 212-355-3345
Web: www.hatsuhana.com
Prices: **$$$**

Lunch Mon – Fri
Dinner Mon – Sat

It's been around since the beginning of time (in NYC Japanese restaurant years) but this is no lesser a destination for excellent sushi. With a retro décor that spans two floors and a business that's run like a machine, Hatsuhana is a go-to for corporate dining.

Though the rave reviews came decades ago, their traditional *Edomae* sushi still holds its own. Fish is top quality, the army of chefs have solid knife skills, and rice is properly prepared. This reliability draws a host of regulars who develop relationships with the *itamae*. Stick to the counter and go omakase: the sushi will be surprisingly impressive with accommodations for the spicy tuna-set. Table service can be bumbling with reduced quality, but there is the menu of cooked items on offer.

Hide-Chan Ramen 🐾

C3

Japanese 🍴

248 E. 52nd St. (bet. Second & Third Aves.)

Subway: Lexington Av - 53 St
Phone: 212-813-1800
Web: N/A
Prices: 🍜

Lunch Mon– Sat
Dinner nightly

There is a meticulous science and culture to this *ramen-ya* that has seemingly perfected the customized noodle experience. Two suggestions to novices: dine during off-hours to avoid their mile-long line; and ponder *exactly* how firm you like your ramen cooked and rich you like your broth before even stepping afoot.

The décor may not say much, but the food speaks volumes in terms of authenticity and flavor. Start with steamed buns of succulent pork or pan-fried *gyoza*, before moving on to enticing mains centered around unbeatable renditions of ramen. *Kuro* ramen features an intensely nourishing and garlicky *tonkotsu* broth bobbing with bits of *char siu*. Meanwhile, health-conscious NYers are in luck, as both vegetable and chicken broth are also on offer here.

Jubilee

D3

French 🍴🍴

948 First Ave. (bet. 52nd & 53rd Sts.)

Subway: Lexington Av - 53 St
Phone: 212-888-3569
Web: www.jubileeny.net
Prices: $$

Lunch & dinner daily

Settled into sleek Sutton Place, Jubilee is New York City's very own version of *Cheers*. Affluent families are in full force here, while friends gather on weeknights to mingle over wine and fine French-Belgian cuisine. The European-inflected nautical décor screams quaint coastal elegance with perpetually packed tables and a bar where everybody knows your name.

A silky, saffron-scented fish soup, accompanied by grated Gruyère, a few croûtes, and pot of *rouille* is deliciously classic and incredibly sumptuous. But before filling up, be sure to sample the sole *meunière*—a delicate fish seared perfectly and served with sautéed spinach leaves. If that doesn't sound like the best way to end a long day, their popular creme brûlée offers the ultimate fix.

Jukai

C3

237 E. 53rd St. (bet. Second & Third Aves.)

Subway: Lexington Av - 53 St
Phone: 212-588-9788
Web: www.jukainyc.com
Prices: $$

Lunch Tue – Fri
Dinner Mon – Sat

With its furtive location, Jukai is a subterranean setting that instantly transports you to Tokyo...on a dime. Styled with various woods and bamboo, this lair is packed with Japanese expats lingering over elaborate meals attended to by an amicable staff.

The menu is traditional, though the chef's unique influences are well expressed in a massive oyster "sashimi" quartered and served with ponzu; or mixed greens mingled with rich foie gras terrine and sliced duck. First-timers should opt for a fixed menu as it allows for sampling of bites like dried cod roe and *tamago*. Shabu-shabu is par excellence with top quality beef—thinly sliced, swished in dashi until perfectly tender, and then served with noodles, tofu, and two delicious sauces for dipping.

Kurumazushi

B3

7 E. 47th St., 2nd fl. (bet. Fifth & Madison Aves.)

Subway: 47-50 Sts - Rockefeller Ctr
Phone: 212-317-2802
Web: www.kurumazushi.com
Prices: $$$$

Lunch & dinner Mon – Sat

The second-floor location up a steep set of stairs may scream Tokyo, but the business clientele and foreign tourists have no problem finding their way to this NYC stalwart of traditional, Edo-style sushi. The room is simple (if outdated) but a warm welcome to your seat at the sushi bar before the extraordinary Chef Toshihiro Uezu is all that's needed. A *washitsu* room is available for private parties.

While à la carte may suffice, Kurumazushi is regaled for its omakase (though there are dramatic variations in pricing, so be sure to communicate a budget). Each taste of this precious sushi—from kampachi and sea scallop to sweet shrimp, giant clam, and uni—holds its place within the upper eschelons of New York sushi dining. The toro is a worthy specialty.

Juni ✿

Contemporary XXX

12 E. 31st St. (bet. Fifth & Madison Aves.)

Subway: 33 St
Phone: 212-995-8599
Web: www.juninyc.com
Prices: $$$$

Lunch Mon – Fri
Dinner Mon – Sat

This elegant hideaway at the recently renovated Hotel Chandler is Chef Shaun Hergatt's current home—and one of midtown's newest shining stars.

Arrive with time to enjoy a cocktail at the bar, where patrons are treated to smoked almonds and a real-time, high-definition view of the kitchen plying its craft. Then make your way to the dining room, where a dark-suited brigade settles diners into a muted scene accented with gold leaf, hammered silver, and photos of fresh produce. A polished slab sits atop each place setting and serves as a stage for Juni's signature elevated cooking. A procession of jewel-like canapés starts the show—think carrot paper dotted with goat cheese—and whets the appetite for Chef Hergatt's creative cuisine.

The foie gras, inspired by the Australian candy bar, Cherry Ripe, is encased in cherry gelée and plated with crispy bits of bitter chocolate. Vividly hued Atlantic salmon is composed with lemon yogurt and spicy granola; and roasted New York state squab bears a crisped skin, lovage chiffonade, and rose petal-infused jus. Perhaps surprisingly, avocado makes a divine dessert when transformed into ice cream and adorned with pineapple "raisins" and juiced fresh mint.

Kajitsu ✿

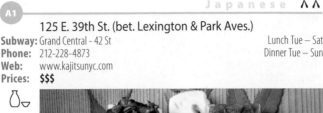

Japanese ✗✗

125 E. 39th St. (bet. Lexington & Park Aves.)

Subway: Grand Central - 42 St
Phone: 212-228-4873
Web: www.kajitsunyc.com
Prices: $$$

Lunch Tue – Sat
Dinner Tue – Sun

Step down from this tree-lined street and into the sunken entrance to Kokage by Kajitsu, with its own menu and specialty tea offerings. Then, proceed to the bright and textured second-floor restaurant, Kajitsu, for a truly unique vegan cuisine rooted in Buddhist tradition.

Straw-colored walls, stone floors, and outdoor views create a rather calm and very quiet ambience. Bare wood tables support the minimalist look and enhance the metallic platters, delicate glass bowls, and hand-glazed pottery used to present each course.

Chef Hiroki Odo's kaiseki offering is equally contemplative and welcoming, beginning with a seasonal vegetable plate of peppers, zucchini, purple okra, tomato, plump berries, and chewy *kaede-fu* presented in the shape of a rainbow. Creativity is paramount in crunchy corn croquettes filled with creamy corn, nestled in slightly charred husks on a smear of savory house-made Worcestershire. That is all served alongside kabocha and dandelion green tempura, with more grilled corn, morels, and bits of cacao. Pronounced flavors are woven through each course, from the thick white celery root soup to the complex broth served with fried yuba, nori-flavored *nama-fu*, and eggplant.

La Grenouille

French 🍴🍴🍴

B2

3 E. 52nd St. (bet. Fifth & Madison Aves.)

Subway: 5 Av - 53 St
Phone: 212-752-1495
Web: www.la-grenouille.com
Prices: $$$$

Lunch & dinner Tue – Sat

A warm, discreet welcome proves proper breeding in gorgeous La Grenouille, which recalls an Old World where true beauty and elegance went hand-in-hand. Imagine handsome suits and coiffed updos amid rich fabric walls, lavish velvet banquettes, accoutered tables, and glorious florals. (Yes, scenes from *Mad Men* have been filmed here, without a single change to the set.)

Their staff is famously gracious and unobtrusive. The very classic French kitchen sets a standard for the Old Guard, assuring that even the tiniest dab of tarragon purée is well placed in *les ravioles de homard a l'estragon*, silky pasta filled with lobster in a butter sauce. *Quenelles "Lyonnaise"* in béchamel are prepared with total precision. *Ouefs à la Niege* are feather-light and divine.

La Mangeoire

French 🍴🍴

C3

1008 Second Ave. (bet. 53rd & 54th Aves.)

Subway: Lexington Av - 53 St
Phone: 212-759-7086
Web: www.lamangeoire.com
Prices: $$$

Lunch Sun – Fri
Dinner nightly

Cozy and warm, La Mangeoire is the French bistro that everyone dreams of having in their neighborhood. Housed on a harried street, this delightful farmhouse feels at once updated and modern with sunlight drenching its floors and French artifacts dotting its walls.

As if to prove their authenticity, they also have a fully French staff who are adept, friendly, and even flirty in their relaying of the classic menu. *Rillettes* of smoked salmon are delicious and rustically served in a little jar with toasted baguette. Still, the roast chicken is the stuff of culinary legends: gorgeously dark, juicy, and crisp-skinned, served with an accompanying pitcher of jus to pour as desired. A rich yet lightly textured milk chocolate mousse is decadence incarnate.

Land of Plenty

D2

204 E. 58th St. (bet. Second & Third Aves.)

Subway: 59 St
Phone: 212-308-8788
Web: www.landofplenty58.com
Prices: $$

Lunch Mon – Fri
Dinner nightly

A sleek, clean, and subterranean space attended to by adept servers, this Chinese haven feels far more nice and elegant than the other Sichuan spots in midtown. Instead of sweet-and-sour pork, crowds of lively, food-savvy diners come for authentic lunchtime specials prepared by a cadre of talented chefs.

The food is just plain stellar, featuring excellent versions of this cuisine's classics, which may start with addictive pickled vegetables or soft pork dumplings paired with sweet soy. While some settle on crunchy conch bathed in roasted chili oil, others opt for smoked duck fried rice to pair with sautéed crispy chicken tossed in chilies and sesame seeds. String beans stir-fried with minced pork and bamboo shoots is a revelatory way to end the affair.

Le Cirque

C2

151 E. 58th St. (bet. Lexington & Third Aves.)

Subway: 59 St
Phone: 212-644-0202
Web: www.lecirque.com
Prices: $$$$

Lunch Mon – Fri
Dinner Mon – Sat

Sirio Maccioni's Le Cirque has been a member of NYC's culinary elite since opening its doors in 1974. Breathing new life into this storied classic is Chef Raphael Francois' (via Hélène Darroze) contemporary carte du jour. Settle in as he orchestrates behind the scenes and surrender to the efficient staff as they guide you through what is sure to be an exciting show.

Highly stylized plates manifest the chef's vision for uplifting riffs on staples and feature chilled lobster garnished with snow peas, blueberries, and crunchy-tart radishes; or perfectly seared Long Island duck breast bathed in a zippy ginger jus. For a timeless treat at the end, the chocolate soufflé is infallible, but also save room for Le Cirque "heritage" items, marked with an asterisk.

Le Relais de Venise

Steakhouse ❌❌

C3

590 Lexington Ave. (at 52nd St.)

Subway: 51 St
Phone: 212-758-3989
Web: www.relaisdevenise.com
Prices: $$

Lunch & dinner daily

There is no menu at Le Relais de Venise L'Entrecôte, a Parisian restaurant with a prime location set along thumping Lexington Avenue. There is only one $28.75 option, but it is a delightful option indeed—green salad with a tangy mustard vinaigrette and walnuts, followed by juicy steak served in two parts (because you wouldn't want the rest of it to get cold, would you?) laced in the house's mouthwatering secret sauce, with all the crunchy frites you can eat.

With a Parisian décor and waitresses darting around in saucy French maid get-ups, this is a lively joint—all the more reason to pluck a glass of *vin* off the extremely affordable list, sit back and relax. By the time the dessert menu rolls around, you'll have forgotten how stressful decisions can be.

Mapo Tofu 😋

Chinese ❌

A1

338 Lexington Ave. (bet. 39th & 40th Sts.)

Subway: Grand Central - 42 St
Phone: 212-867-8118
Web: N/A
Prices: 🥠🥠

Lunch & dinner daily

"How many?" That's the greeting at this temple of "ma la," where enticing aromas are sure to lure you in. Find yourself among executives and locals slurping up a host of chili oil specialties (don't wear white!). This is the kind of place where dragons go to recharge their breath.

Some may peruse the menu—rife with typos—for daily specials, but most blaze their tongues with Sichuan pickles or chilled noodles tossed in an intense sesame vinaigrette. The place is named after a humble dish, but many items surprise with bold flavors like silky fish fillets swimming in a spicy broth with Napa cabbage, or camphor tea-smoked duck. Peppercorns in stir-fried chicken unite subtle sweetness with intense heat, while sponge squash offers a cooling, textural finale.

243

Matisse

French ✗✗

C4

924 Second Ave. (at 49th St.)

Subway: 51 St
Phone: 212-546-9300
Web: www.matissenyc.com
Prices: $$

Lunch & dinner daily

Matisse might be smack dab in midtown, but this tightly packed, sun-filled bistro looks and feels far more downtown. Informal without being casual, this single room restaurant with a front row seat to the action on Second Avenue has that typical New York lack of elbow room, but forever lively and whizzing spirit.

Young and old area denizens are lured by the simple and classic French cooking with a reasonable price tag. The menu presents an appealing range of comfort foods, such as a caramelized onion tarte and croque monsieur. Sunday brunch delivers the goods with omelets and French toast alongside other usual suspects.

Some of the dishes are presented on delightfully rustic wooden boards and exude charm, thereby displaying Matisse's stylish flair.

Mr Chow

Chinese ✗✗

D2

324 E. 57th St. (bet. First & Second Aves.)

Subway: 59 St
Phone: 212-751-9030
Web: www.mrchow.com
Prices: $$$$

Dinner nightly

Oh Mr Chow, how you hook the hordes with your flavorful fusion and fancy prices! Perhaps it's the retro scene decked in black-and-white, lacquered Asian-accented chairs, and glinting mirrors. Or, maybe it's the noodle guy's theatrical display of hand-pulling? Whatever the hype, Mr Chow still has it and Sutton suits along with their wealthy wives party here like it's 1999.

Attentive service and flowing drinks keep everything moving as fans nibble away on the well-priced Beijing duck prix-fixe with four starters plus entrées. Tender orange chicken satay and water dumplings with seafood are tasty, but Dungeness crab sautéed with egg whites, and *ma mignon*, cubes of tender fried beef tossed in a sweet-spicy sauce laced with scallions truly get the crowd going.

Naya

D2

Lebanese ✗✗

1057 Second Ave. (bet. 55th & 56th Sts.)

Subway: Lexington Av - 53 St   Lunch & dinner daily
Phone: 212-319-7777
Web: www.nayarestaurants.com
Prices: $$

Amid this bland stretch of cheap booze and loud beats lies Naya, a tiny and mod neighborhood spot with tasty Lebanese fare. Inside, the streamlined décor feels smart and attractive, with white pleather booths contrasting against shiny dark tables. This sleek aesthetic runs to the back where a large table is best for suit-donning groups.

Most love Naya for its vast choice of Lebanese meze and daily specials featuring home-style food with modern flair. It is clear that this is no amateur show, as obliging waiters present you with the likes of a "quick Naya" lunch special unveiling generous portions of *fattoush*, *labne*, and *baba ghannouj*. A chicken shawarma sandwich reaches epic scopes when paired with their deliciously tangy homemade pickles.

Obikà

B1

Italian ✗✗

590 Madison Ave. (at 56th St.)

Subway: 59 St   Lunch daily
Phone: 212-355-2217
Web: www.obika.it
Prices: $$

Conveniently located in the glass atrium of the IBM building, Obikà exudes an elegant yet casual style that attracts slim suits and sleek shoppers alike. Plentiful sunlight lends an airy feel to the space, which offers counter dining and table seating, smartly separated from the building's lobby with planters.

The focus here is the truly exceptional mozzarella—fresh *bufala*, hauntingly smoked, or tangy *burrata*—which can be paired with a *tagliere* of cured meats and/or grilled vegetables for a perfectly light lunch. The menu ventures on to offer an exceptional rendition of lasagna *tradizionale*, made with delicate layers of pasta, hearty beef ragù, béchamel, and a showering of Parmesan. Come dessert, the tiramisu is another classic.

Osteria Laguna

B1

Italian ✗✗

209 E. 42nd St. (bet. Second & Third Aves.)

Subway: Grand Central - 42 St   Lunch & dinner daily
Phone: 212-557-0001
Web: www.osteria-laguna.com
Prices: $$

A little bit corporate (it is midtown, after all) and a little bit casual (daytrippers from nearby Grand Central), Osteria Laguna has nailed its audience and delivers a perfect blend to suit both worlds. Inside, it's delightfully rustic, complete with the requisite Italian ceramic plates and wooden chairs with rush seating.

Crowd-pleasers like pastas, pizzas from the wood-burning oven, *antipasti*, salads, and grilled meats and fish dishes comprise the menu at this better-than-average Italian. The friendly service can be spotty, but the perfectly crisped wood-fired pizzas are always spot on. The portions are abundant, perhaps even too much given the tiny tables, but the prices aren't, so you can treat your out-of-town friend and keep the change.

Pampano

C3

Mexican ✗✗

209 E. 49th St. (bet. Second & Third Aves.)

Subway: 51 St   Lunch & dinner daily
Phone: 212-751-4545
Web: www.richardsandoval.com
Prices: $$$

Pampano is a proven pick among corporate types craving upscale, seafood-centric Mexican food. An army of hostesses may greet you at the entry but leave you feeling cool. No matter, they might as well have escorted you to Acapulco, otherwise known as a table upstairs—think whitewashed ceilings, giant wicker chairs, and overhead fans. While the bar is very popular at happy hour, the mediocre downstairs "botaneria" seating and menu should be skipped in favor of the superior upstairs setting.

Expect the likes of red snapper-packed *quesadillas de pescado* oozing with Oaxaca cheese and spicy salsas. *Huarache de hongos* topped with mushrooms and goat cheese; or a dark chocoflan with candied peanuts are tasty studies in presentation and texture.

Pera

A4

Turkish 🍴🍴

303 Madison Ave. (bet. 41st & 42nd Sts.)

Subway: Grand Central - 42 St
Phone: 212-878-6301
Web: www.peranyc.com
Prices: $$

Lunch & dinner daily

For fantastically flavorful Turkish food mingled with modern influences, Pera never fails to please. Lunch does big business in this attractive dining room, layered in a chocolate-brown color scheme and packed with corporate groups and visitors looking for a sleek place to roost.

Though dinner is more low-key, the menu always boasts simple and exceptional plates like warm hummus with *pastirma*; lentil and bulgur tartare; as well as watermelon chunks tossed with feta, fresh tomatoes, and a perfect trickle of olive oil. While service can verge on disorganized, all will be forgiven after a forkful of their classic and tender chicken *adana* or lamb burger—a juicy bunful of ground lamb coupled with garlic spread, homemade pickles, and addictively crispy fries.

Phoenix Garden 😊

B1

Chinese 🍴

242 E. 40th St. (bet. Second & Third Aves.)

Subway: Grand Central - 42 St
Phone: 212-983-6666
Web: www.phoenixgardennyc.com
Prices: ⊜⊜

Lunch & dinner daily

This fuss-free and no-frills basement joint shows Chinatown that delicious Chinese food for a great value can exist outside of its borders. Forgo ho-hum lunch deals and pop in at dinnertime for a delectable selection of Cantonese cooking.

The vast menu can take some navigating, so chat up the servers for their expert advice in order to get the goods. Highlights include exquisite salt-and-pepper shrimp, shell on, butterflied, flash-fried and tossed with sliced chilies and garlic; sautéed snow pea leaves in an egg white sauce of sweet crabmeat, carrots, and snow peas; sizzling eggplant casserole studded with minced pork and ham; and crispy Peking duck sliced tableside, rolled up in pancakes, and layered with hoisin, cucumber, and scallions.

P.J. Clarke's

C2

915 Third Ave. (at 55th St.)

Subway: Lexington Av - 53 St
Phone: 212-317-1616
Web: www.pjclarkes.com
Prices: $$

Lunch & dinner daily

Old time and on the ball, P.J. Clarke's drips with New York history—ad men and business execs have patronized this pour house for generations, and with good reason. Besides a dazzling medley of drinks, the kitchen sends out a crowd-pleasing menu showcasing solid technique. Following its repute, the distinct décor spotlights notable artifacts, worn floors, and smartly dressed tables.

Weekends draw a touristy set, but who's complaining with an amazing Bloody Mary so close at hand? Highlights include potato chips with an outrageously gooey blue cheese gratin; braised short rib spring rolls with horseradish-tinged sour cream; and tuna tartare tacos filled with scallion and sesame seeds. The cheeseburger is as classic and on-point as the staff themselves.

Sakagura

B4

211 E. 43rd St. (bet. Second & Third Aves.)

Subway: Grand Central - 42 St
Phone: 212-953-7253
Web: www.sakagura.com
Prices: $$$

Lunch Mon – Fri
Dinner nightly

Without changing, Sakagura continues on as a sought-after sake den. Buried in the basement of an office building, this very Japanese gem requires reservations. The staff is vigilant, but lingering is the name of the game in their vast dining room, elegantly adorned with a counter and lush booths.

Here, lunch is cherished for its fantastic choice and notable value. Nibble your way through perfectly fried chopped shrimp and shredded vegetable *kakiage*, served with radish and dipping sauce; a tasty seaweed salad tossed with ponzu; and *sake ikura don set*—rice topped with salmon sashimi and roe alongside chewy soba with scallions, pickles, and dashi. Dinner is a different ball game with pages upon pages of little bites for savoring with carafes of sake.

2nd Avenue Deli

A1

Deli ✕

162 E. 33rd St. (bet. Lexington & Third Aves.)

Subway: 33 St
Phone: 212-689-9000
Web: www.2ndavedeli.com
Prices: 🅑🅑

Lunch & dinner daily

While the décor may be more deli-meets-deco and there's a tad less attitude, this food is every bit as good as it was on Second Avenue. Ignore the kvetching and know that this is a true Jewish deli filled with personality, and one of the best around by far.

The menu remains as it should: kosher, meat-loving, and non-dairy with phenomenal pastrami, pillowy rye, tangy mustard, perfect potato pancakes, and fluffy matzoh balls in comforting broth. Have the best of both worlds with the soup and half-sandwich combination.

Carve a nook during midday rush, when in pour the crowds. The deli also does takeout (popular with the midtown lunch bunch), and delivery (grandma's pancakes at your door). Giant platters go equally well to a bris or brunch.

Seo 🅖

C3

Japanese ✕✕

249 E. 49th St. (bet. Second & Third Aves.)

Subway: 51 St
Phone: 212-355-7722
Web: N/A
Prices: $$

Lunch Mon – Fri
Dinner nightly

Head to Seo for homey Japanese food. This hospitable hideaway wears no airs and its kitchen is wholly dedicated to the cooking and conservation of their little lair. While westerners may misconstrue it for a sushi bar (peek that wraparound counter), it is anything but. Make your way beyond a steamy kitchen to a neat dining den attired with tables and a glass wall overlooking a garden. Amid this calm, eat your way through salty edamame, followed by *inaniwa udon*, or salmon sashimi atop rice with wasabi. Like its Zen backyard, the red bean green tea ice cream will deliver you far from maddening midtown.

Note to novices: Seo sheds its low-key image for nightly late-night raucous, when it turns into cash-only Ramen Sanshiro, a secret fave among guzzlers.

Sip Sak

C3

Turkish ✗✗

928 Second Ave. (bet. 49th & 50th Sts.)

Subway: 51 St
Phone: 212-583-1900
Web: www.sip-sak.com
Prices: $$

Lunch & dinner daily

The celadon façade of this tiny Turkish treasure with its frosted glass awning and art nouveau look holds its own in mundane midtown. Walls lined with large mirrors and a shiny pressed-tin ceiling stand over an armada of cool white marble-topped tables and bentwood bistro chairs.

The décor seems French, but the cuisine leads to the Eastern Mediterranean with a definite stop in Turkey. A central, fully stocked bar serves as the launching point for Chef Orhan Yegen, who can be seen (and heard) directing his staff as they entice diners with a meze of citrusy olives, delicious hummus, garlicky *cacik*, and creamy *tarama*. House specials like rustic braised lamb chunks set atop a smooth eggplant purée seem straightforward but are deeply comforting.

Smith & Wollensky

C3

Steakhouse ✗✗

797 Third Ave. (at 49th St.)

Subway: 51 St
Phone: 212-753-1530
Web: www.smithandwollensky.com
Prices: $$$$

Lunch Mon – Fri
Dinner nightly

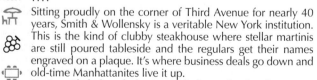

Sitting proudly on the corner of Third Avenue for nearly 40 years, Smith & Wollensky is a veritable New York institution. This is the kind of clubby steakhouse where stellar martinis are still poured tableside and the regulars get their names engraved on a plaque. It's where business deals go down and old-time Manhattanites live it up.

Begin with beloved classics including a beefsteak tomato-and-onion salad finished with house dressing and crumbled blue cheese; or spoon-licking sides like creamed spinach, crispy hash browns, and crunchy onion rings. Then, allow the adept servers to steer you towards the in-house favorite— namely, a beautifully marbled, deliciously fatty, and perfectly tender Colorado rib steak, bone-on and big enough for three.

Soba Totto

B4

Japanese ✗✗

211 E. 43rd St. (bet. Second & Third Aves.)

Subway: Grand Central - 42 St
Phone: 212-557-8200
Web: www.sobatotto.com
Prices: $$

Lunch Mon – Fri
Dinner nightly

It's a jam-packed lunchtime affair here at Soba Totto, where business folks gather and quickly fill the popular space. As the name suggests, everyone arrives in droves for the tasty homemade soba. Dinnertime brings a mellower vibe, and a crowd of beer- and sake-sipping patrons ordering tasty plates of spicy fried chicken and *yakitori* galore.

Midday features several varieties of lunch sets. Tasty appetizers may unveil a salad of assorted pickles and simmered daikon in a sweet ginger dressing. Skip over the fried seafood in favor of the *soba totto gozen* set, which includes the wonderful soba in fragrant *dashi*; or try one of the many delicious *dons* topped with tasty tidbits like sea urchin and salmon roe or soy-marinated tuna, grated yam, and egg.

SushiAnn

B3

Japanese ✗✗

38 E. 51st St. (bet. Madison & Park Aves.)

Subway: 51 St
Phone: 212-755-1780
Web: www.sushiann.net
Prices: $$

Lunch Mon – Fri
Dinner Mon – Sat

Lucky are those who wander into this large, peaceful den helmed by one of the best sushi teams in town—even luckier are those regulars at the counter, who know that despite the Americanized menu options, here there is a depth of authenticity rare in these parts. Such standbys sushi classics as SushiAnn know just how to balance tradition, pleasure, and expectation.

For an adventure, sit at the counter (where there is a $30 minimum) and don't hesitate to express interest in the more authentic items. This is just the right place to go for the omakase: fresh mackerel served with ponzu and minced ginger; fatty bluefin fanned over shiso leaf and kelp; smoky slices of grilled giant clam; or torched sardines—all carefully explained by the knowledgeable staff.

Sushi Yasuda

B4

204 E. 43rd St. (bet. Second & Third Aves.)

Subway: Grand Central - 42 St
Phone: 212-972-1001
Web: www.sushiyasuda.com
Prices: $$$$

Lunch Mon – Fri
Dinner Mon – Sat

Attention rule breakers: this glorious sushi spot ain't for you. Late for your reservation? It will be forfeited. Lingering too long after eating? You will be informed that time is up. Sushi-loving diehards can handle the tough love though, and come back time and time again for their spectacularly fresh fish. Left in the capable hands of Mitsuru Tamura after Naomichi Yasuda's departure, this beloved spot still maintains its loyal following.

Grab a spot at the sleek bamboo sushi counter and give over to the chef's superb recommendations, which will be circled on the menu. Tasty slices of kanpachi (amberjack) and *aji* (mackerel) are brushed with soy sauce and served over rice; while the exquisite *hotate* (scallop) is sprinkled with a touch of sea salt.

Tsushima

B4

210 E. 44th St. (bet. Second & Third Aves.)

Subway: Grand Central - 42 St
Phone: 212-207-1938
Web: N/A
Prices: $$

Lunch & dinner daily

A shiny black awning marks the entrance to this slightly antiseptic yet considerably authentic sushi bar. Having recently relocated to bigger digs (in the former East space), this Japanese den hums with business groups on the run, as well as neighborhood dwellers seeking fantastic value lunches and terrific quality sushi in the evening.

Find a roost at their sushi counter or at a table in the well-lit Japanese-style dining room, attended to by speedy servers. Then, dive into generously sized lunch specials featuring perhaps a colorful *chirashi*, headlining yellowtail, salmon, *tamago*, and amberjack set deftly over well-seasoned sushi rice. Sticky-glazed eel, nicely grilled and plenty fatty, is an absolute must as is the (costlier) omakase for dinner.

Tulsi ✿

C4

Indian 🍴🍴

211 E. 46th St. (bet. Second & Third Aves.)

Subway: Grand Central - 42 St
Phone: 212-888-0820
Web: www.tulsinyc.com
Prices: $$

Lunch Mon – Sat
Dinner nightly

Tulsi sits in a busy area amid heavy-hitting steakhouses and loud construction sites, yet it stands out with a soft-spoken ambience and serene grace. It's hard to pass their vibrant awning and not glance inside, where colorful silks and translucent, billowing fabrics separate private dining booths. Silk light fixtures and artifacts echo the elaborate nature of its cuisine with a look that is somehow glittering yet very tasteful.

The kitchen skillfully brings a delicate, sophisticated, and very authentic touch to each dish, which can be a reminder of what is at the heart of true Indian cooking. Start with *vevichathu*, giant shrimp cooked in a Kerala-style coconut curry fantastically balancing heat and flavor, served over tomato basmati rice. The *baghare baingan* arrives as reconstructed Japanese eggplant: its flesh has been stir-fried with a complex masala, stewed with peanuts, coconut, and onion, then artfully served in the hollowed, roasted eggplant shell. Breads like onion and potato *kulcha* or puffy *parathas* are excellent and ample in size.

Seasonal desserts are a highlight as in an upscale version of mango *falooda* in sweet-spiced milk studded with toasted pistachios and tapioca pearls.

Vitae

Contemporary   XXX

4 E. 46th St. (bet. Fifth & Madison Aves.)

Subway: Grand Central - 42 St
Phone: 212-682-3562
Web: www.vitaenyc.com
Prices: $$$

Lunch Mon – Fri
Dinner Mon – Sat

Vitae may be the epitome of *Mad Men*-chic, from the lively bar scene and sunken dining room to the retro-woven walls and patterned carpets. Thus, it seems only right to begin the night with a Kentucky flip—a roasted peanut-infused cocktail of Bulleit bourbon, honey, cream, egg yolk, and nutmeg that is even creamier and warmer than it sounds.

Once settled into a teal banquette or boxy white leather chair in the glamorous dining room, move on to feather-light yet rich Parker House rolls. Starters may show a tasty personality, as in the pan-roasted quail over Marcona almond couscous, tender carrots, chopped Castelvetrano olives, and preserved cherries. Pastas are wonderfully satisfying as in *chitarra* with tender chicken and ricotta meatballs.

Wild Edibles ⊛

Seafood   X

535 Third Ave. (bet. 35th & 36th Sts.)

Subway: 33 St
Phone: 212-213-8552
Web: www.wildedibles.com
Prices: $$

Lunch & dinner daily

Wild Edibles is just plain neat: this utterly charming Murray Hill fish shop is absolutely flooded with warmth. With a counter in the Grand Central Market, the fabulous retailer remains unequalled—notice a smattering of dark wood tables, subway tiles, and a bar joined to the seafood counter unveiling the freshest (and finest) sea creatures.

Relish the quiet at lunch and do as the regulars do in seeking out straight-from-the-source specials. Take off with an outstandingly warm seafood salad mingling fennel, arugula, and creamy white beans; and then fly high with the Canadian club oyster flight with three pours of wine or beer. The New England (or New Orleans) mussels are sumptuously sopped up by Old Bay fries. Rushed? Take your 'catch' and sauce to-go.

Wolfgang's

A1

Steakhouse ✗✗

4 Park Ave. (at 33rd St.)

Subway: 33 St
Phone: 212-889-3369
Web: www.wolfgangssteakhouse.net
Prices: $$$$

Lunch & dinner daily

Wolfgang's is no stranger to the bustling New York steakhouse scene. From the lunch hour business crowd to the lively, post-work bar scene, Wolfgang's jams in locals and tourists alike—each coming for the classic fare and precise Manhattans. The service can be gruff at times, but they have a good track record of squeezing you into a table or perch at the bar without a reservation.

Once seated, the bone-in Porterhouse, cooked rare, is the only way to go. It arrives sizzling in its own liquid fat and topped with butter. Save space for a slice of bacon—a must-order appetizer—creamed spinach, and crispy German potatoes with yet more salt and fat (at this point, why not?). Just beware: while dishes are sized to share, they're priced like Maseratis.

Midtown West

More diverse than its counterpart Midtown East, but still gritty in parts, Midtown West presents a unique mix of tree-lined streets and ethnic enclaves amid glitzy glass-walled towers. It is also home to numerous iconic sights, including **Restaurant Row**—the only street in all five boroughs to be proudly advertised as such. The fact that it is housed in an area named Hell's Kitchen, and highlights an impressive range of global cuisines, is sealing evidence of this nabe's devotion to great food.

EAT THE STREETS

Also referred to as "Clinton," Hell's Kitchen is a colorful mosaic of workaday immigrants, old-timey residents, and young, affluent families. Gone are the Prohibition-era gangs and grit, now replaced by swanky restaurants, boutique hotels, and hip bars. Steps away from Sixth Avenue is **Little Brazil**, where samba and street food are showcased every summer in all their glory on Brazilian Day. Incredibly popular and teeming with tourists, **Churrascaria Plataforma** is an all-you-can-eat Brazilian steakhouse showing off their wares via waiters donning skewers of succulent roasted meat. Midtown may be choked by traffic and office types on the go, but in true NY-style the residents demand—and streets showcase—outstanding eats in varying venues. Under the guidance of the Vendy Awards and the blog Midtown Lunch, discover a moveable line of speedy but very satisfying street food faves, including delis stocked with Mexican specialties like dried chilies, herbs, and fresh produce. Those in a hurry may hustle over to **Tehuitzingo** for over 17 types of mouthwatering tacos. Others might prefer that tried and true scene at **Tulcingo del Valle**, where exellent tacos and tortas are turned out along with meaty burritos and burgers. Speaking of meat, burger buffs will not be disappointed by those juicy

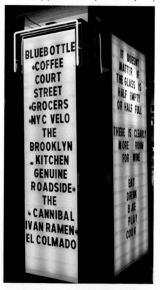

patties laced with crispy fries and thick milkshakes at Le Parker Meridien's delicious **burger joint**.

For a rarer treat, head down to **K-town**—a dark horse-like nabe that has been known to sneak up and stun. Its instant and unapologetically authentic Asian vibe owes largely to the prominence of barbecue and *bi bim bap* joints, karaoke bars, and authentic grocers hawking fresh tofu and handmade dumplings. Macy's is across the street and forever frenzied, but tucked into its quiet crypt is **De Gustibus**, a cooking school and stage for culinary legends. Walk further along these midtown streets only to find that equal attention is tendered to cuisine as to arranging storybook mannequins behind the velvet ropes of glossy stores. Shop till you drop at glitzy Bergdorf, and then stop for caviar and croissants at the very French **Petrossian**. If that isn't luxurious enough, stir things up over lovely libations at the stately **Empire Room** lodged atop the legendary structure of the same name.

Moving from specialty spots to mega markets, **Gotham West** is Manhattan's latest favorite for gourmet eats and treats. Situated along Eleventh Avenue, this culinary complex hosts a parade of chef-driven kiosks and artisanal purveyors preparing charcuterie, tapas, sandwiches, and everything in between. Of special note is the first stateside outpost of **Ivan Ramen**, where the rockstar chef's global fan base slurp down bowlfuls of wispy rye noodles bobbing in a signature, sumptuous broth. Cached beneath the graceful Plaza hotel is the traditionally tasteful **Plaza Food Hall by Todd English**. Here, a dizzying array of comestibles is on full-display and makes for a marvelous attraction—or distraction! Curated by mega-multi personality, Todd English, this 32,000-square-foot space is a perfect meeting place for friends and families looking to sip, savor, and shop. Beginning

257

with caviar, lobster rolls, or sushi and closing with coffee and creamy cupcakes, this veritable tour de force beautifully typifies the city's culinary elite.

FOOD FIXES

A few steps west and Gotham City's eclectic identity reveals yet another facet, where Ninth Avenue unearths a wealth of goodies. A wonderful start (or finale) is certified at **Amy's Bread**, where beautiful, crusty, and fresh-baked baguettes lend countless restaurant kitchens that extra

crumb of culture. However, it is also their famously colorful cakes and aromatic cookies that routinely tempt passersby off the streets and into their sweet surrounds. Across the way, **Poseidon Bakery** is a perpetual winner for authentic Greek delights. It is also the last place around that still crafts their own phyllo dough by hand—a taste of the spanakopita will prove it! Its moniker may depict another district, but **Sullivan Street Bakery's** one and only retail outlet is settled along this stretch, a location so perilously far west in the Manhattan mindset that its success seals its worth in gold. Just as Jim Lahey's luxurious loaves claim a cult-like following, so do the fantastic components (a warm Portuguese-style roll?) at **City Sandwich**.

Theater-lovers and Lincoln Tunnel-bound commuters stuck in traffic know to hit **The Counter** in Times Square, and place their order for delicious hand-crafted burgers said to be a "must try before you die." Meanwhile, locals in the know love the lure of **La Boîte**'s exotic spice blends, as much as the sumptuous *salumi* and soul-warming *formaggi* selection at **Sergimmo Salumeria**. Stroll a few short blocks south of Port Authority Bus Terminal on Eighth Avenue only to unearth an enclave rich with restaurants and brimming with bazaars. Start the feasting at **Ninth Avenue International Foods** proffering such pleasures as olives, spices, and spreads. Among their outstanding spectrum of produce, find the renowned *taramosalata* (as if prepared by the gods atop Mount Olympus themselves) that also stars on the menu of numerous fine dining destinations nearby. Just as **Esposito Meat Market** is a haven for sweet and spicy Italian sausage, a treasure trove of truffles routinely find their way into the shelves of world-renowned **Urbani Truffles**, located on sleek West End Avenue.

TIME WARNER CENTER

Finally, no visit to this district is complete without paying respect to the epicurean feat that is the **Time Warner Center**. Presiding and preening over Columbus Circle, high-flying chefs indulge both themselves and their pretty patrons here with ground-breaking success. Discover a range of delights indoors—from **Bouchon Bakery's** colorful French macarons, to the eye-popping style and sass of **Stone Rose Lounge**. Located on the fourth floor, **Center Bar** (brought to you by Michael Lomonaco) is a sophisticated perch for enjoying a champagne cocktail while taking in the views of Central Park. It's just like classic New York, only more glossy and glamorous.

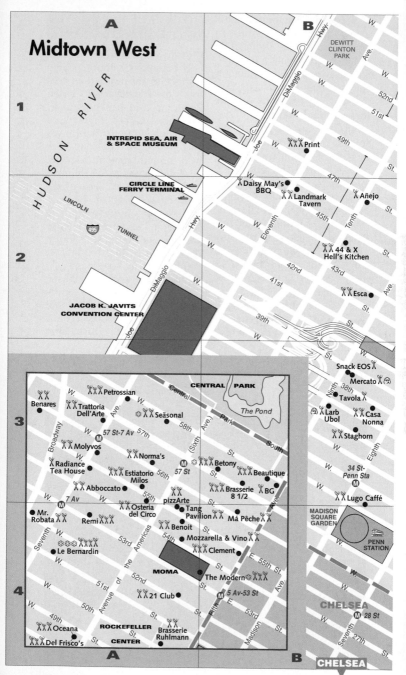

Midtown West

HUDSON RIVER

INTREPID SEA, AIR & SPACE MUSEUM

CIRCLE LINE FERRY TERMINAL

LINCOLN TUNNEL

495

JACOB K. JAVITS CONVENTION CENTER

DEWITT CLINTON PARK

XX Print

Daisy May's BBQ
XX Landmark Tavern
X Añejo

XX 44 & X Hell's Kitchen

XX Esca

Snack EOS X
Mercato X
Tavola X
Larb Ubol ● Casa Nonna
XX Staghorn

34 St-Penn Sta

XX Lugo Caffé

MADISON SQUARE GARDEN

PENN STATION

CENTRAL PARK

The Pond

XX Petrossian
XX Trattoria Dell'Arte
XX Seäsonal
XX Benares
57 St-7 Av
XX Molyvos
XX Norma's
XX Betony
XX Beautique
Radiance Tea House
XX Estiatorio Milos
57 St
XX Brasserie 8 1/2 X BG
XX Abboccato
pizzArte
XX Osteria del Circo
Tang Pavilion XX Má Pêche XX
Mr. Robata XX
Remi XXX
XX Benoit
XX Mozzarella & Vino XX
XX Clement
Le Bernardin

MOMA

The Modern XXX

5 Av-53 St

XX 21 Club

CHELSEA
28 St

XXX Oceana
ROCKEFELLER CENTER
XX Brasserie Ruhlmann
XXX Del Frisco's

CHELSEA

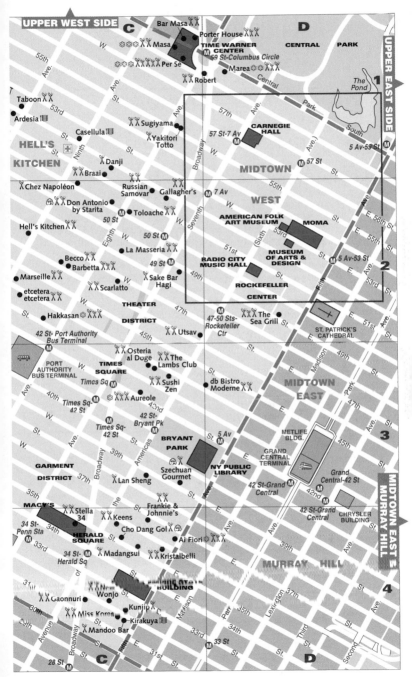

Abboccato

A3

Italian ✗✗

136 W. 55th St. (bet. Sixth & Seventh Aves.)

Subway: 57 St
Phone: 212-265-4000
Web: www.abboccato.com
Prices: $$$

Lunch Mon – Sat
Dinner nightly

It may seem like everyday a new Italian restaurant opens in Manhattan, but Abboccato (owned by the Livanos family, also of Molyvos and Oceana) continues to be a noteworthy recommendation. Adjacent to the Blakely Hotel, the lower street-level dining room is a soothing contrast to the bustling midtown commotion outside. Inside, cream-toned walls and leather furnishings complement inlaid stone floors and a comfortable bar, set off on its own.

The regional spread begins with an array of shareable small plates (*cicchetti*), such as *nonna's* meatballs or polenta-coated *fritti*. The cannelloni is luscious, house-made pasta sheets heartily stuffed with braised pork. Entrées may bring grilled skewered wild shrimp *oreganata* with shaved fennel salad.

Añejo

B2

Mexican ✗

668 Tenth Ave. (at 47th St.)

Subway: 50 St (Eighth Ave.)
Phone: 212-920-4770
Web: www.anejonyc.com
Prices: $$

Lunch Sat – Sun
Dinner nightly

This tasty *cocina* set in Hell's Kitchen is unpretentious and intimate. The house is always full and crowds are convivial, especially while sipping one of Añejo's beloved cocktails. The namesake margarita is an upscale, top-shelf refresher made with fresh lime juice and agave nectar that pairs perfectly with just about anything from the kitchen.

Ceviche, small plates, and tacos are all to be enjoyed with gusto. Start with the guacamole trio featuring traditional, pineapple-chipotle, and tomatillo-charred poblano variations. Then move on to a warm mushroom salad with wilted watercress, brown butter, and Berkshire pork chorizo. Pumpkin tamale is an outstanding deconstructed square of smashed kabocha squash, lamb *barbacoa*, and *crema* inside a banana leaf.

Ai Fiori ✿

Italian 𝆚𝆚𝆚

C4

400 Fifth Ave. (bet. 36th & 37th Sts.)

Subway: 34 St - Herald Sq
Phone: 212-613-8660
Web: www.aifiorinyc.com
Prices: $$$$

Lunch Sun– Fri
Dinner nightly

Elegantly accessed either by a sweeping spiral staircase or the Langham Place hotel elevator, Ai Fiori stands proudly above its busy Fifth Avenue address. Walls of glass windows and espresso-dark polished wood dominate the space. The Carrara marble bar and lounge furnished with silvery tufted banquettes are ideal for solo diners; large florals, brown leather chairs, and square columns adorn the formal dining room. No matter where you sit, the servers are attentive, the linens are thick, chargers are monogrammed with a goldleaf "F" and every last detail is very, very lovely.

As one might expect of a Michael White restaurant, pastas here are masterful. Begin with tender, thin rounds of ravioli filled with smooth, mousse-like pork shoulder bathed in the velvety flavors of *cacio e pepe*. The rack of lamb is a thing of wonder, roasted to perfection with a savory forcemeat combination of rosemary, foie gras and ground lamb, served with crisp balls of potatoes infused with fragrant wood over root vegetable purée.

Dessert offerings are not entirely Italian but nonetheless tasty, like the tropical-inspired millefeuille layering crisp puff pastry with rich coconut pastry cream and a hint of lime zest.

Ardesia

C1

510 W. 52nd St. (bet. Tenth & Eleventh Aves.)

Subway: 50 St (Eighth Ave.)
Phone: 212-247-9191
Web: www.ardesia-ny.com
Prices: $$

Dinner nightly

Ardesia's talented ladies, owner Mandy Oser and Chef Amorette Casaus, have fashioned such a sophisticated, comfortable, and welcoming wine bar that anyone living outside Hell's Kitchen is right to be jealous. Dominated by a white marble counter, the intimate setting feels open amid plate glass windows and high ceilings.

A lounge area accommodates those who come with friends in tow. Be sure to peruse the impressive selection of wines by the glass, listed on the chalkboard-gray walls. Nibbles may feature spiced lamb skewers with mint yogurt sauce, or chicken liver mousse with apple compote and sage. Highlights include slices of perfectly fatty house-cured pastrami atop sauerkraut, braised until it verges on creamy, and excellent toasted rye bread.

Barbetta

C2

321 W. 46th St. (bet. Eighth & Ninth Aves.)

Subway: 50 St (Eighth Ave.)
Phone: 212-246-9171
Web: www.barbettarestaurant.com
Prices: $$$

Lunch & dinner Tue – Sat

Standing proud since its 1906 opening, Barbetta proves that the "new" in New York need not be taken literally. From its gilded furnishings to its candelabra and crystal chandeliers, this dining room celebrates an old-world aesthetic. At the ornate tables, find true-blue New Yorkers who, as regulars, have been treated like family here for more than a century (though outsiders may detect a hint of indifference from the service staff).

Consistency is the theme here, and some of the menu items, such as *minestrone giardiniera*, have been served since the very beginning. Good, traditional Italian food with a few throwbacks, capped off by a selection from the dessert trolley, prove that this just might be your grandfather's favorite Italian restaurant.

Aureole ॐ

Contemporary 𝕏𝕏𝕏

135 W. 42nd St. (bet. Broadway & Sixth Ave.)

Subway: 42 St - Bryant Pk
Phone: 212-319-1660
Web: www.charliepalmer.com
Prices: $$$$

Lunch Mon – Fri
Dinner nightly

A sleek glass façade cuts away the Times Square hullabaloo to fashion the eye-catching entrance to Aureole. The interior is as attractive and soaring as expectation, with lofty ceilings, wines displayed along an elevated catwalk, and high-brow crowds.

The bar room is that sort of idyllic perch where one might pop in for a few *gougères* and cocktails poured into titanium crystal glasses. Beyond this, an upscale dining room has a quieter atmosphere to complement the more elaborate menu options. Servers are accommodating, synchronized, and timely—a boon to anyone with theater tickets.

The contemporary menu brings artful flair and a touch of Americana to each dish, whether served à la carte or as part of a prix-fixe. A three-course dinner may begin with a quivering poached egg, matsutake mushrooms, and lobes of uni in an earthy mushroom broth. Exemplary flavors come alive in the warm corn velouté that finishes pan-roasted Nova Scotia salmon, herbed-potato gnocchi, halved sungold tomatoes, and wax beans. For dessert, the *vacherin* is delectably whimsical; coconut-rum sorbet supports the crisp, light meringue, complemented by compressed pineapple, yuzu gelée, and tiny meringue kisses.

Bar Masa

Japanese ✗✗

C1

10 Columbus Circle (in the Time Warner Center)

Subway: 59 St - Columbus Circle

Lunch & dinner Mon – Sat

Phone: 212-823-9800
Web: www.masanyc.com
Prices: $$$

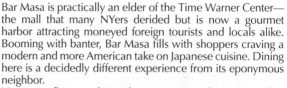

Bar Masa is practically an elder of the Time Warner Center—the mall that many NYers derided but is now a gourmet harbor attracting moneyed foreign tourists and locals alike. Booming with banter, Bar Masa fills with shoppers craving a modern and more American take on Japanese cuisine. Dining here is a decidedly different experience from its eponymous neighbor.

Limestone floors and wood accents warm the space with a convivial aura; a row of tables sit behind billowing fabrics and relaxing perches are set at the bar. The chefs offer no showmanship here: from behind curtains, a masterpiece of oysters bathed in a citrus-mirin sauce, dancing shrimp sprinkled with chili salt, and squat glasses of cocoa- and black sesame-ice cream magically appear.

Beautique

American ✗✗✗

B3

8 W. 58th St. (bet. Fifth & Sixth Aves.)

Subway: 57 St

Dinner nightly

Phone: 212-753-1200
Web: www.beautiquedining.com
Prices: $$$

Descend a staircase next door to the Paris Theater to find this swanky subterranean dining room, where silver velvet seating and a collection of crystal decanters shimmer against rich, dark hues. It's a dressy, adult scene fit for a party.

On the menu, seasonality factors prominently in items like a warm rabbit salad with fennel slices, favas, green grapes, and shaved foie gras. Likewise, king salmon is slow-cooked in olive oil and plated with tart summer squash, steamed potatoes, and a warm buttermilk vinaigrette. Desserts, made fresh in the first-rate pastry kitchen, deserve more from you than "I'll just have a bite" —so waste no time devouring the mini *cannolo* with its perfect strawberries, deconstructed linzer component, and anise-hyssop ice cream.

Becco

C2

italian ✗✗

355 W. 46th St. (bet. Eighth & Ninth Aves.)

Subway: 50 St (Eighth Ave.) Lunch & dinner daily
Phone: 212-397-7597
Web: www.becco-nyc.com
Prices: $$

This Restaurant Row stalwart has no shortage of competition, but Becco is unrivaled when it comes to pleasing diners and theater-goers with reliable and hearty Italian fare. This is all thanks to culinary authority Lidia Bastianich, her impresario son Joe, and longtime Executive Chef William Gallagher.

Becco's pleasing vision of Italian cuisine includes house-made mozzarella *en carozza* sandwiched between fried bread with pesto and tomato sauces; and Belgian-ale roasted pulled pork with salsa verde. The *sarma* (Croatian for stuffed cabbage) honors the family's Istrian heritage with meat-stuffed cabbage in tomato sauce over pan-fried spinach spaetzle.

The wine list features bottles priced at $25, with selections from their own highly regarded label.

Benares

A3

Indian ✗✗

240 W. 56th St. (bet. Broadway & Eighth Ave.)

Subway: 59 St - Columbus Circle Lunch & dinner daily
Phone: 212-397-0707
Web: www.benaresnyc.com
Prices: $$

Christened after the holy city set on the banks of the River Ganges, seafood-centric Benares brings a slice of sacred India to Hell's Kitchen. With scarce competition and a sultry mien, the polished eatery soars to great peaks—picture turmeric-toned chairs and walls dressed in vibrant Benarasi saris. Large green plants feel lush and gold-veined tiles lend a bit of glitz. Accoutrements include a lively kitchen and tasty repertoire of vegetarian dishes like Kashmiri soup with roasted turnips. Meat and (especially) fish seekers can rest easy as these play prominent roles in *saleu gosht*, a Rajasthani special featuring marinated lamb in a cardamom-almond sauce; or *sevai kurma* brimming with seafood.

The FiDi outpost is perfect for suits in need of spice.

Benoit

French ✗✗

60 W. 55th St. (bet. Fifth & Sixth Aves.)

Subway: 57 St
Phone: 646-943-7373
Web: www.benoitny.com
Prices: $$

Lunch & dinner daily

In the former home of the venerated La Côte Basque, Alain Ducasse's Benoit brings new fame to this address. The stunning bistro is rife with elegance through oak-paneled walls, polished brass, and sumptuous red velvet seating, all set off by art nouveau lighting fixtures reclaimed from the previous tenants. Peugeot pepper grinders, bread presented in linen sacks, and espresso served in custom-made Pillivuyt cups add to the opulence.

Chef Philippe Bertineau heads the kitchen, bringing a skilled hand to the likes of *foie de veau,* seared calf's liver paired with potatoes Lyonnaise. Pan-seared monkfish tail is prepared *coq au vin*-style with red wine sauce, lardons, pearl onions, and sautéed mushrooms. Desserts are categorically *magnifique.*

BG

American ✗

754 Fifth Ave. (at 58th St.)

Subway: 5 Av - 59 St
Phone: 212-872-8977
Web: www.bergdorfgoodman.com
Prices: $$$

Lunch daily
Dinner Mon – Sat

On the 7th floor of Bergdorf Goodman, BG offers ladylike posh to the label-conscious clientele of this fashion emporium. The Kelly Wearstler-designed brasserie combines springtime hues with hand-printed Chinoiserie wallpaper, gilded fixtures, and lacquered accents.

Large windows frame killer Central Park vistas and highlight the well-coiffed crowd savoring a number of fine salads. However, the carte du jour offers more vibrant dining with decadent renditions of American comfort favorites, like lobster mac and cheese. The silken tomato basil soup is enriched with just the slightest hint of cream; and Israeli couscous is infused with smoked paprika and stocked with seared black bass and shellfish.

Afternoon tea is a suitably refined affair.

Betony ✿

B3

Contemporary ☓☓☓

41 W. 57th St. (bet. Fifth & Sixth Aves.)

Subway: 57 St
Phone: 212-465-2400
Web: www.betony-nyc.com
Prices: $$$$

Lunch Mon – Fri
Dinner nightly

The successful mixing of business with pleasure is no small feat in the restaurant world, but Betony pulls it off with panache.

Oligarchs of all stripes come to nosh and network in this high-end space, where gilded fixtures and a blown glass chandelier sparkle against exposed brick, inlaid wood flooring, and a rococo plaster ceiling. Adding to the dining room's appeal is a well-orchestrated service team that instinctually adapts to the panoply of personalities that fill it.

While the setting pampers with its soothing luxury, Chef Bryce Shuman's kitchen stimulates the palate. His menu is an à la carte offering—a refreshing change of pace in this world of obligatory tasting menus—and features stunningly creative preparations. Satin-smooth chicken liver mousse sheathed in herb flecked schmaltz is plated with rye bread crumbs, celery curls, and dried apple; while a ring of plump, house-made *cavatelli*, bobbing in powerfully earthy mushroom consommé, cradles a soft-poached farm egg. Short rib with crisped sweetbreads and grilled romaine is an exquisite entrée, and Betony's butterscotch pudding, fortified with Islay whisky and adorned with toasted hazelnuts, is nothing if not swoon-worthy.

Braai

C1

329 W. 51st St. (bet. Eighth & Ninth Aves.)

Subway: 50 St (Eighth Ave.)　　　　　　　　　Lunch & dinner daily
Phone: 212-315-3315
Web: www.braainyc.com
Prices: $$

From its ground floor townhouse home, Braai is adored for its tantalizing South African cuisine. Two tables sit up front in a snug patio, which dovetails into a long and slender dark wood space. Drawing inspiration from its region, wide planks make up the floors while the arched ceiling is thatched with straw. Yet the African-inspired décor in the dining room, set with marble-topped communal tables, is anything but cliché. The menu is resplendent with new and balanced flavors that are at once evident in *frikkadel*, a classic dish of baked meatballs in broth; or calamari drenched in a lovely wine-lemon emulsion. Speaking of mainstays, *bunny chow*, a street treat of lamb curry ladled into a bread bowl, is a favorite here as well as at nearby sib, Xai Xai.

Brasserie 8 1/2

B3

9 W. 57th St. (bet. Fifth & Sixth Aves.)

Subway: 57 St　　　　　　　　　　　　　　　Lunch & dinner daily
Phone: 212-829-0812
Web: www.brasserie8andahalf.com
Prices: $$$

Dress-up, descend that sweeping staircase, and make a grand entrance upon stepping into this well-lit, spacious, grown-up canteen. The serene lounge, with just a handful of tables and walls boasting original works by Henri Matisse and Pablo Picasso, is a rarefied gift that feels worlds away from midtown's cacophony. The masculine, clubby aura of the dining room showcases ivory terrazzo floors, exotic wood veneer-lined walls, polished metal columns, and more artwork.

Talented Chef Franck Deletrain brings a traditional vision of brasserie cooking in items such as coq au vin; or *saucisson chaud*, braised pork sausage nestled in a bed of *lentils du Puy*. Finish with pear poached in spiced red wine, with mascarpone and pistachio financiers.

Brasserie Ruhlmann

French ✗✗

A4

45 Rockefeller Plaza (bet. Fifth & Sixth Aves.)

Subway: 47-50 Sts - Rockefeller Ctr
Phone: 212-974-2020
Web: www.brasserieruhlmann.com
Prices: $$$

Lunch & dinner daily

Named for the French designer, Émile-Jacques Ruhlmann, this stunning brasserie is the work of Jean Denoyer (also of Orsay). Just across from Rockefeller Center's Sunken Plaza, Brasserie Ruhlmann is a glamorous draw for both business and pleasure. Atop its bold mosaic-tiled floors, the space is elegantly wrapped in a glossy faux-ebony veneer, enhancing the glowing silver sconces and red velvet furnishings.

The commendable kitchen honors its classical conceit, yet flirts with contemporary global cuisine. The menu features raw bar treats in addition to beef carpaccio "vitello tonnato-style." NY steak *au poivre* is perfectly seared to specification, presented in a hot cast iron pan, and accompanied by Cognac cream infused with briny green peppercorns.

Casa Nonna

Italian ✗✗

B3

310 W. 38th St. (bet. Eighth & Ninth Aves.)

Subway: Times Sq - 42 St
Phone: 212-736-3000
Web: www.casanonna.com
Prices: $$

Lunch Mon – Fri
Dinner nightly

Quaint sounding Casa Nonna is actually a behemoth of a restaurant run by an international dining group. A boon to garment district workers and suburban commuters, this sprawling, multi-room space is just a few blocks away from bustling Penn Station and the Port Authority bus terminal.

There is a dish for every taste at Casa Nonna, whose attractive menu is replete with satisfying and well prepared Roman and Tuscan fare. Panini and Neapolitan-style pizza are popular during lunchtime, while dinner serves a hearty lineup of *primi* such as *tagliolini frutti di mare*, with fine breadcrumbs clinging the vibrant tomato sauce to the pasta. Entrées feature grilled Cornish hen, spiced *alla diavola*-style with garlic, lemon, and hot pepper.

Casellula

C1

American 🍴

401 W. 52nd St. (bet. Ninth & Tenth Aves.)

Subway: 50 St (Eighth Ave.)   Dinner nightly
Phone: 212-247-8137
Web: www.casellula.com
Prices: $$

 Casellula oozes with warmth in both look and feel. Dark wood tables, exposed brick, and flickering votives are a sight for sore eyes, while the delightful staff is so attentive and friendly, that you may never want to leave.

Small plates are big here, while medium plates feature yummy sandwiches (crunchy *muffulettas* stuffed with fontina and cured meats) and tasty shrimp tacos splashed with *salsa verde*. Pity the lactose intolerant, as cheese (and lots of it) followed by dessert (maybe a pumpkin ice cream "sandwich" pecked with brown butter caramel?) are part and parcel of the special experience at this petite place. Feeling blue? They've got that and much more with over 50 different varieties, perfectly complemented by an excellent and vast wine list.

Chez Napoléon

C2

French 🍴

365 W. 50th St. (bet. Eighth & Ninth Aves.)

Subway: 50 St (Eighth Ave.)   Lunch Mon – Fri
Phone: 212-265-6980   Dinner Mon – Sat
Web: www.cheznapoléon.com
Prices: $$

Oh so popular and family-run by the Brunos since 1982, this atmospheric *bijou* is not to be missed for its unapologetically creamy and butter-dreamy plates of traditional French cuisine. It's not polite to discuss age, but let's just say that Chef/*grandmère*, Marguerite Bruno, has steadily commanded this kitchen for an impressive tenure.

The scene is *magnifique*. Take in the creaky wood floors and parchment-colored walls hung with French-themed jigsaw puzzles, then indulge in chilled silky leeks dressed with the famous house vinaigrette; sautéed veal kidneys in mustard-cream sauce; and steak *au poivre* with black or green peppercorn sauce. Plan ahead when ordering so you have time (and space) for a classic dessert soufflé sided with crème anglaise.

Cho Dang Gol ☺

C4

Korean 🍴

55 W. 35th St. (bet. Fifth & Sixth Aves.)

Subway: 34 St - Herald Sq
Phone: 212-695-8222
Web: www.chodanggolny.com
Prices: ☺☺

Lunch & dinner daily

Among the delicious offerings that comprise the *banchan* welcoming diners to this hopping K-town spot, take note of the tofu. Warm, fluffy, and house-made, it's just one of the reasons why Cho Dang Gol is a standout for Korean cuisine. In fact, the restaurant is named for a South Korean village famous for its soybean curd. Next in line for your attention is the listing of bubbling hot *jjigae* (stew). House varieties of this include short rib with taro and glass noodles; or a wild sesame-and-mushroom casserole.

Though the staff can be brusquely efficient—a product of the high business volume—Korean artifacts and rustic wooden tables lend a sweet sentimentality to the place that, combined with the fresh, high-quality food, make it well worth a visit.

Clement

B4

Contemporary 🍴🍴🍴

700 Fifth Ave. (at 55th St.)

Subway: 5 Av - 53 St
Phone: 212-956-2888
Web: www.peninsula.com/NewYork
Prices: $$$

Lunch daily
Dinner Tue – Sat

This freshly christened bar and dining room is one of the lucky few to call the Peninsula New York home. Created by design firm Yabu Pushelberg, the posh setting includes a series of rooms, each with their own striking touches that sprawl from a thickly carpeted staircase off the lobby. Worth a mention is the book room, with its stacks of bound-linen rag paper, mauve fabrics, and fresh flowers in mercury glasses.

Out in the kitchen, a talented team sends out ambitious preparations like the locally sourced scallop composition pairing carpaccio zested by pink grapefruit and yuzu with seared specimens swiped by sunchoke foam. Another winner is crisp-skinned black bass set beside maitake mushrooms and gussied up tableside with roasted duck broth.

Daisy May's BBQ

Barbecue ✗

B2

623 Eleventh Ave. (at 46th St.)

Subway: 50 St (Eighth Ave.)
Phone: 212-977-1500
Web: www.daisymaysbbq.com
Prices: 🍲🍲

Lunch & dinner daily

Trek to the ends of the earth (known to some as Eleventh Avenue), and the barbecue gods will reward you. Welcome to Daisy May's BBQ—where Chef/owner (and cookbook author) Adam Perry Lang's smoky, succulent 'cue served up in a big old dining hall (think school lunchroom-meets-barn) counts everyone from Oprah and bike messengers to midtown suits as fans.

Three chalkboards list the pig specials: a whole pig for up to 12 people (should you be blessed with so many friends); half a pig; and a few daily specials. The house pulled pork, a mound of tender, glistening sweet and smoky meat, is a fan favorite for good reason. A limited selection of beer and wine is available to wash it all down, but our money's on the irresistibly sweet and minty iced tea.

Danji

Korean ✗

C1

346 W. 52nd St. (bet. Eighth & Ninth Aves.)

Subway: 50 St (Eighth Ave.)
Phone: 212-586-2880
Web: www.danjinyc.com
Prices: $$

Lunch Mon – Fri
Dinner Mon – Sat

The festive spirit at Chef Hooni Kim's Hell's Kitchen baby is thanks to the dominance of communal tables filling up the small, well-designed space. Attractive appointments like silk panels, pottery, and a striking display of spoons are further enhanced by a flattering lighting scheme.

While Danji's menu may have lost some of its luster of late, there's no denying that the Korean small plates prepared here are a refreshed take on specialties. Spicy whelk salad is a pick from the traditional portion of the carte and combines steamed mollusks from Maine with buckwheat noodles and a too sweet-and-spicy dressing accented with herbs. The menu's modern side offers "eggs" over rice, layering warm kernels with cod roe, green onion, and a runny quail yolk.

db Bistro Moderne

D3

Contemporary ✕✕

55 W. 44th St. (bet. Fifth & Sixth Aves.)

Subway: 5 Av
Phone: 212-391-2400
Web: www.dbbistro.com
Prices: $$$

Lunch & dinner daily

A face-lift by Jeffrey Beers has ushered in a contemporary look for Chef Daniel Boulud's midtown canteen. The front lounge is abuzz with post-work and pre-theater gaggles, while well-behaved crowds in the back are seated in a walnut-paneled space dressed with mirrors and black-and-white photography.

Like its setting, the menu has been refreshed and unites classic bistro cooking with market-inspired creations. The lush *pâté en croute* is a buttery pastry encasing layers of creamy country pâté, guinea hen, and foie gras, dressed with huckleberry compote, toasted pine nuts, and pickled enoki mushrooms. Wild rice-crusted fluke presented with Hawaiian blue prawn and sauce *Américaine* demonstrates the kitchen's contemporary leanings.

Del Frisco's

A4

Steakhouse ✕✕✕

1221 Sixth Ave. (at 49th St.)

Subway: 47-50 Sts - Rockefeller Ctr
Phone: 212-575-5129
Web: www.delfriscos.com
Prices: $$$

Lunch Mon – Fri
Dinner nightly

Prime, aged, corn-fed beef is the main attraction at this sprawling, outrageously successful outpost of the Dallas-based steakhouse chain. Portions range from the petite filet to a 24-ounce Porterhouse that will make any Texan proud. The menu begins with a suitably rich feast of cheesesteak egg rolls or white clam flatbread; but then does an about face with knife-and-fork Caesar salad. Lunch is an affordable way to sample their classics.

Complementing its McGraw-Hill Building home, Del Frisco's flaunts a masculine look with a large L-shaped bar, dramatic wrought-iron balcony, wood accents, and towering windows. The mezzanine dining area, accessible by a sweeping staircase, enjoys a quieter ambience.

Also try Del Frisco's Grille in Rockefeller Plaza.

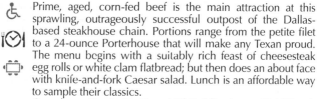

Don Antonio by Starita 🏮

C2

Pizza ✗✗

309 W. 50th St. (bet. Eighth & Ninth Aves.)

Subway: 50 St (Eighth Ave.)
Phone: 646-719-1043
Web: www.donantoniopizza.com
Prices: $$

Lunch & dinner daily

Hell's Kitchen's best pizzeria boasts serious street cred. The namesake original in Naples has been in operation since 1901, while this outpost is run by pizza maestros, Antonio Starita and Roberto Caporuscio. Always busy, the setting features a red-tiled domed pizza oven and walls lined with art depicting volcanoes—this calls to mind the logo of Caporuscio's other pizza hot spot, Kesté.

The lightly-fried, wood-fire finished *montanara Starita* is a house specialty. An array of other fried and filled pies feature a first-rate listing of *pizze rosse, pizze bianchi,* and even gluten-free options. The *speciale* has included the Guiseppe spread with earthy artichoke purée beneath gobs of melted house-made mozzarella, and drizzles of olive oil.

Esca

B2

Seafood ✗✗

402 W. 43rd St. (bet. Ninth & Tenth Aves.)

Subway: 42 St - Port Authority Bus Terminal
Phone: 212-564-7272
Web: www.esca-nyc.com
Prices: $$$

Lunch Mon – Sat
Dinner nightly

Chef David Pasternack's Italian-style seafood has kept this theater district mainstay hopping for fifteen years now. The two-room space is cozy and boasts a rustic charm with its lemon-yellow walls and displayed wine storage.

The steady kitchen turns out consistently impressive cuisine that starts off with a listing of crudo, such as petals of pale pink seabream simply but impeccably dressed with Meyer lemon-infused olive oil, Amangansett sea salt, and black pepper. Other plates reveal seared monkfish liver, custard-soft within, served atop radicchio, organic grains, and candied citrus. The house-made *bucatini* with Rita's spicy octopus sauce is deliciously zesty. Dessert may highlight a semolina pudding with caramel sauce and vanilla yogurt.

Estiatorio Milos

Greek

A3

125 W. 55th St. (bet. Sixth & Seventh Aves.)

Subway: 57 St
Phone: 212-245-7400
Web: www.milos.ca
Prices: $$$

Lunch & dinner daily

This Greek restaurant offers such a deliciously singular focus on the sea that dinner here feels like a relaxing jaunt to the Mediterranean coast. Feast your eyes on the ever-present bounty of iced fish, flown in fresh and displayed in the back of the cavernous room where a well-dressed, business-minded crowd gathers.

Oregano plants atop each table are snipped into bowls of olive oil to accompany the fine bread that precedes the selection of raw bar specialties and grilled fish. The day's bounty may reveal charred *barbouni*, or red mullet, dressed with olive oil, capers, and a sprig of flat leaf parsley. Side dishes unveil *chtipiti*—a mouthwatering spread made from roasted red peppers and barrel-aged feta that you'll want to slather on everything.

etcetera etcetera

Italian 💥💥

C2

352 W. 44th St. (bet. Eighth & Ninth Aves.)

Subway: 42 St - Port Authority Bus Terminal
Phone: 212-399-4141
Web: www.etcetcnyc.com
Prices: $$

Lunch Wed & Sun
Dinner nightly

Cool grey, stone, and dark glossy woods frame the interior of this dining room's chic and contemporary Milanese look. Though etcetera etcetera is open for lunch just once during the week, it remains a huge draw for theatergoers on their way to a matinee.

 A long listing of pasta, available as a half or full portion, includes fine dishes like thin strands of house-made basil-spaghetti tossed with crabmeat, roasted sweet peppers, and a dab of tomato. Untussy cooking is evident in entrées like pan-roasted grouper with cipollini onions, artichokes, fingerling potatoes, and black olives. Excellent rosemary focaccia accompanied by fragrant olive oil, and cookies served with coffee are gracious touches that enhance the dining experience.

44 & X Hell's Kitchen

American ✗✗

B2

622 Tenth Ave. (at 44th St.)

Subway: 42 St - Port Authority Bus Terminal   Lunch & dinner daily
Phone: 212-977-1170
Web: www.44andx.com
Prices: $$

The moniker is a mouthful, but this modern bistro's endearing appeal has attracted eclectic crowds since opening on a block west of no-man's land. Today, this corner of Hell's Kitchen is a solid, mature venue that offers plenty of reason to swing by. Cute servers in black t-shirts are gracious and attentive, presenting updated renditions of spirited comfort food. Lobster tacos with charred tomato salsa, crunchy buttermilk fried chicken accompanied by a chive waffle and maple syrup jus, as well as pan-roasted mahi mahi with lobster and scallop risotto emerge from the skilled kitchen. House-baked apple pie was a lovely sweet special to ward off the chill of an autumn evening.
Sister spot 44 ½ boasts a menu of Asian and Mediterranean influences.

Frankie & Johnnie's

Steakhouse ✗✗

C4

32 W. 37th St. (bet. Fifth & Sixth Aves.)

Subway: 34 St - Herald Sq   Lunch Mon – Fri
Phone: 212-947-8940   Dinner Mon – Sat
Web: www.frankieandjohnnies.com
Prices: $$$

You get a slice of history with your perfectly-seared ribeye at this storied Garment District steakhouse. The renovated townhouse—with its masculine sensibility and cozy wood-paneled library-turned upstairs dining room—used to belong to actor John Drew Barrymore, and it is the second of three sibling restaurants that began in 1926. (The first restaurant is a stone's throw away and the third location resides in Rye, New York.)
Served by a professional, all-male brigade, the food is pure steakhouse bliss: think silky clams casino, topped with crispy bacon and scallions; or tender, bone-in ribeye, seared to rosy perfection and served with irresistibly crisp hashbrowns. Buttery, flaky apple strudel delivered with fresh whipped cream is a knockout finale.

Gallagher's

C2

Steakhouse ✕✕

228 W. 52nd St. (bet. Broadway & Eighth Ave.)

Subway: 50 St (Broadway)
Phone: 212-586-5000
Web: www.gallaghersnysteakhouse.com
Prices: $$$

Lunch & dinner daily

A multi-million dollar renovation hasn't glossed over any of Gallagher's iconic character. Walls covered with photos of horses and jockeys harken back to the 85-year-old stallion's former proximity to the old Madison Square Garden. The menu's "other soup" is a sly reference held over from Prohibition days; and diners still walk past the window-fronted meat locker where slabs of USDA Prime beef are dry-aged.

Gallagher's fresh sparkle is exhibited by the kitchen, on display behind glass panes, which turns out contemporary-minded fare like hamachi crudo plated with a yuzu-jalapeño vinaigrette to go with choice cuts of meat grilled over hickory. The rib steak is a bone-in ribeye that arrives mouthwateringly tender with a side of warm and savory house sauce.

Gaonnuri

C4

Korean ✕✕

1250 Broadway (at 32nd St.)

Subway: 34 St - Herald Sq
Phone: 212-971-9045
Web: www.gaonnurinyc.com
Prices: $$$

Lunch & dinner Mon – Sat

Don't let the security checkpoint, the bland lobby, or the fact that you'll need to take the express elevator up 39 floors dissuade you. A grand entrance and charming hostess await. The modern space is beautifully designed with round windows to emphasize the skyline views from every table, each of which is equipped with its own barbecue and downdraft vent (this is no smoke-filled barbecue joint).

The very fine cuisine is fragrant, approachable, and hewn's back, in addition with classics like sizzling *bibimbap*—rice that develops a tantalizing crust, served in a hot stone bowl topped with tofu, fresh vegetables, kimchi, and a raw egg. Fish dishes include the black cod *jorim jungsik*, simmered until tender, with crunchy daikon in a tangy-spicy sauce.

Hakkasan ✿

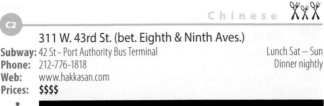

Chinese XXX

C2

311 W. 43rd St. (bet. Eighth & Ninth Aves.)

Subway: 42 St - Port Authority Bus Terminal
Phone: 212-776-1818
Web: www.hakkasan.com
Prices: $$$$

Lunch Sat – Sun
Dinner nightly

This Manhattan outpost of the global and modern Cantonese-dining brand commands a somewhat meh stretch of Hell's Kitchen. But while Hakkasan's understated façade is anything but remarkable, its stunning white Carrara marble-clad corridor opens into a world of over-the-top luxury.

Inside, the massive, cavern-like arena is cut down to human-scale proportions by a series of alcoves and nooks. Ylang-ylang scented candles and jolts of cobalt and fuchsia set dark-toned millwork and silk-embroidered leather banquettes aglow as groups—and the occasional celebrity—pluck stellar dim sum. These immaculate works of edible art are painstakingly formed, cleverly presented, and outstandingly delicious. One bite from the Hakka fried dumplings reveals what all the fuss is about. The menu is an extensive listing of mostly hits, such as crispy rings of tender salt-and-pepper squid showered with bits of fried garlic; and *sha cha* seafood *toban*, a mélange of succulent prawns, scallops, and white fish tossed with green soybeans in a mouthwatering, subtly spicy brown sauce.

For dessert, coconut milk panna cotta with rum-roasted pineapple and pistachio gelato demonstrates the kitchen's multi-disciplinary skill.

Hell's Kitchen

C2 Mexican ✗✗

679 Ninth Ave. (bet. 46th & 47th Sts.)

Subway: 50 St (Eighth Ave.)   Dinner nightly
Phone: 212-977-1588
Web: www.hellskitchen-nyc.com
Prices: $$

This progressive Mexican eatery continues to be a go-to spot for smart south-of-the-border dining. Intimate in scale and tastefully done with dark stone flooring, colorful glass tiles at the bar, and polished copper accents, the dining room often fills up quickly. Delightful preparation is the key to the success at Hell's Kitchen.

This isn't a chips and salsa kind of place; instead, diners are served wedges of cornbread and black bean purée to ward off hunger. The evening's specials may offer a *tlacoyo* trio of griddled masa rounds topped with earthy *huitlacoche*, chorizo crumbles, and shrimp dressed with tomatillo salsa. Entrées have included perfectly caramelized, maple-glazed pork loin sided with roasted *poblano chilaquiles* and spicy salsa.

Keens

C4 Steakhouse ✗✗

72 W. 36th St. (bet. Fifth & Sixth Aves.)

Subway: 34 St - Herald Sq   Lunch Mon – Fri
Phone: 212-947-3636   Dinner nightly
Web: www.keens.com
Prices: $$$

When it comes to steakhouses, Keens is a New York original. Dating back to 1885, these rooms (the Lincoln, Lamb's, and Lillie Langtry) are imbued with Gilded Age charisma. Large tables are closely arranged under low ceilings lined with clay churchwarden pipes—a vestige of Keens' men-only, smoker's club days.

Every night brings a full house of big appetites for belly-busting cuts of meat. Signature favorites include the mutton chop and Porterhouse sized for two or more, dry aged in house to achieve nutty perfection. For the complete experience, cover your table with fantastic sides like creamed spinach and hashbrowns.

The Pub Room pours one of the most extensive selections of single malt Scotch around—happy hour brings complimentary nibbles.

Kirakuya

🍜

C4

2 W. 32nd St. (bet. Broadway & Fifth Ave.)

Subway: 34 St - Herald Sq
Phone: 212-695-7272
Web: www.sakebarkirakuya.com
Prices: $$

Lunch Mon – Fri
Dinner Mon – Sat

Located on the second floor of a nondescript building, this authentic *izakaya* buried in K-town feels exotic and unexpected. Out the elevator and beyond the dim (even dingy) hallway, your welcome will be warm and energetic. The long room is clad in dark brown wood, but bright with large windows and very good service. Take it as an auspicious sign that Japanese is spoken at many of the tables.

Midday is limited to the budget-friendly lunch set, as in a tasty *shio saba* meal of grilled mackerel with a salad, miso soup, and pickles. The wide-ranging evening menu includes overnight dried squid, Berkshire pork belly in a sweet soy sauce, *tsukune* (grilled chicken meatball), and a few Western-influenced snacks like French fries with rosemary salt.

Kristalbelli

🍴🍴

C4

8 W. 36th St. (bet. Fifth & Sixth Aves.)

Subway: 34 St - Herald Sq
Phone: 212-290-2211
Web: www.kristalbelli.com
Prices: $$$

Lunch Mon – Sat
Dinner nightly

Turning up the heat in the dreary Garment District, Kristalbelli is a sexy harbinger of this fast-changing neighborhood. Outside, a gray slate- and marble-façade plus impressive wooden door imply opulence; inside, crystal barbecue grills set on grey marble framed by a jolly gold monk make table-top dining over-the-top. The fun and bling continues upstairs in the young, hip, and hopping lounge.

Yet amid all this glitz and glam is a well-trained service team and very talented kitchen. *Banchan* opens with a superlative assortment that might include green chilies with fermented bean paste, marinated mushrooms, cold egg custard with scallions, and kimchi. A sparkling signature crystal bowl does not distract from the deeply flavored, almost buttery ribeye.

Kunjip

C4

Korean ✗

9 W 32nd St. (bet. Broadway & Fifth Ave.)

Subway: 34 St - Herald Sq
Phone: 212-216-9487
Web: www.kunjip.com
Prices: ⊜⊜

Lunch & dinner daily

One of K-town's better recommendations, this ever-bustling restaurant is open 24-hours a day, seven days a week. Prepare yourself to be immersed in a noisy setting, wafting with food aromas, where orange-shirted servers whiz by, balancing trays heaped with plates of *banchan*, sizzling stone bowls of *bibimbap*, or empty dishes from instantly re-set tables.

You may feel compelled to order right away as the line out the door makes for a less than leisurely ambience, but relax. The staff is pleasant and the vast menu is worth perusing. Find specialties like *mae woon dduk boki*—a saucy stew of pan-fried rice cake tossed with softened white onion, plenty of scallions, mung bean noodles, and fish cake all tossed with spicy, sweet, and rich *gochujang*.

La Masseria

C2

Italian ✗✗

235 W. 48th St. (bet. Broadway & Eighth Ave.)

Subway: 50 St (Eighth Ave.)
Phone: 212-582-2111
Web: www.lamasserianyc.com
Prices: $$

Lunch & dinner daily

La Masseria is a popular and bright Theater District destination, but it's also a wonderfully cozy place where stone, stucco walls, and exposed wood beams add farmhouse-style warmth. The restaurant's convenient location ensures that the large dining room is a routinely full house, and spot-on service delivered by a smartly attired team keeps the conviviality stoked.

When it comes to the food, La Masseria chooses simplicity over theatrics in its Puglia-influenced menu. There are no distractions on a plate of roasted baby artichoke hearts draped with Taleggio *fonduta*, or in a bowl of *grannato* cooked risotto-style stocked with white beans and shellfish. Pasta is *fatta in casa*; and entrées include oven-roasted rabbit with herbs and wine sauce.

The Lambs Club

C3

132 W. 44th St. (bet. Broadway & Sixth Ave.)

Subway: Times Sq - 42 St   Lunch & dinner daily
Phone: 212-997-5262
Web: www.thelambsclub.com
Prices: $$$

On a storied stretch dotted by blue-blooded social institutions and boutique hotels (like the Chatwal which also happens to be its home) find The Lamb's Club, named for the theater group that once resided here. Helmed by Chef/restaurateur Geoffrey Zakarian and reimagined by designer Thierry Despont, this handsome retreat is a glamorous art deco backdrop of ebonized walls and red leather seating set aglow by stainless steel torchieres and a fireplace.

It's a fitting scene for the novel American food that follows. Try slow-poached halibut with crispy frog's legs and licorice herbs, paired with seasonal sides like roasted carrots with prune purée and pecan granola. End with apple crisp "tatin" sandwiching flaky pastry, roasted apples, and caramel mousse.

Landmark Tavern

B2

626 Eleventh Ave. (at 46th St.)

Subway: 50 St (Eighth Ave.)   Lunch & dinner daily
Phone: 212-247-2562
Web: www.thelandmarktavern.com
Prices: $$

Step inside and sense the history. Originally built in 1868, the setting is warm with penny-tile flooring, mahogany woodwork, and stained glass panels. The pub is located in one of the last remaining wild stretches of the island, too far west to attract attention, though gleaming residential towers, boutique hotels, and creative agencies have recently started popping up. Still, service is friendly and speaks with a genuine Irish accent.

The tavern's highly enjoyable pub grub presents bangers and a fluffy mound of mashed potatoes dotted with sweet peas and ladled with brown onion gravy; beer-battered fish and chips; or corned beef with boiled potatoes. End your meal with a boozy coffee, fortified with a wee nip of Irish whiskey or Bailey's.

Lan Sheng

Chinese ⚔

C3

60 W. 39th St. (bet. Fifth & Sixth Aves.)

Subway: 42 St - Bryant Pk
Phone: 212-575 8899
Web: N/A
Prices: $$

Lunch & dinner daily

Midday hordes gathered outside its plain-Jane façade evidences the popularity of this midtown Sichuan stop. The pleasant and comfy interior fashioned from high-backed banquettes, wood-carved wall hangings, and colorful accent lights provides a respite once you make it through the doors. Recent experiences have indicated inconsistent cooking, but the fiery and smoky specialties here are still praiseworthy. Nibble on a crispy pile of camphor tea-smoked duck while waiting for the standout items to arrive. These may include miso- and chili-simmered whole fish showered with green onion; strips of bitter melon dressed with black bean sauce; as well as shredded potatoes shined with oil, vinegar, and hit with dried red plus thinly sliced green chilies.

Larb Ubol 😋

Thai ⚔

B3

480 Ninth Ave. (bet. 36th & 37th Sts.)

Subway: 34 St - Penn Station
Phone: 212-564-1822
Web: www.larbubol.com
Prices: 😋😋

Lunch & dinner daily

Chef Ratchanee Sumpatboon is cooking up her own delicious Isaan-Thai storm in Hell's Kitchen. Inconspicuously lodged between Penn Station and Port Authority, Larb Ubol is tidy, cheerful, and dressed with colorful fabrics.

The *som tom kort muar* is cool and limey yet very spicy with green and red chilies dotting the crunchy mound of lettuce, green papaya, rice noodles, and fried pork rind. Savory and satisfying *pla dook larb*, a spicy ground catfish salad, combines wild ginger, fresh mint, and lime. The deep fried pork belly, *pad puff moo krub*, is rendered crisp yet wonderfully chewy, then stir-fried with chopped eggplant, sweet red pepper, and red curry paste. Cool off with a scoop of coconut ice cream garnished with preserved palm seeds.

Le Bernardin ✽✽✽

Seafood XXXX

A4

155 W. 51st St. (bet. Sixth & Seventh Aves.)

Subway: 50 St (Broadway)
Phone: 212-554-1515
Web: www.le-bernardin.com
Prices: $$$$

Lunch Mon – Fri
Dinner Mon – Sat

Quietly situated at the base of a midtown tower and obscured by shaded windows, Le Bernardin is anything but nondescript. Every aspect of its restful, earthy décor conveys something new: silvery rippled fabric walls to conjure the sea; plush carpeting with subtle rings reminiscent of sea creatures; and the triptych "Deep Water No. 1" as a dramatic focal point. No matter the time or day, there is sure to be a full house of expense account holders and dressy tourists.

While Chef Eric Ripert's signature cooking may combine myriad global accents, this is classically rooted seafood cuisine at its very best. From the "Almost Raw" offerings, find neat rows of sweet scallops and creamy uni contrasted with a brunoise of pickled Granny Smith apple, bits of red chili, chive snips, and Meyer lemon vinaigrette. "Barely Touched" dishes include lobster lasagna composed of fresh pasta sheets, steamed lobster, a touch of roasted tomato, and a luxurious yet not overly rich black truffle-butter sauce.

A clever and highly enjoyable reconfiguration of Chinese flavors is found in the "Lightly Cooked" black bass, amber-brown at the edge and moist within, finished tableside with a riff on hot and sour soup.

Lugo Caffé

B3

Italian 🍴🍴

1 Penn Plaza (entrance on 33rd St.)

Subway: 34 St - Penn Station
Phone: 212-760-2700
Web: www.lugocaffe.com
Prices: $$

Lunch Mon – Fri
Dinner Mon – Sat

In a blah locale that's overshadowed by crowds spilling from Penn Station and Madison Square Garden, Luggo Caffe shines bright as a recommendation for Italian eats. A boisterous scene prevails, as the bar and dining room are overwhelmingly popular among business folk. Light streaming in from the floor-to-ceiling windows shows off a white-tiled bar area and black-and-white photography. A pastel-green Vespa adds an extra dose of charm.

Tables receive a satisfying array of items like warm hand-pulled mozzarella, Neapolitan-style pizza, and zesty entrées like Mediterranean branzino with spicy *puttanesca*. Pasta is deftly prepared and certainly a worthy indulgence, especially the tiny ridged tubes of *rigatoncini* coated with slow-cooked, meaty Bolognese.

Madangsui

C4

Korean 🍴

35 W. 35th St. (bet. Fifth & Sixth Aves.)

Subway: 34 St - Herald Sq
Phone: 212-564-9333
Web: www.madangsui.com
Prices: $$

Lunch & dinner daily

The air is calmer here than at other K-town spots, and it's much fresher too—thanks to a good ventilation system that keeps the smoky scent of Korean barbecue sizzling on those tabletop grills at bay. Upon entering, find shelves displaying numerous cuts of meat, a homely yet authentic touch in an otherwise pleasant setting. The staff is genuinely friendly and eager to please.

Soy marinated ribeye *bulgogi*, a thinly sliced brisket *chadol-baegi*, and fresh pork belly *saeng samgyeopsal* are some of Madangsui's grilling go-to's. Also find a full roster of traditional specialties here, like *nak ji dol sot bibimbap*, a hearty portion of fluffy rice served in a viciously hot stone bowl topped with a saucy-spicy mixture of diced bits of octopus and vegetables.

Mandoo Bar

Korean ✗

C4

2 W. 32nd St. (bet. Broadway & Fifth Ave.)

Subway: 34 St - Herald Sq
Phone: 212-279-3075
Web: N/A
Prices: 🍪

Lunch & dinner daily

Whether steamed, fried, spicy or not, Mandoo is always Korean for "dumpling," and every kind you can dream up is served here as unique, tidy little bundles. This postage stamp-sized K-town favorite keeps its massive number of customers happy with an array of freshly made, unassuming food, dished out fast enough to keep weekend shoppers on the move.

Meals may begin with the likes of pan-fried dumplings filled with pork and vegetables (*goon mandoo*); bite-sized and boiled baby *mandoo*; or the combo *mandoo* with fillings of seafood, vegetables, and pork. Korean-style spicy beef soup (*yuk kae jang*) and acorn or buckwheat flour noodle dishes tossed with a citrus vinaigrette, sesame seeds, scallions, and cilantro are fine and worthy accompaniments.

Má Pêche

Fusion ✗✗

B4

15 W. 56th St. (bet. Fifth & Sixth Aves.)

Subway: 57 St
Phone: 212-757-5878
Web: www.momofuku.com
Prices: $$

Lunch Mon – Sat
Dinner nightly

Midtown's version of Momofuku is a soaring space furnished in blonde wood and located on the lower level of the Chambers hotel. Like all siblings, this "Lucky Peach" family member strives to make its own voice heard—and, thanks to Chef Paul Carmichael, it does so successfully.

Dim sum is the name of the game here, and stimulating small plates are wheeled around the canvas-wrapped expanse. The mega chain's iconic pork buns are presented on their own cart in mini bamboo steamers. A raw bar wagon is stocked with torched sea scallop crudo dressed with yuzu and olive oil; and hot treats include succulent jerk chicken wings. Be sure to save room for dessert, as goodies from Milk Bar star and may include birthday cake truffles, or blueberry-miso soft-serve.

Marea ❀ ❀

Seafood 🍴🍴🍴

D1

240 Central Park South (bet. Broadway & Seventh Ave.)

Subway: 59 St - Columbus Circle   Lunch & dinner daily
Phone: 212-582-5100
Web: www.marea-nyc.com
Prices: $$$$

Idyllically seated at the base of Central Park amid midtown towers, Marea functions like the remote office of the media elite. Service is on the ball and very capable of managing the high-energy crowds of big personalities. The dining room has that certain Manhattan sensibility that is at once dressy and contemporary but never fussy. It screams the kind of money and taste that carries not a glint of flash. To the left of the entrance, find an attractive and popular bar area; if true-blue New York sophisticates sought their ideal venue to speed-date, they'd find it here.

Chef Michael White asserts his genius time and again through signature dishes that are not to be missed. Beautifully cooked octopus may sound excessively complex when paired with smoked potatoes, pickled red onions, chilies, and tonnato sauce, but each element is used in subtle quantity, with a certain restrained harmony that leaves you wanting more. Generous portions of *strozzapretti* bring humble pasta to new heights in a balanced and complementary sauce of briny sea urchin, sweet crab, tomatoes, and basil.

Desserts are elegant and precise, yet manage to layer flavor upon flavor in a contemporary composition of chocolate.

Marseille

French ✕✕

C2

630 Ninth Ave. (at 44th St.)

Subway: 42 St - Port Authority Bus Terminal   Lunch & dinner daily
Phone: 212-333-2323
Web: www.marseillenyc.com
Prices: $$

Marseille marries the charm of a classic French bistro with the inimitable style of New York City. The sexy, soft golden glow, convivial spirit, and superlative Theater District location make it a popular choice for everyone from tourists craving a taste of Broadway to colleagues cooling off after a day's work. The skilled and truly professional kitchen prepares an impressive cuisine bursting with pronounced, balanced flavors. From salads and seasonal specials to more French-formed entrées like steak frites, there is something for everyone. Hungry diners appreciate that the portions lean toward American sensibilities; while the budget-conscious value the prix-fixe lunch and dinner menus. Don't skip out without the frites—they may be the best in the city.

Mercato 😊

Italian ✕

B3

352 W. 39th St. (bet. Eighth & Ninth Aves.)

Subway: 42 St - Port Authority Bus Terminal   Lunch & dinner daily
Phone: 212-643-2000
Web: www.mercatonyc.com
Prices: $$

By virtue of its location on spirited 39th Street, Mercato sees a torrent of visitors filling its invitingly rustic domain. But address aside, this inviting trattoria is routinely mobbed for its very nice and well-priced cuisine prepared with a delicious *Pugliese* accent.

Mercato's look includes a high-ceilinged front bar leading to a cozy back room, all furnished with rustic woods, polished concrete, and exposed brick. The extensive antipasti selection includes fresh and decadent *stracciatella* cheese served with speck; fava bean purée with chicory and extra virgin olive oil; and grilled whole sardines with *salmoriglio*. The long list of excellent pastas has featured a special of house-made fusilli tossed in slow-cooked pork ragú with *cavolo nero*.

Masa ✿ ✿ ✿

C1

10 Columbus Circle (in the Time Warner Center)

Subway: 59 St - Columbus Circle
Phone: 212-823-9800
Web: www.masanyc.com
Prices: $$$$

Lunch Tue – Fri
Dinner Mon – Sat

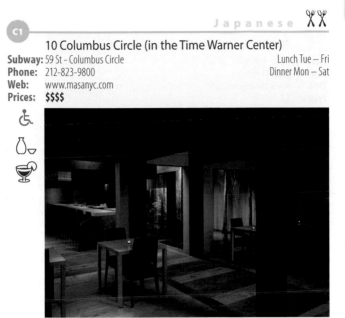

To taste what may be the continent's best sushi, experience the quiet, contemplative, and very exclusive ceremony of Chef Masa Takayama's omakase. Through the heavy wooden door, discover a room that is as unchanging and calming as a river stone, set amid blonde *hinoki* wood and a gargantuan forsythia tree. Yes, you'll forget it's on the fourth floor of a mall.

Attention to detail is unsurpassed; that bespoke Japanese porcelain seems designed specifically for the sweet shrimp it holds. Service displays the same smooth grace, unobtrusive yet at-the-ready with their hot towels, fingerbowls, tea, and touches of pedagogy or insight. Don't let their tendency to upsell extra courses mar your pleasure.

A seaweed salad of vinegar-seasoned jellyfish awakens the palate to the subtle progression of courses that follow. Masterful proportion and elemental balance is unparalleled in the mind-melting toro tartare with oily grains of Californian osetra caviar and toasted bread for crunch. Yet Masa truly distinguishes itself with its parade of sushi showcasing the best of Tokyo's Tsukiji market. Expect phenomenal aji mackerel with grated yuzu, traditional *unagi*, and an indelible finish of toro *temaki*.

Miss Korea

Korean ✗✗

C4

10 W. 32nd St. (bet. Broadway & Fifth Ave.)

Subway: 34 St - Herald Sq   Lunch & dinner daily
Phone: 212-594-4963
Web: www.misskoreabbq.com
Prices: $$

If K-Town were a music arena, Miss Korea would be the headliner. Window-lined and perched above the crowded street level with an ambience that feels equally elevated, it has a unique personality that outshines the competition. Settle into the ground floor or head up a labyrinth of stairs to enter another pleasant dining room filled with tropical accents, tabletop grills, and cozy dining nooks.

This lady is loved by many, so go with a group to really explore the menu and indulge in authentic *japchae* stir-fried with beef and veggies, or flaky seafood pancakes. *Dolsot bibimbap* highlights crusty rice spiced with kimchi and *gochujang*, while pork *mandoo* are extra divine when dunked in light soy. Barbecue pork belly is praiseworthy if not prize-winning.

Molyvos

Greek ✗✗

A3

871 Seventh Ave. (bet. 55th & 56th Sts.)

Subway: 57 St - 7 Av   Lunch & dinner daily
Phone: 212-582-7500
Web: www.molyvos.com
Prices: $$

Enter this popular home to Greek gourmands and Carnegie Hall patrons to find a stacked display of Chef/partner Jim Botsacos' cookbook *New Greek Cuisine*—a confident yet auspicious welcome to Molyvos's laudable cooking. The upscale dining room basks in a creamy palette with touches of warm orange and black-and-white photography. The bar area is more casual, with bare tables and woven placemats.

The menu boasts *mezedes* like lamb pie with *vlahotiri* cheese, and classic *piperies yemistes* that stuff roasted red peppers with a zesty mixture of rice, tomato, dill and *manouri* cheese. Strained yogurt with quince compote and toasted almonds is a sweet finish. An interesting list of Greek wines, Mediterranean beers, and ouzo is deliciously suited to the cooking.

The Modern ✿

Contemporary 🍴🍴🍴

B4

9 W. 53rd St. (bet. Fifth & Sixth Aves.)

Subway: 5 Av - 53 St
Phone: 212-333-1220
Web: www.themodernnyc.com
Prices: $$$$

Lunch Mon – Fri
Dinner Mon – Sat

It goes without saying that The Modern has one of the city's most prized locations, designed to capture the iconic feel of MoMA in which it is seamlessly housed (the entrance can be hard to see). Art enthusiasts appreciate the modernist surrounds, which are as timeless and glorious as the dinnertime chocolate cart with selections available for $8 per person. The bar-lounge is all buzz, while the dining room's sculpture garden views lend tranquility that is conducive to quiet conversation.

Crowds pile in throughout the day, mixing executives with tourists and well-dressed New Yorkers. Service is always warm, well-timed, and hospitable.

The three-course prix-fixe features excellent flexibility and a selection of appealing dishes that showcase neat, clean flavors. Begin with a bright springtime composition of asparagus and peas with foamy buttermilk and snipped chives. Delicate balance and seasonal ingredients are at the heart of a light, lovingly prepared dish of sautéed shrimp with chanterelles, young lettuces, and almonds. For dessert, the caramel "parfait" with mango "ravioli" in a pool of "coconut tapioca" and ten-flavor sorbet may sound complex or aspirational, but is complete pleasure.

Mozzarella & Vino

A4

Italian ✕✕

33 W. 54th St. (bet. Fifth & Sixth Aves.)

Subway: 57 St
Phone: 646-692-8849
Web: www.mozzarellaevino.com
Prices: $$

Lunch Daily
Dinner Mon – Sat

Spoiler alert: as the moniker of this midtown treasure implies, the star of the show here is *mozzarella di bufala*. Bring your appetite to the pretty, narrow space, which features whitewashed brick and taupe walls lined with mirrors and brown leather banquettes, and attempt to choose a version (there are many) of the milky cheese.

Can't decide? Our favorites saw it rolled with grilled sweet peppers hinting of anchovies and presented sliced over arugula; as well as diced and stuffed into a trio of golden-brown, crumb-coated *arancini* filled with sweet pea-studded creamy rice. A salad of avocado and shaved fennel with citrus segments and fresh mint is a refreshing starter, and the short list of entrées indulges with a hearty, oven-baked pasta of the day.

Mr. Robata

A4

Japanese ✕✕

1674 Broadway (bet. 52nd & 53rd Sts.)

Subway: 50 St (Broadway)
Phone: 212-757-1030
Web: www.mrrobata.com
Prices: $$$

Dinner nightly

In an amusing and unexpected feat, humble Mr. Robata somehow thrives within the strip-clubby netherworld of touristy Times Square. Among discerning and discreet of-age adults, this is clearly an entertaining locale. And among foodies, it's a great stop for fusion Japanese. Inside, find two attractive dining areas: one that offers an inviting counter and an auxiliary room decked with well-sized tables.

The food is tasty but less than authentic. Still, Mr. Robata entices with friendly, adept service. Oversized platters shine with powerful flavors, as in fried tuna tacos tossed with crunchy sesame seeds. Wagyu sliders are a generous crowd-pleaser, while the "never too late" maki with soft-shell crab and *robata*-grilled mushrooms and eggplant are fun finds.

New Wonjo

C4

23 W. 32nd St. (bet. Broadway & Fifth Ave.)

Subway: 34 St - Herald Sq   Lunch & dinner daily
Phone: 212-695-5815
Web: www.newwonjo.com
Prices: $$

Smack in the middle of Koreatown, New Wonjo offers a savory respite among the sensory overload of this jam-packed quarter. The simple, well-maintained space offers seating for small parties on the ground level, and a second floor reserved for barbecue-seeking groups to huddle around platters of marinated slices of beef brisket (*chadol baeki*) or spicy squid with pork belly (*o-sam bul goki*) sizzling on table top grills.

Non-barbecue options feature tasty Korean favorites, with starters like *mandoo, japche,* and *pajun*. Sample satisfying stews like *gamba tang*—a bubbling red chili-spiked broth floating slowly simmered and very meaty pork bones with chunks of potato, cabbage, greens, and onions, is wonderfully flavorful but not incendiary.

Norma's

A3

119 W. 56th St. (bet. Sixth & Seventh Aves.)

Subway: 57 St   Lunch daily
Phone: 212-708-7460
Web: www.parkermeridien.com
Prices: $$

Serving heaping platters of breakfast well into the afternoon, Norma's may have been derived from the most humble diner, but rest assured that she is no greasy spoon. A table at this Le Parker Meridien dining room is highly sought after by suits already whirling and dealing over the first meal of the day. Welcoming guests are upscale touches like tables wide enough for a laptop *and* your plate, a polished staff, and gratis smoothie shots. The whimsically worded menu (think "egg cellent" or "Benny sent me" sections) covers all bases and then some: homemade granola; thickly sliced and crispy brioche French toast drizzled with warm, decadent caramel sauce; and gently poached eggs nestled in barbecued pulled pork hash. Savory delights only show up after noon.

Oceana

Seafood 🍴🍴🍴

A4

120 W. 49th St. (at Sixth Ave.)

Subway: 47-50 Sts - Rockefeller Ctr
Phone: 212-759-5941
Web: www.oceanarestaurant.com
Prices: $$$

Lunch Mon – Fri
Dinner nightly

Oceana's doors open to a lavish bounty of seafood on ice—a major tip-off to diners that excess is on the menu. On your way to the dining room, swim past marble-accented seating areas including a casual café and glass-enclosed private rooms (a coveted spot for business lunches). In the center of it all, a two-tier lobster tank cleverly separates the bustling 4,000-square-foot kitchen from the rest of the crowd.

A dizzying array of seafood spans all menus, along with steakhouse-style sides like crisp broccolini. Raw offerings include fresh fluke tartare with a heavy dab of white miso and sweet Korean melon. Entrées play up the presentation factor and include skin-on dorade wrapped in crisp taro strips with vibrant but mild-tasting coconut-cilantro curry.

Osteria al Doge

Italian 🍴🍴

C3

142 W. 44th St. (bet. Broadway & Sixth Ave.)

Subway: Times Sq - 42 St
Phone: 212-944-3643
Web: www.osteria-doge.com
Prices: $$

Lunch & dinner daily

Theater District dining can seem uninspired next to Osteria al Doge. Here, sunny yellow walls, rustic farmhouse tables topped with fresh flowers, and a staff that's genuinely gracious even while attending to the lunchtime throngs make up a completely charming package. As if in defiance of its bustling locale, this authentic *osteria* gives much cause to sit and savor.

The menu offers a taste of Venice in a range of specialties that include risotto *nero*, pan-roasted calf's livers in an onion gravy, and grilled prawns over soft polenta with sweet paprika sauce. Daily specials are another enjoyable way to go, as in the velvet-smooth, dairy-free spinach soup buoyed by a fontina crostini; or *cavatelli* tossed with sausage, sweet peas, and creamy tomato sauce.

Osteria del Circo

Italian ✕✕

A3

120 W. 55th St. (bet. Sixth & Seventh Aves.)

Subway: 57 St
Phone: 212-265-3636
Web: www.circonyc.com
Prices: $$$

Lunch Mon – Fri
Dinner nightly

Step right up to this bold and buzzy midtown destination for a tasteful take on the Big Top, courtesy of the Maccioni family. The setting is a riot of theme and color: a trapeze hangs figurines above the entrance, red-and-white fabrics billow from the tent-like ceiling, harlequin-upholstered seating surrounds tables set with cobalt goblets, and animal sculptures are stationed throughout.

The crackerjack menu highlights thin-crust pizza, Tuscan fish soup (*cacciucco alla Livornese*); as well as wonderful hand-made pastas like silky *tortelli* stuffed with finely chopped radicchio and taleggio, dressed with an earthy mushroom purée and salty speck. Italian-American classics like clams casino, eggplant *Parmigiana*, and chicken Marsala punctuate the lineup.

Petrossian

French ✕✕✕

A3

182 W. 58th St. (at Seventh Ave.)

Subway: 57 St - 7 Av
Phone: 212-245-2214
Web: www.petrossian.com
Prices: $$$

Lunch & dinner daily

Petrossian is not hip. It is classic, continental, and a rare breed in the city. With such exemplary attributes—location, historic setting, and refined staff—this French bastion smacks of bourgeois indulgence. The exterior is unique with detailed stonework that features frolicking cherubs and griffins; a forbidding wrought-iron door guards the entrance. But, the dining room is typical with pink and black granite, a mirrored bar, and crystal sconces.

This costly (or stuffy?) *paradis* clings to the fabric of New York dining, with pleasant and comforting offerings like a tasting of foie gras terrine and smoked fish. Affluent regulars adore pan-roasted lobster risotto with porcini and Parmesan; and a classically rich almond-apple torte with vanilla ice cream.

Per Se ❁ ❁ ❁

Contemporary 🍴🍴🍴🍴🍴

C1

10 Columbus Circle (in the Time Warner Center)

Subway: 59 St - Columbus Circle
Phone: 212-823-9335
Web: www.perseny.com
Prices: $$$$

Lunch Fri – Sun
Dinner nightly

There is no more dramatic departure from the soulless Time Warner Center mall than entering through the iconic blue doors to Per Se. An upscale sense of calm—the kind that only money can buy—instantly soaks the atmosphere. The words posh and exclusive come to mind when admiring the spacious tables, corner banquettes, and stunning views. The crowd is impossibly elegant, moneyed, and could probably take it down a notch. Service is professional and intuitively understands the needs and personality of each table.

Chef Thomas Keller continues to raise the bar with meals that express artistry and seasonality right down to the moment. A classic since day one, the "oysters and pearls" still swim in that bath of luxurious caviar. Supplemental charges are worth every penny once you taste the generous pile of shaved Australian black truffles twirled with hand-cut pasta. Summery flavors reach their peak in the beautiful roulade of veal breast *en persillade*. It may seem that dessert is missing from the parade of courses, but at least you'll have room for the buttery salted caramels.

Those without reservations can stop at the opulent Salon, where much of the menu is available to order à la carte.

pizzArte

Italian 🍴🍴

A3

69 W. 55th St. (bet. Fifth & Sixth Aves.)

Subway: 57 St
Phone: 212-247-3936
Web: www.pizzarteny.com
Prices: $$

Lunch & dinner daily

The serene, slender, bi-level dining room that is pizzArte stands in stark contrast to the workaday bustle outside its doors. A bar and a domed wood-burning pizza oven populate the first floor, while the upstairs is filled with closely set tables and gallery-white walls displaying original art.

Expect the room to be packed with a chic, Italian-accented clientele who flock here for blissfully authentic Neapolitan-style pizzas. These are baked to perfect pliability with a bit of char, topped with impeccable ingredients like creamy *mozzarella di bufala*, broccoli rabe, and sausage. Fine cooking skills are displayed in the *paccheri al baccala*, tossing pasta tubes with cherry tomatoes, plump Sicilian capers, intense Gaeta olives, and firm fillets of cod.

Porter House

Steakhouse 🍴🍴🍴

C1

10 Columbus Circle (in the Time Warner Center)

Subway: 59 St - Columbus Circle
Phone: 212-823-9500
Web: www.porterhousenewyork.com
Prices: $$$$

Lunch & dinner daily

Michael Lomonaco's flagship steakhouse offers unparalleled views of Central Park from its Time Warner Center perch. Here, tables are well-spaced and allow for fine dining, but look for those few intimate booths located in the front bar area—they make for a great escape on busy nights.

The views certainly distinguish this handsome retreat from the pack, as do its carefully selected aged meats, quality fish, and expert sides. The kitchen puts out a tasty helping of sweet and spicy onion rings, buttermilk battered and deep-fried in portions designed for linebackers. The beautifully marbled ribeye is aged for more than 45 days and would be delicious simply seared, though a chili rub adds an aggressive spice. Cool down with a lightly dressed purslane salad.

Print

B1

American ✗✗✗

653 Eleventh Ave. (at 48th St.)

Subway: 50 St (Eighth Ave.)
Phone: 212-757-2224
Web: www.printrestaurant.com
Prices: $$

Lunch & dinner daily

At Print, located in the West Side's hinterlands, a touch of Californian sensibility blooms. Its home, off the lobby of the Ink48 hotel, has an easy-breezy layout that unites lounging and dining in a space that is pleasantly dark and cozy.

The talented team behind this locavore dining room takes its mission seriously: there is a full-time forager on payroll, water is poured into recycled glass, the kitchen composts, and the menu highlights the provenance of its ingredients. Seasonality and simplicity are on show in creations like grilled octopus with Pennsylvania potatoes and homemade chorizo (made from Berkshire pork raised upstate); goat-cheese gnocchi with zucchini and cherry tomatoes; as well as grilled sea bass with wild mushrooms and shell beans.

Radiance Tea House

A3

Asian ✗

158 W. 55th St. (bet. Sixth & Seventh Aves.)

Subway: 57 St - 7 Av
Phone: 212-217-0442
Web: www.radiancetea.com
Prices: $$

Lunch & dinner daily

Radiance Tea House is a delicious midtown curiosity. The workaday locale obscures its presence, but one step inside reveals an unexpected world of green tea and tranquility. Walls are shelved with books about tea and wellness to peruse or purchase, as well as a selection of tea tins and ceramic ware.

Arrive during the lunchtime peak and the scent of rice wine vinegar wafts through the air from tables loaded with dumplings and dipping sauce. A vast selection of loose-leaf blends is offered to be enjoyed alongside chicken wontons with house-made chili oil, green tea soba noodles with sesame sauce, and shrimp-stuffed baby bok choy.

Tea lovers note that a traditional Chinese tea ceremony can be booked one day in advance for a minimum of two persons.

Remi

A4

Italian 𝗫𝗫𝗫

145 W. 53rd St. (bet. Sixth & Seventh Aves.)

Subway: 7 Av
Phone: 212-581-4242
Web: www.remi-ny.com
Prices: $$

Lunch & dinner daily

This well-orchestrated production delights every sense. Designed by Adam Tihany, Remi's slim interior captivates with inlaid wood floors, a striped banquette evoking a gondolier's shirt, Venetian mural, and trio of blown glass chandeliers. A glass wall overlooks a courtyard where seating is offered in warmer weather.

The lengthy menu of Northern Italian specialties is perfectly at home, starting with *carciofi alla Veneziana*—roasted baby artichoke hearts atop a vibrant herb purée, garnished with pitted black olives, roasted garlic cloves, and pecorino. Then, move on to beautifully served *tortelli di zucca* stuffed with roasted squash and *mostarda alla Mantovana*, dressed with drizzles of browned butter, grated cheese, and fried sage.

Robert

D1

Contemporary 𝗫𝗫

2 Columbus Circle (bet. Broadway & Eighth Ave.)

Subway: 59 St - Columbus Circle
Phone: 212-299-7730
Web: www.robertnyc.com
Prices: $$

Lunch & dinner daily

Behold the sweeping views of Central Park from this bright and sexy setting on the ninth floor of the Museum of Art and Design. Be sure to request seating near the north-facing, floor-to-ceiling windows. The interior is almost as pleasing to the eye. splashes of fuchsia and orange perk up a sleek space, where transparent bucket seats, clear-topped tables, and contemporary art installations beautifully reflect the museum to which it belongs.

Drop in for lunch, afternoon tea, or dinner to relish a tuna carpaccio pizza sprinkled with trout caviar, spicy aïoli, and cucumber; or *tagliatelle* with lamb meatballs, mint, and grated *ricotta salata*. Sweet- and sour-braised veal breast atop mashed cauliflower is dabbed with quince relish for a ravishing finish.

Russian Samovar

Russian ✗✗

C2

256 W. 52nd St. (bet. Broadway & Eighth Ave.)

Subway: 50 St (Broadway)　　　　　　　　Lunch & dinner daily
Phone: 212-757-0168
Web: www.russiansamovar.com
Prices: $$

Which came first: the vodka or the celebs? It's hard to say when it comes to this hot spot, which caters to hockey players, Russian intelligentsia, and vodka aficionados alike. Our bets are on that beautiful vodka selection, available in all kinds of flavors, qualities, and sizes (shot, carafe, or bottle). Nestled into the bustling Theater District, Russian Samovar is both quirky and elegant—with low lighting, glass panels, and musicians tickling the piano and violin. The staff, both attentive and sweet, can walk you through delicious fare like fresh salmon-caviar blini, prepared tableside; *pelmeni*, tender veal dumplings served with sour cream and honey mustard; or milk-cured Baltic herring, paired with pickled onions, potatoes, and carrots.

Sake Bar Hagi

Japanese ✗

C2

152 W. 49th St., B1F (bet. Sixth & Seventh Aves.)

Subway: 50 St (Broadway)　　　　　　　　Dinner nightly
Phone: 212-764-8549
Web: N/A
Prices:

This basement *izakaya* can be a challenge to locate—its name is slyly marked on a door that opens to a flight of stairs. Descend to find an unremarkable, brightly lit, and boisterous room tightly packed with wood furnishings and a strong Japanese following.

The space may be small but the menu is vast, so bring friends to ensure a fulfilling experience. Their spot-on small plates are designed to be washed down by beer, sake, or distinctly Japanese cocktails like cassis with oolong tea or soda, or a Calpico sour. Be sure to include wasabi-spiked *shu mai* stuffed with ground pork; or *takoyaki,* deep-fried octopus croquettes with daikon and grated ginger root. Spicy cod roe fried rice and grilled hamachi collar with a light squeeze of lemon are other standouts.

Scarlatto

C2

Italian ✗✗

250 W. 47th St. (bet. Broadway & Eighth Ave.)

Subway: 50 St (Eighth Ave.)
Phone: 212-730-4535
Web: www.scarlattonyc.com
Prices: $$

Lunch & dinner daily

Dip down below street level to find a lovely exposed brick interior displaying rows of wine bottles and glass beaded wall sconces to match the sparkly tiara crowning Audrey Hepburn in a framed still from *Roman Holiday*.

The menu doesn't offer many surprises but this is cooking that—just like a little black dress—never goes out of style. Among the array, search out *polpette al pomodoro*, house-made meatballs in a tomato ragù, or bean soup with fresh pasta. Their *pollo Parmigiana* is a "red sauce" classic, made with breaded and fried chicken breast draped in a bright tomato sugo beneath a bounty of grated and caramelized Parmesan, served atop a mound of al dente spaghetti.

Theater-goers take note: a prix-fixe dinner is offered throughout the evening.

The Sea Grill

D2

Seafood ✗✗✗

19 W. 49th St. (bet. Fifth & Sixth Aves.)

Subway: 47-50 Sts - Rockefeller Ctr
Phone: 212-332-7610
Web: www.patinagroup.com
Prices: $$$

Lunch Mon – Fri
Dinner Mon – Sat

With its dining room overlooking Rockefeller Center's iconic ice-skating rink, The Sea Grill boasts one of the city's most famed locations. A wall of windows frames that view, while sand colored carpeting and gleaming terrazzo cover the floors. This cool aqua-accented setting is the kind of room to dress up for. Understandably, tourists flock here but it is also popular among business folks, especially at lunch when the bar is seated with sharp-looking suits dining on iced lobster tail and tending to business.

As for the food, the kitchen turns out enjoyable cuisine to complement the setting. Offerings are built upon quality seafood dishes such as Block Island golden snapper *a la plancha* dressed with tangy cherry tomato vinaigrette.

Seäsonal ❀

Austrian ✗✗

132 W. 58th St. (bet. Sixth & Seventh Aves.)

Subway: 57 St - 7 Av
Phone: 212-957-5550
Web: www.seasonalnyc.com
Prices: $$$

Lunch Mon – Sat
Dinner nightly

If Seäsonal's longtime devotees suddenly don't recognize its façade, this is because that eternal scaffold has finally been dismantled to reveal its entrance. The interior is attractively austere, with white leather bar stools, dark wood furnishings, and towering fresh florals. Service is professional, if sometimes matter-of-fact and always to-the-point. Such starkness seems to contrast the bright, delicious cuisine.

A sense of class, finesse, and refinement extend to each dish that enters the small dining room. Begin by slathering slices of pumpernickel or rye with an assortment of pumpkin seed and paprika-chive butters to understand how this kitchen elevates a simple dish. Large chunks of juicy and delicious pork sausage stuffed with sharp, melting Austrian cheese are served with roasted fingerling potatoes, toasted sourdough crumbs, and an herb-cabbage salad. Hearty bowls of *kaisergulasch* are comprised of tender veal cheeks in a shimmering pool of paprika broth, topped with lemon zest, orange pepper, and sour cream.

For dessert, the smooth and beautifully glossy *Sacher torte* uses bittersweet chocolate and apricot glaze to delineate layer upon layer of vanilla-tinged chocolate cake.

Snack EOS

Greek ✗

B3

522 Ninth Ave. (at 39th St.)

Subway: 42 St - Port Authority Bus Terminal
Phone: 646-964-4964
Web: www.snackeos.com
Prices: $$

Lunch & dinner daily

Found just steps away from traffic-clogged Port Authority is this boon to the dining landscape of a workaday quarter of Hell's Kitchen. Come for lunch and find suits enjoying a respite in the small cheerful room as they dig into cool salads and hot grilled skewers washed down with mint lemonade. Mediterranean flavors frame the cooking here, so expect to enjoy vibrant items like *melitzanosalata* scooped up with pita chips from the meze selection—a spread of roasted eggplant seasoned with plenty of fresh garlic, red wine vinegar, diced red pepper, and chopped parsley. Delicious *kalamaki* (skewers) of chicken breast, thigh meat confit, and onions are grilled, brushed with lemon-honey vinaigrette, and set over a farro salad studded with sun-dried tomatoes.

Staghorn

Steakhouse ✗✗

B3

315 W. 36th St. (bet. Eighth & Ninth Aves.)

Subway: 34 St - Penn Station
Phone: 212-239-4390
Web: www.staghornsteakhouse.com
Prices: $$$

Lunch Mon – Fri
Dinner Mon – Sat

Does the word "steakhouse" conjure up images of old-school, slightly brusque waiters in white aprons and a no-frills, good-old-boy décor? Well, think again. Staghorn steakhouse takes the bull by its, ahem, horns, and turns it completely on its head. The less-than-thrilling neighborhood may leave something to be desired, but inside, this former warehouse is a wondrous space with an Asian-Zen ambience.

The look is modern but the food is classic, with typical sides like mashed potatoes and creamed spinach. Start with tasty baked clams or the Staghorn salad bursting with Roquefort and tomatoes. From well-aged Porterhouse steaks that ooze with juice to thick and meaty Kansas City bone-in sirloin, it's all about the beef to the chic carnivore at this temple.

Stella 34

C4

Italian XX

151 W. 34th St. (entrance at 35th St. & Broadway)

Subway: 34 St - Herald Sq
Phone: 212-967-9251
Web: www.patinagroup.com
Prices: $$

Lunch & dinner daily

You can find just about anything your heart desires at Macy's flagship Herald Square store, but *pizza Napolitana*? Oh yes, as well as many other Italian delights at this well-designed trattoria accessed by a dedicated elevator for the six-story ride. Step inside to find a spacious layout with large, bright windows and a lush color scheme. A winding counter fronts the open kitchen equipped with three wood-burning ovens.

Run by the Patina Restaurant Group, this dining room tempts with much more than great pizza. Enjoy a rousing array of starters like escarole wilted on the grill; and a fantastic pasta lineup, like *strozzapreti con seppie*, squid ink-tinted twists and tender cuttlefish coated in a creamy red pepper sauce and sprinkled with breadcrumbs.

Sugiyama

C1

Japanese XX

251 W. 55th St. (bet. Broadway & Eighth Ave.)

Subway: 57 St - 7 Av
Phone: 212-956-0670
Web: www.sugiyama-nyc.com
Prices: $$$

Dinner Tue – Sat

Prepare to leave the wilds of midtown behind upon entering Chef Nao Sugiyama's calm and transporting domain. Settle in at a spacious table or front-row counter seat and prepare for a worthwhile Japanese experience.

Several set menu options are offered, including the exemplary modern kaiseki which may unfold with a first bite of tofu enriched with monkfish liver. Seasonal hors d'oeuvres reveal a jewel-like green peach and tiny, wholly edible hard-shelled crab; while sashimi features freshly grated wasabi and specks of gold leaf. *Ishiyaki* (marinated seafood cooked by the diner over a red-hot stone) is another highlight. But for the ultimate conclusion, go for the rice presented in a bamboo leaf, followed by grapefruit gelée drizzled with cream.

Sushi Zen

C3

108 W. 44th St. (bet. Broadway & Sixth Ave.)

Subway: 42 St - Bryant Pk
Phone: 212-302-0707
Web: www.sushizen-ny.com
Prices: **$$$**

Lunch Mon – Fri
Dinner Mon – Sat

Sushi Zen's peaceful interior and intimate scale is a welcomed contrast to its high traffic location. High ceilings and pale earthy hues combine for a soothing look that is accentuated by wood flooring, stone, and an artful tangle of branches.

From behind the U-shaped bar, Chef Toshio Suzuki's team doles out a wide-ranging assortment that might kick off with refreshing wilted spinach *oshitashi*, cooled in dashi and topped with toasted sesame seeds. A colorful seaweed salad is dressed with nasal passage-clearing pickled wasabi skin and *tosazu*, combining rice vinegar, dashi, and soy sauce. The daily nigiri platter has featured generous slices of Spanish mackerel, raw scallop, and black sea bass; as well as very tasty diced tuna and scallion *gunkan-maki*.

Szechuan Gourmet

C3

21 W. 39th St. (bet. Fifth & Sixth Aves.)

Subway: 42 St - Bryant Pk
Phone: 212-921-0233
Web: N/A
Prices: **$$**

Lunch Mon – Fri
Dinner nightly

Come lunchtime, midtown office workers with a jones for the tingly heat of Sichuan peppercorns or the burn of bright red chili oil know exactly where to go. A queue for tables is nearly obligatory, but the pace settles down in the evening and on weekends. Inside, red lanterns and pink linens accent the bustling room and servers fluent in English attend to tables where specialties are piled high.

Though the menu is vast, you can't go wrong by tearing into the best scallion pancakes in town; or cool, hand-shredded chicken draped in a creamy sesame paste and chili oil. Smoked tofu shreds tossed with Asian celery and toasted sesame oil; or wok-tossed jumbo prawns with a crispy shell of peppercorns and spiced salt are the reason for those long lines.

Taboon

C1

Middle Eastern ✕✕

773 Tenth Ave. (at 52nd St.)

Subway: 50 St (Eighth Ave.)
Phone: 212-713-0271
Web: www.taboononline.com
Prices: $$

Lunch Sun
Dinner nightly

Thanks to the restaurant's namesake, a brick-walled, wood-burning oven that sets the whitewashed interior aglow, one is guaranteed a warm welcome at this far western neighborhood gem.

Grazing is the best way to experience this Mediterranean gem's succulent specialties, so you'll want to bring friends—or a big appetite. Peruse the selection over homemade focaccia, served fresh from the *taboon*. Locals know to order the *sambusak*, house bread stuffed with feta and paired with *schoog*, a vibrant paste made from cilantro, garlic, jalapeño, lemon, and spices. (Hint: This Yemenite specialty is also delicious with the marinated shrimp served sizzling in cast iron). For a crisp, refreshing side dish, opt for the baby romaine salad with *labne*, avocado and cucumber.

Tang Pavilion

A4

Chinese ✕✕

65 W. 55th St. (bet. Fifth & Sixth Aves.)

Subway: 57 St
Phone: 212-956-6888
Web: www.tangpavilionchinese.com
Prices: $$

Lunch & dinner daily

This longstanding, elegant Chinese favorite is a delightful contrast to its brassy midtown location. Set foot inside its hushed dining room featuring pale peach walls dressed with black lacquer trim. Jacketed servers dote on a dressy crowd savoring Shanghainese specialties.

The kitchen offers countless delectable house delicacies emphasizing the regional focus. Honey ham Shanghai-style is a sweet and salty treat dressed with dates and lotus seeds. The "eight jewels with hot paste" is a mouthwateringly spiced stir-fry of mushrooms, bamboo shoots, wheat gluten, scallops, chicken, and shrimp. Green beans with tofu sheets is a gorgeously simple combo of soybeans and paper-thin ribbons of bean curd skin judiciously bathed in a light, broth-based sauce.

Tavola

Italian ✗

B3

488 Ninth Ave. (bet. 37th & 38th Sts.)

Subway: 42 St - Port Authority Bus Terminal   Lunch & dinner daily
Phone: 212-273-1181
Web: www.tavolahellskitchen.com
Prices: $$

This Hell's Kitchen pizza and pasta spot is housed in the former Manganaro's Grosseria Italiano, a family-run emporium dating back to 1893. A year after its closing, Chef Nicola Accardi has respectfully repurposed this setting as a convivial destination for an under-served area.

Bright and clean but boasting the patina of its long existence, the dining room now greets guest with a wall of Italian products and skylit pizza station. Here, a wood-burning oven crafted from volcanic clay (from Mt. Vesuvius) produces ten varieties of thin-crust pizza, like the *Calabresa bona*—sporting crushed tomato, fresh mozzarella, dabs of creamy ricotta, basil, and hot slices of *soppressata* from neighboring Esposito's. Pastas include a very fine lasagna *della casa*.

Toloache

Mexican ✗✗

C2

251 W. 50th St. (bet. Broadway & Eighth Ave.)

Subway: 50 St (Broadway)   Lunch & dinner daily
Phone: 212-581-1818
Web: www.toloachenyc.com
Prices: $$

This first location of midtown's Mexican hot spot (with outposts in SoHo and the Upper East Side) remains immensely popular for ample reason. An extensive selection of tequilas flow freely from the spirited bar, chunky guacamole is endlessly mashed from mounds of ripe avocados, and amiable diners emerge from the brick oven in this two-story dining room decked with Talavera tiles, wood-beam ceilings, and stunning copper lanterns.

Toloache puts a contemporary spin on each of its zesty dishes. Tacos begin with tender, excellent masa tortillas amply stuffed with beer-braised beef brisket (*suadero*), tomatillo salsa, and horseradish *crema*. The signature *camarones* Toloache showcase a handful of large, fresh shrimp draped with a vibrant dried *cascabel* salsa.

Trattoria Dell'Arte

A3

Italian ✗✗

900 Seventh Ave. (bet. 56th & 57th Sts.)

Subway: 57 St - 7 Av
Phone: 212-245-9800
Web: www.trattoriadellarte.com
Prices: $$$

Lunch & dinner daily

There's a downright contagious exuberance to Shelly Firemen's always-packed Carnegie Hall classic, Trattoria Dell'Arte. It might be their smart, confident staff, or the overflowing, recession-be-damned antipasto bar. Perhaps it's the cheeky welcome motto ("What's Italian for Carnegie Hall? Trattoria Dell'Arte."), or those Tuscan-styled rooms lined with mahogany wine racks and dripping candles? Whatever it is, people keep returning time and again.

Expect to pay—maybe a bit too steeply—for this kind of *io non lo so*, but the flaky, thin-crust pizzas and heady dishes of finely sauced pastas do not disappoint. Save room for irresistible Italian desserts like an airy cheesecake wrapped in chocolate sponge cake and topped with piping hot chocolate ganache.

21 Club

A4

American ✗✗

21 W. 52nd St. (bet. Fifth & Sixth Aves.)

Subway: 5 Av - 53 St
Phone: 212-582-7200
Web: www.21club.com
Prices: $$$

Lunch & dinner Mon – Sat

Fabled 21 Club has been in business for over 85 years, but there's nothing slowing it down. Opened originally as a speakeasy, this New York institution has wined and dined everyone from movie stars and moguls to moneyed city folk. From its lantern-holding jockeys and townhouse exterior, to the leather- and wood-paneled dining room that feels like a step back in time, this is a classic through and through.

The menu is a perfect accompaniment to the setting with choices like seared foie gras tinged with mango chutney and spread atop toasted brioche; or a splendid and classic rendition of steak tartare paired with a green salad. Upstairs and in the back, the feel is formal—so for a casual bite with prettier prices, head off the main entrance to Bar 21.

Utsav

C2

Indian ✗✗

1185 Sixth Ave. (entrance on 46th St.)

Subway: 47-50 Sts - Rockefeller Ctr
Phone: 212-575-2525
Web: www.utsavny.com
Prices: 🍲

Lunch & dinner daily

Meaning "festival" in Sanskrit, Utsav is an upscale hideaway perched on a suspended corridor between two office buildings. The ground floor features a bar and small plaza with outdoor seating, while the second floor dining room is spacious and has walls covered with floor-to-ceiling windows. Swathes of gold fabric along the ceiling embellish the well-maintained space.

The wallet-friendly and overflowing lunch buffet brings office workers in by the droves, and the early evening prix-fixe is popular with the pre-theater crowd. To whet your appetite, start with a small bite like potato croquettes drizzled in tamarind. Then, move on to *murg xacutti*, a coconut-rich chicken curry from Goa; or *bhindi ki subzi*—okra simmered with tomato, onion, ginger, and cumin.

Yakitori Totto

C1

Japanese ✗

251 W. 55th St. (bet. Broadway & Eighth Ave.)

Subway: 57 St - 7 Av
Phone: 212-245-4555
Web: www.tottonyc.com
Prices: $$

Lunch Mon – Fri
Dinner nightly

To say that this *yakitori-ya* nails authenticity is an epic understatement. Its discreet signage and second floor location feels more Tokyo than Manhattan, J-pop dominates the playlist, and the crowd is a reassuring mix of Japanese-speakers and in-the-know foodies.

Best of all is the aroma of sizzling skewers that are deftly prepared over a charcoal fire. It's all about grilled meats here, like *buta karashi*—pork loin with sweet onion and spicy mustard—but that doesn't mean you should skip *yakumi zaru* tofu, soft cubes dressed with slivered green onion, bonito flakes, ginger, and *ume* salt. For lunch, go for *yakitori don* with skewers of chicken breast and green onion (*negima*) over rice, paired with pickled cucumbers and licked by a sweet *yakitori* sauce.

SoHo & Nolita

SoHo or the area South of Houston and Nolita (North of Little Italy) prove not only that New York City has a penchant for prime shopping and divine dining, but that the downtown scene lives on now more than ever.

SHOPPING IN SOHO

Halfway through the 20th century, SoHo's solid cast iron structures gave way to grand hotels, large theaters, and commercial establishments. Thanks to such large-scale development,

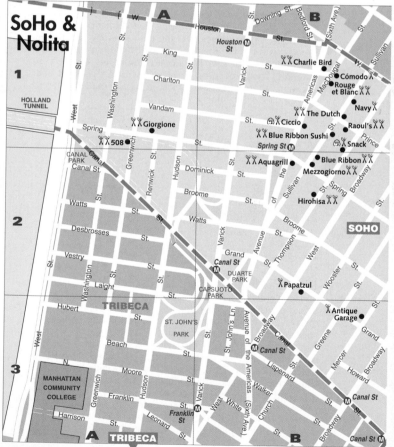

SoHo & Nolita

1

HOLLAND TUNNEL

Houston St.
King St.
Charlton
Vandam
Spring St.
West St.
Washington St.
Greenwich St.

Houston St Ⓜ

Downing St.
Bedford St.
(Sixth Ave.)
W. Sullivan St.

✗✗ Charlie Bird
● Cómodo ●
Rouge et Blanc ✗✗
Navy ✗✗
✗✗ The Dutch
Ⓐ✗ Ciccio ●
Raoul's ✗✗
✗✗ Blue Ribbon Sushi ●
Ⓐ✗ Snack

✗✗ Giorgione
✗✗ 508 ●

Spring St Ⓜ

✗✗ Aquagrill ●
Blue Ribbon ✗✗
Mezzogiorno ✗✗

Hirohisa ✗✗

SOHO

2

CANAL PARK
Canal St.
Watts St.
Desbrosses St.
Vestry St.
Laight St.

Renwick St.
Hudson St.
Dominick St.
Broome St.
Watts St.
Varick St.

Grand St.
Canal St Ⓜ
DUARTE PARK
CAPSUOTO PARK

Broome St.
Avenue of the Americas (Sixth Ave.)
Thompson St.
West St.
Wooster St.
Sullivan St.
Spring St.
Broadway

✗ Papatzul

HUBERT St.
TRIBECA
ST. JOHN'S PARK
Beach St.

St. John's Ln.
Avenue of the Americas (Sixth Ave.)
Broadway
Canal

✗ Antique Garage ●
Grand St.

3

MANHATTAN COMMUNITY COLLEGE
Moore St.
Franklin St.
Harrison St.
Greenwich St.
Hudson St.
Washington St.
West St.

Canal St Ⓜ
Lispenard St.
Walker St.
White St.
Varick St.
Franklin St Ⓜ
Leonard St.

Church St.
Broadway
Mercer St.
Greene St.
Howard St.
Canal St Ⓜ

Canal St Ⓜ

A **TRIBECA**
B

housing costs soared and artists absconded to adjoining Chelsea. And yet, these streets south of Houston remain true to their promise of sun-drenched restaurants and sleek cafés filled with wine-sipping sophisticates, supermodels, and armies of tourists. Locals who are fortunate enough to live in SoHo's pricey condos and lofts, know to stock up on cheese and meats from **Despaña Tapas Café**. They will even prepare a traditional tortilla Española or

octopus platter with advance notice. Follow this up with a fantastic selection of sips at **Despaña Vinos y Mas**, their wine boutique next door.

Scattered with fancy boutiques, these residents are here to stay. Entertaining guests over dinner is bound to be a dream after a visit to **Pino's Prime Meat Market** rife with quality products. The storefront may be simple, but the butchers here know the drill and are

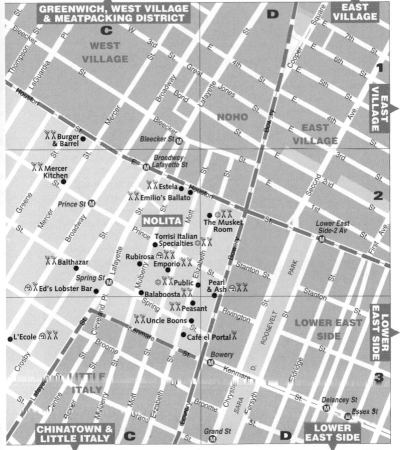

happy to engage rookies as they break down the best game (even deer) in town. On the flip side, vegetarians take great pride in **The Butcher's Daughter**, a meat-free emporium with the sole purpose of treating, cutting, and carving regionally sourced and sustainable produce.

Those seeking Italian specialties should sample the brick oven-baked prosciutto rolls at old-time treasure, **Parisi Bakery**, as well as the signature square pizzas (perhaps the **Prince Perfection**?) or Sicilian arancini at **Prince St. Pizza**. Sugar junkies find their fix at **Vosges Haut Chocolat**, where inventive sweets reach new heights of gratification. Try "The Goose's Golden Eggs" featuring real bacon caramel in half-shelled chocolate eggs for a truly exquisite and decadent experience, before heading over to **MarieBelle**, another renowned cocoa queen, combining exotic ingredients and precise methods to create precious "chocolate jewels."

For New York City's favorite cheeses, coffees, and other condiments, the original Broadway location of **Dean &**

Deluca is always packed with locals and food lovers. This pricey gourmet store is also home to a butcher, baker, and fishmonger, not to mention hordes of hungry office workers fumbling for hors d'oeuvres, entrées, and desserts to keep them going 'till the clock hits happy hour. Speaking of which, the carte at **AstorWines & Spirits** displays an amazing selection and is every barkeep's creed. Weekly tastings and wine-related events focused on unique varietals are exemplary, so plan ahead and book your attendance. Over on Hudson Square, **City Winery** gives urban oenophiles a place to make their own private-label *vino* by providing the grapes, barrels, storage, and expertise. If sweet is the best way to seal a meal, then follow your nose to **Little Cupcake Bakeshop** on Prince Street for a ravishing array of treats. Looking for international accessories with worldly flair? Home shoppers know to frequent **Global Table** whose exquisite selection emphasizes simple lines and vivid finishes. Hunger pangs after a shopping spree should be avoided by stopping at

Smile to Go, a quiet spot merely blocks from Canal Street that serves bold breakfasts and light lunch bites.

NIGHTS OUT IN NOLITA

Nolita may have been an integral part of Little Italy back in the day, but today it is its own, distinctive district and explodes with swanky boutiques, sleek restaurants, and chic bars. Located farther east than tourist-mobbed SoHo, this neighborhood is also home to slightly hipper and well-traveled folks. Not unlike its name, Nolita's eclectic residents shun the typical nine-to-five drill and reject SoHo's scene-y hangouts in favor of smaller spots that invariably begin with the word "café." At the top of this list is **Café Habana**, offering a classic diner vibe and four square meals a day—breakfasts may include sunny-side-up eggs topped with *salsa verde* and *salsa ranchera*. Amazing Mexico City-style corn on the cob is also available for takeout next door at **Café Habana To Go**. **Café Gitane** is another hipster hangout, well-tread at all times

for wonderful, eclectic French-Moroccan food coupled with a lineup of cocktails.

The ethos in Nolita is simple yet resolute: to do a single thing very well. This may have been inspired by **Lombardi's** on Spring Street, which claims to be America's very first pizzeria (founded in 1905). The fact that they still serve coal oven-fired delicacies by the pie and not the slice clearly hasn't caused a stir—find proof in the lines that continue out the door. Hopping countries from Italy to Israel, **Hoomoos Asli** draws a horde of young'uns craving fluffy pitas packed with crispy falafel and outstanding hummus. The décor and service may be elementary, but serious effort goes into the food that is routinely accompanied by tart and refreshing lemonade.

Top off these enticing delights at the aromatic and alluring **Dominique Ansel Bakery**. Formerly an executive pastry chef at Daniel on the Upper East Side, the pastry chef here is now fulfilling his own dessert dreams with specialty cakes, tarts, cookies, and pastries. For a taste of pure bliss, follow instructions and eat the made-to-order "Magic Soufflé" piping hot. Desserts are best matched with coffee, perhaps at **La Colombe**—a Philadelphia-based roaster located merely steps away. If date-night duos aren't closing the deal over one of their exquisite and eco-friendly blends, then find them sweetening it up at **Papabubble**, a stylish spot showcasing candies created with eye-popping design and detail. Flaunting equal parts

including passion fruit as well as goat cheese with orange peel and anise. Cheesecake addicts take note that **Eileen's Special Cheesecake** bears the title "special" for good reason. Embellished with fruit toppings and fun flavors like amaretto or coconut custard, Eileen's divine creations continue to control the downtown scene, chasing those Junior's fans back to Brooklyn.

creative and classic flair, **Rice to Riches** brings comfort food to this edgy nook in bowls of creamy rice pudding. The fact that these are appended with quirky names like "Sex Drugs and Rocky Road" or "Fluent in French Toast" only adds to this dessert den's overall lure. For more such rich and creamy goodness, **A.B. Biagi** brings the craft of traditional Italian gelato-making infused with a taste of Brazil to the heart of Nolita. Their wide range of light yet luscious gelatos and sorbets highlights exotic flavors

One of the greater challenges this neighborhood poses is the decision of where to end the day or night. However, natives know that tucked into these vibrant streets are scores of snug bars, each with its own sleek city feel. Date-friendly **Pravda** presents a tantalizing array of vodkas, while **Sweet & Vicious** pours stellar libations that are bound to leave you starry-eyed. And between these countless dinners and drinks, Nolita also caters to Gotham City's culinary community by virtue of its numerous wholesale kitchen supply stores, all settled along the Bowery.

Antique Garage

B3

Turkish ✗

41 Mercer St. (bet. Broome & Grand Sts.)

Subway: Canal St (Broadway)
Phone: 212-219-1019
Web: www.antiquegaragesoho.com
Prices: $$

Lunch & dinner daily

Bohemian-chic Antique Garage makes for a perfectly discreet rendezvous. Complete with high ceilings and the beat-up bones of a former garage, this sultry spot combines vintage furniture, pendant-like chandeliers, and mirrors galore to create the quintessentially cool hangout. Insanely talented jazz musicians jam in the corner, while gin martinis and Turkish white wines flow as freely as the conversation.

Ottoman cuisine rules here with well-made, welcoming, and wonderful bites—after hitting SoHo's boutiques and galleries, those bowls of spicy olives are the ideal snack for sharing. For heartier fare, try a grilled *halloumi* salad tossed with briny artichoke hearts, or smoky lamb shish kabobs, traditional in presentation and deeply satisfying in flavor.

Aquagrill

B2

Seafood ✗✗

210 Spring St. (at Sixth Ave.)

Subway: Spring St (Sixth Ave.)
Phone: 212-274-0505
Web: www.aquagrill.com
Prices: $$

Lunch & dinner daily

New York is no stranger to oysters but Aquagrill is an institution that puts the other shuckers to shame. A destination for all-things seafood since the 1990s, the menu features as many as 27 types of oysters each day, with patrons holing up at the bar to ingest dozens upon dozens of these bivalves with pitch perfect wines to match.

As always, the kitchen serves a fine lineup of heartier fish dishes including the downright sensual wild *toro* tartare with shiitakes, peppercress, and truffle-soy sauce. Pan-seared red snapper over crispy jasmine rice cakes and sautéed vegetables in ginger-peanut sauce is a show of well-balanced textures and bracing flavors; but a handmade chocolate sampler remains the true starlet, with each morsel as decadent as the next.

Balaboosta

Manhattan ▶ SoHo & Nolita

C2

Middle Eastern 🍴🍴

214 Mulberry St. (bet. Prince & Spring Sts.)

Subway: Spring St (Lafayette St.)
Phone: 212-966-7366
Web: www.balaboostanyc.com
Prices: $$

Lunch Tue – Sun
Dinner nightly

This bright, friendly Middle Eastern café keeps its keen eye on Sephardic Jewish traditions. The room feels cozy and rustic, with windows framing Mulberry Street sidewalks, inlaid wood tables, and walls lined with books and wine bottles. A bar mixes cocktails and pours an inexpensive yet interesting list of organic wines.

The dynamic, all-female kitchen is on full display as they deep-fry green olives and set them atop *labne* with drizzles of harissa oil; toss ribbons of deep-burgundy beet pasta; or blend smoky-creamy eggplant with spices and tahini, then slather it over toasted sourdough with a vividly green herb salad. The hearty Moroccan fish *cazuela* may arrive as a rich and fiery tagine with pepper-paprika sauce, preserved lemon, and chickpeas.

Balthazar

C2

French 🍴🍴

80 Spring St. (bet. Broadway & Crosby St.)

Subway: Spring St (Lafayette St.)
Phone: 212-965-1414
Web: www.balthazarny.com
Prices: $$$

Lunch & dinner daily

As ageless as its beautiful patrons, the brassy and mirrored Balthazar should be called "quintessentially SoHo" because it invented the term. One of the benchmark brasseries from serial restaurateur Keith McNally, the attractive space is housed in a former tannery. Those whiffs of leather have been replaced by red awnings, scents of pastries, and an excellent oyster-filled raw bar completing its Parisian transformation.

It seems as though every other table is topped with their bestselling steak frites—hardly a value but expertly prepared and served with a heaping side of fries. On the delicate side, sautéed skate is served with sweet raisins and tart capers; while silky beef tartare with shallots, herbs, and Worcestershire spreads just like butta.

Blue Ribbon

Contemporary 🍴🍴

B2

97 Sullivan St. (bet. Prince & Spring Sts.)

Subway: Spring St (Sixth Ave.)   Dinner nightly
Phone: 212-274-0404
Web: www.blueribbonrestaurants.com
Prices: $$$

Every New Yorker without a 9-5 job knows that Blue Ribbon serves food until 4 A.M. and is hailed as a chef's canteen for good reason. This classic bistro is genuinely hospitable, lacks pretense, and deserves every bit of its success. The tiny, square space has remained relatively unchanged through the years, and bar seats are still a hot commodity.

The food here is somewhat simple, very memorable, and reliably excellent. Start with the likes of shellfish in smoky dashi broth, bobbing with enoki mushrooms, cilantro, and cubes of white fish spiced with jalapeño. Their fried chicken with silky mashed potatoes and collard greens is a crowd-pleasing platter of pure comfort. The flourless chocolate cake is moist, decadent, and everything you want it to be.

Blue Ribbon Sushi

Japanese 🍴🍴

B1

119 Sullivan St. (bet. Prince & Spring Sts.)

Subway: Spring St (Sixth Ave.)   Lunch & dinner daily
Phone: 212-343-0404
Web: www.blueribbonrestaurants.com
Prices: $$$

Set below street level and just down the block from its eldest sibling, Blue Ribbon Sushi is the famous and successful stalwart whose formula has been reproduced many times over. A sushi bar displays colorful sake bottles and premium spirits as it dominates the space outfitted with polished tables and low, wood-covered ceilings.

While the staff is happy to explain each dish and more Americanized options are available, this is absolutely a place where the $85 omakase is a downright steal. The menu proudly divides its offerings into the *Taiheiyo* ("Pacific") such as the spotted *kohada* atop gently vinegared rice, or a sweet and briny giant clam; and the *Taiseiyo* ("Atlantic"), perhaps featuring fluke fin or spicy lobster knuckle encasing savory egg.

Burger & Barrel

Gastropub ✗✗

25 W. Houston St. (at Greene St.)

Subway: Broadway - Lafayette St   Lunch & dinner daily
Phone: 212-334-7320
Web: www.burgerandbarrel.com
Prices: $$

Comfort food becomes downright elegant at this urbane gastropub, where clubby leather booths, louvered blinds, and requisite chalked-up blackboards stay on the approachable side of chic. When the long bar and closely set tables are at capacity, conversations bouncing off the wood-paneled walls can reach a dull roar. Still, the atmosphere remains relaxed.

The modern pub menu covers all the bases with panache. The griddled Bash burger, slathered with house-made caramelized onion and bacon jam crowned with two crisp onion rings, is a memorable affair. Lighter dishes like a traditional panzanella with chewy-crusty bread cubes and translucent cucumber slices; or chilled sweet-and-tart corn soup with chunks of peekytoe crab are just as satisfying.

Café el Portal

Mexican ✗

174 Elizabeth St. (bet. Kenmare & Spring Sts.)

Subway: Spring St (Lafayette St.)   Lunch & dinner Mon – Sat
Phone: 212-226-4642
Web: N/A
Prices: ☜☜

In an area paved by PR campaigns and flashy restaurants, one authentic Mexican spot trudges on, in a pocket-sized room decked out with the bright colors of a hacienda. While some may view it as kitschy (it's hardly a hipster hangout), foodies gather here for the unique cooking churned out of this genuine kitchen.

The fundamentals that distinguish authentic tacos from the Tex-Mex version are more than adequately covered in the *carnitas taco*. Tortillas, properly warmed on the comal, encase tender pulled pork and jalapeño and are topped with a complex, spicy salsa with just a pinch of cilantro—as fresh as any native could hope to taste. Foodies are equally thankful for the *flor de calabaza* quesadilla drizzled with avocado purée and filled with zucchini.

Charlie Bird

B1

Italian 🍴🍴

5 King St. (entrance at Sixth Ave.)

Subway: Houston St
Phone: 212-235-7133
Web: www.charliebirdnyc.com
Prices: $$$

Lunch Fri – Sun
Dinner nightly

Sixth Avenue teems with trendy spots, but none are as precious as this rustic-chic retreat, flaunting an easy vibe, downtown demeanor, and darling décor. A long bar leads into a super cozy space, adorned with brick walls and vintage-y leather seats. Thumping rap tunes only add to this joint's too-cool feel.

Upbeat servers present diners with fun and rustic cuisine. Technical prowess and judiciously sourced ingredients prevail in soft, spreadable Tuscan chicken liver pâté coupled with crusty bread. Smoky calamari tossed with tender red giant beans and pickled chilies merits a side of roasted cauliflower with crispy pancetta and sliced almonds. Not far behind, a warm *budino* dotted with luscious ice cream guarantees pure bliss—and many repeat visits.

Ciccio

B1

Italian 🍴

190 Sixth Ave. (bet. Prince & Vandam Sts.)

Subway: Spring St (Sixth Ave.)
Phone: 646-476-9498
Web: www.ciccionyc.com
Prices: $$

Lunch & dinner daily

Chef and owner Giacomo Romano defines this brilliant little *alimentaria* as a place where patrons can find an ever-changing menu day or night. Here, that wonderful formula might mean ribollita at lunch, or fresh, heartwarming plates of pasta for dinner. Step inside to find a sun-drenched space outfitted with blonde wood tables, white-washed brick walls, and wood beams.

Expertly prepared dishes include *polpo e ceci*, tender, charred octopus atop chickpea-thyme purée served with fresh bread; a trio of crostini with toppings like lentil and mushroom pâté or tomato, garlic, and oregano; or homemade *tagliatelle* with *polpettine* (tiny meatballs) in tomato ragù. For a fantastic conclusion, try the almond-chocolate tart with mascarpone cream.

Cómodo

B1

58 MacDougal St. (at King St.)

Subway: Houston St
Phone: 646-370-4477
Web: www.comodonyc.com
Prices: $$

Lunch Sat – Sun
Dinner Tue – Sun

After a year of hosting Thursday night "pop-up dinner parties" at their TriBeCa apartment, Chef Felipe Donnelly and his wife, Tamy Rofe, seamlessly transferred their labor of love into this storybook enterprise. Quarters are small and cozy, as diners and staff chat with warm familiarity, lending to the welcoming vibe.

Squeeze into one of the communal tables and get started with juicy lamb sliders on Brazilian cheese bread with chipotle cream sauce; or warm kale and quinoa salad tossed with shiitake mushrooms, dried blueberries, feta cheese, and aged balsamic. Dive into the fantastic three-potato *ajiaco* soup with pulled chicken, sweet corn, avocado, capers, and cilantro; or the *picanha*, a dry-aged Newport steak atop rice and stewed greens.

The Dutch

B1

131 Sullivan St. (at Prince St.)

Subway: Spring St (Lafayette St.)
Phone: 212-677-6200
Web: www.thedutchnyc.com
Prices: $$$

Lunch & dinner daily

Chef Andrew Carmellini's ode to New York in The Dutch is as truly American and distinct as the three rooms it fills nightly. Expect to see Keith Haring among other iconic artists on the walls, handrails inspired by famed local horse stables, and seasonal accents like a vibrant cornucopia strewn throughout. The front rooms are hopping and lure with an oyster bar, while the reservation-only back dining room is warmed with a wood-burning fire.

Start with pleasing appetizers like crisp flatbread paired with creamy-smoky eggplant dip spiced with *za'atar*, before moving onto a perfect plate of fried chicken with honey-buttered biscuits and cool slaw. Their daily pies are not to be missed, as in the fragrant apple-concord grape in a supremely flakey crust.

Ed's Lobster Bar 😊

C2

Seafood 🍴

222 Lafayette St. (bet. Kenmare & Spring Sts.)

Subway: Spring St (Lafayette St.)　　　　　　Lunch & dinner daily
Phone: 212-343-3236
Web: www.lobsterbarnyc.com
Prices: $$

Thanks to Ed's, there's no need to leave the city for an outstanding lobster roll. This seafood-driven favorite is a pitch-perfect encapsulation of the Northeast coast with a lively New York vibe. Inside the white-brick room, the long, gleaming marble bar is definitely the place to sit.

With a mean Bloody Mary, pristine raw bar, and freshly caught daily chalkboard specials, Ed's has amassed a loyal following; aim for off-peak times to avoid the wait.

Shareable appetizers of sweet and briny Ipswich clams are lightly fried for amazing salty-crisp contrast. Pewter caldrons of linguini bathed in olive oil with lemony-garlicky clams and toasted breadcrumbs are terrific. And that signature mayo- and butter-rich lobster roll is worth every calorie.

Emilio's Ballato

C2

Italian 🍴🍴

55 E. Houston St. (bet. Mott & Mulberry Sts.)

Subway: Broadway - Lafayette St　　　　　Lunch & dinner daily
Phone: 212-274-8881
Web: N/A
Prices: $$

This unassuming Houston St. standard is an unsung hero, even if many walk past Emilio's gold- and red-etched window and write it off as some run-of-the-mill red sauce joint. Step inside the narrow, weathered space, where owner Emilio Vitolo offers each guest a personal welcome and a genuine Italian-American experience.

The menu is filled with pasta classics like roman cacio e pepe, tossed with sharp pecorino cheese and freshly ground black pepper. Signature specialties include *pollo Emilio*, a delicately breaded chicken cutlet draped in lemon-caper sauce; and plump clams *oreganata* speckled with garlicky breadcrumbs. Crisp cannoli shells filled with vanilla- and cinnamon-tinged ricotta cream rival any other version found from Palermo to Siracusa.

Emporio

Italian ✗✗

231 Mott St. (bet. Prince & Spring Sts.)

Subway: Spring St (Lafayette St.) Lunch & dinner daily
Phone: 212-966-1234
Web: www.emporiony.com
Prices: $$

Everything at Emporio has been strategically placed, from canned tomatoes by the open kitchen to the pressed-tin ceiling and reclaimed wood accents. It's this Italian-inspired café's attention to detail that has made it a local mainstay, filled with gorgeous crowds and friendly servers. Here, everyone shares conversation over sips set to go with complimentary spreads or "aperitivo" like crispy pancetta with rosemary.

Although the space is small, flavors are huge, and the same attention that went into décor goes into the food—from grass-feed beef to excellent handmade *orecchiette* with cauliflower and shrimp. For a real treat, try a Nutella calzone, its wonderfully thin dough oozing with hazelnut-chocolate and topped with fresh cream and hazelnut crumb.

Estela

Contemporary ✗✗

47 E. Houston St. (at Mulberry St.)

Subway: Broadway - Lafayette St Lunch Sat – Sun
Phone: 212-219-7693 Dinner nightly
Web: www.estelanyc.com
Prices: $$$

This discreet spot (read: minimal signage) is run with élan by the impressive duo of sommelier Thomas Carter and Chef Ignacio Mattos. Their combined skills have crafted a true hot spot that showcases authentic talent and creative cooking. Here, even celery is worthy of applause when transformed into a fantastic salad of shaved stalk and bright leaves kissed by sweet lemon and pecorino shavings. Lamb ribs are crusted with fragrant spices and drizzled with honey. Quivering and delicate ricotta dumplings are sauced with intensely flavorful mushroom broth. Save room for dessert—the chocolate *pot de crème* to be specific.

Small tables, café chairs, and warm lighting from frosted globe ceiling pendants fashion the slim venue's classically downtown vibe.

508

American 🍴🍴

A1

508 Greenwich St. (at Spring St.)

Subway: Spring St (Sixth Ave.)
Phone: 212-219-2444
Web: www.508nyc.com
Prices: $$

Lunch Sun – Fri
Dinner nightly

Not many Manhattan restaurants can lay claim to brewing much of the beer list in-house, but the serious selection at 508 proves they can. Flung among the area's cobblestoned streets and warehouse-lined avenues, this microbrewery offers little frill beyond exposed brick walls, turning all the attention to the malt barley and gastropub cuisine.

The bold dishes have a decadence that holds up to the drinks but never feels unbalanced. Start with the octopus and garbanzo beans, tossed with pancetta, paprika for a smoky tint, and drizzles of olive oil. Then move on to ever-popular deviled eggs topped with a beer-battered oyster. Spiced with jalapeño and bacon, cooling reprieve comes in the form of a horseradish aïoli and pint of Spruce Almighty.

Giorgione

Italian 🍴🍴

A1

307 Spring St. (bet. Greenwich & Hudson Sts.)

Subway: Spring St (Sixth Ave.)
Phone: 212-352-2269
Web: www.giorgionenyc.com
Prices: $$

Lunch Mon – Fri
Dinner nightly

In far west SoHo, beyond Chanel and Balenciaga, find this long-time resident cherished for its quiet location where Spring Street locals enjoy a slower pace—much like Italy itself. Founded by Dean & Deluca's Giorgio Deluca, the stylish and distinctly Italian L-shaped room focuses on straightforward pizza, outstanding pastas, and serious desserts.

You can't go wrong with the handful of pastas on the menu, such as the lovingly crafted pouches of spinach and ricotta ravioli in a light tomato sauce. Delicately grilled lamb chops with *peperonata* and rosemary-roasted new potatoes are simple yet beguiling. Try one (or two) noteworthy desserts, including the flaky *crostata* filled with rich chocolate ganache and bright green *pistachio di Bronte*.

Hirohisa

B2

Japanese ✕✕

73 Thompson St. (bet. Broome & Spring Sts.)

Subway: Spring (Sixth Ave.)
Phone: 212-925-1613
Web: www.hirohisa-nyc.com
Prices: $$$

Lunch Mon – Fri
Dinner Mon – Sat

From its quiet, unmarked address to the muted colors and intensely dedicated staff, Hirohisa verges on monastic (in the best sense of the word). Head for the seats surrounding the kitchen's dining counter, where the meticulous motions of the young chef and his team are best appreciated while preparing kappo cuisine—think braised, grilled, and fried dishes in addition to raw ones.

Distinctive contrast brings brilliant flavors front and center with starters like snow crab, herbaceous okra, and shrimp jelly topped with a demitasse spoonful of caviar. Creamy sesame tofu transcends expectation when offset by dense and flan-like uni, pungent wasabi sauce and crunchy green grilled fiddlehead fern. The rice is imported from Fukui and literally perfect.

L'Ecole 😊

C3

French ✕✕

462 Broadway (at Grand St.)

Subway: Canal St (Broadway)
Phone: 212-219-3300
Web: www.lecolenyc.com
Prices: $$

Lunch & dinner Mon – Sat

Inspired and led by the dedicated students of the International Culinary Center, L'Ecole's creations are naturally insightful; even a dish that feels over-the-top illustrates their desire to succeed. It is a lovely room–welcoming and affable–with an earnest staff. Decorated with colorful walls, black-and-white photos, and circular fixtures, the space feels festive. The large glass windows overlook a bustling intersection, and people-watchers vie for these seats.

The menu features delicious classics, as promised by the surrounding "oohs and aahs." Pretty tables are set with finery, enhancing that roasted spiced monkfish atop green lentils; cured Spanish mackerel beside a warm potato salad; and a gooey chocolate almond cake laced with lemon cream.

Mercer Kitchen

C2

Contemporary 🍴🍴

99 Prince St. (at Mercer St.)

Subway: Prince St   Lunch & dinner daily
Phone: 212-966-5454
Web: www.themercerkitchen.com
Prices: $$$

From its home in the elegant Mercer Hotel, Jean-Georges' mainstay has been sexing up SoHo for over a decade. Once a stronghold for the famous and the fabulous, Mercer Kitchen still draws a well-heeled, mostly European crowd. The bi-level space splits into a café on the top floor and a dining room and lounge on the lower level, where bare tables, sultry lighting, and brick archways lend an air of swank.

Try a refreshing salad mixing plump, steamed shrimp, avocado, white mushroom, and tomato, tossed in a Champagne vinaigrette; or their classic sashimi-grade tuna spring roll, tucked with a layer of tender Napa cabbage and served with a spicy soy bean purée. Bubbly, crisp pear-and-sour cherry crumble, dolloped with crème fraîche, is divine.

Mezzogiorno

B2

Italian 🍴🍴

195 Spring St. (at Sullivan St.)

Subway: Spring St (Sixth Ave.)   Lunch & dinner daily
Phone: 212-334-2112
Web: www.mezzogiorno.com
Prices: $$

Although Mezzogiorno's striking blue awnings arrived on the scene back in the 80s, this pleasing local stalwart has been consistently occupied by pretty people and continues to be a tasteful, timeless SoHo fixture. Those seated inside are charmed by the wood-burning oven, deep-toned wood bar, and walls lined with 100 collages—each one a local artist's unique interpretation of the restaurant's logo.

An Italian-American accent pervades the kitchen's stylish cooking that bursts with flavor. Meals here might include an exceptional *vitello tonnato*, with tuna caught off the coast of Favignana draped with a lusciously creamy sauce, mayo-rich with wonderfully tart, sour capers; and *fiocchetti* pasta stuffed with a beguiling combination of cheeses and pear.

The Musket Room ❀

Contemporary 🍴🍴

D2

265 Elizabeth St. (bet. Houston & Prince Sts.)

Subway: Broadway - Lafayette St
Phone: 212-219-0764
Web: www.themusketroom.com
Prices: $$$

Dinner nightly

The Musket Room is just the kind of restaurant Nolita deserves. Here, whitewashed walls, raw timber, mortar-smeared brick, and Danish modern chairs with blue leather seats and banquettes come together in a farmhouse-chic interior that's as headturning as the willowy young things who call this nabe home. To whet their thirst, wine bottles topping a wall-length table in the back dining room are presented and poured with polish.

Chef Matt Lambert's forte is antipodean cuisine with a contemporary twist, and his masterpieces don't disappoint. To start, jade-green, satiny-smooth broccoli soup is adorned with a crunchy-shelled oxtail croquette and broccoli oil magically transformed into powder. De-constructed steak pie is an excellent entrée that reveals medium rare filet smacked with decadent Taleggio cheese foam, arranged with roasted carrots and celery root, and capped with a disk of golden puff pastry flecked with celery seeds.

Revel in The Musket Room's charismatic ambience by lingering over dessert—specifically the pavlova. The cylinder of stark white, crisp meringue is filled with passion fruit curd and dressed with whipped cream, slivered strawberries, and passion fruit pulp.

Navy

B1

Seafood ✗

137 Sullivan St. (bet. Houston & Prince Sts.)

Subway: Spring St (Sixth Ave.)   Lunch & dinner daily
Phone: 212-533-1137
Web: www.navynyc.com
Prices: $$

Only Navy could pull off a nautical-themed restaurant with repurposed WWII military duffle bags, and panels of distressed copper as well as antique sconces on the walls. Everything is beyond chic here, from the former bowling alley bench banquette, to that massive espresso machine used to serve coffee and pastries to early-to-rise SoHo-ites.

But seafood rules after breakfast, when the raw bar spouts oysters, clams, sea urchin, as well as bright Mediterranean white wine. The menu presents culinary hedonism at its finest, like mussel toast: plump mollusks, paprika, and caper aïoli spread over crunchy sourdough bread. Similarly, soft-shell crabs arrive atop a squash blossom pancake with hints of anchovy, and is accented with a dreamy blend of maple syrup.

Papatzul

B2

Mexican ✗

55 Grand St. (bet. West Broadway & Wooster St.)

Subway: Canal St (Sixth Ave.)   Lunch & dinner daily
Phone: 212-274-8225
Web: www.papatzul.com
Prices: $$

Sangria and salsas rule at Papatzul, a swanky SoHo scene rife with a classically trained chef churning out delightful Mexican cuisine. On any given evening, the cozy and narrow space, decorated with masks and dark wood, is abuzz with drinking buddies getting friendly with tequila offerings and tables of friends diving into five types of salsas—each inspired by a different region in Mexico.

Great care is given to each dish, like chicken flautas made with some of the city's best tortillas, and filled with tender grilled meat, and a dab of salsa *borracha*. For a regal repast, try slow-roasted duck enchiladas featuring a rich, almond-chili *mole*. It rises well above the neighborhood norm, making this spot quite the destination for margarita-fueled fun.

Pearl & Ash 🎭

Contemporary ✗✗

D2

220 Bowery (bet. Prince & Spring Sts.)

Subway: Bowery   Dinner nightly
Phone: 212-837-2370
Web: www.pearlandash.com
Prices: $$

With its close quarters, thumping soundtrack, pretty young things, and a menu of insanely tasty small plates, Chef Richard Kuo's Pearl & Ash is an exuberant slice of today's dining zeitgeist. A sexy ambience pervades the blond wood space, while an array of memorabilia from the chef's travels personalizes the backdrop.

The free-roaming cuisine arranged under the headings raw, small, fish, and meat offer up tantalizing tastes. Start with warm bread paired with an artful smear of maple-butter enriched with chicken fat before moving on to silken tea-cured salmon plated with tamarind paste and seaweed salad; crisped lamb belly and charred eggplant sprinkled with oregano; and fried potatoes dressed with chorizo and umami-packed porcini mayonnaise.

Peasant

Italian ✗✗

C3

194 Elizabeth St. (bet. Prince & Spring Sts.)

Subway: Spring St (Lafayette St.)   Dinner Tue – Sun
Phone: 212-965-9511
Web: www.peasantnyc.com
Prices: $$

Chef and owner Frank DeCarlo keeps getting it right at Peasant—the wine bar downstairs is a perfect mix of cozy and communal, thereby capturing the feeling of being in an authentic *osteria*. But, whether seated upstairs or in the wine room downstairs, the scene is wholly rustic and genuine, showcasing whitewashed brick walls, bare wood tables, and a roster of expert culinary delights.

Try not to fill up on the terrific bread—save it for sopping up the heavenly razor clams *al forno* simmering in garlic sauce. Every bit of the *maltagliati con coniglio* is a perfect ratio of pasta to braised rabbit and fava beans. *Porchetta arrosto*, their excellent rotisserie suckling pig, is wondrously juicy with hints of garlic and rosemary, served with fingerling potatoes.

Public 🏵

C2

210 Elizabeth St. (bet. Prince & Spring Sts.)

Subway: Spring St (Lafayette St.)
Phone: 212-343-7011
Web: www.public-nyc.com
Prices: $$$

Lunch Sat – Sun
Dinner nightly

Smartly designed to embrace its past life as a loading dock, Public is located up a set of metal stairs and behind a garage door. Inside, the space is as multi-faceted and dexterous as the menu. Beyond the entrance displaying vintage *Life* magazines, find a softer dining room with billowing fabrics. Waiting crowds may sip on cocktails at The Daily, where the list changes daily—naturally!

Menus are presented on clipboards and resemble order tickets, lending a certain old-timey appeal. Regulars can have chef-selected artisanal wine delivered monthly to their personal bronzed mailboxes by the entrance.

Public's menu finds a sweet balance between the ambitious and approachable; this is also what keeps the first-come-first-served Sunday Supper popular (go early). Chef Brad Farmerie does not shy away from eye-popping flavors and fusion experiments that marry global ingredients into, say, hibiscus-braised fennel with sea trout. Ingenious, almost meaty carrot Bolognese, cashew nut pesto, and fresh Thai basil add layers of dimension to cloud-like ricotta *cavatelli*. Lamb osso buco braised in achiote apple cider topped with orange gremolata over a bed of crispy chestnut polenta is hauntingly good.

Raoul's

French ✗✗

B1

180 Prince St. (bet. Sullivan & Thompson Sts.)

Subway: Spring St (Sixth Ave.)   Dinner nightly
Phone: 212-966-3518
Web: www.raouls.com
Prices: $$$

Whether by charm or talent, this beloved bistro has survived 30-plus years in one of the fussiest parts of town, somehow remaining popular, sophisticated, and stylishly unpretentious. The authentic French fare is prepared simply, but remains impressive with top ingredients and delicious flavors—as in the steak tartare with quail egg, or seared foie gras with Concord grape purée. The menu, exquisitely handwritten on chalkboards and presented by the amiable waitstaff, still appeals to savvy diners and connoisseurs hungry for meaty steaks and crispy duck fat fries.

The energetic atmosphere in the dimly lit main room is intoxicating, but those seeking a calmer spot for quiet conversation should try the bright upstairs space or tiny covered garden.

Rouge et Blanc

Contemporary ✗✗

B1

48 MacDougal St. (bet. Houston & Prince Sts.)

Subway: Houston St   Dinner Tue – Sun
Phone: 212-260-5757
Web: www.rougeetblancnyc.com
Prices: $$$

Rouge et Blanc features a menu that stirs together the conceits of Vietnamese and French cuisines served amidst a backdrop of Indochine-influenced décor—a burlap-covered ceiling, red lacquered chairs, handcrafted pottery, and plants.

The talented kitchen impresses with salacious specialties like green papaya salad, that everyday favorite, here elevated with homemade green curry vinaigrette and crunchy-fried head-on shrimp. Other items have included cool rice vermicelli dressed with sweet onion sauce and coarse-ground pork sausage; as well as a spicy claypot of tofu and minced chicken braised in rich veal stock. An impressive selection of French wines complement the menu, but a chestnut ale from Corsica, on draught, is a great thirst-quenching option.

Rubirosa 🏵️

C2

Italian ✕✕

235 Mulberry St. (bet. Prince & Spring Sts.)

Subway: Spring St (Lafayette St.)
Phone: 212-965-0500
Web: www.rubirosanyc.com
Prices: $$

Lunch & dinner daily

A no-nonsense approach and unapologetic pride in Italian-American culture leads Rubirosa to success on every level. The rustic wood floors creak with authenticity, the curved marble bar is perfect for people-watching, and the classic menu tastes as if it were passed down through generations of hard-working *nonni*.

Beneath the barrel-vaulted, pressed-tin ceilings, success seems evident on every plate, like the Rubirosa sandwich of fried chicken cutlets with sweet roasted peppers, slathered with excellent pesto. Piping hot and hearty "grandma's braciole" is wonderfully tender beef wrapped around breadcrumbs, cheese, and herbs in a chunky and garlicky tomato sauce that begs to be mopped up with a heel of bread. Grab a slice of pizza from 4-5 P.M. daily.

Snack 🏵️

B1

Greek ✕

105 Thompson St. (bet. Prince & Spring Sts.)

Subway: Spring St (Sixth Ave.)
Phone: 212-925-1040
Web: www.snacksoho.com
Prices: 🍝🍝

Lunch & dinner daily

No need to second-guess the purpose of Snack. It's a casual spot bursting with meze, where shoppers take a break from the jewel-box boutiques that flank this miniscule storefront. Here, juice glasses double as wine goblets, sepia-toned antique photographs line the space, and starting your meal with a baklava is perfectly acceptable. It's no surprise that two sister tavernas have sprouted in the West Village and Hell's Kitchen.

The Mediterranean menu features plenty of signatures including marinated anchovies wrapped in grape leaves, garlicky skordalia, and earthy Macedonian wines. The chalkboard's daily specials are a great starting point, especially the *palpoutsaka*, smoky eggplant stuffed with sirloin and topped with tomatoes and béchamel.

Torrisi Italian Specialties ❀

Italian 🍴🍴

C2

250 Mulberry St. (at Prince St.)

Subway: Spring St (Lafayette St.)
Phone: 212-965-0955
Web: www.torrisinyc.com
Prices: $$$

Lunch Fri – Sun
Dinner nightly

At once fun, serious, professional, and friendly, this celebrated downtown favorite is reinventing Little Italy's past and present with outrageous success. Through the shop-like façade's lacy curtains and wood-framed windows, find shelves lined with Italian-American items like dried pasta and preserved foods. Details like the black- and white-tiled floors, bistro tables, pressed-tin ceiling, Tiffany oyster forks, and Delmonico's crockery are all part of their discourse on yesteryear.

One night, service feels rushed, wrapping up ten tasting dishes in an hour; the next, it is relaxed and comfortable.

Nearly every element from the menu is prepared with modern reinterpretation, and maybe even a bit of Japanese technique. Layers of neighborhood history combine in a single plate of thinly pounded "Tuna Southern Mulberry" bathed in a spicy Sichuan oil, paired with pickled Chinese greens, woodsy shiitakes, and a steamed bun as a nod to nearby Chinatown. Excellent pastas are always a highlight here and may include the supple and beautifully crafted sheep's milk ricotta gnocchi gently showered with butter, ramps, and topped with pecorino. Sweet corn "arancini" are a mind-blowing original.

Uncle Boons

C3

Thai XX

7 Spring St. (bet. Bowery & Elizabeth St.)

Subway: Bowery
Phone: 646-370-6650
Web: www.uncleboons.com
Prices: $$

Dinner Tue – Sun

Join a hip row sipping Singha slushies at this lively hideaway of Chefs Matt Danzer and Ann Redding. Inside, find the tightly set clutch of seats framed by a whimsical albeit kitschy décor. Ignore your table's bitsy size when pondering the husband-and-wife team's passionate fare, which dilates the constraints of traditional Thai food.

Rotisserie chicken (offered as an entrée with green mango salad and sticky rice) is a luscious composition tossed with banana blossoms, cashews, and crispy shallots. *Laab neuh gae* sets chopped lamb ablaze with chilies, lime, mint, and toasted rice powder. Similarly, grilled octopus and *khao soi kaa kai*, homemade noodles in Northern-style golden curry with chicken and preserved greens, are…shall we…killer.

Remember, stars
(❀❀❀ ❀) are awarded
for cuisine only! Elements
such as service and décor
are not a factor.

DRINK AND DINE

TriBeCa is now a bustling commercial center sprinkled with design stores, warehouses-turned-lavish lofts, and trendy drink-cum-dining destinations. Quite simply, this triangle below Canal is a cool place to eat, and its affluent residents can be seen splurging in restaurants whose reputations precede them. Of course that isn't to say that this area's famously wide, umbrella-shaded sidewalks—among the city's top spots for star-gazing—aren't cramped with more modest hangouts such as **Puffy's Tavern**. This friendly neighborhood spot displays five flat-screens for sports fans and happy-hour crowds, who come to devour small bites and hearty sandwiches by the fistful. Over on West Broadway and Leonard, **Square Diner** is a New York institution that takes you back in time via red vinyl booths and a counter serving staples like soups, salads, and sandwiches. Like every other Manhattan neighborhood, TriBeCa claims its own culinary treasures: **Bubby's** is a local delight for comfort food favorites; while **Zucker's Bagels & Smoked Fish** flaunts an updated décor and floors foodies with a taste

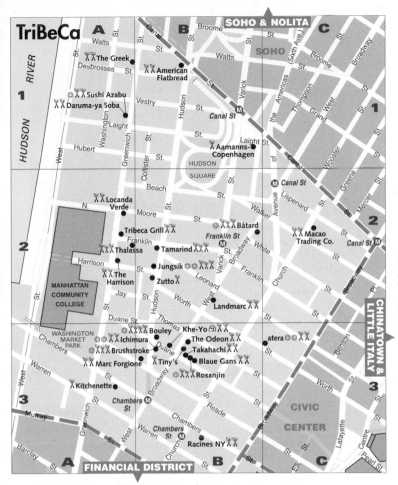

TriBeCa

SOHO & NOLITA

SOHO

HUDSON RIVER

ⅩⅩ The Greek

ⅩⅩ American Flatbread

❀Ⅹ Sushi Azabu

ⅩⅩ Daruma-ya Soba

Ⅹ Aamanns-Copenhagen

HUDSON SQUARE

ⅩⅩ Locanda Verde

❀ⅩⅩ Bâtard

Franklin St

Tribeca Grill ⅩⅩ

ⅩⅩ Macao Trading Co.

ⅩⅩⅩ Thalassa

Tamarind ⅩⅩⅩ

Jungsik ❀❀Ⅹ

Zutto Ⅹ

ⅩⅩ The Harrison

MANHATTAN COMMUNITY COLLEGE

Landmarc ⅩⅩ

WASHINGTON MARKET PARK

❀ⅩⅩⅩ Bouley

Khe-Yo ❀ⅩⅩ

❀❀Ⅹ Ichimura

The Odeon ⅩⅩ

❀ⅩⅩⅩ Brushstroke

Takahachi ⅩⅩ

ⅩⅩ Marc Forgione

Ⅹ Tiny's

Blaue Gans ⅩⅩ

● atera ❀❀ⅩⅩ

❀ⅩⅩⅩ Rosanjin

Ⅹ Kitchenette

Chambers St Ⓜ

CIVIC CENTER

Chambers St Ⓜ

Racines NY ⅩⅩ

CHINATOWN & LITTLE ITALY

FINANCIAL DISTRICT

of *bubbe*'s best. **Dirty Bird To Go** is a mainstay that delivers fresh, all-natural chicken in its many glorious forms—try the buttermilk-fried or slow-roasted rotisserie for instant gratification. And over on North Moore Street, **Smith and Mills** is a charming cocoon presenting fantastic eats along with spectacular drinks.

In keeping with its individuality and cutting-edge spirit, TriBeCa also offers a gourmet experience for any palate

and price tag. Urban groups and wine enthusiasts can be found popping bottles at the always-trending **Bubble Lounge**, a low-lit spot for celebrating any occasion in style. Given its *trés* sophisticated carte of hors d'oeuvres and sips, it's no wonder that city slickers flock here regularly. Otherwise, you may find them delving into the shelves at **Chambers Street Wines** to keep the party going. Those looking for something

to enjoy with their wine will rejoice over the monthly events sponsored by **New York Vintners**. These include free wine and cheese tastings, as well as cooking demonstrations on how to decorate cupcakes with the kids. Sip on a few sparkling varietals while you're at it!

BAKERIES

Work off a hangover at AIRE Ancient Baths, a luxury spa inspired by ancient civilizations and water-induced relaxation. They even offer rituals where you can soak yourself in olive oil, cava, or red wine. The only downside? You can't drink it! Then, take your appetite to one of TriBeCa's numerous (and wonderful) bakeries. **Sarabeth's** is an award-winning jam maker who turned this once humble retail store into the monstrous hit spot it is today. With its impressive spectacle of cookies, cakes, preserves, and pastries, this specialty store knows how to play the culinary game with such solid competitors as **Duane Park Patisserie**, known for pastries and seasonal specialties; or even

Tribeca Treats for a plethora of decadent chocolates. **Birdbath**, an integral part of the City Bakery clan, is admired for its eco-friendly philosophy as well as its unique selection of bites and bevvies. **Takahachi** on Murray Street is a modestly decorated but must-visit treasure for Japanese refreshers. While here, slurp up a *matcha* latte while snacking on a macaron *sakura*.

AROUND THE WORLD

Korin is a culinary haven that flaunts an extensive and exquisite knife collection, plus tableware and gorgeous kitchen supplies. Not only do these products shine in many fine dining establishments, but they also bring to life the essence of food art, leaving cooks hankering for more. Chefs come here to get their blades worked on or to order a specific knife, while others may opt for the gorgeous gift sets, sure to excite a friend or impress a colleague. From top-notch gear to fantastic grub, **Mangez Avec Moi** is a tiny Southeast Asian marvel beloved for its big, bold flavors. Skip the ubiquitous pan-Asian stuff for authentic, homemade Thai or Laotian specials—*nam kao* is a bamboo stew bobbing with mushrooms, fish, and anchovy sauce.

Before this area became associated with top films from varying genres, director Bob Giraldi shot his mob- and food-themed movie *Dinner Rush* at famed eatery, **Gigino Trattoria**. However, thanks to the annual Tribeca Film Festival, a springtime extravaganza created by Robert DeNiro to revitalize the area after 9/11, the 'hood hosts twelve days of great films and plenty of community camaraderie. Gaggles of locals, tourists, and film buffs collect here every year to see the movies and share their views and reviews at hot spots like **Nish Nush**, a sidewalk show-stopper incorporating authentic Israeli hummus and crispy falafel into delicious sandwiches, hearty platters, and healthy salads.

Settled along Franklin Street, **All Good Things** is a simple, sleek, and open market furnishing residents and gourmands with an array of pristine seafood, fresh meat (available at **Dickson's Farmstand**), and hedonistic cheeses from **Cavaniola's Gourmet Cheese Shop**. Coffee, ice cream, fruits, and flowers are also primo, so get here before the clamoring crowds get to you. Speaking of laudable ventures, over on Church Street, Chef David Bouley and team have created **Bouley Botanical**, an imaginative and resourceful event space, designed to entice the senses and committed to celebrating every occasion in style. Equipped with state-of-the-art sound and lighting equipment, as well as an impressive exhibition kitchen, this greenhouse-inspired venue pledges to fit your every mood with the likes of yoga, Pilates, and other wholesome practices.

Aamanns-Copenhagen

Scandinavian ✗

B1

13 Laight St. (at St. Johns Ln.)

Subway: Canal St (Sixth Ave.)
Phone: 212-925-1313
Web: www.aamanns-copenhagen.com
Prices: $$

Lunch & dinner Tue – Sun

Located near the bustling Holland Tunnel, diners would need to dodge the traffic speeding up Sixth before arriving at this striking spot. Phrases like "Danish Eatery" and "RUGBØD PORK" are tattooed on its white-brick façade; while the interior cuts a clean, sleek design with white walls, free form art murals, bare wood tables, and fresh Nordic touches.

The sour, chewy, sweet, and nutty brown bread alone is worth a trip here. Inspired dishes go on to include tangy kale tartare topped with white endive, diced apples, and walnuts; and pan-fried hake *smørrebrød* with green remoulade and herb salad. The trio of herring is a revelation, prepared in mustard-tarragon cream with radish; spicy tomato compote and endive; and pickled juniper, capers, egg, and onion.

American Flatbread

Pizza ✗✗

B1

205 Hudson St. (at Canal St.)

Subway: Canal St (Sixth Ave.)
Phone: 212-776-1441
Web: www.americanflatbread.com
Prices: $$

Lunch & dinner daily

This TriBeCa outpost of the Vermont favorite is the first Flatbread to cross its state's border since its inception. The expansive downtown space is impeccably designed with wraparound windows, plenty of sunlight, and wood-burning ovens put to heavy use.

While they pride themselves on their unique, perfectly formed flatbread crust, the toppings (house-made and organic everything) are the real draw—each ingredient is vibrant, fun, and well balanced. The Mopsy's Kalua Pork is decked with house-smoked shoulder meat, their own mango-barbecue sauce, red onions, pineapple, plus Vermont chevre and whole-milk mozzarella. The New Vermont is layered with juicy maple-fennel sausage, sun-dried tomatoes, caramelized onions, mushrooms, mozzarella, and grana.

atera ✿ ✿

Contemporary 𝕏𝕏

77 Worth St. (bet. Broadway & Church St.)

Subway: Chambers St (Church St.)   Dinner Tue – Sat
Phone: 212-226-1444
Web: www.ateranyc.com
Prices: $$$$

The understated (read: unmarked) façade makes atera easy to overlook. Once inside this large, handsome, and dimly lit space, expect to be served a complimentary cocktail. This is a nice touch, since you'll soon all be sitting together at the slate-gray tasting counter upstairs surrounding the studio-like kitchen.

There is a separate group table milled from the cross-section of a felled tree that is surrounded by grow-walls of lichen for a pleasant, terrarium-like feel. Still, those soft leather counter seats offer priceless views of this young, high-spirited, and deeply talented kitchen.

Chef Matthew Lightner's ambitious set menus begin with a series of genius snacks. Gobble up a beer and buttermilk macaron with sturgeon caviar and crème fraîche; roasted beets with bee's wax in flower petals; or smoked swordfish *lardo*. Outstanding flavor underscores every element of sea urchin with roasted cubes of butternut squash, scoops of chilled sea "pearl" and nasturtium petals and leaves. A mingle of roasted squab breast is artistically arranged with bronze fennel fronds, black garlic purée, autumn olive, elderberries, and huckleberries with a quenelle of chicken liver, heart, and tomato ragout.

Bâtard

Contemporary ✕✕✕

B2

239 West Broadway (bet. Walker & White Sts.)

Subway: Franklin St

Dinner Tue – Sat

Phone: 212-219-2777

Web: www.batardtribeca.com

Prices: $$$

Bâtard is an outright winner among the wealthy downtown throngs and longtime "friends of Drew." Memories of Corton remain behind the gold-painted walls and uncovered tables. Yet its current vibe retains none of that earlier elegance or formality. In fact, it's downright noisy and in total contradiction to Chef Markus Glocker's precise, accurate, and classically European cuisine.

The master brings his perfect training from Gordon Ramsay to this kitchen, but here, the entire experience is more urban than fussy—cue the unremarkable service. Still, every qualm can be quenched by the very reasonably priced and Burgundy-focused wine list, a remnant of Montrachet many moons ago.

Paper-thin slices of cured ocean trout posed beside spicy crème fraîche; and pastrami-treated octopus terrine, topped with creamy potatoes, grainy mustard, and toasty rye crumbles, both flaunt a playful yet intensely pleasant interplay of flavor and texture. Veal tenderloin and asparagus wrapped in a *tramezzini* and trickled with a heady *sauce diable* is a crowd favorite for fitting reason. And, although inelegant to look at, fried caramelized milk bread with fennel yogurt, is an inspired (and delicious) ending.

Blaue Gans

B3

Austrian ✖✖

139 Duane St. (bet. Church St. & West Broadway)

Subway: Chambers St (West Broadway)
Phone: 212-571-8880
Web: www.kg-ny.com
Prices: $$

Lunch & dinner daily

Talented Chef Kurt Gutenbrunner has worked immensely hard to put Austrian food on the Manhattan map, and his Blaue Gans is an unforced, chic home to wonderfully satisfying Austrian cuisine. Regulars flock here to bask in the uniquely European yet downtown setting—like a vintage film poster-lined café in Vienna.

Beyond a glass case of streudel and *kaiserschmarren*, which has you thinking dessert from the moment you enter, lies a menu of authentic tastes. Sample the speck-like South Tyrolian dried ham served with the spicy Liptauer cheese or pretzel-crusted cod with glazed beets, before diving into a creamy chestnut soup with hints of Armagnac and mushroom. The Hugo, a wine-based cocktail with sekt and Grüner Veltliner is refreshing even on chilly days.

Daruma-ya Soba

A1

Japanese ✖✖

428 Greenwich St. (bet. Laight & Vestry Sts.)

Subway: Franklin St
Phone: 212-274-0428
Web: www.darumaya-nyc.com
Prices: $$

Lunch Mon – Fri
Dinner nightly

Known for sensational soba and expert execution, Chef Shuichi Kotani crafts his renowned buckwheat noodles every 30 minutes, cooks them in a mere 20 seconds, and offers an experience as authentic as any you'd find in Japan. Cozy up in a round leather booth in the clubby front area, or take a seat in the more elegant wood and stone dining room.

To truly understand the clearly by, texture, nutty flavors, and the precision that goes into hand-cutting each strand, go for the purest expression of the complex noodles—served in a simple, delicate dashi with scallions, alongside green vegetables and *takuan* (Japanese yellow pickled daikon). Also explore small plates like Japanese fishcake with shiso and wasabi, sushi offerings, or the fixed dinner menu.

Bouley ❀

163 Duane St. (at Hudson St.)

Subway: Chambers St (West Broadway)
Phone: 212-964-2525
Web: www.davidbouley.com
Prices: $$$$

Lunch & dinner Mon – Sat

On the outside, Bouley flaunts the hallmarks of what every successful TriBeCa restaurant should be: an industrial façade with high arches, exposed brick, and oversized windows decked in exceptional silks that when drawn offer streetviews into this remarkably orchestrated kitchen. Inside, hand-painted wallpaper, vaulted ceilings, and custom furnishings make for an operatic setting reminiscent of a château—maybe the same one from which the floors were salvaged (literally).

From a flute of champagne upon arrival to the pound cake guests are gifted upon departure, every detail is planned with warmth and precision. Dining here is a sumptuous and inimitable experience. Of course, this extends to the complex, seasonal, and very contemporary menu. Meals showcase tremendous skill in the yuzu crisp topped with *pommes aligot* and a slice of black truffle from Perigord. Distinct international ingredients are beautifully paired in smile-inducing dishes of sweet Dungeness crab brightened with yuzu, served with warm and earthy porcini flan, and black truffle dashi.

Desserts can be original classics, like the hot caramelized Anjou pear with Valrhona chocolate, biscuit Breton, and hot toffee sauce.

Brushstroke ✹

B3

Japanese 𝕏𝕏𝕏

30 Hudson St. (at Duane St.)

Subway: Chambers St (West Broadway)
Phone: 212-791-3771
Web: www.davidbouley.com
Prices: $$$$

Lunch Tue – Sat
Dinner Mon – Sat

Little parks, cobblestoned streets, and lots of tranquility are the hallmarks of this primo neighborhood corner. The interior embraces an elemental design combining glass, steel, rice paper, and woods—ranging from Canadian white pine and oak counters to rustic reclaimed planks. Even the professional and gracious servers' uniforms seem to complement the space. The result of such painstaking detail is a sense of harmony and beauty throughout Brushstroke.

The kaiseki menu may begin with a custard-like dome of tofu atop wedges of dashi-braised mountain yam, turnip, and pumpkin tucked with sweet Scottish langoustine. Essence of yuzu appears in many guises, notably in the yuzu-perfumed *akamutsu* (a rare deep-sea ruby snapper prized for its oily-tender white meat) over a luscious bed of toro tartare, studded with osetra caviar and crisp ribbons of burdock. Expect intensely flavorful meat courses like sliced pork belly, cooked with myriad techniques for velvety texture, with clear and enticingly sour apple sauce.

Desserts are surprising and delicious—think rich, salty, nutty, caramel-like ice cream flavored with soy sauce topped with a bit of wasabi-induced heat and crunchy buckwheat groats.

The Greek

A1

Greek ✗✗

458 Greenwich St. (bet. Desbrosses & Watts Sts.)

Subway: Franklin St   Lunch & dinner daily
Phone: 646-476-3941
Web: www.thegreektribeca.com
Prices: $$

TriBeCa may offer more highfalutin dining halls than intimate ethnic eats, but one step inside this Greenwich Street haunt transports you to a rustic, cozy den of Greek hospitality. Beyond the impressive mahogany bar and mounted wine barrels, head toward the rear dining room and bask in the relaxed vibe of this very comfortable neighborhood spot.

Start with a trio of excellent, traditional meze, or a whole roasted eggplant drizzled with olive oil. Revel in the land's bounty with the mixed grill, served as a cornucopia of marinated meats like pork and chicken souvlaki with thinly sliced ribeye. End the meal with *kataifi*, shredded phyllo layered with semolina custard, pastry cream, and toasted pistachios, or just sip another glass of Greek wine.

The Harrison

A2

Contemporary ✗✗

355 Greenwich St. (at Harrison St.)

Subway: Franklin St   Lunch Wed – Sun
Phone: 212-274-9310   Dinner nightly
Web: www.theharrison.com
Prices: $$

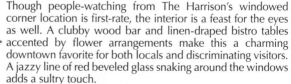

Though people-watching from The Harrison's windowed corner location is first-rate, the interior is a feast for the eyes as well. A clubby wood bar and linen-draped bistro tables accented by flower arrangements make this a charming downtown favorite for both locals and discriminating visitors. A jazzy line of red beveled glass snaking around the windows adds a sultry touch.

The seasonally focused menu changes frequently, but standouts may include a juicy hanger steak with tomato jam-topped corn pudding. A heady "salsa" of chopped Parmesan, herbs, and olive oil arrives with crisply toasted crostini. Desserts are elegant riffs on classic American flavors, including a moist cornmeal biscuit with almonds, cherries, and root beer-infused whipped cream.

Ichimura ✿ ✿

Japanese 🍴

B3

30 Hudson St. (at Duane St.)

Subway: Chambers St (West Broadway)
Phone: 212-791-3771
Web: www.davidbouley.com
Prices: $$$$

Dinner Tue – Sat

This serene little alcove is a special place. It may be located in the shadow of Brushstroke next door, but Ichimura basks in its own rightful glory in a light wood room that fashions an eye-pleasing culmination of Japanese and TriBeCa styles.

Some aspects of service may show a veneer of downtown cool in place of professional polish. But ignore that and settle into your relaxed invitation to the L-shaped counter wrapping around the ever-charming and deeply talented Chef Eiji Ichimura.

Some courses may wander from the confines of omakase tradition with an unexpected progression, self-styled sushi, or cooked dish that is more distinctive than classic, but nothing is sacrificed in that translation. *Chawan mushi* is absolutely luscious beneath a layer of black truffle gelée, mixing sweet Florida crab and minced chives. A succession of *Edo-mae* sushi is the ultimate marriage of exquisite fish and rice that is light, fluffy, and arrives at a temperature that matches your palate with superhuman precision. Each silky slice of supremely fresh, aged, or slightly cured hamachi, fluke, or amberjack tastes as if it were destined for your plate. If given the choice, go for seconds on the double toro.

Jungsik ✿ ✿

B2

2 Harrison St. (at Hudson St.)

Subway: Franklin St
Phone: 212-219-0900
Web: www.jungsik.kr
Prices: $$$$

Dinner Mon– Sat

Cool, chic, and completely urbane, Jungsik is the epitome of contemporary elegance. Inside the large, neatly partitioned space, find rich browns and ivory furnishings with lighting that is flattering yet bright enough to see your food clearly. The chairs are deep and tables are well spaced, but request a plush corner banquette for maximum comfort. Even the place settings have a sculptural beauty, from the dark matte pottery to shiny white porcelain vessels. The clientele is young and hip but the ambience is fairly quiet and somewhat reflective.

The modern Korean cuisine is confident, complex, and profoundly enjoyable. *Bibimbap* is a bowl of toothsome short-grain seaweed rice mingled with layers of diced pickled zucchini, ripe avocado, puffed rice, slivered lettuce, and torched yellowtail cubes. More audacious palates might revel in the crispy red snapper sporting flesh so creamy and flavors so fragrant, balanced, and sensational from a pour of hot oil and accompanying *tom yum* broth.

Soigné presentations feature a whole petite lobster dressed tableside in rich and spicy lobster reduction with seared sea scallop, chewy noodles, daikon chunks, silken tofu, and tiny roulades of Napa cabbage.

Khe-Yo 🏮

B3

Lao 🍴🍴

157 Duane St. (bet. Hudson St. & West Broadway)

Subway: Chambers St (West Broadway)
Phone: 212-587-1089
Web: www.kheyo.com
Prices: $$

Dinner nightly

Khe-Yo brings a breath of fresh, chili-scented air and the fiery, fragrant flavors of Laotian cuisine to TriBeCa. Diners are already packing the place to the gills, sipping cocktails and local craft brews at the bar while waiting for precious banquette seats to open up. Sound skyrockets through the dim, industrial space.

The food is worth braving the wait and the decibel levels, especially with sauces like the Bang Bang with four kinds of Thai chilies, cilantro, fish sauce, and garlic. These same chilies appear in dishes like *nam khao*, which mixes coins of Kaffir lime-pork sausage with crispy, pan-fried coconut rice and crunchy iceberg lettuce wedges for textural contrast. Scallion and prawn toasts sop up every drop of luscious brick-red curry sauce.

Kitchenette

A3

American 🍴

156 Chambers St. (bet. Greenwich St. & West Broadway)

Subway: Chambers St (West Broadway)
Phone: 212-267-6740
Web: www.kitchenetterestaurant.com
Prices: 🍴🍴

Lunch & dinner daily

With its steady stream of moms and financial types looking for a strong cup of fresh brewed coffee, unassuming Kitchenette is a beloved anytime stop for homey food and amazing layer cakes. Everything feels a bit quirky, with sawed off doors doubling as tables, picket fences lining the pink-striped walls, and a time-worn cupboard.

Their famed breakfasts feature egg dishes and freshly baked treats, but the separate milkshake menu (peanut butter-blondie served in a mason jar) is earning equal attention. At other times, find satisfying bowls of chicken noodle soup, or succulent fried chicken drizzled with honey. Desserts here are not to be missed as in moist, fragrant sprinkle cakes slathered in cream cheese frosting and...you guessed it...sprinkles aplenty.

Landmarc

B2

Mediterranean 🗶🗶

179 West Broadway (bet. Leonard & Worth Sts.)

Subway: Franklin St
Phone: 212-343-3883
Web: www.landmarc-restaurant.com
Prices: $$

Lunch & dinner daily

Chef/owner Marc Murphy's Landmarc is *the* TriBeCa destination for meeting friends over casual drinks and food that happens to be rib-sticking delicious. Downstairs, the bi-level space showcases thick steel cables suspending industrial art and a horseshoe bar flanking a large cooking fire that warms the soul and sizzles those lamb chops. The upstairs is more serene.

Meals may start with lighter plates of smoky and blistered shishito peppers flecked with crunchy sea salt. Then, move on to deeply satisfying (and reasonably priced) nightly pasta specials, like thick and buttery spaghetti *alla Bolognese*. "Landmarc classic" cheese plates are a reliable highlight. Miniature desserts mean that there is always room for a lemon-custard tart (or four).

Locanda Verde

A2

Italian 🗶🗶

379 Greenwich St. (at N. Moore St.)

Subway: Franklin St
Phone: 212-925-3797
Web: www.locandaverdenyc.com
Prices: $$$

Lunch & dinner daily

Chef Andrew Carmellini may be a busy man, yet his rustic and gratifying Italian idol remains as trendy as ever. Locanda Verde is coveted as much for its incredible setting as its well-versed lineup of tasty fare. Breakfast verges on divine—think lemon pancakes and apple-cider donuts. No matter the time of day, this Italian brasserie (of sorts) is abuzz and everyone looks beautiful amid low lights, handsome floors, and walls adorned with wine bottles.

Expect to see bare tables packed with diners waxing poetic about marinated beets strewn with pecorino and crushed walnuts, or green fettucine with white Bolognese. Nobody should leave here without sampling one of their superb sweets: a sticky fig-honey upside down cake with fig *sorbetto* shows much flair.

Macao Trading Co.

Macanese ✗✗

311 Church St. (bet. Lispenard & Walker Sts.)

Subway: Canal St (Sixth Ave.)
Phone: 212-431-8750
Web: www.macaonyc.com
Prices: $$

Dinner nightly

A red light marks the entrance to this playful spot, where just beyond the black velvet curtains, a smart clientele packs the dimly lit bar and downstairs dining area. The upstairs space seems to flaunt the opium den-chic of old Macao. Wooden crates sealed in chicken wire hold a collection of decorative items, while dark furnishings and high ceilings complete the look.

The menu is divided into subsections by ingredient and style (Portuguese or Chinese) and includes tasty bites like *tetilla*, cheese-stuffed meatballs in smoked-paprika tomato sauce, topped with chorizo and served with bread chunks for sopping. Seared cuttlefish with sesame noodles may be followed by Chaozhou-style cod, delicately steamed and set atop braised *choy sum* with "sizzling" broth.

Marc Forgione

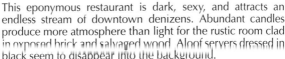

American ✗✗

134 Reade St. (bet. Greenwich & Hudson Sts.)

Subway: Chambers St (West Broadway)
Phone: 212-941-9401
Web: www.marcforgione.com
Prices: $$$

Lunch Sun
Dinner nightly

This eponymous restaurant is dark, sexy, and attracts an endless stream of downtown denizens. Abundant candles produce more atmosphere than light for the rustic room clad in exposed brick and salvaged wood. Aloof servers dressed in black seem to disappear into the background.

The innovative American fare excites with bold flavors, as in barbecued oysters sprinkled with pancetta powder. Montauk fluke *en croute*, set over roasted cauliflower, hazelnuts, and capers topped with a buttery panel of toast, is dressed with *sauce proposal*—so named because the rich brown butter and golden raisin emulsion is said to have earned the chef a few romantic offers. It is delicious, but Chef Forgione deserves equal affection for those amazing butter-glazed potato rolls.

The Odeon

American American ✗✗

B3

145 West Broadway (at Thomas St.)

Subway: Chambers St (West Broadway)
Phone: 212-233-0507
Web: www.theodeonrestaurant.com
Prices: $$$

Lunch & dinner daily

Classic and dry, The Odeon's martinis are among the best in town. Then again, the stylish art deco feel, cascading flowers, and red leather banquettes do just as much to endear this favorite local bistro. In fair weather, the huge, columned space opens to the sidewalk where a handful of tables are set not far from their ice cream cart. It may be thirty-some years young, but the mood is always either fun or ebullient.

The brasserie menu is straightforward and very good, offering crowd-pleasers like hearty onion soup beneath thick slices of bread and a gooey canopy of bubbling Gruyère. Or, try NY strip steaks cooked exactly to order and served with a house-made béarnaise sauce with hints of tarragon. Skip the fries in lieu of crème brulée for dessert.

Racines NY

French ✗✗

B3

94 Chambers St. (bet. Broadway & Church St.)

Subway: Chambers St (West Broadway)
Phone: 212-227-3400
Web: www.racinesny.com
Prices: $$$

Dinner Mon – Sat

A single white orchid atop the wide, marble bar at Racines sums up the theme of this restaurant: beauty in simplicity found through attention to detail. The American outpost of the Parisian originals, Racines produces elegant dishes in an equally sophisticated, yet uncluttered atmosphere that errs on the side of rustic.

Every moment of the meal is well conceived, from the sips of celery velouté spiked with turmeric and offered as an amuse-bouche, to the 800-label strong wine list. The kitchen team's fantastic technique shines in the Oregon wild morels dish—a potpourri of foraged, honeycomb-capped mushrooms, rife with their midnight color and smoky flavors, sitting atop a melting base of Di Palo's burrata, freshly cracked black pepper, and aged balsamic.

Rosanjin ✿

B3

141 Duane St. (bet. Church St. & West Broadway)

Subway: Chambers St (West Broadway) Dinner Mon – Sat
Phone: 212-346-0664
Web: www.rosanjintribeca.com
Prices: $$$$

♿

With windows covered in decorative fabric to impede views inside, Rosanjin appears cloaked in luxury. The stately yet intimate dining room features heavy wood furnishings and opposing walls of olive-colored silks and interlocking pieces of unfinished marble. Tables are covered with unique serving pieces made of gold, turquoise, and cedar chopsticks carved by the finest artisans in Kyoto.

Equally stunning is the impeccable fish, hyperlocal and carefully sourced from a specialty distributor. The nine-course kaiseki may begin with an enticingly subdued starter of pumpkin and tofu in cool bonito dashi with simmered chrysanthemum stem and a tuft of micro-kale. Move on to sashimi featuring *saba* cured in kelp, supremely fresh red snapper, and luscious, sweet-tasting mackerel artistically presented with curlicues of orange carrot, snowy radish, and purple shiso flowers crushed and sprinkled into a tiny pool of soy sauce. Sushi—think thick and creamy uni licked with a "special" soy sauce, pickled ginger, and osetra caviar—is just as masterful.

Rice dishes are compact but brimming with flavor like *do-nabe* with flaky fluke, Chinese sausage, reduced black vinegar, salmon roe, and *oshinko*.

Sushi Azabu ✿

A1

Japanese 🍴🍴

428 Greenwich St. (bet. Laight & Vestry Sts.)

Subway: Franklin St   Dinner nightly
Phone: 212-274-0428
Web: www.darumaya-nyc.com
Prices: $$$

Sushi Azabu has the look and feel of a private den. The space is dim and cozy, yet there are attractively spare embellishments like the pebble-inlaid floor, comfortable curved booths, and the dark, slender painting of a carp behind the counter. Food is not merely prepared but presented with tremendous care: fresh oysters arrive on red lacquer bowls; sushi is set on earthy and metallic pottery; and ebony chopsticks lay on a gold-leaf circular rest.

Service is timely and the chefs' skill are clear as they present each nigiri with earnest explanations.

The procession of omakase may feature a gargantuan and briny oyster from Washington state, cut into quarters and topped with a drizzle of ponzu, slivered scallion, and grated daikon. Sample stellar sashimi including creamy uni, fatty tuna set over shiso leaf and daikon, as well as silver-skinned mackerel over shaven *myoga* ginger. Superb grilled dishes highlight skewered toro chunks with a mouthwatering soy glaze—each nugget virtually melts in the mouth. Before your eyes, a dedicated chef masterfully cuts nigiri like fatty bluefin tuna fresh from Boston, tender Japanese sea eel, and unctuous sweet sea scallop with yuzu salt.

Takahachi

Japanese

B3

145 Duane St. (bet. Church St. & West Broadway)

Subway: Chambers St (West Broadway)
Phone: 212-571-1830
Web: www.takahachi.net
Prices: $$

Lunch Mon – Fri
Dinner nightly

Pop into this quiet neighborhood favorite for an *Oceans 13* or *Perfect Storm*, to name a few of their signature maki. Here, those cinematic titles mean non-traditional rolls featuring excellent products that don't hold back, as in eel, mango, tuna, and salmon, drizzled with spicy mayo and tobiko; or shrimp tempura, cream cheese, and cucumber with black tobiko. Sidle up to the black sushi bar and get started with *beni toro carpaccio*—salmon belly sashimi topped with marinated red onion and cilantro. Follow with a belly-warming bowl of *nabeyaki* soba, full of buckwheat noodles, veggies, and shrimp tempura.

Inside, friendly hosts greet guests behind a wavy white counter, while the serene sounds of water trickling down a stone wall create a calming atmosphere.

Tamarind

Indian

B2

99 Hudson St. (at Franklin St.)

Subway: Franklin St
Phone: 212-775-9000
Web: www.tamarindrestaurantsnyc.com
Prices: $$$

Lunch & dinner daily

After 13 years on E. 22nd Street, owner Avtar Walia has merged both his locations into one fabulous site here on Hudson Street. The softly lit space is as stunning as ever; it hums with energy and is perpetually packed with a mix of gorgeous bankers, locals, and tourists. But, the kitchen may struggle under the weight of a full house.

Meanwhile, the updated menu reflects the style of their original location in Gramercy and features a series of courses that seem to outdo the next. Standards like *saag paneer*, a luscious Kerala fish curry, or any of the choices from the tandoor may not stand out from the other solid Indian cooking in the city, but such specialties as the spinach and garlic rice, broccoli and cheese naan, or *lasuni gobi* are well above par.

Thalassa

Greek

179 Franklin St. (bet. Greenwich & Hudson Sts.)

Subway: Franklin St

Dinner Mon – Sat

Phone: 212-941-7661

Web: www.thalassanyc.com

Prices: $$$

It's fair to say Greek cuisine is part of Thalassa's history—this sprawling venue was once a warehouse used to store Greek food products. Today, it sports classic TriBeCa bones like soaring ceilings and leather seating spread across multiple levels. Sultry candlelight and delicate flowers soften the look. Starched white linens and the suited captain staff are clues to the seriousness of this sleek spot.

Whole fish displayed on ice tempts diners and steers them toward tasting the kitchen's gift with seafood. Portuguese octopus is beautifully grilled with end bits crisped to a tantalizing crunch and simply dressed with red wine vinaigrette. Whole black bass is ultra-fresh, neatly deboned, and plated with tangy herb emulsion and fantastic lemon potatoes.

Tiny's

American

135 West Broadway (bet. Duane & Thomas Sts.)

Subway: Chambers St (West Broadway)

Lunch & dinner daily

Phone: 212-374-1135

Web: www.tinysnyc.com

Prices: $$

The name says it all—Tiny's is indeed tiny, but in that old New York, wood-burning fire and pressed-tin ceiling kind of way. Enter the narrow Federal-style home (c. 1810) and sidle up to the beautiful people along the pew seats overlooking a poster of the Marlboro Man, or head on to the aptly named Bar Upstairs.

The food may be American but seamlessly weaves in Italian influences. Creamy burrata arrives over date purée, glazed in lemon-honey and sprinkled with crushed-tin pistachios. Hake is thickly cut and enticingly flaky, drizzled in brown butter with tart capers, lemon, and parsley, then complemented with both pan-roasted fingerling potatoes and beautifully dressed frisée salad. Even their delicate California chardonnay harkens to old-world flavors.

Tribeca Grill

A2

Contemporary 🍴🍴

375 Greenwich St. (at Franklin St.)

Subway: Franklin St
Phone: 212-941-3900
Web: www.myriadrestaurantgroup.com
Prices: $$$

Lunch Sun – Fri
Dinner nightly

Tribeca Grill is hallowed for its proficient and well-paced service. As a result of this, affluent regulars along with seasoned foodies know to seek their expert sommelier for counsel on a wine list, replete with impressive German and Austrian selections. Less suited for intimate affairs, the Grill exudes a classic quality and is a reliable destination among the beautiful people of NYC.

Diners hold court amid exposed duct work, wall-to-wall windows, and a mighty bar posed in the center. To delight the palate, find rustic veal and mushroom terrine served with raisin-walnut bread and violet mustard. Seared scallops with squash-bacon risotto, subtly spiced pumpkin cheesecake, and a well-plated cheese course unveil a real love for seasonal ingredients.

Zutto

B2

Asian 🍴

77 Hudson St. (bet. Harrison & Jay Sts.)

Subway: Franklin St
Phone: 212-233-3287
Web: www.zuttonyc.com
Prices: $$

Lunch & dinner daily

Distinguishing itself from those Asian smorgasbord restaurants serving every dish under the sun, Zutto focuses on soulful bowls of quality ramen. The interior is a quirky collection of reclaimed woods and practical furnishings that are as pleasing and comfortable as a pub (or *izakaya*). The atmosphere is just plain fun.

Dive into a deep bowl of wasabi *shoyu* ramen, with its steaming base of soy-infused chicken and vegetable stock topped with tofu cubes, simmered bamboo shoots, sprouted daikon seeds, and refreshing shiso, ginger, scallions, and wasabi oil. Other noodle dishes might include cold somen with kimchi and sliced pork belly in a sweet soy-shiitake sauce. Round out those carbs with wonderfully spicy rings of sweet and sour calamari.

Upper East Side

Famously expensive and *trés* charming, the Upper East Side is flanked by glorious Central Park on one side and the East River on the other. If watching barges and boats bob along the water from a dense metropolis doesn't sound like a perfect paradox, know that this prime area is predominantly residential and home to iconic residences like Gracie Mansion. Closest to the park are posh spots catering to expats with expense accounts. But, walk a few steps to the east and discover young families filling the latest *sushi-ya*, artisanal pizzeria, or sidewalk spot. Carnegie Hill's **Lucy's Whey** is cheesy, in a good way—stocked with a wide array of cheeses and accouterments. They also have a sit-down café where you can dig into salads, soup, and

gooey goodness. Think: panini-pressed ciabatta rolls stuffed with Iowa cheddar and local sliced pickles, from Brooklyn, of course! Along First and Second avenues, classic Irish pubs are

packed with raucous post-grads who keep the party alive well through happy hour and into the wee hours.

SHOPPING CENTRAL

The most upper and eastern reaches of this neighborhood were originally developed by famous families of German descent. While here, make sure to join the queue of carnivores at **Schaller & Weber** as they hover over Austro-German specialties including wursts for winter steaming or summer grilling, and a plethora of pungent mustards to accompany them. This region also boasts a greater concentration of gourmet markets than any other nook in town. Each of these emporiums are more packed than the next and make processing long lines an art of inspired efficiency. The presence of **Fairway**, a gourmet sanctuary showcasing everything from fresh produce and glistening meats, to seafood and deli delights, has made shopping for homemade meals a complete breeze. These residents can't imagine living elsewhere especially with such easy access to **Agata & Valentina**, a family-owned and operated food store whose famously cramped aisles are supplied with everything Italian. Complete with delicious gift baskets, recipes, and gfit ideas, this epicurean haven succeeds in delivering an authentic European

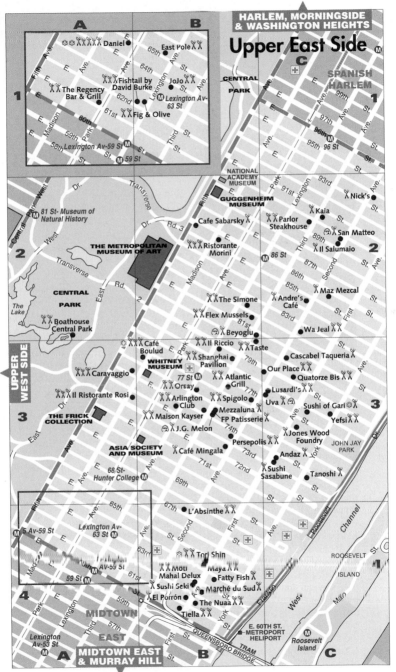

A | **B** | **C**

SPANISH HARLEM

CENTRAL PARK

Daniel
East Pole
Fishtail by David Burke
JoJo
The Regency Bar & Grill
Lexington Av-63 St
Fig & Olive
Lexington Av-59 St
59 St

Nick's
Kaia
Parlor Steakhouse
San Matteo
Il Salumaio

NATIONAL ACADEMY MUSEUM
GUGGENHEIM MUSEUM
Cafe Sabarsky
Ristorante Morini

81 St-Museum of Natural History

THE METROPOLITAN MUSEUM OF ART

Maz Mezcal
Andre's Café
Wa Jeal

CENTRAL PARK

The Simone
Flex Mussels
Beyoglu

The Lake

Boathouse Central Park

UPPER WEST SIDE

Café Boulud
Il Riccio
Taste
Cascabel Taqueria
Our Place
Quatorze Bis
Lusardi's
Uva
Sushi of Gari
Yefsi

Caravaggio
WHITNEY MUSEUM
Shanghai Pavilion
77 St
Atlantic Grill
Il Ristorante Rosi
Orsay
Spigolo
Arlington Club
Mezzaluna
FP Patisserie
Maison Kayser
J.G. Melon
Persepolis
Jones Wood Foundry
Andaz

THE FRICK COLLECTION

ASIA SOCIETY AND MUSEUM
Café Mingala
Sushi Sasabune
Tanoshi

68 St-Hunter College

JOHN JAY PARK

L'Absinthe

Lexington Av-63 St
5 Av-59 St
Lexington Av-59 St
59 St

Tori Shin

Moti Mahal Delux
Maya
Fatty Fish
Sushi Seki
Marché du Sud
El Porrón
The Nuaa
Tiella

ROOSEVELT ISLAND

MIDTOWN EAST

Lexington Av-53 St

QUEENSBORO BRIDGE
E. 60TH ST. METROPORT HELIPORT
Roosevelt Island
TRAM

MIDTOWN EAST & MURRAY HILL

359

experience to the mean streets of Manhattan.

A few steps west, **Citarella** pumps its mouthwatering aroma of rotisserie chickens to entice passersby. Prime meats and rare produce are also on offer here, and contend with the abundant goodness available at **Grace's Marketplace**, a bazaar beloved for its confined corners

gushing with delicious displays. This savory spectacle is bound to leave you starving, so grab a seat at their adjoining trattoria and devour some pasta, pizza, or *pesce* crafted from quality ingredients all carried in the store. At the head of the gourmet game and celebrated as the reigning champion of everything uptown is Eli Zabar and his ever-expanding empire. **E.A.T.** is a Madison Avenue treasure selling all things edible in its casual café. Thanks to its vast offerings and popular appeal, other outposts (like **Vinegar Factory** and mega-mart **Eli's**) began to sprout and continue to prosper in this quarter. Finally, any foodie worth their salt knows that **Kitchen Arts & Letters** flaunts the largest stock of food and wine publications in

the country, and founder Nach Waxman is as good a source of industry insight as any book or blog around.

SUPPER, SWEETS AND SIPS

In spite of such large-scale shopping, still there are smaller purveyors to patronize here. **Lobel's** and **Ottomanelli** are among the finest and time-tested butchers in town; whereas **William Greenberg** continues to bake deliciously moist *babka* as well as New York City's's favorite cookie, the black-and-white. Just as venerable **Ladurée**'s rainbow of pastel-hued macarons brings a slice of the City of Lights to this exclusive quarter, **Glaser's Bake Shop** is reminscent of everything Old World. Just as **Lady M's** haute cakes fit right into its plush setting off Madison Avenue, thirsty travelers will appreciate **Bemelmans Bar**, whose excellent cocktails and sparkling selection are sure to lure you into a tizzy. But for those in the mood for supper and a show, it doesn't get more classic than the storied hotel's, **Café Carlyle**. On the other hand, **Bar Pleiades** at The Surrey is a more contemporary offering, but as elegantly uptown as one would expect with its quilted walls and lacquer finishes.

Andaz

Indian ✗

1378 First Ave. (bet. 73rd and 74th Sts.)

Subway: 77 St
Phone: 212-288-0288
Web: www.andazny.com
Prices: $$

Lunch and dinner daily

Simply stated, Andaz is one of *the* best Indian dining gems in the city's upper quarter. This demure space feels tidy and neutral beneath colorful ceiling pendants and wine shelves. A polite staff attends to the familiar coterie of neighborhood patrons.

The menu specializes in regional dishes that are spiced to your desired level. Sample rich bowls of *keema matar*, a thick and meaty stew of minced lamb and sweet peas in a spicy curry paste of dried red chilies, ginger, coriander, and cloves. Hearty vegetarian options include *paneer makhani*, brimming with cubes of diced house-made cheese in a decadent cream and butter-enriched tomato sauce; or lusciously seasoned and distinctly tart vegetable *vindaloo* stocked with cauliflower, potatoes, and sweet carrots.

Andre's Café

Eastern European ✗

1631 Second Ave. (bet. 84th & 85th Sts.)

Subway: 86 St (Lexington Ave.)
Phone: 212-327-1105
Web: www.andrescafeny.com
Prices: ⊜⊜

Lunch & dinner daily

This charming café details deliciously old-fashioned baked goods from a bakery of the same name established in Queen's in 1976. Tiny, tidy, and welcoming, the exterior proudly boasts this establishment's Hungarian heritage with a red, white, and green awning. A temptingly arranged display of sweet and savory strudels, tortes, and cakes greet guests upon entering. Table service is available in the rear, and before delving into dessert, there is a full menu of hearty old-world fare offered daily.

Weekday meal specials come complete with a salad or soup and choice of three desserts, and can include home spun traditional favorites like chicken *paprikash*, swathed in a luscious paprika cream sauce and accompanied by freshly made *nokedli*.

Arlington Club

B3

Steakhouse ✗✗

1032 Lexington Ave. (bet. 73rd & 74th Sts.)

Subway: 77 St   Lunch & dinner daily
Phone: 212-249-5700
Web: www.arlingtonclubny.com
Prices: $$$

Chef Laurent Tourondel has teamed up with the Tao Group to serve steaks and sushi in this Upper East Side lair. Born and bred in France, he displays an almost wicked flair for both flesh and fish in this handsome, clubby, and cozy dining room, equipped with an oak bar, vaulted brick ceiling, and tufted leather booths.

A hot Gruyère popover is a decadent welcome and classic Tourondel touch, but pace yourself because the kitchen gives plenty of reason to stuff yourself silly. Start light as in a refreshing chopped vegetable salad dressed with Parmesan and lemon vinaigrette; or maki, perhaps with yellowtail, jalapeño, and avocado. Finally, move on to broiled, dry-aged USDA Prime cuts and American Wagyu skirt steak, accompanied by one of the great sides.

Atlantic Grill

B3

Seafood ✗✗

1341 Third Ave. (bet. 76th & 77th Sts.)

Subway: 77 St   Lunch & dinner daily
Phone: 212-988-9200
Web: www.atlanticgrill.com
Prices: $$

This gorgeous Grill's sprawling patio is a seafood oasis in the midst of urban chaos. It seems deceivingly vast until you round the bend to a second, beachy dining room decked with a marble sushi counter and rattan chairs—a taste of tropicana on Third Ave. Despite its name, Atlantic Grill pulls influence from the Pacific (think delicious yet unapologetically unauthentic sushi).

Hints of *sriracha* and ginger keep things bright in bigeye tuna tartare, served in a glass jar glistening with sesame oil and avocado. Soft tacos filled with spicy shrimp and pineapple *pico de gallo* or red-miso Atlantic cod are filling and light at once. Brunch is a hit with twists on traditional fare.

Some whine about the prices, but considering the neighborhood, hush up!

Beyoglu 😋

B2

Turkish ✗

1431 Third Ave. (at 81st St.)

Subway: 77 St
Phone: 212-650-0850
Web: N/A
Prices: $$

Lunch & dinner daily

Upper East Siders can't get enough of the meze at cheerful Beyoglu and its enticing Turkish, Greek, and Lebanese cooking. Vibrant flavors enhanced by garlic and herbs start with chilled platters loaded with hummus, mashed eggplant spread (*patlican salatasi*), and salads like *kisir*, tabbouleh made with cracked wheat. The only other thing you'll need to fully enjoy the Beyoglu experience is a bowl of strained, house-made yogurt. That flatbread is pulled straight from the hot oven only to arrive on your table seconds later, gratis and absolutely gratifying.

Tile-topped tables and pistachio-green walls displaying painted flowers accent the interior. French doors separate the dining room from the sidewalk, but during warm weather both areas fill quickly.

Boathouse Central Park

A2

American ✗✗

The Lake at Central Park (E. 72nd St. & Park Dr. North)

Subway: 68 St - Hunter College
Phone: 212-517-2233
Web: www.thecentralparkboathouse.com
Prices: $$$

Lunch & dinner daily

This unique locale offers Manhattan's only lakeside dining experience. Built in 1954, Loeb Boathouse is a pleasant multi-venue operation that includes a charming outdoor bar perched along the water and a lovely glass-walled dining room offering views of the lake, greenery, and skyline beyond—there isn't a bad seat in the house.

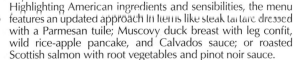

Highlighting American ingredients and sensibilities, the menu features an updated approach in items like steak tartare dressed with a Parmesan tuile; Muscovy duck breast with leg confit, wild rice-apple pancake, and Calvados sauce; or roasted Scottish salmon with root vegetables and pinot noir sauce.

While lunch and brunch are served year-round, note that dinner is only offered during warmer months (April through November).

Café Boulud ✿

B3

French 🍴🍴🍴

20 E. 76th St. (bet. Fifth & Madison Aves.)

Subway: 77 St	Lunch & dinner daily
Phone: 212-772-2600	
Web: www.cafeboulud.com	
Prices: $$$$	

Chef Daniel Boulud's sophisticated vision of food and beverage at the Surrey hotel is comprised of two spaces: the jewel box known as Bar Pleiades, and this luxurious café. Here, posh residents and glam globe-trotters dine in a chic, secluded space complete with low ceilings, plush carpeting, and deep-toned wood accents. Mirrored surfaces and sparkling elements on superbly set tables set off the room's conviviality.

Café Boulud's kitchen displays unwavering consistency under the watch of incoming chef, Aaron Bludorn. The menu remains uniquely constructed, presenting compositions grouped into four categories: La Tradition; La Saison; Le Potager; and Le Voyage.

Decisions never lead to disappointment when they involve ravioli filled with aged Parmesan and presented with a farmer's market bounty of roasted broccoli rabe and caramelized cherry tomatoes. The same is true when the flavors of South America are used to compose a block of steamed halibut with banana leaf, crunchy yucca cake, and creamy, roasted poblano pepper sauce. In the ultimate grand finale, a slender but still decadent chocolate Napoleon layers pistachio genoise with bittersweet ganache and the summer's plumpest Bing cherries.

Café Mingala

B3

Burmese ✗

1393B Second Ave. (bet. 72nd & 73rd Sts.)

Subway: 68 St - Hunter College   Lunch & dinner daily
Phone: 212-744-8008
Web: N/A
Prices: ⊜⊜

Café Mingala is a special destination—not simply because this is the only Burmese restaurant in all five boroughs. The cuisine itself is downright addictive and undeniably unique. This cross-cultural cuisine distills the flavors of Myanmar's neighbors—China, India, Thailand, and Malaysia—into its own luscious specialties.

The pickled green tea leaf salad combines chopped lettuce, bean sprouts, peanuts, sesame seeds, and bits of tea leaf all dressed with spiced oil and fresh lime. Follow this with *mo-goke* pork, from the "land of rubies" made with tender chunks of meat braised in a salty and sweet dark sauce. Café Mingala's signature dish is a flaky "thousand-layer" pancake, or *keema*, topped with ground beef and potatoes in a turmeric-rich curry.

Cafe Sabarsky

B2

Austrian ✗

1048 Fifth Ave. (at 86th St.)

Subway: 86 St (Lexington Ave.)   Lunch Wed – Mon
Phone: 212-288-0665   Dinner Thu – Sun
Web: www.kg-ny.com
Prices: $$

In addition to the renowned art displayed at the intimately scaled Neue Galerie, find Chef Kurt Gutenbrunner's charming café modeled after a late 19th century Viennese *kaffehause*, complete with dark wood-paneled walls and formally attired servers. The museum, housed in a 1914 Beaux-Arts mansion, was conceived by cosmetic mogul Ronald Lauder and art dealer Serge Sabarsky to display their collections of early 20th century Austrian and German art.

The traditional menu features savory taro like smoked bratwurst over riesling sauerkraut, along with an indulgent listing of classic sweets like apple strudel. Beverages include a very interesting selection of German and Austrian wines by the glass, tremendous coffee offerings, and divine hot chocolate.

Caravaggio

Italian 🍴🍴🍴

A3

23 E. 74th St. (bet. Fifth & Madison Aves.)

Subway: 77 St   Lunch & dinner daily
Phone: 212-288-1004
Web: www.caravaggioristorante.com
Prices: $$$

Nestled among Madison Avenue boutiques and commanding a rather formal air, this highbrow Italian dining room is a good reason to dress up and splurge. The slender setting is adorned with silk-lined walls, sleek leather seating, and evocative artwork. The well-dressed staff is serious, but their hospitality is genuine.

The team of highly experienced co-chefs is equally intense in turning out their skilled cooking. Antipasti might include an elegant, warm octopus salad with baby artichoke and crispy potatoes, while heartier options may feature house-made *cavatelli* with jumbo crabmeat and sea urchin. Lunch offers a more pared-down experience, but a bowlful of velvety *pasta e fagioli* stocked with plump *borlotti* beans is a perfect post-shopping tonic.

Cascabel Taqueria

Mexican 🍴

C3

1538 Second Ave. (at 80th St.)

Subway: 77 St   Lunch & dinner daily
Phone: 212-717-8226
Web: www.nyctacos.com
Prices: 😋😋

Inexpensive tacos stuffed with skill and creativity are the reasons this taqueria has been a hit from the start. Highlights begin with the carnitas tacos, slow-roasted pork belly with *chile de arbol* piled high into two masa tortillas sprinkled with pickled onion, *culantro,* and the unorthodox but intriguing crunch from puffed rice. Other choices include burritos served with sweet potato fries, refreshing salads in crisp tostadas, and black beans with quinoa.

Meals are presented on aluminum sheet pans emphasizing the laid-back vibe here. A caddy of salsas—roasted tomato, tomatillo, and very spicy *diablo*—tops and thrills each table. The corner location features a sunny room with exposed brick, bright green accent wall, and retro-style chrome chairs.

Daniel ✿ ✿

French 🍴🍴🍴🍴🍴

A1

60 E. 65th St. (bet. Madison & Park Aves.)

Subway: 68 St - Hunter College
Phone: 212-288-0033
Web: www.danielnyc.com
Prices: $$$$

Dinner Mon – Sat

From its home at the base of the former Mayfair hotel, Daniel is as classic New York as a French restaurant can get. The décor revolves around concentric circles of custom everything; porcelain-tiled chandeliers hang like upside-down wedding cakes over thick, swirling-patterned carpets. Luxury and exclusivity extend from the soaring ceilings to intimate niches, seating a mixed clientele of tourists, celebrants, and expense-account holders. At times, the staff may seem to bear an edge of condescension, but rest assured that your meal will be well-paced and graciously served.

After two decades, Daniel continues to serve one of the city's top French menus; however, flashes of greatness have replaced consistency. Begin with pasta courses like delicate *tagottini* filled with creamy sweet corn purée and presented with poached lobster tail, chorizo oil, and herbaceous lambs quarters. Maine halibut is remarkably soft, gently grilled, spiced with *vadouvan*, and garnished with enticingly bitter braised romaine and smooth dots of lettuce purée.

End with modern and exotic desserts, like the blissful *orchidea vacherin* with calamansi meringue chips, vanilla chantilly, Madagascar sorbet, and fruit coulis.

East Pole

B1

133 E. 65th St. (bet. Lexington & Park Aves.)

Subway: 68 St - Hunter College   Lunch & dinner daily
Phone: 212-249-2222
Web: www.theeastpolenyc.com
Prices: $$$

Just off Park Avenue's pre-war grandeur is this hip addition to the neighborhood, courtesy of the Fat Radish team. The cozy space is on the ground floor of a brownstone, so the setting is understandably narrow. East Pole's front bar is hopping, while black leather booths in the back allow parties to sit and enjoy an eclectic menu in relative peace.

The stimulating cooking here begins with a salad of roasted heirloom carrots with *hijiki*, diced avocado, and soy sauce and sesame seed oil vinaigrette. Then move on to explore Kiev-style chicken, stuffed with garlic butter-enriched broccoli purée, or creamy fish pie stocked with cod, lobster, and fennel. The adult ice cream sundae is a boozy combo of Scotch-chocolate ice cream and Pimm's-soaked cherries.

El Porrón

B4

1123 First Ave. (bet. 61st & 62nd Sts.)

Subway: Lexington Av - 59 St   Lunch & dinner daily
Phone: 212-207-8349
Web: www.elporronnyc.com
Prices: $$

A sleek looking sliver of a spot, El Porrón brings mouthwatering tapas to a traffic-clogged Upper East Side stretch. Dark colors give the space a cloistered feel, amid black-and-white portraits of people drinking from *porróns*—blown-glass wine vessels with tapered spouts.

The kitchen churns out a graceful, all-encompassing array of savory small plates, hearty entrées, and scrumptious paellas that are absolutely worth the 40-minute wait. Sample tapas may include the *puerros del Monasterio*, combining leeks and wild mushrooms softened in garlic and olive oil sauce; or the delicate *empanada del dia*. *Callos Madilenos* is a lusciously unctuous and ambrosial stew of diced beef tripe and pig's foot, *morcilla*, and chorizo served in a bubbling hot *cazuela*.

Fatty Fish

B4

International ✗

406 E. 64th St. (bet. First & York Aves.)

Subway: Lexington Av - 63 St   Lunch & dinner daily
Phone: 212-813-9338
Web: www.fattyfishnyc.com
Prices: $$

Beneath a distinguishing orange awning, Fatty Fish is a bright spot in Yorkville. The comfy space is downright homey with its intimate rooms, creaky wood floors, and a staff that treats everyone like regulars.

The cuisine reflects varied inspiration, but rest assured everything is tempting. From the sushi counter, experience skillfully knifed sashimi, *chirashi*, and maki. Dig into cooked fare like Japanese eggplant and wild mushroom lasagna layered with shredded pork; green curry shrimp and vegetables; or perfectly grilled filet mignon medallions dabbed with spicy Chinese-style mustard gently sweetened with honey, alongside stir-fried bok choy and a tower of crispy onion rings. End with refreshing ginger ice cream studded with strips of candied ginger.

Fig & Olive

B1

Mediterranean ✗✗

808 Lexington Ave. (bet. 62nd & 63rd Sts.)

Subway: Lexington Av - 63 St   Lunch & dinner daily
Phone: 212-207-4555
Web: www.figandolive.com
Prices: $$$

Fig & Olive's exceptional devotion to a single product (olive oil) sets it apart from the nearly countless supply of Mediterranean options. Its burgeoning popularity has enabled expansion, now boasting several branches, including Westchester and Los Angeles.

This original location sits close to fine shopping and offers a sophisticated respite. Rattan seating, a pristine marble dining counter, and warmly lit arrangement of olive oil bottles are squeezed into the slender setting.

Dinners begin with an olive oil trio to sample (though your helpful server will choose which ones you try). One can graze on small plates—crostini, cheeses, or carpaccio or wholeheartedly dig in to the likes of chicken tajine with preserved lemon and plump figs.

Fishtail by David Burke

B1

135 E. 62nd St. (bet. Lexington & Park Aves.)

Subway: Lexington Av - 63 St
Phone: 212-754-1300
Web: www.fishtaildb.com
Prices: $$$

Lunch Sat – Sun
Dinner nightly

This fitting addition to Chef David Burke's oeuvre features an elegant setting through two levels of a cozy townhouse, lending a ritzy, residential feel. The first floor is an oyster bar and lounge popular with the after-work crowds, while the upstairs is a deep red dining room with accents that colorfully convey the ocean theme.

The menu focuses on fish and much is caught by the company-owned boat. Dishes are stamped with the chef's unique touch, whether as salt-baked American red snapper with smoked tomato sauce; shellfish towers; or more creative interpretations like pretzel-crusted crab cakes with lemon-poppyseed mayonnaise. Sunday nights bring a luxe but affordable lobster-themed menu. Regardless of your choice, every item shows ample skill.

Flex Mussels

B2

174 E. 82nd St. (bet. Lexington & Third Aves.)

Subway: 86 St (Lexington Ave.)
Phone: 212-717-7772
Web: www.flexmusselsny.com
Prices: $$

Dinner nightly

Featuring a focused menu of cleverly made, high-quality seafood, it's no surprise that this mussels haven was an immediate success. Still going strong, this setting is routinely packed to the gills, both up front where there is a bar and dining counter, as well as the proper dining room in back, adorned with an abundance of maritime-themed artwork.

Expect to taste plenty of the namesake bivalve, hailing from Prince Edward Island. Priced by the pound and steamed in no fewer than twenty globally inspired broths, they are best with some killer hand-cut skinny fries. Mussels No. 23 refers to the nightly special, perhaps featuring a succulent bath of hot and sour soup bobbing with soft tofu, bits of pork, wood ear mushrooms, and dried red chili flakes.

FP Patisserie

B3

French 🍴

1293 Third Ave. (at 74th St.)

Subway: 77 St
Phone: 212-717-5252
Web: www.francoispayard.com
Prices: $$

Lunch daily
Dinner Mon – Sat

This enticing emporium marks Francois Payard's return to the Upper East Side, where sophisticated sweet-tooths can either grab a box of handmade chocolates or macarons to take home, or stay for an enjoyable meal in the *salon de thé*. Popular among the ladies, this petite room carries a sunny color scheme.

Salads paired with freshly baked bread comprise their fine lighter fare; while heartier appetites will enjoy a choice of *croque monsieur*, or perhaps foie gras- and mushroom *duxelles*-stuffed chicken breast dressed with an intense mushroom jus.

It goes without saying one must save room for dessert. Walk up to the sparkling display case and select any one of the fabulous creations, like the simply stated caramel tart for a salt-flecked piece of heaven.

Il Riccio

B3

Italian 🍴🍴

152 E. 79th St. (bet. Lexington & Third Aves.)

Subway: 77 St
Phone: 212-639-9111
Web: www.ilriccioblu.com
Prices: $$

Lunch & dinner daily

This low-key Italian, and its smiling cadre of charming staff, is just the right spot to recharge after an afternoon of perusing the fabulous neighborhood boutiques or meandering through nearby Metropolitan Museum of Art. Inside, the space offers a cozy feel with warm ochre walls, simple furnishings, and an assemblage of photographs, though regulars know to head back to the enclosed garden to enjoy their meals.

The cooking here is fuss-free, pasta-focused, and lovingly dedicated to the Amalfi Coast. Favored dishes may include an arugula-and-roasted red pepper salad with salty marinated anchovies; spaghetti with crab meat and fresh tomatoes; grilled fish dressed simply with olive oil and lemon; and a straightforward selection of dessert pastries.

371

Il Ristorante Rosi

A3

Italian XXX

903 Madison Ave. (bet. 72nd & 73rd Sts.)

Subway: 77 St
Phone: 212-517-7700
Web: www.salumeriarosi.com
Prices: $$$

Lunch & dinner daily

Madison Avenue has no shortage of shops, but none is more detrimental to your waistline (or wallet) than the Parmacotto *salumi* counter at the front of Il Ristorante Rosi. Further inside discover a very fine-looking restaurant, with dark wood, bursts of red, and a polished décor that's set alongside classically smooth service.

Helmed by Chef Cesare Casella, the menu sticks to Italian favorites including a smoke-heavy version of spaghetti carbonara with the rustic flavors of pork and pecorino. The *pesce del giorno* may feature a Florida red grouper finished with fresh herbs and sautéed hen of the woods mushrooms, set over a bed of cannellini beans. The wine list is well-curated to showcase top Italian producers as well as a few heavy-hitters from France.

J.G. Melon 😊

B3

American X

1291 Third Ave. (at 74th St.)

Subway: 77 St
Phone: 212-744-0585
Web: N/A
Prices: 😊😊

Lunch & dinner daily

Posterity will remember J.G. Melon as a classic and coveted New York institution. Make your way into this cave set upon a cozy Upper East corner, where the timeless vibe and cheery staff make up most of its allure. Drinks are steadily churned out at a dark wood bar, so arrive early to avoid the hordes.

The focus at this multi-generational saloon is the burger—perhaps paired with a lip-smacking Bloody Mary at brunch? The warm toasted bun topped with meat cooked on a griddle to rosy pink is coupled with onions, pickles, and crispy crinkle-cut fries. Be forewarned: you will go through the entire stack of napkins before finishing. Other simple pleasures include standards like salads, steaks, and eggs. Seal the meal with a chocolate chip-studded layer cake.

JoJo

B1

160 E. 64th St. (bet. Lexington & Third Aves.)

Subway: Lexington Av - 63 St   Lunch & dinner daily
Phone: 212-223-5656
Web: www.jojorestaurantnyc.com
Prices: $$$

Chef Jean-Georges Vongerichten's little neighborhood bistro has been serving these affluent residents for nearly a generation, offering proof that although trends may come and go, classics remain steadfast.

Within Jojo's snug townhouse quarters, ritzy locals and well-heeled tourists dine at elegantly dressed tables—think starched linens and polished silver—amid terra-cotta tile floors, plum velvet banquettes, and toile drapery.

The look isn't fresh or exciting, but the cuisine makes up for it. Lunch offers great value for three courses that have featured a salad of warm asparagus with avocado; pan-roasted hake and sautéed wild mushrooms dressed with lime segments and a ginger-scallion condiment; and zucchini cake with pecan ice cream for dessert.

Jones Wood Foundry

Gastropub ✗

C3

401 E. 76th St. (bet. First & York Aves.)

Subway: 77 St   Lunch & dinner daily
Phone: 212-249-2771
Web: www.joneswoodfoundry.com
Prices: $$

Jones Wood Foundry is a stateside take on a classic public house—the kind that Chef/partner Jason Hicks frequented during his childhood in England—that serves the same style of spot-on pub grub. The front bar is a choice spot to sip and savor from the selection of drafts. The space then opens up to a seating area of marble-topped tables, handsome button-tufted brown leather banquettes, and plush red velvet chairs. Beer-battered haddock and chips with tartar sauce, hearty meat pie of the day, and coronation chicken sandwich—the classic mid-century chicken salad dressed with intensely yellow, curry-tinged mayonnaise on toasted baguette—are a few of the true-blue hits. The vibe is charming, but dinner offers much more ambience than midday service.

Kaia

C2

1614 Third Ave. (bet. 90th & 91st Sts.)

Subway: 86 St (Lexington Ave.)   Dinner nightly
Phone: 212-722-0490
Web: www.kaiawinebar.com
Prices: $$

This South African wine bar takes its name from the word for shelter. It is owned by a native South African who chased her dreams of stardom to New York City, while building an impressive resume of work in some of the city's finer dining rooms. The space has a comfortable appeal, spotlighting a lively dining counter as well as high and low wood tables.
Discover a plethora of wines not just from South Africa, but also South America and New York. To accompany your glass, select from the interesting small plates like "spear and shield" of bacon-wrapped asparagus with cheddar-stuffed mushroom caps; or *vark ribbetjies en vark pensie*, pork ribs glazed with honey and *rooibos* tea as well as pork belly braised in Indian pale ale dressed with candied kumquats.

Il Salumaio

C2

1731 Second Ave. (bet. 89th & 90th Sts.)

Subway: 86 St (Lexington Ave.)   Lunch Thu – Sun
Phone: 646-852-6876   Dinner nightly
Web: www.ilsalumaiony.com
Prices: ⊜⊜

Yorkville residents have been doubly blessed by Fabio and Ciro Casella. First, their pizzeria San Matteo arrived on the scene with its wood-fired specialties. Now, the brothers bring more delightfully rustic fare by way of primo panini and pastas, to this underserved neighborhood.
The slender space seats only a handful, but sidewalk tables increase the accommodations. Cured meats and imported cheeses temptingly stocked in a refrigerator display case are skillfully manifested atop luscious plates like the Arthur Avenue—basically a *panino* bursting with ham, *salume*, mortadellla, and provolone. *Paccheri all'Amatriciana* or fat tubes of perfectly cooked pasta in a thick tomato ragù seasoned with onion, pancetta, and Pecorino Romana, is a delight unto itself.

L'Absinthe

B4

French ✕✕

227 E. 67th St. (bet. Second & Third Aves.)

Subway: 68 St - Hunter College
Phone: 212-794-4950
Web: www.labsinthe.com
Prices: $$$

Lunch & dinner daily

Charming the Upper East Side for twenty years now, this is a lovely brasserie that is delightfully impervious to time and trends. Lunch is still a scene where ladies dress up, and there's no shame in ordering a martini (or three). Feel transported to the Left Bank while soaking in the décor, which includes leather banquettes, polished brass fixtures, and etched glass. Chef Jean-Michel Bergougnoux has long been at the helm, turning out authentic meals that start with warm *gougères*. Seasonal offerings may feature slices of vine-ripened tomatoes with lentil salad, pickled cucumber, and shallot vinaigrette. Also explore decadent classic dishes like *coq au vin* garnished *grandmère*-style with lardons, caramelized pearl onions, and sautéed mushrooms.

Lusardi's

C3

Italian ✕✕

1494 Second Ave. (bet. 77th & 78th Sts.)

Subway: 77 St
Phone: 212-249-2020
Web: www.lusardis.com
Prices: $$$

Lunch Mon – Fri
Dinner nightly

With its pumpkin-colored walls, dark woodwork, and vintage posters, this beloved old-school mainstay offers a menu that relishes in decadent Northern Italian cooking. Picture an array of fresh pasta and veal, richly embellished with cream, authentic cheeses, or truffle-infused olive oil.

The *insalata bianca* is a monotone-white yet delightfully refreshing composition of shaved fennel, sliced artichoke ██████, ████████████ ███████, ████████████ ███ ██ ██ ████ ███████ with lemony vinaigrette and *Parmigiano Reggiano*, all singing with black pepper freshly ground tableside. *Paccheri* in *salsa affumicata* presents large pasta tubes draped with plum tomato sauce that has been enriched with creamy smoked mozzarella and strewn with bits of roasted eggplant.

Maison Kayser

B3

1294 Third Ave. (at 74th St.)

Subway: 77 St
Phone: 212-744-3100
Web: www.maison-kayser-usa.com
Prices: $$

Lunch & dinner daily

Maison Kayser is the US flagship of French baker extraordinaire Eric Kayser whose skill with flour and water has yielded him a collection of *boulangeries* that span the globe. Arrive to find a small retail area stocked with temptation and bustling café that comforts guests in an oak-floored, mirror-paneled room staffed with servers sporting Breton tees. Get the ordering out of the way to speed up the arrival of the bread, made from organic New York-grown grain and studded with walnuts or dried fruit, rustically presented in a burlap sack.

From the menu, enjoy the likes of shrimp- and lump crabmeat-topped guacamole; traditional bœuf Bourguignon presented in a cocotte; or pistachio éclair. All are worthy complements to the array of bread.

Marché du Sud

B4

1136 First Ave. (bet. 62nd & 63rd Sts.)

Subway: Lexington Av - 59 St
Phone: 212-207-4900
Web: www.marchedusud.com
Prices: $$

Lunch & dinner daily

Open all day and offering everything from a morning cappuccino to a late evening digestif, Marché du Sud wears many hats—gourmet shop, wine bar, dining room—without a glitch.

Back issues of *Paris Match* (and other French-language titles) double as menu covers. Speaking of which, be sure to peruse the Alsatian *tarte flambée* offerings. *Cette cousine* of pizza features a thin, flaky crust presented with an array of toppings. Traditionalists should go for the *l'authentique* loaded with crème fraîche, lardons, onions, and Gruyère. The remainder of the menu also offers enjoyable specials like sienna-hued *soupe de poisson*, a lush coalescence of seafood, saffron, orange peel, tomato, and herbs. Follow this with roasted chicken draped in zesty mustard-cream sauce.

Maya

B4

Mexican ✗✗

1191 First Ave. (bet. 64th & 65th Sts.)

Subway: 68 St - Hunter College
Phone: 212-585-1818
Web: www.richardsandoval.com
Prices: $$

Lunch & dinner daily

Upscale Mexican dining thrives at Chef Richard Sandoval's *muy* popular Maya. Slick with polished dark wood furnishings, vibrant tiled flooring, and accent walls the color of a ripe mango, this is always a fun scene. Adding to the revelry is the Tequileria, Maya's ajacent bar with a serious focus on agave spirits.

Antojitos, such as squash blossom quesadillas and their trio of salsas, headline as starters. Tasty tacos are stuffed with smoked brisket and creamy chili slaw. Heartier dishes feature *huitlacoche* and wild mushroom enchiladas swathed in a creamy, fire-roasted poblano chile sauce. *Especialidades* like achiote-marinated carne asada with cactus-green bean salad and bacon-wrapped jalapeño display the kitchen's contemporary flair.

Maz Mezcal

C2

Mexican ✗

316 E. 86th St. (bet. First & Second Aves.)

Subway: 86 St (Lexington Ave.)
Phone: 212-472-1599
Web: www.mazmezcal.com
Prices: $$

Lunch Sat – Sun
Dinner nightly

This family-run, longtime favorite still draws its legions of Upper East regulars for satisfying and traditional Mexican fare. Welcomes are personalized and the dining room is filled with guests chatting up the staff about their latest news. The narrow front room is bright with sienna and turquoise walls quirkily decorated with watermelon-themed artwork. The back feels cozier and the bar area seems tucked away.

Commendable specialties have included *camarones en pipian rojo*, shrimp sauced with a blend of dried chiles, ground nuts, and sesame seeds. Finally fish fully combination platters can pair tender fried poblano *chile rellenos* abundantly stuffed with mild cheese, and a crisp, chorizo-filled flauta with tomato-tinted rice and dollop of refried beans.

Mezzaluna

Italian ✗

1295 Third Ave. (bet. 74th & 75th Sts.)

Subway: 77 St
Phone: 212-535-9600
Web: www.mezzalunanyc.com
Prices: $$

Lunch & dinner daily

Time and time again, this Italian idol hits the spot. Just take a look at the jubilant crowd huddled together at pink granite tables throughout the Euro-chic yet cozy room. One wall is yellow while another is completely lined with 77 depictions of the restaurant's name, beneath a sky-blue ceiling painted with clouds.

Neighborhood residents and chic tourists know Mezzaluna's unfussy Italian cooking is guaranteed to be *delizioso*. Take for example the veal Milanese—pounded thin and delicately crunchy, simply topped with peppery wild arugula and sliced cherry tomatoes. Other hits include pizzas that emerge from a wood-burning oven unceremoniously stationed in a corner, or beef carpaccio with a choice of toppings like artichokes and *Parmigiano Reggiano*.

Moti Mahal Delux

Indian ✗✗

1149 First Ave. (at 63rd St.)

Subway: Lexington Av - 63 St
Phone: 212-371-3535
Web: www.motimahaldelux.us
Prices: $$

Lunch & dinner daily

This tempting respite marks the first American location of a fine dining chain that began in Delhi and now boasts outposts throughout India, Nepal, and London. Here in NYC, it's a corner spot with a sidewalk atrium and main dining room decked with stone floors and leather banquettes. The cuisine features a northern accent and traces its origins back to the kitchens of the Mughal Empire, which brought Muslim influences to the Indo subcontinent.

Tasty *tandoori* preparations factor heavily on the menu, as in the delicate *ajwaini machchi tikka* marinated with mustard and carom seeds. Simmered specialties are not to be missed, like their signature *murgh mahkani* (butter chicken) or *dum ke phool*, broccoli florets decadently slow-cooked in a saffron-yogurt sauce.

Nick's

C2

Pizza ✗

1814 Second Ave. (at 94th St.)

Subway: 96 St (Lexington Ave.)
Phone: 212-987-5700
Web: www.nicksnyc.com
Prices: ⊜⊜

Lunch & dinner daily

♿ This Manhattan outpost of the Forest Hills original named for owner Nick Angelis is a cozy setup focused on the pizza station, where dexterous *pizzaiolos* work the gas-fired oven and put on a show. Despite the continuing construction along Second Avenue, a devoted following still seeks out this favored neighborhood pizzeria.

Begin with the spinach salad slicked with hot bacon fat and red wine vinegar before enjoying a thin-crusted but tender and nicely chewy pie, decked with the likes of fennel sausage crumbles, crushed tomatoes, creamy mozzarella, and sweet basil. A delightful finish is Nick's signature cannoli, served as a freshly made *pizzelle* cookie filled upon order with satiny smooth sweetened ricotta and sprinkled with crushed pistachios.

The Nuaa

B4

Thai ✗✗

1122 First Ave. (bet. 61st & 62nd St.)

Subway: 59 St
Phone: 212-888-2899
Web: N/A
Prices: $$

Lunch & dinner daily

The Nuaa brings a certain sexy vibe to a rather blah, trafficky stretch of First Avenue. The room's deep dark palette, with brown leather seating and carved woodwork, pops against abundant gold accents.

The thumping playlist won't be to everyone's liking, but fans of Thai cuisine will find much to enjoy from the well-executed menu. A few nicely pungent salads and noodle dishes give way to creations like char-grilled tiger prawns, served head-on, slicked with ambrosial house-made citrus red curry, plated with stir-fried morning glory; or crispy whole fish with roasted cashew nuts, herb salad, and chili-herb emulsion. Do not miss the braised rice with blue crab, generously stocked with lump meat, green onion, and lemongrass presented in a lotus leaf.

Orsay

B3

1057 Lexington Ave. (at 75th St.)

Subway: 77 St
Phone: 212-517-6400
Web: www.orsayrestaurant.com
Prices: $$

Lunch & dinner daily

With its mahogany paneling, hand-laid mosaic tiles, windows dressed with lacy café curtains, and pewter bar, this luxe brasserie is a painstakingly realized vision of art nouveau. Orsay proves its dedication to French tradition from the sidewalk seating to marble stairs leading up to a private room. Chef Antoine Camin's cheese soufflés sustain much of the well-dressed crowd here, but the classic menu brings much more. *Soupe de poisson* is a richly satisfying fusion of fish, tomatoes, fennel, and herbs; brook trout is presented *à la Grenobloise* with browned butter, capers, and finely diced croutons; and roasted pork tenderloin arrives with savoy cabbage, apples, and hard cider sauce. The soaked *baba au rhum* is as fine a rendition as any *à* Paris.

Our Place

C3

242 E. 79th St. (bet. Second & Third Aves.)

Subway: 77 St
Phone: 212-288-4888
Web: www.ourplace79.com
Prices: $$

Lunch & dinner daily

Reflective of the restaurant's full name, Our Place Cuisines of China, the menu here is expansive and offers pan-regional specialties from Shanghai, Hunan, and Canton. The pleasant room always seems to look new, sporting a wavy green wall, wood furnishings, and tile floors. Friendly servers attend to neighborhood regulars seated at cloth-draped tables.

Go with a group and load up on tasty fare that starts with tangerine beef, pounded flat, crisp-fried, and judiciously finished with dried orange peel and red chili-studded brown sauce. Move on to explore Hunan pork with leeks, and home-style chicken casserole served in an earthenware filled with slices of white meat, mushrooms, and bamboo shoots in an aromatic broth of soy sauce, rice wine, and ginger.

Parlor Steakhouse

C2

Steakhouse 𝖷𝖷

1600 Third Ave. (at 90th St.)

Subway: 86 St (Lexington Ave.)
Phone: 212-423-5888
Web: www.parlorsteakhouse.com
Prices: $$$

Lunch & dinner daily

Set amid subway construction, sexy Parlor Steakhouse has sadly remained under the radar. Boasting top-shelf Belgian and American beers as well as a clubby vibe, this unpretentious steakhouse seems to have it all...including space. Dine here—there's even elbow room for the classically large portions of high-quality beef.

Meat really stands out as does the expert seasoning. Find evidence of this in hand-cut steak tartare, tossed with pickled onions, mustard, and gherkins topped with rye croutons. Served over sweet potato purée with smoked bacon and caramelized onions, the garlicky, herb-crusted Berkshire pork chop is a culmination of divine flavors. Cheesecake crowned with candied pecans and caramel sauce offers an extravagant yet excellent finale.

Persepolis

B3

Persian 𝖷𝖷

1407 Second Ave. (bet. 73rd & 74th Sts.)

Subway: 77 St
Phone: 212-535-1100
Web: www.persepolisnewyork.com
Prices: $$

Lunch & dinner daily

Silky-smooth spreads, homemade yogurt, grilled meats, and fragrantly spiced stews have solidified Persepolis' reputation as one of the city's finest Persian restaurants. Reddish wood furnishings, linen-draped tables, and landscape paintings fashion a setting that is attractive enough to dress up for (or not). Gracious service enhances the convivial scene.

The kitchen's seriousness and skill is revealed in one bite of the house tabbouleh. It arrives as a neatly stacked tower of bulgar wheat and diced vegetables sparked by a bright balance of lemon, garlic, and vibrant green profusion of fresh parsley and mint. The chicken *kubideh* is a hot, juicy kebob of highly seasoned ground chicken alongside fluffy basmati flecked with dried dill and fava beans.

Quatorze Bis

French French 🍴🍴

C3

323 E. 79th St. (bet. First & Second Aves.)

Subway: 77 St
Phone: 212-535-1414
Web: N/A
Prices: $$

Lunch & dinner daily

Savoring a meal at this ever-lovely bistro is like taking a break from the constant evolution that is life In New York City, where tastes change faster than you can Tweet. The red-lacquer façade, claret-velvet banquettes, and sophisticated clientele are all much the same as when Quatorze Bis opened almost 25 years ago.

Though the ambience's timeless appeal is noteworthy, the traditional French cooking is their key to success. Frilly chicory, drizzled with hot bacon fat and red wine vinegar, studded with lardons, croutons, and shallots makes for a very hearty, *très* French salad. Seafood sausage is plump and studded with sweet red pepper and pine nuts. Daily specials keep the menu new, with dishes like striped bass served beside a creamy sorrel sauce.

The Regency Bar & Grill

Contemporary 🍴🍴

A1

540 Park Ave. (at 61st St.)

Subway: Lexington Av - 59 St
Phone: 212-339-4050
Web: www.regencybarandgrill.com
Prices: $$$

Lunch & dinner daily

Following a major renovation, the Loews Regency now serves up a contemporary vision of hotel dining that can stand on its own. Fully-stocked glass and metal shelves at the bar invites passersby to ditch Park Avenue for a cocktail before sinking into the plush dining room, where ivory leather and sky-blue velvet seating is laid out over carpeting inspired by Italian mosaic tiles.

The setting's fresh face is a fitting home for Chef Dan Silverman's au courant cuisine in which shaved radishes and julienned snow peas are combined with pickled shiitakes and sesame dressing for an inspired salad. Grilled double-cut lamb loin chop, cooked perfectly to spec and plated with a stack of panisse- and mint-infused béarnaise sauce, is a sweet dream in the making.

Ristorante Morini

B2

Italian ✕✕✕

1167 Madison Ave. (bet. 85th & 86th Sts.)

Subway: 86 St (Lexington Ave.)
Phone: 212-249-0444
Web: www.ristorantemorini.com
Prices: $$$

Lunch & dinner daily

With its seventh Manhattan venture, The Altamarea Group has claimed some seriously prime real estate: a posh corner of Madison Ave. Thrilled to have a new heavenly body in their galaxy of hot spots, Upper East Siders can be found sipping cocktails at this *ristorante's* lovely street-level bar before heading upstairs to sup in the elegant, window-lined dining room.

Though patrons are free to order à la carte, the menu is best enjoyed as a four-course prix-fixe. Crudo of bigeye tuna with *tonnato* sauce and *bottarga di muggine* is a bracing start, giving way to supple strands of homemade tagliatelle tossed with intense wild mushroom *trifolati*. Next is a rustic presentation of grilled sea bream, and the *tartaleta* of ricotta and honey for dessert is *bellisimo*!

San Matteo 😊

C2

Italian ✕✕

1739 Second Ave. (at 90th St.)

Subway: 86 St (Lexington Ave.)
Phone: 212-426-6943
Web: www.sanmatteopanuozzo.com
Prices: 🍝

Lunch Fri – Sun
Dinner nightly

This tiny pizzeria has made a big splash with its *panuozzo*, a regional specialty hailing from Campania that's a cross between a calzone and *panino*. The puffy plank of tender, salted dough emerges from San Matteo's hand-built, wood-fired oven crusty and smoke-infused before being sliced and stuffed with first-rate ingredients (highlights include the *ortolano's* fresh, house-made mozzarella, grilled eggplant, roasted sweet peppers, and baby arugula).

The room is graciously attended to and perpetually crowded with neighborhood folks stuffing their faces. In addition to the appetizing house signature, other favorites feature fresh salads such as escarole with Gaeta olives, capers, and gorgonzola; Neapolitan-style pizza; or the day's special baked pasta.

Shanghai Pavilion

Chinese ✗✗

B3

1378 Third Ave. (bet. 78th & 79th Sts.)

Subway: 77 St
Phone: 212-585-3388
Web: N/A
Prices: $$

Lunch & dinner daily

Polished Shanghai Pavilion offers plenty of choice, but the slurp-inducing steamed juicy buns are what keeps the crowds returning time and again. Pay attention to the list of chef's picks, which should include firm chunks of grey sole braised in sweet rice wine sauce. This Shanghainese specialty is studded with crisp pea pods and plump goji berries for a memorable combination of subtle elements. Clean, simple flavors underscore every bit of the firm bean curd sheets tossed with fresh soybeans and pickled cabbage. Unique tastes are a highlight in "Hang Zhou" beef presented in a bamboo steamer lined with cabbage, topped with strips of tender beef and slivered green onions, dressed in soy sauce and spicy oil.

Service is as upscale as the attractive room.

The Simone

Contemporary ✗✗

B2

151 E. 82nd St. (bet. Lexington & Third Aves.)

Subway: 86 St (Lexington Ave.)
Phone: 212-772-8861
Web: www.thesimonerestaurant.com
Prices: $$$

Dinner Mon – Sat

 Chef Chip Smith and wife Tina Vaughn prove hospitality isn't dead at their posh dining room, where genuine and forthcoming service—combined with excellent cuisine—has Upper East Siders giddy.

The bonhomie present here sets the perfect tone for astute cooking typified by intricately composed plates. A savory tart to start boasts a shell of perfect house-made *pâté feuilletée* and is luxuriously filled with Gruyère, prosciutto, and a sunny-side up egg. Braised rabbit thigh—dusted with Dijon mustard-smacked breadcrumbs, grilled loin, and fried liver—is presented with pan-fried herbed spaetzle and bacon-wrapped prunes. For an old-fashioned finish, try the Lord Baltimore: a tower of bourbon-soaked sponge, dried fruits, pecans, and torched soft meringue.

Spigolo

B3

Italian ✗✗

1471 Second Ave. (bet. 76th & 77th Sts.)

Subway: 77 St
Phone: 212-744-1100
Web: www.spigolonyc.com
Prices: $$

Dinner nightly

This wildly popular trattoria has moved to a new address merely steps from its old location. Cozy and inviting, the larger setting offers a comfortable bar area and seating in a warm, modern room of knotty pine flooring, white stucco walls, and dark wood beams.

This good-looker's founding husband-and-wife chef team are no longer involved, but the kitchen remains steady in the hands of Chef Joseph d'Angelo, who turns out classic cuisine with a Mediterranean accent. Slices of marinated fluke dabbed with lavender-hued Kalamata olive aïoli is a bracing crudo of the day. Starters include crunchy eggplant "meatballs" nestled in tomato sauce; while chewy *cavatelli* with shredded red wine-braised lamb is just one of the most heartwarming plates on offer.

Sushi Sasabune

C3

Japanese ✗

401 E. 73rd St. (at First Ave.)

Subway: 77 St
Phone: 212-249-8583
Web: N/A
Prices: $$$$

Lunch Tue – Fri
Dinner Tue – Sat

True, Sushi Sasabune has a drab dining room with service that is best described as efficient. That said, everyone comes for their omakase-only menu of pristine fish and skillfully prepared sushi, which deserves every ounce of its high praise. For those who don't already know the drill, abandon any idea of getting a spicy tuna roll—only truly authentic Japanese cuisine is served here. And it happens to be fantastic.

The team sends out the finest from behind the counter and instructs you on exactly how to eat it, as in "soy sauce" or "no soy sauce." Cede control and delight in lean *maguro* drizzled with ponzu, *kurodai* nigiri sprinkled with crunchy sesame seeds, firm *houbou* brushed with hot ginger-soy sauce, and a creamy blue crab hand roll.

Sushi of Gari ✿

Japanese ✗

C3

402 E. 78th St. (bet. First & York Aves.)

Subway: 77 St   Dinner nightly
Phone: 212-517-5340
Web: www.sushiofgari.com
Prices: $$$

The look of this Upper East Side *sushi-ya* may seem typical; the food is anything but. Of Chef Gari's local empire, this is the flagship and *the* place to find sushi prepared with trademark creativity and tremendous skill. The room is efficiently served but always packed. Scoring a reservation can be tricky, so plan on booking in advance.

Be sure to sit at the counter, where each morsel goes straight from the chef's hand to your mouth, just as it is prepared. Furthermore, the excellent omakase includes very interesting creations. The quality of fish is always outstanding, as is the chef's interplay of flavors and textures resulting in a truly original dining experience. Oysters may arrive wrapped in nori or simply baked in their shells. Tuna tartare is placed over a tempura-fried rectangle of nori with toasted pine nuts. Goldeneye snapper is paired with black truffles. Toro may be chopped with marinated daikon or simply barbecued. Unusual and delicious are the hallmarks of any meal here, no matter what may come. The fish imported from Japan is of extraordinary quality, so be sure to explore the impressive array.

Neighbors take note: Sushi of Gari offers a booming takeout business.

Sushi Seki

B4

J a p a n e s e 🍴

1143 First Ave. (bet. 62nd & 63rd Sts.)

Subway: Lexington Av - 59 St   Dinner Mon – Sat
Phone: 212-371-0238
Web: N/A
Prices: $$

An Upper East Side standby that doesn't actually look like much, Sushi Seki combines exceptional sushi and sashimi with a casual vibe that keeps neighborhood loyalists packed in for late-night dinners and take-out. It may seem like a simple restaurant for a very good spicy tuna roll, but their excellent and unique omakase is what put it on the map as a worthy favorite.

The quality and creativity of each bite shows the chef's training at Sushi of Gari, with added twists. Sample excellent toro chopped with ginger that is at once tender, fatty, and crunchy over rice; or slice of fatty salmon with avocado sauce. Don't miss the signature hand roll of toasted nori surrounding juicy chopped scallop with crunchy tempura flakes, tobiko, and spicy mayo.

Tanoshi

C3

J a p a n e s e 🍴

1372 York Ave. (bet. 73rd & 74th Sts.)

Subway: 77 St   Dinner Tue – Sat
Phone: 646-727-9056
Web: www.tanoshisushinyc.com
Prices: $$$

Tanoshi must be appreciated for its simplicity. The menu is focused on omakase (though a few à la carte options are also offered) and seating is limited to three rounds nightly, enabling just a select number to partake in impressive sushi at good value. The small room is tidy and diners are seated in front of a tempting counter.

Chef Toshio Oguma sources excellent fish and presents a distinctive style of sushi that incorporates loosely packed, warm rice seasoned with red *akazu* (sake lees vinegar). For a modest charge, the deluxe menu reveals a bevy of skillfully knifed, seasonal specialties brushed with house-blend soy. Think Kona amberjack; Hokkaido sea scallop; firefly squid; and torched King salmon. Finish off with ginger and shrimp miso soup.

Taste

B3

1413 Third Ave. (at 80th St.)

Subway: 77 St
Phone: 212-717-9798
Web: www.elizabar.com
Prices: $$

Lunch & dinner daily

This little stretch of Third Avenue may as well be nicknamed Eli Zabar's Alley. Stroll past his wine shop, summertime ice cream stand, the namesake emporium displaying fancifully arranged produce, and a flower shop to find the entrance to this elegant sit-down restaurant. The spacious setting combines a striking inlaid tile floor, an earthy palette, Italian linens, and a polished staff chatting it up with the legion of neighborhood regulars.

Seasonal ingredients are the center of every dish. Sample Eli's rooftop greens that star in a salad dressed with Banyuls vinaigrette, before moving on to slow-braised brisket scattered with pomegranate seeds alongside mashed Yukon golds. Finish with a toasted pistachio cake gilded with chunky pistachio ice cream.

Tiella

B4

1109 First Ave. (bet. 60th & 61st Sts.)

Subway: Lexington Av - 59 St
Phone: 212-588-0100
Web: www.tiellanyc.com
Prices: $$

Lunch Tue – Sat
Dinner nightly

Neapolitan specialties and gracious hospitality make Tiella absolutely worth seeking out. This railcar-sized space is set along a traffic-clogged stretch, but once inside, the ambience is sweet with espresso-tinted wood furnishings set against cream walls and exposed brick.

Petite pizzas baked in the wood-fired oven arrive bearing fresh mozzarella, spicy *'nduja*, and fava beans, among other tasty combinations. Starters include *gallette*, chickpea flour fritters stacked with *stracciatella* and shaved prosciutto, drizzled with fig syrup, and stuck with a sprig of rosemary. The enjoyable *primi* include risotto studded with diced artichokes, pancetta, and showered with shaved black truffle. Desserts like the lemon-soaked *delizia al limone* are homespun delights.

Tori Shin ✿

Japanese ✗✗

1193 First Ave. (bet. 64th & 65th Sts.)

Subway: 68 St - Hunter College
Phone: 212-988-8408
Web: www.torishinny.com
Prices: $$

Dinner nightly

Authenticity hangs heavy in the air at this supreme *yakitori-ya*. Settle in and take in the scents of smoke and searing meat as you watch the virtuoso chefs fan *bintochan* embers to achieve the perfect temperature for each and every morsel. Two blends of *shichimi* (one spicy and one mild) for seasoning those succulent Jidori chicken parts, a receptacle to discard the skewers, and a cold towel upon arrival are delightfully proper touches.

The highest quality product is transformed into grilled works of art here, and although one could nibble à la carte, omakase is the choice way to go. Partake in pickled vegetables which tickle the taste buds in preparation for a seasonal dish, like ratatouille, poached shrimp, and mozzarella. Then it's time for the undeniable star of the show: creamy chicken livers, miso-marinated thigh, rich neck meat, and juicy *tsukune* tasting of ginger and accompanied by a runny egg for dipping, are presented along with grilled organic vegetables A refreshing cool down, say crab with vinegar gelée, is served prior to the rice course.

Tori Shin's fan base is sure to grow once the crew sets up shop in a larger, more accessible space midtown, at 362 West 53 Street.

Uva 🐶

Italian ✗

C3

1486 Second Ave. (bet. 77th & 78th Sts.)

Subway: 77 St
Phone: 212-472-4552
Web: www.uvanyc.com
Prices: $$

Lunch Sat – Sun
Dinner nightly

Perpetually packed and always pleasing, this cousin of elegant Lusardi's is a rocking, rustic good time. Votive-filled nooks and fringed sconces cast a flattering light on the inviting room furnished with straw-seat chairs and wooden tables laden with wine bar-themed small plates.

Cheeses, meats, and salads are fine ways to start. The *insalata di manzo* is a tasty hybrid of all three—shaved lean beef topped by peppery young arugula, shaved Parmesan, and pickled mushrooms. Join the crowds at the start of the week for Meatball Mondays offering three courses revolving around…you guessed it. Sample the hearty beef meatball ravioli garnished with sliced artichoke hearts, silky smooth tomato sauce, and a drizzle of extra virgin olive oil.

Wa Jeal

Chinese ✗✗

C2

1588 Second Ave. (bet. 82nd & 83rd Sts.)

Subway: 86 St (Lexington Ave.)
Phone: 212-396-3339
Web: www.wajealrestaurant.com
Prices: $$

Lunch Mon – Fri
Dinner nightly

This Sichuan chili house is not merely weathering the local torrent of Second Avenue subway construction; their spotless room and tasty food will make you forget that the outside world exists. The ambience is upscale and appealing, combining pale walls, prescient images of wicked-red chilies, an engaging staff, and substantial wine list.

The chef's menu specialties reveal the most noteworthy cooking, as in diced fish and crispy tofu stir-fried in a reddish-brown chili sauce speckled with chili seeds and sliced green onions. Sautéed chicken with spiced miso is another pleasure, mixing crisped, boneless pieces, wok-fried with roasted red chilies and charred jalapeños. Tender baby bok choy with garlic is a refreshing contrast to such potent flavors.

Yefsi

Greek XX

C3
1481 York Ave. (bet. 78th & 79th Sts.)

Subway:	77 St	Dinner nightly
Phone:	212-535-0293	
Web:	www.yefsiestiatorio.com	
Prices:	**$$**	

Chef Christos Christou brings a wealth of experience to the kitchen of this Yorkville standout. Having manned the stoves at some of the city's Greek stalwarts, the Cyprus-native knows his way around his Aegean and Mediterranean coastal specialties.

Begin with salads showcasing superb feta or explore the array of luscious meze including zucchini and eggplant chips with tzatziki, octopus braised in *mavrodafni* or wine-spiked tomato sauce, and grilled sausages over black-eyed peas. Entrées entice with freshness and flavor, such as the wow-inducing nightly special of grilled tiger shrimp. Served head-on and lobster-like in size and texture, they are accompanied by a mound of creamy spinach rice and squeeze of fresh lemon—the perfect embellishment.

Look for our category
🍽 small plates.

Upper West Side

The Upper West Side is the epitome of classic New York. Proudly situated between Central Park and the Hudson River, this family-friendly neighborhood is one of the Big Apple's most distinct and upscale quarters, with a near-religious belief in its own way of doing things. Whether it's because these charming blocks cradle some of the best cafés in town, or that life here means constantly tripping over music and theater fans destined for world-renowned Lincoln Center, these residents cannot fathom living elsewhere. Speaking of music, **Dizzy's Club Coca-Cola** is one of the better ways to spend a night on the town. From its alluring ambience and fantastic live jazz shows, to a stirring lineup of Southern food, audiences are entranced by this formidable home to America's equally formdiable art form. This upper west quarter is also considered an intellectual hub (thanks to Columbia University to the north) as well an artistic center, complete with residential

high-rises occupying some of the most coveted real estate. In fact, legendary co-ops like *The Dakota* speak to the area's history, while nourishing respites like **Épicerie Boulud** cater to hungry locals and young'uns on the run with enjoyable food.

ALL IN THE FAMILY

The Upper West Side is also an acknowledged neighborhood for strolling. Its sidewalks are stacked with quaint, pre-war townhouses as well as gorgeous apartments lined with gleaming hardwood floors, beautiful moldings, and bookish locals arguing with equal gusto over the future of opera. When it comes to food, find these deep-rooted residents browsing the shelves at **Murray's** for some of *the* best sturgeon in town, while other, more discerning palates are bound to be gratified at **Cleopatra's Needle**—an old-time jazz club-cum-Middle Eastern eatery named for the monument in Central Park. However, if fantastic live talent and an open mic (on Sunday afternoons!) accompanied by fresh Mediterranean cuisine isn't your speed, keep it easy indoors by stocking up on a selection of delightfully simple sandwiches on offer at **Indie Food and Wine**. Set inside Lincoln Center's Elinor Bunin Munroe Film Center, this inventive café aims to deliver ample pleasure to culture vultures via Italian-inspired

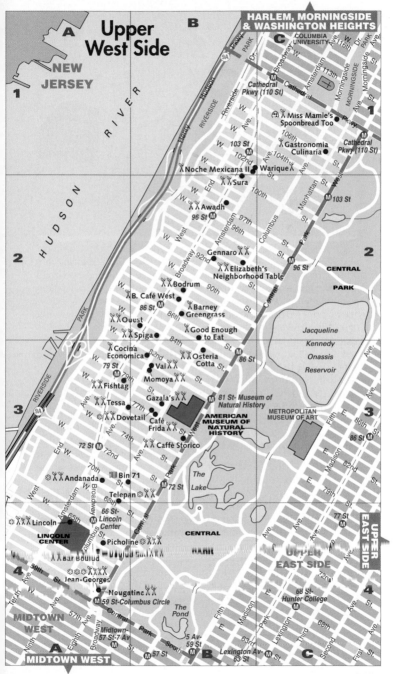

Upper West Side

NEW JERSEY

HARLEM, MORNINGSIDE & WASHINGTON HEIGHTS

COLUMBIA UNIVERSITY

HUDSON RIVER

Cathedral Pkwy (110 St)

Miss Mamie's Spoonbread Too

Gastronomia Culinaria

Cathedral Pkwy (110 St)

103 St

Warique

Noche Mexicana II

Sura

Awadh

96 St

Gennaro

Elizabeth's Neighborhood Table

Bodrum

B. Café West

Barney Greengrass

Ouest

Spiga

Good Enough to Eat

CENTRAL PARK

Cocina Economica

Osteria Cotta

86 St

Vai

Momoya

Fishtag

Gazala's

81 St-Museum of Natural History

Tessa

Dovetail

Café Frida

AMERICAN MUSEUM OF NATURAL HISTORY

METROPOLITAN MUSEUM OF ART

Jacqueline Kennedy Onassis Reservoir

Caffè Storico

72 St

The Lake

Andanada

Bin 71

Telepan

Lincoln

66 St-Lincoln Center

LINCOLN CENTER

Picholine

CENTRAL PARK

UPPER EAST SIDE

Bar Boulud

Jean-Georges

Nougatine

59 St-Columbus Circle

The Pond

68 St-Hunter College

Midtown-57 St-7 Av

5 Av-59 St

57 St

Lexington Av-63 St

MIDTOWN WEST

UPPER EAST SIDE

sandwiches and salads, finished with American flair. A block north, **The Tangled Vine** places fine wine and elegant eats under a warm and accessible spotlight. Showcasing an extraordinary list of organic varietals, this boutique spot is the perfect roost for a sip and small plate before heading south for a Broadway show. Those in the mood for a taste of the past should nestle into a seat at **The Cottage**, a mainstay preparing nostalgic Chinese-American fare for surrounding families and nerdy Ivy Leaguers.

Hopping half way around the world, prepare for an Italian-themed evening by stopping by Cesare Casella's **Salumeria Rosi Parmacotto**, reputed to bring the whole shebang including unique wines, exquisite meats, and other tasty treats. Irrespective of whether you choose to dine in or take out, this Italian idol is sure to knock your socks off. More budget-conscious residents may rest easy as the price is always right at **Celeste**—known for turning out a perfect pizza and Sunday afternoon spread. And

in keeping with this value-meal theme, "Recession Specials" are all the rage at legendary **Gray's Papaya**, the politically outspoken (just check out the window slogans) and quintessentially Upper West hot dog hangout.

BRUNCH AND BAKE

This dominantly residential region jumped on the bakery bandwagon long before its counterparts, and today these sidewalks are rarely short on such calorie-heavy (heavenly?) treats. From rich chocolates at **Mondel** to madeleines at **La Toulousaine**, they flaunt it all. Natives in-the-know get their sweet on at **Levain's** for their legendary chocolate chip cookie; and like one of **Magnolia's** many outposts complete with a cupcake following, **Grandaisy Bakery** is an Italian-inspired confectionary sure to string along sugar fiends. In keeping with its posh surrounds, **Sugar & Plumm** is yet another gem. Here, masterfully created macarons, cookies, and more reach legend status among kids; while adults remain in awe of their brunch hits and sips.

A MEDLEY OF MARKETS

This spirited sense extends to all aspects of life—particularly food—on the Upper West Side. For shopping, the **Tucker Square Greenmarket**—anchored on West 66th and open on Thursdays and Saturdays—is popular for healthy leafy greens and Mexican specialties like *papalo*. Equally celebrated is the original **Fairway**, an ultimate foodie hub rife with well-priced gourmet produce.

Intrepid shoppers should brave its famously cramped elevator to visit the exclusively organic second floor. Finally, no trip is complete without a visit to **Zabar's**—home of all things kosher and wonderful. After ogling their olives, grab a few knishes to nosh on while admiring their line of kitchen supplies. But, rest assured that smaller purveyors not only reside here, but also reign supreme. **Zingone Brothers**, originally a fruit and vegetable stall, is now a fantastic, family-owned and operated grocery that teems with conventional goodies, and treats you like a long-lost friend.

Andanada ⍟

Spanish ❌❌

A3

141 W. 69th St. (at Broadway)

Subway:	72 St	Lunch Sat – Sun
Phone:	646-692-8762	Dinner nightly
Web:	www.andanada141.com	
Prices:	$$$	

Everything is delicious, vibrant, and notably personable at this unselfconscious Spanish powerhouse. Located below street-level, Andanada is laid-back but still formal, with professional, customer-driven servers and a fine-dining menu. The crowd is lively yet very sophisticated, whether seated at the date-friendly bar, pleasant glass atrium, or brick dining room decorated with memorable bullfighting scenes.

Like the surrounds, this noteworthy cuisine arrives much more beautiful than expected—clearly there is modern talent in Chef Manuel Berganza's kitchen. The menu does feature tapas, but each dish is composed with an eye on innovative cooking with classic flavors.

Here, *patatas bravas* are a fascinating mosaic of tender, slowly fried potatoes dotted with *salsa brava* and aïoli to elevate each bite. Fried artichoke hearts combine perfect technique with an enticing showering of salty manchego. The simple-sounding *pulpo a la Gallega* is beguilingly complex, served as tender octopus with olive oil and *pimentòn de la Vera* beneath an impossibly light and almost foamy potato purée. Do not skip pan-seared Iberian pork shoulder with a pastrami-style crust, served hot on a sizzling cast iron platter.

Awadh

B2

Indian 🍴🍴

2588 Broadway (bet. 97th & 98th Sts.)

Subway: 96 St (Broadway)
Phone: 646-861-3604
Web: www.awadhnyc.com
Prices: $$

Lunch & dinner daily

Awadh is out to spice up the Upper West Side. Named after the cuisine of Awadh (in Lucknow), largely influenced by Mughal cooking techniques, Chef Gaurav Anand flaunts his finesse and solid understanding of the provenance in this kitchen.

His parade of carefully plated dishes play with texture and spice, including *Galouti* lamb kebabs served along with a refreshing raita and mint chutney fit for a royal. Though NYC offers myriad versions of butter chicken, his *murgh makhanwala* features the wonderful addition of cashew paste to an insanely fragrant cream sauce, spiced with ginger, *garam masala*, and more. The tender chicken absorbs every bit of the sweet, complex curry, balanced with a kick of green chilies. *Parathas* are perfect to sop up this goodness!

Bar Boulud

A4

French 🍴🍴

1900 Broadway (bet. 63rd & 64th Sts.)

Subway: 66 St - Lincoln Center
Phone: 212-595-0303
Web: www.barboulud.com
Prices: $$$

Lunch & dinner daily

The restaurant that launched Chef Daniel Boulud's Upper West Side trifecta, Bar Boulud's first-class charcuterie and stellar wine list make it an idyllic prelude to any Lincoln Center performance. Sit at the communal table with a hefty pour of a rare wine (ask about specials), and gaze at the tunnel-like dining room, crafted to mimic a barrel and clothed with Vik Muniz photographs of abstract wine spills. The wine-centric motif is as clear as the glassware.

While their array of sips are winning, meat and cheese boards are equally worthy, thanks to the genius of Gilles Verot. He's responsible for the award-winning *fromage de tête* (bright and clean in flavor) as well as the infallible menu of everything from Provençal rabbit to Croatian sheep's cheese.

Barney Greengrass

Deli 🍴

B2

541 Amsterdam Ave. (bet. 86th & 87th Sts.)

Subway: 86 St (Broadway)   Lunch Tue – Sun
Phone: 212-724-4707
Web: www.barneygreengrass.com
Prices: 🍩🍩

Bagels and bialys reign supreme in this culinary institution, set amid a culturally rich stretch dotted with lavish synagogues and purveyors of authentic deli delights. Not all are created equal, though, and little details make all the difference inside this sturgeon king, lauded for its weathered décor featuring muraled walls, a storied past, and service that is as authentically NY as can be. It's the sort of spot families flock to for brunch—imagine a triple-decker (tongue, turkey, and Swiss cheese) on rye paired with a pickle, of course.

Whether you take-out or eat-in, chopped liver with caramelized onions and boiled egg is sure to sate. Finish with a perfect black-and-white cookie, rugelach, or rice pudding, all favorites and fittingly so.

B. Café West

Belgian 🍴

B2

566 Amsterdam Ave. (bet. 87th & 88th Sts.)

Subway: 86 St (Broadway)   Lunch Sat – Sun
Phone: 212-873-0003   Dinner nightly
Web: www.bcafe.com
Prices: $$

Discover a slice of Belgium at this Upper West charmer, where the space may be narrow and deep, but the front bar is always in full swing at happy hour. The dining room is slightly elevated and very warm thanks to cozy bistro-style tables covered in white linen, a pressed-tin ceiling, and beaming waiters.

Posters and brass accents verge on cliché but all misgivings are pardoned upon tasting their fine and familiar favorites. Start with numerous *moules* options like delicious Malay *laksa* (red curry), Pamplona (chorizo), or red Duvel with hot sauce. Crunch your way through beer-battered fish and frites, before savoring a seafood *ostendaise* finished with shallots and cream.

Gaufre de Bruxelles drizzled with chocolate sauce is fit for a Belgian queen.

Bin 71

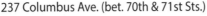

A3

Italian

237 Columbus Ave. (bet. 70th & 71st Sts.)

Subway: 72 St
Phone: 212-362-5446
Web: www.bin71.com
Prices: $$

Lunch & dinner Tue – Sun

An *enoteca* in the true sense of the term, Bin 71 focuses on *vino* with more than 30 varieties by the glass and over 60 by the bottle. A place to discover new blends and producers, this haunt is known to promote wine-focused conversation and amazing Italian-accented cuisine. An all-consuming U-shaped marble bar makes it easy—stay long enough and you're reaching for the menu.

Beyond excellent cheese and charcuterie, dishes feature flavorful herbs that perfume a grilled chicken, which comes on a bed of sautéed spinach with white bean ragout and sweet-sour caponata. Basil-scented North Atlantic cod soup swarming with creamy, thinly sliced potatoes hits the spot, as does dessert—maybe a fanned-out poached pear served with a scoop of *gianduja*-hazelnut gelato?

Bodrum

B2

Turkish

584 Amsterdam Ave. (bet. 88th & 89th Sts.)

Subway: 86 St (Broadway)
Phone: 212-799-2806
Web: www.bodrumnyc.com
Prices: $$

Lunch & dinner daily

Like the white sandy beaches of its namesake fishing village in Turkey, Bodrum has amassed a following of area residents, who stop in for a Mediterranean escape complete with well-made food. Although nearby storefronts lack polish, this retreat breaks the mold with attentive service and charming touches like a brick-covered, wood-burning oven surrounded by blue mosaic-tiled walls.

Wines and spirits are straight out of Turkey, including the refreshing *raki*. Similarly, the menu leans towards classic plates with a few creative additions like pizza or braised leeks with rice. Regulars go for *b'stila djej*, a sweet-savory combo of cinnamon-scented chicken, almonds, and herbs wrapped in phyllo pastry; or stuffed cabbage filled with lamb, rice and dill.

Boulud Sud

Mediterranean ✗✗✗

A4

20 W. 64th St. (bet. Broadway & Central Park West)

Subway: 66 St - Lincoln Center

Phone: 212-595-1313

Web: www.bouludsud.com

Prices: $$$

Lunch & dinner daily

Chef Daniel Boulud indulges his authentic yet modern Mediterranean flair here at Boulud Sud. The decadent menu finds its influences in all sides of the sea, from Morocco to Turkey to Italy and back again. Packed and lively, the dining area is designed with the airy spaciousness of vaulted ceilings, long striped banquettes, and natural lighting.

The semi-open kitchen deftly creates delicacies like homemade lemon-saffron linguine mingled with shaved *bottarga*, dandelion leaves, and cuttlefish so beautifully cooked that it melts on the tongue; or crispy duck duo with aromatic Marsala jus, spring vegetables, and duck confit pastries. Sicilian sabayon is an extraordinary and foamy lemon concoction with bergamot gelato-stuffed tartlets and green tea ice cream.

Café Frida

Mexican ✗✗

B3

368 Columbus Ave. (bet. 77th & 78th Sts.)

Subway: 81 St - Museum of Natural History

Phone: 212-712-2929

Web: www.cafefrida.com

Prices: $$

Lunch & dinner daily

Margaritas and guacamole, the two tentpoles of any good Mexican restaurant, become the standard bearers for all others at this Columbus Avenue fiesta. Guests sample sips from the extensive tequila list at the intricately carved bar, or scoop up chipfuls of tart, chunky guacamole at tables throughout the bi-level space.

Regional specialties on the frequently changing menu let diners explore beyond the typical Mexican dishes, though traditional enchiladas simmered in deep, earthy *mole* are hearty and pleasing. Meanwhile, succulent lamb shank marinated in a *guajillo* sauce, avocado leaf, and olives is tender enough to make steak knives superfluous. Flaming dessert plantains with ice cream replace the same old *sopaipillas* for a new hot-and-cold sensation.

Caffè Storico

B3

Italian ✗✗

170 Central Park West (at 77th St.)

Subway: 81 St - Museum of Natural History
Phone: 212-485-9211
Web: www.caffestorico.com
Prices: $$

Lunch & dinner Tue – Sun

Gone are the days when museum food lacked character, and top Philadelphia restaurateur Stephen Starr's Caffè Storico proves it. Housed in the New York Historical Society, this marble-clad sparkler incorporates the collection into its design, with antique porcelain filling its sky-high shelves and views of the sculpture arcade.

Starr certainly knows how to please a crowd with marvelous salads and Italian-inspired dishes alongside unique wines from some of the country's emerging regions. Though *frittata del giorno* pocked with red peppers, tomato, and mozzarella, as well as panzanella with creamy burrata are eye-poppingly good, save room for a berry *crostata* whose flaky crust is perfectly accompanied by a smidge of vanilla ice cream.

Cocina Economica

B3

Mexican ✗

452 Amsterdam Ave. (bet. 81st & 82nd Sts.)

Subway: 79 St
Phone: 212-501-7755
Web: www.cocinaeconomicamexico.com
Prices: $$

Lunch & dinner daily

Delicious and genuine Mexican fare is served with good cheer here at Cocina Economica. Bedecked with brightly painted walls, Mexican artifacts, and rustic wooden tables, this vibrant little oasis is a welcome addition to the neighborhood.

Nibble on *antojitos* (street snacks) like *pan de elote con aguacate*, cornbread stuffed with creamy avocado, steamed in corn husks; or this dish are almost flaky in grilled empanadas, piping hot and filled with *huauzontle* and oozing Oaxaca cheese, presented alongside pumpkin seed *mole* for dipping. Desserts can be absolute standouts as in their chocolate tart, cut into a dense wedge, studded with toasted walnuts and pecans, served with a scoop of house-made sour cream gelato, all sprinkled with granola.

Dovetail ⛬

B3

103 W. 77th St. (at Columbus Ave.)

Subway: 81 St - Museum of Natural History
Phone: 212-362-3800
Web: www.dovetailnyc.com
Prices: $$$

Lunch Sun
Dinner nightly

A narrow façade belies the roominess and elegance within Dovetail. Walk through a set of gleaming glass doors to arrive at this serious retreat, where the staff is as wonderful and accommodating as the warm and alluring setting itself. Set in a classic brownstone on a tree-lined street, this beautiful space features bare walls embellished with maple veneer panels, soft, muted colors, and intimate banquettes.

Oddly positioned columns may interfere with spatial flow, but creativity and technical aptitude pour out of every item from the kitchen. A smartly bound carte du jour stars such unique hors d'œuvres as cardamom panna cotta infused with orange, fennel, and tart pomegranate gel (a perfect counterpoint to the rich layer beneath). The Carnaroli in Dungeness crab risotto, studded with lemon, crackling poppy seeds, and parsley, is not just creamy and rich but the crowning queen of the dish; while silky swordfish set atop Creole shrimp with smoky chorizo and hot peppers leaves even picky pescetarians quite affected.

For an unforgettable finale, dabble in a dark chocolate crémeux framed by boozy marshmallows and bruléed bananas. Those pretty coffee crumbles on top are a textural tease.

Elizabeth's Neighborhood Table

B2

American 🍴🍴

680 Columbus Ave. (at 93rd St.)

Subway: 96 St (Broadway)
Phone: 212-280-6500
Web: www.elizabethsnyc.com
Prices: $$

Lunch & dinner daily

Picket fencing, a shingled veranda, and mullioned windows might seem more at home in New England than this relatively forgotten nook of the Upper West, but Elizabeth's pops out from the surroundings to embrace her warm and homey name. The décor follows suit with a butcher-block table, white wainscoting, dark walls, and wide, comfortable tables. The kitchen promises a focus on carefully sourced organic and biodynamic ingredients—the kind that Granny used. (Evidently, their foremothers had access to quinoa and excellent feta.) Cobb salad is a pitch-perfect combination of grilled chicken, bacon crumbles, blue cheese, and more in a creamy dressing. End with a seasonal crumble that is tart and cinnamon-sweet with apples, berries, and vanilla ice cream.

Fishtag

A3

Seafood 🍴🍴

222 W. 79th St. (bet. Amsterdam Ave. & Broadway)

Subway: 79 St
Phone: 212-362-7470
Web: www.michaelpsilakis.com
Prices: $$$

Lunch Sat – Sun
Dinner nightly

Refined, charismatic, and comfortable, this sliver of a restaurant instantly feels like an iconic bit of New York, thanks to its classic location tucked amid limestone townhouses. The smartly designed space features a speckled marble bar for dining, earth-toned and exposed brick walls, and an array of seating options (try to snag that large corner booth if you can).

The menu may seem confusing in its organization of lightest to heaviest dishes, but lets diners take control with the help of competent and intuitive servers—in choosing an array of seafood delights. Substantial appetizers might include a *skordalia* brandade "melt" with smoked eggplant and tomato confit. The grilled branzino stuffed with headcheese is a longstanding marvel.

Gastronomia Culinaria

Manhattan ▶ Upper West Side

C1

Italian ✗

53 W. 106th St. (bet. Columbus & Manhattan Aves.)

Subway: 103 St (Central Park West)   Dinner nightly
Phone: 212-663-1040
Web: www.gastronomiaculinaria.com
Prices: $$

From his experience in world-celebrated kitchens, Chef/owner Vincenzo Pezzilli has created this darling Italian restaurant that far exceeds the Big Apple's expectations. A native of Rome, he presides over his talented kitchen nightly, carefully watching over each sous as they transport authentic flavors to a dining room of locals and Ivy League professors. Paintings decorate exposed brick walls, and the soft lighting creates just the scene for satisfying dishes and Italian wines.

Pastas induce swoons, especially the enticingly chewy *strascinati alla norcina* with garlicky pork and porcini bathed in a delectable vegetable ragù. To close, the *tortino ai due cioccolati* (dark chocolate cake filled with white chocolate) is absolutely worth the 20-minute wait.

Gazala's

B3

Middle Eastern ✗✗

380 Columbus Ave. (at 78th St.)

Subway: 81 St - Museum of Natural History   Lunch & dinner daily
Phone: 212-873-8880
Web: www.gazalasplace.com
Prices: $$

Chef/owner Gazala Halabi was born to helm this kitchen and its teeming platters of Druze cuisine (an ancient Muslim offshoot with a vibrant Israeli history). After all, her family owns a restaurant in Israel, from which they still ship spice blends to New York for nearly everything on the menu. Glimpse her work through the Mediterranean-blue framed opening into the kitchen. The big, open dining room glows with natural light from tall windows.

Crêpe-thin like whole wheat handkerchiefs resemble feathery pitas folded with an abundant choice of meze including garlicky fava dip, house-made goat cheese, and spicy *kibbe* stuffed with pine nuts and herbs. Don't miss the flaky and puffy *boureka* pies sprinkled with sesame seeds, which change savory fillings daily.

Gennaro

Italian ✗✗

B2

665 Amsterdam Ave. (bet. 92nd & 93rd Sts.)

Subway: 96 St (Broadway)
Phone: 212-665-5348
Web: www.gennaronyc.com
Prices: $$

Dinner nightly

Despite its age, Gennaro hasn't lost its good looks or popularity—it still packs in hungry locals nightly, who aren't deterred by its borderline gritty surrounds or no-reservations policy. Come early or risk waiting, which isn't so bad considering the bar, whose by-the-glass offerings are vast and very appealing with both familiar and unusual Italian choices. The menu can be overwhelming considering its long list of pastas and daily specials, so trust your gut and you can't go wrong. Start with the polenta gorgonzola, served almost *quattro stagione*-style, with gorgonzola, prosciutto, and a sliced portobello; before twirling your taste buds around chewy *bucatini* showered with pecorino and pepper. The tiramisu is a light, creamy, and fluffy slam dunk.

Good Enough to Eat

American ✗

B2

520 Columbus Ave. (at 85th St.)

Subway: 86 St (Broadway)
Phone: 212-496-0163
Web: www.goodenoughtoeat.com
Prices: $$

Lunch & dinner daily

A mom-and-pop mainstay, Good Enough to Eat has made the most of its fresh digs and the wide sidewalks of Columbus Avenue. Though slightly larger, its vibe remains eternally homey and endearing, with small, thoughtful touches like lots of cow art and a famously friendly staff making this a primo stomping ground among residents.

The food here is unconditionally good, with a daily rotation of down home dishes like roast turkey with gravy, cornbread stuffing and cranberry relish. The standout vegetarian Napoleon combines roasted portobellos, sweet potatoes, peppers, and summer squash cut into a perfect square alongside grilled focaccia. Be sure to sample (extensively) their made-to-order cakes and sweets—especially the sensational coconut custard pie.

Jean-Georges ✿ ✿ ✿

Contemporary 🍴🍴🍴🍴

A4

1 Central Park West (bet. 60th & 61st Sts.)

Subway: 59 St - Columbus Circle
Phone: 212-299-3900
Web: www.jean-georgesrestaurant.com
Prices: $$$$

Lunch & dinner daily

The crown-jewel restaurant of a crown-jewel Trump hotel, Jean-Georges reigns over the Central Park dining scene. Facing its lush grounds and Columbus Circle, the restaurant's separate entrance can be something of a wind tunnel; guests also must pass through buzzing Nougatine to arrive at the silvery gray dining room. Still, those massive windows, columns, and twinkling city lights outside make this a very special place. During weekdays, the feel is more formal and expense account-focused. Weekends bring more tourists, local socialites, and an easier ambience. The highly professional service staff is one well-oiled and smooth machine.

While the contemporary menu may be fixed, the options are numerous and very appealing. The fascinating interplay of flavors can begin with thick hunks of sea trout buried beneath a pillow of olive-oil foam with trout roe and dill purée, all topped with tempura-fried curls of trout skin. Simple but lush elegance underscores Artic char encrusted in Burgundy truffle "crumbs" with paper-thin and crispy parsnips.

Desserts are served as a "sampler" focused on one ingredient, such as chocolate in all its outrageous glory. Save room for marshmallow *mignardises*.

Lincoln ⁣❀

A4

142 W. 65th St. (bet. Amsterdam Ave. & Broadway)

Subway: 66 St - Lincoln Center
Phone: 212-359-6500
Web: www.lincolnristorante.com
Prices: $$$$

Lunch Wed – Sun
Dinner nightly

Lincoln Center not only hosts world-class performers, but it is also home to this sparkling showcase for the culinary arts. The striking exterior appears wrapped in glass and crowned by a swooping turf roof. The drama continues inside, where the chic, cream-colored dining room seems ethereal by day yet sultry at night.

Chef Jonathan Benno and his team, on view in the exhibition kitchen, strive and succeed in honoring Italy's diverse culinary heritage. Each month focuses on a new region, so April's Le Marche gives way to May's Veneto. December's treasures of Piedmont showcase *vitello tonnato* recast as thinly shaven veal terrine set over creamy tuna sauce, given a refreshingly bitter note from torn chicory. Pasta always impresses, as in the *orecchiette di grano arbo* (smoked flour pasta) tossed with shrimp, spicy sausage, and heirloom beans in garlicky tomato sauce and herbed breadcrumbs. Pan-seared cobia is adorned with a streak of arugula pudding, and toasted salsify so perfectly caramelized that it becomes sweet.

Desserts like the fragrant quince *crostata*, uniquely tender and cake-like beneath sweetly spiced brown sugar crumble, demonstrate the all-encompassing talent of this kitchen.

Miss Mamie's Spoonbread Too

Southern ✖️

C1

366 W. 110th St./Cathedral Pkwy. (bet. Columbus & Manhattan Aves.)

Subway: Cathedral Pkwy/110 St (Central Park West)
Phone: 212-865-6744
Web: www.spoonbreadinc.com
Prices: 🍞

Lunch & dinner daily

Come to Miss Mamie's and plan to indulge, Southern style. This tiny institution recently got a makeover in the bright, clean dining room—think comfier wicker chairs, roomier tables, and lots of flowers. Despite its more sophisticated appearance, the kitchen still embraces such tried and true classics as fried chicken thighs with black-eyed peas and collard greens, Louisiana catfish, and a creamy red velvet cake for dessert. Grab a fresh-squeezed lemonade and dive into the sampler, stocked with deep-fried shrimp, fall-off-the-bone beef short ribs, more fried chicken, and probably too many sides of cornbread stuffing and hop 'n John.

End with a cinnamon-scented coffee and start planning a stop by Miss Maude's, the second location in Hamilton Heights.

Momoya

Japanese ✖️✖️

B3

427 Amsterdam Ave. (bet. 80th & 81st Sts.)

Subway: 79 St
Phone: 212-580-0007
Web: www.momoyanyc.com
Prices: $$$

Lunch & dinner daily

A beguilingly simple aesthetic flows through handsome Momoya. The dining room is outfitted in floor-to-ceiling blonde wood, slate floors, and leather booths that exude a subdued masculinity. The front is dedicated to a bar where the drinks flow like a river and the sushi is always tasty.

Appetizers here can be showstoppers, starting with small plates like piping-hot grilled shishitos with yuzu salt, black cod with spinach and kabocha purée, or grilled eggplant with sweet miso. The small sushi counter's strength lies in its creative maki, like a namesake roll combining shiso, cucumber, and ginger topped with beautifully grilled black cod, spicy miso, and sweet potato crisp. Sake offerings are balanced, smooth, and enjoyable to the very last sip.

Noche Mexicana II

B1

Mexican ✗

842 Amsterdam Ave. (at 101st St.)

Subway: 103 St (Broadway)
Phone: 212-662-6900
Web: N/A
Prices: 💲💲

Lunch & dinner daily

If you had a Mexican *tía*, you'd want her to be one of the lovely chefs pounding masa and wrapping tamales at Noche Mexicana II. The tasty corner is dominated by two veranda doors that open onto the sidewalk—a perfect setting for the specialties this talented kitchen sends out routinely. Imagine *huaraches con bistec* topped with tender beef and teeming with refried beans, bright tomatoes, and sour cream. Those who venture uptown are not met with disappointment: *tomate verde mole* is accented with toasted pumpkin seeds and piquant chilies that cover the tender chicken; while brick-red *chilate* boasts plump shrimp swimming in a spicy *guajillo* broth with a sprinkling of cilantro and *queso fresco*. A fresh flan, the only dessert on the menu, is simply excellent.

Nougatine

A4

Contemporary ✗✗

1 Central Park West (at 60th St.)

Subway: 59 St - Columbus Circle
Phone: 212-299-3900
Web: www.jean-georgesrestaurant.com
Prices: **$$**

Lunch & dinner daily

Prestigiously set on the ground floor of the Trump International Hotel, Nougatine proves to be nothing short of lavish. The fresh look is clean and contemporary, bathed in light reflected from its large, unencumbered windows—a world away from the crowded plazas and blaring cabs outside.

Minimalist touches like plush leather banquettes, gleaming light fixtures, and a brushed metal bar convey gentility, making Nougatine an otherworldly spot to rest your weary, globetrotting foot over an aperitif or quick bite. A bowl of verdant green pea soup crested with crispy croutons and Parmesan foam is an elegant standout among other items like succulent skate with aromatic black beans; or a dense slice of sour cream cheesecake with passion fruit compote.

Osteria Cotta

B3

Italian ✗✗

513 Columbus Ave. (bet. 84th & 85th Sts.)

Subway: 86 St (Broadway)
Phone: 212-873-8500
Web: www.cottanyc.com
Prices: $$

Lunch Wed – Sun
Dinner nightly

Osteria Cotta is a reminder that neighborhood restaurants are a precious thing: comfortable, unpretentious, affordable, and ready to welcome a spontaneous visit. The charming interior is warm with wood beams, wrought-iron bannisters, and brick walls that seem so barnyard-chic that you might just forget quite where you are.

The Italian menu may feature an excellent assortment of *verdure*—all wonderfully balanced and full of flavor—as in classic Sicilian sweet-and-sour caponata teeming with *pignoli*. Every taste is good and right in a tender pork chop fanned over grilled yellow squash and zucchini; roasted cauliflower with pickled *peperoncini*; or spaghetti *pomodoro* with chunky, herb-flecked sauce. Their gelato is smooth, creamy, and memorable.

Ouest

B2

American ✗✗

2315 Broadway (bet. 83rd & 84th Sts.)

Subway: 86 St (Broadway)
Phone: 212-580-8700
Web: www.ouestny.com
Prices: $$$

Lunch Sun
Dinner nightly

For the past decade, this contemporary darling has been bringing serious cuisine to the Upper West Side—and those local media celebrities who populate it are loyally grateful. Beyond the narrow front bar, the dining room is sleek and masculine with rather grand ceiling lamps, secluded balconies, and polished everything.

Begin with thick, overlapping slices of flawless smoked sturgeon with poached egg, toast rounds, lardons, and well-dressed frisée. The exceptional taste of fresh, aged goat cheese stuffed into translucent pasta pockets makes for memorable ravioli, bathed in salty-sweet pancetta broth. To finish, the Spanish peanut butter and chocolate "bombe" elevates that old standby dessert with decadence, nostalgia, and lots of warm chocolate sauce.

Picholine ✽

A4

35 W. 64th St. (bet. Broadway & Central Park West)

Subway: 66 St - Lincoln Center

Phone: 212-724-8585

Web: www.picholinenyc.com

Prices: $$$$

Dinner Tue – Sun

Chef Terrance Brennan's Picholine shines once again. The discreet entrance of this grand realm, just steps away from Lincoln Center, ushers swanky theatregoers and discerning sophisticates into a truly plush dining room. Replete with lavish doses of old-world luxury, its posh swagger is defined by glittering fixtures, brocade covered walls, and heavy drapery.

A number of tasting menus showcase a contemporary vision of Mediterranean fare. Risotto is a distillation of seasonal flavors, as in the autumnal concoction of wild mushrooms, black truffle, and sweet cubes of blue Hubbard squash. An ensemble of holistically-raised lamb from Pennsylvania features seared loin and crispy sweetbreads composed with *lentils de Puy*, spiced carrots, thick yogurt, and a sheet of chickpea panisse so delicate it seems to hover.

Turophiles take note: Picholine's cheese service is without peer. Choose to indulge, and the erudite *maître d' fromage* will wheel over the amply laden cart and offer a custom-tailored explanation of the cave-ripened artisanal selection. Should you still have room for something sweet, the *tres leches* cake with brownie ganache and chocolate sorbet is an almost equally impressive finale.

411

Spiga

B2

Italian ✗✗

200 W. 84th St. (bet. Amsterdam Ave. & Broadway)

Subway: 86 St (Broadway)   Dinner nightly
Phone: 212-362-5506
Web: www.spiganyc.com
Prices: $$$

Fantastically authentic Italian is what diners expect at Spiga, the intimate little spot Upper West Siders are lucky to have. Jazzy tunes float through the romantic dining space, replete with distressed brick walls, dark wood tables, shelves of wine bottles, and Italian-speaking servers. The menu is as sophisticated as it is delectable.

Its offerings range from plump grilled scallops over fava bean purée drizzled with a balsamic vinegar reduction, to pan seared duck breast topped with cherry compote and nestled into a mound of sweet potato purée with a side of Brussels sprouts. The pastas are an absolute must, as in lasagna layered with artichokes, béchamel, and Parmesan sauce; or potato and beet gnocchi with melted Taleggio and basil pesto.

Sura

B2

Thai ✗✗

2656 Broadway (bet. 100th & 101st Sts.)

Subway: 103 St (Broadway)   Lunch & dinner daily
Phone: 212-665-8888
Web: www.surathaikitchen.com
Prices: ⊜⊜

Tucked adjacent to the Marrakech Hotel and flanked by some vacant storefronts, Sura offers a bright splash of Bangkok to this residential stretch. Colorful fabrics, mesh-covered lanterns, and wood carvings give it an exotic vibe and support its mission to bring sparky Yaowarat cuisine to this locality's masses.

A tad Americanized but completely delicious, here you will find tasty noodles, sour soups, and refreshing iced coffees. A terrific *massaman* curry with chicken, potatoes, and lotus root offers the perfectly balanced flavors and spice one expects in Thai cooking, blending lemongrass and Kaffir lime with sharp chilies and smooth coconut milk.

Brunch is equally popular with such fantastic fusion dishes as marinated and grilled duck crêpes.

Telepan ॐ

American 🍴🍴

72 W. 69th St. (bet. Central Park West & Columbus Ave.)

Subway: 66 St - Lincoln Center
Phone: 212-580-4300
Web: www.telepan-ny.com
Prices: $$$

Lunch Wed – Sun
Dinner nightly

There is a reason why we all wish that a Telepan would appear in our own neighborhood—this is a thoroughly solid restaurant. With its brownstone charm firmly in place, the impeccable interior has an equally New York feel with cozy rooms, brick, and food-centric artwork decorating the light walls. Every element feels as though it is in smart proportion and lends an airy feel to the space, from the contemporary plates to the petite wood tables. The waitstaff is professional, not overly formal, and genuinely interested in each guest.

Classic American elegance shines in a savory, cake-like chive and potato blini with slices of smoked brook trout with sweet onion cream and chives. Even the legendary and under-hyped hamburger oozes with perfection right down through the volcano of fries and buttery bun that will stand up to a river of juices.

The mouthwatering desserts promise everything that is great in a great dessert. Yes, there is Health connection in a deceptively sophisticated block of peanut butter and gianduja with peanut brittle ice cream and huckleberry gelée; but after one salty-sweet-crunchy bite, you realize the unsung brilliance of a chocolatey peanut butter-and-jelly sandwich.

413

Tessa

A3

Mediterranean 🍴🍴

349 Amsterdam Ave. (bet. 76th & 77th Sts.)

Subway: 79 St
Phone: 212-390-1974
Web: www.tessanyc.com
Prices: $$$

Lunch & dinner daily

An industrial-inspired *enoteca*, Tessa makes a huge, packed room feel intimate enough for a date—a feat in New York. A wine rack made of steel cables, metal security gates across the ceiling, and exposed brick complete the modern *vineria* look that is simply smart and very unique.

Gorgeous French walnut boards holding cheese and *salumi* makes the food even more enticing. Pasta here can be at once luxurious and comforting, as in the *cavatelli* topped with rabbit and pancetta ragù with smoky-sweet cipollini. Grilled entrées may include swordfish steak with a slightly tangy white wine-artichoke *barigoule* and citrusy caper *gremolata*. For dessert, don't miss the thick, cool coffee *pot de crème* topped with cardamom sablé and sweet date purée.

Vai

B3

Mediterranean 🍴🍴

429 Amsterdam Ave. (bet. 80th & 81st Sts.)

Subway: 79 St
Phone: 212-362-4500
Web: www.vairestaurant.com
Prices: $$

Lunch Wed – Sun
Dinner nightly

Warm, cozy, and strikingly attractive, Vai is a casual yet sultry choice for tasty food and wine. The entire space seems to be illuminated by flickering votives bouncing light off cream-colored walls, brown leather seating, and bare wood tables. The small marble bar is superb for solo dining and offers the complete menu, as well as a full view into the hectic kitchen, where Chef Vincent Chirico is at the helm.

On the menu, sample delightful dishes that focus on Mediterranean flavors, as in charred Portuguese octopus with watercress, crisp potato nuggets, and jalapeño "pesto." Then, move on to plump ravioli filled with silky burrata and sweet ricotta, dressed in truffle cream, topped with feathery *parmigiano* and cracked pepper, set over hon shimeji mushrooms.

Warique

Peruvian ✗

B1

852 Amsterdam Ave. (bet. 101st & 102nd Sts.)

Subway: 103 St (Broadway)
Phone: 212-865-0101
Web: www.wariquenyc.com
Prices: $$

Lunch & dinner daily

The façade may not seem to standout against the neighborhood, but their food is straightforward delicious. Two narrow dining rooms flank the semi-visible kitchen at the heart of this restaurant, where the serious yet rib-sticking cuisine is prepared. The staff is helpful and welcoming.

Warique knows how to please its guests with food that they will come to savor time and again. Start with *causa Peruana*— cold, smashed potatoes dressed with mashed avocado, *aji amarillo* (a hellfire-breathing sauce), and then studded with shrimp. Then, try the *papa rellena*, a generous ensemble of potatoes stuffed with tender ground ribeye, chopped egg, raisins, olives, and a smattering of peppers, served with another special *aji* crafted from jalapeños and black mint.

Do not confuse couverts ✗ with stars ❀! ✗ defines comfort, while ❀ are awarded for the best cuisine. Stars are awarded across all categories of comfort.

The Bronx

The Bronx

The only borough attached to the island of Manhattan, the Bronx boasts such awe-inspiring sights as the world-renowned Bronx Zoo, Hall of Fame for Great Americans, and Yankee Stadium. However, it is also revered as a hotbed of culinary treasures. Case in point: The New York Botanical Garden is devoted to education and hosts many garden- and food-related classes. In fact, the Botanical Garden's Bronx **Green-Up** is an acclaimed program aimed at improving inner-city areas by providing them with agricultural advice and practical training.

GOURMET GETAWAY

Located along the west side, Belmont is a residential quarter marked by diverse ethnic and religious communities. Once an Italian hub, its population is now comprised of Hispanics (primarily Puerto Ricans), African-Americans, West Indians, and Albanians. Much of the Bronx today consists of parkland, like Pelham Bay Park with its sandy Orchard Beach. And since a day at the beach is never complete without salty eats, you'll want to step into pizza paradise— **Louie & Ernie's**—for a slice of heaven. Beyond, City Island is a gem of a coastal community teeming with seafood spots. **The Black Whale** is a local fixture frequented for its classic-meets-contemporary cuisine and thirst-quenching cocktails. Sip and savor their offerings, either inside the quirky dining room or out in the garden. When the sun beats down, pop into **Lickety Split** for a cooling scoop of sorbet or ice cream, or both!

Belmont's most renowned street, Arthur Avenue, is home to Italian food paradise—**The Arthur Avenue Retail Market**. This enclosed oasis is a culinary emporium overrun with self-proclaimed foodies as well as famed epicureans, who can be seen prowling for quality pasta, homemade sausages, extra virgin olive oil, notorious heroes, and heirloom seeds. Some begin by diving into a ball of rich, gooey mozzarella at **Joe's Deli** (open on Sundays!). Others may grab them to go with the likes of pistachio-studded mortadella from **Teitel Brothers**, or impressive *salumi* at **Calabria Pork Store**.

Beyond this venerable marketplace, find early-risers ravenously tearing into freshly baked breads from either **Terranova** or **Addeo**—the choices are plenty. Come lunchtime, find a myriad of Eastern European treats. At **Tony & Tina's Pizzeria**, skip the signatures and instead, focus on Albanian or Kosovar *burek* (flaky rolls with sweet pumpkin purée). Just as **Xochimilco Restaurant** is a playground for families with tots in tow, South Bronxite singles may revel in such Ecuadorian delights as *bollon de verde* at **Ricuras Panderia**.

Journeying further south east from the Belmont section, **Gustiamo's** warehouse continues to flourish as a city-wide favorite for regional Italian specialties including olive oils, pastas, and San Marzano tomatoes. Meanwhile, the butchers at **Honeywell Meat Market** can be seen teaching rookies a thing or two about breaking down a side of beef until the end of time. Over on Willis Avenue, Mott Haven's main drag, bright awnings designate a plethora of Puerto Rican diners and Mexican bodegas.

YANKEE STADIUM

Home to the "sultans of swat" (AKA the "Bronx Bombers"), **Yankee Stadium** is *the* place for world-champion baseball. And what goes best with baseball? Big, bold, and serious eats of course, all to be found at the stadium's food court featuring **Lobel's**, the ultimate butcher cart crafting perfectly marbled steak sandwiches to order. Even the boys from Torrisi have set up shop here at **Parm**, seducing

fans with hearty sandwiches and near-heavenly sweets. The bro-mance continues at **Brother Jimmy's**, one of New York's best-selling barbecue chains, proffering the likes of juicy pulled pork sandwiches, fried pickles, baked beans, and more. Extra-refined palates will marvel at the farm-fresh produce from **Melissa's Farmers Market**, just as kids are sure to swoon over the sweets at **Dylan's Candy Bar**.

COMFORT FOODS

A staple among Morris Park residents, **Patricia's** is prized for heart-warming Italian classics (pizzas deserve special praise) crafted from local ingredients. Meanwhile, Eastchester, Wakefield, and Williamsbridge cradle several other communities along with their special eats. After this savory and smoky culinary cornucopia, residents invariably end with something sweet over at **Kingston Tropical Bakery**. Meanwhile, **G & R Deli** pays homage to the neighborhood's deep Italian roots by delivering authentic flavors in sausages and meat sauce sold by the quart. **Sal & Dom's** stick with this line of duty by serving deliciously flaky *sfogliatelle*.

Moving across the globe, it is important to note that Asian food has officially arrived in this borough, with **Phnom Penh-Nha Trang Market** bragging an impressive range of Vietnamese ingredients including rice paper for those famous summer rolls as well as an excellent spread of authentic herbs, sauces, and other condiments necessary to create our own Southeast Asian meal at home. **Sabrosura** offers an excellent blend of Spanish and Chinese inspiration. Even purists can't help but crave their crispy yuca chips paired with sweet crabmeat. And bringing it back to basics, the hamburger craze rages on uptown at **Bronx Alehouse**, rife with a range of beers. Did we say Bronx beer? You bet; and there is an equally ravishing selection to be relished at **Jonas Bronck's Beer Co.** or even **Bronx Brewery** over on East 136th Street.

The Bronx

SHOP 'TIL YOU DROP

Home entertainers keep the party hoppin' and stoves turning by stocking up on pantry staples from **Palm Tree Marketplace**. Find everything you may need here for a Jamaican-themed meal. Another culinary delight vital to NYC's food services is the **Hunts Point Food Distribution Center**—a 329-acre complex of wholesalers, distributors, and food-processing vendors. This expansive center also cradles the **Hunts Point Meat Market** selling every imaginable cut under the sun; the **Hunts Point Terminal Produce Market** supplying patrons with fantastic variety; as well as the **Fulton Fish Market**. This important triumvirate also caters to the city's most celebrated chefs, restaurateurs, and wholesale suppliers. Such mouthwatering cruising is bound to result in voracious cravings, that may be gratified at **Mo Gridder's BBQ**, a classic joint oozing with potent doses of Bronx smoke and flavor.

RIVERDALE

Riverdale is not known for its culinary distinction. However, its winning location as the northernmost tip of the city affords it incredible views, and thereby, lavish mansions. Moneyed residents mingle with inquiring visitors over the retail offerings at **S&S Cheesecake**, or freshly baked babkas at the always-primped **Mother's Bake Shop**. From here, those in need of sips may head to **Skyview Wines**, for an exceptional array of kosher varietals. Then finish with style and flair at **Lloyd's Carrot Cake**, serving divine slices of red velvet or German chocolate cake to the community for over a quarter-century.

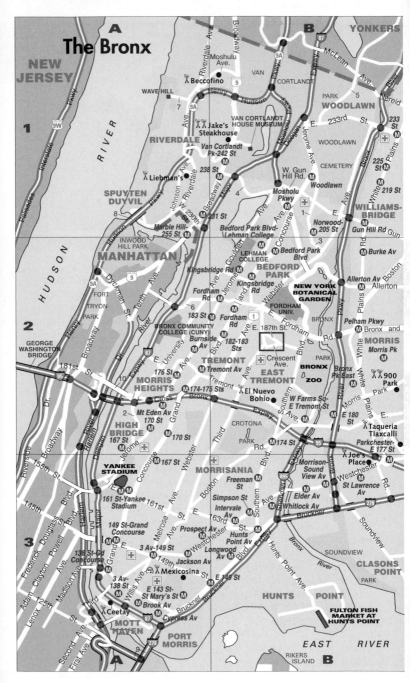

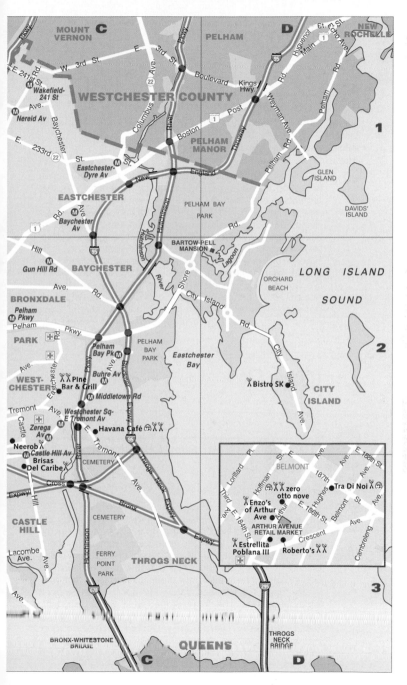

Beccofino

B1

Italian ✗

5704 Mosholu Ave. (at Fieldston Rd.)

Subway: Van Cortlandt Park-242 St
Phone: 718-432-2604
Web: www.beccofinorestaurant.com
Prices: $$

Dinner nightly

An easy, neighborhood darling that is never taken for granted, Beccofino is that earnest sort of Italian-American spot that genuinely cares that each dish is to your liking. The well-kept setting feels charming and no detail is forgotten—water glasses and breadbaskets never remain empty. Strings of holiday lights, exposed brick, and life-sized French posters fashion a rustic bistro look.

Expect starters like cremini mushroom caps stuffed with shrimp, crab, scallops, and garlicky breadcrumbs; or pastas like braised beef ravioli with diced eggplant and tomato sauce. Hearty entrées might include the wonderfully thick center-cut pork chop, served bone-in and pan seared along with sautéed onions, hot cherry peppers, sweet sausage, and white wine.

Bistro SK

D2

French ✗

273 City Island Ave. (bet. Carroll & Hawkins Sts.)

Subway: N/A
Phone: 718-885-1670
Web: www.bistrosk.com
Prices: $$

Lunch Sun
Dinner nightly

City Island locals have a place to call their own at Bistro SK, a sweet mom-and-pop operation making its home in the former Tree House (note the unmovable remnant, a huge glass encased tree trunk). Owners Stephane Kane and Maria Caruso run this delightful French bistro, which flaunts its Gallic charm and stands above those seafood spots that draw in day-trippers. Distressed hardwood floors, flower-topped tables, and sconces on cream-striped walls give a rustic feel. Among the decadent classics, find savory *moules marinières* kissed with parsley, saffron, and garlic; or French onion soup, oozing with Gruyère. Wintry delights include a mushroom, spinach and cheese-stuffed chicken breast with whipped potatoes, apple-brandy sauce, and braised vegetables.

Brisas Del Caribe

C3

Puerto Rican ✗

1207 Castle Hill Ave. (bet. Ellis & Gleason Aves.)

Subway: Castle Hill Av
Phone: 718-794-9710
Web: N/A
Prices: 🍜

Lunch & dinner daily

Fresh, hot, and tasty should be this Bronx native's mantra, set amid a vibrant neighborhood dotted with culinary delights. Boasting years of success, Brisas remains popular among hungry groups who pack its quarters day and night. A steam table laden with Puerto Rican food is in constant motion as the ladies behind the counter plate your order. Towards the back, walls are decked with beach scenes, glossy mirrors, and serve as an ideal backdrop for families tucking into fragrant *arroz con pollo* studded with pigeon peas and served with fried plantains; or tantalizing *chivo guisado*, a garlicky goat stew with fluffy rice and beans.

Seal this savory deal with a sweet *bizcocho Domincano*— vanilla cake layered with pineapples and topped with buttercream.

Ceetay

A3

Asian ✗

129 Alexander Ave. (at Bruckner Blvd.)

Subway: 3 Av - 138 St
Phone: 718-618-7020
Web: www.ceetay.com
Prices: $$

Lunch Mon – Fri
Dinner nightly

Beyond the proliferation of neighborhood juice stands, find a more sophisticated sip along with inventive Asian food in a pleasing ambience at Ceetay. The space is tiny yet handsome with reclaimed wood, metal accents, and a bar that sits only 30. Its location, just a short drive from Hunts Point and The Fulton Fish Market, means that this is a stop for serious seafood.

The sushi bar is a two-chef affair churning out the likes of a Kawasaki roll stuffed with crabmeat, avocado, scallions, and a smear of mayo; or wonderful assortment of striped bass, *shiro maguro, ebi,* and uni. Other items on offer roam through Asia and may reveal such stylistic or regional inflections as brown rice tossed in a fragrant masala of onions, peppers, carrots, and yellow squash.

El Nuevo Bohío

B2

791 E. Tremont Ave. (at Mapes Ave.)

Subway: West Farms Sq - E Tremont Av
Phone: 718-294-3905
Web: www.elnuevobohiorestaurant.com
Prices: ⊜⊜

Lunch & dinner daily

Fixed on a prominent corner and strutting windows tempting passersby with hunks of glistening pork, El Nuevo Bohío is hard to miss. Well-liked by its nearby Puerto Rican community, the front room is minimally adorned with a steam table, prep area (counter laden with authentic dishes), and cash register that is packed with orders at the ready. Snag a seat in the back for friendly table service. Bright walls are flooded with framed photos, and tables are filled with pride thanks to the faithful menu.

Succulent *pernil* heavy on the garlic is roasted until crisp on the outside, juicy on the inside. *Pastelles*, traditional bundles of starchy yucca and rich pork stew; and an array of *sopas* from rice and shrimp to cows' feet, round out the daily offerings.

Enzo's of Arthur Ave

D3

2339 Arthur Ave. (bet. Crescent Ave. & 186th St.)

Subway: Fordham Rd (Grand Concourse)
Phone: 718-733-4455
Web: N/A
Prices: $$

Lunch Mon– Sat
Dinner nightly

It's easy to love Enzo's, a quaint red-sauce throwback on Arthur Avenue. In an area once dominated by Italian-American culture, including a library full of Italian literature, Enzo's sits among longstanding favorites and clearly is welcomed as part of the family. The popular bar invites local business owners and faculty from nearby Fordham University for casual conversation, while the kitchen churns out steaming plates of glistening clams oreganata and rich pastas delivered by a careful service team.

The nostalgic Sunday special—pillow-soft gnocchi topped with tomato gravy and slow-braised pork *braciola* tucked with garlic, parsley, and cheese—is worth an end-of-weekend quest. So is the fresh swordfish steak with wonderfully assertive Livornese sauce.

Estrellita Poblana III

D3

Mexican 🍴

2328 Arthur Ave. (bet. Crescent Ave. & 186th St.)

Subway: Fordham Rd (Grand Concourse) Lunch & dinner daily
Phone: 718-220-7641
Web: www.estrellitapoblanaiii.com
Prices: 🐷🐷

Set against the milieu of the lively Belmont section in the Bronx, this third outpost of the Estrellita family has become an integral member of the diverse community. Fuchsia walls, three huge stars (III) set inside the coffered ceiling, and baby blue accents decorate the small, comfy room. Not only is it friendly and big-hearted, but the food is appetizing yet affordable. This is all ideal for nearby college kids and locals craving something *caliente* with their Coronas.

Tamales may only be available on weekends, but thick, spicy *pancita* (beef tripe soup); wonderfully warm *pozole* made with salty pork; and specials like *bistec* featuring citrus-marinated strips of ribeye sautéed with tart cactus and spicy *pico de gallo* are just as desirable.

Havana Café 😊

C2

Latin American 🍴🍴

3151 E. Tremont Ave. (at LaSalle Ave.)

Subway: N/A Lunch & dinner daily
Phone: 718-518-1800
Web: www.bronxhavanacafe.com
Prices: $$

The Schuylerville area of the Bronx has seen an influx of Latin restaurants, but this longstanding stucco façade still commands a presence. With bright yellow walls, tropical décor, and lazy ceiling fans, Havana Café feels straight out of Cuba, run by three Latin friends who understand the formula for success.

Drinkers and diners pack the U-shaped bar nightly for sports games on the TV's and chewy Cuban *pan de agua*. The dishes range from Caribbean to South American; this cooking is more concerned with taste than authenticity. Try the crispy green plantain *tostones* topped with *ropa vieja* and lime-spiked sour cream, mortar-mashed yucca, or the battered "Pargo" red snapper bathed in garlic, tomato and ever-present pork cracklings.

Jake's Steakhouse

Steakhouse ✗✗

B1

6031 Broadway (bet. Manhattan College Pkwy. & 251st St.)

Subway: Van Cortlandt Park-242 St   Lunch & dinner daily
Phone: 718-581-0182
Web: www.jakessteakhouse.com
Prices: $$$

Lodged across the way from the expansive Van Cortlandt Park, Jake's has claimed its place among the city's finer steakhouses. This multi-floor arena, with its pretty price tags, clubby décor, and a well-stocked bar, is one of the Bronx's better-kept secrets. Servers are personable and very professional.

Mussels *fra diavolo* features meaty mollusks tossed in spicy marinara and paired with crunchy garlic crostini. Porterhouse for two is tender, perfectly marbled, cooked to exact specification, and even better when accompanied by creamy mashed cauliflower flecked with cracked pepper, cheddar, and crispy bacon bits.

Jake's Boston cream pie gilds this robust meal with an addictive layering of moist cake, vanilla pastry cream, and rich chocolate ganache.

Joe's Place

Puerto Rican ✗

B3

1841 Westchester Ave. (at Thieriot Ave.)

Subway: Parkchester   Lunch & dinner daily
Phone: 718-918-2947
Web: www.joesplacebronx.com
Prices: $$

Joe's Place has been a Bronx original since 2003, when it first started serving excellent renditions of New York-Puerto Rican cooking. Locals revel in their numerous dining options, from the kitschy takeout counter and proper dining room to a Bacchanalian lounge (separated from the rest).

Everything on the menu is comforting and satisfying, with sandwiches, *mofongo*, and an array of rice dishes, from pork with peas to seafood paella. Warm the soul with excellent daily *sopas*, perhaps featuring chicken, *bacalao*, or gumbo-like rice and pigeon peas. Sweet-marinated and tender pork chops are a bone-in treat, served with garlic-lime sauce, black beans, and plantains. For dessert, the coconut-infused flan is an addictively good ode to tradition.

Liebman's

A1

Deli 🍴

552 W. 235th St. (bet. Johnson & Oxford Aves.)

Subway: 231 St   Lunch & dinner daily
Phone: 718-548-4534
Web: www.liebmansdeli.com
Prices: 💳

Some things never change (phew!) and Liebman's is definitely one of those things. This iconic kosher deli has been stuffing sandwiches and ladling bowls of matzoh ball soup for over 50 years. Residents wax poetic about the place, but it's nothing special, just a true-blue deli. Walk in and it's like a Smithsonian set for a Jewish deli—a neon sign in the front window, the grill roasting hot dogs, and meat slicing machines.

The food is classic and soulful as in stuffed veal breast, potato latkes, pastrami and tongue sandwiches on nutty rye bread paired with tangy pickles...and even that old standby—noodle pudding. Order to-go, or take a load off and grab a seat at one of the booths. Just don't forget about that bowl of "cure-all" matzoh ball soup.

Mexicosina 😀

A3

Mexican 🍴

503 Jackson Ave. (at E. 147th St.)

Subway: E 149 St   Lunch & dinner daily
Phone: 347-498-1339
Web: www.mexicosina.com
Prices: 💳

Anyone looking for a dazzling spot to impress some adventurous friends with a food odyssey should head here—and it's closer to Manhattan than you probably realize. Set along a rather gritty corner, this large, welcoming, and very personalized gem features whimsical figurines and Mexican artifacts that beam with cultural pride and warmth.

The food remains just as delicious, authentic, and inventive as you'd expect. A thick, complex seafood stew brims with sweet shrimp, catfish, fingerling potatoes, grilled onions, and spicy-smoky-sweet red chili broth. Quesadillas wrap funky *huitlacoche*, charred corn, and habanero sauce for a combination that is as bright as the sun and hot as hell. The intensely fresh corn tortillas are absolutely worth the extra buck.

Neerob

Bangladeshi ✗

C2

2109 Starling Ave. (bet. Odell St. & Olmstead Ave.)

Subway: Castle Hill Av

Lunch & dinner daily

Phone: 718-904-7061

Web: N/A

Prices: 😑◐

The Bangladeshi community may be larger in Queens, but the Bronx now boasts one of their most authentic eateries. Neerob's room is sunny yet conveys a fast food feel with bright lights and clunky furnishings. And while the country itself may be some 53 years young, its cuisine (laden with influences from West Bengal) exudes distinct flavors and seasonings.

On the steam table, find delicacies that celebrate garlic, green chilies, and mustard with spice levels that can seem unrelenting. Dishes include *chandal*, a yellow lentil soup steeped in cumin and ginger; or *gura mas*, pan-fried fish soaked in greens and mustard oil. Fish *illish* or a series of dishes called *bharthas* (maybe the mashed roasted eggplant?) seem to inspire exuberance among the diners.

900 Park

Italian ✗✗

B2

900 Morris Park Ave. (at Bronxdale Ave.)

Subway: Bronx Park East

Lunch & dinner daily

Phone: 718-892-3830

Web: www.900park.com

Prices: $$

900 Park is an easy place to return to regularly. The food is neither fancy nor innovative, but brings those soul-satisfying comforts that we all seek. Myriad seating options make it a great choice for couples settling into the lounge with its roaring fireplace, as well as larger groups gathering in the elevated dining room for platters of hot antipasto. White leather chairs, cotton panels, and rustic tables lend a breezy, calming feel.

The Italian and Italian-American specialties might begin with a classic bowl of *stracciatella*, combining chicken broth and spinach strewn with beaten eggs. Ridged tubes of manicotti are filled with ricotta and pecorino cheese, cooked in a meaty Bolognese, and then topped with rich béchamel for an outstanding dish.

Pine Bar & Grill

C2

Italian ✗✗

1634 Eastchester Rd. (at Blondell Ave.)

Subway: Westchester Sq - Tremont Av
Phone: 718-319-0900
Web: www.pinebargrill.com
Prices: $$

Lunch & dinner daily

Run by the Bronx-based Bastone family (also of the steadfast Pine Tavern), this bi-level stunner is a local favorite. Muted yellow walls showcase black and white photos of the borough's celebrated and lesser known spots, while leafy plants and bright flowers pop against a backdrop of dark wood tables, stairs, and floors.

As testament to the rapidly diversifying local population, the offerings now include Latin influenced delights alongside their wonderfully old-fashion Italian classics. Sample clams casino stuffed with pecorino, breadcrumbs, parsley, and shallots, topped with crispy bacon; or a perfect baked ziti marinara. Then move on to Baja fish tacos and pernil "our way" with roasted, tender pork, fried sweet plantains, and rice with pigeon peas.

Roberto's

D3

Italian ✗✗

603 Crescent Ave. (at Hughes Ave.)

Subway: Fordham Rd (Grand Concourse)
Phone: 718-733-9503
Web: www.roberto089.com
Prices: $$

Lunch & dinner Mon – Sat

You can't miss Roberto's, whose distinctive design falls somewhere between a cozy, welcoming farmhouse and a Mediterranean villa complete with a coral-hued façade and wrought-iron balcony. This storied Italian-American restaurant is the kind of charmer that makes groups feel at home, even as they're sipping their way through a long wait (and wait you will — no reservations here.)

It's also the kind of place that piles on the pasta and takes espresso seriously, whether it's the fettuccine special that features fresh shaved truffle or the ricotta cream that fills an insanely good cannoli. For a real taste of what makes Roberto's shine, let the hearty *tubettini con polipo e fave*, folded with grilled octopus, fava beans, and baby clams speak for itself.

Taqueria Tlaxcalli

B2

2103 Starling Ave. (bet. Odell St. & Olmstead Ave.)

Subway: Castle Hill Av
Phone: 347-851-3085
Web: N/A
Prices: 🍴🍴

Lunch & dinner daily

The exterior may not impress, but the heart of this very sweet little Mexican spot is inviting enough to draw a constant and very diverse stream of locals. Behind the counter set along the narrow space, the smiling staff is machine-gun quick as they prepare each order. Thoughtful details abound, from the fuchsia ribbons that wrap napkins and colorfully painted tortilla baskets to the professional servers who are quick to help anyone not fluent in Spanish.

Made-to-order guacamole is a requisite starter before exploring delicious *sopas*, *carnitas*, and *tortas*. The humbly named soup of the day may be a surprisingly sophisticated shellfish reduction with tender shrimp, earthy root vegetables, and spicy-smoky chipotle. Tacos are excellent and very generous.

Tra Di Noi 😊

D3

622 E. 187th St. (bet. Belmont & Hughes Aves.)

Subway: Fordham Rd (Grand Concourse)
Phone: 718-295-1784
Web: www.tradinoi.com
Prices: $$

Lunch & dinner daily

Tra Di Noi could just happily bask in the overflow from nearby Arthur Avenue. Instead, it is a place where dining is about more than just food; your satisfaction is paramount, and the exceptional lasagna may haunt you. The dining room is humble and immaculate, with crimson walls, decorative accents and frescos.

While the name ("between us") invokes a sense of familial commitment or secrecy, Tra Di Noi draws all and sundry for its solid cooking. Sample the fluffy *gnocchi di patate* in tomato-basil sauce; or carrots, celery, and cannellini beans all cooked to a deliciously creamy whole in *pasta e fagioli*. Look for specials like *muscoletti di vitello*, a hearty veal stew with white wine and rosemary. Homemade cannoli are a sweetheart treat offered daily.

zero otto nove 😊

Italian ✗✗

D3

2357 Arthur Ave. (at 186th St.)

Subway: Fordham Rd (Grand Concourse)
Phone: 718-220-1027
Web: www.roberto089.com
Prices: $$

Lunch Tue - Sat
Dinner Tue – Sun

A powder blue, circa 1960s Fiat 500 set on the sidewalk marks the entry to this Italian icon. If that doesn't clue you in to the genius present here, make your way through wood-framed doors, past a snug bar filled with handsome revelers, into an ample dining room flaunting high ceilings, skylights, and enticing aromas.

In the kitchen, the chefs hover over hearty, rustic dishes inspired by Salerno. Most start with pizza, but the *antipasto* featuring stuffed peppers with eggplant, zucchini, and cauliflower is equally tasty. Tender rings of *calamari alla peperonata* sautéed with peppers and studded with olives; or *pasta al forno*, baked rigatoni layered with a meaty ragù, béchamel, *soppresata*, and mozzarella are classics done with expertise and authority.

Look for the symbol 🍳
for a brilliant breakfast to
start your day off right

433

Brooklyn

Brooklyn

Densely populated with a labyrinth of international enclaves, Brooklyn may well be its own sovereign city. And so it was until 1898 when it merged with the other boroughs to become a vital part of the "City of New York." This big, bold, and bustling locale spotlights a number of exciting dining venues, mom-and-pop stores, and ethnic eateries. Manhattan's young and enterprising culinary talent have set up shop here, but that hasn't stopped the region's more rugged establishments from flourishing. The result? A truly interesting dichotomy. Not far behind, Brooklyn's sustainable food movement is always evolving. Locavores looking to support a neighbor's garden can now get their green thumb going by checking out the handy website (www.eatwellguide.org) for a citywide directory of family farms and farmer's markets.

MEAT AND MORE

Williamsburg—traditionally an Italian, Hispanic, and Hasidic hub—is now a mecca for hipsters and artists. Here in Billyburg, creative culinary endeavors abound which may include several, small-scale diners offering stellar goodies. Case in point: an artisan chocolate line crafted from bean to bar at **Mast Brothers Chocolate**. Bring a big appetite or flock of friends to **Smorgasburg**, where sharing is crucial for a gustatory thrill.

This open-air, all-food market is held on the waterfront from spring through fall and headlines everything from beef sliders and brisket to *bulgogi* and *chana masala*. Or sign up for a cooking class at **Brooklyn Kitchen**, where home cooks can keep up with haute chefs by learning how to pickle, bake, and ferment the likes of kombucha! Over on Metropolitan Avenue, cute

takeout shop **Saltie** serves a brief but tempting list of sandwiches and sweets; while **Pies 'n' Thighs** soothes the soul with heaps of down-home goodness. Close out with a cup of joe from **Toby's Estate** or **Blue Bottle Coffee Co.** on Berry Street. For a different

kind of pick-me-up, head to **Maison Premiere**. The vague signage out front may be of little help, but the line out the door is enough of a clue that this Williamsburg boîte is *the* spot for a drink. Within its beautifully distressed walls, freshly shucked oysters and delish small plates are washed down by absinthe, icy juleps, and other skillfully crafted libations. Inspired by the art of butchery, **Marlow & Daughters** is adored for regionally sourced meat, house-made sausages, and dry goods. Locals who live and breathe by meat and cheese make routine visits to **Best Pizza**, a destination that delivers on what its name proclaims. In keeping with the vibe of the 'hood, this space is disheveled by design, but that doesn't keep crowds from flocking in for a slice of "white." **Fette Sau** brings rudimentary comfort but ravishing roadhouse-style barbecue to Brooklyn's residents; and **BrisketTown** on Bedford Avenue has been winning over hearts and palates for some time now. California on a mission venture west to Gowanus where **Fletcher's Brooklyn Barbecue** proffers tons of variety and quality; while Bensonhurst best-seller **Bari Pork Store** sticks to perfecting the pig. Even flesh fiends need some sweet, preferably at **Four & Twenty Blackbirds**, a bakeshop brought about by sisters Melissa and Emily Elsen. Their black bottom oatmeal pie is rightly raved about.

SPECIALTY FOODS

The Brooklyn Navy Yard is a hub for commercial business and houses over 200 tenants including the expansive **Brooklyn Grange Farm**. Besides DUMBO's stellar views, stroll down cobblestoned Water Street and straight into **Jacques Torres** for a taste of chocolate bliss. Bordering Prospect Park, quaint Park Slope brags of fancy trattorias set amidst effortlessly chic cafés filled with stroller-rolling parents. The **Park Slope Food Coop** is a member-operated and owned venture selling locally farmed produce, grass-fed meat, and free-range poultry. Lauded as the largest of its kind in the country, membership is offered to anyone willing to pay a small fee and work a shift of less than three hours each month. Carry on this charming culinary excursion to Carroll Gardens, a historically Italian-American neighborhood identified by a flurry of family-owned butchers and bakers along Court Street. Here, **D'Amico** deals an impressive range of specialty coffees and teas; while **Caputo's** has locals returning for sandwiches packed with supreme *salumi*. **Ferdinando's Focacceria** may be an age-old haunt, but it successfully keeps step with the times by cooking classic food straight from Palermo. As Court Street blends into family-centric Cobble Hill, find **Staubitz Market**, the most sociable butcher in town moving meticulously cut meat, cheese, and charcuterie. Looking for a change in mood...and food? Shift "hills" from Cobble to Boerum to feast on Middle Eastern hits at **Sahadi's** or **Damascus Bakery** in Vinegar Hill.

Red Hook rests on Brooklyn's waterfront, where diligent locals and responsible residents have transformed this region's aged piers and deserted warehouses into über-cool breweries, bakeries, and bistros. **Red Hook Lobster Pound** is a popular haunt for seafood cliques. But, if in need of a bit of sweet, head to **Baked**; followed by **Steve's Authentic Key Lime Pie**; and finish at **Cacao Prieto's**, known and loved for their family farm-sourced chocolates and spirits. Just as **Red Hook Village Farmers' Market** (open

on Saturdays) brings pristine produce from its Community Farm to the locality, trucks and tents in **Red Hook Ball Fields** cater to natives in the know with *delicioso* Central American and Caribbean food trucks. Dining destinations in their own right, these diners-on-wheels may only be parked on weekends from May through October, but they certainly leave an impression that lasts through the year.

GLOBAL TABLE

Brooklyn is big on international eats and its nooks are perpetually overflowing with exciting feasts. Saunter to Fort Greene for a taste of African delicacies—maybe Ethiopian at **Bati's** or South African at **Madiba**? Then stop over at Sunset Park to savor spicy, mouthwatering Mexican flavors, before cooling off with an original ice pop (*paleta*) at **Sley Deli**—a genuine Mexican grocer booming with business in Borough Park. Across from Maimonides Medical Center, **Fei Long Market** is a giant emporium that buzzes with Asian foodies in search of vegetables, dried squid, and all kinds of sauces. Slightly south, where Mexico meets China, sidewalks teem with vendors steaming tofu and fishmongers purveying wonderfully offbeat eats—bullfrog anyone? In a flock of kosher restaurants, **Di Fara** is a popular pizzeria with a mini offshoot (**MD Kitchen**) also in Midwood. **Totonno's Pizza** is sought-after for Neapolitan-style pies; and **Joe's of Avenue U** is divine for deliciously fried chickpea *panelle*.

At the southernmost end of Brooklyn is Brighton Beach, best known for its borscht and blintzes. This hugely publicized Russian district is also home to Ukranian hot spot **Café Glechik**, churning out staples for its patrons packed within. But for a true alfresco snack to tote, **Gold Label International Food** remains unrivaled. Bakery buffs should take a time out at **Toné Café**, where an ancient tandoor-

and free-spirited revelers. This same old-time vibe is nothing if not a virtue at **Tortilleria Mexicana Los Hermanos**—a bustling machine in Bushwick churning out tortillas—and corresponds to the nostalgic scene at **Octopus Garden** in Gravesend. Italian regulars have been flocking here for upwards of 30 years to stock up on goods for their famous Christmas Feast of the Seven Fishes. While strolling through this Eastern European area, sojourn to **Mansoura**, a Syrian institution proudly preparing pastries, artisan chocolates, and other Middle Eastern confections. Speaking of which, **Le Sajj** dishes up faithful Lebanese food with live classical tunes (on Saturday nights) to Bay Ridge residents. Across the way, East New Yorkers trek to local

like oven turns out impeccable Georgian bread (*shoti*) crafted from flour, water, yeast, and salt. Athletic-types hike north to Bed-Stuy where **SCRATCHbread**'s goodies are swallowed up by the loaf. Pair these killer carbs with links of kielbasa from **Jubilat Provisions** for a real deal treat. Classic customs, traditions, and cuisine come alive in **Moldova**, a culinary bastion that favors Moldavian elders over young

sensation, **Lindenwood Diner** for liberally spiced Cajun cuisine And while there is no confusing the Chesapeake with Sheepshead Bay, **Randazzo's Clam Bar** will provide you with a similarly superior seafood experience. Just keep in mind that beef is always king here and reigns supreme, with big flavors and bold bites to be had at **Brennan & Carr**—where the menu doesn't change, but NY'ers love it all the same.

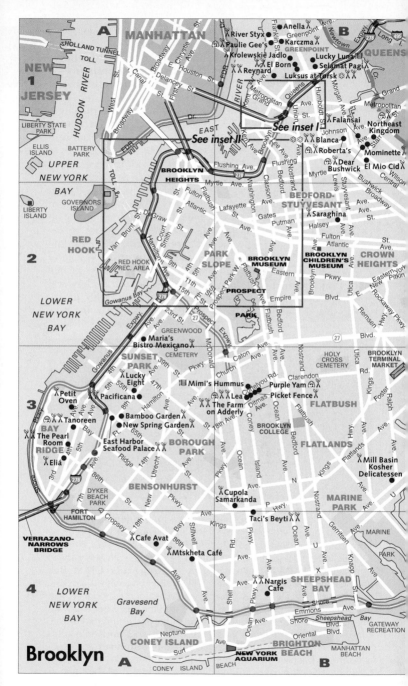

Brooklyn

MANHATTAN

NEW JERSEY

A **B**

1

SHOLLAND TUNNEL
TOLL

HUDSON RIVER

LIBERTY STATE PARK

ELLIS ISLAND

UPPER NEW YORK BAY

LIBERTY ISLAND

BATTERY PARK

GOVERNORS ISLAND

West St.
Broadway
Canal St.
Delancey St.
Houston St.
Christie St.
Essex St.
First St.

EAST RIVER

Kent Ave.
Metropolitan Ave.
Grand St.
Wythe Ave.
Bedford Ave.
Berry St.
Driggs Ave.
Union Ave.
Humboldt St.
Morgan Ave.

Anella
River Styx
Paulie Gee's
Krolewskie Jadlo
Reynard
El Born
GREENPOINT
Greenpoint Ave.
Newtown
Karczma
Lucky Luna
Selamat Pagi
Luksus at Tørst

QUEENS

Long Island Expwy
I-278
I-495

Grand Ave.
Metropolitan Ave.

Falansai
Northeast Kingdom
Mominette
El Mio Cid

See inset I

Johnson Ave.

Blanca
Roberta's
Dear Bushwick

Flushing Ave.
Nostrand Ave.
Classon Ave.
Myrtle Ave.
Lewis Ave.
Stuyvesant Ave.
Broadway
Bushwick Ave.
Wilson
Central Ave.

See inset II

BROOKLYN HEIGHTS

BROOKLYN NAVY YARD
Flushing Ave.
Myrtle Ave.
Fulton St.
Atlantic Ave.
Lafayette Ave.
Gates Ave.
Putman Ave.

DeGraw St.
Court St.
Smith St.

2

LOWER NEW YORK BAY

RED HOOK

RED HOOK REC. AREA

Van Brunt St.
Hamilton Ave.
9th St.
2nd Ave.
4th Ave.
5th Ave.
11th St.
15th St.

Gowanus Bay

I-278

23rd St.

PARK SLOPE

BROOKLYN MUSEUM

Prospect Park W.
Flatbush Ave.
Eastern Pkwy.

PROSPECT PARK

Empire Blvd.

BROOKLYN CHILDREN'S MUSEUM

BEDFORD-STUYVESANT

Fulton St.
Atlantic Ave.

Saraghina
Halsey St.

CROWN HEIGHTS

Eastern Pkwy.
Utica Ave.
Rockaway Pkwy.
Remsen Ave.
Pitkin Ave.

3

GREENWOOD CEMETERY

Maria's Bistro Mexicano

SUNSET PARK

Gowanus
4th Ave.
39th St.
47th St.
55th St.

Lucky Eight
Pacificana

Petit Oven
Tanoreen

The Pearl Room

BAY RIDGE

Elia

Bamboo Garden
New Spring Garden
East Harbor Seafood Palace

BOROUGH PARK

Hamilton Ave.
65th St.
Ridge Blvd.
14th Ave.
Utrecht Ave.

Prospect Expwy.
McDonald Ave.
Prospect Park
Coney Island Ave.

Mimi's Hummus
Lea
The Farm on Adderly
Church Ave.
Ditmas Ave.
Clarendon Rd.

Purple Yam
Picket Fence

FLATBUSH

Caton Ave.
Ocean Ave.
Nostrand Ave.
Flatbush Ave.

BROOKLYN COLLEGE

HOLY CROSS CEMETERY

Foster Ave.

BROOKLYN TERMINAL MARKET

Flatlands Ave.
Ralph Ave.

FLATLANDS

Kings Hwy.

Mill Basin Kosher Delicatessen

BENSONHURST

New Utrecht Ave.
86th St.

DYKER BEACH PARK

FORT HAMILTON

Cropsey Ave.
18th Ave.
Bay Pkwy.
Stillwell Ave.

Cupola
Samarkanda
P Hwy.

Taci's Beyti

Ocean Pkwy.
Kings Hwy.
Nostrand Ave.
Gerritsen Ave.
Knapp St.

MARINE PARK

MARINE PARK

VERRAZANO-NARROWS BRIDGE

Shore Pkwy.
I-278

Cafe Avat
Mtskheta Café

86th St.
Bay Pkwy.
Shell Rd.

4

LOWER NEW YORK BAY

Gravesend Bay

Neptune Ave.
Surf Ave.

CONEY ISLAND

Nargis Cafe

SHEEPSHEAD BAY

Shore Pkwy.
Emmons Ave.
Shore Blvd.
Sheepshead Bay
Oriental Blvd.

BRIGHTON BEACH

MANHATTAN BEACH

GATEWAY RECREATION

NEW YORK AQUARIUM

CONEY ISLAND BEACH

A **B**

440

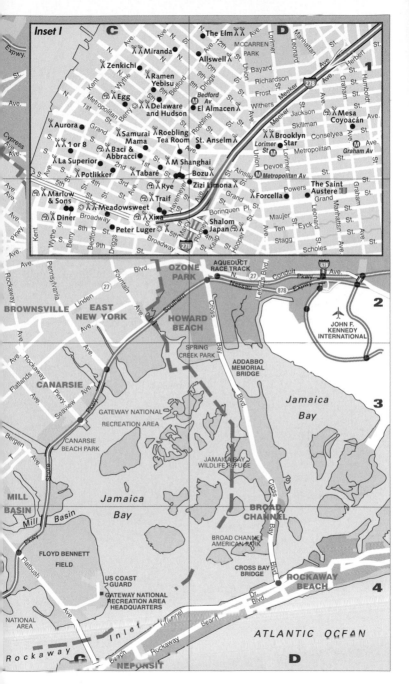

Inset I

C   **D**

Expwy.

St.

Ave.

Cypress Ave.

Ave.

Ave.

Ave.

Ave.

Ave.

Pkwy.

X The Elm **XX**

X Miranda

X Zenkichi

X Ramen Yebisu

Egg

X Delaware and Hudson

X Aurora

X Samurai Mama

X 1 or 8

X Baci & Abbracci

X La Superior

X Potlikker

X Tabaré

Marlow & Sons

Meadowsweet

X Diner

Peter Luger

X Allswell

El Almacen

Roebling Tea Room

St. Anselm **X**

X M Shanghai

Bozu **X**

Zizi Limona **X**

X Rye

X Traif

X Xixa

Shalom Japan **X**

MCCARREN PARK

Leonard

Manhattan

St.

Herbert

St.

Humboldt

St.

Graham

St.

Richardson

Frost

Withers

Jackson

Skillman

Conselyea

Metropolitan

Devoe

Ainslie

Grand

Powers

Mauger

Ten

Stagg

Scholes

X Mesa Coyoacán

XX Brooklyn Star

X Forcella

The Saint Austere

OZONE PARK

AQUEDUCT RACE TRACK

678

JOHN F. KENNEDY INTERNATIONAL

BROWNSVILLE

EAST NEW YORK

HOWARD BEACH

SPRING CREEK PARK

ADDABBO MEMORIAL BRIDGE

Jamaica Bay

CANARSIE

GATEWAY NATIONAL RECREATION AREA

CANARSIE BEACH PARK

JAMAICA BAY WILDLIFE REFUGE

BROAD CHANNEL

MILL BASIN

Jamaica Bay

BROAD CHANNEL AMERICAN PARK

FLOYD BENNETT FIELD

US COAST GUARD

GATEWAY NATIONAL RECREATION AREA HEADQUARTERS

CROSS BAY BRIDGE

ROCKAWAY BEACH

NATIONAL AREA

Rockaway

Inlet

ATLANTIC OCEAN

C   **D**

NEPONSIT

1

2

3

4

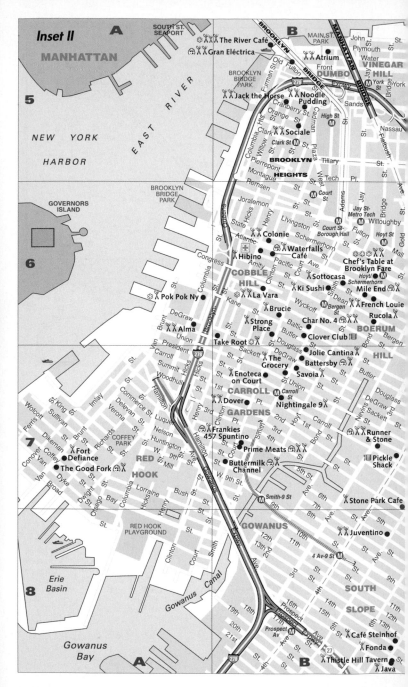

Inset II

A · B

MANHATTAN

SOUTH ST SEAPORT

The River Café
Gran Eléctrica
Atrium

MAIN ST PARK
John St.
Plymouth St.
Water St.

DUMBO
VINEGAR HILL
York St.
Bridge
York

NEW YORK HARBOR

EAST RIVER

Old Fulton St.
Front St.

BROOKLYN BRIDGE PARK
Furman St.

Jack the Horse
Noodle Pudding
Cranberry St.
Orange St.
Sociale
Clark St.
Columbia Hts.
Willow St.
Pierrepont
Montague
Remsen
Joralemon
State St.
Hicks St.
Henry St.

BROOKLYN HEIGHTS

High St.
Clark St.
Cadman Plaza
Sands St.
Nassau
Tillary St.
West St.

Court St.
Livingston St.
Schermerhorn St.
Atlantic Ave.
Adams St.
Jay St.
Bridge St.

Jay St-Metro Tech
Willoughby
Fulton
Hoyt St.
Gold St.
Mall

Court St-Borough Hall

GOVERNORS ISLAND

BROOKLYN BRIDGE PARK

Congress St.
Columbia St.

Colonie
Hibino
Waterfalls Café
Pacific St.

COBBLE HILL
Amity St.
Clinton St.
Court St.

Chef's Table at Brooklyn Fare
Sottocasa
Mile End
Hoyt/Schermerhorn

Pok Pok Ny
DeGraw St.
Brunt St.
Kane St.
La Vara
Ki Sushi
Dean St.
Bergen St.
French Louie
Rucola

Alma
Union St.
Van Brunt
Brucie
Baltic St.
Char No. 4
Clover Club
Butler St.

BOERUM HILL
Wyckoff St.
Bond St.
Nevins St.

Strong Place
Take Root
Sackett St.
Douglass St.

Bergen St.
Douglass St.
DeGraw St.
Sackett St.
Butler St.

President St.
Summit St.
Woodhull St.

The Grocery
Jolie Cantina
Battersby
Savoia
Enoteca on Court

Carroll St.

CARROLL GARDENS

Dover
Nightingale 9
Carroll St.
1st Pl.
2nd Pl.
Hoyt St.
Bond St.

Frankies 457 Spuntino
Prime Meats
Buttermilk Channel

RED HOOK

COFFEY PARK
Imlay St.
Commerce St.
Delavan St.
Verona St.
Nelson St.
Huntington St.
W. 9th St.
Luquer St.
Hamilton Ave.

Runner & Stone
Pickle Shack

Fort Defiance
The Good Fork

Wolcott St.
King St.
Sullivan St.
Dikeman St.
Coffey St.
Ferris St.
Conover St.
Van Brunt
Van Dyke St.
Beard St.
Dwight St.
Richards St.
Otsego St.
Columbia St.
Hicks St.
Henry St.
Clinton St.
Court St.
Smith St.

3rd St.
4th St.
5th St.

Smith-9 St
Stone Park Cafe
6th St.
7th St.
8th St.

RED HOOK PLAYGROUND

GOWANUS
9th St.
10th St.
11th St.
12th St.
13th St.

Juventino
4 Av-9 St

Erie Basin

Gowanus Canal
Lorraine St.
Bush St.
Bay St.
Broad St.

3rd Ave.
16th St.
14th St.
15th St.
18th St.
19th St.
20th St.
21st St.

SOUTH SLOPE
5th Ave.
6th Ave.
11th St.
12th St.
13th St.

Prospect Expwy.
Prospect Av
17th St.

Café Steinhof
Fonda
Thistle Hill Tavern
Java

Gowanus Bay

278

27

Gowanus

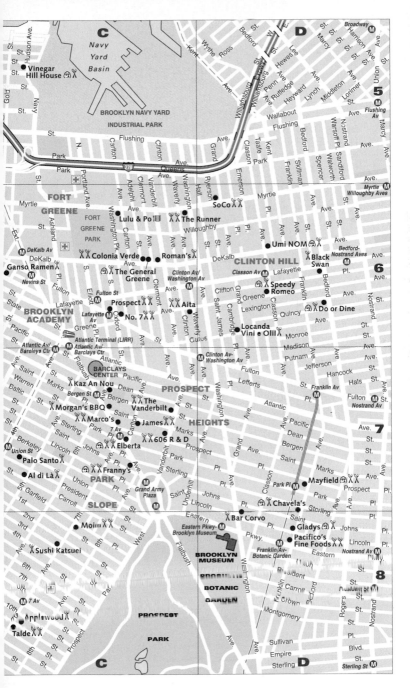

Aita

Italian ✗✗

C6

132 Greene Ave. (at Waverly Ave.)

Subway: Clinton - Washington Avs
Phone: 718-576-3584
Web: www.aitarestaurant.com
Prices: $$

Lunch Fri – Sun
Dinner nightly

Tucked into a cozy corner, this quintessential trattoria echoes the beauty and charm of Cobble Hill. Amid a robust culinary scene, Aita finds a niche with its warm (never effusive) service and equally comforting décor of antique mirrors, wood paneling, and lacy curtains.

Chef/co-owner Roberto Aita certainly has a way with pasta, crafting thick, homemade noodles twirled with flavorful sauces, such as the *taglierini* with buttery clam broth that is slightly sweet with melted leeks and strewn with irresistibly briny littlenecks. Italian tradition echoes through beguilingly simple desserts, like a bowl of plump fresh berries with nothing more than a dollop of cream and end-of-meal biscotti.

The wines are as deliciously approachable as the cooking itself.

Al di Là

Italian ✗

C7

248 Fifth Ave. (at Carroll St.)

Subway: Union St
Phone: 718-783-4565
Web: www.aldilatrattoria.com
Prices: $$

Lunch & dinner daily

This long-loved Park Slope gem from husband-and-wife team Emiliano Coppa and Chef Anna Klinger (of the Crown Heights café Lincoln Station) has been deliciously consistent over the years. Inviting and lived-in, its wooden pew seating, dainty wallpaper, and blown glass chandelier is both comfortable and chic enough for a romantic dinner *a due*.

Al di Là's Italian delights are northern in spirit and include enticing preparations. A salad of roughly chopped escarole is tossed with thinly shaved Jerusalem artichokes, slivers of red onion, diced crisped pancetta, toasted walnuts, and a warm sherry vinaigrette. When offered, the *lasagna alla Bolognese*, fashioned from sheets of fresh pasta and served hot from the oven with crisped edges, is a must.

Allswell

D1

Gastropub ✗

124 Bedford Ave. (at N. 10th St.)

Subway: Bedford Av
Phone: 347-799-2743
Web: www.allswellnyc.com
Prices: $$

Lunch & dinner daily

It's all good at this all-day Williamsburg tavern, where the vibe is welcoming and the setting is comfortable. Come as you are for friendly service amidst a patchwork of vintage wallpaper, then settle in to choose from the enjoyable selection listed on the wall-mounted blackboard.

In keeping with the cozy atmosphere, brunch is served every day of the week. Offerings include eye-opening chorizo and beans with poached eggs; and smoked whitefish toast—house-baked brioche topped with fresh ricotta and large chunks of infused fish, sided by a perfect boiled egg and parsley salad. Dinner brings yet more comfort fare like orecchiette with lamb ragù and fava beans; grilled chicken with lentils; or divine sweets like a tall wedge of seed-crusted cinnamon cake.

Alma

A6

Mexican ✗✗

187 Columbia St. (at Degraw St.)

Subway: Carroll St
Phone: 718-643-5400
Web: www.almarestaurant.com
Prices: $$

Lunch Sat – Sun
Dinner nightly

This festive stalwart with a renowned rooftop has come a long way since its early days along this rather unromantic waterfront. Mexican artifacts and mirrors line the brick walls of this multi-story spot with a margarita-fueled vibe and food that puts a smile on every face.

Alma's pleasing Mexican cooking focuses on good, clean ingredient combinations in a nuanced menu of simple, flavorful dishes. Go for a delicious standard like plump, tender short rib enchiladas in soft, flour tortillas with roasted *ranchero*, Gouda cheese, and pumpkin seed sauces. Be sure to add on baked *arroz con queso*, a side of baked rice with tomato, poblano, and sharp cheddar. The classic palate-cooling flan is topped with an enticingly sticky mantel of caramel.

Anella

Contemporary ✗

B1

222 Franklin St. (bet. Green & Huron Sts.)

Subway: Greenpoint Av
Phone: 718-389-8100
Web: www.anellabrooklyn.com
Prices: $$

Lunch Sat – Sun
Dinner nightly

Tucked away in Greenpoint, just a few blocks from the East River, Anella hosts diners in an intimate rough and tumble space boasting a sliver of a dining room, charming back patio, and welcoming bar fashioned out of a reclaimed work bench from the Steinway & Sons piano factory.

The kitchen is on display and sends forth a menu of ambitious creations, beginning with a loaf of bread freshly baked and served in a clay flowerpot. Smoke was a recent inspiration as seen in a slice of brisket afloat in a lusciously fluid risotto of spinach and garlic. Other preparations have included seared striped bass paired with lentils and cauliflower that was roasted and whirled into a purée; and a finale of apple *crémeux* atop almond cake sided by rum ice cream.

Applewood

American ✗

C8

501 11th St. (bet. Seventh & Eighth Aves.)

Subway: 7 Av (9th St.)
Phone: 718-788-1810
Web: www.applewoodny.com
Prices: $$

Lunch Sat – Sun
Dinner Mon – Sat

With its stately façade, wrought-iron fencing, and box planters, Applewood really is that quintessential Brooklyn charmer. Inside find pale yellow walls holding shelves of old books, sturdy maple tables, and a fireplace at the center that fosters its family-friendly vibe.

Go for the reasonable prix-fixe, or indulge in à la carte choices like a summery vegetable pan roast of garlic scapes and zucchini tossed in a spicy curry oil and set over a crisp polenta cake. Succulent fillet of haddock is pan-fried then served with lovely onion soubise over a bed of marinated cucumbers, alongside purslane, radish greens, and sourdough panzanella lending palate-cleansing crunch. Deliciously high-minded desserts may include a warm zucchini cake with basil ice cream.

Atrium

B5

Contemporary 🍴🍴

15 Main St. (bet. Plymouth & Water Sts.)

Subway: York St
Phone: 718-858-1095
Web: www.atriumdumbo.com
Prices: $$$

Lunch & dinner daily

This industrial bi-level space has a rather iconic setting along the waterfront, between the Brooklyn and Manhattan bridges. Dark wood dominates the light-filled interior, amid metal accents and walls that sprout greenery to soften the room.

The food may have a farm-to-table focus, but a contemporary tilt is clear in everything that emerges from Atrium's bustling open kitchen. Elegant "baby greens" arrive as enticingly charred root vegetables over peppery arugula coulis; whereas crisply seared red snapper served over wild rice with dashi-simmered baby turnips, meaty mushrooms, and finished with a rich fumet makes the chef's (Laurent Kalkotour) French heritage abundantly clear. The chocolate-dipped crème fraîche and quark cheesecake is deservedly popular.

Aurora

C1

Italian 🍴

70 Grand St. (at Wythe Ave.)

Subway: Bedford Av
Phone: 718-388-5100
Web: www.aurorabk.com
Prices: $$

Lunch & dinner daily

This charming trattoria has long been a popular dining choice for residents of this dynamic stretch of Williamsburg. Stocked with wood furnishings, the rustic brick and plaster room is dressed up with vintage knickknacks and features a pretty ivy-covered outdoor area that doubles the seating capacity of the corner setting.

Aurora's enjoyable Italian cuisine speaks to the power of simplicity with minimally dressed market greens, expertly prepared pastas, and roasted meats. One can't go wrong with a meal of plump house-made sausage with lightly sautéed broccoli rabe and pickled Calabrian pepper; silky agnolotti stuffed with ricotta, spring peas, and fresh mint; or *affogato* with chocolate crumb-coated vanilla gelato, all offered at impressive value.

Baci & Abbracci

Italian ✗

C1

204 Grand St. (bet. Bedford & Driggs Sts.)

Subway: Bedford Av
Phone: 718-599-6599
Web: www.baciny.com
Prices: $$

Lunch Sat – Sun
Dinner nightly

This upbeat Williamsburg eatery features Italian cuisine with a wholehearted emphasis on pizza. With more than twenty permutations of pies baked in their wood-burning oven from Naples, these smoky-chewy crusts may be the foundation for sauce and freshly made mozzarella, or even *focaccia tartufata*—two thin layers filled with *robiola* cheese and topped with truffle oil. Beyond this, the adept kitchen also boasts homemade bread, enjoyable pastas, and an impressive short list of *secondi* like juicy lamb chops with a crisp potato-rosemary crust.

The intimate space sports a contemporary design framed by a concrete floor, sleek furnishings, and glazed-tile accents. A charming little patch of backyard makes an especially popular setting for weekend brunch.

Bamboo Garden

Chinese ✗

A3

6409 Eighth Ave. (at 64th St.)

Subway: 8 Av
Phone: 718-238-1122
Web: N/A
Prices: ⊜⊜

Lunch & dinner daily

This bustling establishment confirms that there is impressive dim sum to be found in Brooklyn. The large setting may look a bit tattered but it is clean and boasts a generous number of large, round, linen-draped tables; during the day the space is jam-packed with a gregarious flock of local residents.

The tables are attended to by Cantonese-speaking ladies, dressed in fuchsia blouses and red vests, pushing carts of steaming treats through the hungry hordes. Resist the urge to stock your table all at once; instead, survey the delicacies and pace yourself for a spectrum of fresh, delish dumplings, buns, and pastries. The feast also includes some refreshingly unique preparations (perhaps braised tofu with salted fish?) that steer away from the standard lineup.

Bar Corvo

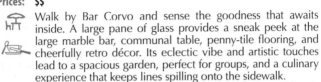

D8

Italian

791 Washington Ave. (bet. Lincoln & St John's Pls.)

Subway: Eastern Pkwy - Brooklyn Museum
Phone: 718-230-0940
Web: www.barcorvo.com
Prices: $$

Lunch Sat – Sun
Dinner nightly

Walk by Bar Corvo and sense the goodness that awaits inside. A large pane of glass provides a sneak peek at the large marble bar, communal table, penny-tile flooring, and cheerfully retro décor. Its eclectic vibe and artistic touches lead to a spacious garden, perfect for groups, and a culinary experience that keeps lines spilling onto the sidewalk.

Here, a house-made aïoli adds a horseradish kick to sublimely tender beef tongue fries—braised in a chicken stock, tossed in a beer and rice-flour batter, and finally fried to perfection. The savory *pesce al forno* starts with a base of fingerling potatoes and continues with a lightly breaded fillet of hake, baked with cherry tomatoes, black olives, and finished with garlic and herb *salmoriglio*.

Battersby ⊕

B7

Contemporary

255 Smith St. (bet. Degraw & Douglas Sts.)

Subway: Bergen St (Smith St.)
Phone: 718-852-8321
Web: www.battersbybrooklyn.com
Prices: $$

Dinner nightly

This bright spot along well-endowed Smith Street is the domain of Chefs Joseph Ogrodnek and Walker Stern. The intimate space has a homey, fuss-free feel, and tiny open kitchen. Squeeze in and glimpse the team at work in their petite but well-equipped corner.

Battersby's sophisticated cooking offers the likes of an ultra-seasonal mélange of spring peas, comprised of pods, young snap peas, shelled sweet peas, and a thicket of pea greens dressed with a touch of lemon and olive oil, showered with sweet pecorino. Heartier dishes include *fregola Sarda*, bead-shaped pasta from Sardinia prepared with unctuous bits of tripe braised in tomato and sprinkled with Grana Padano. Come dessert, the rhubarb galette with Stilton and Port ice cream is very, very nice.

Black Swan

D6

1048 Bedford Ave. (bet. Clifton Pl. & Lafayette Ave.)

Subway: Bedford - Nostrand Avs
Phone: 718-783-4744
Web: www.blackswannyc.com
Prices: $$

Lunch & dinner daily

You can't go wrong at Black Swan, so slide into a dark wooden booth, order a craft beer, and strike up a conversation with the other diners crammed into the deep, long space. As young as this American gastropub is, it feels as comfortable and rustic as a well-worn pair of jeans—just right for settling into a fast-paced match on TV.

True to its pub spirit, the food keeps pace with the ample beer list with a crackling, tender, and moist crab cake, fried until golden and topped with a deeply spiced remoulade. Deep bowls of turkey chili are rich and hearty, with loads of ground turkey, cumin, and bits of smoky bacon served with fluffy white rice and cornbread. Sea bass with wild mushroom ragout, cilantro, and grapefruit is effortlessly enjoyable.

Bozu

C1

296 Grand St. (bet. Havemeyer & Roebling Sts.)

Subway: Bedford Av
Phone: 718-384-7770
Web: www.oibozu.com
Prices:

Dinner nightly

An enticing selection of Japanese tapas—with many pleasing vegetarian options—is buttressed by a gracious staff and laid-back vibe at this upbeat, hip, and tasty spot. The slim wood and brick space is dressed in grey and installed with an L-shaped counter, a row of tables, and back patio. Brings friends and order a lot.

The sushi bar tempts with the *yakko* roll filled with silken house-made tofu and green onion; spicy mushroom roll dabbed with tomatillo purée; and *gunkanzushi* topped with sweet sea scallop and plump salmon roe alongside soy sauce pre-seasoned with wasabi. Cooked dishes bring on the likes of deep-fried *gyoza* filled with tomato, and fantastically intense nuggets of fried chicken thigh marinated for 48 hours in garlic and soy sauce.

Blanca ✿ ✿

Contemporary 🍴🍴

B1

261 Moore St. (bet. Bogart & White Sts.)

Subway: Morgan Av
Phone: 347-799-2807
Web: www.blancanyc.com
Prices: $$$$

Dinner Wed – Sat

As humble and welcoming as that taste of local beer to open your meal, Blanca is beyond cool. But never too cool. Don't let the compound's graffiti-covered corrugated metal deceive you. Enter through the ruckus of Roberta's to escape into this epitome of urban elegance in a gleaming warehouse kitchen. Inside, vibey vinyl records play the blues and camel-colored leather stools sit center stage before the immaculate open kitchen. There is just enough light to let the foodies ogle over each plate.

This nightly menu of 20-something courses is bold, intense, masterful, and innovative. Exceptional simplicity is clear in squiggles of sweet shrimp topped with poppy seeds and a light bath of blood orange. Tender octopus with gently seasoned fish displays Japanese culinary expertise. Pasta courses are equally strong, especially Chef Carlo Mirarchi's signature *nduja*-filled ravioli. Even a roast chicken is wow inducing. Memorable cheese plates may feature frozen smoked ricotta, pine-nut gelato, and lime syrup showcasing a genius interplay of temperature, flavor, and texture.

Be forewarned: the unpublished daily menu makes no dietary accommodations and dishes arrive on time. Pictures are verboten.

Brooklyn Star

D1

593 Lorimer St. (at Conselyea St.)

Subway: Lorimer St - Metropolitan Av
Phone: 718-599-9899
Web: www.thebrooklynstar.com
Prices: $$

Lunch Sat – Sun
Dinner nightly

Chef Joaquin Baca's handiwork at Brooklyn Star displays a fun and creative streak that yields admirable results. Pork chops are brined with molasses, striped bass is poached in duck fat, and roasted chicken is glazed with sweet tea and plated with dirty rice. Gluttony will convince you to bolster a meal here with bacon-jalapeño cornbread or buttermilk biscuits. But, let restraint chime in with a tasty raw kale salad. Starring golden raisins, toasted peanuts, lemon vinaigrette, and a lacy cheddar crisp on top, it's pleasure on a plate.

Though the focus is on the eats, the room is comfortably outfitted with brick red terrazzo floors and grey-trimmed walls. Blonde wood tables are set with bottles of hot sauce, pepper vinegar, and wild flowers.

Brucie

B6

234 Court St. (bet. Baltic & Kane Sts.)

Subway: Bergen St (Smith St.)
Phone: 347-987-4961
Web: www.brucienyc.com
Prices: $$

Lunch Sat – Sun
Dinner nightly

Despite the tough guy name, this local canteen proudly claims the distinctly female touch of Chef/owner Zahra Tangorra. The pleasantly thrown-together space seats a diverse selection of patrons, many with kids in tow. Step in to find a smattering of tables, copper-topped dining counter, and shelves lined with canned products, jars, and bottles.

Old-world inspiration combines with new-world sensibility and results in product-driven, mostly Italian creations like *tagliatelle* with Brussels sprouts, tomato butter, and house-made *burrata*. Then, savor the brined and barbecued chicken basted with earthy stout- and maple syrup-enriched sauce.

Try the chef's signature lasagna service: drop off your empty pan and pick it up filled and ready to feed a crowd.

Buttermilk Channel 🐾

B7

524 Court St. (at Huntington St.)

Subway: Smith - 9 Sts.
Phone: 718-852-8490
Web: www.buttermilkchannelnyc.com
Prices: $$

Lunch Sat – Sun
Dinner nightly

The talented duo of Doug Crowell and Chef Ryan Angulo have steered this lovely spot from new kid on the block to a charmer that Brooklynites are proud to call their own.

Pale yellow walls and a chic, simple décor are ideal for unwinding with a brew at the bar before moving back to the seating area to dig into their array of clever fare. Expect the likes of barbecued oysters, gently warmed yet still slurpable, seasoned with green onion, bits of smoked bacon, and a splash of Worcestershire. Equally impressive is the pan-roasted East Coast flounder, served whole, dressed with lentils and a chunky pistachio vinaigrette. Also find a rotating list of such lovely daily specials as Monday's $30 prix-fixe, Friday's lobster, and tasty vegetarian options.

Cafe Avat

A4

2158 Bath Ave. (bet. Bay 29th St. & Bay Pkwy.)

Subway: Bay Pkwy
Phone: 718-676-4667
Web: N/A
Prices: 🍝

Lunch & dinner daily

At this immaculate little outpost, sweet and hospitable Cafe Avat valiantly serves the Central Asian cuisine of Kyrgyzstan (the original location in Bishkek is still going strong). The décor is limited to ceramic-tiled floors, a wood-framed window overlooking Bath Avenue, and tables arranged with *very* spicy condiments. Its greatest feat may be authenticity— note the refrigerator stocked with sparkling waters from all along the Silk Road.

Even if the flat-screen looping music videos is distracting, keep your focus on *manti*, steamed mutton dumplings served with chopped dill; and flaky, golden Uzbek-style round breads filled with cumin-spiced ground lamb. *Chim-cha* is a spicy cabbage salad that should be joined with shish kebabs for a match made in heaven.

Café Steinhof

B8

422 Seventh Ave. (at 14th St.)

Subway: 7 Av (9th St.)
Phone: 718-369-7776
Web: www.cafesteinhof.com
Prices: 🍷🍷

Lunch Tue – Sun
Dinner nightly

Austrian flavors abound at this winsome Park Slope café. Dominating the space is an affable bar, where a selection of beers on draught, generously measured libations, and fruit brandies are poured; and any of these would be a fine accompaniment to the traditional and hearty Central European cooking. Dark wood furnishings and old-timey signage promoting Austrian provisions hung on the walls frame the space. The scene is more laid-back during the day but just as enjoyable.

Small plates and house specialties, imbued with old-world relish include the likes of golden chicken consommé with crêpe slivers and chives; black sausage strudel; tender bread dumplings with wild mushroom fricassee; and chicken in paprika-seasoned cream sauce.

Char No. 4 🏵

B6

196 Smith St. (bet. Baltic & Warren Sts.)

Subway: Bergen St (Smith St.)
Phone: 718-643-2106
Web: www.charno4.com
Prices: $$

Lunch Fri – Sun
Dinner nightly

The discreet façade of this 20th century row house in Cobble Hill is neither notoriously beautiful nor polished, but shields a truly welcoming spot. A backlit bar is focused on service and the wall of bourbon and "brown" spirits that it displays.

The dining room has comfy booths towards the back, tables for two, and fierce pride in its Southern fare. This is a serious home to smoked meats, so try their thinly sliced, house-cured lamb pastrami: a little smoky, a little sweet, served with coriander aïoli and enhanced with pickling spices. For dessert, the baked Macoun apple kissed with nutmeg and cinnamon and paired with Fontinella ice cream is heavenly. Brunches here are near legendary, as are Mardi Gras, the Kentucky Derby, and other special events.

Chavela's 🐶

Mexican ✗

D7

736 Franklin Ave. (at Sterling Pl.)

Subway: Franklin St
Phone: 718-622-3100
Web: www.chavelasnyc.com
Prices: 💰💰

Lunch & dinner daily

Look for the light blue dome and wrought-iron doors to enter Chavela's and discover an absolute riot of color inside. From the bar's Mexican tiles to the wall of ceramic butterflies, the room is an explosion of artistic sensibilities.

Guacamole is just as pleasing as the setting, whether going for a traditional or creative version mixed with flaky smoked trout, *pico de gallo*, and *morita chile* salsa. Small, crisp *taquitos de cangrejo* filled with the perfect balance of sweet crabmeat, salsa verde, white cheese, and *crema Mexicana* are irresistible. *Costilla en salsa verde* (deliciously tender, mild pork short rib stew) is studded with nopales swimming in a thick, verdant sauce, and served with a delectable mountain of yellow rice and refried black beans.

Clover Club

American 🍽️

B6

210 Smith St. (bet. Baltic & Butler Sts.)

Subway: Bergen St (Smith St.)
Phone: 718-855-7939
Web: www.cloverclubny.com
Prices: $$

Lunch Sat – Sun
Dinner nightly

A former shoe store is now an atmospheric rest stop that fashions a spot-on vintage vibe with mosaic-tiled floors, glove-soft leather banquettes, and pressed-tin ceilings dangling etched-glass pendants that glow as warmly as single malt. The glossy mahogany bar (furnished with leather-upholstered bar stools) is overseen by natty bartenders artfully shaking and pouring a stellar selection of libations like the namesake Clover Club—a mixture of gin, dry vermouth, lemon, and raspberry syrup.

An excellent savory carte is a perfect counterpoint to such liquid indulgences. Highlights may include herb-marinated hanger steak over toasted baguette spread with horseradish cream; duck fat-fried potato crisps; oysters on the half-shell; and American caviar service.

Chef's Table at Brooklyn Fare ✿✿✿

B6

Contemporary 🍴🍴

200 Schermerhorn St. (bet. Bond & Hoyt Sts.)

Subway: Hoyt-Schermerhorn

Phone: 718-243-0050

Web: www.brooklynfare.com

Prices: $$$$

Dinner Tue – Sat

At 7 P.M. this storefront attached to a gourmet grocer becomes something new and remarkable. Here, Chef César Ramirez—the bespectacled authoritarian—stands center stage, surrounded by sous chefs and state-of-the-art everything. He personally welcomes every guest to his "table" which is actually a gleaming steel counter. In his kitchen just behind, each copper pot is watched-over and each porcelain vessel is cooled or warmed to match the temperature of the food it holds. The bar for painstaking detail seems to rise with each dish.

The courses arrive as a thoughtful composition of art, texture, and taste. From the very first bite of *kinmedai* flown in from Japan, with its gentle base of miso cream and drop of yuzu juice, it's clear that this will be an extraordinary meal. Oysters arrive obscenely creamy, perhaps to be balanced with foamy mushroom reduction. Resist the urge to nibble and prolong the experience; just pop that Hokkaido uni into your mouth all at once. It literally melts to mingle with the truffle coin and buttery brioche, yielding otherworldly pleasure.

Desserts involve shattering crystalline sugar domes to reveal wintry spice ice cream that's so light it almost seems whipped.

Colonia Verde

219 DeKalb Ave. (bet. Adelphi St. & Clermont Ave.)

Subway: Clinton - Washington Avs
Phone: 347-689-4287
Web: www.coloniaverdenyc.com
Prices: $$

Lunch Sat – Sun
Dinner Tue – Sun

The historic blocks with row homes on Fort Greene's DeKalb Ave. make for an equally appealing restaurant row. Thanks to a sunken front room that flanks the open kitchen's wood-fired oven, plus a glassed-in "greenhouse" that transitions to a pebbled outdoor garden, locals stroll into Colonia Verde no matter the time of year. And why not? The banter is lively and meals rewarding.

Its menu is a Brazilian-esque expression of the owners of Cómodo in SoHo. Curiously named dishes like poblano pepper fettuccine stars pasta tossed with a spicy, satisfying ragù made from roasted poblanos, pecans, and ground beef. For dessert, the Brooklyn Mess sweetens the deal: three scoops of coffee ice cream topped with mango, dulce de leche syrup, and toasted manioc flour.

Colonie

127 Atlantic Ave. (bet. Clinton & Henry Sts.)

Subway: Borough Hall
Phone: 718-855-7500
Web: www.colonienyc.com
Prices: $$

Lunch Sat – Sun
Dinner nightly

The low-slung edifices that line this commercial strip of Brooklyn Heights make discreet homes for brick-walled hot spots like Colonie. Well-ensconced in the local culinary scene, this seasonally focused gem serves innovative American dishes to couples seated by lovely windows overlooking Atlantic Avenue.

The greenery decorating the small space and open kitchen echo the purity of the food, which although may appear straightforward and expected for this neighborhood, is always expertly prepared: plump roasted chicken towers sit atop braised mustard greens and hedgehog mushrooms. Classic desserts feature a spiced apple crumble with allspice-ginger ice cream. This is the kind of food that can banish a dreary wet day, leaving you satisfied and restored.

Cupola Samarkanda

Central Asian 🍴

1797 McDonald Ave. (at Ave. P)

Subway: Avenue P
Phone: 718-375-7777
Web: N/A
Prices: $$

Lunch & dinner daily

To say that this feels like a glitzy invention by Tony Manero—the star character from *Saturday Night Fever* with a fancy for Brooklyn discos—is surely no exaggeration. Nor is it an exaggeration to claim that here you'll find some of the most memorable *manti* in the city. The strobe lights are flickering, the keyboard wants tuning, and the back-up singer is wobbly, but this is precisely what makes Cupola Samarkanda so desirable, bizarre, and fun.

Among the local Georgians, Uzbeks, and Azerbaijani denizens, this gem offers perfect bites of home in the form of *cheburek*, plump, subliminal layers of flaky dough filled with cheese; and *geez-beez*, a classic sauté of tender, pouty liver cubes served in a cracker-like vessel and crowned with onion rings.

Dear Bushwick

Contemporary 🍴

41 Wilson Ave. (bet. George & Melrose Sts.)

Subway: Morgan Av
Phone: 929-234-2344
Web: www.dearbushwick.com
Prices: $$

Lunch Sat – Sun
Dinner nightly

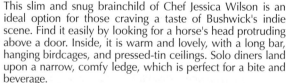

This slim and snug brainchild of Chef Jessica Wilson is an ideal option for those craving a taste of Bushwick's indie scene. Find it easily by looking for a horse's head protruding above a door. Inside, it is warm and lovely, with a long bar, hanging birdcages, and pressed-tin ceilings. Solo diners land upon a narrow, comfy ledge, which is perfect for a bite and beverage.

Accentuating the vintage vibe are portraits of men in mustaches who seem to be contemplating diners as they devour hard-boiled eggs in a pool of glistening horseradish butter. Or, try a refreshing and dainty dish of baby artichokes "crudo" with farmhouse cheddar and mushrooms. Finish with a scoop of rich chocolate pâté crowned with sea salt, pink peppercorns, and crème fraîche.

Delaware and Hudson ✿

American 🍴🍴

C1

135 N. 5th St. (bet. Bedford Ave. & Berry St.)

Subway: Bedford Av

Lunch & dinner Tue – Sun

Phone: 718-218-8191

Web: www.delawareandhudson.com

Prices: $$

This little newcomer is quickly becoming a shining star in its increasingly unaffordable yet still-edgy neighborhood. Inside the spare, narrow space, gray walls are decorated with color photographs of farm animals and produce, while honey-toned wood tables are set with a spray of wildflowers. The look clearly iterates this kitchen's locally minded sensibilities.

The low-key vibe and spirited, personal cuisine expresses the kind of food that Chef Patti Jackson might serve in her own home.

The generous fixed menu may begin with a series of appetizers to share like a petite slice of chickweed pie in a flaky, golden-brown double crust filled with creamy, mild greens. This is followed by a first course, such as pillow-soft farmers' cheese dumplings tossed in arugula pesto, finished with slivers of pickled cherries and matchstick-like bits of Virginia ham. Main dishes include seared black bass with a springtime assortment of wild dandelions and plump fava beans. Desserts are always pleasant, like the dense almond cake with roasted figs or a tiny coin of steamed chocolate cake with mint anglaise. Don't be surprised if the chef herself comes out with mignardises to personally thank each guest.

Diner 😋

American ✗

C2

85 Broadway (at Berry St.)

Subway: Marcy Av
Phone: 718-486-3077
Web: www.dinernyc.com
Prices: $$

Lunch & dinner daily

Williamsburg's restored 1920s-era diner is a modern day hipster hangout complete with swivel stools lining the counter and wood-slat booths in the dining room. In lieu of a menu, the cool-looking servers handwrite Diner's concise carte directly onto paper-topped tables, all the while explaining each item in detail.

A fried chicken sandwich or grass-fed burger are thoroughly appropriate fare for the setting, but it's the less expected plates that really wow. Take for example the grilled chicory, served charred and wilted, and plated with a fluffy dollop of ricotta cheese, crispy bacon lardons, and toasted walnuts. An equally impressive fillet of pan-seared trout boasts caramelized cipollini onions, poached currants, and a smear of strained yogurt.

Do or Dine 😋

Contemporary ✗

D6

1108 Bedford Ave. (bet. Lexington Ave. & Quincy St.)

Subway: Bedford - Nostrand Avs
Phone: 718-684-2290
Web: www.doordinebk.com
Prices: $$

Lunch Sat — Sun
Dinner nightly

Under a yellow awning advertising Caribbean takeout lies Do or Dine, a groovy, psychedelic trip into fine dining under a disco ball. Teacups serve as lampshades next to graffiti art in this hodgepodge chic, Bed-Stuy restaurant, started by four chef-friends who wanted more for this neighborhood.

Leave inhibitions behind when digging into the Nippon nachos, a cross of Japanese and Tex-Mex that tops crisp *gyoza* with cheddar cheese, *pico de gallo*, and *masago*-infused sour cream. "You've got quail" and truffle polenta primes you for more cheeky dishes, such as habanero chicken and "woffals" (waffles enriched with chicken liver) or a deep-fried foie gras doughnut. Get "drank" at the bustling bar with George and Gingers, the signature bourbon mule.

Dover

Contemporary 🍴🍴

B7

412 Court St. (at 1st Pl.)

Subway: Carroll St
Phone: 347-987-3545
Web: www.doverbrooklyn.com
Prices: $$$

Lunch Sat – Sun
Dinner nightly

Chefs Walker Stern and Joe Ogrodnek, the duo behind Battersby, are also working their culinary magic at this larger new offering. Candlelit Brooklynites favor this spare, tastefully appointed establishment for a creative carte that's precluded by gifts from the kitchen and warm bread to start.

Expect seared sea scallops arranged with carrots (shaved raw ribbons and al dente wedges), orange segments, and Marcona almonds; or lamb ribs which have been slow-cooked in duck fat before a turn on the grill. The meaty morsels are then plated Thai-style with crispy fried shallots and silken eggplant tasting of lime juice, fish sauce, and palm sugar. An updated take on Brooklyn blackout cake is sided by a surprising scoop of beet ice cream—and it totally works.

East Harbor Seafood Palace

Chinese 🍴🍴

A3

714-726 65th St. (bet. Seventh & Eighth Aves.)

Subway: 8 Av
Phone: 718-765-0098
Web: N/A
Prices: $$

Lunch & dinner daily

Come for dim sum to this behemoth that rocks with joyful chatter and gleeful moans from tables devouring impressive morsels. *Cha siu bao* (barbecue pork buns); *cha siu soh* (barbecue pork puff pastry); *zha liang* (fried crullers wrapped with *cheung fun* skin); and other treats are stocked on steaming carts that constantly circulate the room.

However, come sundown the setting is sparsely occupied. But that shouldn't deter you from making dinner here a consideration; quite the contrary in fact. The warm welcome is genuine and suggestions are forthcoming when requested. They may reveal tender stir-fried beef tossed with long beans and cashew nuts; or a succulent sea scallop gently steamed in its shell and topped with chopped garlic-studded glass noodles.

Egg

C1

109 N. Third St. (bet. Berry St. & Wythe Ave.)

Subway: Bedford Av
Phone: 718-302-5151
Web: www.eggrestaurant.com
Prices: ⊜⊜

Lunch daily

It was only a matter of time before owner George Weld would have to find larger digs for his home of the city's best biscuits. Egg's ravenous following is now accommodated in a much larger location that's light and bright with seating at a number of counters and ample table space; yet it's still common to be faced with a queue.

Breakfast is served all day, every day, and stars those fantastic buttermilk biscuits. The fresh-baked beauties are split open and smothered with pork sausage-studded sawmill gravy, stacked with country ham, house-made fig jam, and Vermont cheddar cheese; or simply accompanied by molasses, honey, or jelly. Lunchtime brings savory fare like Carolina kale wilted in a spicy tomato broth poured over a wedge of crumbly cornbread.

El Almacen

D1

557 Driggs Ave. (bet. N. 6th & N. 7th Sts.)

Subway: Bedford Av
Phone: 718-218-7284
Web: www.elalmacennyc.com
Prices: $$

Lunch Sat – Sun
Dinner nightly

This Argentinian grill is a carnivore's delight with its menu of meaty entrées from the grill (*de la parrilla*) like the *parrillada* featuring hearty ribeye and chorizo with truffle fries; or the "kitchen" offerings (*de la cocina*) which might include malbec-braised short ribs with sweet potato purée and Brussels sprouts. These hearty creations are best followed by *dulce de leche* in one of its several guises.

El Almacen, which means general store in Spanish, boasts a dark, rustic, and atmospheric setting replete with creaking wood furnishings, shelves of bric-a-brac, and cast iron skillets mounted on a brick wall. The bar is inviting, amply stocked with wine bottles, and set against a backdrop of creamy white tiles warmed by the candlelit room.

Elberta 😋

Southern ✗✗

C7

335 Flatbush Ave. (bet. Park & Prospect Pls.)

Subway: 7 Av (Flatbush Ave.)
Phone: 718-638-1936
Web: www.elbertarestaurant.com
Prices: $$

Lunch Sat — Sun
Dinner Tue — Sun

Elberta has certainly found her groove. This soulful speakeasy that pays homage to a jazz singer and the fuzzy Elberta peach drink, also dedicates nights to live music and creative cocktails. Her approachable vibe leads right into a Southern-inspired menu, featuring elegant interpretations of the usual suspects, including dessert: fantastic brioche doughnuts stuffed with sweet potato, caramel, and chocolate sauce.

But before the sweet tooth kicks in, try curry goat-stuffed ravioli in a creamy, cauliflower-based sauce; or Creole fisherman's stew dominated by whole prawns, scallops, mussels, and octopus. Use toasted sourdough or dirty rice loaded with gizzards and chicken liver to sop up the cherry-red tomato base, spiked with peppers, herbs, and spices.

El Born

Spanish ✗✗

B1

651 Manhattan Ave. (bet. Nassau & Norman Aves.)

Subway: Nassau Av
Phone: 347-844-9295
Web: www.elbornnyc.com
Prices: $$

Dinner Tue — Sun

Hip and happening Greenpoint is a highly appropriate location for this tapas den named after the equally trendy Barcelona district of El Born. The slender expanse of red brick and concrete is brightened by a neon squiggle suspended from the ceiling, red Shaker-style chairs, and a kitchen-fronting wall clad with encaustic cement tile.

A tray of crostini, simmered tomato, and garlic cloves is served gratis, for a do-it-yourself *pan con tomate* to stimulate the palate for what's to come. Enjoy *croquetes* oozing goat cheese and served with apple compote; or shaved summer squash with *ibérico* ham, blueberries, and padrón pepper vinaigrette. Stone-grilled octopus seasoned with olive oil, thyme, and paprika is a pretty plate packed with big flavors.

Eliá

Greek

8611 Third Ave. (bet. 86th & 87th Sts.)

Subway: 86 St	Dinner Tue – Sun
Phone: 718-748-9891	
Web: www.eliarestaurant.com	
Prices: $$	

Oh my, Mykonos? Nope, it's Bay Ridge, but Eliá's weathered plank floors and whitewashed walls decorated with wooden shutters will have you convinced otherwise. And that's before you have even seen the charming backyard patio.

This sure isn't a weak Greek with plenty of top-of-the-mind classics (grilled shrimp, octopus) and a few newbies (house-made ravioli filled with shredded braised lamb) thrown in for good measure. Appetizers, like the tender pork ribs marinated in ouzo and roasted with Greek herbs, are large enough to count as entrées, but with so many tempting choices, don't stop there. Definitely go for the pan-seared sheep's milk cheese *saganaki*, doused with a shot of ouzo for (ta-da!) flaming fun. Who doesn't love dinner and a show?

The Elm

Contemporary

160 N. 12th St. (bet. Bedford Ave. & Berry St.)

Subway: Bedford Av	Lunch Sun
Phone: 718-218-1088	Dinner nightly
Web: www.theelmnyc.com	
Prices: $$$	

The openness of the dining room, kitchen, and bar bring a lofty feel to this hotel restaurant. Even the heavy glasses and Japanese ceramics are of-the-moment. It's all very cool, but decidedly grown up and in contrast to some of the more self-consciously hip local joints.

Hearty steak frites and burgers may be popular, but measure this kitchen by its pitch-perfect foie gras terrine, or *gnocchetti* with blue crab, *bottarga*, and buttery bits of braised summer squash with zucchini foam and essence. From Thursday through Sunday, their "Little Elm" dining counter serves a tasting menu only and is one of the city's best-kept secrets. Reserve a seat here and begin to understand the extraordinary talent, personality, and vision of this kitchen.

El Mio Cid

B1

50 Starr St. (at Wilson Ave.)

Subway: Jefferson St   Lunch & dinner daily
Phone: 718-628-8300
Web: www.elmiocidrestaurant.com
Prices: $$

In contrast to the popular tapas spots sweeping the city, this is an old guard Iberian stalwart, deep in the heart of Bushwick. The interior bears a Mediterranean sensibility, with idyllic murals of the Spanish countryside, dark wood tables, and huge vessels of refreshing sangria.

The best way to explore this menu is through the tapas, salads, and daily soups rather than entrées. The Spanish tortilla is an old-timey classic of crisp potatoes and fluffy eggs, sliced into perfect, warm triangles. Their soups can be exceedingly fortifying, as in the traditional Galician bowl of gently smoked pork, white beans, and collard greens. Interesting desserts include bread soaked in spiced wine with vanilla ice cream; or poached pear and raspberry coulis.

Enoteca on Court

B7

347 Court St. (bet. President & Union Sts.)

Subway: Carroll St   Lunch & dinner daily
Phone: 718-243-1000
Web: www.enotecaoncourt.com
Prices: 🍸🍸

From the folks who run the old-school but revived Marco Polo Ristorante located just next door, comes this fresh-hearted take on *la cucina Italiana*. The wine bar-inspired room dishes out wood and brick details and serves as a cozy spot in which to enjoy a long line of snacks that include Italian cheeses, panini, and *marinati* (olives, roasted peppers, or eggplant).

The wood-burning oven is used to prepare the majority of offerings that highlight baked pastas; *carciofo ripieno* (stuffed artichokes), and an array of pizzas topped with a regionally influenced composition of ingredients. The *spiedini* are worthy of consideration—meaty skewers filled with the likes of house-made sausage, onions, and peppers, finished with a red wine reduction.

Falansai

Vietnamese ✗

112 Harrison Pl. (at Porter Ave.)

Subway: Morgan Av
Phone: 347-599-1190
Web: www.falansai.com
Prices: $$

Lunch Tue – Fri
Dinner Tue – Sun

This wonderful Vietnamese kitchen gives you reason to trek out to Bushwick—or is it East Williamsburg? Bay Area transplants listen up: Chef/owner Henry Trieu who once cooked at The Slanted Door has arrived and he's here to stay. Falansai's serene home—highlighting aqua walls and orchids lining the windowsills—is a pretty respite from the 'hood's grit. Find the likes of *bánh mì*, crusty baguettes slathered with black olive pâté, fermented mustard greens, green papaya slivers, and crunchy veggies; or excellent shrimp summer rolls served with a smooth peanut sauce.

For more redolence, order the *ca kho*; these catfish fillets are cooked in a claypot filled with an ambrosial broth scented with burnt sugar and stocked with red pepper, carrots, and green onions.

The Farm on Adderley

B3

American ✗✗

1108 Cortelyou Rd. (bet. Stratford & Westminster Rds.)

Subway: Cortelyou Rd
Phone: 718-287-3101
Web: www.thefarmonadderley.com
Prices: $$

Lunch & dinner daily

This hot spot perfectly exemplifies its diverse neighborhood, where eco-conscious residents refurbish old Victorian homes and support the most profitable food co-op in the city. Kid-friendly and cocktail-ready with a small heated patio and exposed brick, this farm-to-table respite creates seasonal dishes that are both delicious and healthy. Surprise yourself by digging into nourishing roasted spaghetti squash with aged goat feta and pumpkin seeds; or thinly pounded and crispy fried beef heart slices set atop a knoll of cheesy grits. Otherwise, stick to the classics with a poached farm egg over quinoa pocked with almonds.

This "Farm" is so popular that it spun off the Sycamore and set up an expanded bakery on Church Ave., proffering a variety of loaves.

Fonda

B8

434 Seventh Ave. (bet. 14th & 15th Sts.)

Subway: 7 Av (9th St.)
Phone: 718-369-3144
Web: www.fondarestaurant.com
Prices: $$

Lunch Sat – Sun
Dinner nightly

Bright colors and bold artwork adorn this cheery Park Slope favorite for creative Mexican cooking. The staff radiates hospitality, and speaking of warmth, when the sun is out, the tiny dining room is augmented by seating out back, which regulars know is *the* place to be.

Fonda's menu is endowed with a skilled spin, evident in items like a refreshing salad of diced watermelon and cucumber embellished with mild yet creamy *queso fresco* and the crunch of crushed *pepitas*. A lighter take on *chile rellenos* reveals roasted poblanos stuffed with spinach, raisins, and pine nuts, and dressed with a tomato-chipotle sauce and knob of epazote-seasoned goat cheese.

Chef Roberto Santibañez lets Manhattan in on the fun at his well-loved offshoot in the East Village.

Forcella

D2

485 Lorimer St. (bet. Grand & Power Sts.)

Subway: Lorimer St - Metropolitan Av
Phone: 718-388-8820
Web: www.forcellaeatery.com
Prices: ෨

Lunch & dinner daily

The original location of a trio of outposts, this favored pizzeria offers a convivial vibe in a quaint setting complete with white stucco walls and brass sconces.

The wood-burning domed pizza oven, encrusted with shards of black tile, is the heart of Forcella. It pumps out a listing of signature pies built upon disks of moist chewy dough charred in all the right places, like the *pignarocca*. A sauce-less pizza *Bianca*, it's strewn with bits of caramelized onions, crumbles of fennel sausage, and gobs of fresh mozzarella and fontina. Also try the *montanara*, a house specialty crust that's fried before being decked and baked as a traditional Margherita. If that doesn't do the trick, create your own pie with any combination from their wide array of toppings.

Fort Defiance

A7

365 Van Brunt St. (at Dikeman St.)

Subway: Smith - 9 Sts (& bus B61)
Phone: 347-453-6672
Web: www.fortdefiancebrooklyn.com
Prices: $$

Lunch daily
Dinner Wed – Mon

Young, likeable, and very resilient, Fort Defiance proves that a place named for a Revolutionary War fort and focused on favorites like deviled eggs as well as a handful of daily specials, makes for a great Southern tavern (of sorts). Then again, those spectacular cocktails including The Pundit with coffee-infused Scotch make everything all the warmer. The gamut of beers on tap is equally impressive.

Meals might seem progressively delicious, beginning with beautifully crisped sweetbreads set on a bed of parsnip purée with meaty shiitake mushrooms, fried capers, and a sweet Marsala *demi-glace*. Great skill and care is evident in the wonderfully spiced skate fried in a cornmeal crust with fresh cranberry bean ragout and buttery spinach.

Frankies 457 Spuntino ☺

B7

457 Court St. (bet. 4th Pl. & Luquer St.)

Subway: Smith - 9 Sts
Phone: 718-403-0033
Web: www.frankiesspuntino.com
Prices: ☕☕

Lunch & dinner daily

The ever-expanding empire of Frank Castronovo and Frank Falcinelli (the Franks) has its origins in this hands-down Carroll Gardens favorite.

Loosely translated as "snack," the menu of this home-styled Italian spot offers a selection of deliciously fuss-free fare. Headliners include fresh salads like shaved Brussels sprouts pocked with diced Castelrosso cheese and slicked with the house's golden-hued olive oil. The signature meatballs are studded with pine nuts and raisins; and sublime pastas like sweet potato-filled ravioli glide in a Parmesan broth.

Cooking is initially done in the basement kitchen, but dishes are finished upstairs behind stacks of charcuterie and crusty breads gracing the utterly charming brick-lined and wood-furnished space.

Franny's 😋

C7

Italian ✕✕

348 Flatbush Ave. (bet. Sterling & St. John's Pls.)

Subway: Grand Army Plaza   Lunch & dinner daily
Phone: 718-230-0221
Web: www.frannysbrooklyn.com
Prices: $$

Despite Franny's bigger digs, the wait for a table here has barely shortened. A voracious crowd is still the norm, but no matter. Grab a cocktail at the bar, decked with white subway tiles, and then strike up a conversation with a new best friend. While patio dining is a thing of the past, Franny's now offers a lower level that doubles as a private party room. Upstairs, keep your eyes on the open kitchen equipped with two wood-burning ovens used to produce the majority of the menu. Feast on a succulent assortment of charred snow peas, roasted broccoli with garlic and sunflower seeds, or orecchiette with velvety *borlotti* beans. And then there's that pizza—which is just as puffy, tender, light, and delicious as ever, not unlike their sensational clam pie.

French Louie

B6

Mediterranean ✕✕

320 Atlantic Ave. (bet. Smith & Hoyt Sts.)

Subway: Hoyt-Schermerhorn   Dinner nightly
Phone: 718-935-1200
Web: www.frenchlouienyc.com
Prices: $$

From the team behind Buttermilk Channel, French Louie combines a candlelit vibe with rustic touches and a dominantly Mediterranean menu in a welcoming setting that's become *the* neighborhood hideaway. Whether you perch at the mahogany bar or in the spacious backyard, be sure to come hungry for the splurge-worthy cheese plate and profiteroles—golden, puffy and encapsulating a fennel pollen-flavored ice cream.

For a dish to share, try the Le Grand socca, not normally found outside Liguria (where's it's called *farinata*) or the South of France. A bit thicker than the traditional, this pizza-sized crêpe arrives topped with a shelled-bean stew, charred asparagus, *freekeh*, and spiced lemon yogurt, with just the right amount of smokiness from the skillet.

Ganso Ramen

C6

Japanese ✗

25 Bond St. (bet. Fulton & Livingston Sts.)

Subway: Nevins St   Lunch & dinner daily
Phone: 718-403-0900
Web: www.gansonyc.com
Prices: 🍜

A welcome sight amid the sneaker stores and pizza joints peppering the commercial Fulton Mall, this sleek respite is a sure sign that things are changing in downtown Brooklyn. Inside, wood booths and tables sit atop stone floors, while those forever buzzing chefs are visible through encased glass. Thank cookbook author and owner Harris Salat for taking the plunge.

Thanks are also due to the kitchen for a killer menu of *ippin* and ramen. The former features a range of salads, spring rolls, and steamed buns including *buta* kimchi mingling pork belly and a spicy bean paste. Meanwhile, the ramen craze continues to rage on with several varieties, so get slurping on the likes of *tori shio* with soy-braised chicken *chashu*; or spicy *soboro* miso with ground pork.

The General Greene 👻

C6

American ✗

229 DeKalb Ave. (at Clermont Ave.)

Subway: Lafayette Av   Lunch & dinner daily
Phone: 718-222-1510
Web: N/A
Prices: $$

Despite the fact that this sounds like Grandpa's pet-name for his antique tractor, The General Greene is a space that nicely straddles rusticity and hipness while serving three satisfying meals a day. Everything seems cool here, if perhaps a bit aloof, from the perfectly ambient lighting, comfy banquettes, and leather bar stools to that highly prized espresso machine and free WiFi for your iPad.

The menu has a playful Southern slant, as seen in a warm haricot vert salad tossed with dates, almonds, and orange segments with an extra chive-buttermilk biscuit; or mac and cheese melting Vermont cheddar, Gruyère, and Parmesan folded with *cavatelli*. Ham-and-Gruyère bread pudding is custard-like and brutally addictive. Homemade cookies seem to fly out the door.

Gladys 😊

D8

Caribbean 🍴

788 Franklin Ave. (at Lincoln Pl.)

Subway: Franklin Av
Phone: 718-622-0249
Web: www.gladysnyc.com
Prices: $$

Lunch Fri – Tue
Dinner nightly

A popular sandwich shop turned Caribbean joint, Gladys makes it possible to sip a custom cocktail and live the Caribbean dream without leaving Crown Heights. Michael Jacober and Chef Matteo Potenza have transformed this corner location into a festive, turquoise destination, with a kitchen full of cooks roasting, grilling, and pan-frying jerk specialties, including fresh lobster.

It's no surprise that the wood-fired, whole porgy makes for a delicious and generous dish, with its smoky notes and accents like refreshing cucumber, pickled onion, and mango. Whale-sized, unshelled, and peppered shrimp arrive head-on with traditional Jamaican garlic, habanero, and a flirtatious dash of allspice. Dishes are remarkably luscious and flavor-packed at budget prices.

The Good Fork 😊

A7

Contemporary 🍴

391 Van Brunt St. (bet. Coffey & Van Dyke Sts.)

Subway: Smith - 9 Sts (& bus B61)
Phone: 718-643-6636
Web: www.goodfork.com
Prices: $$

Lunch Sat – Sun
Dinner Tue – Sun

The Good Fork is a destination restaurant, and foodies know that it's well worth the journey. Located on the food-centric Van Brunt Street near the Red Hook Waterfront, this inviting spot swaps New York pretense for pure passion—it's the dream of a married couple who built the restaurant from scratch, literally. Co-owner Ben Schneider crafted the space, while his classically trained wife, Chef Sohui Kim, helms the kitchen.

Her cuisine reflects the team's commitment to the locality, as seen in such original dishes as pan-seared cod reclining on squid rings braised in a spicy kimchi broth; or hot and crisp manchego *arancini* cooled with yogurt and a fennel-tomato marmalade. A *tres leches* cake with fresh berry compote is a crowning way to close this meal.

Gran Eléctrica 🐶

Mexican 🍴🍴

5 Front St. (bet. Dock & Old Fulton Sts.)

Subway: High St
Phone: 718-852-2700
Web: www.granelectrica.com
Prices: $$

Lunch Sat – Sun
Dinner nightly

Located in the shadow of the Brooklyn Bridge and just blocks from the riverfront in DUMBO, Gran Eléctrica epitomizes tech-savvy *nouveau* Brooklyn. Inside, the helpful staff keeps the tables turning, so settle into their lovely bar, savor a zesty margarita (some rave over the "beet" version), or just take in the vaguely European, shabby-chic décor, mixing modern accents with a bit of kitsch.

Whether seated in a cozy dining nook or in the lush outdoor garden, start with a tomato-based seafood *coctel* spiked with jalapeño and lime. Then, perhaps move on to a classic *gordita*, a light and crisp tortilla shell encasing strips of decadent *chicharrón*, *crema*, and *queso fresco*. Vibrant flavors come alive in crunchy, spicy, and tangy pickled vegetables *en escabeche*.

The Grocery

American 🍴

288 Smith St. (bet. Sackett & Union Sts.)

Subway: Carroll St
Phone: 718-596-3335
Web: www.thegroceryrestaurant.com
Prices: $$

Dinner Tue – Sat

There's plenty to love about Smith Street's quintessential neighborhood restaurant. Open for over a decade, The Grocery's longevity is commendable. And justly so— the quaint space framed by sage green walls is an always welcoming scene, though regulars know to make a beeline for the luxuriant backyard when the weather warms.

Co-chefs Charles Kiely and Sharon Pachter attend to the kitchen and take turns venturing out into the dining room to chat up the devoted clientele. The vibe is unmistakably cordial. Sit back and relish the facile cooking that renders appetizing items like a salad of sautéed squid, shaved fennel, and kalamata olives dressed with a lemon-scallion vinaigrette; or tender and flavorful slow-roasted duck with red wine sauce.

Hibino

B6

333 Henry St. (at Pacific St.)

Subway: Borough Hall
Phone: 718-260-8052
Web: www.hibino-brooklyn.com
Prices: 💲💲

Lunch Mon – Fri
Dinner nightly

This Cobble Hill treat is demure in appearance, but the warm welcome provided by a gaggle of female servers is a fitting prelude to the hospitality that will unfold. Once seated, a small blackboard is brought tableside where guests peruse the list of *obanzai* (Kyoto-style tapas). The evening may bring marinated and fried chicken thigh with tartar sauce; *chikuzen ni* (simmered chicken); or roasted oysters with spicy gazpacho. The menu items change daily but their tastiness remains constant.

Hibino's regional dedication is also evident in its offering of Osaka's traditional *hako* sushi. This box-pressed preparation might be served as a layering of excellent quality rice, shiso, *kanpyo* (preserved gourd), and fresh salmon.

The menu is pared-down at lunch.

Jack the Horse

B5

66 Hicks St. (at Cranberry St.)

Subway: High St
Phone: 718-852-5084
Web: www.jackthehorse.com
Prices: $$

Lunch Sun
Dinner nightly

This sleepy American tavern rife with exposed brick has been a favorite of Brooklyn Heights for years. As if to check everything off the list of what it takes to succeed in Brooklyn, Jack the Horse ups the ante with ten flavors of bitters and quite the selection of Vermont and New York cheeses. The mixologist at the well-stocked bar produces a thrillingly professional Old Fashioned with barrel-strength bourbon, and other drinks that can stand up to rich quality appetizers. Start with a smoked trout salad arranged around warm fingerling potatoes before indulging in ricotta- and butternut squash-ravioli covered in brown butter and Grana Padano. Mains prove just as savory, like a decadent JtH burger layered with Gruyère and caramelized bourbon onions on focaccia.

James

C7

605 Carlton Ave. (at St. Marks Ave.)

Subway: 7 Av (Flatbush Ave.)
Phone: 718-942-4255
Web: www.jamesrestaurantny.com
Prices: $$

Lunch Sat – Sun
Dinner nightly

This phenomenal little jewel of a restaurant feels as though it has been presiding over this corner for a hundred years. Pressed-tin ceilings and creaky wood floors make it a nostalgic spot, with modern touches like the Dutch Lucite chandelier lending a chic, romantic vibe.

The owners take every detail seriously, from the herb garden on the roof to that wonderful "Cecil & Merl" cheesecake they sell online. The contemporary American cooking highlights top ingredients handled with great care, as in delicate celery root soup topped with silky smoked trout and sharp wasabi sprouts. Generous pastas include enticingly chewy *trofie* enrobed in a pale sauce of puréed greens balancing tart Meyer lemon, earthy sautéed mushrooms, and sharp *Pecorino sardo* shavings.

Java

B8

455 7th Ave. (at 16th St.)

Subway: 7 Av (9th St.)
Phone: 718-832-4583
Web: N/A
Prices: 😊😊

Dinner nightly

Java's corner in Park Slope has been an enduring first choice for the exotic eats of Indonesia since 1992. Tiny yet tidy, this dark wood-furnished space is brightened by tall windows covered in golden drapery, native artwork, and the smiles of a friendly staff wearing batik aprons.

A nibble from the bevy of fried appetizers is certainly recommended. Begin with *bakwan* or golden-fried corn fritters, but don't forget about the mouthwatering *sate*— charred skewers of chicken, meat, or seafood brushed with *kecap manis* and topped with diced tomato and crispy fried shallots. The array of saucy, simmered options includes *sambal goring udang*: excellent batter-fried shrimp doused in turmeric-tinted coconut milk infused with lemongrass, ginger, and basil.

Jolie Cantina

B7

Fusion ✗

241 Smith St. (at Douglass St.)

Subway: Bergen St (Smith St.)   Lunch & dinner Tue – Sun
Phone: 718-488-0777
Web: www.joliecantina.com
Prices: $$

A marriage of French and Mexican sensibilities is the guiding force behind Jolie Cantina's novel cuisine. The kitchen sates diners all-day with spins on the classics like a hot *croque señor* made with roasted poblanos, chorizo, melting Comté, and (*bien-sûr*) accompanied by excellent fries. The range of fascinating creations also includes Mexican steak tartare dressed with pickled jalapeños, tequila, and capers; as well as the Cantina cassoulet comprised of black beans and *chicharrónes*.

The walls of this Cobble Hill corner spot feature whimsical artwork like a red-and-blue mural of roosters and piñatas, in a room furnished with bright red and yellow enameled chairs. Reiterating its French leaning, the bar hangs a sign that reads: "Hecho en France."

Juventino

B8

Contemporary ✗✗

370 5th Ave. (bet. 5th & 6th Sts.)

Subway: 4 Av - 9 St   Lunch daily
Phone: 718-360-8469   Dinner Tue – Sun
Web: www.juventinonyc.com
Prices: $$

This lovely storefront feels like a transplant from a seaside New England town. The sun-drenched space dons natural wood tables lined with aged newspapers and cheery flower arrangements, while white shelves stocked with an impressive collection of cookbooks stretch across the walls.

The delightful menu includes crispy cornmeal-crusted oysters with wilted greens and a verdicchio-sardo cream sauce; a salad tossing Neuroälhı mushrooms, whole grains, and Explorateur cheese in pumpkin seed vinaigrette; and meatballs mixing veal, beef, pork, and *sardo* simmered in a six-hour tomato sauce. Brunch highlights Mexican favorites like *huevos rancheros* and chorizo breakfast sandwiches. Be sure to try the freshly baked biscuits, made in house, Monday-Friday.

Karczma

Polish ✗

B1

136 Greenpoint Ave. (bet. Franklin St. & Manhattan Ave.)

Subway: Greenpoint Av
Phone: 718-349-1744
Web: www.karczmabrooklyn.com
Prices: 🍲🍲

Lunch & dinner daily

Located in a slice of Greenpoint that still boasts a sizeable Polish population, Karczma offers a lovely old-world ambience that may belie its age (opened for five-plus years) but perfectly matches its very traditional, budget-friendly menu. Hearty offerings may include peasant-style lard mixed with bacon and spices, or a plate of Polish specialties piled high with pierogies (three varieties, steamed or fried, topped with sliced onions and butter), kielbasa, potato pancakes, hunter's stew, and stuffed cabbage. Grilled plates can be prepared for two or three, while others, like the roasted hocks in beer, could easily feed an army.

The quaint, farmhouse-inspired interior is efficiently staffed with smiling servers in floral skirts and embroidered vests.

Kaz An Nou

Caribbean ✗

C7

53 6th Ave. (bet. Bergen & Dean Sts.)

Subway: Bergen St (Flatbush Ave.)
Phone: 718-938-3235
Web: www.kazannou.com
Prices: $$

Dinner Tue – Sun

This tiny, dark, and lovable outfit is sought for its fantastic take on French-Caribbean fare. The name aptly means "our house" in Creole. The Rastafarian-inspired space is filled with red tables, comfy banquettes, bright walls hung with artwork, and touches that couldn't be more inviting.

The mouthwatering menu represents the roots of husband and wife team, Sebastien Aubert (who hails from Guadeloupe) and Michelle Lane. Stop in to sample the likes of mashed sweet plantains mixed with basil béchamel and topped with a melting layer of Emmentaler cheese. Specialties include the *dombré crevette*, a traditional dish of insanely spiced little dumplings, deeply flavored and smoky shellfish broth, sweet shrimp, and vegetables. The spicy chocolate cake is a must.

Ki Sushi

B6

Japanese ✗

122 Smith St. (bet. Dean & Pacific Sts.)

Subway: Bergen St (Smith St.)
Phone: 718-935-0575
Web: N/A
Prices: $$

Lunch Mon – Sat
Dinner nightly

Smith Street offers plenty of dining option to choose from, but Ki is this strip's sushi standout. Low-key and proffering good value, it is also a neighborhood favorite. At lunch, find downtown Brooklyn professionals taking a respite from the day's proceedings. At night, young couples and families routinely pack the room that brandishes a dim and earthy mien.

Sample an array of cold and hot appetizers like yellowtail tartare with yuzu-ginger vinaigrette or rock shrimp tempura with creamy-spicy sauce. Follow this with creative maki, or better yet, the sushi deluxe platter. The skillfully constructed nigiri lineup features an array of fluke, sea bream, amberjack, and mackerel, as well as a roll stuffed with lean and deliciously unadulterated tuna.

Krolewskie Jadlo

B1

Polish ✗

694 Manhattan Ave. (bet. Nassau & Norman Aves.)

Subway: Nassau Av
Phone: 718-383-8993
Web: www.krolewskiejadlo.com
Prices: ☜☜

Lunch Mon – Fri
Dinner nightly

Krolewskie Jadlo ("king's feast" in Polish) sits in a Greenpoint enclave that was once home to a large number of Polish immigrants. Although the size of the community has decreased through the years, the area still thrives with a distinct Eastern European soul.

The room is pleasant and routinely packed with crowds basking in the enjoyable authenticity. The Polish plate brings all one could hope for in a hearty old world platter. cabbage rolls stuffed with ground beef and braised in tart tomato sauce; pan-fried potato pierogis; and a link of smoky kielbasa. Other items are just as tasty, like the pounded pork shoulder steak, grilled and brushed with honey, and served with pickled cabbage and beets.

A second outpost is located in Ridgewood, Queens.

La Superior

C1

295 Berry St. (bet. S. 2nd & S. 3rd Sts.)

Subway: Bedford Av
Phone: 718-388-5988
Web: www.lasuperiornyc.com
Prices: 🐷🐷

Lunch & dinner daily

This south Williamsburg taqueria is as loved for its lip-smacking selection of tacos as it is for its budget-friendly prices and rock-star vibe. A handful of tables add seating beyond the tiny bar, decorated with vintage wallpaper, brightly painted chili-red walls, and a mounted Mexican flag. Tacos anchor La Superior's menu, and include *lengua*, creamy *rajas*, or *carne asada* to be wrapped in excellent tortillas. However, other options also tempt like the *torta ahogada*—a "drowned" sandwich served as toasted sourdough bread stuffed with roasted pork drenched in *chile de arbol* and tomato sauce. A specialty of Guadalajara, the *cebollitas chambray* is a great side dish made with fat scallions that have been grilled until blistered, tender, and sweet.

Lea

B3

1022 Cortelyou Rd. (at Stratford Rd.)

Subway: Cortelyou Rd
Phone: 718-928-7100
Web: www.leabrooklyn.com
Prices: $$

Lunch Sat – Sun
Dinner nightly

From its prime corner location with sidewalk seating to its all-glass façade, Lea is quite the looker. But its substance lives up to the pretty face, with a breezy vibe and eccentric accents like reclaimed wood and dismantled water tower segments that cover the ceiling.

The food is an equally lovely collection of Italian dishes made with a degree of deference to the country's regional cuisines. Don't miss the expert cannelloni served Neapolitan style: stuffed with ricotta and braised lamb, covered with a sensational *ragù di pomodoro*, and baked to the perfect texture in a wood-burning oven. On the lighter side, try the smartly made panzanella that pairs braised squid with root vegetables and a fragrant, herb-laced sheep's milk yogurt dressing.

La Vara

Spanish

B6

268 Clinton St. (at Verandah Pl.)

Subway: Carroll St
Phone: 718-422-0065
Web: www.lavarany.com
Prices: $$

Lunch Sat – Sun
Dinner nightly

Set in quiet and charming Cobble Hill, La Vara is as alluring as its surrounds. Inside, hip singles get down to business around a sleek marble bar; while PYT's looking to party it up migrate to curved leather booths or a wooden alcove up front. In the dining room, white tables set with contemporary crockery are just the right contrast to rustic brick walls.

From beautiful lighting and personable service, to immaculately prepared food and inventive presentations, this convivial respite never misses a beat. Embark on a journey to culinary Shangri-La with *alcachofa* or crispy artichokes sloshed in anchovy aïoli, before lingering over creamy, golden-brown *croquetas* studded with *jamón Serrano*. Then, sail on to *mar y montaña* highlighting smoky pork strips and Maine shrimp swimming in a lush pool of pimento-topped *ajo blanco*.

With luck on your side, *cochinillo* (slow-cooked, amber-hued suckling pig with crackling skin and rose-quince sauce); or *tortilla de calabacín* (a green squash "pancake" with "pisto" and gingered yogurt) may star on the menu. If not, rest easy as you can still have your cake (maybe a *torta Santiago* dusted with powdered sugar and preserved cherries) and eat it too!

479

Locanda Vini e Olii

Italian ✗

D6

129 Gates Ave. (at Cambridge Pl.)

Subway: Clinton - Washington Avs

Phone: 718-622-9202

Web: www.locandany.com

Prices: $$

Dinner nightly

This elder statesman of Clinton Hill feels like it was dreamed up by the charming townhouses and tree-lined neighborhood it has served for over a decade. Through lace-covered windows, the dining room flickers its candlelight with unabashed romance. The room is actually a repurposed 19th century apothecary that awakens such historic details as rolling ladders and small wooden drawers.

Begin with diverse antipasti, including custardy cauliflower *sformato di cavolfiore* set atop puréed spinach. Unusual *paste* include tiny house-made gnocchi tossed with clams, mussels, and tender shrimp over perfectly braised broccoli rabe. Move on to a restrained and luscious Hudson Valley duck breast, then finish with a warm chocolate torte topped with caramel sauce.

Lucky Eight

Chinese ✗

A3

5204 Eighth Ave. (bet. 52nd & 53rd Sts.)

Subway: 8 Av

Phone: 718-851-8862

Web: N/A

Prices: 🥢🥢

Lunch & dinner daily

Eat well for a Cantonese song at Lucky Eight, though first you'll need to find it buried among Chinese pastry shops, grocers spilling goods onto the sidewalk, and the throng of pedestrians populating this stretch of Eighth Avenue south of Sunset Park.

Everything is small and bustling. A front counter proffers the menu to-go, while those who dine in are swiftly greeted, ushered to a table (or empty seat), and presented with a laminated menu displaying an array of dim sum that is a departure from the standard set (think fish skin dumplings and pork knuckles). The Cantonese line-up offers barbecued meats over rice; a savory tangle of noodles like *e-fu* tossed with XO sauce and dried scallops; and vegetables like *choy sum* steamed to emerald green.

Lucky Luna

B1

Fusion

167 Nassau Ave. (at Diamond St.)

Subway: Nassau Av
Phone: 718-383-6038
Web: www.luckyluna-ny.com
Prices: ⊛

Dinner Tue – Sun

There's no other restaurant around like Lucky Luna. Seriously. Their delicious menu is a hybrid of Taiwanese and Mexican cuisine. The pizzazz on the plate is served in a simple yet tidy assemblage of glossy black tables, and an ambitious beverage program makes the small bar a total draw.

Mom's sweet-and-sour cucumber salad, flavored with ginger and garlic, is a bracing start for Peking duck confit *bao* spread with hoisin mayonnaise, garnished with crispy duck *chicharrònes* and duck fat popcorn dusted with Chinese five spice. Another hit: the taco of "reverse" carnitas is a pile of succulent pork shoulder that's been seared *then* braised in a broth of beer, oranges, and tomatoes, and finally topped with crunchy bits of radish and spicy pickles.

Lulu & Po

C6

American

154 Carlton Ave. (at Myrtle Ave.)

Subway: DeKalb Av
Phone: 917-435-3745
Web: www.luluandpo.com
Prices: $$

Dinner nightly

On the approach, Lulu & Po isn't quite charming—it sits a bit beyond Fort Greene Park's historic brownstones and closer to the hardscrabble storefronts—but it is a great find for a consistently tasty selection of small plates. The interior features an open kitchen, the huge image of a bright, happy rooster, and ample windows to make the diminutive space seems larger. The room remains packed; watch as those tables for two manage to accommodate three. Or even four. Impeccably timed plates might begin with grilled pizza dough topped with basil purée and homemade ricotta. Move on to try warm corn tortillas served with tender roasted bone marrow augmented by a parsley-caper salad and *sriracha;* or slices of pickled beef tongue with a red pepper-herb emulsion.

Luksus at Tørst ✿

Contemporary 🍴🍴

615 Manhattan Ave. (bet. Driggs & Nassau Aves.)

Subway: Nassau Av   Dinner Tue – Sun
Phone: 718-389-6034
Web: www.luksusnyc.com
Prices: $$$$

Enter through Tørst, wander to the back, and find Luksus—it's like unearthing a little boudoir behind a beer bar. The small, highly Instagrammable room has a Scandinavia-via-Brooklyn look, with a choice marble dining counter for chef viewing and smattering of tables. Sure, the crowd is heavily tattooed and tight-shirted, but this is no place for poseurs. Luksus has an artsy edge that cements Greenpoint's status as the hotbed of NY cool. Cue the *Girls* location scouts.

The young staff may be hipsters, but everyone is passionate, friendly, and can recite beer history like it's their catechism. Absolutely go for the pairing.

The cuisine is firmly rooted in Scandinavian techniques and ingredients, with inspiration from afar. An elegant, hybrid dish of mackerel is served sweet, banishing all traces of fishiness with slices of watermelon radish and bacon dashi. Lush and slow-poached in butter, skate is a supple contrast to crisp sunchoke chips and swipe of kohlrabi. A pub-like dish of beef tongue gets twist and flair from firm garbanzo beans and a green sauce, vivid with watercress. Desserts push the envelope with combinations that can be decadent, arresting, and not necessarily for everyone.

Marco's

Italian ✗✗

C7

295 Flatbush Ave. (bet. Prospect Pl. & St. Marks Ave.)

Subway: Bergen St (Flatbush Ave.) Lunch Sat – Sun
Phone: 718-230-0427 Dinner nightly
Web: www.marcosbrooklyn.com
Prices: $$$

Clearly, someone is taking countrified Italian-ish food seriously. Beyond the glass façade, over the white marble bar, and into the back of this informal trattoria lies a small, open kitchen with a serious objective. Owners Andrew Feinberg and Francine Stephens have carefully crafted their Italian-inspired dishes with local ingredients into an overnight sensation in Prospect Heights.

Pitch-perfect pasta honors the technical savviness of the chef while smart flavor combinations—think: wonderfully finessed *colatura*, walnuts, herbs, and olive oil—prove the kitchen's creativity and Brooklyn frame of mind. Desserts include wedges of sweet poached quince, dense and delicious, with two scoops of creamy vanilla gelato topped with fragrant biscotti crumbles.

Maria's Bistro Mexicano

Mexican ✗

A2

886 Fifth Ave. (bet. 37th & 38th Sts.)

Subway: 36 St Lunch & dinner daily
Phone: 718-438-1608
Web: www.mariasbistromexicano.com
Prices: $$

Head to Sunset Park for some great Mexican cuisine—those who call this vibrant Brooklyn pocket home consider themselves lucky to have such a bright spot in the neighborhood. The cozy space complete with backyard seating pops with color and is warmed by the genuinely hospitable light cast by Maria herself.

Dig into a hearty bowlful of *pozole* or tortilla soup before delving into appetizing preparations like a thick-cut grilled pork chop with *salsa roja Oaxaqueño* or *enchilada mi bandera* topped with a trio of sauces. This *chile poblano* combo is a delicately fried one-two punch: one plumped with a savory combination of cheeses, the other stuffed with a beguilingly sweet mixture of chicken, almonds, diced plantains, and apple.

Marlow & Sons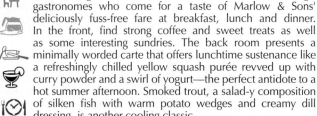

C2

81 Broadway (bet. Berry St. & Wythe Ave.)

Subway: Marcy Av   Lunch & dinner daily
Phone: 718-384-1441
Web: www.marlowandsons.com
Prices: $$

This enticing den is manna for the denizens of Williamsburg's gastronomes who come for a taste of Marlow & Sons' deliciously fuss-free fare at breakfast, lunch and dinner. In the front, find strong coffee and sweet treats as well as some interesting sundries. The back room presents a minimally worded carte that offers lunchtime sustenance like a refreshingly chilled yellow squash purée revved up with curry powder and a swirl of yogurt—the perfect antidote to a hot summer afternoon. Smoked trout, a salad-y composition of silken fish with warm potato wedges and creamy dill dressing, is another cooling classic.

Dinner features the succulent, bronze-skinned brick chicken, a menu mainstay, as well as oysters, cheeses, and an oft-changing list of specials.

Mayfield

D7

688 Franklin Ave. (bet. Park & Prospect Pls.)

Subway: Park Pl   Lunch & dinner daily
Phone: 347-318-3643
Web: www.mayfieldbk.com
Prices: $$

Mayfield (named for the R&B legend) has rightfully earned each one of its many devotees. Expertly run by co-owners Chef Lev Gewirtzman and Jacques Belanger, this Southern-inspired, rustic, yet hip eatery combines a sexy art deco style, soul-stirring soundscape, and unapologetic, expertly made cuisine. Inside, distressed brick walls and sleek tiles outfit the space, while brass mermaid door handles keep the look very playful.

Try the buttermilk-fried quail, dainty, bone-in, and supremely tender, paired with honey dipping sauce, served alongside cornmeal spoonbread and ultra-porky collards. Then, move on to the pork chop saltimbocca, charred and juicy, served with savory-sweet farro salad, caramelized onions, and grilled red radicchio.

Meadowsweet ❀

Mediterranean 🍴🍴

C2

149 Broadway (bet. Bedford & Driggs Aves.)

Subway: Marcy Av   Dinner nightly
Phone: 718-384-0673
Web: www.meadowsweetnyc.com
Prices: $$

Much to the delight of the locals, Meadowsweet has returned the old Dressler space to its rightful place as one of the borough's most stellar dining venues.

A soaring, glass-fronted façade, whitewashed brick walls, and reclaimed pine furnishings illuminate the restored dining room, while original mosaic-tiled floors lend a stunning, old-timey accent and hearken back to the building's former life as a print shop. But the real magic happens in the kitchen—a space that deserves newfound praise thanks to Chef Polo Dobkin.

Its menu can be described as enticingly familiar and temptingly novel Americana, with whiffs of the Mediterranean woven throughout. Every composition is beautifully plated, including a tender crêpe purse clutching smoked trout, horseradish, and dressed with green apple and frisée. Hand-rolled sheets of pasta bear mint-infused ricotta, sweet peas, and a flavorful Parmesan broth; whereas perfectly pink, pan-seared Colorado lamb loin is fanned over plump beans, crisp, salty lamb ribs, and a lick of lush romesco. For dessert, the frozen—not firm—wedge of coconut ice cream pie, dotted with raspberries in a crumbly cookie crust, is a sophisticated sweet with a fun side.

Mesa Coyoacán 🦛

D1

372 Graham Ave. (bet. Conselyea St. & Skillman Ave.)

Subway: Graham Av
Phone: 718-782-8171
Web: www.mesacoyoacan.com
Prices: $$

Lunch & dinner daily

Not that Brooklyn is wanting for exciting dining options, quite the opposite actually, but Chef Ivan Garcia's tempting establishment has been greeted with open arms (and mouths). The Mexico City native ruled the roost previously at Barrio Chino and Mercadito, and has now settled into this glass-fronted slab where wolfish appetites are sated.

It's not just the swank interior, outfitted with richly patterned wallpaper, snug banquettes, and communal tables, but the mouthwatering Mexican food that makes this place such a pleasure. Partake in tacos, perhaps the *carnitas*—braised Berkshire pork D.F.-style stuffed into handmade tortillas—or a choice from the *platos fuertes* that include *enchiladas de mole*, made from the chef's secret family recipe.

Mile End 🦛

B6

97A Hoyt St. (bet. Atlantic Ave. & Pacific St.)

Subway: Hoyt-Schermerhorn
Phone: 718-852-7510
Web: www.mileendbrooklyn.com
Prices: 🫘

Lunch & dinner Tue – Sun

Boerum Hill's most bodacious deli (head to Mile End Sandwich for the delish Manhattan offshoot) serves up killer smoked meat and so much more. The tiny space gets lots of traffic, and those who can't find a seat along the counter or trio of communal tables can feast at home with takeout procured from the sidewalk window.

Now for the food: a cured and smoked brisket sandwich, stacked onto soft rye bread and smacked with mustard, is the stuff that dreams are made of. Eclectic and vegetarian-friendly, the menu also reveals pouitne (owner Noah Bernamoff is a Montreal native), roasted eggplant *brik* dotted with capers, pine nuts, and raisins; Sunday-only Chinese specialties; as well as fresh-baked desserts like almond cake with house-made vanilla ice cream.

Mill Basin Kosher Delicatessen

D e l i 🍴

B3

5823 Ave. T (bet. 58th & 59th Sts.)

Subway: N/A
Phone: 718-241-4910
Web: www.millbasindeli.com
Prices: $$

Lunch & dinner daily

This middle-aged Brooklyn treasure is as old-school as it gets, and though it's a bit of a trek to Mill Basin, anyone looking for a real Jewish deli won't think twice. Part deli counter, part artsy dining room, and part party hall, Mark Schachner's beloved spot serves up all the classics from beef tongue sandwiches to gefilte fish.

The wildly overstuffed sandwiches (all served with homemade pickles and coleslaw) are a home run, as in the pastrami, which is steamed not once but twice, leaving the meat juicy yet hardly fatty. Dive into a Rueben—an open-face and intense pile of juicy corned beef, Swiss cheese, and tart sauerkraut on toasted rye bread, topped with Russian dressing. The pastrami eggroll is a serious, cultish favorite.

Mimi's Hummus

M e d i t e r r a n e a n

B3

1209 Cortelyou Rd. (bet. Argyle & Westminster Rds.)

Subway: Cortelyou Rd
Phone: 718-284-4444
Web: www.mimishummus.com
Prices: 😊😊

Lunch & dinner daily

Mimi Kitani whips up a mean hummus that is just as creamy and delicious as ever, not to mention complete with a variety of tasty toppings—even mushrooms! But partner Avi Shuker has expanded his mini operation to include an adjoining Middle Eastern market and The Castello Plan—an inviting bar located two doors down, complete with live music, and named for the first map of New York.

Drop by for joyful banter with the über friendly staff along with an Iraqi sandwich piled with fried eggplant and boiled egg; roasted beet salad with an avalanche of onion and parsley; or well-spiced lamb stuffed into bright red peppers. Large windows, wood panels, and a bustling kitchen create an industrial aspect, while maintaining a sleek tone throughout.

Miranda

C1

80 Berry St. (at N. 9th St.)

Subway: Bedford Av
Phone: 718-387-0711
Web: www.mirandarestaurant.com
Prices: $$

Lunch & dinner Wed – Mon

The cuisines of Latin America and Italy join for a splendid union at this Williamsburg trattoria, run by husband-wife team Sasha and Mauricio Miranda. The pretty space is illuminated with jewel-toned votives and boasts a cement floor inlaid with oak, straw seat chairs, and exposed brick. Beyond this, the chef puts her impressive experience to work in the open kitchen.

The house-made *pappardelle* is a perfect example of Miranda's unique approach: the wide delicate strands of pasta clutch on to bits of slow-cooked lamb in a dark, earthy, *mole* tasting of dried chilies, sweet spices, and bitter chocolate. Other items may include grilled baby octopus with avocado and jalapeño, or roasted pork tenderloin with tomato and cumin-scented Arborio rice.

Moim

C8

206 Garfield Pl. (at Seventh Ave.)

Subway: 7 Av (Flatbush Ave.)
Phone: 718-499-8092
Web: www.moimrestaurant.com
Prices: $$

Lunch Sat – Sun
Dinner Tue – Sun

In a step-down space along a tree-lined Park Slope street, Moim is a fun and easy place to tuck into an array of Korean fare. The name translates as "gathering," so go with a group and prepare to share in the generous portions of traditional *pajun* chock-full of scallions and seafood, or *bibimbap* with marinated sirloin. Chunky tables, sloping wood panels, and concrete brick walls keep the look simple yet modern.

Begin with at least one round of plump, pan-fried *mandoo*, filled with lean pork and a restrained amount of kimchi, along with sesame-soy dipping sauce. Then, move on to entrées like *ssang-sun gui*, which arrives as a whole grilled branzino topped with thick scallion-ginger sauce tinted red thanks to *gochujang*, and accompanied by sticky rice.

Mominette

B1

French 🍴

221 Knickerbocker Ave. (bet. Starr & Troutman Sts.)

Subway: Jefferson St
Dinner nightly
Phone: 929-234-2941
Web: N/A
Prices: $$

Enter through the swinging wooden doors to discover that the less-than-glitzy surroundings seem a world away. Inside, Mominette's highly romanticized glow is impossible to ignore—picture wallpaper crafted from sepia-toned newspapers along with risqué photos of women amid vintage chandeliers. Add to that a familial staff and fantastic food...*et voilà*...a fun, energetic, instant favorite!

There is a reason why each newcomer becomes a regular: the food is surprisingly delicious and very authentic. The menu focuses on classics like escargots deliciously baked with tomatoes and garlic; a fresh kerchief of puff pastry filled with tender roast duck infused with wine and tart cranberries; followed by braised pork tenderloin set atop nutty lentils.

Morgan's BBQ

C7

Barbecue 🍴

267 Flatbush Ave. (at St. Marks Ave.)

Subway: Bergen St (Flatbush Ave.)
Lunch & dinner daily
Phone: 718-622-2224
Web: www.morgansbrooklynbarbecue.com
Prices: $$

Barbecue has been having a New York moment, mixing up sauces ranging from the vinegar-heavy Eastern NC-style to sweeter Tennessee renditions. At Morgan's, it's all about Texas, where there is an unparalleled emphasis on the quality of meat and smoke. The bare wood tables, plastic bottles, and industrial rolls of paper towels provide no dining frills not that they are missed.

Come hungry for slow-smoked brisket with a spicy and inspired rub that's straight out of Austin. Hard to find outside the state, the Hill Country specialty of deep-fried turkey tails is especially tender, served over porky collard greens and salty-sweet cornbread with pepper jelly. Sides are to die for; same goes for the signature pecan "cutie pie" made with Widow Jane bourbon.

M Shanghai

C1

292 Grand St. (bet. Havermeyer & Roebling Sts.)

Subway: Bedford Av
Phone: 718-384-9300
Web: www.newmshanghai.com
Prices:

Lunch & dinner daily

Look at the steamer full of luscious soup dumplings on just about every table in this notable Williamsburg Chinese café, and there should be little doubt of the best way to begin a meal here. Plump full of hot pork broth magically encased in scalloped wonton wrappers, they are sheer pleasure. Vegan and vegetarian treats include fried tofu with sweet peppers and black bean sauce; or cool, silken batons of eggplant salad dressed with plenty of garlic, soy, and a hint of sweetness. The scallion pancakes are fantastically large, hot, and shatteringly crisp wedges accompanied by a dipping sauce prepared tableside.

The low-key room is accented by whitewashed brick walls, honey-toned bamboo slats, and ceiling lights fashioned out of birdcages.

Mtskheta Café

A4

2568 86th St. (bet. Bay 41st St. & Stillwell Ave.)

Subway: 86 St
Phone: 718-676-1868
Web: N/A
Prices:

Lunch & dinner Thu – Tue

Deep in the heart of Brooklyn bordering Bath Beach, Mtskheta Café pumps out Georgian classics in a green-hued, faux-brick dining room complete with paper napkins, a campy jungle mural, and television looping foreign music videos. While the décor may lack, the service and food excel, setting this impossible-to-pronounce restaurant apart from the nearby bodegas and elevated subway tracks.

Whether or not you can deduce what's on the Cyrillic menu, friendly servers standby, directing guests to native dishes like *badrijani*, an almost overwhelming helping of eggplant stuffed with fluffy walnut purée. It's light compared to the mutton *bozbashi*, though—a heady soup of tarragon, cilantro and lamb fat that adds a layer to any blustery day.

Nargis Cafe

B4

2818 Coney Island Ave. (bet. Kathleen Pl. & Ave. Z)

Subway: Sheepshead Bay
Phone: 718-872-7888
Web: www.nargiscafe.com
Prices: $$

Lunch & dinner daily

This industrial strip is ground zero for Central Asian hot spots, where Nargis Cafe endures as a real treat. Composed of a front bar area and larger, brighter dining room, the entire space is brought together with marvelous Persian rugs and exotic pierced-metal sconces.

Nargis hits a strong stride among the locals for its convivial vibe and unique repertoire of dishes that may include a *bojon* salad of smoky eggplant tossed with garlic, peppers, carrots, and cucumber. Kebabs are taken seriously here, so try the succulent lamb with chopped onion and dill. Uzbek *plov* studded with chickpeas, lamb, and raisins is simple but imperative. For dessert, the honey-sweet *chak-chach* is fried but surprisingly light and exquisitely indulgent.

New Spring Garden

A3

912 65th St. (bet. Fort Hamilton Pkwy & Ninth Ave.)

Subway: Fort Hamilton Pkwy
Phone: 718-680-2289
Web: N/A
Prices: $$

Lunch & dinner daily

This dim sum palace offers additional evidence that Dyker Heights continues to swell in its slew of Chinese dining. Seating more than 500, the setting inside doesn't break new ground in décor—find fully carpeted floors and bold red-accented walls affixed with gold dragons. And yet, more often than not, every seat is filled and the space rings from the buzz of chatty crowds.

Carts rolling past are stacked with temptations and marvels. Pile your table high with *ngao yuk kao*, beef meatballs flecked with cilantro, steamed goji balls, braised duck feet, or steamed banana leaf wrapped around sticky rice pocked with mung beans, chicken, dried fish, and lotus nuts. For a sweet and unexpected finish, try the green-tinted pastries filled with durian custard.

Nightingale 9

B7

Vietnamese ✗

329 Smith St. (bet. Carroll & President Sts.)

Subway: Carroll St   Dinner Tue – Sun
Phone: 347-689-4699
Web: www.nightingale9.com
Prices: $$

Smith Street's fresh take on Vietnamese cuisine is the brainchild of Chef Robert Newton. Nightingale 9's new home is the old Seersucker space, and the larger digs better accommodate the stream of neighborhood families out for something different. Its curious name refers to the old Brooklyn telephone exchange.

Meanwhile, the ingredient-driven menu offers a subtle take on shredded green papaya salad that is accented by nuggets of house-dried beef, mint, and crispy shallots. Grilled beef meatballs are wonderfully chewy, flavorful, and fun in your mouth. They are in turn accompanied by sheets of rice paper and water; diners moisten these sheets until they become soft, pliable, and ready to roll with meat and herbs, before being dunked in spicy *nuoc cham*.

Noodle Pudding

B5

Italian ✗✗

38 Henry St. (bet. Cranberry & Middagh Sts.)

Subway: High St   Dinner Tue – Sun
Phone: 718-625-3737
Web: N/A
Prices: $$

With Dean Martin and Frank Sinatra rotating on the playlist and a dark wood bar full of regulars, Noodle Pudding embodies all the essential qualities of a winning neighborhood spot. It's the type of place to kick back and relax, dine on consistently good food, and even sit solo but never feel "alone."

The kitchen has mastered Italian-American classics, with honest ingredients and great preparation, like the balance of acidic and sweet components in the gently poached cod *Livornese*. The tantalizing eggy-cheesy, slightly smoky-sweet, and creamy carbonara that bathes toothsome mezze rigatoni, fava beans, and tiny pork sausage meatballs is "dynomite."

Top it all off with the exemplary (and shareable) house-made cheesecake and a perfect shot of espresso.

Northeast Kingdom 😊

American 🍴

B1

18 Wyckoff Ave. (at Troutman St.)

Subway: Jefferson St
Phone: 718-386-3864
Web: www.north-eastkingdom.com
Prices: $$

Lunch & dinner daily

The importance of each ingredient's provenance is more than a policy or marketing ploy here at this Northeast Kingdom of über-local, farm-to-table cooking. Inside, it is cottage-like (if cramped) and charming with vintage chairs, exposed brick, and bare tables. Downstairs, find their wine and cocktail bar. Chef Kevin Adey's menu is immersed in sustainability and changes as frequently as the greenmarket offerings. Standouts include burgers with duck-fat fries and pot pies perhaps filled with chunks of Clawhammer Farm pork and meltingly tender root vegetables encased in a buttery and savory pastry crust. Whole animal butchery might be celebrated as the focal point of a multi-course dinner featuring a 10-month old pig raised upstate on kale and acorns.

No. 7

American 🍴🍴

C6

7 Greene Ave. (bet. Cumberland & Fulton Sts.)

Subway: Lafayette Av
Phone: 718-522-6370
Web: www.no7restaurant.com
Prices: $$

Lunch Sat – Sun
Dinner nightly

This is the type of place where you sit down, look at the menu, and say, "Does that really work?" And as far as No. 7 is concerned, it does—most of the time. With its worn-in good looks, casual vibe, and horseshoe-shaped banquettes, this perpetually packed spot accomodates group dinners.

Feast your eyes on the open kitchen, where the talented team crafts obsession-worthy dishes like the double decker broccoli tacos. The exemplary combination of flavors and textures is simply brilliant: both a soft and a crisp taco shell (with just the right grease-tinged crunch) hold a mixture of cooked broccoli, salty feta, creamy beans, and fried shallots. To balance the earthy flavors, sink into the salted chocolate and corn puff tart, served with peanut butter ice cream.

1 or 8

C1

66 S. 2nd St. (at Wythe Ave.)

Subway: Bedford Av
Phone: 718-384-2152
Web: www.oneoreightbk.com
Prices: $$

Dinner Tue – Sun

Step inside this chic Williamsburg hideaway to find a lofty and dramatically appointed room. A stark white palette complements the setting's industrial bones, which even made an appearance in an episode of *The Good Wife*.

1 or 8's kitchen turns out impressive cooked food organized as small plate appetizers. It's an ideal destination for group dining, but smaller parties should make a beeline to the impressive sushi counter. Score a seat, request the omakase, and revel in the pieces Chef Kazuo Yoshida sets before you. Soy-marinated bluefin tuna, wild Alaskan sockeye salmon, and sea scallop sprinkled with yuzu and sea salt are but a few of the piscine delights to be enjoyed. Dark miso soup poured over house-made tofu concludes the impressive meal.

Pacificana

A3

813 55th St. (at Eighth Ave.)

Subway: 8 Av
Phone: 718-871-2880
Web: N/A
Prices: $$

Lunch & dinner daily

You can thank Sunset Park's growing Asian population for the influx of excellent Chinese restaurants into this far-flung pocket of Brooklyn. Among the best of the lot is Pacificana, a bright, airy restaurant—think vaulted ceilings, jumbo windows, and an open kitchen sporting floor-to-ceiling fish tanks—tucked into a second floor space off bustling Eighth Avenue.

Dim sum carts packed to the gills roll by like temptations-on-wheels and dinner guests tuck into traditional fare like the rich, fragrant South China duck casserole alongside other treats like crispy pork over jelly fish, and tender shrimp dumplings. Chicken with crunchy mustard greens, paired with preserved black beans and a steaming bowl of fluffy white rice is nothing short of heartwarming.

Pacifico's Fine Foods

D8

Latin American 🍴🍴

798A Franklin Ave. (bet. Eastern Pkwy. & Lincoln Pl.)

Subway: Franklin Av
Phone: 917-966-2670
Web: www.pacificosfinefoods.com
Prices: $$

Lunch Sat – Sun
Dinner nightly

Gentrification has come to Crown Heights. Though 99-cent stores and West Indian eateries still dot Franklin Avenue, newcomers like the well-designed Pacifico's Fine Foods are finding a foothold in the neighborhood. Single fresh flowers add cheer to every table, and lively chatter streams from the white-walled room through open windows.

In the kitchen, Chef Shanna Pacifico, formerly of Back Forty, turns out simple but sensational dishes. Market vegetables—a smattering of lemony baby radishes, spring peas, and delicate celery—become memorable when tossed with flower petals and toasted Brazil nuts. Crispy battered chicken is tender beneath the crunch, accompanied by a thatch of lime-squeezed cilantro and Pacifico's signature fiery *piri piri* sauce.

Palo Santo

C7

Latin American 🍴

652 Union St. (bet. Fourth & Fifth Aves.)

Subway: Union St
Phone: 718-636-6311
Web: www.palosanto.us
Prices: $$

Lunch Sat – Sun
Dinner nightly

Nestled among Park Slope's brownstones, Palo Santo's ground floor space feels delightfully homey. Handmade wood furnishings, tiled flooring, and an amber-hued counter set the warmly shaded scene. The kitchen, stocked with neatly arranged produce, is set behind the counter and framed by copper pots and colorful pitchers.

The eclectic Latin cuisine utilizes local ingredients gathered from the Grand Army Plaza Greenmarket as well as those grown in the rooftop garden. The day's *anticuchos* has featured skewers of rich grilled pork liver dusted with spices; and entrées list a hearty plate of pan-roasted bluefish accompanied by sweet plantain, roasted whole in the skin and garnished with shredded cabbage slaw dressed in red wine vinegar and jalapeños.

Paulie Gee's 😀

B1

Pizza ✗

60 Greenpoint Ave. (bet. Franklin & West Sts.)

Subway: Greenpoint Av
Phone: 347-987-3747
Web: www.pauliegee.com
Prices: 😋

Dinner nightly

Owner Paul Giannone, aka Paulie Gee, channeled a lifelong love of pizza into this charmingly delicious spot that feels as if it has been around forever. Rustic in appearance, the room's cool concrete and brick are warmed by the glow of the wood-burning oven imported from Naples. From here, Giannone and his son work their magic.

The addictive crust is beguilingly moist and chewy, perfumed with smoke, and adroitly salted. Killer wood-fired pies dominates the menu with tempting combinations, excellent ingredients, and whimsical names. Offerings may include the Harry Belafontina—fontina, tomatoes, beefy meatballs, cremini mushrooms, and golden raisins. Vegans get equal respect here, with an added menu of vegan cheese and house-made vegan sausage.

The Pearl Room

A3

Contemporary ✗✗

8201 Third Ave. (at 82nd St.)

Subway: 86 St
Phone: 718-833-6666
Web: www.thepearlroom.com
Prices: $$

Lunch & dinner daily

With its jumbo garden and bright, sun-streaked dining room, this Brooklyn steady is a solid choice year-round. Most days, you'll catch a glimpse of the charming Chef/owner Anthony Rinaldi floating around, working his magic back in the kitchen and out in the dining room.

The Pearl Room is known for its vast seafood spread, and Rinaldi's wheelhouse is intricately designed fish plates like pan-fried, pine nut-crusted lemon sole or ravioli stuffed with Maine lobster, ricotta, and fresh herbs in cream sauce. But don't discount his other offerings. The menu boasts starters like house-made mozzarella with roasted peppers and marinated golden tomatoes, vegetarian and meat dishes ample enough to split, as well as a few tongue-wagging desserts.

Peter Luger ⁂

Steakhouse 🍴

178 Broadway (at Driggs Ave.)

Subway: Marcy Av
Phone: 718-387-7400
Web: www.peterluger.com
Prices: $$$$

Lunch & dinner daily

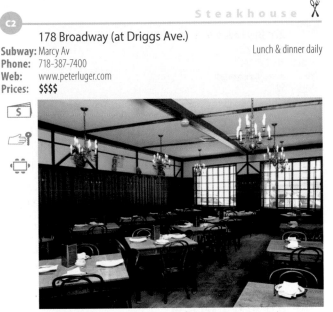

Venerated Peter Luger resides in an expansive space reminiscent of old New York and early German ale houses—an endless line of visitors only serves to reiterate how special a place this truly is. Add to that a series of imposing pane windows, wood-paneled walls, and decorative old steins, and find yourself utterly smitten.

Begin with thrillingly fatty, thick-cut bacon nearly sweet on the outside, or shrimp cocktail in a rich tomato dressing. But, what truly leaves diners speechless is that delightfully succulent Porterhouse for two, three, or four. These slabs of beautifully naked meat are simple but their marbling is a thing of complexity and perfection, sizzling in drippings. The wedge salad sets a new standard: it is an enormous and crisp slice of iceberg drowned in blue cheese dressing, chopped tomato, and more bacon. The carnivorous feast is complete when sanctified by crispy French fries or excellent creamed spinach. Properly prepped servers are cordial, yet informal and honoring.

A hunk of NY cheesecake, creamy, tart, and served with schlag, is every bit as classic as one imagines. Equally marvelous and dressed to the nines is a "Holy cow sundae"—the title speaks for itself!

Petit Oven

French 🍴

A3

276 Bay Ridge Ave. (bet. Ridge Blvd. & Third Ave.)

Subway: Bay Ridge Av
Phone: 718-833-3443
Web: www.petit-oven.com
Prices: $$

Dinner Wed– Sun

Unassuming but worth your attention, this little Bay Ridge site offers a petite, tidy room that is simply done and fills quickly. The ambience here brings a gracious welcome, and the air wears a palpable note of authenticity.

Chef/owner Katarzyna Ploszaj styles her agreeable and refreshingly relaxed cuisine through a classic French lens. Appetizers may include a novel riff on Greek salad composed of thinly shaved Brussels sprouts mingled with diced feta, a handful of black olives, sliced red onion, and a sprig of fragrant oregano all licked with olive oil and a bright hit of lemon juice. Expect equally impressive entreés like a cooked duck breast, crisped and rosy, with red onion-ginger marmalade, and duck fat-roasted potatoes scented with thyme.

Picket Fence

American 🍴

B3

1310 Cortelyou Rd. (bet. Argyle & Rugby Rds.)

Subway: Cortelyou Rd
Phone: 718-282-6661
Web: www.picketfencebrooklyn.com
Prices: $$

Lunch & dinner daily

The glory days of Ditmas Park have returned, as moneyed families refurbish their old Victorian homes lining the avenues and restaurants like Picket Fence fill the need for a no-fuss, all-American meal. This tiny café, complete with an intimate garden, bursts with friendly service that's as comforting as the food.

Families dine here over healthy salads and plates of well-made fries. Homey, delicious food headlines with walnut and honey-dressed baked brie, or a tender, gravy-covered turkey meatloaf on a brioche roll topped with loads of cheddar cheese and sweet, caramelized onions. Pair that with a tall frosted glass of Brooklyn Lager, and you may never leave.

Excellent desserts highlight a triple-layer carrot cake with vanilla-cream cheese frosting.

Pickle Shack

B7

256 Fourth Ave. (bet. Carroll & President Sts.)

Subway: Union St   Lunch & dinner daily
Phone: 347-763-2127
Web: www.pickleshacknyc.com
Prices: ⊜⊜

Start with a menu that highlights the small-batch handiwork of Brooklyn Brine Co., then add an extensive assortment of beers from Dogfish Head Craft Brewery. Toss in wood tables, inviting counter seating, and dusky blue walls, and you have this enticing pub.

Chef Neal Harden has put together a menu of suds-friendly food consisting of vegetarian snacks (think fried hop pickles with preserved lemon aïoli), and salads such as grilled romaine and Tuscan black kale with beluga lentils. Pickle Shack's lighter fare is rounded out by hearty, imaginative sandwiches crafted from local ingredients and purveyors. To that end, order the crusty artisan baguette filled with warm cannellini bean purée, grilled asparagus, and fennel-pickled beets.

Potlikker

C1

✗

338 Bedford Ave. (bet. S. 2nd & S. 3rd Sts.)

Subway: Bedford Av   Lunch & dinner Tue − Sun
Phone: 718-388-9808
Web: www.potlikkerbrooklyn.com
Prices: $$

Chef/owner Liza Queen serves up cooking with a side of Williamsburg's signature devil-may-care attitude. Though the room is bright and cheerful with pistachio-green furnishings poised against lemon-yellow walls, custom-designed warning signs are sure to elicit chuckles.

Lunchtime fare is primarily a selection of sandwiches, but even so it's clear this kitchen does everything with pride. Take the Cobb, for example, with its grilled chicken breast tucked between thick toast spread with crushed avocado and blue cheese dressing, completed by shredded lettuce and crisp, meaty bacon. Come dinnertime, the kitchen turns up the heat with a short list of seasonally inspired entrées like lamb chops paired with sweet pea flan and mint-pinot blanc jelly.

Pok Pok Ny ✿

127 Columbia St. (bet. Degraw & Kane Sts.)

Subway: Carroll St
Phone: 718-923-9322
Web: www.pokpokny.com
Prices: $$

Lunch Sat – Sun
Dinner nightly

Now housed just a few doors down from its original home on the waterfront, Pok Pok Ny is still serving its trademark wonders. The expanded space is clad in salvaged wood, exposed brick, and has a sizeable back garden. The crowds have died down enough to end those painfully long wait times.

Low key yet very serious, this remains one of the city's penultimate foodie scenes. Chef Andy Ricker has a scholarly approach and deep knowledge of Isaan culinary traditions; however, his American hand and farm-to-table ethos do leave their traces with excellent local ingredients and spice levels toned down for Brooklyn tastes. Every flavor is carefully crafted here—right down to those crowning and very complementary beers and cocktails.

A wild mushroom salad begins with a fantastic assortment of stir-fried chanterelles and creminis dressed with soy sauce, lime, mint, cilantro, and little rings of lemongrass with rice powder for crunch. Superb execution and pronounced flavors are clear in the creamy coconut curry floating with flaky, finely ground fish, thin and delicate rice noodles, as well as toasted dried chilies that are crushed tableside, lending texture and heat to this memorable dish.

Prime Meats 😊

European ✗✗

B7

465 Court St. (at Luquer St.)

Subway: Smith - 9 Sts.
Phone: 718-254-0327
Web: www.frankspm.com
Prices: $$

Lunch & dinner daily

Prime Meats stands tall and proud as a true original and local gem for German eats set to American beats. The booths in front are bright and snug, while bentwood chairs and net curtains tied into a knot add to that brasserie feel. A warm vibe and cheery servers complete the picture.

Hand-crafted sausages and burgers are all the rage here. Nibble away on homemade pretzels while perusing the lunch menu, which may be simple and sandwich-focused, but always showcases a gutsy edge. Bold flavors shine through in a creamy roasted squash soup; *jagerwurst*, a lightly charred, delicately smoky, and meaty sausage with red cabbage casserole; or Jen's German potato salad tossing waxy potato slices, chopped herbs, and thick bacon lardons in a pickled dressing.

Prospect

American ✗✗

C6

773 Fulton St. (bet. Oxford & Portland Aves.)

Subway: Lafayette Av
Phone: 718-596-6826
Web: www.prospectbk.com
Prices: $$

Dinner Mon – Sat

This Fort Greene standout offers delicious cooking and just so happens to be pretty cool, too. Barrel-aged negronis are among the offerings from a white marble bar that provides much needed real estate. Walls are lined with reclaimed planks of the Coney Island boardwalk, and genuinely hospitable service tames the perpetually packed house.

Quality trumps quantity in the streamlined selection of product-driven creations. Silken strands of house-made fettucine twirled with lemon beurre blanc and finely grated Parmesan make an enticing starter, while pan-seared skate garnished tableside with coconut milk broth redolent of lemongrass and Persian lime is an inspired entrée. Finish off with a *tres leches* cake topped with salted sugar cookie crumbs.

Purple Yam

Asian ✗

1314 Cortelyou Rd. (at Rugby Rd.)

Subway: Cortelyou Rd
Phone: 718-940-8188
Web: www.purpleyamnyc.com
Prices: $$

Lunch Sat – Sun
Dinner nightly

Filipino food authorities Amy Besa and Romy Dorotan serve up a deliciously freewheeling array of Southeast Asian treats at this inviting café, named for their homeland's adored tuber. Located in lovely Ditmas Park, a neighborhood extoled for its Victorian homes, the interior charms with soothing colors and a view of the kitchen at work.

Filipino favorites abound, as in chicken *adobo*—the bone-in pieces are browned and braised in a complex-tasting sauce of coconut sap vinegar, coconut milk, and soy sauce. Standouts might include *pancit bihon* made with rice vermicelli stir-fried with roast pork, bok choy, and bean sprouts. Other tasty options depart from the Philippines, such as sweetly spiced goat curry with fresh mango chutney.

Ramen Yebisu

Japanese ✗

126 N. 6th St. (bet. Bedford Ave. & Berry St.)

Subway: Bedford Av
Phone: 718-782-1444
Web: www.ramenyebisu.com
Prices: ⊜

Lunch & dinner daily

At this popular Williamsburg *ramen-ya*, Chef and Hokkaido native Akira Hiratsuka ladles signature bowlfuls of Sapporo-style ramen, characterized by its seafood-infused broth and wavy noodles aged for 48-hours. The results are distinct and delicious. Among the host of options to be tried are *shoyu* (soy-based), *shio* (salt-based), or the special house ramen brimming with a bounty of shellfish. A recent unique offering featured a fiery broth infused with a blend of 12 spices and fish sauce and filled with bone-in pork rib, cabbage, and red chilies.

Slurp your soup at one of two seating options in the moody, dark-walled space: perched atop tall tables or at a counter looking into the kitchen, where a refrigerator unit is stocked with custom-made noodles.

Reynard

American ✗✗

B1

80 Wythe Ave. (at N. 11th St.)

Subway: Bedford Av
Phone: 718-460-8004
Web: www.reynardsnyc.com
Prices: $$

Lunch & dinner daily

Inside Williamsburg's Wythe hotel, find this fun and *très* Brooklyn-chic dining room, thanks to restaurateur Andrew Tarlow (of Diner and Marlow & Sons). The setting's former life as a century-old cooperage is proudly honored in myriad details like original masonry and cast iron columns. Parchment-colored walls and mosaic-tile floors enhance the throwback mien. Even in the cool light of day, over a bowl of strained house-made yogurt, drizzled in golden honey and topped with granola, Reynard feels sexy.

The kitchen—equipped with a wood-burning oven— produces intriguing creations such as warm olives or red kale tossed with smoked Caesar dressing to snack on while awaiting hake chowder. Hearty entrées include oyster stew or rabbit with whole grain mustard.

River Styx

Contemporary ✗

B1

21 Greenpoint Ave. (near West St.)

Subway: Greenpoint Av
Phone: 718-383-8833
Web: www.riverstyxny.com
Prices: $$

Lunch Sat – Sun
Dinner nightly

Walk down Greenpoint Avenue and keep walking until you almost hit the East River to reach this newly launched venture. The setting is an undeniably cool combination of rough-hewn timber ceiling beams, tables embedded with shards of glazed ceramic tile, and an open kitchen installed with a wood-burning oven.

Take a look at the menu and final items like hake with raw almond butter. Sound familiar? This is the handiwork of Chef Dennis Spina, also of Roebling Tea Room. Choose from a tempting lineup and enjoy anchovies sitting by a fire; *raviolo* stuffed with Taleggio afloat in a bright green nettle broth; or morsels of braised pork dabbed with spicy tomatillo salsa. Vanilla panna cotta with blueberry and black vinegar compote is a lovely finish.

The River Café ✿

Contemporary ✕✕✕

B5

1 Water St. (bet. Furman & Old Fulton Sts.)

Subway: High St
Phone: 718-522-5200
Web: www.therivercafe.com
Prices: $$$$

Lunch Sat – Sun
Dinner nightly

Owner Buzzy O'Keefe has painstakingly restored this dreamy dwelling, in one of the most divine nooks in town. In fact, The River Café has bounced back to its very special self, despite the havoc inflicted by Hurricane Sandy. Perks that were part of its original glory remain, including free parking and an incredibly romantic space, complete with breathtaking vistas cherished by city birds and foodies from all corners of the world.

Chef Brad Steelman is still onboard, cooking his solid-as-ever cuisine. Find proof of this on the crest of well-dressed tables attended to by smooth and professional servers. Lofty windows overlooking the river and FiDi skyline just beyond serve as an ideal backdrop for such fine cuisine as sweet, creamy Dungeness crab tossed in a citrus marinade and topped with fragrant ribbons of basil. The same elegance, simplicity, and supreme freshness rule the roost in Pacific Blue shrimp prepared "Oscar Style" with a creamy Maltaise sauce and paired with white poached asparagus.

Rose bouquets atop every table are as wonderfully extravagant as the café's chocolate *marquise*, crowned with thin dark chocolate formed into the "Brooklyn Bridge" and kissed with raspberry mousse.

Roberta's

B1

Contemporary ✗

261 Moore St. (bet. Bogart & White Sts.)

Subway: Morgan Av   Lunch & dinner daily
Phone: 718-417-1118
Web: www.robertaspizza.com
Prices: $$

Bushwick's love affair with Roberta's seems stronger each year—and for good reason. With its industrial-rustic space, underground Bohemian vibe, homegrown garden, and very own Heritage Radio Network broadcasting from their backyard studio, everything here epitomizes Brooklyn-chic. Queens native Chef Carlo Mirarchi leads a talented kitchen, which headlines a variety of creatively named pizzas (Cheesus Christ), tasty sandwiches, and a smattering of fresh vegetables harvested from their rooftop garden. Start with a salad of black radishes, organic greens, glazed baby turnips, and diced apples dressed in a delicate sesame vinaigrette. Then, move on to the decadent sliced pork-collar sandwich served on house-made *bâtard* spread with spicy *gribiche*.

Roebling Tea Room

C1

Contemporary ✗

143 Roebling St. (at Metropolitan Ave.)

Subway: Lorimer St - Metropolitan Av   Lunch & dinner daily
Phone: 718-963-0760
Web: www.roeblingtearoom.com
Prices: $$

Cuisine that bristles with creativity keeps the foodie crowd coming to this rough-hewn Williamsburg café. A popular bar anchors the room's layout, which is rustically appointed with absinthe-green ceramic tiles, rusted window frames, and pale beige painted-over brick accented by vintage wallpaper. Lunch starts early and includes eye-opening options like the big pancake. Really, it's huge—baked in a cast iron skillet, laden with thinly sliced apples, and accompanied by warm maple syrup. Steak tartare with fried chickpeas and Kewpie mayonnaise satisfies savory cravings; and creamy grits and egg yolk stuffed ravioli, slicked with shrimp infused "flamingo butter" sauce, is a specialty that successfully sums up the kitchen's distinct personality.

Roman's

Italian ✗

C6

243 DeKalb Ave. (bet. Clermont & Vanderbilt Aves.)

Subway: Lafayette Av
Phone: 718-622-5300
Web: www.romansnyc.com
Prices: $$

Lunch Sat – Sun
Dinner nightly

Romans is another beloved member of that prolific restaurant family that spawned Reynard, Marlow & Sons... and counting. It's idyllically situated on one of those quaint but never quiet Brooklyn arteries, populated by freelancers, nannies, and parks.

This is a coveted area with sidewalk seating for sipping iced coffee with almond milk. The simple, small interior flickers with candlelight and serves everything its affluent clientele dreams of finding in an Italian home. House cocktails—one bitter, one sweet—are a memorable start to a meal that might include fresh *maccheroni* with cauliflower, pancetta, and porcini; or perfectly seasoned cannellini beans with *scungilli*. Some wonderfully chosen cheeses augment the pleasant desserts.

Rucola

Contemporary ✗

B6

190 Dean St. (at Bond St.)

Subway: Bergen St (Smith St.)
Phone: 718-576-3209
Web: www.rucolabrooklyn.com
Prices: $$

Lunch & dinner daily

Nestled among the brownstone-lined streets of beautiful Boerum Hill, this inviting trattoria is open all day. Rucola's attractive interior rocks that prototypical rusticity of reclaimed wood and aged mirrors, while tables are set with sprigs of fresh wild flowers.

Yogurt and granola with local honey is part of the kitchen's repertoire, but the restaurant's Northern Italian influence fully comes into focus in the evenings. Vegetable antipasti, like spicy spears of pickled fennel, are offered alongside cured meats and imported cheeses. Arugula (that's *rucola in Italiano*) is tossed with shaved radish and a celery seed vinaigrette. Enjoyable entrées include a neat block of lasagna layering pasta sheets and hearty pork ragù with a creamy béchamel sauce.

The Runner

C6

A m e r i c a n 🍴🍴

458 Myrtle Ave. (bet. Washington & Waverly Aves.)

Subway: Clinton - Washington Avs — Lunch Sat – Sun
Phone: 718-643-6500 — Dinner nightly
Web: www.therunnerbk.com
Prices: $$

Part cocktail bar, part farm-to-table restaurant, The Runner has that low-lit industrial cool that draws in passersby both day and night. With a rustic aesthetic and modern touches, it's a lovely spot to cozy up with a craft beer at the bar, where the bartender is on a first-name basis with regulars.

The menu prizes top ingredients that skew local, as in the tender L.I. fluke with succulent mussels *marinière*, made even heftier with a creamy, garlic-buttery broth of white wine, parsley, and shallots. Don't even try to share that dish; instead, greedily sop it all up with an order of hot and gently crisped "tongue bread." Finish with pistachio frangipane tart, blending sweet and nutty flavors with a dense crust and scoop of vanilla ice cream.

Runner & Stone

B7

C o n t e m p o r a r y 🍴🍴

285 Third Ave. (bet. Carroll & President Sts.)

Subway: Union St — Lunch & dinner daily
Phone: 718-576-3360
Web: www.runnerandstone.com
Prices: $$

An innate sense of purpose pervades this ambitious Gowanus operation. The name refers to the two stones used to grind grain; the location is just blocks away from where the city's first tide-water grist mill once stood; and the dining room is backed by a fantastic bakery headed by an alum of Per Se. Inside, the theme continues with walls constructed out of flour sack-formed concrete blocks.

For lunch, sandwiches on mouthwatering bread include grilled cheddar with roasted and pickled peppers on whole wheat *pain au lait*, or falafel-inspired broccoli fritters swaddled in a warm pita with shots of *harissa* and walnut-yogurt sauce. Impressive house-made pastas and the likes of roasted chicken with soft buckwheat dumplings are crowd-pleasers at dinnertime.

Rye 🐾

American 🍴

C1

247 S. 1st St. (bet. Havemeyer & Roebling Sts.)

Subway: Marcy Av　　　　　　　　　　　Lunch Sat – Sun
Phone: 718-218-8047　　　　　　　　　　Dinner nightly
Web: www.ryerestaurant.com
Prices: $$

Rye's Classic Old Fashioned—a carefully crafted swirl of liquid amber—is the perfect personification of Chef Cal Elliott's beloved establishment. Like the signature pour (strong, satisfying, and comforting), the mien of this discreetly marked spot follows suit with a space that is anchored by a reclaimed mahogany bar and accented by creaky plank flooring and exposed filament lighting.

The succinct menu boasts adept touches reflecting the kitchen's chops. An entrée of skewer-grilled shrimp and scallops was dressed with a spicy Thai-inspired vinaigrette and set upon a salad of avocado and grapefruit revealed a highly enjoyable inspiration. For dessert, molten chocolate cake was another classic that was lovingly partnered with pistachio ice cream.

The Saint Austere

Contemporary 🍴

D2

613 Grand St. (bet. Leonard & Lorimer Sts.)

Subway: Lorimer St - Metropolitan Av　　　　Dinner Mon – Sat
Phone: 718-388-0012
Web: www.thesaintaustere.com
Prices: 🍺🍺

Sometimes all one needs is a fine glass of wine and a little snack (or three). For this, The Saint Austere fits the bill nicely. Platings bring on far-flung influences—as in the *bánh Mi(lano)*, pork terrine, thinly-shaved mortadella, and house-pickled vegetables sandwiched into a toasted baguette moistened by a chili-flecked dressing. However, the menu's truest muse is a general coupling of Italian and Spanish flavors, such as pork belly *croquetas* accompanied by a dipping sauce of crushed chicken livers; or slow-cooked polenta topped with sweet onions caramelized in sausage drippings.

The spartanly adorned room offers a hospitable bar in addition to three communal tables. And the wine list proffers a gently priced selection of mostly European labels.

Samurai Mama

C1

Japanese ✕

205 Grand St. (bet. Bedford & Driggs Aves.)

Subway: Bedford Av
Phone: 718-599-6161
Web: www.samuraimama.com
Prices: 😊😊

Lunch & dinner daily

Chef Makoto Suzuki (also of Momo Sushi Shack and Bozu) dishes up an appetizing composition of mostly cooked fare at this whimsical Williamsburg gem. The Japanese vibe and flavor are quaint and impressively authentic, and diners tend to partake in preparations that include *konbu dango* (deep-fried seaweed and soybean croquettes). Chewy, salty flying fish jerky topped with pickled daikon shards, and salmon *negi* sushi "taco" cradled in a sheet of toasted nori are other highlights.

A series of quirky paintings frame the seasonally dressed communal table which may unveil such delicacies as *kinoko tsukejil* "dipping-style" udon, featuring handmade noodles crafted from California-milled flour bobbling alongside wild mushrooms in a rich and complex broth.

Saraghina

B2

Italian ✕

435 Halsey St. (at Lewis Ave.)

Subway: Utica Av
Phone: 718-574-0010
Web: www.saraghinabrooklyn.com
Prices: $$

Lunch & dinner daily

Much more than a pizzeria, Saraghina is a welcome addition to this gentrified part of Bushwick. The multi-room setting is fun and kitschy with old butcher signs, marmalade jars, and restroom signs that read "Women and children, only."

There may be no better start to an autumnal afternoon than with a grilled butternut squash, endive, radicchio, and frisée salad in a lemon-ginger dressing enjoyed in their foliage-filled back garden. Classic dishes include *fave e cicoria*, a thick purée of fava beans folded with exceptional olive oil and a nest of wilted dandelion greens; while their perfectly charred and puffy pizzas verge on legendary.

Freshly baked breakfast treats and perhaps the most epic espresso in the city also await at Saraghina.

Savoia

Italian ✕

B7

277 Smith St. (bet. Degraw & Sackett Sts.)

Subway: Carroll St   Lunch & dinner daily
Phone: 718-797-2727
Web: www.savoiarestaurant.com
Prices: $$

With its young at-home moms, lunching construction crews, and savvy foreign visitors, all walks of life are drawn to this Smith Street charmer, pastorally furnished with wooden tables and straw-seat chairs. Exposed brick and colorful tiles complement the two-room setting equipped with a wood-burning pizza oven.

Fittingly, Savoia devotes a large portion of its menu to manifold pizza offerings made in the Neopolitan tradition. There is also an ample selection of gratifying homemade pastas, like the organic buckwheat *maltagliati* with porcini mushrooms, *bresaola*, and truffle oil; as well as heartier items like the roasted pork chop with eggplant caponata and grilled *orata* with sun dried tomatoes.

Affable service adds to Savoia's casual vibe.

Selamat Pagi

Indonesian ✕

B1

152 Driggs Ave. (bet. Humboldt & Russell Sts.)

Subway: Nassau Av   Lunch Sat – Sun
Phone: 718-701-4333   Dinner Tue – Sun
Web: www.selamatpagibrooklyn.com
Prices: ⊜⊜

This curious little café in the far reaches of Greenpoint is owned by the folks behind Van Leeuwen artisanal ice cream. The whitewashed room has limited seating between the wood plank banquette and metal chairs. Dining here is utterly charming, unique, and cheap.

Selamat Pagi means "good morning" in Balinese and it greets the 'hood with coffee, pastries, and brunch; but the concise menu of fragrant and flavorful cooking keeps people coming back. Dishes include luscious compositions like *nasi campur*—chopped long bean *lawar* dressed in lime juice, galangal, and toasted coconut, served with prawn crackers, shaved red chili—and Bali fish salad seasoned with turmeric and shallot. For dessert, choose a scoop of sticky black rice or lemongrass ice cream.

Shalom Japan ⚫

D2

Fusion ✗

301 S. 4th St. (at Rodney St.)

Subway: Marcy Av
Phone: 718-388-4012
Web: www.shalomjapannyc.com
Prices: $$

Lunch Sat – Sun
Dinner Tue – Sun

A unique fusion of Jewish and Japanese cuisines is astutely realized at this Williamsburg newcomer. Husband-and-wife team Aaron Israel and Sawako Okochi have an impressive resume between them, and their charming dining room is attended to with gravitas.

Small plates progress to a handful of entrées, and a blackboard display of specials offers further enticements like *abura-age*, or fried tofu pockets filled with oozing raclette cheese and dressed with green tomato relish. Chicken breast is a pastrami-stuffed beauty presented with melted cabbage, diced potatoes, and mustard seed jus. Be sure to save room for the divine chocolate-banana bread pudding, which is made from house-baked sake *kasu* challah and sauced with decadent whiskey caramel.

606 R & D

C7

American ✗✗

606 Vanderbilt Ave. (bet. Prospect Pl. & St. Marks Ave.)

Subway: 7 Av (Flatbush Ave.)
Phone: 718-230-0125
Web: www.606rdbklyn.com
Prices: $$

Lunch Sat – Sun
Dinner nightly

A Sunday supper to end the weekend feels just right at this expanded farm-to-table restaurant, featuring a gardener's green accents and wood wainscoting. Rustic planter's boxes simply reinforce the mission. This refreshed space is narrow and deep, flanked with mirrors on one side and an open kitchen on the other.

The cuisine follows suit with seasonal vegetables and local charms that keep patrons returning for more. A (pricey) favorite among wealthy regulars, rotisserie chicken is a signature, arriving as a whole or half, bristling with watercress and yogurt. Vegetarians and carnivores alike savor the nourishing black bean soup with root vegetables and a dab of cream. Seasonal tarts like the chunky rhubarb folded with almond paste are memorable.

Sociale

B5

72 Henry St. (at Orange St)

Subway: High St
Phone: 718-576-3588
Web: www.socialebk.com
Prices: $$

Lunch & dinner daily

Although the name evokes a swinging place with cocktails and conversation, Sociale proves much more than a neighborhood social club. With true Italian hospitality and a cozy corner location across from a throw-back cinema, Sociale has become the Brooklyn Heights spot to spend a lively Friday night. Regulars wedge up to the bar for glasses of mineral-rich Italian whites or crowd into a charming, lair-like dining room, where the table inches away from yours may host your newest companion.

The menu sticks to classics, with perfectly cooked spaghetti in fresh and chunky *pomodoro* sauce; or veal loin wrapped in pancetta and drizzled with great veal jus. Come dessert, the banana and date bread pudding with Guinness gelato is absolutely delicious.

SoCo

D6

509 Myrtle Ave. (bet. Grand Ave. & Reyerson St.)

Subway: Classon Av
Phone: 718-783-1936
Web: www.socobk.com
Prices: $$

Lunch Fri – Sun
Dinner Tue – Sun

Hailing from longtime NYC favorite Negril, SoCo's kitchen (like its moniker) oozes with Southern Comfort. Yet, unlike that frat-fave liqueur, this Myrtle Avenue standout is quite grown-up. The urbane dining room grooves to a soulful soundtrack and features cement floors, walls hung with mirrors, and a popular bar beneath a yellow glow, where Edison bulbs playfully shine a spotlight on sleek young crowds.

Dishes with cheeky names and outstanding flavors have been known to steal the show—think crisp-smoked "F-Que" wings with creamy *tzatziki*. Nola's garlic-steamed mussels arrive with deliciously meaty andouille sausage and spicy habanero cream.

Bonuses range from a delectable caramel martini with vanilla-infused vodka to live music performances.

Sottocasa

B6

Pizza ✗

298 Atlantic Ave. (bet. Hoyt & Smith Sts.)

Subway: Hoyt-Schermerhorn
Phone: 718-852-8758
Web: www.sottocasanyc.com
Prices: $$

Lunch Sat – Sun
Dinner nightly

Harried Atlantic Avenue is home to this refreshingly simple spot, whose terrific Neapolitan-style pies have sent pizza aficionados into a complete tizzy. Here, Luca Arrigoni makes his magic in a two-ton clay oven imported from Naples—this traditional, wood-burning wonder is set in the tiny, open kitchen. Other accents like bare wood tables and whitewashed brick walls convey a relaxed mood, while the mini bar showcases a selection of wines.

Antipasti may include *tonno e ceci*, a zesty concoction of silky tuna, chickpeas, and capers. Pizzas hail from the Napoli—a crispy crust crowned with crushed tomatoes, salty anchovies, and creamy mozzarella—to the *Verdure* with eggplant, sweet caramelized onions, tomatoes, and mushrooms.

Speedy Romeo 😊

D6

American ✗

376 Classon Ave. (at Greene Ave.)

Subway: Classon Av
Phone: 718-230-0061
Web: www.speedyromeo.com
Prices: $$

Lunch & dinner daily

Named for a racehorse and just as focused and quick, Speedy Romeo is in for a successful run. Part tavern, part roadside grill, its kitschy décor and modern touches transform this former automotive shop into a surprisingly attractive spot.

The owner launched much of the Jean-Georges empire, and that intelligence and experience is conveyed through the smart accents and the whimsical menu that begins with Italian ingredients. Look to the wood-burning oven for smoky, meaty artichoke halves topped with lemon aïoli, sourdough crumbs, mint, and peppery arugula. Take a chance on the non-traditional but utterly fantastic pizza combinations, such as the St. Louis, layering a proper crust with meats, pickled chillies, and Midwestern Provel cheese.

St. Anselm

D1

355 Metropolitan Ave. (bet. Havemeyer and Roebling Sts.)

Subway: Bedford Av   Dinner nightly
Phone: 718-384-5054
Web: N/A
Prices: $$

Look to this roughhewn Williamsburg café for a meal of grilled, meaty satisfaction. Loud and proud carnivores, this one's for you.

The perpetually rollicking kitchen embraces grilling as its preferred method of cooking to turn out a commendable bill of fare. Razor clams, sardines, artichokes, or *haloumi* comprise the offering of sizzling "smalls," while "bigs" are founded on cuts of hormone-free meats procured from small ranches, and have included a dinner plate-sized lamb blade steak—scorched, enjoyably fatty, and deliciously salted—topped with a coin of mint-gremolata butter. Other options can include a sweet tea-brined chicken; sides like decadent spinach gratin; or Mason jar of chocolate *pot de crème* topped with *fleur de sel* and whipped cream.

Stone Park Cafe

B7

324 Fifth Ave. (at 3rd St.)

Subway: Union St   Lunch Tue – Sun
Phone: 718-369-0082   Dinner nightly
Web: www.stoneparkcafe.com
Prices: $$

At this corner location, large windows peer onto Park Slope's vibrant Fifth Avenue thoroughfare and small park, attracting neighborhood couples and families seeking worldly and creative cuisine.

A three-course, $35 prix-fixe Market menu offers excellent value and admirable cooking. Expect small plates like grilled baby octopus with Spanish chorizo, fingerling potatoes, and preserved lemon. Fresh pastas and hearty entrées such as grilled hanger steak with black pepper spätzle and balsamic-veal reduction also star here.

The light, airy interior has exposed brick, pale sage walls, a long bar near the entrance for pre-dinner cocktails, and a candlelit, sunken dining room with linen-topped tables. Weather permitting, alfresco sidewalk seating is available.

Strong Place

B6

270 Court St. (bet. Butler & Douglass Sts.)

Subway: Bergen St (Smith St.)
Phone: 718-855-2105
Web: www.strong-place.com
Prices: $$

Lunch Fri – Sun
Dinner nightly

Strong Place is a Cobble Hill favorite for its epic beer list, which offers more than 20 brews on tap plus over ten bottled options. Kick back, unwind, and drink up; the vibe is chill, and chunky tables with metal seating render a comfortable, vaguely industrial look.

The snacks pair perfectly with their frosty pints—imagine spicy duck fat edamame, Cajun boiled peanuts, or a platter of iced shellfish from the raw bar. Stay on for dinner, because the menu offers plenty of proper options. Smooth asparagus and fennel soup sprinkled with crushed bacon gains its silken texture from puréed red bliss potatoes; while the thick, juicy lamb burger is topped with creamy feta cheese and accompanied by sun-dried tomato ketchup and rosemary-salt tossed French fries.

Sushi Katsuei

C8

210 Seventh Ave. (at Third St.)

Subway: 7 Av (9th St.)
Phone: 718-788-5338
Web: www.sushikatsuei.com
Prices: $$

Lunch Sat – Sun
Dinner nightly

Park Slope's serious sushi den is the kind of place where the *itamae* will adamantly decline requests for soy sauce. But rest assured it comes from a place of love, because that beautiful piece of nigiri has already been brushed with soy sauce, sprinkled with yuzu and sea salt, or dabbed with *yuzu koshu*. In other words, it's fantastic as is.

A handful of straightforward cooked items like free range chicken teriyaki or tempura udon are great if the kids are in tow, but the real focus is sushi best enjoyed in an omakase that won't break the bank. Be sure to choose the option that includes sashimi and begin this repast with velvety slices of medium fatty tuna and sparkling sea bass, followed by a maki of mackerel, slivered cucumber and pickled ginger.

Tabaré

C1

221 S. 1st St. (bet. Driggs Ave. & Roebling St.)

Subway: Bedford Av
Phone: 347-335-0187
Web: www.tabarenyc.com
Prices: $$

Lunch Sat – Sun
Dinner nightly

Spanish tuna and black olive empanadas, homemade pastas, and the market-driven likes of a summery chilled soup made of Cubanelle peppers all deliciously co-exist at the charming Tabaré, where the cuisine of Uruguay headlines the delightful roster. Attractively rustic, the compact dining room is lined by slats of unpolished wood, and provides seating along a colorful fabric-covered banquette. The bar—like the back patio—is an inviting roost.

Tabaré's cooking uses local product and represents the Italian-Spanish influences that color the kitchen's creations. This includes *malfatti*, luscious ricotta dumplings adorned with squash blossoms wilted under a drizzle of hot butter and white truffle oil; or grass-fed skirt steak sided by savory *chimichurri*.

Taci's Beyti

B4

1955 Coney Island Ave. (bet. Ave. P & Quentin Rd.)

Subway: Kings Hwy (16th St.)
Phone: 718-627-5750
Web: www.tacisbeyti.com
Prices: $$

Lunch & dinner daily

Find safety from the evil eye at Taci's Beyti, a bright Turkish spot tucked into a busy thoroughfare in Midwood, where smiling strangers chat at communal tables amid dozens of *nazar boncugu* amulets. Homey and cozy, families dig into rustic dishes as servers spring to and fro with platters of golden, fresh, fragrant food and pile tables high with *pide*, *tabuli*, grape leaves, and almond-stuffed apricots.

Turkish options are few and far between in this predominately Orthodox neighborhood, and dishes here reflect this mergence of ethnicities, as in the unexpected but appealing combination of hummus topped with pastrami. Indulge in dishes that focus on vivid Aegean flavors, like the artichoke heart salad with potatoes and sweet peas (a meal unto itself).

Take Root ✿

B6

Contemporary ✗

187 Sackett St. (bet. Henry & Hicks Sts.)

Subway: Carroll St
Phone: 347-227-7116
Web: www.take-root.com
Prices: $$$$

Dinner Thu – Sat

New York foodies seeking a breath of fresh air should make their way to Take Root for one of the most personal culinary endeavors they'll ever experience.

Chef Elise Kornack and wife Anna Hieronimus have produced a homey setting that accommodates a mere handful of lucky patrons each night. The dining room, accented with pale sage walls, bamboo flooring, and potted greenery, is the domain of Ms. Hieronimus, while Chef Kornack oversees the immaculate kitchen. The team works in tandem when it comes to presenting the uniquely composed plates, and what results is that rare gem of a restaurant where the head chef prepares every morsel from start to finish.

Substitutes are not offered on the solitary tasting menu, but there's little chance you'll want to miss out on what's to come. A stimulating salt and vinegar potato croquette is the opening act for the likes of salt-roasted golden beets nestled in slow-cooked egg yolk; or velvety macadamia nut soup with coriander sprouts. Hand-rolled tortellini stuffed with English pea purée in a Parmesan consommé, or seared quail over wheatberry salad dressed with lobster jus is deliciously sealed by a pink grapefruit sponge cake with chamomile ice cream.

517

Talde

Asian ✗✗

C8

369 Seventh Ave. (at 11th St.)

Subway: 7 Av (9th St.)
Phone: 347-916-0031
Web: www.taldebrooklyn.com
Prices: $$

Lunch Sat – Sun
Dinner nightly

This corner of Park Slope is the domain of Chef Dale Talde, whose forte for cooking creative pan-Asian delights at glitzy hot spots has been astutely translated here. Carved woodwork and figurines define this sexy venue that, by virtue of its location, is also family-friendly.

His menu invokes the flavors of China, Japan, Thailand, Korea, as well as the Philippines. Wonton noodle soup is not to be missed: pork-and-chive dumplings poached in a rich, cloudy broth stocked with springy noodles, tender pork shoulder, wilted greens, and a six-minute egg. Miso-marinated salmon is plated with puffed bulgur, pickled plums, and *salsa verde*; while local corn is tossed with long beans and lemongrass-Kaffir lime butter for a light yet delightful bite.

Tanoreen 😊

Middle Eastern ✗✗

A3

7523 Third Ave. (at 76th St.)

Subway: 77 St
Phone: 718-748-5600
Web: www.tanoreen.com
Prices: $$

Lunch & dinner Tue – Sun

One of the city's finest Middle Eastern experiences is tucked into an unassuming Bay Ridge corner and run by Chef/owner Rawia Bishara and her daughter.

Meals graciously commence with pickled vegetables and *za'atar*-dusted flatbread and are followed by a tableful of unique plates brimming with flavors and colors. Turkish salad is actually a bright red tomato spread shot with *harissa* and dressed with bits of diced cucumber and a drizzle of excellent olive oil. Appetizers are numerous, but try to fit in the chicken *fetti*: an entrée of basmati rice pilaf studded with toasted, broken vermicelli and topped with spicy bits of chicken, slivered toasted almonds, a generous drizzle of yogurt-tahini sauce, and chopped parsley for a fresh, final note.

Thistle Hill Tavern

B8

American ✕

441 Seventh Ave. (at 15th St.)

Subway: 15 St - Prospect Park
Phone: 347-599-1262
Web: www.thistlehillbrooklyn.com
Prices: $$

Lunch Sat – Sun
Dinner nightly

At this offshoot from the team behind Talde, you can also expect highly creative cooking, but this time the accent is decidedly American. Set along a corner, this is a fine spot for dining alfresco; inside, find a charming assemblage of sports memorabilia and servers flitting around.

Locals head to this South Slope tavern to fill up on hearty cooking that hints of the Mediterranean but is best typified by the likes of pulled pork sliders tucked between a bun, stuffed with pickled ramp and spicy mayonnaise; or crunchy fried chicken, drizzled with black pepper country gravy and sided by a cheddar biscuit. Wrap up the contemporary flavors offered here with apple pie. The deep-fried pocket is accompanied by a buttery apple cider sauce and cinnamon gelato.

Traif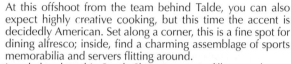

C2

Contemporary ✕

229 South 4th St. (bet. Havemeyer & Roebling Sts.)

Subway: Marcy Av
Phone: 347-844-9578
Web: www.traifny.com
Prices: $$

Dinner Tue – Sun

Small plates smacked with flavor are the dishes du jour at this rollicking eatery. The moniker translates to "forbidden" in Yiddish, and the renegade menu displays an affinity for pork and shellfish. From the open kitchen, Chef Jason Marcus and his team send a steady stream of solid creations like cornmeal-dusted fried green tomatoes with Old Bay aïoli and Tabasco sauce. Head-on prawns, pan-roasted in foie gras fat with wild mushrooms and spring onion, are served on a slice of toast thick enough to absorb all the savory drippings. For dessert, try the homemade praline layered with rosemary ice cream and chopped hazelnuts.

The narrow space is muted with pale grey walls but enhanced by a mural of cartoon colors and an especially pleasant back patio.

Umi NOM

D6

433 DeKalb Ave. (bet. Classon Ave. & Taaffe Pl.)

Subway: Classon Av
Phone: 718-789-8806
Web: www.uminom.com
Prices: $$

Lunch Sat
Dinner Mon – Sat

Discerning Pratt students likely inspired the team behind Umi NOM, a fun and adventurous area standout. Outfitted in wood paneling and pew-like benches, the narrow space incorporates intriguing design elements and bamboo ornaments to keep the eyes as pleased as the palate—and rises well above the typical takeout joints that line this unremarkable block.

The lack of a liquor license is all but forgotten with a sip of the thirst-quenching calamansi juice to pair with fusion tacos stuffed with strips of pig's ear, pickled onions, smoked spicy salsa, and more. Don't miss the *pad krapow* made with ground beef, long beans, Thai chilies, and clove-like holy basil. Pork belly adobo, braised for three hours in coconut milk and spices, is a thing of beauty.

The Vanderbilt

C7

570 Vanderbilt Ave. (at Bergen St.)

Subway: 7 Av (Flatbush Ave.)
Phone: 718-623-0570
Web: www.thevanderbiltnyc.com
Prices: $$

Lunch Sat – Sun
Dinner nightly

Casual dining with a serious pedigree should be no surprise when Saul Bolton and Ben Daitz are involved. Nothing is stuffy, but each dish is skillfully prepared with much dependability. Servers are engaged and fire up great conversation without overstaying their welcome. The bar is perfect for solo dining, while upholstered seats and weathered-wood panels complete the corner space. The chef's talents with charcuterie make the kielbasa near-obligatory; pork belly with grits and fried green tomatoes is also super tasty. Weekday happy hour brings a great roster of cocktails, rum punch, wine, and cheap bites like fried pickles or hushpuppies.

Brooklyn Bangers is their spin-off that creates all the sausages served here as well as at a handful of other spots.

Vinegar Hill House 🐾

C5

American ✗

72 Hudson Ave. (near Water St.)

Subway: York St
Phone: 718-522-1018
Web: www.vinegarhillhouse.com
Prices: $$

Lunch Sat – Sun
Dinner nightly

Find this carriage house just steps from the historic Commandant's House and Navy Yard, in a neighborhood that is quickly becoming a beacon for artisans. After its full recovery from Superstorm Sandy, this one-time butcher shop and ever-popular haunt is again as distinguished and delicious as ever.

Packed to the rafters with locals, this "house" boasts quality, sustainable products prepared in a wood-burning oven. A wonderfully broiled grapefruit topped with puffed rice mixed with shrimp paste, or liver pâté topped with pistachios display an inventive mix of global ingredients. Favorites like pappardelle with shad roe and lemon zest, or caramelized pork chops with creamy grits are flooded with flavor.

Big bonus: Hillside resides only doors away.

Waterfalls Café 🐾

Middle Eastern ✗

B6

144 Atlantic Ave. (bet. Clinton & Henry Sts.)

Subway: Borough Hall
Phone: 718-488-8886
Web: N/A
Prices: 😊😊

Lunch & dinner daily

There is no shortage of excellent mint tea and warm pita being offered in this diverse borough, but Waterfalls Café keeps patrons returning for its meticulously prepared cuisine and genuine hospitality. The dedicated and benevolent owner watches over his small, colorful restaurant accented with intricate wood carvings and shelves of vases.

The menu begins with shareable appetizers like well-made hummus and lesser known dishes such as a Syrian salad spotlighting fresh mint. Everything here is made-to-order, including the delicious spiced lamb *lahmbajin* "pizza" on a flat pita, and the *moujadarra*, a lentil salad perfumed with cumin, allspice, and nutty cracked wheat topped with fried onions. Wonderful desserts include the sticky-sweet honey cake, *basbousa*.

Xixa ⊗

C2

241 S. 4th St. (bet. Havemeyer & Roebling Sts.)

Subway: Marcy Av   Dinner Tue – Sun
Phone: 718-388-8860
Web: www.xixany.com
Prices: $$

Chef Jason Marcus' follow-up to Traif (just down the street) is a Mexican-accented romp flaunting the chef's trademark whimsy. The beverage list is arranged by style, so sparkling wines appear under the heading of Liberace and seductive reds like pinot noir under the title Scarlet O'Hara.

As for the food, the extensive menu has fun too. The array offers the likes of *chiles rellenos*, served as a mélange of roasted peppers slicked with sweet juices and house-made burrata; or grilled carrots *elote*, dressed with honey butter, sprinkles of grated feta, and lime. Their mad scientist version of fish tacos features an *achiote*-rubbed hamachi collar plated with pounded and fried sweet plantain coated with masa, Brussels sprouts slaw, and pickled onions.

Zenkichi

C1

77 N. 6th St. (at Wythe Ave.)

Subway: Bedford Av   Dinner nightly
Phone: 718-388-8985
Web: www.zenkichi.com
Prices: $$

This exceptional Japanese brasserie in Williamsburg bears an utterly unique setting. Pay attention, or you'll miss the entry— the wood-armored façade is a sly indication of its existence. Step inside and receive warm greetings all around, followed by an escorted journey to your private dining booth on one of the floors above. Each booth is sequestered by bamboo shades, while dark wood and minimal lighting further elevate the sense of intimacy. When you need assistance, ring the tabletop buzzer.

Zenkichi's omakase is a big draw, but items may also be ordered à la carte. These may highlight house-made tofu drizzled with chilled dashi; *maguro* carpaccio arranged over shredded carrots and dressed with a ginger sauce; or grilled *jidori* chicken with *yuzu kosho*.

Zizi Limona

D2

Mediterranean ✗

129 Havemeyer St. (at S. 1st St.)

Subway: Lorimer St - Metropolitan Av

Phone: 347-763-1463

Web: www.zizilimona.com

Prices: ⊛⊛

Lunch Fri – Sun
Dinner nightly

This inviting and low-key café is a luscious addition to Williamsburg's already diverse array of dining options. A trio of skilled partners have come together to highlight the home-style cooking of Israel and Morocco.

The shawarma wrap is a necessary lunchtime indulgence, made with bits of chicken cooked in lamb's fat, spiced with gusto, and wrapped with a spread of incredible hummus, charred red onion, and preserved lemon. Begin with starters like grilled baby eggplant with arugula and feta; or try the hearty 5-hour *bureka* stuffed with slow-cooked oxtail, black olives, and crushed tomato.

Colorful tile lends a distinctive flair to the inviting room embellished with shelves of product for sale such as spices, olive oil, and rosewater.

Avoid the search for parking. Look for ⊜.

Queens

Queens

Nearly as large as Manhattan, the Bronx, and Staten Island combined, Queens covers 120 square miles on the western end of Long Island. Reputedly the most ethnically varied district in the world, its diversified nature is reflected in the thousands of immigrants who arrive here each year for its affordable housing, strong sense of community, and cultural explosion. Such a unique convergence of cultures results in this stately borough's predominantly global and very distinctive flavor. Though Hurricane Sandy was especially damaging to the Rockaways, the streets of Queens continue to prosper with amazing and affordable international eats even today.

GLOBE-TROTTING

Begin your around-the-world feast in Astoria, a charming quarter of old-world brick row houses and Mediterranean groceries. Stroll through its quaint streets to discover grilled octopus bookended by baklava at one of the many terrific Greek joints. Prolong your culinary spree over juicy kebabs at **Little Egypt** on Steinway Street; or chow on equally hearty Czech *tlačenka* at the ever-popular **Bohemian Hall & Beer Garden**. On lazy days, brew buffs can be found at Astoria's hottest beer havens— think **Sweet Afton** for an intimate setting with a serious selection or the sublime **Studio Square** for the ultimate alfresco experience. Order a dish from their Garden Grill menu and find an airy corner to sip from their selection of suds. Showcasing equally exquisite beverages alongside beautifully baked goods, **Leli's Bakery** may be a relatively new arrival to Astoria's scene but

offerings as **Shake Shack** courtesy of restaurateur, Danny Meyer, and **Uptown Brasserie** from the much raved about **Red Rooster** chef/owner, Marcus Samuelsson. Frequent flyers with refined palates will appreciate Dave Cook's *Eating in Translation*, a daily newsletter citing fantastic food finds at unusual locations—including, yes, airports!

hooks its troops with age-old roots—their commercial kitchen in the Bronx has been supplying fine dining establishments with a wealth of sweetness since time immemorial. Founded in 1937, **La Guli** is an acclaimed Italian *pasticceria* whose expert talent has been feeding families with rich and creamy cakes and cookies. Staying true to tradition, **The Lemon Ice King of Corona**, brought to you by Family Benfaremo, is a nostalgic ode to Italian ice complete with sugar-free selections for health-embattled hordes hooked on sweet.

Travelling south east, **La Boulangerie** brings a tantalizing part of France to Forest Hills by means of fresh-baked loaves of white bread and crusty, piping-hot baguettes. Of course, cheese couples best with bread, and the choices are abundant at **Leo's Latticini** in Corona. Perhaps surprisingly, eating in **Terminal C** at La Guardia Airport is now considered a gastronomic delight with wonderful food and beverage outposts churned out by star chefs like Andrew Carmellini, Michael Lomonaco, and many more. Hopping airports, JFK's **Delta Terminal 4** is fast becoming known as a culinary emporium replete with such acclaimed

Moving from terminals to terrific art galleries, **M. Wells Dinette** housed inside MoMA PS 1 delivers some insanely inventive offerings to artistically curious visitors and the lucky locals of Long Island City. Proffering an imaginative blend of diner signatures, Quebecois favorites, and "are you serious!?" combos, this sequel to the original, very outstanding diner continues to charm crowds by simply doing their thing. Further enhancing this quarter's global repute is **Güllüoglu**, a Turkish bakery and café whose elegant space and tasty bites bring Istanbul to life. But for a taste of home in this dominantly diverse stretch, cozy **Café Norma** is every Ridgewood

resident's go-to destination for classic comfort food.

ASIA MEETS THE AMERICAS

Flushing still reigns as Queens' most vibrant Asian haven and locals are always dropping in for dim sum, Henan specialties, or a savory bowl of hot *pho* like you'd find street side in Saigon. Food vendors at Flushing's mini-

malls offer feasts from far flung corners of China that are light on the pockets but big on flavors. Of both local note and city-wide acclaim, **New World Mall Food Court** is a clean and airy space serving excellent Asian fare. You'll find everything at these inviting stalls from hand-pulled noodles (at **Lanzhou**) and fiery Sichuan dishes at **Chengdu Snacks**, to Taiwanese shaved ice for the end of the night. And the Chinese offerings don't stop here. Over on Main Street, vegans are tendered love and care at **New Bodai Vegetarian** where such kosher-friendly dishes as vegetarian duck and seaweed sesame rolls have the crowds returning. Meanwhile, **Mingle Beer House** keeps the party hopping with a unique brew of bottles poppin' and karaoke

screens flashing. Make your way east to find **Queens County Farm Museum**, considered one of the largest working farms in the city that supports sustainable farming, farm-to-table meals, and is rife with livestock, a greenhouse, and educational programs. Speaking of livestock, **Chand Halal Meat** is a small, specialty market where the butchers know your name and game: beef, goat, or lamb. From Flushing to Floral Park, **Real Usha Sweets & Snacks** cooks India's favorite street eats from first-rate ingredients. If home is where your heart is, then have them cater your next party with such treats as *chana chor, papadi,* and banana chips—a Kerala specialty. Also reminiscent of flavors from this sub-continent, **Singh's Roti Shop and Bar** prepares Caribbean delicacies like curry chicken, saltfish, and *aloo pie* to gratify its contiguous community. Shifting gears from the south to the core of the continent, as many as 40,000 Central Asians immigrated to New York after the fall of the Soviet Union. They staked their claim in Forest Hills, and **King David Kosher Restaurant** remains a paragon among elder statesmen as well as their large, loud, and vibrant families craving Bukharian specialties.

Energy and variety personify Elmhurst, the thriving hearth to immigrants primarily from Latin America, China, and Southeast Asia. **The Royal Kathin**, a celebration that occurs at the end of Thailand's rainy season, pays homage to the spirit of Buddhist monks. While Elmhurst's adaptation of this festival may lack the floods, it certainly proffers a bounty of authentic Thai bites. Whitney Avenue is home to a booming restaurant row with an array of small Southeast Asian storefronts. Indulge your *gado gado* yearning at **Upi Jaya** before getting your *laksa* on at **Taste Good**. Elmhurst spans the globe, so if the powerful and pungent flavors of Southeast Asia don't fit your bill, relocate from Asia to the Americas by indulging in thick, creamy Greek yogurt at **Kesso Foods**, founded in 1986. This mini shop in East Elmhurst caters to area residents; whereas **Cannelle Patisserie**'s unapologetically decadent goodies keep carb-addicts returning and locals buzzing.

Jackson Heights is home to a large South Asian community. Take in the bhangra beats blaring from cars rolling along 74th Street, a dynamic commercial stretch of Indian markets, Bengali sweet shops, and Himalayan-style eateries serving *tandoori* specialties and steaming Tibetan *momos*. Following the fact that Latin Americans make up a large part of the demographic here, Roosevelt Avenue swarms with authentic taquerias, aromatic Colombian coffee shops, and sweet Argentinean spots as if to satiate their assorted tastes.

WANDERING THROUGH WOODSIDE

Take this thriving thoroughfare west to Woodside, where Irish bars mingle with spicy Thai spots. Once home to an enormous Irish population, Woodside now shares its streets with Thai and Filipino communities even if kelly green awnings of decade-old pubs continue to dot these blocks and clover-covered doors advertise in Gaelic. Positioned alongside **Donovan's**, an age-old Irish respite grilling up one of the best burgers in town, is **Little Manila**—an eight-block stretch of Roosevelt Avenue where you can find Filipino groceries galore. Find these same folks join the lines outside **Jollibee**, an ultra-popular fast-food chain serving up flavors from home. If Filipino sounds too funky, then rest assured that **Piemonte Ravioli** carries every choice of fresh-made pasta for an Italian *cena con la famiglia*. Down south in Sunnyside, eat your way through Korea, Columbia, Mexico, Romania, China, and Turkey. And every year in late June, **The New York City Food Film Festival** features food and film enthusiasts eager to view screenings of food films while noshing on a variety of lip-smacking nibbles.

Queens

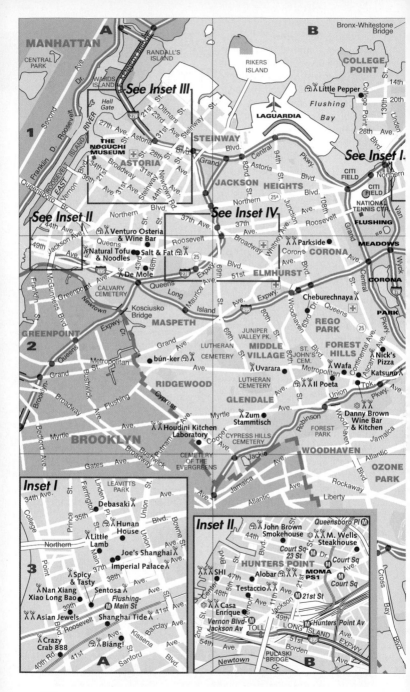

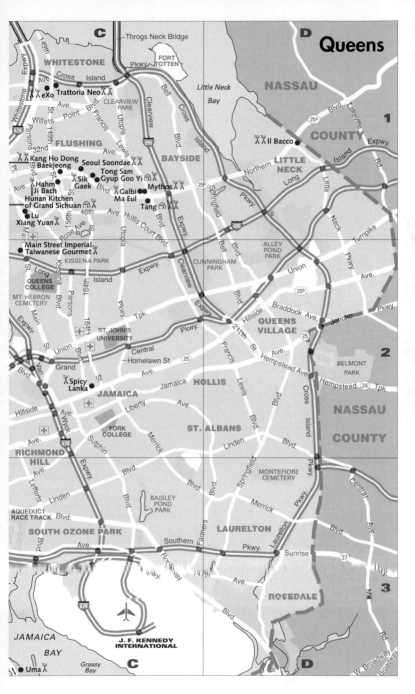

C Throgs Neck Bridge

D Queens

WHITESTONE

FORT TOTTEN

NASSAU

Cross Island Pkwy.

149th Ave.

Ave.

Whitestone Expwy.

I-678

Parsons

X eXo
XX Trattoria Neo

Point Blvd.

Francis Lewis Blvd.

CLEARVIEW PARK

Willets Ave.

Utopia

Clearview Expwy.

I-295

Bell Blvd.

Cross Island Blvd.

Little Neck Bay

BAYSIDE

Blvd. Lakeville

25A

COUNTY

1

Long Island Expwy.

LITTLE NECK

XX Il Bacco

149th Ave.

FLUSHING

32nd Ave.

XX Kang Ho Dong
Baekjeong

Parsons Blvd.

Ave.

56th Ave.

X Hahm
Ji Bach

X Sik
Gaek

Seoul Soondae XX
Tong Sam
Gyup Goo Yi X

X Galbi
Ma Eul

Mythos X X

Northern Blvd.

Springfield Blvd.

Little Neck Pkwy.

Long Island Expwy.

495

Turnpike

Hunan Kitchen
of Grand Sichuan X
X Lu
Xiang Yuan X

46th Ave.

Hollis Court Blvd.

Utopia Blvd.

Rose Ave.

Main St.

Tang XX

Clearview Expwy.

ALLEY POND PARK

25A

Main Street Imperial X
Taiwanese Gourmet X

KISSENA PARK

Kissena Blvd.

Island

Expwy.

CUNNINGHAM PARK

Union Tpke.

25B

Long Island Expwy.

QUEENS COLLEGE

164th St.

Parsons Blvd.

MT. HEBRON CEMETERY

St.

Main St.

Union Blvd.

ST. JOHN'S UNIVERSITY

Central

Homelawn St.

Tpke.

212th St.

Francis Lewis Blvd.

Hillside Ave.

Braddock Ave.

QUEENS VILLAGE

Jericho

Hillside Ave.

25

2

Van Wyck Expwy.

Grand Ave.

Ave. 25

BELMONT PARK

JAMAICA

X Spicy
Lanka

Jamaica Ave.

HOLLIS

Hempstead Ave.

Cross Island Pkwy.

Hempstead Tpk. 24

NASSAU

Hillside Ave.

Liberty Ave.

ST. ALBANS

Lewis Ave.

Springfield Blvd.

COUNTY

RICHMOND HILL

I-678

York College

Sutphin Blvd.

Merrick Blvd.

Linden Blvd.

Linden Blvd.

AQUEDUCT RACE TRACK

Lefferts Blvd.

Linden Blvd.

Van Wyck Expwy.

Blvd.

BAISLEY POND PARK

Farmers Blvd.

MONTEFIORE CEMETERY

Springfield Blvd.

LAURELTON

Merrick Blvd.

Laurelton Pkwy.

Central Ave.

Blvd.

SOUTH OZONE PARK

Southern Ave.

Rockaway Blvd.

Sunrise

27

3

I-678

X4th Ave.

ROSEDALE

JAMAICA BAY

X Uma

Grassy Bay

J. F. KENNEDY INTERNATIONAL

C

D

W. Broadway
Broadway

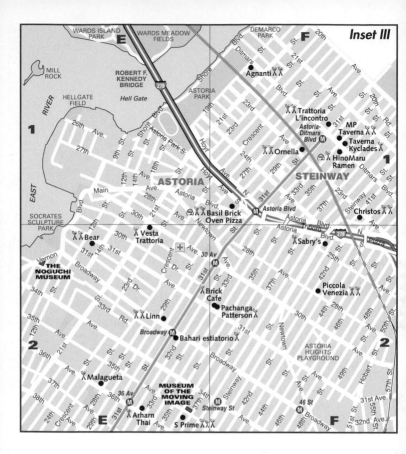

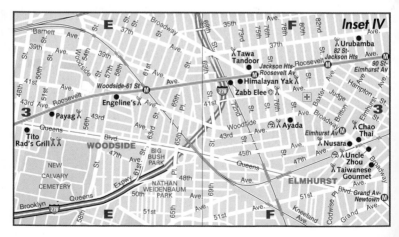

Agnanti

Greek ✕✕

F1

19-06 Ditmars Blvd. (at 19th St.)

Subway: Astoria - Ditmars Blvd
Phone: 718-545-4554
Web: www.agnantimeze.com
Prices: $$

Lunch & dinner daily

Situated on a corner lot, this taverna offers stunning panoramas of midtown, the Queensboro Bridge, and Astoria Park; on sunny days, outdoor tables speckle the front area. The view alone sets this darling apart from the host of Greek restaurants that popularized Astoria as a dining destination.

Yet the food offers its own view of Greek cuisine. Here, East meets West in a menu section reserved for Turkish classics with a unique spin, such as *midia dolma* or mussels with pine-nut studded rice. Other usual suspects also make an appearance including tzatziki with cucumber, lemon, and garlic—a marvelous accompaniment to zucchini-and-cheese croquettes. But don't fill up until you've sampled smoky swordfish kabobs basted with rosemary and lemon sauce.

Alobar 🐵

American ✕✕

B3

46-42 Vernon Blvd. (bet. 46th Rd. and 47th Ave.)

Subway: Vernon Blvd - Jackson Av
Phone: 718-752-6000
Web: www.alobarnyc.com
Prices: $$

Lunch Wed – Sun
Dinner Tue – Sun

Hailed for its inventive cooking and talented butchering, Alobar boasts a vast and deep dining room adorned with antiques and slate floors. Blonde wood ceilings offer a great contrast to worn wood tables, but all eyes are fixed upon the open kitchen packed with helpful servers and zealous cooks. You may find them preparing an assortment of pickles as a prelude to smoky seared foie gras and potato pierogies with an apple- horseradish- and cheese-sauce; or a finger-licking masterpiece of fried chicken with chipotle honey for dipping. Orecchiette and cheese with cubes of pancetta is an elevated version of mac and cheese carbonara; while warm salted caramel bread pudding with vanilla custard evokes classic Americana infused with an expert Italian twist.

Arharn Thai

Thai ✗

E2

32-05 36th Ave. (bet. 32nd & 33rd Sts.)

Subway: 36 Av
Phone: 718-728-5563
Web: www.thaiastoria.com
Prices: 😊😊

Lunch & dinner daily

Dishes burst with delightfully refreshing flavor here at Arharn Thai. The small space is bright and clean, arranged with glass-topped tables, decked with artifacts from the motherland, and equipped with two flat screen TVs.

An organized kitchen spins out goodies like *khaum jep*: steamed dumplings stuffed with ground chicken, shrimp, crabmeat, and meaty mushrooms, served with a wonderfully sticky- garlicky- and salty-dipping sauce. The exquisitely tender *gob kra prow* (frog legs) are marinated and fried until golden, then cooked with garlic, chili peppers, onions, coconut milk, and Penang curry paste. Roasted eggplant arrives white, silky, and sublime, tossed in a light and vibrant salad of citrus-lime sauce, then crowned with flaky dried shrimp.

Asian Jewels

Seafood ✗✗

A3

133-30 39th Ave. (bet. College Point Blvd. & Prince St.)

Subway: Flushing - Main St
Phone: 718-359-8600
Web: www.tunseng.com
Prices: $$

Lunch & dinner daily

Arguably the best dim sum in Flushing, this spectacular gem is an absolute must for anyone seeking serious seafood and very authentic Cantonese cooking. A longtime resident of 39th Avenue, the expansive dining room is outfitted with round, banquet-style tables, bamboo plants, and ornate chandeliers.

Let the feasting begin with memorable crab-and-pork soup dumplings, before moving on to the thrill-inducing dim sum carts. Taste the likes of steamed rice rolls with honey-roast pork; pork spareribs with rice starch and black beans; chicken and ham wrapped in yuba; and poached jellyfish with scallions and sesame. The signature Dungeness crab—steamed and stir-fried with ginger and green onions, served with Japanese eggplant and garlic—is simply outstanding.

Ayada 😊

F3

Thai 🍴

77-08 Woodside Ave. (bet. 77th & 78th Sts.)

Subway: Elmhurst Av
Phone: 718-424-0844
Web: N/A
Prices: $$

Lunch Mon – Fri
Dinner nightly

Warm, family-focused, and just a stone's throw from a prominent Buddhist temple, Ayada is as dedicated to Thai cuisine as those sepia-toned photos of the royal family displayed on its celadon walls. Hailing from the Phichit province in Northern Thailand, owner Duangjai Thammasat brings an affinity for balancing the sweet, sour, salty, and spicy in complex curries and noodles to her quiet corner space.

Made with pristine ingredients, each dish showcases the kitchen's creativity, such as the deeply flavored Penang duck in an addictive orange curry—abundant coconut milk calms the fiery notes. Pungent *kaeng som* is a sour curry that weaves lemongrass, Kaffir lime leaves, ginger, and galangal with broccoli, shrimp, and eggs for deliciously complex results.

Bahari estiatorio

E2

Greek 🍴

31-14 Broadway (bet. 31st & 32nd Sts.)

Subway: Broadway
Phone: 718-204-8968
Web: www.bahariestiatorio.com
Prices: $$

Lunch & dinner daily

Go hungry to Bahari estiatorio, a classic Greek-American restaurant where families gather for solid dishes with a hint of rusticity. Not trying to be anything more, the simple décor—featuring dozens of shutters hanging on bright blue walls—is refreshing rather than indifferent, as clear thought went into making the two open rooms feel embracing.

Head straight to the *Mageirefta* portion of the menu, a collection of traditional casserole dishes showcased at the front of the restaurant. Though pre-prepared, glorious kabobs and plates like *gemista me kima*-stuffed tomatoes with rice, herbs, and beef can make for an entire meal. Daily dessert specials like a custardy *galaktoboureko* pie provide the perfect ending to this big, fat, Greek feast.

Basil Brick Oven Pizza

F1

Italian ✗✗

28-17 Astoria Blvd. (bet. 28th & 29th Sts.)

Subway: Astoria Blvd   Lunch & dinner Thu – Tue
Phone: 718-204-1205
Web: www.basilbrickoven.com
Prices: $$

Astoria now has dibs on some of the best pizza around, thanks to this recently expanded little pizzeria-cum-restaurant. In addition to quadrupling capacity and adding a lovely garden patio, Chef Barbos has augmented the already massive pizza menu with a handful of hearty pastas and entrées.

Masterfully done *pizzucca*, topped with herbed pumpkin walnut sauce, homemade mozzarella, pancetta, and *Parmigiano Reggiano* is a luscious choice. Or, go for *il polpettone*, a wonderfully puffy and golden brown *panino*, stuffed with beef meatballs, tomato sauce, and olive oil. The *lasagna* verde—a unique potato-pesto version topped with mozzarella and a sprinkling of breadcrumbs—is served with pesto, mascarpone, and marinara to reflect the colors of the Italian flag.

Bear

E2

Eastern European ✗✗

12-14 31st Ave. (bet. 12th & 14th Sts.)

Subway: Broadway   Lunch & dinner Tue – Sun
Phone: 917-396-4939
Web: www.bearnyc.com
Prices: $$

Tucked away on a side street in vibrant Astoria, Bear may not be an obvious destination for a distinctive meal. But, take the time and look around to find dark glossy walls, fresh flowers, and a host of diners feasting on chef *extraordinaire* Natasha Pogrebinsky's order-in-advance tasting menu. Appearances aside, this place is serious.

Start with a cleverly crafted libation—the St. Dill martini has become a much buzzed about pour—before delving into a carte of items that adeptly parodies old-world foundation with new-world panache. Dinner has yielded smoked fish pâté deviled eggs; Ukrainian-style borscht boosted with vodka and *salo*; and a rich mushroom stroganoff starring slow-roasted mushrooms, deliciously enhanced by garlic and cream.

Biáng! 🐾

A3

Chinese ✗

41-10 Main St. (bet. 41st Ave. & 41st Rd.)

Subway: Flushing - Main St
Phone: 718-888-7713
Web: www.biang-nyc.com
Prices: $$

Lunch & dinner daily

Biáng! isn't exotic by accident. In fact, Chef/owner Jason Wang's cuisine interplays contrasts and textures with the intention to excite. Tucked into Flushing's main artery, the setting is boisterous and tables are busy, but shabby-chic details like a plate-glass exterior are the first sign that you're in for an unencumbered and unique treat. Dark walls and floors cover the inside, but gentle lighting and lofty ceilings add dimension to the narrow space.

Strong flavors and fiery oils star in dishes like crispy lotus root tossed in an earthy sesame vinaigrette; fresh buckwheat noodles mingled with cucumber, soy, and mustard oil; and *chang*, hot, creamy tofu with pickled vegetables. Lamb burgers seasoned with jalapeños and cumin are a fitting signature.

Brick Cafe

F2

Mediterranean ✗

30-95 33rd St. (at 31st Ave.)

Subway: Broadway
Phone: 718-267-2735
Web: www.brickcafe.com
Prices: $$

Lunch Sat – Sun
Dinner nightly

This neighborhood *bijou* is beloved for its big flavors and small, rustic space. From lace curtains and weathered floors, to a yellow façade with a "stained" glass pane, everything at Brick Cafe invokes the charming French countryside including its olive-tinted walls set beneath a hand-crafted tin ceiling. It's all very quaint to the point of being precious, but nonetheless appealing.

To match a lovely wine list, the menu highlights such well-made items as cucumber salad tossed with tomatoes, olives, and yogurt; or specials like goat cheese and asparagus-stuffed chicken wrapped in speck, roasted until crisp, and poured with a Parmesan cream set over mashed potatoes. Light and fluffy crêpes filled with berries offer the perfect end to such decadence.

537

bún-ker ☺

A2

V i e t n a m e s e ✗

46-63 Metropolitan Ave. (at Woodward Ave.)

Subway: Grand St (& bus Q54)
Phone: 718-386-4282
Web: www.bunkervietnamese.com
Prices: 🅑

Lunch Sat – Sun
Dinner Tue – Sun

Finding bún-ker is tricky and the journey isn't pretty, but this sweet and sunny "coffee shop" shines with a bright yellow façade. Inside, find the owners flitting amid burnt-orange walls, mismatched chairs, and plaid curtains laid atop white-framed windows. Know that this is not simply a spot for cheap eats: bún-ker is skillfully crafting solid Vietnamese food from quality ingredients, and they're here to stay.

Find pure harmony in mushroom *pho* with rice vermicelli and a plate of symphonic herbs and accompaniments. Perfect *bánh mì* are filled with melting smoked Gouda and pickled vegetables. *Ca ri ga* (chicken curry with lemongrass and coconut); and *cha cha* (turmeric-bathed fried salmon topped with peanuts and chilies) are both excellent.

Chao Thai

F3

T h a i ✗

85-03 Whitney Ave. (bet. Broadway & Macnish St.)

Subway: Elmhurst Av
Phone: 718-424-4999
Web: N/A
Prices: 🅑

Lunch & dinner daily

Thanks to the delectable eats, snug setting, and generous spirit, tiny Chao Thai's loyal following makes perfect sense. The LIRR rumbles nearby, but green-painted walls and a lofty window help soothe the setting. In an area teeming with Southeast Asian eateries, Chao Thai thrives as a wonderful destination for die-hard foodies.

Their seemingly silent existence has afforded the kitchen the liberty to create such faithful renditions as a mouth-numbing jungle curry balanced with coconut milk, lemongrass, and rich pork strips. Start with tiny fish cakes (*tod man*) with chili sauce before launching into sour fish stir-fried with a pungent curry paste.

Nearby and larger, Chao Thai Too also parades a deliciously unapologetic use of heat and spice.

Casa Enríque ✿

M e x i c a n 🍴🍴

B3

5-48 49th Ave. (bet. 5th St. & Vernon Blvd.)

Subway: Vernon Blvd - Jackson Av

Phone: 347-448-6040

Web: www.henrinyc.com

Prices: $$

Lunch Sat – Sun
Dinner nightly

Authenticity is the refrain at Casa Enríque, whose haute take on Mexican cuisine is a welcome blend of creativity and tradition. Comely picture windows mark the entrance to this lovely, laid-back dining room. Step in and find yourself engulfed by warm, hospitable servers; then consider the sleek décor featuring a stainless steel counter, cement floors, and contemporary white chairs, and know this is a *muy* welcoming lair infused with urban flair.

As for the kitchen? It churns out a host of faithful, consistently flavorful, and enjoyable eats. It's tough to narrow down the cornucopia here, so start with anything that can escort their incredible house salsas. Then there's the guac with spicy jalapeños—a guaranteed good time. *Mole de piaxtla* poured over tender chicken is a brilliant Pueblan version, rife with flavor complexity and mystery. But, if that doesn't spark your tongue, a deeply satisfying *posole de mi tía, chiles rellenos,* or any one of the enchiladas (perhaps with that plate-licking mole) are just the ticket to thick, flavorful, and fun flavor.

The *tres leches* cake may be the best in town, but don't forget about their vast list of margaritas adding to the tequila fueled fun...*vamos*!

Cheburechnaya

B2

92-09 63rd Dr. (at Austin St.)

Subway: 63 Dr - Rego Park
Phone: 718-897-9080
Web: N/A
Prices: 😊😊

Lunch Sun – Fri
Dinner Sat – Thu

♿ This may be a kosher spot with no bagel in sight, but one look at its counter loaded with layers of bowl-shaped *noni toki* bread and you quickly realize that a meal here is a dining adventure. Specializing in Bukharian (Central Asian) cuisine, longstanding Cheburechnaya has been a neighborhood pioneer.

The focused menu is more engrossing than the décor, and it's easy to want every cumin- and paprika-laced item on it. Bring your own vodka and start with the house specialty, *chebureki*, an empanada-like deep-fried wrap stuffed with either hand-cut lamb seasoned with cumin, chili, cilantro, and paprika; or fennel-sparked cabbage. It may serve as the perfect complement to smoky lamb fat, tender quail, veal heart, and seared beef sweetbread kebabs.

Christos

F1

41-08 23rd Ave. (at 41st St.)

Subway: Astoria - Ditmars Blvd
Phone: 718-777-8400
Web: www.christossteakhouse.com
Prices: $$$

Dinner nightly

☞ This beloved Astoria steakhouse has a lot going for it, but its cause for celebration is that authentic Greek accent that imbues the everything here. Excellent quality beef, as in the signature prime wedge for two, is dry-aged in-house, charbroiled to exact specification, and finished with sea salt and dried oregano. Vibrant starters and sides underscore the Aegean spirit at play with pan-fried *vlahotyri* cheese, charred octopus with roasted peppers and red wine dressing, and smoked feta mashed potatoes.

Christos has a commanding presence on a quiet tree-shaded corner just off of bustling Ditmars Blvd. Mixing shades of brown, the cozy and elegant dining room has a separate bar area and is lined with fish tanks stocked with live lobsters.

Crazy Crab 888

A3

B u r m e s e ✗

40-42 College Point Blvd. (bet. 40th Rd. & 41st Ave.)

Subway: Flushing - Main St   Lunch & dinner daily
Phone: 718-353-8188
Web: N/A
Prices: $$

You may second-guess your arrival to Crazy Crab 888 when you see the tarred-over landscape and autobody shops, but one step inside this downright delicious gem dispels any and all reservations. A sort of Burmese-Chinese seafood shack with influences from India and Thailand, the food offers recognizable ingredients in creative combos worthy of its wacky title—per Chinese culture, the number 8 is known to bring much good luck.

The pickled ginger salad packs a punch-crunch of fried garlic with cilantro, and makes for a cooling lead into the seafood 888 platter of Dungeness crab and crawfish—complete with a bib! For more spice, Yunnan sliced pork, straight from the face of a pig, combines fleshy meat with peanuts and chilies for a funky, must-try delight.

Debasaki

A3

K o r e a n ✗

33-67 Farrington St. (bet. 33rd & 35th Aves.)

Subway: Flushing - Main St   Dinner nightly
Phone: 718-886-6878
Web: www.dbsknyc.com
Prices: $$

Its own sort of Asian hipster lounge, Debasaki defies the norm. Located in an industrial section of Flushing, it's packed until 2 A.M. nightly. To combat those blasting beats dominating the room, there's a call button at every private booth to send over a server with another frozen soju-lychee cocktail or draft beer.

Even though you may not be able to see through the pitch-dark space, every table is surely covered with another plate of deep-fried, garlic- and soy-glazed chicken wings stuffed with creamed corn, shrimp, or hot poppers. Give in, order another drink, and accept that this food is good to the point of bawdry. A curious and unforgettably delish version of kimchi fried rice renders flavors that are at once tart, funky, and fantastically spicy.

Danny Brown Wine Bar & Kitchen ✿

Mediterranean 🍴🍴

B2

104-02 Metropolitan Ave. (at 71st Dr.)

Subway: Forest Hills - 71 Av   Dinner Tue – Sun
Phone: 718-261-2144
Web: www.dannybrownwinekitchen.com
Prices: $$

Metropolitan Avenue may surge with restaurants, but none are as *magnifique* as this beau. Beyond the handsome doors flanked by large windows and seasonal planters, this bright room radiates elegance and festivity. Muted colors let the expertly lit artwork and sultry soundtrack steal the scene.

Make your way through the well-appointed room only to be greeted by servers who are genuine and very helpful. Crisp linen-covered tables are set with sparkling cutlery and well-spaced for privacy, lending a note of intimacy to the couples and families smiling over each dish. Ever the consummate and passionate professional, Chef Danny Brown delivers a serious cuisine that never misses its mark. Begin with crispy Yukon Gold potato blinis topped with delicately smoked Irish salmon, American sturgeon caviar, and tart crème fraîche. Relish in the wild and unmistakably creamy flavors of fresh sea urchin, enriched by shaved *bottarga* and twirled with chewy linguine. Thick slabs of pork belly simmered in an intensely smoky bacon broth are beautifully balanced by braised red cabbage.

Soft, spicy, and simple desserts like rum raisin-carrot cake with frothy cream cheese mousse are unmissable.

De Mole

A2

Mexican ✗

45-02 48th Ave. (at 45th St.)

Subway: 46 St - Bliss St
Phone: 718-392-2161
Web: www.demolenyc.com
Prices: 🍜

Lunch & dinner daily

If the words sweet, competent, clean, and Mexican come into mind, you're most likely thinking of this heart-warming haunt for delightful Mexican. Albeit a tad small, with a second dining room in the back, rest assured that De Mole's flavors are mighty, both in their staples (burritos and tacos) and unique specials—seitan fajitas anyone?

This Mexican pearl rests on a corner of low-rise buildings where Woodside meets Sunnyside, yet far from the disharmony of Queens Boulevard. Fans gather here for hearty *enchiladas verdes con pollo*, corn tortillas smeared with tomatillo sauce and *queso blanco*. Crispy chicken *taquitos* are topped with rich sour cream; steamed corn tamales are surprisingly light but filled with flavor; and the namesake *mole* is a must.

Engeline's

E3

Filipino ✗

58-28 Roosevelt Ave. (at 59th St.)

Subway: Woodside - 61 St
Phone: 718-898-7878
Web: N/A
Prices: 🍜

Lunch & dinner daily

This may be the place for your local Filipino gossip. A breakfast, lunch, and dinner hangout for the neighborhood's growing Filipino population, this bakery-restaurant invites conviviality. A taste of the soft, flan-like cassava cake alone is worth the visit. Head to the well-maintained dining room for a more thorough introduction.

Discerning just what's in each dish can prove challenging, but find straightforward pleasure in the *sarsiadong bangus*, fried milkfish steaks simmered in garlic, tomatoes, green onion, a subtle yet flavorful fish sauce, and then topped with scrambled eggs. The *chicharon bulaklak* and the accompanying house-made *suka*, coconut-sugarcane vinegar steeped with bird chilies, gives quite the kick to sinfully crispy fried chicken skin.

eXo

Greek XX

C1

15-16 149th St. (at 15th Rd.)

Subway: N/A
Phone: 718-767-4396
Web: www.exorestaurant.com
Prices: $$

Lunch & dinner Tue – Sun

With a name that translates as "outside," this classically Mediterranean restaurant is located not far from the Long Island Sound. Featuring an airy patio, marvelous fig tree loaded with sweet fruit, and murals of exotic dancers, this is a casual space that invites sunshine.

With a new chef and updated menu, eXo continues to showcase delicious Greek fare. The wonderful wild duck breast is roasted until beautifully pink, fanned over a disc of spicy eggplant-kissed risotto, and finished with thin spears of asparagus and olive compote. The expertly prepared fish of the day keeps true to its roots: simply grilled branzino arrives light and succulent with an herb-olive-lemon dressing, roasted cauliflower, and red bliss potatoes in lemon-butter sauce.

Galbi Ma Eul

Korean X

C1

194-03 Northern Blvd. (bet. 194th & 195th Sts.)

Subway: Flushing - Main St (& bus Q12)
Phone: 718-819-2171
Web: N/A
Prices: $$

Lunch Mon – Fri
Dinner nightly

While Flushing has a good number of Korean spots, the lines outside Galbi Ma Eul never seem to fade. Locals and visitors gather here around tabletops equipped with traditional wood-burning charcoal barbecue pits clamoring perhaps for their tantalizing house-specialty, *galbi*—a mountain of perfectly marinated beef short ribs and pork belly with an array of tasty sides. Other than these tabletop feasts, the space itself is nondescript, with large planters and a blaring television.

The menu goes on to offer an excellent second specialty, *agoo jjim*, a gargantuan pot of spicy monkfish stew with spring onions and bean sprouts in a perfect balance of sweet, salty, and spicy flavors. *Banchan* may include octopus in *gochujang* and crab in chili sauce.

Hahm Ji Bach

C1

41-08 149th Pl. (bet. Barclay & 41st Aves.)

Subway: Flushing - Main St   Lunch & dinner daily
Phone: 718-460-9289
Web: N/A
Prices: $$

 A healthy assortment of *banchan* is usually a good indicator of a serious Korean restaurant. And you'll find no shortage of them here, at Hahm Ji Bach—a delicious Korean barbecue joint buried down a nondescript side street in the blossoming K-town that has sprung up near Queens' Murray Hill LIRR station.

This unassuming room won't woo you with its plain-Jane décor, but the patient, oh-so-knowledgable service staff more than makes up for it. Not to mention the kitchen, which scores major points for masterful specialties. *Daeji bulgogi*, marinated pork ribs in a chili-garlic sauce sprinkled with bright scallions; or *boyang jeongol*, a traditional hot pot of lamb, dumplings, and vegetables swimming in a rich, spicy beef broth are some of the favorites here.

Himalayan Yak

F3

72-20 Roosevelt Ave. (bet. 72nd & 73rd Sts.)

Subway: 74 St - Broadway   Lunch & dinner daily
Phone: 718-779-1119
Web: www.himalayanyak.com
Prices: $$

Broadly appealing yet truly unique, Himalayan Yak transports diners to a fantastical world of intricately carved wooden doors, mask-covered walls, and miniature stuffed yaks. It reflects an area of Central Asia where a hybrid cuisine of Nepalese, Tibetan, and Indian specialties rules.

Lassi here is made from scratch and an absolute highlight of any meal. Start with an order of tandoor cooked dumplings filled with ground pork, scallions, cilantro, ginger, and cabbage. For an exotic array of tastes, try the *phaparko dhendo* combination platter with buckwheat flour roti used to scoop up Nepali-style goat curry; or dig into the mound of *tse shogo ngopa* (sautéed potatoes, spinach, mushrooms and bell pepper) with grated radish pickles and tart yogurt sauce.

HinoMaru Ramen 😊

Japanese 🍴

33-18 Ditmars Blvd. (bet. 33rd & 34th Sts.)

Subway: Astoria - Ditmars Blvd
Phone: 718-777-0228
Web: www.hinomaruramen.com
Prices: $$

Lunch & dinner daily

A trip to this Japanese "tapas" and ramen bar doesn't take much convincing. The simple spot forgoes fussy décor for a chalkboard menu, friendly service, and energetic open kitchen. Grab a Sapporo on tap or cold jasmine tea, and dig into a collection of small plates, including seriously crispy strips of pig ears; wonderfully juicy and spicy chicken wings (*nagoya tebasaki*); as well as *buta kimchi*—pork belly with sautéed kimchi and bonito flakes. The other real focus here is a big, slurp-worthy bowl of ramen. In addition to superbly traditional pork and miso stocks, HinoMaru also offers an excellent vegetarian ramen showcasing a soy milk base and teeming with carrots, ginger, and broccoli.

Midtown residents: an offshoot has opened on East 53rd.

Houdini Kitchen Laboratory

Pizza 🍴🍴

15-63 Decatur St. (at Wyckoff Ave.)

Subway: Halsey St
Phone: 718-456-3770
Web: N/A
Prices: 😊😊

Lunch & dinner daily

Houdini's Kitchen Laboratory rests in an industrial neighborhood near Queens' massive cemeteries. But despite its character-less setting, the inventive restaurant more than lives up to its creative name. A large, airy space complete with an impressive cement dome oven, Houdini's whips up a small but selective menu of excellent pastas and unique pizzas with daily specials.

The generous spirals of tagliatelle bathed in a meat ragù make for a very satisfying start. Sure, it's carb-heavy, but when in Rome—right? Follow that up with the popular, 18-month-old Monte Poro pecorino, or go all in with the sensational *habanera* pizza: crazy spicy peppers and strips of spicy pork loin in one fiery, mozzarella- and tomato sauce-topped pie. Who says Queens isn't hot?

Hunan House 😊

Chinese 🍴

A3

137-40 Northern Blvd. (bet. Main & Union Sts.)

Subway: Flushing – Main St
Phone: 718-353-1808
Web: www.hunanauthentic.com
Prices: 😊😊

Lunch & dinner daily

This quieter stretch of Northern Boulevard is NY's rising (and reigning) Chinatown and is sure to fire up any spice-seekers willing to brave the trek. Here, Hunan House is a plain but tidy spot serving heartwarming Hunanese fare, and reminding all of its phenomenal complexity. The menu reads like a textbook of this region's cuisine; its authenticity is paramount.

Many dishes, like braised fish head, are seafood-centric, though they often share Sichuan's affinity for chilies. Expect the likes of steamed spare ribs, thick and lean, in a hollowed bamboo branch teeming with a powerful sauce of fermented black beans and red chili oil. White chili-preserved beef is an ingenious dish of dried bean curd and a mix of five-spice, star anise, and beefy broth.

Hunan Kitchen of Grand Sichuan 😊😊

Chinese 🍴

C1

42-47 Main Street (bet. Blossom & Franklin Aves.)

Subway: Flushing – Main St
Phone: 718-888-0553
Web: N/A
Prices: 😊😊

Lunch & dinner daily

As New York's Sichuan renaissance continues apace, this pleasant and unpretentious Hunanese spot has popped up on Flushing's Main Street. The look here is tasteful and uncomplicated; the cooking is fiery and excellent.

The extensive menu of Hunan specialties includes the likes of the classic regional dish, pork "Mao's Style" simmered in soy sauce, Shaoxing wine, oil, and stock, then braised to tender perfection. Boasting heat and meat in equal amounts, the spicy-sour string beans with pork expertly combines rich and savory aromatics, vinegary beans, and fragrant pork with tongue-numbing peppercorns. The barbecue fish Hunan-style is a brilliant menu standout.

Smaller dishes, like winter melon with seafood soup, round out an expertly prepared meal.

Il Bacco

D1

Italian XX

253-24 Northern Blvd. (bet. Little Neck Pkwy & Westmoreland St.)

Subway: N/A
Phone: 718-224-7657
Web: www.ilbaccoristorante.com
Prices: $$

Lunch & dinner daily

With its dulcet Mediterranean-esque façade, crimson awnings, and rooftop garden, Il Bacco is hard to miss. This Little Neck-by-way-of-Tuscany gem shows off a stylish setting; the fact that it is bolstered by a popular catering operation augments its overall appeal.

This kitchen dutifully honors Italian-American classics with skill and top-notch ingredients. The pizza oven is a beauté that produces perfect pies, while tables pile up with *gamberetti infernali*, shrimp in a drink-worthy sauce of white wine, garlic, and red pepper flakes; or *spaghetti picchi paccu*, tossed with crushed plum tomatoes, basil, and pecorino. *Pollo Gelsomina* is chicken scaloppine beautifully finished with a chunky sauce of mushrooms, artichoke hearts, and roasted peppers.

Il Poeta

B2

Italian XX

98-04 Metropolitan Ave. (at 69th Rd.)

Subway: Forest Hills - 71 Av
Phone: 718-544-4223
Web: www.ilpoetarestaurant.com
Prices: $$

Lunch Mon – Fri
Dinner nightly

Even if nothing further is said about Il Poeta, let one thing be clear—this family-run charmer knows how to hit Italian specialties out of the park. Perched on a quaint corner and edged with lofty windows, their white curtains contrasted against pink and orange walls seem to capture the soul of Tuscany. The suited staff and vibrant artwork make Il Poeta much more than just a trattoria.

Venerable creations are pitch-perfect, as in calamari *dorati* superbly supple and fried to golden perfection; or outstanding *linguine alla puttanesca con tonno* dressed with tomato sauce studded with tuna, olives, and capers. The *pollo spezzatino* may well resemble the classic *cacciatore*, but is nonetheless stellar starring peppers, sausage, and hints of herbs.

Imperial Palace

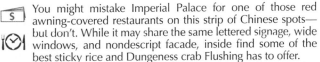

Chinese 🍴

A3

136-13 37th Ave. (bet. Main & Union Sts.)

Subway: Flushing - Main St
Phone: 718-939-3501
Web: N/A
Prices: $$

Lunch & dinner daily

You might mistake Imperial Palace for one of those red awning-covered restaurants on this strip of Chinese spots—but don't. While it may share the same lettered signage, wide windows, and nondescript facade, inside find some of the best sticky rice and Dungeness crab Flushing has to offer.

Seafood is front and center, with servers promptly presenting everything from deep-fried jumbo shrimp tossed with candied sesame walnuts to shrimp-stuffed tofu with slices of conch. It's easy to plow through all the fresh shellfish dishes with a chilled beer and sweet rice, but try to leave room for the clam casserole: a spicy broth full of Cantonese flavors, loads of onions, and small, briny clams, finished with a sprinkling of crisp coriander stems.

Joe's Shanghai

Chinese 🍴

A3

136-21 37th Ave. (bet. Main & Union Sts.)

Subway: Flushing - Main St
Phone: 718-539-3838
Web: www.joeshanghairestaurants.com
Prices: $$

Lunch & dinner daily

Patience is a virtue at Joe's Shanghai, where a hectic rush to snag a table precedes a visit for the soup dumplings. As with most Flushing restaurants, flavor outdoes the interior decoration, with walls in need of fresh paint and dated furnishings.

What the atmosphere lacks, the food fulfills as the kitchen swiftly prepares delicate *xiao long bao*, that despite stiff competition, still stand a head above the rest. The chefs have perfected the art of wrapping hot liquid into these soft, thin pouches, complete with spiraled shoulders. To bite into a soup dumpling it recommend that diners don't even bother to glance at the flat-screens hanging in the dining room. While the menu offers fried bean curd and smoked fish, nothing sticks like the dumplings.

549

John Brown Smokehouse 😊

Barbecue ✗

10-43 44th Dr. (bet. 10th & 11th Sts.)

Subway: Court Sq - 23 St
Phone: 347-617-1120
Web: www.johnbrownseriousbbq.com
Prices: $$

Lunch & dinner daily

While this western tip of Queens may still be in transition, the food scene is here to stay. Case in point: John Brown Smokehouse. This barbecue boss showcases an expansive dining room, whose simple décor unveils a bustling front area, framed photos of a bearded man (perhaps John Brown himself?), as well as an outdoor beer hall complete with live music.

Still, everyone is here for their truly authentic and very addictive Kansas City-style barbecue and peachwood-smoked treats that may include the likes of rib tips (meat candy, really) with burned ends enticingly seasoned with sugar and ground coffee. Other favorites reveal spicy kimchi radish, smoky lamb sausage, and *el chupacabra* with roast pork and barbecue sauce—a righteous daily special.

Kang Ho Dong Baekjeong

Korean ✗✗

152-12 Northern Blvd. (bet. 153rd & Murray Sts.)

Subway: Flushing - Main St (& bus Q13)
Phone: 718-886-8645
Web: N/A
Prices: $$

Lunch & dinner daily

The Korean barbecue of the moment is a short LIRR trip away, and well worth the ride. This is the first East Coast branch of (Korean wrestler and TV personality) Kang Ho Dong's growing restaurant empire—and it is already among the best in the city.

The menu is focused, the space is enormous, the air is clean, and the service is friendly. Start your grill off with steamed egg, corn, cheese, and more to cook along the sides while marbled pork belly or deeply flavorful marinated skirt steak strips sizzle at the center. Their *bibimbap* is a classic rendition, mixing beef seasoned with red pepper paste (*gochujang*), vegetables, sesame, nori, and crisp sprouts in a hot stone bowl—so hot that it sears the bottom rice to golden while cooking the raw egg on top.

Katsuno

Japanese ✗

B2

103-01 Metropolitan Ave. (at 71st Rd.)

Subway: Forest Hills - 71 Av   Dinner Tue – Sun
Phone: 718-575-4033
Web: www.katsunorestaurant.com
Prices: $$

To find Katsuno, look for the white lantern and those traditional *noren* curtains. Featuring less than ten tables, what this Japanese jewel lacks in size it makes up for in flavor and attitude. The owner's wife greets each guest at the door, while Chef Katsuyuki Seo dances around the miniscule kitchen crafting precise Japanese dishes from top-quality ingredients. His elegant plating of sashimi may reveal the likes of amberjack topped with a chiffonade of shiso, luxurious sea urchin, translucent squid crested with needle-thin yuzu zest, as well as supremely fresh fluke, tuna, and mackerel. Meanwhile, carb fans will enjoy a warm bowl of soba in duck broth with tender duck breast; or the fantastically brothy *inaniwa udon*, served only on special nights.

Linn

Japanese ✗✗

E2

29-13 Broadway (bet. 29th & 30th Sts.)

Subway: Broadway   Dinner Tue – Sun
Phone: 718-204-0060
Web: www.linnnyc.com
Prices: $$

With its art gallery-like setting and authentic Japanese fare, Linn is one of Astoria's many hidden gems. A museum-worthy wall features track lighting and oil-painted canvases, while its dishes are brushstrokes of pure talent. Head Chef Tanaka Shigenori, formerly of Masa, is the master behind homey, slow-braised delights like broiled yellowtail cheek. But, also on offer and very popular is the omakase featuring pork belly in a warm soy- ginger- and sake-broth, octopus from Hokkaido, sardines from Japan's Inland Sea, and a delicate dashi with turbot and yams.

From the usual suspects are divine sushi maki, alongside wasabi and pickled ginger with salmon and red snapper; while miso soup, dotted with tofu, seaweed, and scallions, is sumptuous and slurpable.

Little Lamb

A3

36-35 Main St. (bet. 37th Ave. & Northern Blvd.)

Subway: Flushing - Main St
Phone: 718-358-6667
Web: www.thebesthotpot.com
Prices: 💰💰

Lunch & dinner daily

 Even though English proves challenging for the staff here, that's no reason to fret—especially since "pointing" works just fine at this charming spot for hot pots. Not to be confused with Little Sheep, unique Little Lamb's website handle (the best hot pot!) inspires confidence as does the astonishing roster. Find over 70 varying items to be dunked into bubbling broth, which is available "spicy red," (bobbing with capsicum and Sichuan peppercorns) "non-spicy white," or "half-and-half."

The combos are endless, but it's all a treat: thinly sliced lamb, head-on shrimp, and chewy udon to name a few. Thrill-seekers will devour other unmentionable animal parts; while a refreshing trio of cucumber, bitter melon, and shredded potato is a cool palate cleanser.

Little Pepper

B1

18-24 College Point Blvd. (bet. 18th & 20th Aves.)

Subway: Flushing - Main St (& bus Q20A)
Phone: 718-939-7788
Web: N/A
Prices: 💰💰

Lunch & dinner Fri — Wed

Set on an ordinary block of residences and businesses is Little Pepper, a tiny yet extraordinary rendition of Sichuan cooking. The room wears a delicate vibe with hand-painted murals, marble-tiled floors, and a cozy service bar. But, the real focus remains on the food, which is honest, bold, and always on-point.

Sample soft and yielding *mapo* tofu, sweet with minced pork, fiery with chilies, and smoky with ground peppercorns sinking into a thick, oily gravy; or shredded pork tossed with potato strands and pickled cabbage to truly appreciate their excellent (if occasionally) underrated food. Pine nuts sautéed with corn and snow pea leaves is marvelous for mellow palates, while chicken stir-fried with dried red chilies is a hit among those on a spice trip.

Lu Xiang Yuan

C1

Chinese 🍴

42-87 Main St. (bet. Blossom & Cherry Aves.)

Subway: Flushing - Main St
Phone: 718-359-2108
Web: N/A
Prices: 😋

Lunch & dinner daily

S

The ambience appears unassuming and ordinary, but Lu Xiang Yuan is an outstanding choice for tasty, affordable, regional Qingdao fare. The crowds have calmed, so tables are often available at peak meal times.

This is the place to hit for deep bowlfuls of restorative Chinese noodle soups that could carry you through the day—picture translucent bean threads, long slices of dried tofu, and morsels of lamb bobbing among fragrant cilantro, Chinese wolfberries, and black tree mushrooms in a broth enhanced with smoky chili paste. Other intriguing dishes unveil delicate kingfish steaks that have been subtly smoked, gently spiced, and served chilled. The black bone chicken and *ginseng* soup showcases the dark flesh and deep flavor of its ingredients.

Main Street Imperial Taiwanese Gourmet

C2

Chinese 🍴

59-14A Main St. (bet. 59th & 60th Aves.)

Subway: Flushing - Main St (& bus Q44)
Phone: 718-886-8788
Web: N/A
Prices: 😋

Lunch & dinner daily

S

It's a real journey to this Taiwanese treasure—not only in its trek from the closest subway stop, but more importantly, in the experience. Here, the staff speaks their mother tongue for the most part, incense wafts from an altar, and the food is otherworldly.

Dishes present dazzling, authentic flavors, easily savored in the peaceful atmosphere. Sweet, head-on shrimp arrive steamed and still in the shell, housing juice that accentuates the concentrated flavor when dipped in soy sauce. Likewise, the stinky tofu (a traditional delicacy) gets its flavor from a light sauté and a pinch of blue bit crybs pickles. And if you're any sort of fan of the famed oyster pancake, this outstanding version will remain in your memory long after the lengthy ride home.

Malagueta

E2

✗

25-35 36th Ave. (at 28th St.)

Subway: 36 Av
Phone: 718-937-4821
Web: www.malaguetany.com
Prices: $$

Lunch & dinner Tue – Sun

A longstanding spot for authentic Northeastern Brazilian fare, Malagueta's pop of color and spice stands out from its residential surroundings. From its personable and dedicated staff to the warm and unassuming setting, this culturally rich retreat keeps locals and destination diners returning to this tiny spot and settling into a bistro chair.

The kitchen plays with smoky, sour, hot, and salty flavors stewed to mellowness to strike just the right balance. Even the humble *arroz y feijao* is a deeply satisfying blend of tender beans with pearly white rice. *Picanha* features grilled slices of sirloin topped with *farofa* (toasted manioc flour), enhanced by a citrus-herb vinaigrette, and accompanied by rice and beans. Finish with an excellent coconut flan.

MP Taverna

F1

✗✗

31-29 Ditmars Blvd. (at 33rd St.)

Subway: Astoria - Ditmars Blvd
Phone: 718-777-2187
Web: www.michaelpsilakis.com
Prices: $$

Lunch & dinner daily

This sprawling, multi-level hot spot has diners and drinkers from all around the city hopping the N or Q line to Astoria. Lively and raucous, the main level is dressed in an urban style of slate walls, steel touches, and wood paneling. The second floor is more luxurious with its ornate chandeliers, leather chairs, and floor-to-ceiling windows.

Brought to you by Michael Psilakis, this outpost is one of three sister locations, all serving up the same tasty menu. Offerings include chopped bulgur salad of dates, green olives, and red onions, studded with pomegranate and pistachio; a hearty mix of grilled lamb sausage, pork tenderloin and chicken basted in oregano and lemon; or fantastic walnut-and-parsnip cake with candied nut rubble and ice cream.

M. Wells Steakhouse ⸂

B3

Gastropub ✕✕

43-15 Crescent St. (bet. 43rd Ave & 44th Rd.)

Subway: Court Sq - 23 St
Phone: 718-786-9060
Web: www.magasinwells.com
Prices: $$$$

Dinner Wed – Mon

Yes, you have the correct address (the entrance is across from the posh high-rise). Once inside, bask in the warm, urban, and distinctly styled space featuring brick, wood, and a semi-open kitchen. Steel gates roll down on one side; floral gold and black wallpaper line the ceiling; and a '60s documentary on Quebequois lumberjacks is projected on the red-accented wall. Somehow, this former auto body shop pulls it all together with very attractive results. Service is professional yet maintains a quirkiness that mirrors the all-around fun vibe.

Trademark personality and creativity shine right from the start in a Caesar salad showered with grated smoked mackerel. A whole roasted chicken is perfectly seasoned and crisped for an enticing interplay with the finely textured liver and *croûtes* that accompany it. Expertly cooked lamb chops with a fascinating North African spice rub are served over a mound of couscous and a gorgeous slice of belly meat that can only be described as lamb bacon.

Outstanding desserts like the *Paris-Brest*—eggy-crisp pastry filled with hazelnut cream then studded with hazelnuts and crumble—prove the seriousness behind this fun, sparky, and distinctive cooking.

Mythos

C1

Greek ✗✗

196-29 Northern Blvd. (bet. 196th St. & Francis Lewis Blvd.)

Subway: N/A
Phone: 718-357-6596
Web: www.mythosnyc.com
Prices: $$

Lunch & dinner daily

Set upon the eastern end of Northern Boulevard's stretch of Korean eateries is this Greek favorite for dishes of impeccably fresh fish, grilled to juicy perfection. The welcoming white façade is splashed with a dark blue awning and red paneled doors flanked by oversized windows. The interior is simply done in white linen-topped tables and dark wood floors, with a lower-level private party room.

Start off with *bekri meze*, a warm appetizer combination of crispy codfish served with garlic dip; pan-fried *Kasseri* cheese; roasted red peppers in wine sauce; and *loukaniko*, grilled Greek sausage. Pair a plate of fresh grilled asparagus, zucchini, and eggplant with a whole grilled porgy, *tsipoura*, that is crispy on the outside and perfectly delicate within.

Nan Xiang Xiao Long Bao

A3

Chinese ✗

38-12 Prince St. (bet. 38th & 39th Aves.)

Subway: Flushing - Main St
Phone: 718-321-3838
Web: N/A
Prices: ☯☯

Lunch & dinner daily

Also known as Nan Xiang Dumpling House, it is easily found among a strip of restaurants reflecting the diversity of Flushing's dominant Asian population. Simply decorated, the comfortable dining room features rows of closely set tables and a mirrored wall that successfully gives the illusion of space.

The enjoyable and interesting menu focuses on noodle-filled soups, toothsome stir-fried rice cakes, and the house specialty, juicy dumplings. These are made in-house and have a delicate, silky wrapper encasing a flavorful meatball of ground pork or crab and rich tasting broth. Eating the specialties may take some practice, but take your cue from the slurping crowd: puncture the casing on your spoon to cool the dumplings and avoid scalding your mouth.

Natural Tofu & Noodles

A2

40-06 Queens Blvd. (bet. 40th & 41st Sts.)

Subway: 40 St
Phone: 718-706-0899
Web: N/A
Prices: $$

Lunch & dinner daily

This is the sort of place you've walked by a hundred times and never noticed. But it's time to look up, because the house-made tofu here is unrivaled. The space may be more functional than cozy, but this staff knows how to treat its customers, from happily adjusting a dish's spice level to presenting the bill with melon-flavored Haitai gum.

They also clearly know the many secrets of tofu—the kitchen makes its own, then deploys it in a series of silken *soondubu* (soft bean curd stews) like the funky Korean favorite "kimchi soft tofu." The fragrant and rich "seafood tofu" arrives in a small cauldron of bubbling broth with steel tongs for serving oysters, shrimp, clams, mushrooms, and scallions with the most custardy tofu on this side of Queens Boulevard.

Nick's Pizza

B2

108-26 Ascan Ave. (off Austin St.)

Subway: 75 Av
Phone: 718-263-1126
Web: N/A
Prices: 😊😊

Lunch & dinner daily

For all the historic touches and architectural details at Nick's Pizza, the 20-year-old spot has the feel of a '50s diner that happens to live among the Tudor-style homes of Forest Hills. This is true not only of the ornate tin but also the marble tabletop, and a *caffè* from the antique brass espresso machine.

Wearing an old-school New York pizza attitude, Nick's shuttles pies to and from the oven at unbelievable speeds, keeping each table loaded. The terrific crust delivers a deliciously smoky flavor that's heightened by the crisp texture and any number of toppings—from salty anchovies to tender meatballs. The signature calzone is also worth a bite, with tangy mozzarella and ricotta oozing like slow lava and a cup of red sauce on the side for dipping.

Nusara

F3

Thai ✗

82-80 Broadway (at Whitney Ave.)

Subway: Elmhurst Av   Lunch & dinner daily
Phone: 718-898-7996
Web: www.nusarathaikitchen.com
Prices: $$

Tucked between an array of eateries and a sprawling supermarket, little Nusara's excellent Thai dishes make it a welcoming spot for a satisfying meal. The exterior looks more like a shop than a restaurant, but inside the attractive yet simple décor and colorful sketches that line the walls are trumped by your dive into the extensive two-page menu.

Begin with the pork strips soaked in fish sauce and lime marinade, deep-fried for perfect salty-sweet contrast, and served with a chili dipping sauce. The *khao mon gai* is a Thai take on Haianese chicken, where the remarkably tender and pale white meat is poached in ginger and rice wine, set over fragrant rice, and eaten with a spicy ginger-chili dipping sauce and a bowl of marvelous chicken broth.

Ornella

F1

Italian ✗✗

29-17 23rd Ave. (bet. 29th & 31st Sts.)

Subway: Astoria - Ditmars Blvd   Lunch & dinner daily
Phone: 718-777-9477
Web: www.ornellatrattoria.com
Prices: $$

Ornella and Giuseppe Viterale are always at home in their small and warm trattoria, settled in the middle of vibrant Astoria. The friendly service here includes Giuseppe swinging by tables and talking about the farmhouse event space he runs upstate. Ornella's orange-striped awning, stained glass sconces, and mural-lined walls give it a kitschy, fairy-tale feel that mirrors the Italian-American menu.

Here, you'll find tasty and popular duck meatballs in an orange-brandy reduction (think duck *à l'orange* in Italian) or braised short ribs with Madeira sauce. For a filling treat, try the *imbustata*, pasta filled with ground veal, chicken mushroom, mascarpone, and a knob of mozzarella that's drenched in a chunky sauce of tomatoes, onions, and fresh basil.

Pachanga Patterson

F2

Mexican ✗

33-17 31st Ave. (at 34th St.)

Subway: 30 Av
Phone: 718-554-0525
Web: www.pachangapatterson.com
Prices: $$

Lunch Sat – Sun
Dinner nightly

This unassuming spot for tasty Mexican food with a twist has been a smash from the start. The vibe inside is always a feel-good one, with floor-to-ceiling windows, fairy lights, and quirky artifacts adorning the space. While the décor is subtle, the fuchsia-painted kitchen brims with bold flavors and superb textures as seen in soft tortillas folded with sweet grilled pineapple, spicy habanero salsa, and adobo-marinated shrimp. In a salad of red beets, salty crumbled *cotija* deliciously offsets those tangy chunks of pickled watermelon; and empanadas are a particular treat, filled with meaty portobellos and creamy potatoes.

End with crispy sweetbreads *con mole coloradito*, redolent of cumin, *guajillo*, and chocolate, and find yourself thinking— dessert what?

Parkside

B2

Italian ✗✗

107-01 Corona Ave. (bet. 108th St. & 51st Ave.)

Subway: 103 St - Corona Plaza
Phone: 718-271-9871
Web: www.parksiderestaurantny.com
Prices: $$$

Lunch & dinner daily

Set upon a landmark corner beyond the Corona Italian Ice King, Parkside's interior evokes a golden era of Italian-American dining, circa 1978. Waiters don tuxedos, regal archways are the norm, and walls boast classic photos or plaques etched with names of the city's elite above the more desirable tables.

The energy and celebratory atmosphere is contagious, amid linen-topped tables laden with the likes of a thinly worthy lentil soup, or colossal crabmeat cocktail with melted butter and zesty black pepper. Try tender slices of prime steak *pizzaiola* with a chunky-garlicky tomato sauce strewn with herbs, paired with meltingly soft potato croquettes. Finish with a house-made tiramisu served in a glass trifle with powdered chocolate and chewy cocoa bits.

Payag

Filipino ✗

51-34 Roosevelt Ave. (at 52nd St.)

Subway: 52 St   Lunch & dinner daily
Phone: 347-935-3192
Web: www.payagrestaurant.com
Prices: $$

Thoughtfully crafted with ingenuity and spirit, Payag is intended to feel like a home. From the open and light design that evokes a *bahay kubo* (Tagalog for "house") to the chatty and knowledgeable servers, this restaurant brings a welcoming air to this quiet corner. With bamboo touches and live Filipino music on the weekends, Payag strives to preserve a cultural identity both on and off the menu.

The dishes showcase a regional approach to the multi-island nation's cuisine. National favorite *kinilaw na isda*, a sour ceviche of delicate white fish, ginger, and cucumber, is a refreshing start to the meal. Then move on to the beautiful *bulalo*, a tender beef shank specialty from Batangas, gently simmered in a broth with yellow corn, cabbage, and baby bok choy.

Piccola Venezia

F2

Italian ✗✗

42-01 28th Ave. (at 42nd St.)

Subway: 30 Av   Lunch Mon – Fri
Phone: 718-721-8470   Dinner nightly
Web: www.piccola-venezia.com
Prices: $$$

Piccola Venezia deserves its landmark status: this old-time idol has been going strong ever since opening in 1973. With Italian-American cooking so rampant in the city, it is wholly refreshing to happen upon a classic of such welcoming comfort. The décor is outdated, but the white tablecloths are clean and crisp. The glasses gleam at the prospect of great wine varietals, and the walls are adorned with watercolors depicting Venetian scenes.

With a distinctly macho mien and crowd, well-versed waiters follow suit. They make you nostalgic for *yota*, a heartwarming bean-and-cabbage soup loaded with bacon; *fusi* swirled in a grappa- mushroom- and Grana-sauce; or *trippa alla Triestina*, succulent tripe in a light tomato sauce served with smashed-fried potatoes.

Sabry's

F2

Seafood ✕

24-25 Steinway St. (bet. Astoria Blvd. & 25th Ave.)

Subway: Astoria Blvd   Lunch & dinner daily
Phone: 718-721-9010
Web: N/A
Prices: $$

Among the hookah lounges of Astoria's Steinway St., Sabry's offers authentic Egyptian seafood and friendly service. A strictly Muslim (no alcohol) establishment, the focus here is on tradition—one bite of the complimentary hot, puffy, deliciously chewy, and totally enjoyable Egyptian pita with sesame dipping sauce proves the team attends to every detail. Take a seat near wood-framed doors that open to the street for people-watching, or by the open kitchen for chef-watching. Then, prepare for hearty items beginning with impossibly tender and smoky grilled octopus. An icebox labeled "Day's Catch" features a daily roster of whole fish, cooked-to-order and served with lemon and rice. *Taojine* with scallops laden in a fragrant tomato sauce is a savory thrill.

Salt & Fat 😊

A2

Contemporary ✕

41-16 Queens Blvd. (bet. 41st & 42nd Sts.)

Subway: 40 St   Dinner Tue – Sun
Phone: 718-433-3702
Web: www.saltandfatny.com
Prices: $$

This city-wide favorite just keeps getting better. Thank neighborhood native Chef Daniel Yi for his expert vision and execution, as well as his highly skilled staff, both in front and back of the house. The narrow storefront is tidy and warm, the food is contemplative and fun.

Bacon fat popcorn might be a prelude to the spicy BLT piled with a thick square of beautifully caramelized Berkshire pork bacon, cherry tomatoes, pickled veggies, shredded romaine, and onion on *bao* slathered with spicy-sweet mayo. Paired with a smoked porter from upstate New York, the dish is unbeatable. Yellowtail tartare combines a swoosh of yuzu gel, dots of smoky ancho-*sriracha* mayo, and cassava chips to showcase distinct flavors and extraordinary pleasure.

Sentosa

Queens

A3

Malaysian

39-07 Prince St. (at 39th Ave.)

Subway: Flushing - Main St   Lunch & dinner daily
Phone: 718-886-6331
Web: www.sentosausa.com
Prices:

Sentosa is a nirvana of sorts for die-hard Southeast Asian food fans. Set at the base of a building where the foot traffic never ceases, this Malaysian marvel is firmly planted amid Chinese banquet halls and eateries hawking Cantonese roast meats and Vietnamese *pho*. The inside is immaculate, airy, and modern in a muted sort of way with natural light bouncing from teak walls to stone-tiled floors.

The courteous and friendly staff is eager to educate and delight you with any number of dishes from the well-explained menu—from firm and fiery pickled vegetables to the refreshing watermelon juice. Expect *poh piah* packed with jicama, tofu, and bean sprouts; or the ever-authentic *nasi lemak* mingling coconut rice, anchovies, chicken curry, and hard-boiled eggs.

Seoul Soondae

C1

Korean

158-15 Northern Blvd. (at 158th St.)

Subway: N/A   Lunch & dinner daily
Phone: 718-321-3231
Web: N/A
Prices: $$

In the heart of Northern Boulevard, among Korean boutiques, groceries and barbecue joints, is Seoul Soondae—New York City's first outpost for this small-chain restaurant.

What gives this delicious gem the edge is its unique regional menu offering a variety of well-made delights. The gargantuan house specialty, *soondae naejang bokeum*, is a rich example: it arrives as a plate of peppery blood sausage, pork intestine, tongue, ears, and a heap of shredded vegetables, all tossed in toasted sesame oil, and ready to be cooked at the table. Other options include fragrant *gamja tang*, pork and potato stew; or *jjol myun* noodles, served cold and topped with carrots, cabbage, pickled cucumber, bean sprouts, and boiled egg, crowned with a hot and spicy sauce.

Shanghai Tide

A3

Chinese ✗

135-20 40th Rd. (bet. Main & Prince Sts.)

Subway: Flushing - Main St

Lunch & dinner daily

Phone: 718-661-0900

Web: N/A

Prices: $$

Shanghai Tide may not be new, but it is rising to the top here in Flushing, perhaps leading a new wave of regional restaurants to replace those mélange of generic Chinese spots. The space is simply appointed with ropes of twinkly Christmas lights, dark rugs, and well-spaced tables run by a helpful (if slow) staff.

The vast menu is reliably good, but their hot pots are worthy of big love. Picture huge bubbling pots sitting like centerpieces at each table, filling the restaurant with a spicy sort of aromatherapy, and brimming with marbled meats, mung bean sheets, abalone, prawns, octopus, vegetables... you name it. Beyond this, try silky dried bean curd tossed with soybeans and snow cabbage, or bitter melon with preserved black beans.

SHI

B3

Asian ✗✗✗

47-20 Center Blvd. (bet. 47th & 48th Aves.)

Subway: Vernon Blvd - Jackson Av

Lunch & dinner daily

Phone: 347-242-2450

Web: www.eatdrinkshi.com

Prices: $$

SHI makes the most of its extraordinary location with expansive floor-to-ceiling windows that display stellar views of the United Nations and Manhattan skyline. The dramatic dining room alone may literally blow you away. The front lounge offers banquettes, a sleek bar, and crystal chandeliers. In addition to the setting, Asian-American, Chinese, and Japanese specialties attract a steady crowd of affluent professionals and local families.

The menu highlights sentimental favorites, like crab Rangoon combining flaky crab, oozing cream cheese, and scallion in crisp wontons, or Buddhist delight, a wonderful vegetarian ensemble of bean threads, noodles, bamboo shoots, and tofu. Also sample an array of maki like the *tohru* roll filled with eel teriyaki.

Sik Gaek

C1

161-29 Crocheron Ave. (bet. 161st & 162nd Sts.)

Subway: Flushing - Main St (& bus Q12) Dinner Tue – Sun
Phone: 718-321-7770
Web: N/A
Prices: $$

There may be glitzier Korean spots in town, but insanely delicious, exceedingly simple Sik Gaek assures a good time, every time. Dressed in silly costumes, the staff is always having a blast in this seasonally decorated shack-like dining room featuring corrugated metal roofs, street lights, buckets for shells, and walls papered in dollar bills. Booths along the edge are filled with noisy regulars.

The kitchen serves the ocean's bounty, starting with a deliciously crisp and gargantuan pancake, *pajeon*, studded with seafood and kimchi begging to be dipped in enticingly salty soy-sesame sauce. A cloudy soup bobbing with tofu arrives piping hot, boasting that sharp, nutty, telltale flavor of fermented bean curd, and seems to have its own restorative powers.

Spicy Lanka

C2

159-23 Hillside Ave. (bet. 160th St. & Parsons Blvd.)

Bus: Parsons Blvd Lunch & dinner daily
Phone: 718-487-4499
Web: N/A
Prices:

Walk through the door at Spicy Lanka, and—BAM!—the heady aroma of spice might just knock you off your feet. It's worth the trek to this far-out Jamaica restaurant, full of hip-hop music, brightly colored murals of palm trees, and an unbridled enthusiasm for heat and colliding Sri Lankan flavors.

The biryani is steamed for hours in a bubbling blend of cardamom, nutmeg, paprika, bay leaves, and star anise, then tossed with garlic- and ginger-marinated chicken and okra—a blast of flavor on the palate. Further rock your world with the string hopper *kothu*, mutton curry filled with noodles and a fistful of herbs and spices—think cardamom, cloves, and turmeric. To cool off, treat your tongue to the *watalappam* coconut custard, spiked with bits of buttery cashew.

Spicy & Tasty

A3

Chinese ✗

39-07 Prince St. (at 39th Ave.)

Subway: Flushing - Main St
Phone: 718-359-1601
Web: www.spicyandtasty.com
Prices: ⊖⊜

Lunch & dinner daily

Spicy & Tasty has found its home in this bustling pocket of Queens, where a dizzying array of restaurants, bakeries, and stores jockey to win the favor of Flushing's booming Asian population. Its local love is clear in the diverse ethnicities scattered across the clean, contemporary, and spacious dining room, as well as in the cuisine—though it does seem to restrain its punchy Sichuan heat for fear of scaring the newbies.

Nonetheless, this food is thoroughly enjoyable. It is likewise fun to watch the warm, knowledgeable staff walk first-timers through steaming plates of dumplings, plump with a spicy red chili sauce and minced meat; broad noodles in a powerful, rich, meaty sauce dancing with scallions and peppers; or a tender and fiery cold tripe salad.

S Prime

E2

Steakhouse ✗✗

35-15 36th St. (bet. 35th & 36th Aves.)

Subway: 36 Av
Phone: 718-707-0660
Web: www.sprimenyc.com
Prices: $$$$

Dinner Tue – Sat

You can take the steakhouse out of Manhattan, but you can't take Manhattan out of the steakhouse. At this slick Astoria joint, beef rules and the same New York service applies: rough around the edges but not without its charm. Here, a neighborhood crowd packs into the loud bar and industrial-style dining room, toasting to another happy hour or date-night.

While the menu offers some contemporary dishes beyond the classics, aficionados know to stick to the solid sides and aged cuts of meat. That ribeye is dry-aged with Himalayan sea salt onsite for 60 days, which results in heavily flavored beef that pairs excellently with classic accompaniments. Think: traditionally prepared béarnaise sauce, creamy spinach, and a crispy pancake of grated hashbrowns.

Taiwanese Gourmet

F3

Chinese ✗

84-02 Broadway (at St. James Ave.)

Subway: Elmhurst Av
Phone: 718-429-4818
Web: N/A
Prices: 😂😂

Lunch & dinner daily

A truly local spot, Taiwanese Gourmet puts diners in the mood with its semi-open kitchen (a rarity for Chinese restaurants) and tasty food. Natural light floods the walls, which showcase an impressive collection of ancient warrior gear, all beautifully framed as if museum-ready. Menu descriptions are minimal but the staff is happy to elaborate.

Excellent technique shines through the Taiwanese specialties, notably in strips of "shredded beef" sautéed in a dark, meaty paste, and tossed with dried tofu that balances complex flavors with fresh Chinese celery—a hands down winner on the menu. Likewise, the stir-fry of wonderfully briny clams and basil offers a perfect balance of sweet and salty flavors with oyster sauce, soy sauce, rice wine, and red chilies.

Tang

C1

Korean ✗✗

196-50 Northern Blvd. (at Francis Lewis Blvd.)

Subway: N/A
Phone: 718-279-7080
Web: www.gammeeok.com
Prices: $$

Lunch & dinner daily

This 24-hour Northern Boulevard standout is an absolute must-visit for anyone seeking authentic Korean specialties. Connected to an art gallery, Tang has an impeccably cool style, starting with its angled exterior ablaze in beams of yellow light, and an interior done in brick walls and bare-wood tables.

The menu offers a handful of *bibimbap*, tofu dishes, and barbecue platters, as well heavenly soups like *seolleongtang*, made with ox-bone and paired with two outstanding varieties of kimchi—radish and Napa cabbage. But the main attraction is the sensational *jeon*, traditional Korean pancakes grilled to order (weekends and dinner, only). Try the perilla leaf *jeon* stuffed with seasoned pork; or *nok du jeon* of ground mung bean, sprouts, and minced pork.

Taverna Kyclades

F1

Greek ✗

33-07 Ditmars Blvd. (bet. 33rd & 35th Sts.)

Subway: Astoria - Ditmars Blvd   Lunch & dinner daily
Phone: 718-545-8666
Web: www.tavernakyclades.com
Prices: ⊜⊜

Forget the no-frills surroundings and focus instead on the fantastically fresh fish. This beloved Greek spot has folks happily dining elbow to elbow in a tiny yet lively space where the bustling kitchen is in view and seafaring scenes paint the walls. Quick, straightforward servers may address you in Greek if you look the part—that's just how local it gets here. Grab a seat on the enclosed patio for some serenity and get things going with garlicky and bubbling hot crab-stuffed clams; or the cold, classic trio of powerful *skordalia*, cooling tzatziki, and briny *taramosalata* served with toasted pita triangles. Order a side of *horta* (steamed escarole and dandelion) to accompany a plate of sweet and delicate mullets, served with a side of lemon potatoes.

Tawa Tandoor

F3

Indian ✗

37-56 74th St. (bet. Roosevelt & 37th Aves.)

Subway: Jackson Hts - Roosevelt Av   Lunch & dinner daily
Phone: 718-478-2730
Web: N/A
Prices: $$

There is a very good reason to stop and taste something deliciously unexpected, amid this strip of Indian diners and shops with windows dressed in sumptuous saris and jewelry. The solid Indian menu not only towers above local curry shops but offers fusion dishes honoring the culinary legacy of Chinese immigrants who settled in Calcutta and Bombay eons ago. The narrow, deep room dons dark hues, coffered ceilings, comfy seats, and lures crowds with its lunch buffet. *Aloo tikki chole* with fluffy potatoes, tender chickpeas, and tangy yogurt tossed in tamarind chutney keep regulars happy. Heat-seekers will adore such Indo-Chinese items as *hakka* chili chicken, highly spiced and with the concentrated flavors of star anise, cilantro, ginger, and scallions.

Testaccio

B3

Italian ✗✗

47-30 Vernon Blvd. (at 47th Rd.)

Subway: Vernon Blvd - Jackson Av
Phone: 718-937-2900
Web: www.testacciony.com
Prices: $$

Lunch & dinner daily

Elegant yet rustic, this Roman-inspired *ristorante* is a standout among its Vernon Boulevard neighbors. The bi-level space is filled with high, arched ceilings, distressed brick walls, antique mirrors, and dark wood tables against leather banquettes for a sophisticated vibe. Grab a seat at the fantastic bar, and choose a glass from the ample Frascati wine selection.

Comforting, well-made dishes define the food, starting with the likes of marinated artichoke wrapped in thin slices of lamb carpaccio, served over arugula salad. The *gnocco alla romana* baked in rich tomato sauce with basil and Parmesan are light, delicate, and sure to melt in your mouth. Excellent braised oxtail with mushroom ragout and rosemary mashed potatoes is supple and hearty.

Tito Rad's Grill

E3

Filipino ✗✗

49-10 Queens Blvd. (bet. 49th & 50th Sts.)

Subway: 46 St - Bliss St
Phone: 718-205-7299
Web: www.titorads.com
Prices:

Lunch & dinner daily

This eclectic resto's move to bigger digs gives it that much more space to seduce with its innovative fusion yet hearty flavors. The new dining room, clad in rough white marble and dark wood, includes several cozy touches including a framed photo of the original Tito's and white butcher paper atop the tables. The décor is just the right balance between contemporary and familiar, one that perfectly encapsulates the unique Malay-Spanish-Chinese- and Japanese-inspired menu.

Intensity abounds in every dish, from the fiery kick of the spicy *laing taro* leaves with pork and chicken, to the *lechon kawali*'s crispy pork belly skin. If it's available, be sure to try the *tortang dilis*, a puffball-like torta that's stuffed with tiny silver anchovies called *dulong*.

Tong Sam Gyup Goo Yi 🐷

C1

162-23 Depot Rd. (bet. Northern Blvd. & 164th St.)

Subway: Flushing – Main St (& bus Q13)   Lunch & dinner daily
Phone: 718-359-4583
Web: N/A
Prices: $$

Flushing is no stranger to Korean food, but this prized, pig-loving barbecue destination is always packed. Inside, the bright room's décor forgoes all frills to focus on regional specialties. Smiling servers are earnest and hospitable.

Begin with the usual but very exquisite *banchan* like pickled turnips, fermented bean paste soup, and specially aged house kimchi—funky, garlicky, and a total pleasure. Bowls of glassy *naengmyun* noodles dancing in a chilled broth with kimchi are just as popular. Yet what makes this place unique is that barbecue grill on each table, used for sizzling slices of flavorful duck with miso, garlic cloves, and bean sprouts; spicy, tender bits of octopus; and sweet, fatty pork with soy sauce, red chili paste, and scallions.

Trattoria L'incontro

F1

21-76 31st St. (at Ditmars Blvd.)

Subway: Astoria - Ditmars Blvd   Lunch & dinner Tue – Sun
Phone: 718-721-3532
Web: www.trattorialincontro.com
Prices: $$

Locals fancy Trattoria L'incontro for proudly dishing out the best in Italian-American cuisine. If you're imagining patrons with tucked napkins clinking glasses and filling the airy room with heartfelt laughter, then you're right on track. The space combines coral walls with frescos depicting a range of idyllic Italian landscapes, and sweet, attentive service.

In the back rests an oven that churns out deliciously blistered pizzas and a long, breathless list of specials. Sample the likes of *portobello in cartoccio* baked with herbs atop a sprightly green salad; or *pollo 4 funghi*, strips of silky chicken tossed with and thyme-sauce. The *pizza al cioccolato* oozing Nutella is worthy of framed accolades.

Trattoria Neo

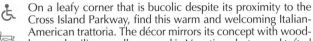

C1

15-01 149th St. (at 15th Ave.)

Subway: N/A	Lunch & dinner daily
Phone: 718-767-1110	
Web: www.trattorianeo.com	
Prices: $$	

On a leafy corner that is bucolic despite its proximity to the Cross Island Parkway, find this warm and welcoming Italian-American trattoria. The décor mirrors its concept with wood-beamed ceilings, walls covered in Venetian plaster, and tufted banquettes the color of wine.

Of course, pastas are a highlight and may include pillowy spinach-potato gnocchi bathed in sharp and creamy Gorgonzola sauce that is fragrant with basil and just a hint of tomato. The *arancini* are surprisingly inventive, mixing rice with marinara sauce and eggplant purée that lends an enticingly smoky flavor to the deep-fried morsels. *Pollo con salsiccia* demonstrates skilled cooking through succulent chicken with sausage crumbles in light brown sauce over pan-fried broccoli rabe.

Uma

C3

Central Asian ✗

92-07 Rockaway Beach Blvd. (bet. Beach 92nd & 94th Sts.)

Subway: Beach 90 St	Lunch & dinner daily
Phone: 718-318-9100	
Web: N/A	
Prices: $$	

Like any other seaside area, Rockaway Beach boasts a number of surfer hangouts with a laid-back vibe, one that extends to the hospitable Uma. Here, time is relative, and a chef's break is truly relished, but that doesn't mean he isn't working hard.

Behind a rusty brick façade, this Central Asian gem cooks up such delightful and generous specialties as *moshova*, a vegetarian soup with mung beans, rice, and finished with tart yogurt. Since many dishes err on the heavy side, start with their light yet filling signature salad tossing red peppers, cubes of fried eggplant, herbs, and feta. Then continue with butternut squash *manti*. Typically filled with meat, this delightful vegetarian version comes in a thin wrapper and is topped with caramelized onion sauce.

Uncle Zhou 😊

Chinese ✗

83-29 Broadway (at Dongan Ave.)

Subway: Elmhurst Av   Lunch & dinner daily
Phone: 718-393-0888
Web: N/A
Prices: 😊😊

Gifted cooks have been trekking to Elmhurst to show off their skills, but the chef/visionary of this modestly decked, massively popular Hainanese gem has been a fixture from the start. Seat yourself inside the butterscotch-hued room, surrender to the affable staff, and await a memorable feast.

Opening this culinary show are pickled cucumbers and briny bamboo shoots with mushrooms, followed by pan-seared lamb dumplings or hugely fortifying "Dial oil" noodles sautéed with dried red chilies. For the consummate finale, pre-order "Taosibao," an impressive showpiece of rice-stuffed quail inside a squab, inside a chicken, inside a duck. Not only is this trumped-up version of *turducken* technically superb, but every element is flavored by an aromatic broth.

Urubamba

Peruvian ✗

86-20 37th Ave. (at 86th St.)

Subway: 82 St - Jackson Hts   Lunch & dinner daily
Phone: 718-672-2224
Web: N/A
Prices: $$

Named for Peru's intensely beautiful river, the Rio Urubamba, this hacienda-inspired space features indigenous paintings and artifacts that echo the rustic fare pouring out of the kitchen.

On weekends, the eatery serves traditional *desayuno*, a gut-bursting feast of *chanfainita* beef stew, and other hearty favorites. Here, tamales are a broad and flat banana leaf wrapped and stuffed with chicken and olives a tasty contrast to the familiar Meso-American counterpart. For ultimate comfort, go for the *seco de cabrito*, a fantastically tender lamb and *aji panca* stew served with chunks of cassava and extra sauce in a tiny clay kettle. The dense *alfajor* cookie sandwich filled with dulce de leche and *crema volteada* flan is a perfectly decadent ending.

Uvarara

B2

79-28 Metropolitan Ave. (at 80th St.)

Subway: Middle Village - Metropolitan Av (& bus Q54)   Dinner Tue – Sun
Phone: 718-894-0052
Web: www.uvararany.com
Prices: $$

From its quirky mismatched chairs and gothic arches to the curtain created out of strings of wine corks, Uvarara is intimate, comfortable, and very homey. Tucked away in the quaint, residential neighborhood of Middle Village, this restaurant is the work of the Iadicicco family, who hail from Caserta and have created an authentic atmosphere akin to the *osterie* of their native country.

The kitchen consistently spins out delectable dishes, such as baked gnocchi over butter and *Parmigiano* sauce, with touches of sage and pepper; or broiled portobello mushroom caps stuffed with pork sausage, garlic, cheese, and parsley, topped with toasted breadcrumbs and balsamic reduction. The *basa* fish special arrives flaky and beautifully fried, with a standout lentil salad.

Venturo Osteria & Wine Bar 🐷

A2

44-07 Queens Blvd. (bet. 44th & 45th Sts.)

Subway: 46 St - Bliss St   Lunch & dinner daily
Phone: 718-406-9363
Web: www.venturovino.com
Prices: $$

From the moment it opened its doors in the summer of 2013, Venturo has amassed a loyal following of Italian food fiends in Queens. Original canvas paintings dress the Aegean-blue walls and distressed wood accents reinforce the calm Mediterranean vibe—even at peak times.

Chef Michelle Vido helms a dedicated kitchen that surprises with excellence and generosity. House-made defines every dish, from freshly baked focaccia to the honey yogurt drizzled upon a lemon tart. Plump P.E.I. mussels in a fiery, serrano-tomato broth make for a great snack. But, for a fuller meal, try chewy ribbons of whole-wheat fettuccine tossed with hedgehog mushrooms, leeks, and pancetta; or roasted leg of lamb stuffed with garlicky herbs over braised chickpeas and escarole.

Vesta Trattoria

E2

Italian ✗

21-02 30th Ave. (at 21st St.)

Subway: 30 Av
Phone: 718-545-5550
Web: www.vestavino.com
Prices: $$

Lunch Sat – Sun
Dinner nightly

Astoria favorite, Vesta Trattoria, still attracts neighborhood foodies to its postage stamp-sized room—modestly dressed with sage-green banquettes—for a respectable wine list and ever-changing daily specials. Not only does this Italian idol walk the line between classic and contemporary cooking with seasonal ingredients, but it also boasts a wine on tap program.

The extremely appetizing menu includes light bites like sugar snap peas tossed with brown butter yogurt. Keeping it in the "pea" family is a chilled English pea soup topped with spiced *labneh*, perfectly tailed by pappardelle laced with a luscious veal-and-tomato sauce and Grana Padano. It screams for more forkfuls, not unlike a spiced Baby Jesus Cake—light, spongy, and covered in caramel sauce.

Wafa

B2

Middle Eastern ✗

100-05 Metropolitan Ave. (bet. 70th Ave. & 70th Rd.)

Subway: Forest Hills - 71 Av
Phone: 718-880-2055
Web: www.wafasfood.com
Prices: $$

Lunch & dinner Wed – Mon

One cannot know the sheer joy and passion that goes into homemade Lebanese food without a visit to Wafa. Nestled among the mom-and-pop shops of Forest Hills' main strip, this pocket-sized spot appears shy on décor but bold on authenticity.

The smiling owner, Wafa Chami, runs the kitchen and her falafel still ranks among the best in town—these perfect orbs of chickpeas and "secret Wafa spices" are stuffed in a fluffy pita with hummus, pickled turnips, and *har* hot sauce. Primo specials range from stuffed eggplant and zucchini, to ground lamb steeped in garlicky tomato sauce. Meat pies sound pedestrian but should be sampled—these light-as-air flatbreads are topped with minced beef, sautéed with onions, tomatoes, and her infamous spice mix.

Zabb Elee 🌸

Thai 🍴

71-28 Roosevelt Ave. (bet. 70th & 72nd Sts.)

Subway: 74 St - Broadway
Phone: 718-426-7992
Web: N/A
Prices: 🍜

Lunch & dinner daily

Easily accessed by subway and much more impressive from the inside, this humming storefront looks simple enough, but is actually one of the city's most complex Thai restaurants. The inviting dining room displays a bit of elegance in the patterned tile floor, mirrors surrounded by pale green shutters, shiny metal-topped tables, and white bird cages arranged over the small bar.

This kitchen is unapologetically authentic and isn't afraid to cook like it's in Northeast Thailand instead of Jackson Heights. The majority of patrons are expats; non-Thai minority should expect to be quizzed about spice levels. Know that in order to taste true Isaan flavors, you'll need to insist on real heat. Just assure those kindly, sympathetic servers that you want accurate spicing.

Fasten your seatbelt, find a hand to hold, and start with an outrageously funky Lao green papaya salad tossing preserved blue crab, pickled fish, crisp pork rinds, and Thai eggplant all spiked with a spicy-sour-tart sauce of ginger and fermented fish. Then, move on to the wonderful slow burn of yellow curry with crunchy bamboo shoots and delicate poached shrimp. Sweet and flaky grilled catfish with "Thai herbs" is a revelation.

Zum Stammtisch

German 🍴

B2

69-46 Myrtle Ave. (bet. 69th Pl. & 70th St.)

Subway: N/A
Phone: 718-386-3014
Web: www.zumstammtisch.com
Prices: $$

Lunch & dinner daily

Family owned and operated since 1972, this unrelenting success story has expanded over the years and welcomed Stammtisch Pork Store & Imports next door.

Zum Stammtisch hosts a crowded house in a Bavarian country inn setting where old-world flavor is relished with whole-hearted enthusiasm. The goulash is thick and hearty, stocked with potatoes and beans, but that's just for starters. Save room for *sauerbraten, jägerschnitzel,* or a platter of succulent grilled sausages that includes *bratwurst, knockwurst,* and hickory-smoked *krainerwurst* served with sauerkraut and potato salad. The *Schwarzwälder Kirschtorte* (classic Black Forest cake) layers dense chocolate sponge with Kirsch-soaked cherries and cream, and is absolutely worth the indulgence.

Sunday brunch plans?
Look for the 🛏 !

Staten Island

Staten Island

Staten Island may be the least populated borough of NYC, but the erection of the Verrazano-Narrows Bridge ended its previously bucolic existence. This fact is especially apt because one of the strongest, most accurate simplifications is that this "island" is home to a large Italian-American population, and no self-respecting foodie would visit here without picking up a *scungilli* pizza from **Joe & Pat's**, or slice from **Nunzio** and **Denino's**. This borough's shores, marinas, and waterfronts, once in shambles thanks to Hurricane Sandy, are slowly but surely recovering. Case in point: **Skippy's**, originally a famous food truck, continues to sell its hot dogs prepared in various regional styles to residents of Mariner's Harbor right on Richmond Terrace. To that end, anyone with preconceived notions about this "forgotten borough," can leave them at the ferry door. Though deemed at one time the largest landfill in the world, Staten Island is currently being transformed into a verdant and very vast public park.

CULINARY CORNUCOPIA

While this region is revered as an Italian-American hub, today it continues to surprise visitors with its ethnically diverse communities. Take a culinary tour of the eastern Mediterranean at **Dinora**, proffering an abundance of olives, cheeses, and freshly butchered meat. Otherwise, stop by those coveted old-time Polish delis, which seem to comfortably thrive on their takeout business and tasty homemade jams. It may not have **Cangiano's** bread recipe missed by many around here, but **Giuliano's Prodotti Italiani** promises to keep patrons happy with such homey, old country classics as handmade pizzas, pastas, calzones, and more.

Spice heads will rejoice at the fantastic Sri Lankan food finds in the area surrounding Victory Boulevard. A spectrum of restaurants (more like storefronts) are scattered here and include **New Asha**, serving this country's fiery food including flavorful fish buns and pungent vegetable stews. In keeping with South Asian cuisine, customs, and culture, Staten Island is also home to Jacques Marchais Museum of Tibetan Art, a reputed institution aimed at advancing Tibetan and Himalayan art. Steps from these subcontinent gems, discover authentic taquerias and a large Liberian outdoor market in the vicinity of Grasmere, where a small but special selection of

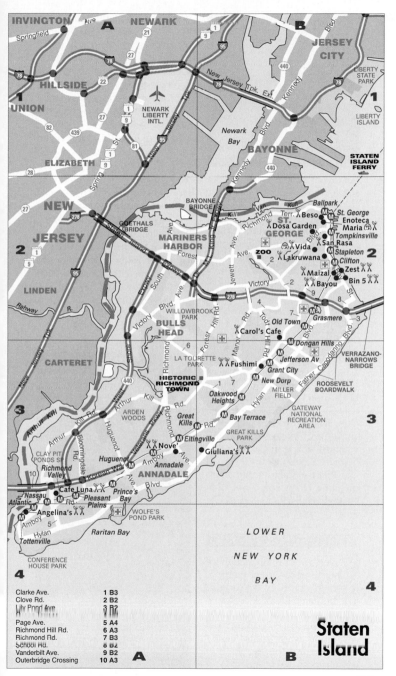

Staten Island

purveyors supply West African staples and regional delights. Take these treats back home for dinner or cook up a fresh spread with fantastic, locally farmed produce from **St. George Greenmarket**, open on Saturdays. Historic Richmond Town is an homage to Staten Island's sustainable food movement by organizing the family-focused festival **Uncorked!**, featuring the best in homemade cuisine and wine. They even offer recipes for traditional favorites and American classics. For rare and more mature varietals, **Mission Fine Wines** is top-notch, but if in need of calorie-heavy (AKA heavenly) eats, **The Cookie Jar** is way above par. Opened in 2007, this youngest sibling of **Cake Chef**, a beloved bakeshop up the road and **Piece-A-Cake** further south on New Dorp Lane, not only incites but engages its audience in a riot of sweet selections.

FOOD, FUN & FROLIC

Given its booming culinary scene and cultural merging, it should come as no surprise that the Staten Island of the future includes plans for a floating farmer's market, aquarium, and revamped waterfronts, giving residents and tourists another reason to sit back and savor a drink at one of the bars along Bay Street. Sips need to be tailed by savories which can be found in abundance at **Adobe Blues**, a cantina preparing sumptuous Southwestern food and prettified with a cozy fireplace, clay walls, and collectables depicting the island's rodeo days…yee-haw! Residents love this local haunt for its modest demeanor coupled with gratifying grub, and are likely to endorse it till the end of time. After dawdling on Lafayette Avenue, drive through some of the city's wealthiest zip codes starring mansions rife with magnificent views of Manhattan and beyond. Whether here to glimpse the world's only complete collection of rattlesnakes at the zoo; or seek out the birthplaces of such divas as Christina Aguilera and Joan Baez, a visit to Staten Island is nothing if not interesting.

Angelina's

A4

399 Ellis St.

Bus:	N/A	Lunch Mon– Sat
Phone:	718-227-2900	Dinner nightly
Web:	www.angelinasristorante.com	
Prices:	$$$	

It's no secret that Angelina's is Staten Island's place to celebrate Italian-American culture. Packed by 7:00 P.M. and boasting stunning river sunset views, it also offers live music and a massive atrium attracting revelers from near and far.

The multi-level Victorian may conjure New Orleans, but Angelina's keeps the focus clearly on Italian-American cooking with excellent pastas and plush red wines. The classic baked clams oreganata have that idyllic blend of butter and garlic. *Spaghettini al pomodoro* is as lovely as it sounds, with long-simmered tomato ragù, basil, and sprinkling of Parmigiano. The popular *trenette nere con frutti di mare* piles a mountain of shrimp, clams, mussels, and scallops on to thick squid ink pasta bathed in chunky tomato sauce.

Bayou

B2

1072 Bay St. (bet. Chestnut & St. Marys Aves.)

Bus:	51, 81	Lunch & dinner daily
Phone:	718-273-4383	
Web:	www.bayounyc.com	
Prices:	$$	

Southern fare isn't novel to the city, but Cajun food on Staten Island is a whole new realm, which Bayou delivers with its veritable setting and spread. The space may seem a bit bawdy with gold and green accents, but linen-covered tables, luminous mirrors, and luxe chandeliers lend refinement. Live music on some nights adds fun.

Cajun offerings begin with a wonderfully complex jambalaya, rice tucked with smoky Tasso ham, tomato, and sweet shrimp, served with a lemon-basil mayonnaise; or roast beef po'boy with caramelized onions. Blackened catfish is soul-satisfying in every sense, served in a skillet beside a pile of fluffy rice. Bananas Foster with rum and brown sugar are tasty, but turn heavenly when paired with one of the many boozy, rich coffees.

Beso

Staten Island

Spanish ✗

B2

11 Schuyler St. (bet. Richmond Tr. & Stuyvesant Pl.)

Bus: N/A

Lunch & dinner daily

Phone: 718-816-8162

Web: www.besonyc.com

Prices: $$

Well-located? Yes, just off the ferry. Good food? Helpful staff? Of course. Great for both parties and solo diners? You know it. Lovely Beso seems to have it all, including an interior that spotlights quaint accents like antique sideboards and an intricately carved U-shaped bar. While grazing menus are all the rage, the larger dishes (*platos fuertes*) are also worth exploring.

Their tapas selection is vibrant—starting with *fundito*, a richly flavored green chili-tomato sauce topped with melted Mahón cheese and studded with chorizo. Follow with the *elote de cangrejo*, crab cakes with roasted corn over a bracing horseradish aïoli; or flautas filled with roasted mushrooms and melted *cobrales*. Close with sweets like coconut flan cloaked in caramel.

Bin 5

Contemporary ✗✗

B2

1233 Bay St. (bet. Maryland & Scarboro Aves.)

Bus: 51, 81

Dinner Tue – Sun

Phone: 718-448-7275

Web: www.bin5nyc.com

Prices: $$

At this intimate bistro in Rosebank, dinner comes with a view of the twinkling Manhattan skyline. Complete with teardrop chandeliers, exposed brick, and a walled, outdoor garden, Bin 5's romantic setting has for long drawn locals seeking consistently good food and quiet conversation (plus that fantastic panorama!).

The playful menu—complete with solid daily specials—ranges from the perfectly chilled crab martini, a ceviche of top-notch crabmeat, avocado, cilantro, and mango, to fluffy knobs of ricotta gnocchi tossed with a sweet pear sauce, caramelized onions, and toasted pignoli nuts. Try the grilled pork loin, a truly fantastic dish which is cooked to medium, cut into three slices, and drizzled with a hoisin- ginger- and sweet chili-barbecue sauce.

Cafe Luna

A3

31 Page Ave. (bet. Boscombe Ave. & Richmond Valley Rd.)

Bus: 74   Lunch Mon – Fri
Phone: 718-227-8582   Dinner nightly
Web: www.cafelunanyc.com
Prices: **$$**

This well-run local institution proves that one should never judge a restaurant by its strip mall cover. With its Italian-American cooking, romantic fireplace, enclosed wine room, and covered veranda, Cafe Luna has a friendly, warm, and familial air thanks to the Sicilian owners who hail from Palermo.

Their perfectly prepared pastas mean the standards are taken care of, and it's easy to leave here satisfied. Start with short little corkscrews of fresh fusilli *puttanesca* in a strong, plum tomato sauce enhanced by anchovies, red chili flakes, garlic, basil, and black olives. Deliciously fresh red snapper *marechiaro* combines briny clams and sweet mussels with a fresh fish fillet and light tomato sauce with hints of chili flakes and lots of fresh parsley.

Carol's Cafe

B2

1571 Richmond Rd. (at Four Corners Rd. & Seaview Ave.)

Bus: 74, 76, 84, 86   Dinner Wed – Sat
Phone: 718-979-5600
Web: www.carolscafe.com
Prices: **$$**

Dining here is like dining in Chef/owner Carol Frazzetta's kitchen—almost literally, because she lives on the premises. Her delightful personality fills the space, from the fresh flowers and pink linens, to shareable dishes and that homemade chocolate stout triple layer cake.

Not only has Frazzetta owned the building since the 1970s, but she clearly knows her neighbors, many of whom flock to the café for a roster of daily specials (top hits include "wild game of the day" like grilled buffalo ribeye and a marvelous prosciutto- and tomato-stuffed bread). The chef's slow-cooked *spaghetti al pomodoro* is another fan fave, topped with a chiffonade of basil and peppered with Parmesan, before serving. Like everything else, it's simple, well-made, and *delizioso*.

Dosa Garden

B2

Indian ✗

323 Victory Blvd. (bet. Cebra Ave. & Jersey St.)

Bus: 46, 48, 61, 66
Phone: 718-420-0919
Web: N/A
Prices: ⊖⊖

Lunch Tue – Sun
Dinner nightly

The spicy, complex, and fragrant *dosas* of Dosa Garden make this casual stop a thoroughly impressive hidden gem. The ambience feels more storefront eatery than sit-down restaurant, with just a few hints of South Asian décor, but the warm, made-to-order dishes and aromas from the kitchen are transporting.

The kitchen boasts a tandoor oven but also churns out an array of elaborate *dosas*, like the tantalizingly crisp Mysore masala served with a sour yogurt sauce, spread with spicy chutney, and folded with potatoes, peppercorns, curry leaves, chili, and cumin. Don't miss the unique *rasa vada*, crunchy lentil doughnuts soaked in a deliciously spicy *rasam*. Curries are amazingly delish, like the shockingly deep brown Chettinadu fish, accented with mustard seeds.

Enoteca Maria ☺

B2

Italian ✗

27 Hyatt St. (bet. Central Ave. & St. Marks Pl.)

Bus: N/A
Phone: 718-447-2777
Web: www.enotecamaria.com
Prices: $$

Dinner Wed – Sun

⬜ S ⬜

No need to venture far on Staten Island for excellent Italian food—Enoteca Maria is just two blocks from the ferry terminal. With its Carrera marble and lively vibe, this tiny spot could easily be wedged into Greenwich Village. Thankfully, it's not—anywhere else its certain authenticity would be sacrificed.

Each night, the menu changes depending on which *nonna* is presiding over the kitchen, as in Teresa from Sicily, who might serve an oxtail ragù or grilled artichokes glistening with good olive oil and a squeeze of lemon—simple yet great. *Coniglio alla cacciatora* arrives as diverse cuts of tender rabbit swimming in an inspired sauce of braised tomatoes, root vegetables, herbs, and a sweet-wine reduction with rosemary and garlic.

Fushimi

Fusion ✗✗

B3

2110 Richmond Rd. (bet. Colfax & Lincoln Aves.)

Bus: 51, 81
Phone: 718-980-5300
Web: www.fushimi-us.com
Prices: $$$

Lunch & dinner daily

Fushimi is the ultimate spot for hungry locals in search of a dependable club scene sans commute. On any given night, its cozy booths are packed with islanders slinging back colorful cocktails and digging into architecturally designed sushi and sashimi from the Asian-fusion menu. Presentation is a knockout here, and the creativity and precision extends to the quality and combination of ingredients as well. Case in point: the aptly named Staten Island, a shrimp tempura roll topped with thin slices of seared filet mignon and dollops of mint-honey mustard and spicy aïoli.

Sink your teeth into the long-braised short ribs, which is fall-off-the-bone tender and served with Korean *galbi* sauce and "pee wee" potato chips made from those adorably tiny tubers.

Giuliana's

Italian ✗✗

B3

4105 Hylan Blvd. (at Osborn Ave.)

Bus: 54, 78, 79
Phone: 718-317-8507
Web: www.giulianassi.com
Prices: $$

Lunch & dinner Tue – Sun

Staten Island may swarm with Italian eateries, but Giuliana's does a masterful job in keeping its kitchen distinct and the patrons loyal. This queen bee rests amid shops, catering halls, and ample competition. The interior is modest and charming, with framed pictures of smiling patrons and a fully stocked bar.

Meals should begin with a taste of their freshly made mozzarella, or perhaps the *carciofi Giuliana*, perfectly seasoned, crispy artichoke hearts with a rich and intensely flavored Gorgonzola sauce. Sesame seed-crusted tuna in a balsamic jus is served with sautéed spinach and a restrained kiss of garlic. Sunday suppers featuring a traditional Southern Italian *ragù del macellaio* simmered with meatballs and *braciole*, are a draw in their own right.

Lakruwana

B2

Sri Lankan ✗

668 Bay St. (at Broad St.)

Bus:	51, 76
Phone:	347-857-6619
Web:	www.lakruwana.com
Prices:	⊛⊛

Lunch & dinner Tue – Sun

S

Prepare for a sensory overload the moment you set foot into Lakruwana—the Sri Lankan hot spot is covered from floor-to-ceiling in murals, sculptures, flags, and more. The bright kaleidoscope of textures and colors is a welcome sight in an otherwise downtrodden part of the borough, as is the energetic owner who drifts from table to table.

Those familiar with Indian food will love Lakruwana's abundance of curries, green chili-spiked *kuttu roti*, as well as refreshingly salty-and-sour *lassi*. But their flavorful fare is considerably spicier, packing heat into everything from fiery red chili *lunu miris* chutney to devilled chicken. Loaded with ginger and garlic, this stellar tomato-based chicken specialty comes with cooling *raita* and tangy vegetable curry.

Maizal

B2

Mexican ✗

990 Bay St. (bet. Lynhurst & Willow Sts.)

Bus:	51, 81
Phone:	347-825-3776
Web:	www.maizalrestaurant.com
Prices:	$$

Lunch Sun
Dinner nightly

Amid a wealth of Italian options, lovely Maizal is a sweet, attractive, and welcomed addition to this corner of the city. Large, solid wood tables, a marble-topped bar, bright walls, seasonal flowers, and semi-open kitchen in the back fashion a very comfortable atmosphere. Live, contemporary music on weekends enhances the fun of dining here.

Begin with a refreshing salad mingling fennel, crispy bacon, and manchego; or intensely spicy and "angry jalapeños" stuffed with gooey goat cheese and served alongside grapes and mango for sweet, contrasting flavors. Look for daily specials like tacos stuffed with deliciously seared skirt steak, pickled onions, and creamy slaw. The roast lime chicken may sound simple, but is beautifully arranged, silky, and supple.

Nove'

A3

Italian ✕✕

3900 Richmond Ave. (bet. Amboy Rd. & Oakdale St.)

Bus: 59, 79
Phone: 718-227-3286
Web: www.noveitalianbistro.com
Prices: $$$

Lunch & dinner Tue – Sun

Hipsters stay clear—Nove' is an ardent, old-school *ristorante* where couples of a certain age are as well-dressed as the staff and reservations are long-standing. The space is ornamented yet never gaudy, and makes a bold statement with burnt-orange walls, carved wood moldings, and pocket doors separating the warm lounge from the main dining room. Elegant custom cabinets are arranged with fine wines for pairing.

Tasty offerings begin with incredibly tender calamari rings tossed with bits of sweet red pepper, arugula, fennel, and *peperoncini* dressing; or *sacchettini*, beggar's purse pasta filled with a blend of cheese, pears, and greens in a brown butter-and-sage sauce. Their veal chop *grottino* with spring pea-and-leek risotto is an original classic.

San Rasa

B2

Sri Lankan ✕

226 Bay St. (bet. Hannah St. & Victory Blvd.)

Subway: 51
Phone: 718-420-0027
Web: www.sanrasa.com
Prices:

Lunch & dinner Wed – Mon

San Rasa may require both a ferry ride and an open mind, but this authentic Sri Lankan favorite is absolutely worth it—and absolutely delicious. Conveniently situated just a short walk from the ferry landing, this ace location doesn't exactly mind its appearence (the décor can seem busy with odd gadgets and carved items; the views nonexistent). Focus on the smells and tastes of the feast before you.

Ideally, go with a group to explore the menu and savor the likes of *lamparis*, banana leaf purses filled with fragrant yellow rice and silky chicken. *Appams*, made from flour and coconut milk, are best for sopping up a fiery goat curry infused with turmeric, chilies, and cumin seeds. The Sunday lunch buffet is an extraordinary bargain for intrepid foodies.

Vida 😊

American ✗

B2

381 Van Duzer St. (bet. Beach & Wright Sts.)

Bus: 78   Dinner Tue – Sat
Phone: 718-720-1501
Web: www.vidany.com
Prices: $$

⟦S⟧ Run by owner Silva Popaz, whose infectious warmth and delightful dishes keep regulars coming back for more, Vida is a truly enchanting local haven. The bright and immaculate room is hung with stunning artwork (which is not for sale). Menu items can be found on an easel, and the friendly staff is dedicated to high-quality hospitality.

From the menu, nosh on the likes of batter-fried eggplant rolled with tart goat cheese, and baked in chunky tomato sauce with mozzarella and herbs; decadent gumbo of smoked sausage, shrimp, and chicken; and organic brown rice and braised lentil cake topped with tahini and spinach, set over grilled portobello mushroom. Satiate the sweet craving with bread pudding, oozing with cinnamon and nuts and served with ice cream.

Zest

French ✗✗

B2

977 Bay St. (bet. Lynhurst & Willow Sts.)

Bus: 51, 81   Dinner Tue – Sun
Phone: 718-390-8477
Web: www.zestaurant.com
Prices: $$

Whether seated inside or out, the surroundings are verdant and lush here at Zest. The outdoor garden is a perfect destination for warm nights, while the elegant interior glows with goldish hues and is outfitted in dark woods, vintage vases, blown glass light fixtures, and handsome greenery.

Begin with a tasty vegetable terrine, layering creamy goat cheese, roasted artichoke, eggplant, zucchini, red peppers, fine herbs, and presented with garlic aïoli. The veal tenderloin Cordon Blue is richly stuffed with ham and Gruyère, drizzled with red pepper sauce, and then fanned over potato gratin and a trio of vegetables. Specials may include dill and vodka-cured gravlax over micro arugula alongside silver-dollar potato pancakes and horseradish-spiked sour cream.

Where to **Eat**

Indexes

Alphabetical List of Restaurants

Indexes ▲ Alphabetical List of Restaurants

Indexes ▶ Alphabetical List of Restaurants

Indexes ▶ Alphabetical List of Restaurants

Indexes ▶ Alphabetical List of Restaurants

Restaurants by Cuisine

American

Joseph Leonard	🍴	155
Juni	❀ 🍴🍴🍴	239
Juventino	🍴🍴	475
Le Cirque	🍴🍴🍴🍴	242
Left Bank	🍴🍴	159
Louro	🍴🍴	161
Luksus at Tørst	❀ 🍴🍴	482
Mas (farmhouse)	🍴🍴🍴	164
Mercer Kitchen	🍴🍴	327
Modern (The)	❀ 🍴🍴🍴	293
Momofuku Ko	❀❀ 🍴	72
Momofuku Ssäm Bar	⊛ 🍴	73
Musket Room (The)	❀ 🍴🍴	328
Narcissa	🍴🍴	74
NoMad	❀ 🍴🍴🍴	121
North River	🍴	75
Nougatine	🍴🍴	409
Pearl & Ash	⊛ 🍴🍴	330
Pearl Room (The)	🍴🍴	496
Perilla	🍴🍴	170
Perry Street	⊛ 🍴🍴	171
Per Se	❀❀❀ 🍴🍴🍴🍴🍴	298
Piora	❀ 🍴🍴	172
Prune	⊛ 🍴	77
Recette	🍴🍴	173
Regency Bar & Grill (The)	🍴🍴	382
Resto	🍴	124
River Café (The)	❀ 🍴🍴🍴	504
River Styx	🍴	503
Robert	🍴🍴	301
Roberta's	⊛ 🍴	505
Roebling Tea Room	🍴	505
Rosette	🍴	213
Rouge et Blanc	🍴🍴	332
Rucola	🍴	506
Runner & Stone	⊛ 🍴🍴	507
Saint Austere (The)	🍱	508
Salt & Fat	⊛ 🍴	561
Saxon + Parole	🍴🍴	175
Simone (The)	🍴🍴	304
Skál	🍴🍴	215
Standard Grill	🍴🍴	178
Stone Park Cafe	🍴	514
Take Root	❀ 🍴	517
Tocqueville	🍴🍴	126
Traif	⊛ 🍴	519
Trestle on Tenth	🍴🍴	30
Tribeca Grill	🍴🍴	357
Vitae	🍴🍴🍴	254

Deli

Barney Greengrass	🍴	398
Katz's	⊛ 🍴	211
Liebman's	🍴	429
Mile End	⊛ 🍴	486
Mill Basin Kosher Delicatessen	🍴	487
2nd Avenue Deli	🍴	249

Eastern European

Andre's Café	🍴	361
Bear	🍴🍴	536
Kafana	🍴	65
Oda House	🍴	75

Ethiopian

Zoma	⊛ 🍴	201

European

Marrow (The)	🍴🍴	163
Prime Meats	⊛ 🍴🍴	501

Filipino

Engeline's	🍴	543
Maharlika	🍴	69
Payag	🍴	560
Tito Rad's Grill	🍴🍴	568

French

Artisanal	🍴🍴	227
Balthazar	🍴🍴	318
Bar Boulud	🍴🍴	397
Benoit	🍴🍴	268
Bistro SK	🍴	424
Bistro Vendôme	🍴🍴	229
Brasserie Ruhlmann	🍴🍴	271
Buvette	🍱	142
Café Boulud	❀ 🍴🍴🍴	364
Cédric	🍴🍴	192
Chez Napoléon	🍴	272
Daniel	❀❀ 🍴🍴🍴🍴	367
DBGB Kitchen & Bar	⊛ 🍴🍴	56
FP Patisserie	🍴	371
Jubilee	🍴🍴	237

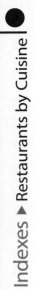

Jamaican

Japanese

Indexes ▶ Restaurants by Cuisine

Peruvian

Panca	𝗫	168
Urubamba	𝗫	571
Warique	𝗫	415

Pizza

American Flatbread Co.		𝗫𝗫	340
		𝗫	19
Don Antonio by Starita	⊛	𝗫𝗫	276
Forcella		𝗫	467
Houdini Kitchen Laboratory		𝗫𝗫	546
Kesté Pizza & Vino	⊛	𝗫	156
Luzzo's		𝗫	69
Motorino		𝗫	73
Nick's		𝗫	379
Nick's Pizza		𝗫	557
Paulie Gee's	⊛	𝗫	496
Sottocasa		𝗫	513

Polish

Karczma	𝗫	476
Krolewskie Jadlo	𝗫	477

Puerto Rican

Brisas Del Caribe	𝗫	425
El Nuevo Bohío	𝗫	426
Joe's Place	𝗫	428

Russian

Mari Vanna	𝗫𝗫	119
Russian Samovar	𝗫𝗫	302

Scandinavian

Aamanns-Copenhagen		𝗫	340
Aquavit	❀❀	𝗫𝗫𝗫	226

Seafood

Aquagrill	𝗫𝗫	317
Asian Jewels	𝗫𝗫	534
Atlantic Grill	𝗫𝗫	362
Blue Water Grill	𝗫𝗫	102
Crave Fishbar	𝗫𝗫	232
Cull & Pistol	𝗫	22
Ed's Lobster Bar ⊛	𝗫	323
Esca	𝗫𝗫	276

Fishtag		𝗫𝗫	403
Fishtail by David Burke		𝗫𝗫𝗫	370
Flex Mussels		𝗫𝗫	370
John Dory Oyster Bar (The)		𝗫	115
Le Bernardin	❀❀❀	𝗫𝗫𝗫𝗫	286
Marea	❀❀	𝗫𝗫𝗫	289
Mary's Fish Camp		𝗫	164
Mermaid Inn (The)		𝗫	70
Navy		𝗫	329
Oceana		𝗫𝗫𝗫	296
Pearl Oyster Bar		𝗫	169
Sabry's		𝗫	561
Sea Grill (The)		𝗫𝗫𝗫	303
Wild Edibles	⊛	𝗫	254
ZZ's Clam Bar	❀	𝗫	184

Senegalese

J. Restaurant Chez Asta	⊛	𝗫	196

South African

Braai	𝗫𝗫	270
Kaia	𝗫	374

Southern

Elberta	⊛	𝗫𝗫	463
Melba's		𝗫	197
Miss Mamie's Spoonbread Too	⊛	𝗫	408
SoCo		𝗫𝗫	512

Spanish

Alcala		𝗫𝗫	225
Andanada	❀	𝗫𝗫	396
Bar Jamón		🍴	100
Barraca		𝗫𝗫	138
Beso		𝗫	583
Boqueria	⊛	𝗫𝗫	103
Casa Mono	❀	𝗫𝗫	106
Cata	⊛	𝗫𝗫	207
Degustation		𝗫𝗫	57
El Born		𝗫𝗫	463
El Mio Cid		𝗫	465
El Porrón		𝗫	368
El Quinto Pino		𝗫𝗫	24
Huertas		𝗫𝗫	63

La Nacional	✕	25
Las Ramblas	📇	158
La Vara	✿ ✕✕	479
Salinas	✕✕	28
Sevilla	✕	176
Socarrat	✕	28
Tertulia	☺ ✕	181
Tía Pol	📇	29
Toro	📇	30
Txikito	✕✕	31

Sri Lankan

Lakruwana	✕	587
San Rasa	✕	588
Sigiri	✕	80
Spicy Lanka	✕	564

Steakhouse

Arlington Club	✕✕	362
BLT Prime	✕✕	101
BLT Steak	✕✕✕	228
Christos	✕✕	540
Del Frisco's	✕✕✕	275
Frankie & Johnnie's	✕✕	278
Gallagher's	✕✕	279
Jake's Steakhouse	✕✕	428
Keens	✕✕	281
Le Relais de Venise	✕✕	243
MarkJoseph	✕✕	89
Nebraska Steakhouse	✕✕	90
Parlor Steakhouse	✕✕	381
Peter Luger	✿ ✕	497
Porter House	✕✕✕	299
Prime & Beyond New York	✕	77
Ricardo Steakhouse	✕✕	199
Smith & Wollensky	✕✕	250
S Prime	✕✕	565
Staghorn	✕✕	305
Wolfgang's	✕✕	255

Thai

Arharn Thai	✕	534

Ayada	☺ ✕	535
Chao Thai	✕	538
Kin Shop	✕✕	156
Larb Ubol	☺ ✕	285
Nuaa (The)	✕✕	379
Nusara	✕	558
Pok Pok Ny	✿ ✕	500
Somtum Der	☺ ✕	81
Sura	✕✕	412
Uncle Boons	✕✕	335
Zabb Elee	✿ ✕	574

Tibetan

Himalayan Yak	✕	545

Turkish

Antique Garage	✕	317
Beyoglu	☺ ✕	363
Bodrum	✕✕	399
Pera	✕✕	247
Sip Sak	✕✕	250
Taci's Beyti	✕✕	516
Turkish Kitchen	☺ ✕✕	127

Vegan

Blossom	✕✕	18
Pure Food and Wine	✕✕	123

Vegetarian

Dirt Candy	☺ ✕	58
Gobo	✕✕	149

Vietnamese

bún-ker	☺ ✕	538
Falansai	✕	466
Nightingale 9	✕	492
Pho Băng	✕	43
Thái Sơn	✕	45
Xe Lua	✕	45

MANHATTAN

Chelsea

American
Colicchio & Sons	✗✗✗	20
Cookshop	✗✗	20
Red Cat (The)	✗✗	27
Tipsy Parson	✗✗	29

Asian
Chop-Shop	✗	19

Chinese
Legend Bar & Restaurant	✗✗	25

Contemporary
Americano (The)	✗✗	18
Foragers City Table	✗✗	24
Trestle on Tenth	✗✗	30

Italian
da Umberto	✗✗	22
Del Posto	❀ ✗✗✗✗	23
Pastai	✗✗	26

Japanese
Naka Naka	✗	26

Latin American
Coppelia	✗	21

Mexican
Crema	✗✗	21
Rocking Horse Cafe	✗	27

Pizza
Co.	✗	19

Seafood
Cull & Pistol	✗	22

Spanish
El Quinto Pino	✗✗	24
La Nacional	✗	25
Salinas	✗✗	28
Socarrat	✗	28
Tía Pol	▦	29
Toro	▦	30
Txikito	✗✗	31

Vegan
Blossom	✗✗	18

Chinatown & Little Italy

Chinese
A-Wah	✗	35
Bo Ky	✗	35
Dim Sum Go Go	☺ ✗	36
Golden Unicorn	✗	37
Grand Harmony	✗	37
Great N.Y. Noodletown	✗	38
Nom Wah Tea Parlor	☺ ✗	40
Oriental Garden	✗	41
Peking Duck House	✗	42
Royal Seafood	✗	43
Shanghai Café	☺ ✗	44
Shanghai Heping	✗✗	44

French
Parigot	✗✗	42

Gastropub
Brinkley's	✗	36

Italian
Il Cortile	✗✗	38
Il Palazzo	✗✗	39

Malaysian
New Malaysia	☺ ✗	40
Nyonya	▦ ✗	41

Mexican
La Esquina	✗	39

Greenwich, West Village & Meatpacking District

Harlem, Morningside & Washington Heights

Upper East Side

Starred Restaurants

*W*ithin the selection we offer you, some restaurants deserve to be highlighted for their particularly good cuisine. When giving one, two, or three Michelin stars, there are a number of elements that we consider including the quality of the ingredients, the technical skill and flair that goes into their preparation, the blend and clarity of flavours, and the balance of the menu. Just as important is the ability to produce excellent cooking time and again. We make as many visits as we need, so that our readers may be assured of quality and consistency.

A two or three-star restaurant has to offer something very special in its cuisine; a real element of creativity, originality, or "personality" that sets it apart from the rest. Three stars – our highest award – are given to the choicest restaurants, where the whole dining experience is superb.

Cuisine in any style, modern or traditional, may be eligible for a star. Due to the fact we apply the same independent standards everywhere, the awards have become benchmarks of reliability and excellence in over 20 countries in Europe and Asia, particularly in France, where we have awarded stars for 100 years, and where the phrase "Now that's real three-star quality!" has entered into the language.

The awarding of a star is based solely on the quality of the cuisine.

🏵🏵🏵

Exceptional cuisine, worth a special journey

One always eats here extremely well, sometimes superbly. Distinctive dishes are precisely executed, using superlative ingredients.

Chef's Table at Brooklyn Fare	XX	456
Eleven Madison Park	XxxX	109
Jean-Georges	XxxX	406
Le Bernardin	XxxX	286
Masa	XX	291
Per Se	XxXxX	298

🏵🏵

Excellent cuisine, worth a detour

Skillfully and carefully crafted dishes of outstanding quality.

Aquavit	XxX	226	Jungsik	XxX	348
atera	XX	341	Marea	XxX	289
Blanca	XX	451	Momofuku Ko	X	72
Daniel	XxXxX	367	Soto	XX	177
Ichimura	XX	347			

🏵

A very good restaurant in its category

A place offering cuisine prepared to a consistently high standard.

Ai Fiori	XxX	263	Casa Mono	XX	106
Aldea	XX	97	Caviar Russe	XxX	233
Andanada	XX	396	Danny Brown		
Aureole	XxX	265	Wine Bar & Kitchen	XX	542
Babbo	XX	137	Delaware and Hudson	XX	459
Bâtard	XxX	342	Del Posto	XxxX	23
Betony	XxX	269	Dovetail	XX	402
Blue Hill	XX	140	15 East	XX	110
Bouley	XxxX	344	Gotham Bar and Grill	XxX	151
Breslin (The)	X	104	Gramercy Tavern	XxX	112
Brushstroke	XxX	343	Hakkasan	XxX	280
Café Boulud	XxX	364	Jewel Bako	X	64
Café China	XX	231	Juni	XxX	239
Carbone	XX	143	Junoon	XxX	116
Casa Enrique	XX	539	Kajitsu	XX	240

Bib Gourmand

This symbol indicates our inspectors' favorites for good value.
For $40 or less, you can enjoy two courses and a glass of wine or a dessert (not including tax or gratuity).

Indexes ▶ Bib Gourmand

Brunch

Late Dining

Credits

Michelin is committed to improving the mobility of travellers

ON EVERY ROAD AND BY EVERY MEANS

Since the company came into being – over a century ago – Michelin has had a single objective: to offer people a better way forward. A technological challenge first, to create increasingly efficient tires, but also an ongoing commitment to travelers, to help them travel in the best way. This is why Michelin is developing a whole collection of products and services: from maps, atlases, travel guides and auto accessories, to mobile apps, route planners and online assistance: Michelin is doing everything it can to make traveling more pleasurable!

Sustainable mobility
→ *is clean mobility... and mobility for everyone*

Sustainable mobility means enabling people to get around in a way that is cleaner, safer, more economical and more accessible to everyone, wherever they might live. Every day, Michelin's 113,000 employees worldwide are innovating:

• by creating tires and services that meet society's new needs.

• by raising young people's awareness of road safety.

• by inventing new transport solutions that consume less energy and emit less CO_2.

→ *Michelin Challenge Bibendum*

Sustainable mobility means allowing the transport of goods and people to continue, while promoting responsible economic, social and societal development. Faced with the increasing scarcity of raw materials and global warming, Michelin is standing up for the environment and public health. Michelin regularly organizes 'Michelin Challenge Bibendum', the only event in the world which focuses on sustainable road travel.

Manhattan
Bus Map
April 2014

©2014 Metropolitan Transportation Authority Unauthorized duplication prohibited.

The Michelin strategy:
→ multi-performance tires

Michelin is synonymous with safety, fuel saving and the capacity to cover thousands of miles. A MICHELIN tire is the embodiment of all these things – thanks to our engineers, who work with the very latest technology.

Their challenge: to equip every tire – whatever the vehicle (car, truck, tractor, bulldozer, plane, motorbike, bicycle or train!) – with the best possible combination of qualities, for optimal overall performance.

Slowing down wear, reducing energy expenditure (and therefore CO_2 emissions), improving safety through enhanced road handling and braking: there are so many qualities in just one tire – that's Michelin Total Performance.

MICHELIN
Total Performance

Every day, **Michelin** is working towards sustainable mobility

OVER TIME, WHILE RESPECTING THE PLANET

Michelin
→ *innovation in movement*

Created and patented by Michelin in 1946, the belted radial-ply tire revolutionized the world of tires. But Michelin did not stop there: over the years other new and original solutions came out, confirming Michelin's position as a leader in research and innovation.

→ *the right pressure!*

One of Michelin's priorities is safer mobility. In short, innovating for a better way forward. This is the challenge for researchers, who are working to perfect tires capable of shorter braking distances and offering the best possible traction to the road. To support motorists, Michelin organizes road safety awareness campaigns all over the world: "Fill up with air" initiatives remind everyone that the right tire pressure is a crucial factor in safety and fuel economy.

→ Michelin Apps

Because the notions of comfort and security are essential, both for you and for us, Michelin has created a package of six free mobile applications—a comprehensive collection to make driving a pleasure!

→ **Michelin MyCar** • *To get the best from your tires; services and information for carefree travel preparation.*

→ **Michelin Navigation** • *A new approach to navigation: traffic in real time with a new connected guidance feature.*

→ **ViaMichelin** • *Calculates routes and map data: a must for traveling in the most efficient way.*

→ **Michelin Restaurants** • *Because driving should be enjoyable: find a wide choice of restaurants, in France and Germany, including the MICHELIN Guide's complete listings.*

→ **Michelin Hotels** • *To book hotel rooms at the best rates, all over the world!*

→ **Michelin Voyage** • *85 countries and 30, 000 tourist sites selected by the Michelin Green Guide, plus a tool for creating your own travel book.*

A tire...
→ what is it?

Round, black, supple yet solid, the tire is to the wheel what the shoe is to the foot. But what is it made of? First and foremost, rubber, but also various textile and/or metallic materials... and then it's filled with air! It is the skilful assembly of all these components that ensures tires have the qualities they should: grip to the road, shock absorption, in two words: 'comfort' and 'safety.'

1 TREAD
The tread ensures the tire performs correctly, by dispersing water, providing grip and increasing longevity.

2 CROWN PLIES
This reinforced double or triple belt combines vertical suppleness with transversal rigidity, enabling the tire to remain flat to the road.

3 SIDEWALLS
These link all the component parts and provide symmetry. They enable the tire to absorb shock, thus giving a smooth ride.

4 BEADS
The bead wires ensure that the tire is fixed securely to the wheel to ensure safety.

5 INNER LINER
The inner liner creates an airtight seal between the wheel rim and the tire.